BLACK HERITAGE IN SOCIAL WELFARE 1860-1930

compiled and edited

by

EDYTH L. ROSS

The Scarecrow Press, Inc.
Metuchen, N.J. & London
1978

Library of Congress Cataloging in Publication Data

Main entry under title:

Black heritage in social welfare, 1860-1930.

Bibliography: p.
Includes index.
1. Afro-Americans--Social work with--History--Addresses, essays, lectures. 2. Afro-Americans--Charities--History--Addresses, essays, lectures. 3. Social service--United States--History--Addresses, essays, lectures. I. Ross, Edyth L., 1916-
HV3181.B55 362.8'4 78-8403
ISBN 0-8108-1145-6

Manufactured in the United States of America

This book is dedicated to my husband, Hubert B. Ross, for his endless and untiring support, and to my children, Susan and Michael Ross.

FOREWORD

Out of Atlanta University's School of Social Work now has come a second major work in the study of Black social welfare enterprise. This volume by Edyth Ross, a professor in the University's School of Social Work, concentrates on the period from 1860 to 1930. Its immediate predecessor was the 1973 Alton Childs Series publication which was concerned with the antebellum period. Professor Ross enlarged her purposes to seek both synthesis and integration--synthesis of the history of Blacks in social welfare thought and activities, and integration of the matrix into the general fabric of social welfare enterprise in this country.

That a scholar who is Black and who works in a university which is predominantly Black has produced this work speaks eloquently to the need for the "Black" university as well as to the century-old traditions at Atlanta University of scholarship about Blacks but in the interests of the general national welfare as well. It is hardly likely that this kind of compilation would have been made yet at a university that is predominantly "White" in the United States.

It is likewise significant and relevant that this work developed within the environment of the oldest accredited School of Social Work for Blacks in the United States. Formed in 1920, accredited in 1928, this School of Social Work has been enriched by such men as John Hope, Forrester B. Washington, Jesse O. Thomas, E. Franklin Frazier, and Whitney Young, as well as other creative and supportive people.

Atlanta University's Professor Ross has responded well to the challenge posed by using documents as a medium of synthesis and integration. She has unearthed some documents that are brought together for the first time and published in a coherent fashion. Not only social workers but also historians, politicians, social scientists, and laymen will find nuggets or gems of information in these documents.

Documents on the life of Blacks in the Sea Islands off the coast of Georgia ("site of the first United States government program in social welfare") and the great Port Royal experiment during the post-Civil War period present a panorama of detail which is at one and the same time edifying and highly effective. The story of the "Exoduster"--Black migrants to Kansas at the end of the last century--is searchingly revealed by rare documents. There is a great variety of documents relating to the role of individuals who initiated or supported social service programs through their own expertise and creativity. There are documents illustrative of the beginning of the Carrie Steele (Pitts) Orphans Home in Atlanta; the famous Ida B. Wells Barnett exposé on American racism reflected in contemporary analyses of rapes; of individual and group movements against segregation in the post-Plessy v. Ferguson period; of Negro efforts to escape the oppression of segregation by migrating to African shores or to California; and perhaps most momentous of all, W. E. B. DuBois' summary of social service developments and needs among the Black communities of the nation. The documents shed new light on conditions of Blacks in Southern peonage, in rural life, and in urban areas such as Durham, North Carolina. They speak of the role of the Black church as a social service agency and of kindergartens for Black children.

Social work efforts on the national scene are not neglected. Widespread activities of individual Blacks and of nationally organized groups are documented as shown in the anti-lynching campaigns, the early twentieth-century race riots, housing, crime, public health, labor unions, voting rights, Black YWCA's, war relief, etc. Both national and regional organizations are given a share of the limelight.

Edyth Ross provided a narrative linkage for these documents which reflects artistry and sensitivity. She allowed the documents to tell the story and by their selection made the story both poignant and meaningful. There is little doubt that the volume will serve as a milestone in the history and analysis of social work. As a source of information for this body of knowledge, it has not been matched in the field. Scholars of all kinds will find it useful and highly suggestive. It will contribute to the long and distinguished history of significant scholarly works done by Atlanta University scholars and is in the tradition of Atlanta University's constant concern with excellence and the search for truth without limitations of race or color.

Prince E. Wilson
Vice President for Academic Affairs
Atlanta University

PREFACE

This textbook was devised and developed as a corrective for omissions and deficiencies in the existing literature on Social Welfare, and especially by the absence of any extensive body of materials illustrative of the black heritage and experience in this area of knowledge. It was also deemed necessary to prepare a pioneer compilation of new and unpublished documentary source materials which reveal the social welfare activities undertaken by individuals and groups who have been typically neglected in conventional studies. Finally, the need was seen to bring to the attention of the public (in line with the current trend of defining social welfare not in terms of those roles and institutions which have functions residual to the normal operation of the economy, policy and society but rather in accordance with the posture that social welfare concerns and activities are an integral part of the functioning of a viable society), that, rooted in the necessities of sheer survival, these concepts had an earlier inception in the thoughts and activities of black leaders who deserve recognition for their pioneer roles in contributing to the emergence, organization and development of social welfare enterprise.

The documentary evidences provide a historical overview of the general and specific responses of Blacks to the situational and personal problems facing them.

I wish to acknowledge and thank the following persons for the intrinsic assistance given in bringing this study to fruition:

The Lois and Samuel Silberman Fund for an initial grant to undertake the project; Dr. Charles Sanders, Project Director; Consultants Dr. Inabel Lindsay; Dean Emeritus, Howard University School of Social Work; Dr. Ralph Pumphrey; George Warren Brown,

School of Social Work, Washington University; Dr. Philip Foner, Historian, Lincoln University; Mrs. Willie Bolden, Historian, Clark College; Dr. Hubert Ross, Anthropologist, Atlanta University; Dean Genevieve Hill, Atlanta University School of Social Work; Mr. Casper L. Jordan, Librarian, Atlanta University; Mrs. Lee Alexander, Archivist, Atlanta University; Mrs. Lillian Lewis, Curator, Negro Collection, Atlanta University; Dr. Clifton H. Johnson, Archivist, Amistad Collection, Dillard University; Mrs. Dovie Patrick, Librarian, Clark College; Ms. Claudette Rivers, Atlanta University School of Social Work; Mrs. Dorothy Beatty and Mrs. Elzora Andrews, Atlanta University Center Undergraduate Program in Social Welfare and Mrs. Lynn Suruma, Institute of the Black World.

My deepest appreciation is also extended to the many persons, heirs, relatives and friends who granted permission to use the documents in this publication.

E. L. R.

TABLE OF CONTENTS

Foreword v
Preface viii
List of Documents xiii

PROLOGUE

Introduction 1
Slavery as an Institution 6
Colonial America: Slave and Free 12
The Antebellum Period 14

I FROM HOPE TO DESPAIR: 1861-1877

Introduction 39
Transition from Slavery 42
Stabilization of Family and Community Life 78
Laws Affecting Social Welfare 98

II SURVIVING EMERGENT SEGREGATION: 1877-1896

Introduction 109
Colonization 111
Establishment of All-Black Towns 114
Emigration to North and West 117
Welfare Interests of the Black Church 132
Emergence of Multiple Function Social Welfare Agencies in the Black Community 133
Emergence of Single Function Social Welfare Agencies in the Black Community 143
Emergence of Black Labor Organizations 150
W. E. Burghardt DuBois: Social Science in the Service of Social Welfare 152
The Role of Women 162
Segregation Enshrined 167

III RENEWAL AND RESURGENCE: 1895-1915

Introduction 177

Building All-Black Communities by Migration and Colonization 181
The Emergence of New Leadership for Social Movements 192
The Rural Scene 209
Surveying Conditions Fifty Years After Emancipation 216
The Urban Scene 225
The Atlanta Experience: A Case Study 243

IV THE GREAT MIGRATION AND ITS CONSEQUENCES: 1915-1930

Introduction 283
The Urban Migration 288
The All-Black Community 300
Colonization: The "Back-to-Africa" Movement of Marcus Garvey 304
The Concept and Consciousness of the "New Negro" 311
Problems Requiring National Attention 319
- a) Lynching and the Anti-Lynching Campaign 320
- b) Race Riots 323
- c) Welfare Problems 335
- d) Health Problems 342

Organizational Responses to Problems of National Import 350
- a) Labor 351
- b) The National Association for the Advancement of Colored People 370
- c) The Commission on Interracial Cooperation 373
- d) Roles and Activities of Black Women 379
- e) Roles and Activities of Black Men 398
- f) The Black Church in Social Service 406
- g) Specific Practices of Social Welfare Agencies 412

Social Work Education for Professional Practice 422

EPILOGUE 465

Bibliography 471
Index 479

LIST OF DOCUMENTS

PROLOGUE

1. St. Clair Drake, "Afro-American and African-American Cultures." 15
2. John H. Russell, "Origin of the Free Negro Class." 20
3. Loren Miller, "Slavery in the Constitution of the United States." 22
4. Benjamin Banneker, "To Thomas Jefferson"--1791. 24
5. Laurence Foster, "The Seminole Wars and the Removal West." 27
6. John W. Lyda, Lost Creek Settlement, Vigo County, Ind. 28
7. Wilson Armistead, Anthony Benezet. 29
8. Minutes of the Conference of the Third Annual Convention for the Improvement of the Free People of Colour of the United States.... Philadelphia, 1833. 30
9. King E. Davis, "Chronological Development of Black Fund-Raising Organizations (1775-1855)" (Appendix I of "Black Fund Raising:...") 31
10. Robert Austin Warner, New Haven Negroes, A Social History. 33
11. Delilah L. Beasley, "Mammy Pleasants" in The Negro Trail Blazers of California. 33

I FROM HOPE TO DESPAIR: 1861-1877

1. W.E.B. DuBois, Black Reconstruction in America, 1860-1880. 42
2. Joseph T. Wilson, Emancipation, Its Course and Progress, 1882. 44
3. E. L. Pierce, "The Freedmen at Port Royal," Atlantic Monthly, XII, September, 1863. 46
4. James E. Yeatman, Report to the Western Sanitary Commission in Regard to Leasing Abandoned Plantations, with Rules and Regulations Governing the Same, 1864. 63
5. Charlotte L. Forten, The Journal of Charlotte Forten, A Free Negro in the Slave Era. 70
6. Susie King Taylor, Reminiscences of My Life in Camp with the 33rd United States Colored Troops Late 1st S.C. Volunteers, 1902. 73
7. Edyth L. Ross, "Robert Smalls" in "Black Heritage in Social Welfare ... 1861-1905." 74

8. Inabel Burns Lindsay, "Some Contributions to Welfare Services, 1865-1900," Journal of Negro Education. 77
9. George Hendricks, "Union Army Occupation of the Southern Seaboard, 1861-1865." 79
10. Letters of Teachers and Superintendents of the New England Educational Commission for Freedmen, 1864; Letters from AMA Archives in Amistad Collection, Dillard University, New Orleans, La. 79
11. G. W. Hubbard, History of Colored Schools of Nashville, Tennessee, 1874. 88
12. "Condition of the Colored People," Baltimore, Md., New York Tribune, 1870. 89
13. General W. T. Sherman, Field Order #15, War Department Archives, 1865. 93
14. Letter from General W. T. Sherman to President Andrew Johnson, 1866. 95
15. "War Department, Bureau of Refugees, Freedmen and Abandoned Lands," Circular No. 15, 1865. 96
16. Mary Ames, From a New England Woman's Diary in Dixie in 1865. 98
17. XIII Amendment to the United States Constitution, December 18, 1865. 98
18. XIV Amendment to the United States Constitution, July 20, 1868. 102
19. XV Amendment to the United States Constitution, March 30, 1870. 102
20. Proceedings of the Constitutional Convention of South Carolina, Vol. I, 1868. 103
21. "Liquidation of the Freedmen's Bureau," The Christian Recorder, 1873. 105

II SURVIVING EMERGENT SEGREGATION: 1877-1896

1. Henry McNeal Turner's speech in Africa and the American Negro, 1896. 112
2. J. Fred Rippy, "A Negro Colonization Project in Mexico, 1895," Journal of Negro History, 1921. 113
3. Stanley Cisby Arthur, biographical sketch of Isaiah T. Montgomery. 115
4. Letters from Ministers Encouraging Migration to Kansas, Christian Recorder, 1873. 118
5. Report and Testimony of the Select Committee of the United States Senate to Investigate the Causes of the Removal of the Negroes from the Southern States to the Northern States, 1880. 120
6. Glen Schwendemann, "St. Louis and the Exodus of 1879," Journal of Negro History, 1931. 125
7. Debate on Relief to Exodusters. Proceedings and Debates of the 46th Congress, 1880. 128
8. Benjamin Singleton, Testimony, Report of the Select Committee of the Senate, 1880. 131
9. Monroe N. Work, "The Negro Church and the Negro Community," Southern Workman, 1908. 132

10. L. H. Hammond, "A Woman Banker," In the Vanguard of a Race, 1922. 133
11. R. L. Smith, "An Uplifting Negro Cooperative Society," World's Work, 1908. 136
12a. E. R. Carter, "Mrs. Carrie Steele Logan," The Black Side, 1894. 143
12b. Petition of Carrie Steele, et al., to Superior Court, Fulton County, Ga., to establish a home for "indigent colored orphan children," 1888. 145
13. E. R. Carter, "The Good Samaritan Order," The Black Side, 1894. 146
14. E. R. Carter, "Rev. N. J. Jones, Founder of the Colored Men's Protective Association," The Black Side, 1894. 146
15. E. R. Carter, "I.O. of O.F. St. James Lodge No. 1455," The Black Side, 1894. 148
16. E. R. Carter, "The Colored Protective Association," The Black Side, 1894. 149
17. "The Organization of Negroes in the Knights of Labor," John Swinton Papers, 1886. 151
18. W. E. Burghardt DuBois, "The Study of the Negro Problem," Publications of the American Academy of Political and Social Science, 1897. 154
19. W. E. Burghardt DuBois, The Philadelphia Negro, A Social Study, 1899. 155
20. Some Efforts of American Negroes for Their Own Social Betterment, Atlanta University Publications, 1898. 157
21. Letter to Second Annual Atlanta University Conference from Frederick Howard Wines, editor of Charities Review, 1897. 161
22. Ida Wells Barnett, A Red Record, 1895. 162
23. Josephine St. Pierre Ruffin, "An Open Letter to the Educational League of Georgia." 165
24. Congressman Benjamin F. Butler, letter to Robert Harben, Jr., Washington, D.C., 1875. 168
25. Charles L. Black, Brief for Appellants, Supreme Court of the United States, 1953. 170

III RENEWAL AND RESURGENCE: 1895-1915

1. William E. Bittle and Gilbert L. Geis, "Alfred Charles Sam and an African Return," Phylon, 1962. 182
2. Delilah L. Beasley, The Negro Trail Blazers of California, 1919. 189
3. Booker T. Washington, "The Atlanta Exposition Address," 1900. 193
4. J.W.E. Bowen, An Appeal to the King, Atlanta, 1895. 194
5. "The Niagara Movement" (Editorial), The Voice of the Negro, 1905. 198
6. W.E.B. DuBois, "The Niagara Movement," The Voice of the Negro, 1905. 198
7. J. Max Barber, "The Niagara Movement at Harper's Ferry," The Voice of the Negro, 1906. 202

8. W. E. Burghardt DuBois, "The National Association for the Advancement of Colored People," The Horizon, 1910. 206
9. "The Peonage Law Upheld," The Voice of the Negro, 1905. 209
10. Rossa B. Cooley, "The Regeneration of Colored Population in the Rural South," Proceedings of the National Conference of Charities and Corrections, Boston, 1911. 211
11. W. E. Burghardt DuBois, "Play for Negroes," The Survey, 1912. 215
12. George E. Haynes, "The Basis of Race Adjustment," The Survey, 1913. 217
13. W. E. Burghardt DuBois, "Social Effects of Emancipation," The Survey, 1913. 219
14. W. E. Burghardt DuBois, "The Upbuilding of Black Durham," World's Work, 1912. 226
15. Fannie B. Williams, "Growth of Social Settlement Idea," The New York Age, 1905. 231
16. Fifth Annual Report of the Free Kindergarten Association for Colored Children, 1900. 233
17. George E. Haynes, "Cooperation with Colleges in Securing and Training Negro Social Workers for Urban Centers," Proceedings of the National Conference of Charities and Corrections, Boston, 1911. 236
18a. Bulletin of National League on Urban Conditions Among Negroes, 1912-1913. 240
18b. "Results of the 1912-1913 Program," Bulletin of National League on Urban Conditions Among Negroes, 1913. 242
19. Henry Hugh Proctor, Between Black and White, 1914. 243
20. Merlissie R. Middleton, "Residential Distribution of Members of an Urban Church," 1953. 251
21. David A. Russell, Jr., "The Institutional Church in Transition," 1971. 251
22. Louie D. Shivery, "The History of the Gate City Free Kindergarten Association." 258
23. Louie D. Shivery, "The Neighborhood Union, A Survey of the Beginnings of Social Welfare Movements Among Negroes in Atlanta." 264
24. Louie D. Shivery, "The History of Organized Social Work Among Atlanta Negroes, 1890-1935," Appendixes. 269

IV THE GREAT MIGRATION AND ITS CONSEQUENCES: 1915-1930

1. "Letters of Negro Migrants of 1916-1918," Journal of Negro History, 1919. 288
2. "Negro Migration as the South Sees It," The Survey, 1917. 292
3. George E. Haynes, "Negro Migration, Its Effects on

Family and Community Life in the North," Opportunity, 1924. 293
4. George Edmund Haynes, "Negroes Move North," The Survey, 1919. 297
5. Jesse O. Thomas, "A Social Program to Help the Migrant," Opportunity, 1924. 299
6. R. Edgar Iles, "Boley (An Exclusively Negro Town in Oklahoma)," Opportunity, 1925. 300
7. "Aims and Objects of Movement for Solution of Negro Problem" in Philosophy and Opinions of Marcus Garvey, or Africa for the Africans. 305
8. E. Franklin Frazier, "The Garvey Movement," Opportunity, 1926. 307
9a. "The New Negro: What Is He?" (Editorial) The Messenger, 1920. 311
9b. Alain Locke, "The New Negro," Survey Graphic, 1924-25. 314
10a. Anti-Lynching Petition, Atlanta, 1918. 320
10b. "Lynchings Increase" (Editorial) Opportunity, 1926. 322
11. Reports of Race Riots. Negro Year Book, 1918-19. 323
12. Stanley R. Norvell and William M. Tuttle, Jr., "Views of a Negro During 'The Red Summer' of 1919," Journal of Negro History, 1966. 324
13. George E. Haynes, "Race Riots in Relation to Democracy," The Survey, 1919. 331
14. Monroe N. Work, "Problems of Negro Urban Welfare," The Southern Workman, 1924. 336
15a. Eugene Kinckle Jones, "The Negro's Struggle for Health," Proceedings of the National Conference of Social Work, Washington, D.C., 1923. 342
15b. T. J. Woofter, Jr., "Organization of Rural Negroes for Public Health," Proceedings of the National Conference of Social Work, Washington, D.C., 1923. 347
16. George E. Haynes, "The Negro Laborer and the Immigrant," The Survey, 1921. 352
17. T. Arnold Hill, "Recent Developments in the Problem of Negro Labor," Proceedings of the National Conference of Social Work, Chicago, 1921. 357
18a. A. Philip Randolph, "The Truth About the Brotherhood of Sleeping Car Porters," The Messenger, 1926. 362
18b. "The Brotherhood of Sleeping Car Porters," The Social Service Bulletin of the Methodist Federation for Social Services, 1927. 364
19. J. A. Jackson, "Colored Actors' Union," The Messenger, 1925. 369
20. Nixon v. Herndon, et al., 273 U.S. October Term, 1926. 370
21a. "Interracial Group," Ms. Neighborhood Union Papers, 1918, Atlanta University. 373
21b. Will W. Alexander, "Phylon Profile, XI: John Hope," Phylon, 1947. 374
22. Francis A. Kellor, "Assisted Emigration from the South," Charities, 1905. 380

23. Alice Dunbar Nelson, "Negro Women in War Work," The American Negro in the World War, by Emmet J. Scott, 1919. 385
24. Emmet J. Scott, "Social Welfare Agencies," The American Negro in the World War, 1919. 398
25. George E. Haynes, "The Church and the Negro Spirit," Survey Graphic, 1925. 406
26. A. Clayton Powell, "The Church in Social Work," Opportunity, 1923. 411
27a. Report of the Negro Civic Welfare Committee of the Council of Social Agencies, Cincinnati, Ohio, 1921. 412
27b. Eugene Kinckle Jones, "Building a Larger Life," Opportunity, 1923. 417
28. John Marshall Ragland, "A Hospital for Negroes with a Social Service Program," Opportunity, 1923. 425
29. Robert C. Dexter, "The Negro in Social Work," The Survey, 1921. 427
30. Minutes of a Meeting Called to Discuss the Organization of the Atlanta School of Social Work, My Story in Black and White, by Jesse O. Thomas. 430
31. Announcement, Atlanta School of Social Service at Morehouse College, Atlanta, Georgia, 1920. 433
32. Charter Incorporating the Atlanta School of Social Work, Superior Court, Fulton County, Georgia, May 22, 1924. 437
33. Edward Franklin Frazier, "The Pathology of Race Prejudice," Forum, 1927. 439
34. Forrester B. Washington, "What Professional Training Means to the Social Worker," Annals of the American Academy of Political and Social Science, 1926. 445
35. Bulletin, Atlanta School of Social Work, 1929-30, Announcements, 1930-31. 450
36. Eugene Kinckle Jones, "Social Work Among Negroes," The Annals of the American Academy of Political and Social Science, 1928. 456

PROLOGUE

INTRODUCTION

If, in the words of Romanyshyn, the concept of social welfare may be defined "as including all those forms of social intervention that have a primary and direct concern with promoting both the welfare of the individual and of the society as a whole," it is most relevant to reexamine the social welfare heritage of the citizens of African ancestry and descent with special attention to "those provisions and processes directly concerned with the treatment and prevention of social problems, the development of human resources, and the improvement of the quality of life." Such reexamination will reveal that, contrary to uninformed popular opinion, members of the black population, both singly and in groups, developed on their own initiative, "social services to individuals and families," and engaged as well in "efforts to strengthen or modify social institutions," which often imposed intolerable constraints against them, and which were sanctioned by both custom and law.[1*]

In pursuit of this objective, namely the reexamination of the black heritage in social welfare, it is necessary to probe far back into the hidden recesses of American history. Also, in many instances, it is necessary to reanalyze the then-emerging system of British imperialism in order that we recover as much documentary evidence as is possible of the significant contributions of black people to social welfare policies, programs and institutions. It is amazing that in many cases we can reclaim some part of this her-

*Footnotes to the Prologue begin on page 35.

itage, but it should not be surprising to anyone that it was there to be uncovered. Surely blacks, whose tenure in involuntary servitude has been longer than that of any other ethnic group in the New World, have of necessity had to be concerned with efforts to improve the conditions under which they might enjoy life, liberty and the pursuit of happiness. In such cases only a goal of mere survival within the social system was attainable. It will be seen however, that, while many records of the unceasing struggle are irretrievably lost, much information is still available and remains to be recovered, especially from the memories of those still living and often still contributing to social welfare objectives.

One of the functions of this reader, then, is to make available to the general public, as well as students and social welfare practitioners, the previously ignored documentary evidence which will accord to black men and women the recognition long overdue for their worthy achievements. In the process we become familiar with the persons who have pioneered the development of social welfare programs for blacks in those many instances where social services for the black population were not made available from the overall resources of the dominant communities. It should be noted that the existence of a black heritage in social welfare in no way diminishes the valued contributions of members of other ethnic groups in behalf of, or in cooperation with, blacks. Rather, it augments, complements and enriches the total history of social welfare as it has emerged in the United States. We also become aware of the tremendous struggle to create new institutions to serve the general needs of any people, and the particular needs of the black population.

In this volume, the major emphasis is placed upon the recovery and presentation of documents relative to the period of American history beginning in 1861 and ending in 1929. The most significant efforts by blacks in the field of social welfare were not made until the Thirteenth, Fourteenth and Fifteenth Amendments to the United States Constitution were ratified. These are the policy enactments which changed the legal status of blacks in the United

States. However, the participation of blacks in social welfare enterprise both antedates and postdates our self-imposed period of re-examination.

It is also important to recognize that, in the antebellum period which comprises the colonial era and the era of early nation-building, members of the black population, on their own initiative, planned and implemented viable institutions of social welfare, some of which have survived into the present. These institutions provided the oppressed black population with the social and ideological supports necessary for survival in the face of onerous burdens imposed by the constraints of involuntary servitude and institutionalized racism. False stereotypes of black behavior and racist ideologies were advanced to mask the efforts of those who had attained some modest success. Alongside the rudimentary structure of social welfare which the government erected, presumably for the benefits of all, blacks developed, wherever possible, a complementary structure of institutions. These institutions enabled black people to cope with existing conditions, particularly where black participation in which institutions was denied or forbidden.

Today, when blacks place so much emphasis upon their cultural identity, the omnipotent presence of the black community can be ascertained by the constructive efforts to develop relevant economic, political and social structures. There is, however, the tendency to think of the black community as a monolithic entity. Such unity as exists has been achieved by the emergence and evolution of a large and homogeneous black community which emanated from individual and group enterprises. These eclectic enterprises are representative of the multitude of small, isolated communities. These individuals and groups have built upon a black heritage which includes the following elements: 1) a common identification on the basis of African ancestry; 2) a common experience of involuntary removal from Africa; 3) a common experience of involuntary servitude in the New World; and a multitude of 4) common experiences emerging from the need to improvise techniques and strategies for survival in the face of the manifold subtleties of ethnic prejudice, ethnic discrimination, and institutionalized racism, as well as the constraints of administrative, judicial, and legislative decisions, enforced by the domestic police on local, state and national levels of governmental organization.

Prior to the present effort, there has been no major attempt to organize and synthesize in a systematic fashion the history of blacks in social welfare. Nor has there been any major effort to integrate materials relating the black experience to the larger context of social welfare enterprise in the United States, certainly none of which has exceeded the efforts of the Pumphreys.[2] Thus the task of achieving such synthesis and integration are major objectives for this volume. We should take note, however, of a publication which attempts to encourage research into the history of black social welfare enterprise in the antebellum period.[3] This work comprises four papers, originally presented at the 1972 sessions of the National Conference on Social Welfare. The first, by Miss Joanne V. Rhone,[4] argues for the recognition of "a unique 'social service delivery system'--a system of self-help" in the antebellum black community, which is in turn defined as a "slave community." One may quarrel with the attempt to apply the concept of a social service delivery system to a "slave community" which operates within a plantation system. However, many of the points made by Miss Rhone have been elaborated in a recent publication by John W. Blassingame.[5] In a second paper, Drs. Charles L. Sanders and William S. Jackson[6] consider the role of the abolition movement in social welfare enterprise, asserting that "within the abolition movement, there were social welfare services offered by the societies, the underground railroad, and the national convention organizations." Next, Charles L. Sanders[7] discusses the activity of the black church, characterizing it as "a community service center where a series of social, recreational, educational, economic and political needs of the community were reflected," while the final paper of Jackson[8] stresses the social welfare efforts of beneficial or mutual aid societies and secret fraternal orders and describes an instance of the mobilization of emergency health services by the black community of Philadelphia to cope with the yellow fever epidemic of 1793. These commendable papers are efforts to recover the social welfare history of blacks in antebellum days, and it is to be hoped that they will stimulate others to recover other instances of black social welfare in this period of American history. As mentioned above, some social scientists may quarrel with the conceptualization in some of these papers but, nevertheless, the effort of the authors to apply a model of a social service delivery system to the interpretation of black welfare enterprise is intellectually stimulating and suggestive of future research possibilities.

It is pertinent here to refer to Dr. W. E. B. DuBois, perhaps the greatest of all black scholars, not only for the strength of his intellectual leadership, but also for his commitment to purposive social action. DuBois once characterized freedom as the most valued objective of purposive endeavor undertaken by blacks, and defined this concept as embracing "full economic, political and social equality with American citizens, in thought, expression and action, with no discrimination based on race or color."[9]

It is the tragedy of the black heritage and experience that after some four hundred years of purposive endeavor, freedom remains a dream rather than a fulfillment. It is significant, however, that the possession of this dream has probably been part of the heritage of every African slave brought to American soil, and that the hope for its fulfillment has been transmitted to all of Africa's descendants in the new world. The pursuit of this dream has at some time or other been the objective of every black American, influencing each decision he has had to make in order to cope with the problems of survival in an alien and basically hostile world. No African transported to the New World is alleged to have made the voyage voluntarily. Melville J. Herskovits[10] has exposed the "myth of the Negro past" intellectually, and the civil rights movement of the sixties has exposed it pragmatically. No person of African descent has been adjusted to a perpetual condition of abasement.

SLAVERY AS AN INSTITUTION

Africans were imported, specifically, to serve as agricultural laborers on the plantations established under the sovereignty of British, Dutch, French, Spanish and Portuguese governments, in the period when these nations vied for control of the high seas and overseas markets. In the early seventeenth century the control of the territory along the Atlantic seaboard had not yet been achieved by the British, and the coast was shared with Dutch and Spanish intruders into the lands of the aboriginal Amerindian nations. All of the sovereign powers were rivals and all were aware of the tremendous potential for agricultural, commercial and industrial development which would flow from the settlement and colonization of these lands. In fact, all were so supremely confident of their ability to do this that their sovereigns arrogantly allocated rights to settle and colonize these Amerindian territories to small groups of privileged proprietors or to chartered companies. It is usually alleged that the systems which evolved to recruit, supply, and control the labor of European ethnics by indenture proved inadequate; that attempts at enslavement of the Amerindian populations proved impossible; and, that the superior adaptability of the Africans for sustained agricultural labor in the tropics paved the way for their importation as slaves. But, there was more to the exploitation of Africans than these commonly cited allegations reveal.

Initially, it was possible to achieve the permanent subjugation of a labor supply of African descent only because, unlike European ethnics who were at least sustained by ties of language and culture, the Africans of diverse cultural traditions, captured and transported into an alien land and forced to learn an alien culture, lacked the support of any military, naval or domestic police power capable of intervening in their behalf. No African nation was a maritime power, nor did any have the technological knowledge to develop a countervailing military power which could compete in the New World with any of the aggressive European powers for the commercial, agricultural or industrial exploitation of the territories and populations of the New World. This was true of Asian nations as well. As pointed out by Carlo M. Cipolla, guns, sails and empires made possible European expansion overseas.

> The gunned ship developed by Atlantic Europe in the course of the fourteenth and fifteenth centuries was the contrivance that made possible the European saga. It was essentially a compact device that allowed a relatively small crew to master unparalleled masses of inanimate energy for movement and destruction. The secret of the sudden and rapid European ascendency was all there; in the skill acquired by Atlantic nations, in the use of their sailing ships and in their having understood that "sea fight in these days come seldom to boarding or to great execution of bows, arrows, small shot and the sword but are chiefly performed by the great artillery.'[11]

Again,

> Thanks to the revolutionary characteristics of their man-of-war, it took only a few decades for the Europeans to establish their absolute predominance over the oceans. Because their advantage resided in their man-of-war, for almost three centuries their predominance was confined to the seas.[12]

He points out that "maps show better than any verbal description that until the eighteenth century European possessions the world over consisted mostly of naval bases and coastal strongholds,"[13] and that even in Africa "the position of Europeans ashore was no less precarious than in Asia."[14]

In the New World, however, the lack of an African presence to support the legitimate dreams and aspirations of African ethnics was the decisive factor which permitted the exploitation of their labor and their encapsulation in the defenseless conditions of slavery. The fact seems well established that Africans, originally imported into Virginia and Maryland, were assigned a social status similar to that of the indentured servants imported from Europe. But in the absence of any kind of cultural and social structural support from African sources, their vulnerability to exploitation and their eventual reduction to a status of slavery was clearly inevitable.
It may be, as Lerone Bennett[15] has argued, that the decision of the European and the Euro-American to exploit the African and African-

American was delayed somewhat longer than most persons realize. Nonetheless, his conclusion is similar: the mobilization of law and domestic police power, sanctioned by the kind of customary practices described as "institutionalized racism," proved sufficiently powerful to deny free status and equality of opportunity to the African and to his creole descendants in the New World, setting in motion a train of consequences which plague this nation to the very present.

But, it is also necessary to view this matter in the international perspective. The overseas expansion of Atlantic Europe linked Africa and America in a chain of economic interdependence, and stimulated the depopulation of Africa, eventually fashioning upon it the shackles of colonial dependence. In the words of historian Lawrence H. Gipson:

> ... the importance to the (British) Empire of Guinea in the eighteenth century can hardly be overemphasized--abhorrent as was the institution of slavery even to many contemporaries. Its coasts helped to maintain the New England rum industry and offered perhaps the greatest market for the coarse fabrics furnished by the United East India Company to traders who exchanged these commodities for slaves, gold and ivory. It has been estimated that in the exploitation of the human resources of the Gulf of Guinea area and the adjacent parts of Africa, between the years of 1680 and 1786, over two million blacks were received within the Empire. These slaves were held to be an essential element in the production of the sugar of the West Indies, the rice and indigo of South Carolina, and the tobacco of Chesapeake Bay; further, their presence in these parts guaranteed the prosperity of the provision trace of Ireland and of Pennsylvania, as well as the prosperity of the Massachusetts Bay fisheries by furnishing a market for the lower grades of fish. To Malachy Postlethwayt, writing in 1745, the African trade was 'the fundamental prop and support' of the Empire.[16]

Gipson offers another quote to the same effect:

> The vast importance of the African trading posts was expressed by one writer in 1763 as follows: 'The trade carried on between Great Britain, Ireland, North America, the West Indies, and Africa is of greater advantage to this country (Great Britain), than all other trades whatsoever, arising from the great exportation of British manufacturers, East India goods, provisions as well as linens from Ireland, which are paid for by specie, sugar, tobacco, rice and cotton and other plantation products; and

> with the commodities of Africa, such as gold-dust, bees-wax, elephant's teeth, gum Senegal, various sorts of dying woods, and particularly Negroes for the plantation.' The author insisted that the above two-thirds of all British shipping was dependent upon this triangular trade and that a continuous supply of Negroes was 'the chief and fundamental support of the British Empire.'[17]

Although Africans appear earliest in the New World in the company of the Portuguese and the Spaniards, they were to be found as slaves in Europe in pre-Columbian times, especially in cities such as Seville and Lisbon. According to Ruth Pike,

> Sixteenth century Sevillians found nothing new or unusual about the existence of numerous slaves in their cities. Negro slavery had been a part of its life for many centuries. We do not know when the first Africans were introduced into Seville after its reconquest from the Moslems in 1248, but the Chroniclers tell us that by the end of the fourteenth century many Negro slaves had been brought there by merchants engaged in the trans-Saharan trade. During this period the municipal authorities tried to ease the rigors of servile life by allowing the Negroes certain privileges, such as the right to gather together on feast days and perform their own dances and songs. Eventually it became customary for one of them to be named by the city officials as mayoral (steward) over all the rest, with authority to protect them from their masters, defend them before the courts of law, and settle their quarrels. In a similar manner the Church, although primarily interested in conversion, tried to ameliorate the physical conditions of slavery. During the last years of the fourteenth century the Church expressed its charitable intentions by establishing the Hospital of Our Lady of the Angels in the parish of San Bernardo to serve the Negro population. A short time later the Church made the further gesture toward incorporating Negroes into the spiritual fold by creating a Negro religious confraternity to run this hospital. In subsequent years many wealthy Sevillians helped to maintain Our Lady of the Angels; a notable donor was the Duke of Medina Sidonia, who at his death left in 1463 one thousand marvadis for the poor of this institution.[18]

The presence of a large black population in Seville, however, soon aroused fears and posed problems of security:

> Although most slaves were well behaved, the existence of a large servile population created security problems for the municipal government. The city fathers feared that the urban slaves, led by the Moriscos, might band together and seize the town, and the unofficial uneasiness on

> this score found expression in a series of municipal ordinances restricting the movements of slaves.[19]

In addition, tensions and conflicts were engendered by the economic competition of whites and blacks. Pike tells us that "chronic unemployment and severe food shortages were the realities of life for the majority of Sevillians throughout the sixteenth century," and that "competition for jobs strained relations between freedmen and the white Sevillian laborers."

> Besides domestic slavery there existed in Seville (as well as in the rest of Andalusia) the systematic exploitation of slave labor for profit. Many Sevillians considered the ownership of slaves an excellent capital investment and a profitable source of income. Some people were totally dependent on the earnings of their slaves, for they had no other way of earning their living. The use of slaves to earn money for their owners added another class of laborers to the city's large unskilled working force....[20]
>
> Although most Sevillian Negroes were slaves, the city also contained a significant free Negro population. Enfranchisement was not a step toward economic and social betterment, however, for Negroes and mulattoes remained on the lowest rungs of the social ladder, whether slaves or freedmen. Ex-slaves continued to work in unskilled and menial jobs and to reside in the same neighborhoods as before their emancipation. A combination of discrimination and unfavorable economic conditions prevented freedmen from rising in society. The artisans feared Negro competition and jealously excluded them from the few skilled positions which the inadequate Sevillian industry afforded.[22]

The relevance of the Sevillian experience to the American experience is that it provides us with data useful for comparing and evaluating social welfare policy and practice, which was actually applied to the needs of the black population. The Sevillian experience antedates the American experience by some hundred odd years. There occurred in Seville the emergence of a plantation system based upon slave labor. It was not until later that a sizable population permitted the establishment of townships and cities. It is significant, however, that with the emergence of urban life, there appeared similar problems and similar solutions to problems, except that the concern for the social welfare of the slave was not encouraged and was less tolerated in British America than in Spanish America. This has been discussed in lucid fashion by Herbert S. Klein in his comparative study of slavery in Cuba and Virginia.[22] "It was in sixteenth century Spain," Klein informs us, "that the first abolitionists of modern history gave voice to the question of Negro rights and Negro freedom," citing as evidence the writings of the Dominican Fr. Bartolome de las Casas, Alfonso de Montufar, the Archbishop of Mexico, and Fray Tomas de Mercado, and the missionary activity of friars Pedro Claver and Alonso de Sandoval.[23]

Klein holds that in both Virginia and Cuba the slave code differed from that in Europe. In the following excerpt he differentiates clearly the structural distinctions between the slave systems in English-speaking and Spanish-speaking America, particularly those related to the legal structure and from which comparative analysis permits the drawing of significant conclusions which distinguish the policy and practice of social welfare undertakings in behalf of African slaves. While he agrees that the first Africans introduced into Virginia in 1619 appear to have been treated as indentured servants, Klein points out that

> ... with the beginning of direct heavy African importations after 1640, the colored population of Virginia began to be increasingly divided between the fourth decade being immediately reduced by the planters who bought them to servitude 'for life.' It also became increasingly difficult for the Negro servant to prove his right to freedom, and the class dwindled rapidly. For the colonial leaders early recognized that they could possess the labor of the Negro for his lifetime with little opposition from any outside power. Doing this, they were about to provide themselves with a form of labor that was the cheapest that they had been able to obtain. Compared to the short terms of the white indentured servant, an enslaved Negro might be held for life and his progeny forever, all for only one initial outlay. Negroes could more easily be controlled and policed, thrive on cheaper fare, and live in poorer dwellings. Finally, there would be no payment of freedom dues, which were a heavy and periodic financial burden on the planter.[24]

It follows from Klein's distinction between the systems of slavery in Virginia and Cuba that any actions which might be interpreted as contributions to the social welfare of blacks, whether slave or free, were contrary to the prevailing mores and were minimal in Virginia. The conclusions of Klein may perhaps be pessimistic when he states that

> The more the slave regime settled into its mold the more the Freedmen became an anomaly and an irritating element in the well-ordered view of the races held by pre-Civil War southern whites. For this mold required that every colored person be a dependent being who could not function without a white master, and that he be considered part of an inferior race predestined to slavery by a superior white who would lead him to civilization. In such a world view, the conception of an independent, self-sufficient, and seemingly coequal colored person was impossible. The masters could deny the slaves access to non-slaves, to literacy, and to mobility, and they could mold the personality of the slave in the direction of docility and subservience, ruthlessly destroying those who would not bend, but they could not so control the freedmen.

And, perhaps, he goes too far in his assertion that

> ... the only threat--economic, political, social or military--that they exercised was to the stability of the colored slave population in that they indicated an alternative life to slavery, and this alternative example the white planters justifiably feared. Like their hostility to the freer patterns of urban slavery, the planters opposed the free Negro as an example to the slave Negro. To picture him as a challenge to their own status would have been literally inconceivable.

For history written from a planter's point of view this is, perhaps, true. However, it is our intention to present evidence for another historical perspective, that blacks, slave or free, never ceased to struggle for true freedom.

COLONIAL AMERICA: SLAVE AND FREE

The first objective was to attain freedom. Since limitations were placed upon owners who wished to manumit, the possibility of purchasing one's freedom was another alternative. If this alternative was blocked, there were several others: 1) to take one's freedom by organized application of group force, (and we know this was attempted), or 2) to achieve freedom by flight. This was not only

attempted but achieved when conditions were favorable and escape was feasible, particularly in frontier areas.

In cases where freedom had been attained, some were able to realize a degree of wealth and to invest some of this in the aid of other blacks, principally by participating in some form of institution-building: churches, fraternal orders, print media. For others there was the option to emigrate to Africa or to move in the direction of the frontiers, north and west. For some, the objective of such migration would be to group together with other blacks in communities apart from whites; for others, to attempt integration in existing townships and cities. Despite apparent helplessness and dependency, there were alternatives and there were blacks who opted to exercise them. It is in their history that we find the seeds of black heritage which took root in social welfare.

A limited number of blacks, notably those arriving earliest in colonial Virginia, were incorporated into the labor force in the same manner as most European ethnics who had been lured to North America, that is, in the status of indentured servants, which included "all persons bound to labor for various periods of years as determined either by agreement or by law, both minors and adults, and Indians and Negroes as well as white."[25] Such persons were never slaves, for their release from bondage was merely conditional upon satisfactory completion of service and, as far as blacks were concerned, this was generally the case prior to the 1660's. But about that time there came a change such that, subsequently, blacks were received into the labor force as slaves, and therefore kept in the status of involuntary servitude. In other colonies many blacks had been imported and sold as slaves, after having been brought either "seasoned" from the West Indies or directly from Africa. For these blacks the attainment of free status was virtually impossible, except by manumission or, in some cases, self-purchase. Nonetheless, there was a small and evergrowing nucleus of free blacks who, if no barriers or impediments to free social intercourse had been placed in their way, might have become worthy and honored persons in their communities, enjoying the rights and privileges and discharging the duties and obligations of citizenship. But this was not to be. Over a period of time such freedom as blacks enjoyed became progressively more nominal than real, and the invidious manifestations of both overt and institutional racism took their toll.[26] It does appear to be the case, as argued by Lerone Bennett, Jr., that the so-called "race problem," was invented in order to control the labor supply of captive blacks.[28]

In the perspective of contemporary scholarship, the birth of America was a series of events which eased the social welfare problems of northwestern European nations, and especially the British, by fostering emigration to the colonies. In the process it relieved these nations of some of the responsibilities of providing services for impoverished populations, the Georgia colony being a case in point.

In colonial America it soon became evident that, as the fortunes of persons of European descent rose, those of persons of African descent declined. The few blacks who earned or inherited their freedom were hedged in with restrictive legislation, institutionalized racism, and the contemptuous behavior customarily afforded the poor in the eighteenth century. By what may be termed "the constitutional racism" of the Dred Scott Decision, those enslaved in colonial America were ultimately reduced to a depressed caste without any civil rights whatsoever.

Nevertheless, blacks, slave and free, endured physically and culturally throughout the period of slavery. The enslaved developed a culture of survival, characterized by spiritual and aesthetic creativity of high order, and particularly sustained and reinforced by persistence of black music styles. The free blacks, sometimes in collaboration with whites, but often in the face of white opposition, pioneered the development of community organization, institution building, and development of voluntary associations with social welfare objectives.

THE ANTEBELLUM PERIOD

Pointing out the trauma of the Middle Passage across the

Atlantic and the indignity of slavery, Drake discusses the cultural resources at the disposal of newly arrived Africans and their mobilization to create a new "Creole" culture plantation, which sustained the slaves during the period of their ordeal.

Document 1*

St. Clair Drake, "Afro-American and African-American Cultures," from his The Redemption of Africa and Black Religion, (Chicago: Third World Press or Atlanta: Institute of the Black World, 1970), pp. 12-18.

Once the degrading experience of the Middle Passage was over and the indignity of being cold like an animal in the slave mart was behind him, each newly imported African became a member of some New World social system on a plantation, in a mining camp, or in a town. Each individual had been torn out of a familiar cultural setting in which his obligations to his fellowmen and his reciprocal rights and privileges were well-defined, even if he happened to be a slave. In Africa, he was bound by ties of affection and reciprocity to kinsmen and friends, and, even if a slave, was adopted into a kin group where time softened, and sometimes totally wiped out, the individious distinction. He was not a "chattel." The rules of the game were set by tradition and everyone knew what the characteristics of a "virtuous" man or woman were, whatever the station in life in African society. The mold was shattered as soon as he became one of that nameless mass of individuals designated for the Middle Passage. There was no need in Africa, even under the mild forms of slavery to which a few people were subjected, for them to sing in lamentation. But it is no mystery why, out of the traumatic experience of the trans-Atlantic slave trade and subsequent enslavement, American Negroes came to sing:

> Sometimes I feel like a motherless child;
> Sometimes I feel like a motherless child--
> A l-o-n-g w-a-y-y-y from home.

When the fact has been accepted that African slaves were men and women like all other human beings, it is not difficult to imagine the depths of their fears, the agony of their anxieties, and the profundity of their great griefs and sorrows when they were forcibly expatriated. We are fortunate in having a few personal accounts to confirm our empathy, written by some exceptional human beings who survived the experience, rose above it and left the legacy of their words.

No one can question the fact that some Africans--and perhaps most--resented being torn out of the familiar matrix of existence

*Reprinted by permission of the author.

for a voyage across the sea to live an alien mode of life. The mutinies and suicides aboard ship and the refusals to take food; the cases of "tongue-swallowing" and suicide on the plantation; the sullen demeanor of many slaves on the auction block; the flight of some to the backlands and mountains to become Maroons; the high incidence of "salt water Negroes" among the leaders of revolts--all of this gives convincing testimony that the initial reaction to enslavement was one of intense hostility and sometimes of extreme personal disorganization. What happened immediately after being purchased and handed over to a "master," however, depended upon the social situation in which the individual found himself and of these there was a great variety. The extremes in North America might be illustrated by the difference between the fate of the Senegalese slave girl bought by a couple in Boston who became the first American Negro poetess, Phillis Wheatley, and some nameless black girl bought by a Southern planter to be taken to his plantations to sate the passions of himself and his cronies. In the West Indies the extremes may be measured by the fate of a house servant on the estate of a resident planter in Barbados as contrasted with that of a canecutter in Jamaica on a plantation owned by an absentee landlord and managed by a ruthless drunken "attorney."

Out of the ranks of the favored few came the spies and the informers, but out of this stratum, too, also came creative individuals like the Haitian leader, Toussaint L'Ouverture. The great mass of the slaves had to construct for themselves a society that could put some meaning into their existence other than that of being producers of commodities and of a new generation of slaves for their masters. No longer bound together as family and village units growing food for themselves, they were alienated from the productive process. Land and the cultivation of it could no longer be the critical focus of their interest and emotions as in Africa. The men of honor and prestige, similar to them in color and culture--their elders and chiefs--were now replaced by white men with different values and standards--masters and overseers--with black subalterns to carry out their will toward other black men. Most of the exiled Africans were destined to live out their lives as participants in a new type of society--a plantation system--where one man, an owner or estate manager, had absolute control over every aspect of their lives, could sell them as individuals instead of family groups, and could even take their lives for disobedience if he wished to do so. For slaves who chose compliance rather than defiance--and these understandably were in the majority--the rational reaction was to do the job assigned (though not necessarily well) in return for food and shelter, and to avoid punishment, as well as to size up the situation to see what scanty special awards were available to those who played the game astutely, and to count the costs to be payed for bucking the system. In Africa, such calculations of one's personal welfare were always made with reference to the effect upon kinsmen and in consultation with them. For newly landed slaves these bonds had been ripped asunder. It was each for himself. The cultures of Africa provided no cues for coping with slave-traders and newly acquired "masters."

Men, however, cannot live as completely atomized individuals. Where individuals from the same tribe were placed together in New World work situations, the "tribe," the ethnic group, provided one natural primordial base for binding men together--even though they were not kinsmen. Ethnic solidarity and a sense of ethnic identity persisted wherever it was not deliberately disrupted by the masters or was made impossible by the accident of extreme heterogeneity within a given group of slaves. But, from the beginning, a new bond of solidarity is also apparent on the plantations, a supratribal bond, the tie between "shipmates," the solidarity of those who defined themselves as "We who went through the ordeal of the Middle Passage together." Dyadic relations were quickly established, too, between individuals of the same sex who became friends, and between men and women who pleased each other (though there were seldom enough women to allow all men to find a mate during the first generation), or when new increments of slaves were thrown into a plantation society. Out of the relations between mothers and the children born to them matrifocal family clusters took root, but where possible men and women formed the types of household units in which they had been reared in Africa.

On every plantation a "Creole" culture emerged--a blending of African and European cultural elements with modifications and reinterpretations of material from both sources. Once such a local culture had come into being, any new Africans who were imported were inducted into that culture and did not face the same difficult adjustments as the original group. The extent to which they modified the Creole culture depended upon the size of the new group introduced as well as upon the type of African culture they brought, the roles they were assigned by the master, and the types of personalities among them. In Haiti and Jamaica there was a clear tendency for elements from a variety of African cultures to fuse and form a subculture with a system of religion and magic that drew heavily from Dahomey in the case of Jamaica. The configurations were less highly integrated in other Caribbean areas but African "cultural survivals" everywhere provided fixed points of reference for social relations and for philosophical and theological orientation. Occasionally, a common plantation culture welded the slaves together for united action, but always, for the ordinary individual, it provided a scheme of living that put order and meaning into life, allowed people to maintain a sense of worth despite their subordination, and guaranteed them a measure of "enjoyment" if not contentment.

But all individuals in the plantation subculture were not "ordinary" individuals. Some social scientists--notably Elkins, in his book, Slavery--have attempted to prove that slavery generated a personality type in the American South, childlike, obsequious, compliant and "devious"--the "Sambo" type and that most of the slaves were "Sambos." Orlando Patterson feels that an equivalent type can be defined for Jamaica, the "Quarshie." (The actual statistical incidence of the type has not been ascertained.) Both point out, however, that under Portugese and Spanish slave systems this type was probably not in the majority. But whatever type formed the majority in a plantation population, there is abundant evidence to indicate that there were always other social types present, too, artisans who were assigned responsibility and elicited respect from both masters and slaves; those endowed with great intelligence and wisdom to whom lesser men turned for counsel and advice; "bad niggers" as well as "Uncle Toms." Such people expressed, in their total personality, wishes and moods not obvious on the surface that existed as minor aspects of every slave's personality. Their presence on the plantation made them agents of social change.

Of all the social types produced in these New World social systems none were more crucial in the process of social change than the house servants. Exposed to a way of life totally different from that of the slave quarters, thrown into a nexus of interpersonal relations that involved intimacy and affection, they developed as a group apart, marginal and ambivalent in their attitudes toward their cruder fellows and jealously guarding their own privileges. Out of the relations between masters and black women in this stratum, groups of mulattoes came into being who prized their lighter skin color as the symbol of their higher status. On some plantations, mulattoes born from white men's matings with black women of the field did not achieve a privileged status, but exerted an unsettling influence due to their marginal position. In the French West Indies, a "free colored" group formed a distinct social stratum with well-defined privileges not accorded to the blacks. All house servants and free colored persons were bound to the white segment of plantation society by similarity of culture and outlook, and sometimes by kinship. They were both admired and hated by "field Negroes," and were, themselves, often divided in mind and spirit by conflicting loyalties.

But, whatever the fate of an African was to be after he had become a part of plantation society, in the initial stages of enslavement all shared a common experience. At home in Africa, Kofi not only had a name that was of symbolic significance to him, but also had an unambiguous group identity, and was respected as an individual. To make a slave of Kofi he had first to be transformed from a tribesman into a "worthless nigger," a "heathen black." The slave factories and the baracoons on the coast of Africa and the indignities of the Middle Passage were calculated to begin the process. Then the "black" had to be reduced almost to the level of an animal--eyed and poked and felt and bid for in the New World slave marts. The aim was not really to dehumanize him, however, but only to degrade him, to change him from one kind of human being into another, from an autonomous individual rooted in a culture into a tractable, pliant, human being always responsive to the command of a master or a mistress. The processes of capture and sale were what anthropologists call rites of separation, the first stages in an initiation process. There were acts designed to "kill" the old man, a death preparatory to rebirth.

The "seasoning" process was the first step in a rite of transition, in the making of a new man out of Kofi, often a man with a new scoffing name like Caesar, Prince or Pompey, a name without the rich and sometimes mystical meaning of the African name. Planters as well as visitors to plantations have left us numerous accounts of the "breaking-in" or "seasoning" process, but we have a few accounts of it by ex-slaves who were subject to it or witnessed it. The slaves already there, after the plantation had been organized, the bearers of the Creole culture, were allotted a role in the seasoning process. This was never precisely what the masters intended it to be, however, for while the members of the plantation community taught the newcomer how to be a good slave, how to fit in, they also taught him how to maintain his humanity if not always his dignity, and the tricks of survival and of working against the system by subtle sabotage and malingering, about which a great deal of evidence has been compiled.

Occasionally, too, the confrontation between Creoles and "salt water Negroes" became a dialogue about how men should react to enslavement, for, in some cases, the baracoons and the Middle Passage and the auction block had not been traumatic and psychologically devastating enough to break Kofi, to make him accept the status of "worthless nigger" or chattel. Thus, the smooth working of the "seasoning" process was sometimes disturbed by the flight of Creoles to the hills and backlands under Kofi's leadership or participation in rebellions led by him. All of this created folk heroes whose names and exploits were handed down from one generation of plantation dwellers to another and these spread throughout the New World as slaves were sold from plantation to plantation, Caribbean island to Caribbean island, and from the West Indies into North America. In addition to Ananse the Spider, Brer Rabbit and those other clever animals who outwitted the strong ones, the names of clever people became a part of the black subculture of the New World. We can be sure that even Sambos and Quarshies had a sneaking admiration for them. Thus, while the folk culture operated to stabilize the plantation system it also carried within itself elements to reinforce group rebellion in times of crisis.

In addition to a common African-American culture that took form in the Caribbean and South America among the mass of the slaves, and an Afro-American culture in North America, where pressures for Europeanization were stronger, a sense of black consciousness emerged throughout the world of Diaspora. In Africa, men continued to think of themselves primarily as members of specific tribes. Here and there in the New World, ethnic identification remained, but over-arching and over-riding the tribal focus of identity was an imposed identity. White men defined all Africans as "blacks," "les noirs." They might try to divide and rule by favoring one tribe against another on a specific plantation; they might have their stereotypes about which tribes were brave or pusillanimous or produced exciting and seductive women, but in their buying and their selling of men, their suppression of rebellion, and their verbalizations when expressing anger, all were simply "blacks." The slaves' counter-image of themselves was that they were Africans. The people of the Diaspora eventually defined Africa as their "home," not some specific local spot from which they came or where their tribe or that of their ancestors lived, but Africa. The word, Guinea, in some places, came to symbolize the continent. When a man died his spirit went "home"--to "Guinea" or to Africa--the land of black men.

It was inevitable that, given the shifting of slaves from island to island throughout the Caribbean and from the Caribbean to North America, and vice versa, an awareness of their wide distribution in the Diaspora would emerge, and that as leaders mobilized black consciousness in a bid for black power in local situations through risings and the formation of Maroon communities, sentiments of Pan-Negroism would emerge--the solidarity of all Africans, of all black men. Two goals began to take shape as to what Black Power should be used for: to return "home," to Africa; and to wrest the land where they toiled from the men who kept them in subjection--an extension of the Maroon pattern into black nationalism. Toussaint, Dessalines and Christophe, by 1804 had made the first conquest of New World soil by black men in the form of a nation-state.

The earliest Africans in Virginia were sold into indentured servitude and, after serving the contracted period, became free men, in some instances later becoming slaveholders themselves. From this group, by natural increase and manumission, emerged the class of free Negroes. Eventually, these blacks, in urban and rural communities, pioneered in many aspects of social welfare, community organization, institution-building, and the formation of voluntary associations for social welfare purposes.

Document 2*

John H. Russell, "Origin of the Free Negro Class," excerpt from Chapter II of his The Free Negro in Virginia, (New York: Dover Publications, 1969, pp. 39-41; originally published by the Johns Hopkins Press, Baltimore, 1913).

The upper limit of the period in which it was possible for negroes to come to Virginia as servants and to acquire freedom after a limited term is the year 1682. A law of 1670 was intended to enslave all negroes brought in after its enactment, but in practice it permitted a few to escape. In 1678 two men of African blood were sold for terms of seven years by inhabitants of Boston to residents of Virginia. Under the provisions of the law of 1670 "all servants not being Christians imported into this colony by shipping" were to be slaves for their lives, but such servants as came by land were to "serve, if boys and girls until thirty years of age, if

*Reprinted by permission of the publisher.

men or women, twelve years and no longer." After this act had been in force twelve years, the preamble of a new act asserted that "many negroes, Moors, mulattoes and others" born in a heathen country and of heathen parents had, before coming to Virginia, been converted to the Christian faith, and that such persons, when sold in Virginia, had to be sold as servants for a limited term. Hence an act was passed repealing the law of 1670 and making slaves of all persons of non-Christian nationalities thereafter coming to the colony, whether they came by sea or land and whether or not they had been converted to Christianity after capture.

After the enactment of this law the free negro population in Virginia received from imported negroes no more recruits of which we have any record until after the non-importation act of 1778. By 1662 other means of growth had been opened up to this class. For the next two hundred years the free colored population was increased by five classes of colored persons springing from the population already existing. The classes may be enumerated as follows:

(1) Children born of free colored parents. The rule of partus sequitur ventrem was applied consistently from 1662 to 1865, and natural increase or procreation was throughout this period an important factor in the growth of the free negro population.
(2) Mulatto children born of free colored mothers.
(3) Mulatto children born of white servant or free women.

The most numerous class of the mulattoes was of slavewomen parentage, but such children were slaves. Both classes of free mulattoes were the product of illegitimacy, since the laws prohibited the intermarriage of whites and negroes, bond or free. Under the provisions of the law of 1691 free mulatto bastards were bound by the church wardens as apprentices to responsible white persons for a term ending upon their attaining the age of thirty years. In the revision of this act in 1705 one year was added to the period of apprenticeship. By 1774 this long term apprenticeship had come to be regarded as bearing "an unreasonable severity toward such children," and it was shortened to twenty-one years for males and eighteen years for females. After the disestablishment of the Anglican church in 1785 this class of persons were bound out by the overseers of the poor as they had been previously by the church wardens.

(4) Children of free negro and Indian mixed parentage. If such children had no visible means of support, they were bound out as apprentices, just as were free mulatto children. The offspring of all colored apprentices born during the apprenticeship became, by mere force of the law, apprentices to the masters of their mothers on terms similar to those under which the mothers were bound. All colored apprentices were counted with the free colored population even during their apprenticeship.
(5) Manumitted slaves. Manumission was the most important of all the methods by which the free colored population was increased in numbers. In an act of 1670 occurred the words "negroes manumitted and otherwise free,"....

Manifestations of overt racism appeared early in colonial history, for example in the 1630's in Virginia. Over time and through devious instrumentalities, there developed an institutionalized racism which placed barriers, both customary and legal, to the possibility of equal opportunity and achievement. Indentured servants who were black were often reduced to slavery, and free Negroes were denied the fruits of freedom by denial of the franchise, restrictions on mobility, and by other means. And in the Constitution of the United States discriminatory practices against blacks were so masked and disguised that we may speak of the disabilities of "constitutional racism" in the antebellum period.

Document 3*

Loren Miller, "Slavery in the Constitution of the United States," an excerpt from Chapter I of his The Petitioners, The Story of the Supreme Court of the United States and the Negro, (New York: Pantheon Books, 1966), pp. 23-25.

The astute Founding Fathers were well aware of the contradictions implicit in recognition of slavery in the Constitution side by side with the guarantees of individual rights. That they glossed over these contradictions does not convict them of hypocrisy. The belief in the inferiority of Negroes was widespread and deeply rooted. Even Jefferson vacillated; giving it support and sanction more often than not. The Founding Fathers could not be sure that Negroes were capable of exercising the rights of, or shouldering the responsibilities of, citizenship. Time would tell. Time, it was also hoped, would bring the demise of slavery and acquit Negroes of its disabilities, and there was also vague hope that as slaves became free men, they would become persons in reality as well as in constitutional fiction. But slavery did not die, and the perceptive Jefferson ultimately cried out that it was the Rock on which the Union would break. That lay in the future in 1787.

There were fitful denunciations of the slavery compromises when the Constitution was submitted to the people, but objections never assumed serious proportions. The proud young nation embarked on its voyage with a Constitution that (1) ordered the counting of three fifths of all slaves in the apportionment of congressmen, (2) forbade congressional interference with the foreign slave trade until 1808, (3) prohibited Congress from taking slavery out of existence, and (4) provided that a slave who escaped to a free state should be returned to his master. Cutting deeper than these obvious accommodations to political realities was the fact that the Constitution implicitly recognized the existence of slavery in the several states and the correlative right of slave states to its exclusive control and regulation within their borders.

Important questions were left unanswered. The Constitution specified that a slave escaping to a free state should be "delivered up on Claim of the Party" by whom he was held in slavery, but it did not specify the duty, or lack of it, of the asylum state in the case where a fugitive was demanded. Similarly, the Constitution gave Congress the power to regulate foreign and interstate commerce, but it was silent on the question of whether or not the states could control interstate commerce in slaves, although such commerce was extensive at the time the Constitution was framed and adopted. Article IV, Section 2, provided that, "The Citizens of each State shall be entitled to all Privileges and Immunities of Citizens in the several States," but there was no definition of citizenship in the Constitution and no specific language to indicate whether free Negroes were, or were not, citizens vested with these priceless privileges and immunities in the states of their residence. Obviously, slaves were not citizens of a free republic, but if free Negroes had that status in one state, did they have national citizenship? Could they exercise their state citizenship rights in another state? Or could the slave states exclude free Negroes altogether? The Constitution did not say. Nor did the Constitution vest Congress with specific power to enact fugitive slave legislation, control the flow of slave property in interstate commerce, determine the citizenship status of free Negroes, or define their rights in slave states. It could have been predicted that a weak central government would leave such matters to state comity, while a strong, or stronger, central government would insist on its own solution.

There was an unanswered question of another hue. Congress was given power to "make all needful Rules and Regulations respecting" the territory belonging to the United States, but that provision was not as complete as it seemed. The issue would arise as to whether it applied only to territory then owned by the United States or to territory that the nation might acquire in the future. Indeed, there was no constitutional warrant for acquiring new territory. When new territory was acquired, despite constitutional silence, by the Louisiana Purchase and the Mexican War, the question arose as to the extent of congressional control over slavery in that new territory. Slaveholders soon asserted a right to take their slaves into new territory, with the argument that slaves were property and that the Constitution protected the right of every citizen to hold property in federal territories and empowered them to invoke constitutional protection against impairment of property rights. Opponents of slavery answered that congressional protection or recognition of slavery in such territories amounted to establishment of slavery where it did not exist, and they argued that neither Congress nor any other agency of the federal government had any such power. New territory meant new states; another ambiguity was added. Could the citizens of a new territory organize for statehood and apply for admission to the Union as a slave state, and would the admission of a new state as a slave state amount to federal establishment of slavery?

The Constitution did not resign resolution of these unanswered questions to the Supreme Court in so many words. Nor did it specifically take them away from Congress. What the Constitution did do was to provide that it should be the Supreme Law of the Land and binding on all state judges, that the judicial power of the United States should be vested in a Supreme Court and such inferior courts as Congress might establish, and that the judicial power should extend to all cases arising under the Constitution, laws, and treaties of the United States. The exact meaning of that provision became a matter of debate, but regardless of what it meant when the Framers wrote it, the Court gradually expanded it to mean that the judiciary was clothed with exclusive power to interpret the Constitution and, ultimately, to invalidate congressional enactments found to be in conflict with the notions of the meaning of the Constitution.

Whether slavery was debated in Congress or in the courts, the slaveholding states adopted as their central theme the proposition that the Constitution left the whole matter to the states. That constant harping on the rights of states in respect to slavery nourished the growth of the states rights doctrine which, of course, had roots as well. In its final form, the state's rights doctrine asserted that the states had entire control over slavery within their own borders; that interstate commerce in slaves was beyond the control of Congress; that free Negroes held no national citizenship and hence were not beneficiaries of the privileges-and-immunities clause; that slaveholders had a right to take their property into all federal territories, and that residents of territories applying for statehood had a right to secure admission of new states as slave states.

In short, this doctrine resolved every constitutional ambiguity in favor of slavery and the slave states....

Free blacks were concerned with the plight of the slaves. In this next document Benjamin Banneker, a free black, petitions, in fact challenges, Thomas Jefferson to apply to blacks the principles of the Declaration of Independence.

Document 4

Benjamin Banneker, "To Thomas Jefferson," Letter written August 19, 1791, Baltimore County, Maryland.

I am fully sensible of that freedom, which I take with you in the present occasion; a liberty which seemed to me scarcely allowable, when I reflected on that distinguished and dignified station in which you stand, and the almost general prejudice and prepossession, which is so prevalent in the world against those of my complexion.

I suppose it is a truth too well attested to you, to need a

proof here, that we are a race of beings, who have long labored under the abuse and censure of the world; that we have long been looked upon with an eye of contempt; and that we have long been considered rather as brutish than human, and scarcely capable of mental endowments.

Sir, I hope I may safely admit, in consequence of that report which hath reached me, that you are a man less inflexible in sentiments of this nature than many others; that you are measurably friendly, and well disposed towards us; and that you are willing and ready to lend your aid and assistance to our relief, from those many distresses, and numerous calamities, to which we are reduced.

Now Sir, if this is founded in truth, I apprehend you will embrace every opportunity, to eradicate that train of absurd and false ideas and opinions, which so generally prevails with respect to us; and that your sentiments are concurrent with mine, which are, that one universal Father hath given being to us all; and that he hath not only made us all of one flesh, but that he hath also, without partiality, afforded us all the same sensations and endowed us all with the same faculties; and that however variable we may be in society or religion, however diversified in situation or color, we are all in the same family and stand in the same relation to him.

Sir, if these are sentiments of which you are fully persuaded, I hope you cannot but acknowledge, that it is the indispensable duty of those, who maintain for themselves the rights of human nature, and who possess the obligations of Christianity, to extend their power and influence to the relief of every part of the human race, from whatever burden or oppression they may unjustly labor under; and this, I apprehend, a full conviction of the truth and obligation of these principles should lead all to.

Sir, I have long been convinced, that if your love for yourselves, and for those inestimable laws, which preserved to you the rights of human nature, was founded on sincerity, you could not but be solicitous, that every individual, of whatever rank or distinction, might with you equally enjoy the blessings thereof; neither could you rest satisfied short of the most active effusion of your exertions, in order to the promotion from any state of degradation, to which the unjustifiable cruelty and barbarism of men may have reduced them.

Sir, I freely and cheerfully acknowledge, that I am of the African race, and in that color which is natural to them of the deepest dye; and it is under a sense of the most profound gratitude to the Supreme Ruler of the Universe, that I now confess to you, that I am not under that state of tyrannical thraldom, and inhuman captivity, to which too many of my brethren are doomed, but I have abundantly tasted the fruition of those blessings, which proceed from that free and unequalled liberty with which you are favored; and which, I hope, you will willingly allow you have mercifully received, from the immediate hand of that Being, from whom proceedeth every good and perfect Gift.

Sir, suffer me to recall to your mind that time, in which the arms and tyranny of the British crown were exerted, with every powerful effort, in order to reduce you to a state of servitude: look back, I entreat you, on the variety of dangers to which you were exposed; reflect on that time, in which every human aid appeared unavailable, and in which even hope and fortitude wore the aspect of inability to the conflict, and you cannot but be led to a serious and grateful sense of your miraculous and providential preservation; you cannot but acknowledge, that the present freedom and tranquility which you enjoy you have mercifully received, and that it is the peculiar blessing of Heaven.

This, Sir, was a time when you clearly saw into the injustice of a state of slavery, and in which you had just apprehensions of the horror of its condition. It was now that your abhorrence thereof was so excited, that you publicly held forth this true and invaluable doctrine, which is worthy to be recorded and remembered in all succeeding ages: 'We hold these truths to be self-evident, that all men are created equal; that they are endowed by their Creator with certain unalienable rights, and that among these are, life, liberty, and the pursuit of happiness.'

Here was a time, in which your tender feelings for yourselves had engaged you thus to declare, you were then impressed with proper ideas of the great violation of liberty, and the free possession of those blessings, to which you were entitled by nature; but, Sir, how pitiable is it to reflect, that although you were so fully convinced of the benevolence of the Father of Mankind, and of his equal and impartial distribution of these rights and privileges, which he hath conferred upon them, that you should at the same time counteract his mercies, in detaining by fraud and violence so numerous a part of my brethren, under groaning captivity, and cruel oppression, that you should at the same time be found guilty of that most criminal act, which you professedly detested in others, with respect to yourselves.

I suppose that your knowledge of the situation of my brethren, is too extensive to need a recital here; neither shall I presume to prescribe methods by which they may be relieved, otherwise than by recommending to you and all others, to wean yourselves from those narrow prejudices which you have imbibed with respect to them, and as Job proposed to his friends, 'put your soul in their souls' stead'; thus shall your hearts be enlarged with kindness and benevolence towards them; and thus shall you need neither the direction of myself or others, in what manner to proceed herein.

Both Indian and black slaves escaped to Florida and freedom under the Spanish crown. Later, blacks assumed leadership among the Seminoles, contributing to the maintenance of the Seminole way of life, participating in the wars waged by the United States, and in the removal of the Seminoles to Arkansas and Oklahoma. This excerpt is concerned with activity on the original frontier.

Document 5*

Laurence Foster, "The Seminole Wars and the Removal West," excerpt of Chapter II of his Negro-Indian Relationships in the Southeast, (Philadelphia, 1935), pp. 19-20.

In the early colonial days, South Carolina claimed a vast extent of territory embracing most of Florida. The adjudication of this claim, which the Spanish Crown denied, involved the colonists in many heated disputes. There were other questions involved besides more land. Chief among them was the question of slavery. The Carolina colonists held many slaves, both Negroes and Indians. Indian slavery was common in the South in those days, but it reached its height in South Carolina. In 1708, when the total population of South Carolina was 9,580, there were 2,900 Negro slaves and 1,400 Indian slaves. Charleston, the chief city maintained markets in which both types of slaves were sold. At length, the Indians began to escape to Florida where under the Spanish crown they could be freed. The Negroes soon followed their example. The attitude of the Spanish crown toward slavery vexed the colonists. Many efforts were made on the part of the colonists to have the crown return the exiles, but all were unsuccessful.

At length, a boundary line was established between South Carolina and Florida. The territory of what is now Georgia was then inhabited by the Creeks. This was generally interpreted as free territory. In a few years this territory became known as the colony of Georgia and was later established as the free state of Georgia and thereupon it prohibited slavery.

Immediately the Carolinians attempted to have Georgia declare itself a slave state. After many efforts and much pressure, they succeeded. It was said that slavery helped to Christianize the heathen, and many leaders, including James Habersham, consented to it partly on these grounds. In the meantime, the Negroes and Indians continued to escape into Florida where they could be free, and where they were protected by the Spanish Crown.

In 1736, the numbers were sufficiently large to be well formed into companies which established many settlements. Among the Negro settlements were those known as the Mulatto Girl, King Hejah, and the Big Hammock settlements. In 1738 the colonial government of South Carolina demanded from the Spanish Crown a return of the runaway slaves. The demand was rejected, and the runaway slaves remained in Florida. The Negro runaways were now free, and began to cultivate the lands given to them by the Spanish Crown. "They manifested much judgment in the selection of their land for cultivation,--locating their own principal settlements on the rich

*Reprinted by permission.

bottoms lying along the Appalachicola and the Sewanee Rivers. Here they opened plantations and many of them became wealthy in flocks and herds." They also cultivated the friendship of their neighbors, the Indians. It is believed that these slaves taught the Indians how to improve their farming and how to select that part of the land which was best adapted to agriculture. They also advised them in their councils. It is safe to say that the slaves served as advisors to the Indians in most of their activities.

Free Negroes from North Carolina emigrated to Indiana and founded an all-black settlement, Lost Creek. Opposed to colonization in Liberia by the American Colonization Society and harassed by whites, free Negroes often sought refuge in the establishment of all-black communities.

Document 6*

John W. Lyda, Lost Creek Settlement, Vigo County, Indiana, MS. papers of Claude Barnett.

Shortly before 1827 Bowen Roberts was sent by his people in North Carolina to seek a haven from the persecution which free Negroes were then suffering there. He passed through what is now Lost Creek Township, Vigo County, Indiana, and was very favorably impressed thereby. On his return home he said to the people, "Fat hogs are roaming the forest with knives and forks in their backs." This account so impressed those who heard it that they decided to migrate to Lost Creek Township to make their future homes. Those who owned ox-carts loaded them with their modest belongings while the many who were not so fortunate decided to make the journey on foot. Those composing the caravan were the Andersons, Archers, Chavises, Roberts, Stewarts, and Trevens. George Anderson, Sr., and his sons with the exception of Jordan, stopped briefly in Tennessee. Jordan continued the journey to Lost Creek and was its first settler.

The other families composing the caravan stopped in Orange County, Indiana, where they remained three years before coming to Lost Creek. Moses Archer and Richard Roberts came to the Lost Creek Settlement during the early years of its history. They were soon followed by Jerry Anderson, Kinchin Roberts, and Dixson Stewart.

According to the records of Vigo County, Jeremiah Anderson, Hezekiah, Richard and Kinchin Roberts all purchased land in Lost Creek Township from the Federal Government between 1832 and 1835.

These pioneers after having purchased land set to work at

*Reprinted by permission.

once to build cabins of logs for dwellings and other uses, to clear the land for the cultivation of crops, to fight wild animals, and to contend with diseases. They had to suffer the privations common to all pioneers at that time and in addition to endure many legal and economic disabilities on account of their race.

That these early settlers were very much interested in higher and better things in life is proven by the fact that they held a meeting soon after their arrival to establish a school for the education of their children. They were not admitted to the public school at that time and not until 1869. The land on which the first schoolhouse was built was purchased from Kinchin and Nancy Roberts, his wife. It was located at the intersection of Stop 10 and Fort Harrison roads and was built of logs like practically all other private and public buildings at the time. It was supported by tuition paid by parents of the children who attended. Abel Anderson who had received the rudiments of an elementary education in North Carolina, his old home, was the first teacher. The religious life was not neglected. Reverend Paul Quinn of the A. M. E. Church organized a church of that denomination in 1840, and Reverend L. Anderson a church of the Baptist faith two years later. The land on which the A. M. E. church was located was donated by Kinchin Roberts and his wife, Nancy, and that on which the Baptist church was built by Jeremiah Anderson, who also donated the land on which School No. 3 was built. School No. 8 in Otter Creek Township, north of Lost Creek township; was donated by William Chandlier.

The first frame house and the first cook stove seen in the community were the property of William Chandlier. These so awakened the curiosity of the early settlers that they traveled for miles around to see them.

In this excerpt is told the story of the founding of a school for free blacks by Anthony Benezet in Philadelphia, a distinguished Quaker who was representative of the best interests of white philanthropy. James Foster, father of Charlotte Foster, attended this school.

Document 7

Wilson Armistead, Anthony Benezet, from the original memoir, revised with additions by Wilson Armistead, (London: A. W. Bennett, Bishopsgate Street, 1859; Philadelphia: Lippincott and Co., 1859).

White and Black Philanthropy

With his enlightened and unbounded philanthropy, it was to be expected that the degraded and suffering condition of the negroes would occupy a large share of Benezet's notice and sympathy. About the year 1750, it was observed that his feelings were deeply affected with the iniquity of the slave trade, the unlawfulness of carrying negroes into captivity, and the cruelties exercised by those who purchased and employed them. The impulses of duty then, for the first time, brought him from the retirement of private life before the world, to lift up his voice in behalf of an oppressed and wretched portion of his fellow-beings. Perhaps no man in any age, or in any country, could have been better adapted to the great office of an advocate for the violated rights of a people, than was Anthony Benezet, by his peculiar capacity for being profoundly sensible of their wrongs. And when the astonishing effects of his labours in this work of mercy are reviewed, no doubt can be entertained, that his commission to "plead the cause of the oppressed," proceeded from on High.

Among the earliest proofs of his compassion toward the African race, were the exertions he employed for the promotion of their welfare. In Philadelphia, the number of these objects of his regard was considerable, and he adopted the most rational course that could have been devised for their benefit, the establishment of an evening school, which he taught gratuitously himself. And when a more enlarged plan of this nature was determined upon, by his brethren in religious professions, he contributed liberally towards it from his own limited income, and was indefatigable in soliciting donations from his opulent fellow-members, for the erection of a school for the instruction of black people.

Much of the two last years of Benezet's life were devoted to a personal attendance on this school, being earnestly desirous that they who came to it might be better qualified for the enjoyment of that freedom to which great numbers of them had thus been restored. To this he sacrificed not only the superior endowments of his former school, but his bodily ease also, for the weakness of his constitution demanded more indulgence. By his last will he directed, that after the decease of his widow, his whole little fortune (the savings of the industry of fifty years) should, except a very few legacies, be applied to the support of it....

"I can," said Benezet, "with truth and sincerity declare, that I have found amongst the negroes as great variety of talents, as among a like number of whites; and I am bold to assert, that the notion entertained by some, that the blacks are inferior in their capacities, is a vulgar prejudice, founded on the pride or ignorance of their lordly masters; who have kept their slaves at such a distance as to be unable to form a right judgment of them."

This brief excerpt is a statement of the aims of the Convention for the Improvement of the Free People of Colour of the United States. It clearly details and illustrates the concern for building viable agencies of social welfare on the initiative of blacks themselves.

Document 8

Minutes of the Conference of the Third Annual Convention for the Improvement of the Free People of Colour of the United States.... Philadelphia, June 3-13, 1833. New York, 1933, p. 40.

This Society will aim to accomplish the following objects. To visit every family in the Ward, and make a register of every coloured person in it--their name, sex, age, occupation, if they read, write and cipher,--to induce them, old and young and of both sexes, to become members of this society, and make quarterly payments according to their ability;--to get the children out to infant, Sabbath and week schools, and induce the adults also to attend school and church on the Sabbath,--to encourage the females to form Dorcas Societies to help clothe poor children of colour if they will attend school, the clothes to be loaned, and to be taken away from them if they neglect their schools; and to impress on their parents the importance of having the children punctual and regular in their attendance at school,--to establish circulating libraries formed in each ward for the use of people of colour on very moderate pay,--to establish mental feasts, and also lyceums for speaking and for lectures on the sciences, and to form moral societies,--to seek out young men of talents, and good moral character, that they may be assisted to obtain a liberal education,--to report to the Board all mechanics who are skilful and capable of conducting their trades,--to procure places at trades and with respectable farmers for lads of good moral character--giving a preference to those who have learned to read, write, and cipher,--and in every other way to endeavor to promote the happiness of the people of colour, by encouraging them to improve their minds, and to abstain from every vicious and demoralizing practice.

In the following extract, King E. Davis has compiled data relating to fund-raising for black causes by both blacks and whites in the antebellum period. While neither complete nor exhaustive (the philanthropy of the Quakers and of the abolitionists is omitted), it reveals how free blacks created voluntary associations to provide for special social welfare objectives.

Document 9* [see chart, page 32]

King E. Davis. "Black Fund-Raising:..." (unpublished Ph.D. dissertation, Brandeis University, 1972). Appendix I: "Chronological Development of Independent Black Fund-Raising Organizations (1775-1855)," pp. 335-338.

Individual philanthropy was practiced by blacks such as Hannah Gray, who bequeathed her home for aged black women; and Bias and Margaret Stanley, who left their accumulated savings for the education of black youth.

*Reprinted by permission of the author.

Chronological Development of
Black Fund-Raising Organizations (1775-1855)

Year	Methods	Organization	Race of Givers	City	Recipient	Purpose
1775	Dues, fees	Masons	Blacks	Boston	Blacks	Protection, insurance, economic uplift
1787	Dues, fees, Dinners	Free African Society	Blacks	Philadelphia	Blacks and Whites	Health, welfare aid migrants, sickness
1790	Membership, dinners	Brown Fellowship	Blacks	Charleston	Black widows, children	Insurance, relief burial, debts
1798	Dues, Membership	Sons of Africa Society	Blacks	Boston	Blacks, widows	Relief, burial, insurance
1800	Weekly dues, initiation	Free Men of Color	Blacks	Petersburg	Wives, children	Emergency economic support, relief
1810	Initiation fees, dues	Free School, Negroes	Blacks	Charleston	Black children	Education
1824	Membership, Contributions	Knights Liberty	Blacks	Charleston	Slaves	Emancipation, escape underground railroad
1835	Dues, fees, membership	Benevolent Society	Blacks	Philadelphia	Black families	Burial, investment, emergency aid
1840	Bequests, fees	Ecole des Orphans	Blacks	New Orleans	Black children	Education
1843	Membership fees	Order of Odd Fellows	Blacks	Boston	Black families	Social and economic uplift
1848	Contributions	American Missionary	Whites	Philadelphia	Blacks, Freedmen	Distribution of the Bible, education
1854	Contributions	Presbyterian Church	Whites	Philadelphia	Blacks	Education, building of Lincoln University
1855	Contributions, Tithes	Church	Whites	Wilberforce	Blacks	Development of Wilberforce University

Document 10*

Robert Austin Warner, New Haven Negroes, A Social History, (New Haven: Yale University Press, The Institute for Human Relations, 1940), pp. 80, 97.

Some time before 1820 Simeon Jocelyn, white middle class member of the Center Congregational Church, of which the Reverend Nathaniel Taylor was the pastor, was moved by Christian benevolence to assist the Negroes. He held regular Sunday services with some of them, in spite of white opposition, and in 1824, having obtained a meeting house on Temple Street, his group formed the "African Ecclesiastical Society." Of the officers, the clerk was Prince Duplex, the grandfather-to-be of the first Negro physician in New Haven, Dr. Creed; and the treasurer was Bias Stanley, to whom many Negro youths were to be indebted for aid in their education ...." (p. 80)

One thing, however, the abolitionists had achieved. Psychological conditions for the New Haven Negroes had been bettered, and the improvement was reflected in the lives of men and women. Hannah Gray, who found time from her hard daily labor to collect money for the support of a Negro missionary worker among the fugitives in Canada, at her death left her house to be used as a home for indigent, aged colored females. Bias and Margaret Stanley, by a lifetime of devotion to Connecticut standards of frugality and industry, saved almost $10,000 which, as their tombstone announced, "they gave to Christ for the education of youth and the support of his church among their people...." (p. 97)

Delilah Beasley relates the fascinating story of Mammy Pleasants, who financed the activities of John Brown, prior to her emigration to California.

Document 11†

Delilah L. Beasley, "Mammy Pleasants," an excerpt from her The Negro Trail Blazers of California, (Los Angeles, 1919, pp. 95-97; reprinted by Greenwood Press, a division of Williamhouse-Regency, Inc.).

While speaking of slavery in California, and the numerous laws to prevent Free Negroes from coming to or residing in the State, and the number of colored people who left the State and went to live in Canada, and afterward returned to fight it out in California, there was one Negro woman who left the State also to go to Canada. Any of the pioneer colored people, when asked concerning her, immediately begin to tell all sorts of queer stories about her, and usually end by saying: "She always wore a poke bonnet and plaid

*Reprinted by permission of the publisher.
†Reprinted by permission of the publisher.

shawl," and "she was very black, with thin lips," Then sometimes they will also add: "She handled more money during pioneer days in California than any other colored person."

It will not interest the average colored person of today, in California, whether this strange woman was a witch or a great financier, but the following story concerning her activities with the hero, John Brown, of Harper's Ferry, will interest more than one. While the general public may have criticized her life, as they thought they knew it, nevertheless, if the story which I am relating be true, she was in disguise a modern "Queen Esther."

This story was given to the writer by a Mr. William Stephens, of Oakland, California (now at Del Monte), who said: "While on the private car of Mr. Crocker, and while the car was at one time in the railroad yards at Point Levy, Quebec, Canada, I was engaged in conversation with the foreman of the yards, who, after learning that we were from San Francisco, asked if I had ever seen 'Mammy Pleasants', I said I had, and he then told me that his father had been a Canadian Labor Commissioner before the Civil War, and also had been connected with the Underground Railroad (a society organized to assist Negro slaves to Canada). When the slaves reached Canada, his father, as Labor Commissioner, had seen to their securing work, that they might not become public charges."

This foreman of the railroad yards further told Mr. Stephens that his father had seen "Mammy Pleasants" give John Brown a large sum of money, and that this money was used by John Brown in financing his raid on Harper's Ferry. Mr. Stephens said that he had never heard anyone in California say that "Mammy Pleasants" had been to Canada. But a number of years afterward, at the death of "Mammy Pleasants", there appeared in the San Francisco Chronicle and Call a wonderful biography of the woman which Mr. Stephens saved, and from which the writer was permitted to make the following copy:

(San Francisco Call, January 4, 1904)

> Her epitaph is written; the tombstone of 'Mammy Pleasants' will express her loyalty to the hero of Harper's Ferry. Tribute to John Brown, remains of woman who gave him financial assistance are borne to last resting place. The remains of 'Mammy Pleasants' who died early Monday morning at the home of Lyman Sherwood, on Filbert Street, will rest tonight under the soil of the little cemetery in the town of Napa, to which her body was taken this morning. One last request of 'Mammy Pleasants' was that there be placed above her grave a tombstone bearing her name, age, nativity, and the words: 'She was a friend of John Brown's.' One of the many interesting stories of her eventful career, told by Mrs. Pleasants, was her experience during the exciting times preceding the outbreak of the Civil War. With the money inherited

from her first husband, she came to California, and was here in 1858, when the first news of John Brown's efforts to free the slaves of the South were conveyed to San Francisco. Being in full sympathy with the movement, she conceived the idea of lending him financial assistance for the undertaking, and April 5, 1858, found her eastward bound with a $30,000 United States Treasury draft, which had been procured for her through the aid of Robert Swain, John W. Coleman and Mr. Alford.

Reaching Boston, Mrs. Pleasants arranged for a meeting with John Brown in Windsor, Canada. Before leaving Boston, Mrs. Pleasants had her draft exchanged for Canadian paper which she converted into coin and finally turned over to Brown. After a conference in Canada, it was agreed between them that he should not strike a blow for freedom of the Negro until she had journeyed to the South and had aroused the feelings of rebellion among her people. Disguised as a jockey, she proceeded to the South, and was engaged in her part of the plot when she was startled by the news that Brown had already made his raid on Harper's Ferry and had been captured. Learning that the authorities were in pursuit of Brown's accomplices, Mrs. Pleasants immediately fled to New York, and, after remaining in hiding for some time, assumed another name and made her way back to California.

When Brown was captured, there was found on his person a letter reading: 'The ax is laid at the root of the tree. When the first blow is struck, there will be more money to help.' The message was signed 'W. E. P.' For months the authorities vainly searched for the author of the message. In later years it developed that Mrs. Pleasants had written the letter, but in signing it she had made her first initial 'M' look like 'W'. Mrs. Pleasants always blamed Brown for hastening his attack at Harper's Ferry, which she claimed cost her in all over $40,000. Among her effects are letters and documents bearing upon the historical event in which she played a secret and important part.

NOTES--PROLOGUE

1. In these paragraphs are included all of the essential elements of the definition of social welfare used by John M. Romanyshyn in his book, <u>Social Welfare, Charity to Justice</u>, (New York: Random House and Council on Social Work Education, 1971), p. 3. To the above he adds the observation that "looking at it from a sociological point of view, social welfare functions to maintain the social system and to adapt it to changing social reality. From an ideological

point of view, it is society's answer to that ancient and ever-recurring question, 'Am I my brother's keeper?'"

2. Ralph E. Pumphrey and Muriel W. Pumphrey, eds., The Heritage of American Social Work. (New York: Columbia University Press, 1961).

3. William S. Jackson, Joanne V. Rhone and Charles L. Sanders, Social Service Delivery System in the Black Community During the Antebellum Period (1619-1860). Alton M. Childs Series, Atlanta University School of Social Work (Atlanta, 1973).

4. Joanne V. Rhone, "Social Service Delivery System Among Slaves (1619-1790)" in W. S. Jackson, et al., op. cit., pp. 3-11.

5. John W. Blassingame, The Slave Community, Plantation Life in the Ante-Bellum South. (New York: Oxford University Press, 1972).

6. Charles L. Sanders and William S. Jackson, "Role of the Abolition Movement During the Ante-Bellum Period," in W. S. Jackson, et al., op. cit., pp. 12-24.

7. Charles L. Sanders, "The Black Church as a Social Welfare Institution During the Ante-Bellum Period," in W. S. Jackson, et al., op. cit., pp. 25-32.

8. William S. Jackson, "Social Services Among Mutual Aid Systems and Emergency Health Services," in W. S. Jackson, et al., op. cit., pp. 33-41.

9. W. E. Burghardt DuBois, "My Evolving Program for Negro Freedom," in What the Negro Wants, ed., Rayford W. Logan, (Chapel Hill, N. C.: University of North Carolina Press, 1944), p. 65.

10. Melville J. Herskovits, The Myth of the Negro Past, (New York: Harper & Brothers, 1941).

11. Carlo M. Cipolla, Guns, Sails, and Empires: Technological Innovation and the Early Phase of European Expansion, 1400-1700, (New York: Pantheon Books, 1965), p. 171.

12. Ibid., p. 140.

13. Ibid., p. 143.

14. Ibid., p. 141.

15. Lerone Bennett, Jr., "The Road Not Taken," The Making of Black America, Part III, Ebony (XXV 110), August, 1970.

16. Lawrence Henry Gipson, The British Empire Before the American Revolution. Vol. II, The British Isles and the American Colonies: The Southern Plantations, 1748-1754, (New York: A. A. Knopf, 1960), pp. 267-68.

17. Lawrence Henry Gipson, The British Empire Before the American Revolution. Vol. XIII, The Empire Beyond the Storm, 1770-1776, (New York: A. A. Knopf, 1967), p. 57.

18. Ruth Pike, "Slavery in Seville at the Time of Columbus," From Reconquest to Empire: The Iberian Background to Latin American History, (Edited with Introduction by H. B. Johnson, Jr.), (New York: A. A. Knopf, 1970), p. 87.

19. Ibid., p. 92.

20. Ibid., p. 94-95.

21. Ibid., p. 97.

22. Herbert S. Klein, Slavery in the Americas: A Comparative Study of Cuba and Virginia, (Chicago: University of Chicago Press, 1967).

23. Ibid., p. 12.

24. Ibid., pp. 41-42.

25. Richard B. Morris, Government and Labor in Early America, (New York: Octagon Books, Inc., 1965), p. 310.

26. John H. Russell, The Free Negro in Virginia, 1619-1865, (New York: Dover Publications, Inc., 1969; originally published in 1913 by the Johns Hopkins Press, Baltimore).

27. Lerone Bennett, Jr., "The Making of Black America," Part I, XXIV (8), Ebony, June, 1969, pp. 31-43.

PART I

FROM HOPE TO DESPAIR: 1861-1877

INTRODUCTION

The social upheavals created by the War between the States fostered more than just the need to re-cement the territorial boundaries and the political relations between the Union and the Confederacy. The more urgent need called for solutions to the manifold social, economic, and political problems posed by the emancipation of some four million enslaved blacks who, previously, had been denied the options and alternatives afforded others to provide a more bountiful life for themselves and their descendants.

The active intervention of the Federal Government in their behalf was necessary and, for a brief period at least, of great assistance. It was the noble intention of most members of the post-war Congresses to assist the newly freed citizens in overcoming both their dependency and their poverty. Thus, the provisions of the Thirteenth, Fourteenth and Fifteenth Amendments to the Constitution remain monuments to this intention to provide freedom, due process and equal protection of the law, and the right to responsible citizenship through use of the ballot. It is true that often these Amendments have been subverted to sanction policies detrimental to the interests and values of the black population. But, overall, their effect has been more beneficial than detrimental to the black cause. In addition to these legislative enactments, active governmental intervention in the social process made this period one of great social experimentation, providing models for policies and programs relevant to future periods of social crisis.

Perhaps the greatest significance of this period, however, resides in the determination of blacks to ensure their survival and welfare by assuming as much responsibility as was permitted them for coping in their own ways with their own peculiar and singular social problems. Long established customary behavior was enshrined in restrictive legislative enactments, enforced by executive decree, and sanctioned by judicial judgments. This institutionalized racism had so shackled the minds and dulled the perceptions of the white majority that, however massive the contribution of government and private philanthropy, solutions to the varied problems faced by blacks had to be envisaged, proposed, initiated and actualized by blacks themselves. For the victims of the social process were considered by the majority group to be "the problem," indeed, "the Negro problem." It will be seen, then, that as federal and state actions on behalf of blacks lagged or were inhibited, it became imperative for blacks to develop self-help institutional arrangements which, though primarily designed to alleviate the problems of blacks (for there is a great distinction between "the problems of Negroes" and "the Negro problem"), were also of such broad conceptualization as to provide solutions beneficial to other ethnics in similarly deprived situations. Although success was modest, blacks did attempt to redefine their roles, rights and responsibilities; to exercise their capabilities to ensure group as well as individual survival; and, to fulfill desirable group aspirations. Sometimes it was feasible to collaborate with whites who were able to empathize and act in concert with them; at other times it was more feasible to act on their own initiative. In any event, what was required were the intellectual skills and the emotional maturity of responsible, aware citizens, who needed to redefine both the nature of their problems and their necessary solutions in terms of new concepts of interdependence and interrelatedness with <u>all</u> Americans.

This was the posture adopted and pursued as most useful and viable in the long run, and it engendered a broadened view of social welfare enterprise. This concept of social welfare emphasized the need to develop social technologies which could minister to the aspirations and values of the group rather than to those of the individual and which would be geared to the development and fulfillment of group and community objectives above individual objectives. Not only did the basic physical and biological imperatives of food, clothing and shelter have to be met for all, but new social roles had to be learned, roles which responded to an aesthetic enhancement of life. Where this was not understood, programs and policies resulted which were not only unsatisfactory but were basically inimical to the interests and values of blacks, and which served to bottle up rather than release their creativity.

Perhaps in advance of others blacks realized that the solution to their problems required a new concept of social welfare, one based upon a free citizenry devoid of racist distinctions but appreciative of ethnic pluralism. Responding as was necessary, learning primarily by trial and error, members of the black community pioneered this new kind of social welfare expertise, which remains viable today for resolving recurrent problematic social conditions. For these ideas undergird the tenacity necessary to create and strengthen life and to creatively construct a future.

In essence, then, the period beginning with the onset of the Civil War witnessed, for the first time, the participation of blacks in the resolution of their own peculiar problems, problems which arose not because they were black, but because the society within which they must live decreed that being black was being less than human. In this chapter, we discuss developments of the period, 1861-1877, designated herein as a period in which the black population began a new, collective life in hope but which concluded in an atmosphere of uncertainty and despair. As noted above, there arose in this period a tremendous need for a new kind of social experimentation, unique heretofore in United States history, to serve the needs of some four million blacks soon to be freed from slavery.

This experiment began in the Sea Islands off the coast of South Carolina and the adjacent mainland centering about the town of Beaufort. The exigencies of war singled out this area as the site of social experimentation under the cooperative aegis of the federal government and private philanthropy, together devising creative solutions to the economic, political and social problems of the freedmen. To one who carefully peruses the documents selected to describe and illustrate this endeavor it will be apparent that the experiment was not always or completely successful. Unfortunately, in many instances, there was a lack of policies, programs and services which would move the black population to total freedom and complete independence, unhampered by racist contraventions. The federal government did improvise solutions, but it was basically unclear and ambiguous as to the direction in which it ought to move, making decisions and reversing them in accordance with the fluctuations of political fortune. In the case of private philanthropic enterprise, those individuals involved in the implementation of policies and programs more often seem bent upon adapting blacks to the status quo than in addressing themselves to the problems of raising the freedmen to whatever requisite level of social and economic competitiveness that would enable them to truly be free and independent. Nevertheless, there was social response to social crisis, and this new experimentation in social welfare ultimately reordered the structure of American society and redefined the concept of social welfare.

TRANSITION FROM SLAVERY

Perhaps the first great problem confronting officers of the Union Army was the disposition of slaves who fled from abandoned plantations to Union Army camps as refugees. The first instance of record occurred at Fortress Monroe, Virginia in 1861, when the coming of the refugees forced the commanding general, Benjamin F. Butler, to provide minimal labor and social services for those slaves who had fled from surrounding plantations. In the first document, W. E. B. DuBois describes this confrontation and characterizes it as analogous to a "general strike." In any case, the action of blacks on their own initiative is emphasized.

Document 1*

W. E. B. DuBois, Black Reconstruction in America, 1860-

*Reprinted by permission of the publisher.

1880, (New York: Atheneum Press, 1969), pp. 63-64.

The Southern worker, black and white, held the key to the war; and of the two groups, the black worker raising food and raw materials held an even more strategic place than the white. This was so clear a fact that both sides should have known it. Fremont in Missouri took the logical action of freeing slaves of the enemy round about him by proclamation, and President Lincoln just as promptly repudiated what he had done. Even before that, General Butler in Virginia, commander of the Union forces at Fortress Monroe, met three slaves walking into his camp from the Confederate fortifications where they had been at work. Butler immediately declared these men "contraband of war" and put them to work in his own camp. More slaves followed, accompanied by their wives and children. The situation here was not quite so logical. Nevertheless, Butler kept the fugitives and freed them and let them do what work they could; and his action was approved by the Secretary of War.

> On May twenty-sixth, only two days after the one slave appeared before Butler, eight Negroes appeared; on the next day, forty-seven, of all ages and both sexes. Each day they continued to come by twenties, thirties and forties until by July 30th the number had reached nine hundred. In a very short while the number ran up into the thousands. The renowned Fortress took the name of the 'freedom fort' to which the blacks came by means of a 'mysterious spiritual telegraph.' [Brown, Junius H., 1865]

In December, 1861, the Secretary of the Treasury, Simon Cameron, had written, printed and put into the mails his first report as Secretary of War without consultation with the President. Possibly he knew that his recommendations would not be approved, but "he recommended the general arming of Negroes, declaring that the Federals had as clear a right to employ slaves taken from the enemy as to use captured gunpowder." This report was recalled by the President by telegraph and the statements of the Secretary were modified. The incident aroused some unpleasantness in the cabinet.

The published report finally said:

> Persons held by rebels, under such laws to service as slaves, may, however, be justly liberated from their constraint, and made more valuable in various employments, through voluntary and compensated service than if confiscated as subjects of property.

Transforming itself suddenly from a problem of abandoned plantations and slaves captured while being used by the enemy for military purposes, the movement became a general strike against the slave system on the part of all who could find opportunity. The trickling streams of fugitives swelled to a flood. Once begun, the general strike of black and white went madly and relentlessly on like some great saga.

Another perspective is provided by Wilson, who gives us the genesis of the great Port Royal experiment from a military point of view. The legal status of a refugee from an abandoned plantation was ambiguous. At first accepted only as contraband of war, the refugees later became active participants in the war as a part of the military.

Document 2

Joseph T. Wilson, Emancipation, Its Course and Progress, Hampton, Virginia, 1882, pp. 63-64.

Three Negro men, Shepard Mallory, Frank Baker, and James Townsend, property of Colonel Mallory Hampton entered line of General Butler at Fortress Monroe on May twenty-second--forty days after the surrender of Fort Sumter, seeking protection.

Mallory was a Confederate Officer and was about to send them away to work on rebel fortifications. Butler held them as contraband of war and instructed the quarter-master to put them to work. Others came in....

On May twenty-seventh--wrote Lt. Gen. Scott--"Slave property a serious magnitude. Virginia using Negroes in the batteries and preparing to send their women and children South." [Butler responded]: "Escapers are numerous. Squads of women and children came in this morning. Heretofore families arrived employed ablebodied, issued proper food support for others, charging against services of heads of families the expense and care and sustenance of non-labor--keeping strict account of service and expenditures, board of survey determining worth of services and cost of expenditures." [He continued]:

> As a matter of property to the insurgents it will be of very great moment--the number that I now have amounting to what in good times would be of the value of $60,000. Twelve escaped from batteries of Sewell's Point, which fired upon my expedition. As a means of offense in the enemy's hands these Negroes when able-bodied are of great importance. Without them the batteries could not have been erected. As a military question it would seem to be a measure of necessity to deprive the masters of their services.
>
> How can this be done? As a political question and as a question of humanity can I receive the services of a father and mother and not take the children? Of humanitarian--no doubt--of political--no point to judge. There-

> fore submit all this to your better judgment--duplicated political aspect and forwarded to Secretary of War,
>
> B. N. Butler May Twenty-seven

General Cameron, Secretary of War, clearly defined the administration's position in reply:

> To Major General Butler,
>
> Sir
> Your action in respect to the Negroes who came within your lines from the service of rebels is approved. Department sensible of the embarrassment which must surround officer conducting military operation in a state by the laws of which slavery is sanctioned. The government cannot recognize the rejection of any state of its Federal obligations resting upon itself, among these Federal obligations, however, no one can be more important than that of suppressing and depressing any combination of the former for the purpose of overthrowing its constitutional authority. While therefore you will permit no interference by persons under your command with the relation of persons held to service under the laws of any state, you will on the other hand, so long as any state within which your military operations are conducted remains under the control of such above combinations, refrain from surrendering to alleged masters any person who came within its lines. You will employ such persons in the services to which they will be best adapted keeping an account of the labor by them performed, of the value of it, and the expenses for their maintenance. The question of their final disposition will be reserved for future determination. (p. 45)

Wilson also cites Vattel's definition of "contraband" as follows:

> That in time of war if it be a just war and there be a people, who have been oppressed by the enemy and that enemy be conquered, the victorious party cannot return that oppressed people to the bondage from which they have rescued them. (p. 49)

Because Butler sought the advice of Lt. General Scott and of General Cameron, the Secretary of War, E. L. Pierce was asked to establish and supervise a program of work for the able-bodied refugees and to provide social services for their women and children at Fortress Monroe. His program proved so successful that, on the basis of his operations in this area, Pierce was called upon by the President and the Secretary of War to devise a program for the many refugees who were located in those areas of the Sea Islands and the adjacent mainland where there were plantations abandoned by their owners. How he did this is recounted in his article, "The Freedmen at Port Royal", from which we have excerpted the following. (The article also documents the participation and activities of blacks as teachers, land developers, owners of plantations and the like.)

Document 3

E. L. Pierce, "The Freedmen at Port Royal," Atlantic Monthly, XII, (September, 1863), pp. 291-315.

The capture of Hilton Head and Bay Point by the navy, November 7th, 1861, was followed by the immediate military occupation of the Sea Islands. In the latter part of December, the Secretary of the Treasury, Mr. Chase, whose foresight as a statesman and (of) humane disposition naturally turned his thoughts to the subject, deputed a special agent to visit the district for the purpose of reporting upon the condition of the negroes who had been abandoned by the white population, and of suggesting some plan for the organization of their labor and the promotion of their general well-being. The agent, leaving New York January 13th, 1862, reached that city again on his way to Washington on the 13th of February, having in the meantime visited a large number of the plantations, and talked familiarly with the negroes in their cabins. The results of his observations, in relation to the condition of the people, their capacities and wishes, the culture of their crops, and the best mode of administration, on the whole favorable, were embodied in a report. The plan proposed by him recommended the appointment of superintendents to act as guides of the negroes and as local magistrates, with an adequate corps of teachers. It was accepted by the Secretary with a full indorsement, and its execution intrusted to the same agent. The agent presented the subject to several members of Congress, with whom he had a personal acquaintance, but, though they listened respectfully, they seemed either to dread the magnitude of the social question, or to feel that it was not one with which they as legislators were called upon immediately to deal. The Secretary himself, and Mr. Olmsted, then connected with the Sanitary Commission, alone seemed to grasp it, and to see the necessity of immediate action. It is doubtful if any member of the Cabinet, except Mr. Chase, took then any interest in the enterprise, though it has since been fostered by the Secretary of War. At the suggestion of the Secretary, the President appointed an interview with the agent. Mr. Lincoln, who was then chafing under a prospective bereavement, listened for a few moments, and then said, somewhat impatiently, that he did not think he ought to be troubled with such details,--that there seemed to be an itching to get negroes into our lines; to which the agent replied, that these negroes were within them by the invitation of no one, being domiciled there before we commenced occupation. The President then wrote and handed to the agent the following card:

> I shall be obliged if the Secretary of the Treasury will in his discretion give Mr. Pierce such instructions in regard to Port Royal contrabands as may seem judicious.
>
> A. Lincoln
> February 15, 1862

The President, so history must write it, approached the great question slowly and reluctantly; and in February, 1862, he little dreamed of the proclamations he was to issue in the September and January following. Perhaps that slowness and reluctance were well, for thereby it was given to this people to work out their own salvation, rather than to be saved by any chief or prophet.

Notwithstanding the plan of superintendents was accepted, there were no funds wherewith to pay them. At this stage the "Educational Commission", organized in Boston on the 7th of February, and the "Freedmen's Relief Association", organized in New York on the 20th of the same month, gallantly volunteered to pay both superintendents and teachers, and did so until July 1st, when the Government, having derived a fund from the sale of confiscated cotton left in the territory by the Rebels, undertook the payment of the superintendents, the two societies, together with another organized in Philadelphia on the 3rd of March, and called the "Port Royal Relief Committee", providing for the support of the teachers.

When these voluntary associations sprang into being to save an enterprise which otherwise must have failed, no authoritative assurance had been given as to the legal condition of the negroes. The Secretary, in a letter to the agent, had said, that, after being received into our service, they could not, without great injustice, be restored to their masters, and should therefore be fitted to become self-supporting citizens. The President was reported to have said freely, in private, that negroes who were within our lines, and had been employed by the Government, should be protected in their freedom. No official assurance of this had, however, been given; and its absence disturbed the societies in their formation. At one meeting of the Boston society action was temporarily arrested by the expression of an opinion by a gentleman present, that there was no evidence showing that these people, when educated, would not be the victims of some unhappy compromise. A public meeting in Providence, for their relief, is said to have broken up without action, because of a speech from a furloughed officer of a regiment stationed at Port Royal, who considered such a result the probable one. But the societies, on reflection, wisely determined to do what they could to prepare them to become self-supporting citizens, in the belief, that, when they had become such, no Government could ever be found base enough to turn its back upon them. These associations, it should be stated, have been managed by persons of much consideration in their respective communities, of unostentatious philanthropy, but of energetic and practical benevolence, hardly one of whom has ever filled or been a candidate for a political office....

On the morning of the 3rd of March, 1862, the first delegation of superintendents and teachers, fifty-three in all, of whom twelve were women, left the harbor of New York, on board the United States steam-transport Atlantic, arriving at Beaufort on the 9th. It was a voyage never to be forgotten. The enterprise was new and strange, and it was not easy to predict its future. Success or defeat might be in store for us; and we could only trust in God that our strength would be equal to our responsibilities. As the colonists approached the shores of South Carolina, they were addressed by the agent in charge, who told them the little he had learned of their duties, enjoined patience and humanity, impressed on them the greatness of their work, the results of which were to cheer or dishearten good men, to settle, perhaps, one way or the other, the social problem of the age,--assuring them that never did a vessel bear a colony on a nobler mission, not even the Mayflower, when she conveyed the Pilgrims to Plymouth, that it would be a poorly written history which should omit their individual names, and that, if faithful to their trust, there would come to them the highest of all recognitions ever accorded to angels or to men, in this life or the next,--"Inasmuch as ye have done it unto the least of these, ye have done it unto Me."

This first delegation of superintendents and teachers was distributed during the first forthnight after their arrival at Beaufort, and at its close they had all reached their appointed posts. They took their quarters in the deserted houses of the planters. These had all left on the arrival of our army, only four white men, citizens of South Carolina, remaining, and none of those being slaveholders, except one, who had only two or three slaves. Our operations were, therefore, not interfered with by landed proprietors who were loyal or pretended to be so. The negroes had, in the mean time, been without persons to guide and care for them, and had been exposed to the careless and conflicting talk of soldiers who chanced to meet them. They were also brought in connection with some employes of the Government, engaged in the collection of cotton found upon the plantations, none of whom were doing anything for their education, and most of whom were in favor of leasing the plantations and the negroes upon them as adscripti glebae, looking forward to their restoration to their masters at the close of the war. They were uncertain as to the intentions of the Yankees, and were wondering at the confusion, as they called it. They were beginning to plant corn in their patches, but were disinclined to plant cotton, regarding it as a badge of servitude. No schools had been opened except one at Beaufort, which had been kept a few weeks by two freedmen, one bearing the name of John Milton, under the auspices of the Reverend Dr. Peck. This is not the place to detail the obstacles we met with, one after another overcome,--the calumnies and even personal violence to which we were subjected. These things occurred at an early period of our struggle, when the nation was groping its way to light, and are not likely to occur again. Let unworthy men sleep in the oblivion they deserve, and let others of better natures, who were then blind, but now see, not be taunted with their inconsiderate acts. The nickname of Gibeonites, applied to the colonists, may, however, be fitly remembered. It may now justly claim rank with the honored titles of Puritan and Methodist. The higher officers of the army were uniformly respectful and disposed to cooperation. One of these may properly be mentioned. Our most important operations were in the district under the command of Brigadier-General Isaac I. Stevens, an officer whose convictions were not supposed to be favorable to the enterprise, and who, during the political contest of 1860, had been the chairman of the National Breckenridge Committee. But such was his honor as a gentleman, and his sense of the duty of subordination to the wishes of the Government that his personal courtesies and official aid were never wanting. He received his mortal wound at Chantilly, Virginia, on the first of September following, and a braver and abler officer has not fallen in the service.

Notwithstanding our work was commenced six weeks too late, and other hindrances occurred, detailed in the second report of the agent, some eight thousand acres of esculents,--a fair supply of food,--and some four thousand five hundred acres of cotton (after a deduction for overestimates) were planted. This was done upon one hundred and eighty-nine plantations, on which were nine thousand and fifty people, of whom four thousand four hundred and twenty-nine were fieldhands, made up of men, women, and children, and equivalent, in the usual classification and estimate of the productive capacity of laborers, to three thousand eight hundred and five and one-half full hands. The cotton-crop produced will not exceed sixty-five thousand pounds of ginned cotton. Work enough was done to have produced five hundred thousand pounds in ordinary times; but the immaturity of the pod, resulting from the lateness of the planting, exposed it to the ravages of the frost and the worm. Troops being ordered North, after the disasters of the Peninsular campaign, Edisto was evacuated in the middle of July, and thus one thousand acres of esculents, and nearly seven hundred acres of cotton, the cultivation of which had been finished, were abandoned. In the autumn, Major-General Mitchell required forty tons of corn-fodder and seventy-eight thousand pounds of corn in the ear, for army-forage. These are but some of the adverse influences to which the agricultural operations were subjected.

It is fitting here that I should bear my testimony to the superintendents and teachers commissioned by the associations. There was as high a purpose and devotion among them as in any colony that ever went forth to bear the evangel of civilization. Among them were some of the choicest young men of New England, fresh from Harvard, Yale and Brown, from the divinity-schools of Andover and Cambridge,--men of practical talent and experience.

On the first of July, 1862, the administration of affairs at Port Royal having been transferred from the Treasury to the War

Department, the charge of the freedmen passed into the hands of Brigadier-General Rufus Saxton, a native of Massachusetts, who in childhood had breathed the free air of the valley of the Connecticut, a man of sincere and humane nature; and under his wise and benevolent care they still remain. The Sea Islands, and also Fernandina and St. Augustine in Florida, are within our lines in the Department of the South, and some sixteen or eighteen thousand negroes are supposed to be under his jurisdiction.

The negroes of the Sea Islands, when found by us, had become an abject race, more docile and submissive than those of any other locality. The native African was of a fierce and mettlesome temper, sullen and untamable. The master was obliged to abate something of the usual rigor in dealing with the imported slaves. A tax commissioner, now at Port Royal, and formerly a resident of South Carolina, told me that a native African belonging to his father, though a faithful man, would perpetually insist on doing his work in his own way, and being asked the threatening question, "A'nt you goint to mind?" would answer, with spirit, "No, a'n't gwine to!" and the master desisted. Severe discipline drove the natives to the wilderness, or involved a mutilation of person which destroyed their value for proprietary purposes. In 1816, eight hundred of these refugees were living free in the swamps and everglades of Florida. There the ancestors of some of them had lived ever since the early part of the eighteenth century, rearing families, carrying on farms, and raising cattle. They had two hundred and fifty men fit to bear arms, led by chiefs brave and skillful. The story of the Exiles of Florida is one of painful interest. The testimony of officers of the army who served against them is, that they were more dangerous enemies than the Indians, fighting the most skillfully and standing the longest. The tax-commissioner before referred to, who was a resident of Charleston during the trial and execution of the confederates of Denmark Vessey, relates that one of the native Africans, when called to answer to the charge against him, haughtily responded,--"I was a prince in my country, and have as much right to be free as you!" The Carolinians were so awestruck by his defiance that they transported him. Another, at the execution, turned indignantly to a comrade about to speak, and said, "Die silent, as I do!" and the man hushed. The early newspapers of Georgia recount the disturbances on the plantations occasioned by these native Africans, and even by their children, being not until the third generation reduced to obedient slaves.

Nowhere has the deterioration of the negroes from their native manhood been carried so far as on these Sea Islands,--a deterioration due to their isolation from the excitements of more populous districts, the constant surveillance of the overseers, and their intermarriage with each other, involving a physical degeneracy with which inexorable Nature punishes disobedience to her laws. The population with its natural increase was sufficient for the cultivation of the soil under existing modes, and therefore no fresh blood was admitted, such as is found pouring from the Border States into the sugar and cotton regions of the Southwest. This unmanning and depravation of the native character of had been carried so far, that the special agent, on his first exploration, in January, 1862, was obliged to confess the existence of a general disinclination to military service on the part of the negroes; though it is true that even then instances of courage and adventure appeared, which indicated that the more manly feeling was only latent, to be developed under the inspiration of events. And so, let us rejoice, it has been. You may think yourself wise, as you note the docility of a subject race; but in vain will you attempt to study it until the burden is lifted. The slave is unknown to all, even to himself, while the bondage lasts. Nature is ever a kind mother. She soothes us with her deceits, not in surgery alone, when the sufferer, else writhing in pain, is transported with the sweet delirium, but she withholds from the spirit the sight of her divinity until her opportunity has come. Not even Tocqueville or Olmsted, much less the master, can measure the capacities and possibilities of the slave, until the slave himself is transmuted to a man.

But the features in the present condition of the freedmen bearing directly on the solution of the social problem deserve most consideration.

And, first, as to education. There are more than thirty schools in the territory, conducted by as many as forty or forty-five teachers, who are commissioned by three associations in Boston, New York, and Philadelphia, and by the American Missionary Association. They have an average attendance of two thousand pupils, and are more or less frequented by an additional thousand. The ages of the scholars range in the main from eight to twelve years. They did not know even their letters prior to a year ago last March, except those who were being taught in the single school at Beaufort already referred to, which had been going on for a few weeks. Very many did not have the opportunity for instruction till weeks and even months after. During the spring and summer of 1862 there were not more than a dozen schools, and these were much interrupted by the heat, and by the necessity of assigning at times some of the teachers to act as superintendents. Teachers came for a brief time, and upon its expiration, or for other cause, returned home, leaving the schools to be broken up. It was not until October or November that the educational arrangements were put into much shape; and they are still but imperfectly organized. In some localities there is as yet no teacher, and this because the associations have not had the funds wherewith to provide one.

I visited ten of the schools, and conversed with the teachers of others. There were, it may be noted, some mixed bloods in the schools of the town of Beaufort,--ten in a school of ninety, thirteen in another of sixty-four, and twenty in another of seventy. In the schools on the plantations there were never more than half a dozen in one school, in some cases but two or three, and in others none.

The advanced classes were reading simple stories and didactic passages in the ordinary school-books, as Hillard's Second Primary Reader, Willson's Second Reader, and others of similar grade. Those who had enjoyed a briefer period of instruction were reading short sentences or learning the alphabet. In several of the schools a class was engaged in an elementary lesson in arithmetic, geography, or writing. The eagerness for knowledge and the facility of acquisition displayed in the beginning had not abated.

On the 25th of March I visited a school at the Central Baptist Church on St. Helena Island, built in 1855, shaded by lofty live oak trees, with the long, pendulous moss everywhere hanging from their wide-spreading branches, and surrounded by the gravestones of the former proprietors, which bear the ever-recurring names of Fripp and Chaplin. This school was opened in September last, but many of the pupils had received some instruction before. One hundred and thirty-one children were present on my first visit, and one hundred and forty-five on my second, which was a few days later. Like most of the schools on the plantations, it opened at noon and closed at three o'clock leaving the forenoon for the children to work in the field or perform other service in which they could be useful.

One of the teachers of this school is an accomplished woman from Philadelphia. Another is from Newport, Rhode Island where she had prepared herself for this work by benevolent labors in teaching poor children. The third is a young woman of African descent, of olive complexion, finely cultured, and attuned to all beautiful sympathies, of gentle address, and, what was specially noticeable, not possessed with an overwrought consciousness of her race. She had read the best books, and naturally and gracefully enriched her conversation with them. She had enjoyed the friendship of Whittier; had been a pupil in the Grammar-School of Salem, then in the State Normal School in that city, then a teacher in one of the schools for white children, where she had received only the kindest treatment both from the pupils and their parents, and let this be spoken to the honor of that ancient town. She had refused a residence in Europe, where a better social life and less unpleasant discrimination awaited her, for she would not disever herself from the fortunes of her people; and now, not with a superficial sentiment, but with a profound purpose, she devotes herself to their elevation.

In a school at St. Helena village, where were collected the Edisto refugees, ninety-two pupils were present as I went in. Two ladies were engaged in teaching, assisted by Ned Lloyd White, a colored man, who had picked up clandestinely a knowledge of reading while still a slave. One class of boys and another of girls read in the seventh chapter of St. John, having begun this Gospel and gone thus far. They stumbled a little on words like "unrighteousness" and "circumcision"; otherwise they got along very well. When the Edisto refugees were brought here, in July, 1862, Ned who is about forty or forty-five years old, and Uncle Cyrus, a man of seventy, who also could read, gathered one hundred and fifty children into two schools, and taught them as best they could for five months until teachers were provided by the societies. Ned has since received a donation from one of the societies, and is now regularly employed on a salary. A woman comes to one of the teachers of this school for instruction in the evening, after she has put her children to bed. She had become interested in learning by hearing her younger sister read when she came home from school; and when she asked to be taught, she had learned from this sister the alphabet and some words of one syllable. Only a small proportion of the adults are, however, learning.

A few freedmen, who had picked up an imperfect knowledge of reading, though a want of proper training materially detracts from their usefulness in this respect. Ned and Uncle Cyrus have already been mentioned. The latter, a man of earnest piety, has died since my visit. Anthony kept four schools on Hilton Head Island last summer and autumn, being paid at first by the superintendents, and afterwards by the negroes themselves; but in November he enlisted in the negro regiment. Hettie was another of these. She assisted Barnard at Edisto last spring, continued to teach after the Edisto people were brought to St. Helena village, and one day brought some of her pupils to the school at the Baptist Church, saying to the teachers there that she would carry them no farther. They could read their letters and words of one syllable. Hettie had belonged to a planter on Wadmelaw Island, a kind old gentleman, a native of Rhode Island, and about the only citizen of Charleston who, when Samuel Hoar went on his mission to South Carolina, stood up boldly for his official and personal protection. Hettie had been taught to read by his daughter; and let this be remembered to the honor of the young woman.

Such are the general features of the schools as they met my eye. The most advanced classes, and these are but little ahead of the rest, can read simple stories and the plainer passages of Scripture; and they could even pursue self-instruction, if the schools were to be suspended. The knowledge they have thus gained can never be extirpated. They could read with much profit a newspaper specially prepared for them and adapted to their condition. They are learning that the world is not bounded north by Charleston, south by Savannah, west by Columbia, and east by the sea, with dim visions of New York on this planet or some other,--about their conception of geography when we found them. They are acquiring the knowledge of figures with which to do the business of life. They are singing the songs of freedmen. Visit their schools; remember that a little more than a twelve month ago they knew not a letter, and that for generations it has been a crime to teach their race; then contemplate what is now transpiring, and you have a scene which prophets and sages would have delighted to witness. It will be difficult to find equal progress in an equal period since the morning rays of Christian truth first lighted the hill-sides of Judea. I have never looked on St. Peter's, or beheld the glories of art which Michael Angelo has wrought or traced; but to my mind the spectacle of these poor souls struggling in darkness and bewilderment to catch the gleams of the upper and better light transcends in moral grandeur anything that has ever come from mortal hands.

Next as to industry. The laborers, during their first year under the new system, have acquired the idea of ownership, and of the security of wages, and have come to see that labor and slavery are not the same thing. The notion that they were to raise no more cotton has passed away, since work upon it is found to be remunerative, and connected with the proprietorship of land. House-servants, who were at first particularly set against it, now generally prefer it. The laborers have collected the pieces of the gins which they destroyed on the flight of their masters, the ginning being obnoxious work, repaired them, and ginned the cotton on the promise of wages. Except upon plantations in the vicinity of camps, where other labor is more immediately remunerative, and on unhealthy excitement prevails, there is a general disposition to cultivate it. The culture of the cotton is voluntary, the only penalty for not engaging in being the imposition of a rent for the tenement and land adjacent thereto occupied by the negro, not exceeding two dollars per month. Both the Government and private individuals, who have become owners of one-fourth of the land by the recent tax-sales, pay twenty-five cents for a standard day's-work, which by a healthy and active hand by noon; and the same was the case with the tasks under the slave system on very many of the plantations. As I was riding through one of Mr. Philbrick's fields one morning, I counted fifty persons at work who belonged to one plantation. This gentleman, who went out with the first delegation, and at the same time gave largely to the benevolent contributions for the enterprise, was the leading purchaser at the tax-sales, and combining a fine humanity with honest sagacity and close calculation, no man is so well fitted to try the experiment. He bought thirteen plantations, and on these has had planted and cultivated eight hundred and sixteen acres of cotton where four hundred and ninety-nine and one twelve-hundreth acres were cultivated last year,--a larger increase, however, than will generally be found in other districts, due mainly to prompter payments. The general superintendent of Port Royal Island said to me,--"We want to restrain rather than to encourage the negroes to take land for cotton." The general superintendent of Hilton Head Island said, that on that island the negroes had, besides adequate corn, taken two, three and in a few cases four acres of cotton to a hand, and there was a general disposition to cultivate it, except near the camps. A superintendent on St. Helena Island said, that, if he were going to carry on any work, he should not want better laborers. He had charge of the refugees from Edisto, who had been brought to St. Helena village, and who had cleared and fenced patches for gardens, felling the trees for that purpose.

The laborers do less work, perhaps, than a Yankee would think they might do; but they do about as much as he himself would do, after a residence of a few years in the same climate, and when he had ceased to work under the influence of Northern habits. Northern men have sometimes been unjust to the South, when comparing the results of labor in the different sections. God never intended that a man should toil under a tropical sun with the same energy and constantly as in our bracing latitude. There has been less complaint this year than last of "a pain in the small of the back," or of "a fever in the head,"--in other words, less shamming. The work has been greatly deranged by the draft, some features of which have not been very skillfully arranged, and by the fitfulness with which the laborers have been treated by the military authorities. The work both upon the cotton and the corn is done by the women, children, and disabled men. It has been suggested that field work does not become women in the new condition; and so it may seem to some persons of just sympathies who have not yet learned that no honest work is dishonorable in man or woman. But this matter may be left to regulate itself. Field-work, as an occupation, may not be consistent with the finest feminine culture or the most complete womanliness; but it in no way conflicts with virtue, self-respect, and social development. Women work in the field in Switzerland, the freest country of Europe; and we may look with pride on the triumphs of this generation, when the American negroes become the peers of the Swiss peasantry. Better a woman with the hoe than without it, when she is not yet fitted for the needle or the book.

The negroes were also showing their capacity to organize labor and apply capital to it. Harry, to whom I referred in my second report, as "my faithful guide and attendant, who had done for me more service than any white man could render," with funds of his own, and some borrowed money, bought at the recent tax-sales a small farm of three hundred and thirteen acres for three hundred and five dollars. He was to plant sixteen and a half acres of cotton, twelve and a half of corn, and one and a half of potatoes. I rode through his farm on the 10th of April, my last day in the territory, and one-third of his crop was then in. Besides some servant's duty to an officer, for which he is well paid, he does the work of full hand on his place. He hires one woman and two men, one of the latter being old and only a three-quarters hand. His wife works also, of whom he said, "She's the best hand I got;" and if Celia is only as smart with her hoe as I know her to be with her tongue, Harry's estimate must be right. He has a horse twenty-five years old and blind in both eyes, whom he guides with a rope,--carrying on farming, I thought, somewhat under difficulties. Harry lives in the house of the former overseer, and delights, though not boastingly, in his position as a landed proprietor. He has promised to write me, or rather dictate a letter, giving an account of the progress of his crop. He has had much charge of Government property, and when Captain Hooper, of General Saxton's staff, was coming North last autumn, Harry proposed to accompany him; but at last, of his own accord, gave up the project, saying, "It'll not do for all two to leave together."

Another case of capacity for organization should be noted. The Government is building twenty-one houses for the Edisto people, eighteen feet by fourteen, with two rooms, each provided with a swinging board-window, and the roof projecting a little as a protection from rain. The journeymen-carpenters are seventeen colored men, who have fifty cents per day without rations, working ten hours. They are under the direction of Frank Barnwell, a freedman, who receives twenty dollars a month. Rarely have I talked with a more intelligent contractor. It was my great regret that I had not time to visit the village of improved houses near the Hilton Head camp, which General Mitchell had extemporized, and to which he gave so much of the noble enthusiasm of his last days.

Next as to the development of manhood. This has been shown, in the first place, in the prevalent disposition to acquire land. It did not appear upon our first introduction to these people, and they did not seem to understand us when we used to tell them that we wanted them to own land. But it is now an active desire. At the recent tax-sales, six out of forty-seven plantations sold were bought by them, comprising two thousand five hundred and ninety-five acres, sold for twenty-one hundred and forty-five dollars. In other cases the negroes had authorized the superintendent to bid for them, but the land was reserved by the United States. One of the purchases was that made by Harry, noted above. The other five were made by the negroes on the plantations combining the funds they had saved from the sale of their pigs, chickens, and eggs, and from the payments made to them for work,--they then dividing off the tract peaceably among themselves. On one of these, where Kit, before mentioned, is the leading spirit, there are twenty-three field-hands, who are equivalent to eighteen full hands. They have planted and are cultivating sixty-three acres of cotton, fifty of corn, six of potatoes, with as many more to be planted, four and a half of cowpeas, three of pea-nuts, and one and a half of rice. These facts are most significant. The instinct for land--to have one spot on earth where a man may stand, and whence no human being can of right drive him--is one of the most conservative elements of our nature; and a people who have it in any fair degree will never be nomads or vagabonds.

This developing manhood is further seen in their growing consciousness of rights, and their readiness to defend themselves, even when assailed by white men. The former slaves of a planter, now at Beaufort, who was a resident of New York when the war broke out, have generally left the plantation, suspicious of his presence saying that they will not be his bondmen, and fearing that in some way he may hold them, if they remain on it. A remarkable case of the assertion of rights occurred one day during my visit. Two white soldiers, with a corporal, went on Sunday to Coosaw Island, shot a chicken belonging to a negro. The negroes rushed out and wrested the gun from the corporal, to whom the soldier had handed it, thinking that the negroes would not take it from an officer. They then carried it to the superintendent, who took it to headquarters, where an order was given for the arrest of the trespasser. Other instances might be added, but these are sufficient.

Another evidence of developing manhood appears in their desire for the comforts and conveniences of household life. The Philadelphia society, for the purpose of maintaining reasonable prices, has a store on St. Helena Island, which is under the charge of Friend Hunn, of the good fellowship of William Penn. He was once fined in Delaware three thousand dollars for harboring and assisting fugitive slaves; but he now harbors and assists them at a much cheaper rate. Though belonging to a society which is the advocate of peace, his tone is quite as warlike as that of the world's people. In this store alone--and there are others on the island, carried on by private enterprise--two thousand dollars' worth of goods are sold monthly. To be sure, a rather large proportion of these consists of molasses and sugar, "sweetening," as the negroes call it, being in great demand, and four barrels of molasses having been sold the day of my visit. But there is also a great demand for plates, knives, forks, tin ware, and better clothing, including even hoop skirts. Negro-cloth, as it is called, osnaburgs, russet-colored shoes,--in short, the distinctive apparel formerly dealt out to them, as a uniform allowance,--are very generally rejected. But there is no article of household furniture or wearing apparel, used by persons of moderate means among us, which they will not purchase, when they are allowed the opportunity of labor and earning wages. What a market the South would open under the new system! It would set all the mills and workshops astir. Four millions of people would become purchasers of all the various articles of manufacture and commerce, in place of the few coarse, simple necessaries, laid in for them in gross by the planters. Here is the solution of the vexed industrial question. The indisposition to labor is overcome in a healthy nature by instincts and motives of superior force, such as the love of life, the desire to be well clothed and fed, the sense of security derived from provision for the future, the feeling of self-respect, the love of family and children, and the convictions of duty. These all exist in the Negro, in a state of greater or less development. To give one or two examples. One man brought Captain Hooper seventy dollars in silver, to keep for him, which he had obtained from selling pigs and chickens,--thus providing for the future. Soldiers of Colonel Higginson's regiment, having confidence in the same officer, intrusted him, when they were paid off, with seven hundred dollars, to be transmitted by him to their wives, and this besides what they had sent home in other ways,--showing the family-feeling to be active and strong in them. They have also the social and religious inspirations to labor. Thus, early in our occupation of Hilton Head, they took up, of their own accord, a collection to pay for the candles for their evening meetings, feeling that it was not right for the Government longer to provide them. The result was a contribution of two dollars and forty-eight cents. They had just fled from their masters, and had received only a small pittance of wages, and this little sum was not unlike the two mites which the widow cast into the treasury. Another collection was taken, last June, in the church on St. Helena Island, upon the suggestion of the pastor that they should share in the expenses of worship. Fifty-two dollars was the result,--not a bad collection for some of our Northern churches. I have seen these people where they are said to be lowest, and sad indeed are some features of their lot, yet with all earnestness and confidence I enter my protest against the wicked satire of Carlyle.

Is there not here some solution of the question of prejudice or caste which has troubled so many good minds? When these people can no longer be used as slaves, men will try to see how they can make the most out of them as freemen. Your Irishman, who now works as a day laborer, honestly thinks that he hates the negro; but when the war is over, he will have no objection to going South and selling him groceries and household-implements at fifty per cent. advance on New York prices, or to hiring him to raise cotton for twenty-five or fifty cents a day. Our prejudices, under any reasonable adjustment of the social system, readily accomodate themselves to our interests, even without much aid from the moral sentiments.

Let those who would study well this social question, or who in public trusts are charged with its solution, be most careful here. Every motive in the minds of these people, whether of instinct, desire, or duty, must be addressed. All the elements of human nature must be appealed to, physical, moral, intellectual, social, and religious. Imperfect indeed is any system which, like that at New Orleans, offers wages, but does not welcome the teacher. It is of little moment whether three dollars or thirty per month be paid the laborer, so long as there is no school to bind both parent and child to civil society with new hopes and duties.

There are some vices charged upon these people, or a portion of them, and truth requires nothing be withheld. There is said to be a good deal of petty pilfering among them, although they are faithful to trusts. This is the natural growth of the old system, and is quite likely to accompany the transition-state. Besides, the present disturbed and unorganized condition of things is not favorable to the rigid virtues. But inferences from this must not be pressed too far. When I was a private soldier in Virginia, as one of a three-months' regiment, we used to hide from each other our little comforts and delicacies, even our dishes and clothing, or they were sure to disappear. But we should have ridiculed an adventurous thinker upon the characteristics of races and classes, who should have leaped therefrom to the conclusion that all white men or all soldiers are thieves. And what inferences might not one draw, discreditable to all traders and manufacturers, from the universal adulteration of articles of food! These people, it is said, are disposed to falsehood in order to get rations and small benefits,--a natural vice which comes with slavery, and too often attends on poverty without slavery. Those of most demonstrative piety are rarely better than the rest, not, indeed, hypocritical, but satisfying their consciences by self-depreciation and indulgence in emotion,--psychological manifestations which one may find in more advanced communities. They show no special gratitude to us for liberating them from bonds. Nor do they ordinarily display much exhilaration over their new condition,--being quite unlike the Italian revolutionist who used to put on his toga, walk in the forum, and personate Brutus and Cassius. Their appreciation of their better lot is chiefly seen in their dread of a return of their masters, in their excitement when an attack is feared, in their anxious questionings while the assault on Charleston was going on, and in desire to get their friends and relatives away from the Rebels,--an appreciation of freedom, if not ostentatious, at least sensible.

But away with such frivolous modes of dealing with the rights of races to self-development! Because Englishmen may be classified as hard and conceited, Frenchmen as capricious, Austrians as dull, and the people of one other nation are sometimes thought to be vain-glorious, shall these therefore be slaves? And where is that model race which shall sway them all? A people may have grave defects, but it may not therefore be rightfully disabled.

During my recent visit, I had an opportunity, on three different occasions, to note carefully Colonel T. W. Higginson's colored regiment, known as the First Regiment of South Carolina Volunteers. Major-General Hunter's first regiment was mainly made up of conscripts, drafted May 12th, 1862, and disbanded August 11th, three months afterwards, there being no funds wherewith to pay them, and the discharged men going home to find the cotton and corn they had planted overgrown with weeds. On the 10th of October, General Saxton, being provided with competent authority to raise five thousand colored troops, began to recruit a regiment. His authority from the War Department bore date August 25th, and the order conferring it states the object to be "to guard the plantations, and protect the inhabitants from captivity and murder." This was the first clear authority ever given by the Government to raise a negro regiment in this war. There were, indeed, some ambiguous words in the instructions of Secretary Cameron to General Sherman, when the original expedition went to Port Royal, authorizing him to organize the negroes into companies and squads for such services as they might be fitted for, but this not to mean a general arming for military service. Secretary Stanton, though furnishing muskets and red trousers to General Hunter's regiment, did not think the authority sufficient to justify the payment of the regiment. The first regiment, as raised by General Saxton, numbered four hundred and ninety-nine men when Colonel Higginson took command of it on the 1st of December; and on the 19th of January, 1863, it had increased to eight hundred and forty-nine. It has made three expeditions to Florida and Georgia,--one before Colonel Higginson assumed the command, described in Mrs. Stowe's letter to the women of England, and two under Colonel Higginson, one of which was made in January up the St. Mary's, and the other in March to Jacksonville, which it occupied for a few days until an evacuation was ordered from head-quarters. The men are volunteers, having been led to enlist by duty to their race, to their kindred still in bonds, and to us, their allies. Their drill is good, and their time excellent. They have borne themselves well in their expeditions, quite equalling the white regiments in skirmishing. In morale they seemed very much like white men, and with about the same proportion of good and indifferent soldiers. Some I saw of the finest metal, like Robert Sutton, whom Higginson describes in his report as "the real conductor of the whole expedition at the St. Mary's," and Sergeant Hodges, a master-carpenter, capable of directing the labors of numerous journeymen. Another said, addressing a meeting at Beaufort, that he had been restless, nights, thinking of the war and of his people,--

that, when he heard of the regiment being formed, he felt that his time to act had come, and that it was his duty to enlist,--that he did not fight for his rations and pay, but for his wife, children and people.

These men, as already intimated, are very much like other men, easily depressed, and as easily reanimated by words of encouragement. Many have been reluctant to engage in military service,--their imagination investing it with the terrors of instant and certain death. But this reluctance has passed away with participation in active service, with the adventure and inspiration of a soldier's life, and the latent manhood has recovered its rightful sway. Said a superintendent who was of the first delegation to Port Royal in March, 1862,--a truthful man, and not given to rose-colored views,--"I did not have faith in arming negroes, when I visited the North last autumn, but I have now. They will be not mere machines, but real tigers, when aroused; and I should not wish to face them." One amusing incident may be mentioned. A man deserted from the regiment, was discovered hidden in a chimney in the district where he had lived, was taken back to camp, went to Florida in Higginson's first expedition, bore his part well in the skirmishes, became excited with the service, was made a sergeant, and, receiving a furlough on his return, went to the plantation where he had hid, and said he would not take five thousand dollars for his place.

But more significant, as showing the success of the experiment, is the change of feeling among the white soldiers towards the negro regiment, a change due in part to the just policy of General Saxton, in part to the President's Proclamation of January 1st, which has done much to clear the atmosphere everywhere within the army-lines, but more than all to the soldierly conduct of the negroes themselves during their expeditions. I had one excellent opportunity to note this change. On the 6th day of April, Colonel Higginson's regiment was assigned to picket-duty on Port Royal Island,--the first active duty it had performed on the Sea Islands,--and was to relieve the Pennsylvania Fifty-Fifth. When, after a march of ten miles, it reached the advanced picket-station, there were about two hundred soldiers awaiting orders to proceed to Beaufort. I said, in a careless tone, to one of the Pennsylvania soldiers, who was looking at Higginson's regiment as it stood in line,--"Isn't this rather new, to be relieved by a negro regiment?"

"All right," said he. "They've as much right to fight for themselves as I have to fight for them."

A squad of half a dozen men stood by, making no dissent, and accepting him as their spokesman. Moving in another direction, I said to a soldier,--

"What do you think of that regiment?"

The answer was,--

"All right. I'd rather they'd shoot the Rebels than have the

Rebels shoot me;" and none of the bystanders dissented.

As one of the negro companies marched off the field to picket a station at the Ferry, they passed within a few feet of some twenty of the Pennsylvania soldiers, just formed into line preparatory to marching to Beaufort. The countenances of the latter, which I watched, exhibited no expression of disgust, dislike, or disapprobation, only of curiosity. Other white soldiers gave to the weary negroes hominy left from the morning meal. The major of the Fifty-Fifth, highest in command of the relieved regiment, explained very courteously to Colonel Higginson the stations and duties of the pickets, and proffered any further aid desired. This was, it is true, an official duty, but there are more ways than one in which to perform even an official duty. I rode back to Beaufort, part of the way, in company with a captain of the First Massachusetts Calvary, who was the officer of the day. He said "he was'nt much of a negro-man, but he had no objection to their doing our fighting." He pronounced the word as spelled with two gs; but I prefer to retain the good English. Colonel Montgomery, who had a partly filled regiment, most of whom were conscripts, said that on his return from Jacksonville he sent a squad of his men ashore in charge of some prisoners he has taken. Some white soldiers seeing them approach from the wharf, one said,--

"What are those coming?"

"Negro soldiers," (word pronounced as in the former case,) was the answer.

"Damn 'em!"

But as they approached nearer, "What have they got with 'em?" was inquired.

"Bully for the negroes!" (the same pronunciation as before) was then the response from all.

So quick was the transition, when it was found that the negroes had demonstrated their usefulness! It is, perhaps humiliating to remember that such an unreasonable and unpatriotic prejudice has at any time existed; but it is never worthwhile to suppress the truth of history. This prejudice has been effectually broken in the Free States; and one of the pageants of this epoch was the triumphal march through Boston, on the 28th of May, on its way to embark for Port Royal, of the Fifty-Fourth Regiment of Massachusetts Volunteers, the first regiment of negro soldiers which the Free States have sent to the war. On the day previous, May 27th, a far different scene transpired on the banks of the Mississippi. Two black regiments, enlisted some months before in Louisiana under the order of Major-General Butler, both with line and one with field officers of their own lineage, made charge after charge on the batteries of Port Hudson, and were mown down like summer's grass, the survivors, many with mutilated limbs, closing up the thinned ranks and pressing on again, careless of life, and mindful only of honor and duty, with a sublimity of courage unsurpassed in the annals of war, and leaving there to all mankind an immortal record for themselves and their race.

Homeward bound, I stopped for two days at Fortress Monroe, and was again among the familiar scenes of my soldier-life. It was there that Major-General Butler, first of all the generals in the army of the Republic, and anticipating even Republican statesmen, had clearly pointed to the cause of the war. At Craney Island I met two accomplished women of the Society of Friends, who, on a most cheerless spot, and with every inconvenience, were teaching the children of the freedmen. Two good men, one at the fort and the other at Norfolk, were distributing the laborers on farms in the vicinity, and providing them with implements and seeds which the benevolent societies had furnished. Visiting Hampton, I recognized, in the familiar faces of those who, in the early days of the war, had been for a brief period under my charge. Their hearty greetings to one whom they remembered as the first to point them to freedom and cheer. When with its prospect could hardly be received without emotion. But there is no time to linger over these scenes.

Such are some of the leading features in the condition of the freedmen, particularly at Port Royal. The enterprise for their aid, begun in doubt, is no longer a bare hope or possibility. It is a fruition and a consummation. The negroes will work for a living. They will fight for their freedom. They are adapted to civil society. As a people, they are not exempt from the frailties of our common humanity, nor from the vices which hereditary bondage always superadds to these. As it is said to take three generations to subdue a freeman completely to a slave, so it may not be possible in a single generation to restore the pristine manhood. One who expects to find emancipated slaves perfect men and women, or to realize in them some fair dream of an ideal race, will meet disappointment; but there is nothing in their nature of condition to daunt the Christian patriot, rather, there is everything to cheer and fortify his faith. They have shown capacity for knowledge, for free industry, for subordination to law and discipline, for soldierly fortitude, for social and family relations, for religious culture and aspirations; and these qualities, when stirred and sustained by the incitements and rewards of a just society, and combining with the currents of our continental civilization, will, under the guidance of a benevolent Providence which forgets neither them nor us, make them a constantly progressive race, and secure them ever after from the calamity of another enslavement, and ourselves from the worse calamity of being again their oppressors.

The Yeatman Report includes copies of the rules and regulations set up by the government for leasing abandoned plantations and employing the freedmen. The success of the Western Sanitary Commission and the American Missionary Association provided the kind of information needed to establish the Freedmen's Bureau, which was created by the Federal Government, March 3, 1865.

The responses to this organized attempt at massive social experimentation were vacillating, because, as noted previously, there was no clear cut definition of the legal status of the emancipated slave between 1861 and the adoption of the XIII Amendment to the Constitution in 1865, which finally provided the definitive action to free all of the slaves in rebellious territory. Thus the activities undertaken by Pierce and others in their improvised associations were accomplished for a population with ambiguous legal status. Furthermore, blacks had to overcome, as best they could, a lack of real and genuine acceptance of their potential, if not their capacity, to initiate and develop programs on their own behalf. Thus, regardless of the existence of ample evidence to the contrary, they were forced to proceed on their own and did so, despite the fact that, lacking great financial resources, it was necessary for them to operate on a shoestring.

Document 4

James E. Yeatman, Report to the Western Sanitary Commission in Regard to Leasing Abandoned Plantations, with Rules and Regulations Governing the Same, St. Louis: Western Sanitary Commission Rooms, No. 10 North 5th St., 1864.

Lease:

This Agreement, made this _______ day of _______ 1864, by and between the United States of America, by William P. Mellen, Supervising Special Agent of the Treasury Department, in the first Agency, and _______ in the State of _______.

That in pursuance of instructions from the Secretary of the Treasury of the United States, and of orders from the Secretary of War, concerning the leasing of abandoned houses, tenements and lands in States declared in insurrection, the said Agent for in behalf of the United States, agrees, upon the terms hereinafter contained, to lease to the said _______ from the date hereof to the first day of January, 1865, the following described lands and premises, viz:

The said _______ having taken and filed the prescribed oath hereunto annexed, hereby agrees to pay to the said Agent, as rent for the above described lands and premises _______ cents per pound on all cotton and a proportionate sum upon all other products raised by him, which payment shall be made as provided for, and in pursuance of the Rules and Regulations for leasing Abandoned Plantations, and employing Freedmen, hereunto annexed: and in all cases where freed labor is employed, the said_______further agrees to contribute or pay to the said Agent the sum of one cent per pound on all cotton, and a proportionate sum on all other products grown on said premises, for the purposes set forth in Section V of said Rules and Regulations.

And the said_______further agrees that, during the continuance of this lease, he will keep employed No. 1 man, or the equivalent thereto in men, women or children, as classified in said Rules for each twelve acres of tillable land occupied by him under this lease, it being hereby agreed that said premises contain_______ acres, and require_______No. 1 hands, or other equivalent in other grades.

And the said Leasee further agrees to furnish to the persons so employed, suitable tenements, with separate quarters for families who may desire the same; and that to each family of four or more persons he will set apart for their sole use and benefit not less than one acre of ground suitable for garden purposes, and fuel sufficient for the use and comfort of each family, all of which shall be without charge to such persons or the Government.

Said Lessee hereby further agrees that no freed person shall be employed on the said premises, except under contracts made with such person; and no contract for freed labor shall be valid without the sanction of the Superintendent of the Freedmen's Home Farm, who shall in each case designate the proportion of each grade or sex to be employed.

Said Lessee further agrees to pay each freed person so employed according to the terms set out and established in Section X of the said Rules and Regulations.

Said Lessee further agrees to pay at least one-half the amount of the monthly wages during each and every month, said payment to be in cash, food, clothing, or other necessaries, at the option of the laborer; all food, clothing, or other articles so furnished to be of good quality, and not to be charged at more than 15 per cent. advance on wholesale invoice prices at St. Louis, Chicago, Cincinnati, or Louisville, or New Orleans for southern products purchased there.

It is further agreed that the parties of this contract shall be subject to the observance of the rules and regulations hereto subjoined.

Signed, sealed, and delivered in presence of--

_______(L. S.)

____

_______(L. S.)

STATE OF________)
________) ss:
COUNTY OF_______)

I_______do solemnly swear that I will bear true faith and allegiance to the Constitution and Government of the United States, any law, constitution or ordinance of any State to the contrary notwithstanding; that I have no part, and will take no part in the existing rebellion against the Government of the United States, and will in no way give aid, comfort, or countenance to any person engaged therein; that I will obey and observe all laws of Congress touching slaves and the conditions of slavery, and all Proclamations of the President of the United States relating to the same subject, and that I will do what in me lies to induce all others within the circle of my influence to do the same.

Sworn to and subscribed before me this) ____________
)
________day of________186)

Rules and Regulations for Leasing Abandoned Plantations and Employing Freedmen:

I. Said Plantations, or such portions thereof as may be required, will be leased to good and loyal citizens, who have taken the oath subjoined to the foregoing contract.

II. Preference will be given to those wishing small tracts of land.

III. No lessee will be allowed to lease more than one abandoned plantation, and all shall be obliged to furnish satisfactory evidence of ability to stock and cultivate the quantity of land applied for.

IV. Owners of plantations who have taken the prescribed oath may occupy the same, and no charge will be made, except in cases where they employ the labor of freedmen, when payment of one cent per pound will be charged on all cotton grown by them, and a proportionate charge upon all other products of their labor, which will be applied to the support of aged, infirm and helpless freed people, and for sanitary and educational purposes.

V. On all lands the lessee shall pay a rent of one cent per pound on all cotton, and a proportional charge upon other products grown by him, and in all cases where freed labor is employed, the lessee shall, in addition to the stipulated rents, contribute one cent per pound on all cotton grown by him, and a proportionate sum upon all other products of their labor, to the fund for the support of helpless and aged freed people, for education and other purposes connected therewith.

VI. Freedman's Home Farms shall be established at convenient locations, which shall be under a superintendent appointed for the purpose, and shall be places--

First, Where all freed persons of the respective districts in which they are located, shall be registered and employed, until engaged or hired by other employers.

Second, As homes for the aged and infirm freedmen, and motherless children unable to perform labor.

VII. Planters, farmers, and other employers requiring laborers, shall make application to the Superintendent of the Freedmen's Home Farms, who will furnish such as may be required. Persons employing fathers or mothers, must take with them such children or near relatives as may be dependent upon them, and desire to go.

VIII. All freed persons over the age of twelve years, who are capable of performing labor, will be required to work.

IX. All laborers shall be classified by the Superintendent as follows: 1. Sound persons from twenty to forty years of age, inclusive, shall be called No. 1 hands. 2. From fifteen to nineteen inclusive, and from forty-one to fifty, inclusive, shall be called No. 2 hands. 3. From twelve to fourteen, inclusive, and over fifty, No. 3 hands. Persons suffering from any physical defect or infirmity shall be classified by the Superintendent, and wages for them designated.

X. Application for hands shall be made to Superintendents, with certificate or copy of contract showing number of acres leased and hands required. One No. 1 hand, or the equivalent in other grades of hands, shall be employed for every twelve acres of tillable land. The Superintendent to designate the proportionate numbers and grades of each sex to be selected, and the wages of No. 1 males shall be $25 per month; No. 2, $20; No. 3, $15; Nos. 1, 2, and 3 females, $18, $14, and $10.

In case any person employing freed persons to labor on plantation, shall wish to give any of those employed an interest in the profits resulting from the working the same, in lieu of the regular wages above specified, and such persons shall desire to make a contract with the employer for a stipulated portion of such profits in lieu of other wages, it may be done: Provided, however, that all such contracts shall be approved by the Superintendent of the Freedman's Home Farm, at which they are employed, or nearest which they may be located, and also by the Agent of the District, and that one cent per pound on all cotton raised, and a proportionate amount upon other products, shall be contributed for the support of the helpless, as provided in case of stipulated wages, and also that all necessary supplies for the employed shall be furnished to them by the employer, upon the same terms, and subject to the same conditions as in cases of payment of the regular wages above provided for.

XI. When lessees wanting laborers shall have made their selections, lists shall be prepared, and the employer and employee shall each sign a contract in duplicate in presence of a witness, one copy of which shall be retained and filed by the Superintendent.

XII. At the end of the year of period of time for which such contracts shall be made, the lessee shall return the hands to the Farm from which they were taken, or account for them, and a full settlement shall then be made, he paying to his hands in cash such balance as may be due; and no cotton shall be sold or shipped without previous written permit of the Special Agent of the District, or the certificate of the Superintendent of the Farm from which they were hired, that wages have been fully paid.

XIII. Lessees shall provide, without charge, good and sufficient quarters for laborers employed, a separate tenement for each family, with proper regard for sanitary conditions, a sufficient supply of food, one acre of ground to each family of four or more persons, and also to others requiring it, in same proportion.

XIV. The lessee shall provide and keep on hand a sufficient supply of wholesome food, and suitable clothing for the employees and their families, which shall be sold to the laborers at the wholesale cost price, and fifteen per cent. thereon, keeping an account of the items with each laborer, which account shall be settled and approved by the Superintendent at the close of the year, at which time the balance due shall be paid. All accounts and invoices shall be open to inspection of the Superintendent and the Special Agent of the District at all proper times.

XV. Laborers to be paid for full time unless they shall be sick, or voluntarily neglect to work. In cases of such sickness or neglect, the employer may report it to the Farm Superintendent within ten days after the end of the month, who, upon being satisfied of such sickness or neglect, shall endorse the proper deduction therefor upon the contract. In case a person fails to labor as contemplated by the contract, the Superintendent upon being satisfied of the fact, shall receive him or her back at the Farm, and cancel the contract, upon payment by the employer of the amount properly due. Should a hand quit voluntarily, without consent of lessee, before the end of the term, the balance of wages to be forfeited, half to the employer, and half to the Government.

XVI. Where the lessee fails to furnish a proper supply of food, clothing, or does not furnish proper quarters, or overtasks his laborers, or otherwise abuses them, or violates his agreement, they shall have the right to appeal to the Superintendent, who may have the same corrected, by declaring the contract forfeited, and taking possession of the land, or by releasing the employees from their contract, in which latter case the lessee shall be required to pay all wages due, and shall be held responsible for half wages until other employment for the released employees can be obtained.

XVII. There shall be employment provided on the Freedman's Home Farms, for all who are able to work, for which no wages shall be paid; food and clothing being considered as an equivalent therefor; the labor performed being for the benefit of the occupants of the Farm, and the general good. The Superintendent may establish such rules for police and other purposes, as may be proper in conducting the Farm, and governing the persons connected therewith.

XVIII. Lessees shall only be required to pay half the monthly wages, either in money, provisions, or clothing, until the crops are sold. The first lien upon the crops shall be for the wages of the laborer, and provision will be made by the Superintendent, to secure the prompt payment of the same.

XIX. The Supervising Agent, or such officer as shall be designated by him for that purpose, will from time to time examine invoices and accounts of lessees, and see that the rules are complied with.

XX. The use of the lash, paddle, and all other cruel modes of punishment shall not be permitted or inflicted by lessees, or any one in their employment, upon the persons of any of the employees or their families.

XXI. Schools will be established in convenient localities, and all children between the ages of six and twelve years shall be required to attend them.

XXII. Persons desiring to employ mechanics, wood-choppers, or other laborers, must apply to the Superintendent of the Freedman's Home Farm, and all contracts for such labor shall be subject to his approval.

XXIII. All persons living together as husband and wife shall be legally married; they shall assume a family name, and Registers of marriages, births, and deaths shall be kept by the Superintendents, to whom the same shall be reported by the employers. And also the and location of all employers, together with the names of the persons employed by them, and of those living with them.

XXIV. All persons taking leases, either by bid at a public letting, or without competition, will be required to work the hands awarded to them under their own supervision or that of a substitute accepted by the proper Assistant Special Agent or Superintendent of a Freedman's Home Farm, and no transfer will be permitted or recognized in which an assignee shall pay, or agree to pay, a bonus.

Wm. P. Mellen,
Supervising Special Agent,
First Agency.

This contract, made this________day of________, 186 , between________, employer, and________, ________freed laborers.

Witnesseth: That said________agrees to employ said laborers on his________from the________day of________, 1864, to the________ day of________, 186 , on the terms prescribed in the code of Rules and Regulations for leasing abandoned property, and hiring freed men; and the said laborers agree to be diligent and faithful hands while in his employ; it being understood and agreed that this Contract is subject to the provisions of said code, by which all parties hereto agree to be governed.

In presence of--

________,

________,

________,

________,

________.

Cotton grown and shipped from Goodrich's Landing, raised by colored men, who leased ground and worked same on their own account:

	Bales		Bales
Solomon Johnson	7	Edward Maxwell	28
Samuel Howard	47	Contraband	12
Wm. Goodin	3	Tom Taylor	4
Henry Johnson	6	Moses Wright	6
Wm. Gibson and Forst	5	Chas. Bowman	2
Geo. Washington	4	Nat Brooks	1
York Hardin & J. Hardin	4	Alex. Hamilton	1
Thomas Taylor	1	James Fisher	1
Archy Stewart	5	Lewis Jackson	4
Sam'l Tousey and Son	4	Richard Walker	1
Peter Boyes	2	Lewis White and Charles	5
	88		65
			88
			153

	Bales	Bales Sold	Netting
Silas Stepheny	27	6	$1,401.35
Robert Cookley	7	3	790.43
York Horton	2	2	504.84
Sancho Lynch	75	29	6,897.43
Henry Harris	31	9	2,251.69
Sol Richardson	10	7	1,642.13
	152	56	$13,487.87

	Bales	Bales Sold	Netting
Luke Johnson	11	9	$2,061.18
Richard Walker	5	5	1,247.60
Ben Mingo	14	2	580.61
Wm. Goodin	4	4	1,023.94
L. White	28	25	5,838.60
	62	45	$10,751.93
	152	56	
	153	101 sold	
Whole no. bales raised	367		

Net proceeds of	56	bales sold	$13,487.87
" "	45	" "	10,751.93
	101		$24,239.80
Average of	276	" at $240	66,240.00
	367		$90,479.80

It is clearly apparent that an examination of the lives of individuals who early participated in the varied efforts to assist the freedmen, men and women who had in some instances attained varying degrees of success for themselves, shows that they were not selfishly oriented, but desired and worked for the attainment of similar accomplishments by other blacks. Of those who have left written records of their activities, two women and one man remain outstanding personages in the period of transition from slavery to freedom. They were Charlotte L. Forten (1838-1914) who later became the wife of the Reverend Francis J. Grimké; Susie King Taylor (1848-?); and Robert Smalls.

Charlotte L. Forten, the granddaughter of James Forten, one of the greatest black abolitionists, member of a family of free Negroes residing in Philadelphia, herself educated in New England, came to Port Royal under the same auspices as many missionary whites. The following pages of her diary show how she utilized her skills, knowledge and talents with warmth and compassion to help provide a new vision of life for her young students and their families.

Document 5*

Charlotte L. Forten, The Journal of Charlotte Forten, A Free Negro in the Slave Era, edited, with an introduction and notes by Ray Allen Billington, (New York: Collier Books, 1953), pp. 149-153, 155, 169-170.

Thursday, Nov. 6. Cut out a dress to-day for an old woman--Venus,--who thanked and blessed me enough. Poor old soul. It was a pleasure to hear her say what a happy year this has been for her. "Nobody to whip me nor dribe me, and plenty to eat. Nebber had such a happy year in my life before." Promised to make a little dress for her great-grandchild--only a few weeks old. It shall be a bright pink calico, such as will delight the little free baby's eyes, when it shall be old enough to appreciate it. [p. 149]

Thursday, Nov. 13. Talked to the children a little while to-

*Reprinted by permission of the editor.

day about the noble Toussaint (L'Ouverture). They listened very attentively. It is well that they sh'ld know what one of their own color c'ld do for his race. I long to inspire them with courage and ambition (of a noble sort) and high purpose. [p. 150]

Tuesday, Nov. 18. After school went to The Corner again. Stopped at old Susy's house to see some sick children. Old Susy is a character. Miss T(owne) asked her if she wanted her old master to come back again. Most emphatically she answered. "No indeed, missus, no indeed dey treat we too bad. Dey tuk ebery one of my chilen away from me. When we sick and c'ldn't work dey tuk away all our food from us; gib us nutten to eat. Dey's orful hard Missis." When Miss T(owne) told her that some of the people said they wanted their old masters to come back, a look of supreme contempt came to Susy's withered face. "Dat's 'cause dey's got no sense den, missus," she said indignantly. Susy has any quantity of children and grandchildren, and she thanks God that she can now have some of them with her in her old age. [p. 151-2]

Sunday, Nov. 23. After the sermon an old negro prayed a touching and most effective prayer. Then the minister read Gen. Saxton's Proclamation for Thanksgiving--which is grand--the very best and noblest that c'ld have been penned. I like and admire the Gen. more than ever now.

Six couples were married to-day. Some of the dresses were unique. Am sure one must have worn a cast-off dress of her mistress's. It looked like white silk covered with lace. The lace sleeves and other trimmings were in rather a decayed state and the white cotton gloves were well ventilated. But the bride looked none the less happy for that. Only one had the slightest claim to good looks. And she was a demure little thing with a neat, plain silk dress on. T'was amusing to see some of the headdresses. One, of tattered flowers and ribbons, was very ridiculous. But no matter for that. I am truly glad that the poor creatures are trying to live right and virtuous lives. As usual we had some fine singing. It was very pleasant to be at church again. For two Sundays past I had not been, not feeling well. "Down in the Lonesome Valley" so well sung. [p. 153]

After an appropriate prayer and sermon by Rev. Mr. Phillips, Gen. Saxton made a short but spirited speech to the people--urging the young men to enlist in the regiment now forming under Col. T. W. Higginson. That was the first intimation I had had of Mr. Higginson being down here. I am greatly rejoiced thereat. He seems to me of all fighting men the one best fitted to command a regiment of colored soldiers. The mention of his (name) recalled the happy days passed last summer in Massachusetts, when day after day, in the streets of W(orcester) we used to see the indefatigable Capt. H(igginson) drilling his white company. I never saw him so full of life and energy--entering with his whole soul into his work--without thinking what a splendid general he w'ld make. And that too may come about. Gen. Saxton said to-day that he hoped to see him commander of an army of black men. The Gen. told the people how nobly Mr. H(igginson) had stood by Anthony Burns, in the old dark days, even suffering imprisonment for his sake; and assured (them) that they might feel sure of meeting no injustice under the leadership of such a man; that he w'ld see to it that they were not wronged in any way.

Then he told them the story of Robert Small(s), and added. To-day Rob(ert) came to see me. I asked him how he was getting on in the store which he is keeping for the freed people. He said he was doing very well--making fifty dollars a week, sometimes, "But" said he "Gen. I'm going to stop keeping store. I'm going to enlist." "What," said I. "Are you going to enlist when you can make fifty doll(ar)s a week keeping store?" "Yes Sir," he replied "I'm going to enlist as a private in the black regiment. How can I expect to keep my freedom if I'm not willing to fight for it? Suppose the Secesh sh'ld get back here again? What good w'ld my fifty doll(ar)s do me then? Yes, I sh'ld enlist if I were making a thousand dollars a week."

Beside the Gen. and Mrs. G(age) there were several other strangers present;--ladies from the North who come down here to teach. [p. 155]

Friday, Dec. 26. Kept store nearly all day. I like it occasionally. It amuses and interests me. There was one very sensible man in today, whose story interested me much. He had been a carpenter, and had been taken up by his master on the mainland, on "the main," as they call it, to help build houses to which the families of the rebels might retreat when the Yankees w'ld come. His master sent him back again to this island to bring back a boat and some of the people. He was provided with a pass. On reaching the island, he found that the Union troops had come, so he determined (indeed he had determined before) to remain here with his family, as he knew his master did not dare to come back after them. Some of his fellow servants whom he had left on the "main," hearing that the Union troops had come resolved to try to make their escape. They used a boat of the master's out of which a piece about six feet square had been cut out. In the night, secretly, they went to the boat which had been sunk near the edge of the creek, measured the hole, and went to the woods and, after several nights' work, made a piece large enough to fit in. With this they mended the boat by another night's work, and then sunk it in the same position in which they had found it. The next night five of them embarked, and after passing through many perils in the shape of the enemy's boats, near which they were obliged to pass, and so making very slow progress, for they c'ld travel only at night, and in the day time, ran their boat close to the shore, out of sight--they at last passed the enemy's lines and reached one of our gunboats in safty (sic). They were taken on board, and their wants attended to, for their provisions had given out and they were much exhausted. After being there some time they were sent to this island, where their families, who had feared they w'ld never see them again welcomed them rejoicingly. I was much interested in the story of their escape, and give it for your especial benefit, Dear A. [p. 169-70]

In contrast to Charlotte Forten, daughter of a free and wealthy Negro family, who had been provided with an education equal to that enjoyed by the most fortunate of white women of her day, Susie King Taylor, was born in slavery in Liberty County, Georgia. Reared in Savannah by her grandmother, she was able to contract for her labor and to live apart from her master, a privilege for a slave. In the early pages of her memoirs we can discern the strength with which familial relations functioned, despite the constraints placed upon the family by the slave system. Her service represents perhaps a higher level of achievement, for she had not the advantages of a Charlotte Forten, nor was she prepared to function in the Port Royal Experiment at the same level. Nevertheless, her ability to teach and to nurse, and her willingness to do this without the compensation due her, reveals a mature woman who made an equally compassionate contribution to her fellows.

Document 6

Susie King Taylor, Reminiscences of My Life in Camp with the 33rd United States Colored Troops Late 1st S. C. Volunteers, Boston: The Author, 1902, p. 21.

I taught a great many of the comrades in Company E to read and write, when they were off duty. Nearly all were anxious to learn. My husband taught some also when it was convenient for him. I was very happy to know my efforts were successful in camp, and also felt grateful for the appreciation of my services. I gave my services willingly for four years and three months without receiving a dollar. I was glad, however, to be allowed to go with the regiment, to care for the sick and afflicted comrades.

The singular accomplishments of Robert Smalls highlight his self-help activities and his total involvement in bettering the lives of others. He originally achieved fame as the man who was able to take charge of a Confederate vessel and pilot it into the Union's possession. Later, his actions in the Port Royal area, specifically in Beaufort, South Carolina, resulted in the provision of schools and homes for the poor. In addition, through his participation in the South Carolina Constitutional Convention of 1868, he assisted other black assemblymen to develop new social welfare laws designed to correct and alleviate the problems not only of blacks, but of poor people in general. He is a signal example that nothing could deter the forward momentum of blacks themselves in participating in the society which was new for them. The involvement of blacks like Charlotte Forten, Susie King Taylor and Robert Smalls, all contributing in accordance with their capabilities, imparted great significance to the Port Royal Experiment. It became the model which provided guidance to Congress, which established the Freedman's Bureau in May, 1865. This organization, a federal bureaucracy hastily improvised, may justifiably be called the "war on poverty" of its day. It was an umbrella-type of social service delivery system which, hopefully, intended to serve a multiple number of needs of the free, but poor people. Supreme command resided in the military, but the execution of the program was aided by the organization of many private voluntary associations, such as, the American Missionary Association among others. It was truly a joint effort of both the federal government and private philanthropy.

Document 7

Edyth L. Ross, "Black Heritage in Social Welfare, Survival Through Adaptation to Specific Questions, 1861-1905," Unpublished manuscript, 1973, pp. 17-20.

Robert Smalls was born in Beaufort, South Carolina, and was the slave of John H. McKee, who had been nursed by Small's mother. At the age of twelve, his master moved to Charleston, where Smalls began work as a waiter. He later worked as a stevedore and then as a deckhand and wheelsman on the steamer, *Planter.* All but one dollar of his earnings had to be paid to his master's widow.

The steamer on which he worked became a part of the Confederate navy in 1861, under Captain Hamilton, who had surveyed all of the bars on the coast of South Carolina, Georgia and Florida. In this manner Smalls became thoroughly familiar with the coastal waters also.

Although the lot of Smalls as a slave had been better than most, he had learned early the dehumanizing consequences of the system and yearned to be free. His opportunity arose in 1862, when the *Planter* became the dispatch boat and flagship of the Confederate commander, General Ripley. Smalls and his slave companions worked on a plan for quitting the Southern Confederacy and taking refuge on the "Lincoln Gunboat". On May 13, 1862, while all officers were ashore, Smalls executed his plan. He picked up his wife and children, four other women and one other child and, with the assistance of nine fellows he successfully turned the steamer over to the Federal fleet. Smalls was allowed $1,500 as his share of prize money and was appointed by General Saxton, first as a second lieutenant, detailed to the Navy, later a Captain, in the Quartermaster Department of the Army.

This deed not only made Smalls a hero to blacks but also served to direct national policy toward enlisting Port Royal freedmen into the Union Army and paying for their services. All who enlisted were declared forever free. Smalls returned to Beaufort to help in the enlistment effort.

Smalls also was very effective in promoting the social experiment at Port Royal. He solicited money, books, and clothing in the North and was prominently acclaimed in the white press.

Never exposed to formal education, he was self-taught. One of his main interests was the education of the Sea Islanders. In 1867, at a government tax-sale, he purchased a two-story building and deeded it to the colored children of the town of Beaufort. He, as President of the School Board, and with his wife, Mrs. Hannah Smalls, Treasurer of the Ladies Fair, a voluntary association formed to advance the social life of the area, made many appeals to Northerners for school funds.

Smalls also displayed financial acumen. He bought his former mate's home, joined with several veterans of the First South Carolina Volunteers to buy and operate, cooperatively, a steamer under his command, and bought the Beaufort County Poor Farm and several town lots. His financial success enabled him to sponsor his educational projects, combining business economic enterprise with meeting the needs of his people.

Although the Emancipation Proclamation in 1863 officially freed them, the Sea Islanders early recognized the need for political action. In the spring of 1864 they held a rally in Beaufort and elected Smalls as one of the black delegates to the National Convention of the Republican Party to be held in Baltimore. Although these delegates were not officially received, it was obvious that the fight for freedom was far from over, and insured his selection later as a delegate to the famous South Carolina Convention of 1868. Here he significantly contributed to the framing of the South Carolina Constitution which remained in effect for twenty-eight years.

These examples of black achievement in the Sea Islands occurred within the larger framework of vacillating national and local policies which affected their lives. For, as pointed out by Willie Lee Rose, the conflicting policies between the land commissioner, Rufus Saxton, and others were predicated on shifting governmental policies.

From an institutional frame of reference, the significance of the Port Royal Experiment is that it became the model which provided guidance to the Congress which established the Freedmen's Bureau in 1865. The Freedmen's Bureau, technically entitled Bureau of Refugees, Freedmen and Abandoned Lands, was an umbrella type of social service system designed to meet a multitude of needs of free but poor people. Again, it was a joint effort of the Federal Government and of private and philanthropic organizations. Supreme command resided in the military, but the execution of the program was fostered by these organizations and by many cooperating Freedmen's aid societies and, particularly, the American Missionary Association.

The Freedmen's Bureau, according to W. A. Low,[1*] had four clearly defined aims and objectives, namely,

> relief: by providing food, clothing, shelter and medical care for freedmen and refugees; the administration of justice: by protecting the political and civil rights of black men; protection: by defending freedmen from physical violence or fraud, by military arms, if necessary; and by education: by cooperating with agencies, individuals, and local officials in providing schools and teachers for freedmen. In the border states, however, the Bureau's most significant work was performed in the field of education.

It enjoyed variable success in the attainment of one or another of its objectives, according to such factors as status of military occupation; of land policy; of black access to political power; of white support; etc. Perhaps the greatest success was in the field of education, for educational institutions founded under its aegis are still viable today, these being "the glory" of its first director, Major General O. O. Howard, for whom Howard University is named.

These programs are well described in the doctoral dissertation of Inabel Lindsay which is entitled "The Participation of Negroes in the Establishment of Welfare Services, 1865-1900." This work also delineates the overall organizational patterns and structures evolved to meet legal, economic, and social needs. Despite vacillating and ambiguous policies primarily resulting from the assassination of

---

*Footnotes to Part I begin on page 106.

President Lincoln and the assumption of the Presidency by Andrew Johnson, they served everywhere in the South as the instrumental means for setting in motion developments in education, public health care of the destitute and other helpless populations, and eventually came to have enduring significance. Some of the basic functions of the Freedmen's Bureau and the contributions of significant individuals are detailed in the following adaptation of Dr. Lindsay's dissertation.

Document 8*

Inabel Burns Lindsay, "Some Contributions to Welfare Services, 1865-1900," Journal of Negro Education, No. 25, Winter, 1956, pp. 15-24.

Despite marked reluctance and only after months of bitter congressional debate, the Federal government finally, in March, 1865 established a facility to supervise the transition of slave to free citizen; to administer aid, also to white refugees; and to assume custody of abandoned lands. Its tenuous existence was extended only year by year for less than a decade, with various of its activities eliminated or curtailed before they were well under way. In view of the uncertainty of its existence and the hostile atmosphere in which it existed, it is surprising that the Bureau operated with even a modicum of effectiveness. However, its activities in relief and rehabilitation and its support of educational programs were comparatively effective. The first Bureau Act provided that military personnel might be assigned to administer the program, but carried no appropriation for its operation. Consequently, the effectiveness of its services reflected the varying attitudes of compassion and hostility of the military supervisors.

The lack of preparation and opportunity for the majority of Negroes to assume positions of responsibility were factors limiting their participation in the operation of the Bureau. Nevertheless, a fair degree of participation was evident. In addition to such indirect services as supplying land, building school houses and paying their teachers salaries, Negroes were identified among the ranks of agents and officers of lesser rank. John M. Langston, colored lawyer of Ohio, was appointed in April 1867, a general inspector of the Bureau. Dr. Martin Delany, of Pittsburgh, was assigned in August 1865 to command the Bureau's affairs at Hilton Head, South Carolina. Dr. Charles B. Purvis and Dr. Alexander T. Augusta of Washington were engaged as physicians for the freedmen. Sojourner Truth, that rare old crusader against slavery and fighter in the causes of woman suffrage and temperance, had been appointed a "counselor

*Reprinted by permission of the publisher.

to the freed people of Arlington Heights, Virginia," and in September 1865 an Assistant to the Surgeon in charge of the newly established hospital for freedmen in Washington.

Besides these well-known Negro leaders, others, more obscure, were also in their humble assignments, instrumental in the implementation of the Bureau's program. These workers included "employment agents," "missionary teachers," "matrons," and designated community supervisors for the freedmen's villages. One of the "Agents" was Christian Fleetwood, who had served with distinction in the Union Army and was motivated by a desire to continue his service to his race. A native of Maryland, he had moved to Washington and there undertook his work as employment agent for the Bureau. A "Miss Ellis," a colored teacher in the freedmen's village at Arlington was "sustained by a Village Society". Maria W. Stewart, a matron of the Freedmen's Hospital, in connection with her duties, visited the destitute children nearby to offer help and, with the help of Dr. Rayburn, then superintendent of the hospital, raised funds to buy a building in which to conduct a Sabbath School for seventy-five scholars.

In the short span of six or seven years, the Bureau did much to further the rehabilitation of the needy and the reorganization of a disrupted society. Negro participants in its program aided in the limited ways open to them.

STABILIZATION OF FAMILY AND COMMUNITY LIFE

Observations made in letters, newspaper articles and other documents indicate that the central concern of blacks was with the quality of family life. Contradicting the many myths which stereotyped the behavior of the freedmen as carefree, improvident, incompetent, and irrational, there are records which demonstrate clearly that there was serious concern for what we now call social welfare activities. These documents exhibit evidence of a desire for stable family living, and for services to those unable to fend for themselves.

Of considerable interest is Dr. Hendricks' assertion that blacks refused to work in gang-type labor forces but preferred to work only if family-type plots were made available. This attests to the fact that perhaps the relation between family and land--in the African case between lineage and land--had some effect still in the minds of the black population, and also attests to the survival of familial-type bonds in the period of slavery, despite the fact that the slave codes had stripped the slave of his right to have a legally sanctioned family structure.

Document 9

George Hendricks, "Union Army Occupation of the Southern Seaboard, 1861-1865," Abstract, unpublished Ph.D dissertation, Columbia University, 1954.

In the winter of 1861-1862 a joint expedition of the Union Army and Navy occupied Port Royal, Fernandina, and St. Augustine in order to provide bases for the South Atlantic Blockading Squadron. The white people left the South Carolina Sea Islands when the Union forces came, abandoning their plantations and slaves.

General T. W. Sherman, commander of the Union army, assumed responsibility for the slaves. He published a plan for superintendence and education. He and others appealed for public support. Charitable societies were formed in New York, Philadelphia, and Boston, and throughout the war these agencies sent superintendents and teachers to the Sea Islands. The Treasury Department directed their work in the spring of 1862. The War Department took over the direction through a special mission headed by General Rufus Saxton in the summer of 1862.

The superintendents at first tried simply to add money wages to the tasks and gang system of labor peculiar to the Islands. The Negroes resisted gang labor and the plantations were in anarchy in the summer of 1862. In this anarchy the family plot system--still for money wages, and not for a share of the crop--was worked out. In the fields, this assignment of plots to families for cultivation was the basic change from slavery to freedom.

The Civil War direct tax laws created a surprising possibility of turning the family plots into homesteads owned by the Negroes. The direct tax on land was not paid in the islands and the plantations were sold for taxes. There was great wrangling between two per-homestead factions, and in the end just under a thousand Negro families were granted small tracts of about ten acres for $1.25 per acre.

The following letters and newspaper article document the varied means by which the freedmen sought to secure for themselves a measure of social stability. The overwhelming emphasis is on their desire to not only care for themselves individually, but to extend care toward their families, those dependent within their communities, and on building lasting institutions, even in their poverty.

Document 10

Letters of Teachers and Superintendents of the New England

Educational Commission for Freedmen, Fourth Series, (Boston: David Clapp, 1864), pp. 6, 12, 14. [Letters "b" through "h" excluding "f," are from AMA Archives in Amistad Collection, Dillard University, New Orleans, La.]

a) Letter from A. B. Plimpton.

Ashdale, near Beaufort, S. C.
July 8, 1863

The colored people are doing well generally. They are quite industrious, and well informed in all that appertains to raising the cotton and all the other productions of their subsistence. They are laboring assiduously to procure in the coming harvest sufficient to supply all the wants of the body, with some amount to sell. The Governor of this department in the spring cut off the clothes and rations from all the people that were able to labor in the fields, it has proved one of the most efficient means of promoting industrious habits among them. So long as they saw before them a source from which they could draw food and clothes, they were contented, and these contributions had a deleterious effect upon them. Now they are aware that if they do not produce sufficient to support themselves, they must suffer, and they are quite ambitious to get as much as possible. It is quite surprising to see the ingenuity and tact with which many of them exhibit to accomplish that end.

They certainly have imbibed largely the spirit of trade and commerce, by which they increase their revenue. Their little fields are guarded with the strictest care, and the growth of all the products watched with much eagerness, and the profits calculated by them, as much as the cargo and the profits to accrue there from are, by the great shippers of our commercial marts. They are fast learning the value of money, and are acquiring an idea of property, whether it be in a horse or land. There is a growing desire among them to become owners of land.

Hundreds of them are guarding their little stores with jealous care and adding to their stock all they can, in order to have sufficient money to make purchases at the next sales of land. To be able to receive all the proceeds of their labors, is one of the heights of their ambition. The adjoining plantation to the one where I live, was purchased last year by the negroes. They have exhibited all the skill, thus far, of those that have been worked by the Government. They have a large field of cotton, and a larger one of corn. I see them frequently, and converse with them about it. They are as proud of their labors as are any of the farmers of the North when success follows a period of industry. They have planted and brought to good growth by the necessary working three acres of cotton, each of which is, I am told, the maximum of one person's allotment, when other crops are worked by the same hand to the maximum. This condition of that plantation excites the emulation of all the surrounding people, and they frequently say that if they could work this land in the same way we could see some great crops. I have no doubt that if the negroes owned the land and could work it with the expectation of receiving all the proceeds, the cotton crops would have been increased one-third, if not one-half.

So far as the question of subsistence is involved with these people, there is not the least doubt about it. They are abundantly competent and able and willing to support themselves, and in a short time many of them will acquire a competence that will enable them to demand and supply themselves with many of the comforts of civilized life.

b) Letter from E. S. Philbrick to Alpheus Hardy, Treasurer of the Committee for Aid to the Freedmen of the West.

Beaufort, S. C.
December 28, 1863

I employ about 500 laborers--women and children mostly, having a population of 920 on my lands. They have raised for me 73,000 pounds of Sea Island cotton this year, worth 50d. sterling in Liverpool, besides their own provision crops, above referred to. This has been done in hearing of Gen. Gilmore's big guns on Morris Island, surrounded by camps, with no civil law, and without the help of the able-bodied men, who were all pressed into the military service, leaving and the plantations with none but old men, women and children. I have no paupers, all the old and infirm being fed and clothed by their friends, and children.

c) Letter from E. F. Ayer to Reverend George Whipple.

Atlanta, Georgia
February 15, 1866

The Freedmen seem to be doing all they can for themselves. I think they have had a contribution for some important object every Sabbath since we have been here. On the first Sabbath they had two objects in view. The first was to put windows in their house, the African Church, so as to have one school there and the other to furnish a hospital for colored strangers; so that no more of them should die naked, starving and friendless in the streets, "Brethren" said one, "rather than such a thing should happen again I would give all my living." The rebels are already trying to get all they can against us to prove that we were better off in bondage than we are in freedom. We must do all we can. The leaders seemed to know who would be likely to have a little money, and where they could not pass the hat for the crowd, they called individuals by name "Tom, if you've got any money come and put it in." "Jim, you come right along and put in what you've got. That ain't enough; haint you got any more?" "Go to Alice, she can give you something;" and so on, till of their poverty they got over $20. Most of the slaves here were "run off" by their masters before Sherman entered the city. Those who had anything became poor and those who were poor, became still poorer.

d) Letter from E. W. Douglas to Mr. Whiting, 67 John Street, N. Y. Grove Hill, Ogeechee Dist., Chatham Co., Ga., April 23, 1866, AMA Archives No. 19802.

We applied for aid in building an orphan house in Wilmington. I read to the Freedmen here. They were very much interested and wished to give their mite. Though they are poor and need help themselves, yet I thought best to encourage their desire to help others. Those having no money have given eggs. One of their number has written a letter to you which I enclose. I am sorry that I did not know of it in season to give him a clean sheet of paper. Fifteen cents worth of eggs have been given since the letter was written. This with five dollars (a part of some money sent to me to use for the Freedmen) that I think I can use this way as well as any makes the whole amount seven dollars twenty-five cents. $7.25. Place this sum to the donation for the Orphan House and deduct the same from the amount due to me.

e) Letter from Frederick Ayer to Reverend George Whipple, Atlanta, Georgia.

April 15, 1866

The poor creatures were thrown on their own resources, and had to begin life, not only under new, but very trying, circumstances but the idea of "freedom" of independence of calling their wives and their children, and, little hut their own, was a soul-animating one, that buoyed up their spirits, and inspired strong hopes, and influenced them to persistent efforts for self-preservation, and human elevation.

Husbands and wives and children of the same family were scattered broadcast over the South. On learning that they were free they sought each other, and after a separation of months and even many years, many large households would be gathered, and begin the struggle of life together in a little hut, built with their own hands, of any rough materials they could possess, leasing grounds on the outskirts of the city, for 1, 2 or 3 years.

Others would rent a room or small hut or shanty at an enormous rate per month, buildings being put up of the most primitive style by whites expressly for securing a great profit.

Many of the whites are making most vigorous efforts to retrieve their broken fortunes and display a most commendable, energy and perseverance in, rebuilding their dwellings and shops on their former sites. This furnished employment to a larger number of colored people as Masons, Carpenters, Teamsters, and common workmen. This is the center of the lines of railroads. A large number of Freedmen get employment as draymen, waiters, and laborers at the depot; also as mechanics at manufactories.

So notwithstanding, their wages are less than that of whites and, advantages often taken of their necessities and ignorance and the prices of all commodities enormously-high-yet many of them are improving their circumstances enough to buy a small building lot, and their own poor, to a considerable extent cared for by them.

For two months past the small pox has made fearful ravages among them. Hundreds have died of it. The Freedmen have aided in building a hospital for their sick, and of late hired ten of their own number to act as ward master and nurses at an expense of $200.00 per month.

f) New Orleans Picayune, December 12, 1865

Many freedmen have been seen coming into the State from further up North. They invariably reply to the question where they are going by answering: to rejoin their women and children. They have in many cases only a remote idea where their women and children might be, but they feel confident that they are soon to rejoin them. It is most pathetic to see numerous cases of black men scanning faces of passersby in the hope of recognizing their own kin. They frequently stop strange freedmen and ask if they recall hearing of a certain woman who came from Charleston with three children six or seven years ago.

g) Letter from E. P. Smith of Cincinnati, Ohio to Reverend Strieby in Atlanta, Georgia. AMA 19810.

Cincinnati
April 28, 1866

Rev. Mr. Strieby,
Dear Brother.

I wrote you a few days since respecting an Orphan Home for Colored Children at Atlanta. I have now another plea to file. At all our schools, and in many places I have visited south, I have found the want--a higher grade of education than we are yet offering. There are young men who have already mastered the elementary branches, and want to take a course of instruction that shall fit them for teachers and preachers. These two professions seem to cover the whole field of ambition for the present. We cannot give such minds proper attention in connection with our elementary schools. Besides they need to be brought together and put under the best of home influences, so as to be trained into a proper conception of the true social and domestic life. Such a school must be within reach of all worthy youth of both sexes, but must not be a charity school. Both the expenses and the effect upon the scholars, make the charity system undesirable. The class we wish most to reach cannot afford to pay tuition and the ordinary cost of board. If tuition and quarters can be furnished, and twenty-five acres of land for gardening purposes, by working four hours per day, and having vacation in the busy season, when labor commands the highest prices, the scholars can largely work their own way through the school year. Many of these young men who are pushing their way into an education have already learned a trade of some sort. They are from the class of the quickest and most enterprising minds,--for these, the many manufacturing establishments of Atlanta will afford opportunity for good wages in all hours that can be spared from study. For this reason, and for others the school ought not to be over a mile from the city limits. The high ridge overlooking Atlanta on the east offers a most desirable site. Five acres there will cost $4,000. (The rest of the land can be bought further from the city at less price.) For five thousand more, buildings can be erected that will accomodate teachers and scholars for a school of 200. Ten thousand, in all, will set the school in full operation, and on a basis ready to invite permanent endowment by the friends of the race. I would, by all means open the school to all without distinction of color. Practically, the whites will exclude themselves for a while--not long--for I am confident we can make it such a school as will attract them over the high wall of prejudice, and, in the course of years, will grow to the character and power of a school like Oberlin.

We ought to begin next fall. I met, during my tour South, at every point, with young men who are waiting for such an opening. On the cars from Nashville a bright faced youth told me he had laid up $250 and learned to read, the last year and now he wants to go to school five years. He wants to preach, and said he thought a man who was going to talk about the great things of religion all his life "had a right (ought) to know a heap of things."

Another, just mustered out of the U. S. service showed his 7:30's and how well he could read. "That's what I got for soldiering, and now I want to do something for myself and my people." I suggested that he go to South Alabama in a colony just then buying lands. He shook his head--He would rather buy schooling. Neither of these men have money enough to come North and stay at school, but in Georgia, and on the plan I have proposed, they could begin at once and go through a thorough training. In Macon I found the son of a baptist preacher, a wheelwright by trade, in great solicitude for an education. He has been studying Latin lessons this winter, reciting to one of our teachers after work hours. At one of our school meetings in Macon, a young Presbyterian minister--ex slave of Horace Cobb, was called upon unexpectedly, for a speech. He spoke briefly and modestly, but with such appropriateness and point and gracefulness, as mark him to be a natural orator. He has one of the finest forms and faces in Georgia, and is, in every way most promising and a man of marked influence, if he can get the education he is sighing for. His eye glistened with moisture, as he caught my hand in grateful emotion, when I told him I would try to find a way for him to study. He is the young preacher, who, during the war became "burdened" for the country, and gathering some of the church together secretly, told them it was not enough to pray for the Union alone, they ought to offer united prayer,--but how to do it and not be arrested they did not see.

After several meetings for consultation, they lit upon this plan--They were to call the Union, Lion. During the war, from that time, a stranger in the congregation would be at a loss to understand the fervent amens and hallelujahs with which the congregation responded to the earnest prayers of Gen. Cobb's slave, that "Lion" might go forth from conquering to conquer--that all her foes might be smitten and confounded, and her starry banner wave, in triumph all over the land.

Fifty such men as I have described will answer to the roll call in Atlanta, next November, if notice can go out that they will receive help to the extent I have indicated, and this number will rapidly grow to any dimensions on which you can afford to plan the Industrial School.

I am satisfied there are worthy good people in the North, who want to do some such thing as this for the colored people, and Christ's kingdom, and are only waiting for responsible parties to assume the general management, and they will furnish the means.

The participation of blacks in institution-building is well illustrated in the following documents: 1) the letter of Henry McNeal Turner to the Reverend George Whipple, soliciting books for the Sabbath Schools founded by the A. M. E. Church; and 2) in the report describing the origins of the Savannah schools. Both documents also emphasize as significant the leadership which came out of the black church. Henry McNeal Turner was a self-taught preacher who later became both a bishop in the A. M. E. Church and a member of the Georgia State Legislature. He was among those blacks who, as legislators, were first ousted and then reinstated during the Reconstruction.

h) Letter from Henry McNeal Turner to Rev. Geo. Whipple.

New York
Aug. 27th 1866

Rev. George Whipple

Sir, I am on tour in this city for the purpose of Soliciting books in behalf of several Sabbath Schools under the auspices of the African M. E. Church, and which Sabbath Schools have been either organized by myself of the ministers under my supervision in the State of Georgia. In Columbus, Ga., there is a School under Rev. E. L. Bailey of 374 children, which is conducted without a dozen books, and over one-third of these children can read the Bible if they had them.... And I most respectfully ask you Sir, to give us all the aid you can, for the children are nearly crazy for books to learn in on the Sabbath. The appeals that these children sometimes make to me, in behalf of books are heart ravishing not to mention the disheartened teachers, who have to entertain their pupils by telling anecdotes, and little stories, when they should be otherwise engaged. I am directing Elder of all above named places, and several more. But I only mention the points which most need books. If you can give us any Bibles, Testaments, or catachisms, you can forward them to the ministers named or to my headquarters, Macon, Georgia, And I will send them out as they average in size, and according to their advancement.

May the great head of the church bless your noble interprize, and aid that which has aided so many.

i) Letter from W. L. Richardson to Rev. George Whipple AMA Archives 19356, Fisk University.

The Freedmen of Savannah

There are some eight or ten thousand persons who have been transferred from bondage to freedom, since the approach of Gen. Sherman's grand army.

In general appearance and intelligence, they are evidently much above those who come in from the rice, and cotton plantations.

They have given proof of their intelligence, and ability, by what they have done among themselves within the past few days, with some advice from their friends.

"Savannah Educational Association"

This is the name of an organization first formed by the colored people of Savannah. It is an association composed of the Pastors, Preachers and others, for the purpose of establishing free schools for themselves and their children.

The energy and activity, evinced by them, in pushing forward this enterprise, is truly surprising. On my arrival in Savannah on the ninth I found steps had already been taken by the brethren of the colored churches and others, towards the formation of this association.

A large and enthusiastic meeting of the people was held the same afternoon in the First African Baptist Church. Short addresses were made at this meeting by Rev. J. W. Alvord, Sect. of the Boston Tract Society, Rev. James Lynch, Missionary at Port Royal, and Rev. W. T. Richardson, Supt. of Schools for the American Missionary Association in S. C. and Florida; after which, a well drafted constitution was presented as the basis of the proposed association and after some discussion, was unanimously adopted.

I copy one or two articles. Article 8th. --Any person may become a yearly member of this association by paying the sum of three dollars, and a monthly tribute of twenty-five cents. A life member, by the payment of ten dollars and the same amount monthly. Article 13th.,--This Association may cooperate with any association organized in the Loyal States, for the education of freedmen.

After the adoption of the constitution, the following resolution was presented, and cordially adopted:

> Whereas this association may need protection from Government and more advanced teachers than of themselves they are able to furnish--and whereas the American Missionary Association from its long tried antislavery character, has our entire confidence, therefore resolved that we hereby respectfully invite the patronage and assistance of the American Missionary Association in the great work, now evolving upon us.

In reply to the above Rev. W. T. Richardson thanked the people for their expression of esteem and confidence in the Am Miss Ass. and pledged their aid and cooperation in this work.

At this point of the meeting, a call was made by the chairman for the people to come forward with their names and money. The scene was novel and intensely interesting! Men and women came to the table with a grand rush--much like the charge of the Union soldiers on a rebel battery.

Fast as their names could be written by a swift penman, the greenbacks were laid upon the table in sums from one to ten dollars, until the pile footed up the round sum of seven hundred and thirty dollars, as the cash receipt of the meeting.

Grand Rally of the Children!

Tuesday morning we met some five hundred of them in the lecture room of the church. After the proper arrangements were made they were marched forth through the streets of the city, to the buildings assigned for schools. This army of colored children moving through the streets, seemed to excite feeling and interest, second only to that of Gen. Sherman's army.

Such a gathering of Freedmen's sons and daughters that proud city had never seen before.

Many of the people rushed to the doors and windows of their houses, wondering what these things could mean! This they were told, is the onward march of Freedom.

A goodly number of these children we found were able to read and spell, others evinced considerable knowledge of arithmetic, geography and writing. The project is very encouraging for the free schools of Savannah. Fifteen colored teachers are already engaged in these schools, and other teachers from the north, will soon join them in this noble work.

These halls in which the poor slave mother has often groaned in the anguish of her Soul, as she has seen her darling babes, one after another torn from her embrace, and sold forever from her sight--are now resounding with the merry shouts of happy school children.

I am most happy to see these noble efforts put forth by the Freedmen of Savannah in their own behalf, but we must not suppose that they will be able of themselves, to bear the whole burden.

They have given in their poverty for the support of these schools. God grant, that the abundance of our liberality may abound towards them in temporal and spiritual things.

Beaufort, Jan. 25th, 1865

During the 1860's black political activity began with involvement in government, not only on local, but state and federal levels also. Well aware of the urgent need to address the basic problems which faced them, blacks helped to pass legislation beneficial to the welfare of both races. Thomas E. Miller,[2] who represented South Carolina in the Congress of the United States, eloquently summed up this achievement in the following words:

> We were eight years in power. We had built school houses, established charitable institutions, built and maintained the penitentiary system, provided for the education of the deaf and dumb, rebuilt the jails and the court houses, rebuilt the bridges and re-established the ferries. In short, we had reconstructed the state and placed it on the road to prosperity and, at the same time by our acts of financial reform, transmitted to the Hampton government an indebtedness not greater by more than $2,500,000 than was the bonded debt of the state in 1868, before the Republican Negroes and their white allies came into power.

As an example of the positive policy in behalf of blacks, we offer this document reporting the action of the city council of Nashville, Tennessee, providing for free public school education.

Document 11

G. W. Hubbard, History of Colored Schools of Nashville, Tennessee, (Nashville, Tenn.: Wheeler, Marshall and Price Printers, 1874), p. 28.

Nashville was one of the first, if not the first city in the South to provide free Public Schools for colored children.

In June, 1867, the City Council passed an ordinance providing for the establishment of colored schools, which were to enjoy the same privileges, and be governed by the same regulations as the white schools then in operation.

The Belle View building, situated at the corner of Summer and Jackson streets, was purchased at an expense of $10,000 in city checks, which were then selling at a considerable discount.

This building is seventy feet long, forty feet wide, and two stories in height; there are four school rooms on the first floor, and the second story contains a large study hall and three recitation rooms. The whole building will comfortably seat about 350 children.

The Belle View School was opened September, 1867.

Mr. T. H. Hamilton was the first principal.

In December the Cumberland School which had been previously supported by the Pittsburg Freedmen's Aid Commission, was transferred to this building, and G. W. Hubbard placed in charge of the consolidated schools, which position he has occupied until the present time....

As in the other city schools, the regular course of study occupies seven years.

One class has completed this course, and nearly all of the pupils belonging to this class expect to teach next year.

The total number of children that have attended this school since it first opened is about 2,500.

The following statistics are for the school year ending June, 1873:

Total Enrollment	587
Average number belonging	359
Percent of attendance	95.88

An excellent example of black organizational activity developed in an urban setting is illustrated in the efforts of the skilled laborers of Baltimore, Maryland.

Document 12

"Condition of the Colored People," Baltimore, Md., Aug. 8, New York Tribune, September 1, 1870.

Maryland, and especially Baltimore, contains a larger proportion of skilled colored labor than any portion of the country, New Orleans not excepted. We may, therefore, hope to see its colored citizens, take and hold a leading position in all that tends to make them useful. One of the best evidences of thrift and enterprise I have noticed, so far, are the building and other self-help associations which exist here. The first-named societies were inspired by the successful economy and activity of the Germans. There are at least 25 colored societies in the city. There are several known as "The National Relief Association No. 1," etc. The admission fee is $2.50 and ten cents a week is required thereafter....

Among the noteworthy efforts is an operative brickyard, owned in five-dollar shares, and run by the shareholders themselves. It is doing well, but I have been unable to get its balance-sheets, and we cannot state the amount and results of business done.

At various times, during the past four or five years, attempts have been made to establish cooperative stores, but they have not succeeded, chiefly because the parties engaged have not the knowledge or patience to carry out such experiments. The most interesting movement I have found is that known as the Chesapeake Marine Railway and Dry Deck Company, which, as it illustrates the tyranny of caste and the manner by which it can be defeated, when even energy, industry, skill and determination (are) combined, deserves some extended notice. The company, or rather its lending corporators, have already attained more than a local fame, from the fact that from among them came the movement which resulted in the recognition last year at the Philadelphia Labor Congress of colored labor delegates, and subsequently of the organization at Washington in December following of the National Colored Labor union. Now for the origin of this enterprise. Baltimore, had always been famous as a ship-building and repairing entrepot. In slave times a large portion of the ship caulkers especially were colored men, as were also many ship-carpenters. In all other trade connected with this interest, a considerable share of the skilled, and nearly all of the unskilled labor, was colored. As a rule they were and are excellent mechanics. Frederick Douglass once worked in the very yard now owned by colored men. When last in Baltimore, he visited the yard, and took the caulker's tool in hand once again. The slave power was strong enough to protect these colored mechanics, many of them being slaves. When the war terminated, however, the bitter hostility, hitherto, suppressed, against colored labor, manifested itself in violent combinations. As Mr. Gaines, the present manager of the company, informed me, extermination of colored mechanics was openly declared to be the aim of their white rivals. The combination was against all labor, but manifested mostly in the shipbuilding trades. The white mechanics all struck, even refusing to work, where colored cartmen and stevedores were employed. There was no antagonism or complaint on account of wages, as the colored men were as strenuous as the whites in demanding full pay. The Trades Unions, to which, of course, colored men were not admitted, organized the movement. In the yards on one side of the Patapace River the colored caulkers were driven off in 1865. In 1866 the general strike was organized. The bosses did not sympathize with the white mechanics, and to the credit of many, be it said, they stood out as long as possible. Very soon the strike threatened to become general against all colored labor, mechanical or otherwise; the violence threatened to be extended even to hotel waiters of the prescribed race. The atrocious movement was industrially fermented by the active men in Andrew Johnson's reaction.

At least the leading colored caulkers, carpenters, and mechanics, seeing what the crusade meant, determined on a vigorous protective effort. Their conclusion was reached in the organization of the Maryland Mutual Joint Stock Railway Company, whose capital was to consist of 10,000 shares at $50. About 2000 shares were taken within a few days, and $10,000 subscribed, 100 shares being the largest amount taken by any one person. Most of the shares were taken in ones, twos, and threes, by mechanics, caulkers, laborers, even the barbers and washerwomen being represented. The shipyard and marine railway they now own belonged to Jas. L. Mullen and Son, earnest Union men and warm defenders of equal rights to their workmen. They offered to sell and asked no more than the place was worth--$40,000. The bargain was closed; another honorable gentleman, Capt. Sipplegarth, ship-owner, builder, and navigator, came forward and loaned them the remaining $30,000, on six years' time, at moderate interest, with the privileges of paying at any time within the six years, taking a mortgage on the property itself.

It is interesting to note their progress from this fair start. The plan embraced only ordinary business rules, and their managers have never attempted the introduction of either the industrial partnership idea, or more distinctive cooperative principles. The value of the enterprise, however, is in the lesson it teaches of what quiet energy and industry will do toward conquering prejudices and combinations.

The Company was organized and got to work by Feb. 2, 1866, employing at first 62 hands, nearly all skilled men, and some of them white. Business was depressed, the outrageous strike having driven it away from the port, and the work did not average for some months more than four days per week, at the average wages of $3 per day. At the present time the Company are able to employ, full time, 75 hands. From Feb. 2, 1866, to Jan. 1, 1867, its business amounted to about $60,000, on which the profits were nearly or quite 25 percent or $15,000. The next year was better for them, though business was generally very dull. In carrying out their work and paying their men, they had to resort to borrowing as a rule. They never had a note protested. Within four years from organization they completed the payment for their yard and railway, lifting the mortgage in June last. In 1868 they were incorporated by the title I have given, having done business previously under the firm name of John H. Smith and Co. Most of their trade is with Eastern ship-owners and masters. At the present time they do, and have done for three years past, more repairing than any other company on the Patapace River. This success has not been achieved without serious trouble. Intimidation has been practiced on their patrons. In two instances, where profitable jobs were pending, they have been driven off by white mobs; in one case a white man who took charge of their working force was shot dead. What added point to the act was the fact that he was ordinarily one of their bitterest antagonists. On another occasion having hired the Canton Marine Railway to take up a large ship which they were caulking and repairing, the whites threatened to strike, and so the Railway Company refused to allow its use. Still they have perservered, and today are masters of the situation. They have had some good contracts, in one case repairing Government dredges and tugs.

The managers think the feeling against them decidedly subsiding. They accredited this fact mainly to their ability to employ labor and pay for it promptly. They think that men have been forced to a sense of shame by finding no resentments cherished on the part of the corporators of the Chesapeake Company. To some extent, more recently, they believe that the dread of Chinese labor, induces the ultra-trades unionists to desire their (the colored mechanics') favor. It is worth noting that they are not, and never have been members of the trades unions. Their business rules, as stated to be by the manager, are simple. Asking why they did more ship work than other firms or companies possessing equal facilities, the reply was: 1st, because our labor is of the best; the men we employ are thoroughly skilled, and 2nd, we seek to retain custom as well as make money. We have never lost a patron except by outside intimidation. We try to accomodate, work hard and overtime to finish jobs, and always use the best materials. These are good rules, and this is a good record....

The ownership of their works, buildings, and machinery valued at $40,000, and a business valued at not less than $65,000, and a business of at least $75,000 per annum is no bad result of a movement designed to resist caste and race oppression. If, new, these stockholders would go further and recognize labor as entitled to profits equally with capital, if only in the partial principle of the famous Briggs Colliery (England), it would become still more a shining mark, and have as the noblest laurels the generous fact that it taught here the solution of the labor and capital problem. In one sense, even now, the material projected by the builder has become the corner-stone; but if this corporation of working men could be induced to do the larger thing, and establish an industrial co-partnership, how much more truly would the old Scriptural illustration be realized.

The positive responses to the hopes of the Freedmen were reflected in the previous documents, but the seeds of despair culminating in the withdrawal of federal troops from the former Confederacy in 1877, were sown early. Alongside positive measures, which improved the welfare of the freedmen, emerged negative actions, restricting, inhibiting and modifying the hoped-for gains. The final documents in this section will illustrate this enveloping mood of despair, as positive measures offering hope are countered by negative measures which nullify these hopes.

In order to provide for the needs of the multitude of refugee slaves which followed in the train of his advancing army, General W. Y. Sherman, as a temporary measure of relief, issued his famous Field Order no. 15, confiscating certain islands and lands along the southeastern coast for the resettlement of the refugees. This action was interpreted by blacks as a means by which they could make a living for their families by farming the lands. However, General Sherman's action was challenged and, later, he wrote a letter in which he explained why he had substantially reneged on the promise which his original field order had made to the blacks. The final action, though, which led to complete despair was that of President Andrew Johnson, who rescinded the order of confiscation and restored the plantations to their former owners. The reaction of blacks to all of this is recorded in Mary Ames' report of a meeting of freedmen with General O. O. Howard on Johnson's land policy, October 19, 1865.

Document 13

Field Order No. 15, War Department Archives, Mil. Div. of the Mississippi. Savannah, Georgia, January 16, 1865.

I. The islands from Charleston, south, the abandoned rice fields along the rivers for thirty miles back from the sea, and the country bordering the St. John's River, Florida are reserved and set apart for the settlement of the negroes now made free by the acts of war and the proclamation of the President of the United States.

II. At Beaufort, Hilton Head, Savannah, Fernandina, St. Augustine, and Jacksonville, the blacks may remain in their chosen or accustomed vocations, but on the islands, and in the settlements hereafter to be established, no white person whatever, unless military officers and soldiers, detailed for duty, will be permitted to reside; and the sole and exclusive management of affairs will be left to the freed people themselves, subject only to the United States military authority and the acts of Congress. By the laws of war and orders of the President of the United States the negro is free, and must be dealt with as such. He cannot be subjected to conscription or forced military authority of the department, under such regulations as the President or Congress may prescribe. Domestic servants, blacksmiths, carpenters, and other mechanics, will be free to select their own work and residence, but the young and able-bodied negroes must be encouraged to enlist as soldiers in the service of the United States, to contribute their share towards maintaining their own freedom, and securing their rights as citizens of the United States.

III. Whenever three respectable negroes, heads of families, shall desire to settle on lands and shall have selected for that purpose an island or a locality clearly defined, within the limits above designated, the inspector of settlements and plantations will himself, or by such subordinate officer as he may appoint, give them a license to settle such island or district, and afford them such assistance as he can to enable them to establish a peaceable agricultural settlement. The three parties named will subdivide the land, under the supervision of the inspector, among themselves and such others as may choose to settle near them, so that each family shall have a plot of not more than forty (40) acres of tillable ground, and when it borders on some water channel, with not more than 800 feet water front, in the possession of which land the military authorities will afford them protection until such time as they can protect themselves, or until Congress shall regulate their title. The quartermaster may, on the requisition of the inspector of settlements and plantations, place at the disposal of the inspector one or more of the captured steamers, to ply between the settlements and one or more of the commercial points heretofore named in orders, to afford the settlers the opportunity to supply their necessary wants, and to sell the products of their land and labor.

IV. Whenever a negro has enlisted in the military service of the United States he may locate his family in any one of the settlements at pleasure, and acquire a homestead and all other rights and privileges of a settler, as though present in person. In like manner negroes may settle their families and engage on board the gunboats, or in fishing, or in the navigation of the inland waters, without losing any claim to land or other advantage derived from this system. But no one, unless an actual settler as above defined, or unless absent on government service, will be entitled to claim any right to land or property in any settlement by virtue of these orders.

V. In order to carry out this system of settlement, a general officer will be detailed as inspector of settlements and plantations, whose duty it shall be to visit the settlements, to regulate their police and general management, and who will furnish personally to each head of a family, subject to the approval of the President of the United States, a possessory title in writing, giving as near as possible the description of boundaries, and who shall adjust all claims or conflicts that may arise under the same, subject to the like approval, treating such titles altogether as possessory. The same general officer will also be charged with the enlistment and organization of the negro recruits, and protecting their interests while absent from their settlements, and will be governed by the rules and regulations prescribed by the War Department for such purposes.

VI. Brigadier General R. Saxton is hereby appointed inspector of settlements and plantations, and will at once enter on the performance of his duties. No change is intended or desired in the settlement now on Beaufort Island, nor will any rights to property heretofore acquired be affected thereby.

Document 14

Letter from General W. T. Sherman to President Andrew Johnson, February 2, 1866.

Congressional Globe, House of Representatives, 39th Congress. 1st Session, February 2, 1866, p. 83; and National Anti-Slavery Standard, February 10, 1866.

Congress, General Sherman and the Freedmen

The letter below from Gen. Sherman shows that his order, relative to his occupancy of the Sea Islands by the Freedmen, was conditional only. But it is evident that both he and the Secretary of War supposed that they were doing a work which Congress would confirm for all time. The action of that body, yesterday, however, shows how wildly they judged of its constitution and quality. They did all in their power by giving the best title they could confer, and by carefully avoiding in the order any language which might throw doubt upon the validity of the claims. It was universally understood that these islands were confiscated forever; and none more fully believed it than their rebel owners who had fled from them. No shadow of a suggestion ever was breathed that they would or could be restored to them. The problem of the Federal Government soon brought thirty thousand loyal, laboring men and women to possess and improve them. And although surrounded by every form of discouragement, hardship and suffering, they soon dotted the lands with their school houses, and churches, and the Islands began to blossom again like the rose.

And now, after all this, while the poor settlers were jubilant with hope, even in the most despondent conditions in many respects, and were looking forward to a millenium of liberty, a brighter paradise on earth, than they had ever prayed for even in Heaven, behold a Republican Congress by a majority of one hundred and thirty-six to thirty-three, dashing all those bright anticipations to the ground forever! Human language fails here. So with the letter of Gen. Sherman, the subject must rest for the present.

Washington, February 2, 1866

To Andrew Johnson, President of the United States:

Sir: I have the honor to acknowledge the receipt last evening of your letter of Feb. 1, and in compliance with your request, enclose herewith a copy of field order No. 15 of 1863, with this brief history of its origin and the reasons for making it:

The Hon. E. M. Stanton, Secretary of War, came to Savannah

soon after its occupation by the forces under my command, and conferred with me as to the best methods to provide for the vast number of negroes who had followed the army from the interior of Georgia, as also for those who had already congregated on the Islands near Hilton Head, and were still coming into our lines. We agreed perfectly that the young and able-bodied men should be enlisted as soldiers, or employed by the Quartermaster in the necessary work of unloading ships, and for other army purposes. But this left in our hands the old and feeble, the women and children, who had necessarily to be fed by the United States. Mr. Stanton summoned a large number of the negroes, mostly preachers, with whom he had a lengthy conference, of which he took down notes. After the conference he was satisfied the negroes could, with some little aid from the United States, by means of the abandoned plantations of the Sea Islands and along the navigable waters, take care of themselves. He requested me to draw up a plan that would be uniform and practical. I made the rough draft, and we went over it very carefully. Mr. Stanton making many changes, and present Orders No. 15 resulted and were made public.

I knew, of course, we could not convey title to land and merely provided "possessory" titles to be good so long as war and military power lasted. I merely aimed to make provision for the negroes who were absolutely dependent upon us, leaving the value of their possessions to be determined by after events and legislation.

At that time, January, 1865, it will be remembered that the tone of the people of the South was very defiant, and no one could foretell when the period of war would cease. Therefore, I did not contemplate that event as being so near at hand. I am, Sir, with great respect your obedient servant.

(Signed) W. T. Sherman, Maj.-Gen.

Document 15

"War Department, Bureau of Refugees, Freedmen and Abandoned Lands," Washington, September 12, 1865. Circular No. 15.

I. Circular No. 13, of July 28, 1865, from this Bureau, and all portions of Circulars from this Bureau conflicting with the provisions of this Circular are hereby rescinded.

II. This Bureau has charge of such "tracts of land within the insurrectionary states as shall have been abandoned, or to which the United States shall have acquired title by confiscation, or sale, or otherwise," and no such lands now in its possession shall be surrendered to any claimant, except as hereinafter provided.

III. Abandoned lands are defined in Section 2, of the Act of Congress, approved July 2, 1864, as lands, "the lawful owner whereof shall be voluntarily absent therefrom, and engaged, either in arms, or otherwise, in aiding or encouraging the rebellion."

IV. Land will not be regarded as confiscated until it has been condemned and sold by decree of the United States Court for the District in which the property may be found, and the title thereto thus vested in the United States.

V. Upon its appearing satisfactorily to any Assistant Commissioner that any property under his control is not abandoned as above defined, and that the United States has acquired no title to it, by confiscation, sale, or otherwise, he will formally surrender it to the authorized claimant or claimants, promptly reporting his action to the Commissioner.

VI. Assistant Commissioners will prepare accurate descriptions of all confiscated and abandoned lands under their control, keeping a record thereof themselves, and forwarding, monthly, to the Commissioner, copies of those descriptions, in the manner prescribed in Circular No. 10, of July 11, 1865, from this Bureau.

They will set apart so much of said lands as is necessary for the immediate use of loyal Refugees and Freedmen, being careful to select for this purpose those lands which most clearly fall under the control of the Bureau, which selection must be submitted to the Commissioner for his approval.

The specific division of lands so set apart into lots, and the rental or sale thereof, according to Section 4, of the law establishing the Bureau, will be completed as soon as practicable, and reported to the Commissioner.

VII. Abandoned lands, held by this Bureau, may be restored to owners, pardoned by the President, by the Assistant Commissioner, to whom applications for such restoration should be forwarded, so far as practicable through the Superintendent of the Districts in which the lands are situated.

Each application must be accompanied by:

1st. Evidence of special pardon by the President, or a copy of the oath of amnesty prescribed in the President's Proclamation of May 29, 1865, when the applicant is not included in any of the classes therein excepted from the benefits of said oath.

2d. Proof of title

Officers of the Bureau through whom the application passes, will endorse thereon such facts as may assist the Assistant Commissioner in his decisions--stating especially the use made by the Bureau of the land.

VIII. No lands under cultivation by loyal Refugees or Freedmen will be restored under this Circular, until the crops now growing shall be secured for the benefit of the cultivators, unless full and just compensation be made for their labor and its products, and for their expenditures.

O. O. Howard,
Major General, Commissioner

Approved:
Andrew Johnson,
President of the United States

Document 16

Mary Ames, From a New England Woman's Diary in Dixie in 1865. Springfield, Mass. (n.p.), 1906.

Meeting of Freedmen with General O. O. Howard on Johnson's Land Policy, October 19, 1865.

In October Mr. Alden was told to bring the people together that General Howard might talk to them about their future. On the 19th a calvacade of twenty negroes, mounted on horses and mules of all kinds and sizes, rushed down to the landing, and formed two lines, through which General Saxton and General Howard, with the other gentlemen, passed, receiving the horsemen's salute.

The church was crowded. General Howard, in simple words, said that he, being their friend, had been sent by the President to tell them that the owners of the land, their old masters, had been pardoned, and their plantations were to be given back to them; that they wanted to come back to cultivate the land, and would hire the blacks to work for them.

At first the people could not understand, but as the meaning struck them, that they must give up their little homes and gardens, and work again for others, there was a general murmur of dissatisfaction. General Howard's task grew more painful. He begged them to lay aside their bitter feelings, and to become reconciled to their old masters. We heard murmurs of "no, never." "Can't do it." General Howard proposed that three men be chosen to represent the people to consult and report to him.

LAWS AFFECTING SOCIAL WELFARE

The adoption of the Thirteenth Amendment, December 18, 1865, federally sanctioned a new legal status for blacks, deeming all slaves constitutionally free.

Document 17

XIII Amendment to the United States Constitution, December 18, 1865.

Section 1. Neither slavery nor involuntary servitude, except as a punishment for crime whereof the party shall have been duly convicted, shall exist within the United States, or any place subject to their jurisdiction.

Section 2. Congress shall have the power to enforce this article by appropriate legislation.

Unfortunately, however, the passage of this Amendment alone

did not resolve the manifold problems, political, economic or social of the freedmen. Particularly in those states comprising the former Confederacy, whole governments had been restored under the relatively lenient plans of Presidential reconstruction and along lines proposed by both Lincoln and Johnson. The freedmen encountered difficulties which threatened to keep them in much the same second-class citizenship status which had been the lot of the free people of color in antebellum times. Between 1865 and 1868, when the Fourteenth Amendment was ratified, numerous laws, known as the Black Codes, were enacted by Southern legislatures to prevent the realization of true economic, political and social equality for blacks. The purpose of these codes was to retain as much social control over the freedmen as was possible.

An excellent summary statement relevant to this point is that of Kenneth Stampp:[3]

> The crucial point about these codes was their ultimate purpose. They were not designed to help the Negro through the admittedly difficult transition from the status of a slave to that of a responsible freedman. They were not intended to prepare him for a constructive role in the social, political and economic life of the South. Rather, the purpose of the Black Codes was to keep the Negro, as long as possible, exactly where he was: a propertyless rural laborer under strict controls, without political rights, and with inferior legal rights. As Schurz quite accurately explained them, they were 'a striking embodiment of the idea that although the former owner has lost his individual right of property in the former slave, "the blacks at large belong to the whites at large".' To put it bluntly, the Black Codes placed the Negro in a kind of twilight zone between slavery and freedom.

As such, they contributed to the beginnings of despair and disenchantment, which destined to increase during what Lincoln in his last address called the "reinauguration of the national authority--reconstruction."[4]

The intention to maintain racial boundaries, both overt and institutional, early on was made quite explicit. In 1865, for example, South Carolina passed a law that "although such persons (Negro) are not entitled to social or political equality with white persons, they might hold property, make contracts, etc...." The constitution of

Mississippi, as amended August 1, 1865, abolished slavery and gave the legislature power to make laws for the protection and security of the persons and property of the freedmen, and to protect "them and the State against any evils that may arise from their emancipation."[5]

Many states placed restrictions upon the mobility of freedmen, especially requiring that those who had migrated from other states upon arrival must register and be bonded as a security for their good behavior. As in Mississippi, there were restrictions on the renting or leasing of lands, except where these lands were located in the corporate limits of a town. "Under this same statute, every free man, Negro, or mulatto was required to have on January 1, 1866, and annually thereafter, a lawful home and employment with written evidence thereof."[6] As was the case in the slave codes, the sale of firearms and liquor was in most instances forbidden. "In general it was specified that all contracts for personal service with persons of color should be in writing and properly attested by some white person."[7] Children of freedmen, or orphans, were regularly apprenticed under strict regulation, sometimes to their former owners, and in states such as Mississippi and South Carolina, these laws were applied only to freedmen. A test of the apprenticeship law of Maryland in 1867 found it in violation of the XIII Amendment, since its conditions were of virtual slavery.

Of particular relevance were enactments relating to vagrancy and pauperism, both designed to penalize broad categories of people.

> The Mississippi vagrancy list was almost as extensive as that of South Carolina, with the addition, 'that any freedmen, free Negroes, or mulattoes, over eighteen years of age, found on the second Monday of January, 1866, or thereafter, with no lawful employment or business, or found unlawfully assembling themselves with freedmen, free Negroes, or mulattoes ...' on terms of equality or living in adultery or fornication with a freedwoman, free negro or mulatto, should be considered vagrants.[8]

Finally, "the close of the war found the South facing the problem of how to meet its paupers, white and Negro. A large part of the property of whites had been swept away, or had been greatly depreciated in value. The Negroes, with few exceptions, had no property to lose. They lost their right to look to the white people for sustenance. The legislatures of the South adopted the plan for levying a tax upon each race for the support of its own indigents."[9]

It is plain from the citations made above that the legislatures of the former Confederate states clearly intended to limit the potential of former slaves to compete equally in the labor market; to contract labor and services freely; to move freely to places offering more advantageous employment and residence; and, to subject freedmen to police harassment when settled and employed, as well as when migrant and unemployed. These black codes had several kinds of consequences. On the positive side, they granted to blacks certain new legal and political rights: to sue and be sued, to marry, to sign contracts, and to testify in court cases in which only blacks were parties. But, more perniciously, the contained provisions which reintroduced elements of the former slave codes which penalized them and returned them to their former status of slavery. As noted above, vagrancy was punishable by fine. But if the alleged offender had not the ability to pay the fine, he or she was liable to be bonded out to work for whomever paid the fine in his or her stead, obviously an act of involuntary servitude in contravention of the intention of the XIII Amendment.

Urban governments in the north responded to the codes by publishing the oppressive conditions protested by free blacks. Details of one of the most oppressive was published in a Cincinnati newspaper about a system of detention in Richmond, Virginia. Blacks were being detained for minor offenses (or for no offense at all) in what was called the Negro bullpen. These blacks felt that their situation had actually deteriorated since the end of the war and the abolition of slavery in the XIII Amendment.

The breach of faith of the restored southern government as reflected in the black codes led many in the North, and many who were members of the Congress, to come to the realization that the mere abolition of slavery was not sufficient; and that, if the black man were to prosper at all in southern society, there must be provisions for congressional support for black reconstruction. This kind of thinking led some northern senators and representatives to attempt to provide further guarantees for blacks to the extent that they should actually be able to participate in the politics of the South as a means of securing their newly gained freedom. As a result of these new attitudes, the XIV and XV Amendments were added to the Constitution. The Fourteenth Amendment, 1868, provided for the citizenship of all blacks and for the exercise of due process and equal protection of the law, none of which had been provided for previously for all citizens. The XV Amendment, adopted in 1870, extended to the freedmen the right to vote.

Document 18

XIV Amendment to the United States Constitution, July 20, 1868.

Section 1. All persons born or naturalized in the United States and subject to the jurisdiction thereof, are citizens of the United States and of the State wherein they reside. No state shall make or enforce any law which shall abridge the privileges or immunities of citizens of the United States; nor shall any State deprive any person of life, liberty, or property, without due process of law; nor deny to any person within its jurisdiction the equal protection of the laws.

Section 5. The Congress shall have power to enforce, by appropriate legislation, the provisions of this article.

Document 19

XV Amendment to the United States Constitution, March 30, 1870.

Section 1. The right of citizens of the United States to vote shall not be denied or abridged by the United States or by any State on account of race, color, or previous condition of servitude.

Section 2. The Congress shall have the power to enforce this article by appropriate legislation.

The first restored governments of the former Confederate states were all declared invalid by the Congress, except for the government of the State of Tennessee. To be restored to the Union all these states had to meet new conditions. Congressional reconstruction, as it is known, required that the southern states write new constitutions to be approved by the Congress, after which, and only after which, the states should be restored to the Union. The political participation of blacks guaranteed in the XIV Amendment and also guaranteed by the Reconstruction Act of 1867, which placed the South under military rule, brought blacks for the first time into the political arena. They participated in the constitutional conventions in the southern states and attempted to draft constitutions which would provide blacks with some measure of economic security.

Some statements from the South Carolina Constitutional Convention of 1868 furnish evidence of the thinking of blacks on the importance of developing the entire black community as a means of removing the badge of servitude. Both R. H. Cain and F. L. Cardoza proposed that southern plantations be divided up and sold in small plots to farmers, black and white. Insofar as blacks were concerned, Cain's selection shows that he felt that the dole, as practiced by the Freedmen's Bureau, was actually a dead end street. It would not in itself solve any of the freedmen's problems, for what was critically needed was land ownership.

Document 20

Proceedings of the Constitutional Convention of South Carolina, Vol. 1, (Charleston, S. C., Dening and Perry Printer, 1868), pp. 380-383.

(Rep. R. H. Cain is speaking)

But a people without homes become wanderers. If they possess lands they have an interest in the soil, in the State, in its commerce, its agriculture, and in everything pertaining to the wealth and welfare of the State. If these people had homes along the lines of railroads, and the lands were divided and sold in small farms, I will guarantee our railroads will make fifty times as much money, banking systems will be advanced by virtue of the settlement of the people throughout the whole State. We want these large tracts of land cut up. The land is productive, and there is nothing to prevent the greatest and highest prosperity. What we need is a system of small farms. Every farmer owning his land will feel he is in possession of something. It will have a tendency to settle the minds of the people in the State and settle many difficulties. In the rural districts now there is constant discontent, constant misapprehension between the parties, a constant disregard for each other. One man won't make an engagement to work, because he fears if he makes a contract this year, he will be cheated again as he thinks he was last year. We have had petitions from planters asking the Convention to disabuse the minds of the freedmen of the thought that this Convention has any lands at its disposal, but I do desire this Convention to do something at least to relieve the wants of these poor suffering people. I believe this measure, if adopted and sent to Congress, will indicate to the people that this Convention does desire they shall possess homes and have relief....

I do not desire to have a foot of land in this State confiscated. I want every man to stand upon his own character. I want these lands purchased by the government, and the people afforded an opportunity to buy from the government. I believe every man ought to carve out for himself a character and position in this life. I believe every man ought to be made to work by some means or other, and if he does not he must go down. I believe if the same amount of money that has been employed by the Bureau in feeding lazy, worthless men and women, had been expended in purchasing lands, we would to-day have no need of the Bureau. Millions upon millions have been expended, and it is still going on ad infinitum. I propose to let the poor people buy these lands, the government to be paid back in five years time. It is one of the great cries of the enemies of reconstruction, that Congress has constantly fostered laziness. I want to have the satisfaction of showing that the freedmen are as capable and willing to work as any men on the face of the earth. This measure will save the State untold expenses. I believe there are hundreds of persons in the jail and penitentiary cracking rock to-day who have all the instincts of honesty, and who, had they an opportunity of making a living, would never have been found in such a place. I think if Congress will accede to our request, we shall be benefited beyond measure, and save the State from taking charge of paupers, made such by not having the means to earn a living for themselves.

I can look to part of my constituency, men in this hall, mechanics, plasterers, carpenters, engineers, men capable of doing all kind of work, now idle because they cannot find any work in the city. Poverty stares them in the face, and their children are in want. They go to the cotton houses, but can find no labor. They are men whose honesty and integrity has never been called in question. They are suffering in consequence of the poverty-stricken condition of the city and State. I believe the best measure is to open a field where they can labor, where they can take the hoe and axe, cut down the forest, and make the whole land blossom as the Garden of Eden, and prosperity pervade the whole land.

Now, the report of Major General Howard gives a surplus of over seven millions in the Freedmen's Bureau last year. Out of that seven millions I propose to ask Congress to make an appropriation of one million, which will be properly distributed and then leave several millions in that Department, my friend from Barnwell notwithstanding.

I think there could be no better measure for this Convention to urge upon Congress. If that body should listen to our appeal. I have no doubt we shall be benefited. This measure of relief, it seems to me, would come swiftly. It is a swift messenger that comes in a week's time after it is passed; so that in the month of February or March, the people may be enabled to go to planting and raising crops for the ensuing year. One gentleman says it will take six months or a year, but I hope, with the assistance of the Government, we could accomplish it in less time.

Cain's colleague, Francis L. Cardoza, agreed with him on the importance of land, but he also saw the necessity to break up the plantation as a means of removing the psychological impact of slavery. He equates the plantation system and its replacements, lien cropping and sharecropping, as continuing the system of slavery. He wanted the vestiges of slavery to be erased by breaking up the plantations, allowing for the purchase of the small plots carved out of these plantations by blacks as well as whites. A number of blacks in Charleston had been able to buy large tracts of land at a greatly reduced amount by pooling their purchases of small plots.

The issuance of the XIV and XV Amendments, however, was not to produce the millenium, as many blacks thought they should or would. It seemed, rather, that the southern states were able to regain control of the government by a variety of means. For example, Georgia expelled her black representatives from the legislature. Later they were ordered reinstated, but soon they were again expelled by the "redeemers". The massive federal program mounted by the Freedmen's Bureau was finally dismantled and liquidated.

Document 21

"Liquidation of the Freedmen's Bureau," The Christian Recorder, February 27, 1873.

When Congress ordered General Howard to turn over what there was of the Freedmen's Bureau to the War Department, it had no idea, that its instructions would be so literally carried out. It seems, however, that things were turned over, or overturned, as you may be pleased to have it, with a vengeance. From a communication which General Howard has made to the Committee on Military Affairs, and a copy of which he was kind enough to send us, this very severe turning over, is accounted for.

> Gen. Vincent kindly sent wagons, messengers, laborers and clerks [says the communication] to take the archives. My own clerks were irritated and disappointed, having been suddenly cut off from Government employment, and,

as it seemed to them, treated as if in disgrace, though they were as able and upright as their successors. Books and papers were taken with little regard to order, and tumbled into the carts.

O ye naughty clerks, could'nt you watch with your master one hour. Were it only the loaves and the fishes ye were after? Did ye not know that ravenous wolves were on the track, hungry for blood. Yet, forsooth, ye were for the moment dropped from the employ of the government, ye were willing to turn over the very records by which he was to defend and justify himself. Ye very naughty clerks, account it to the goodness of his heart, rather than to the judgment of his head, that he says you, "were as able and upright as their successors." Possibly it is so, but to our minds, ye could not have shown how able you were more effectively than helping to carry those Archives to Vincent's teams, and have seen.... After all, it is not O. O. Howard that they want. It is the man of the Freedmen's Bureau who was the strength of the negro in the perilous moment of his transition--the man that taught him to wipe away his reproach, and stand up like a man--it is the Commissioner, for whose blood they thirst. In the faith that God will defend the right, he can afford to go before his countrymen, who will believe that he has performed much labor well.

Loren Miller[10] has described and documented the part played by the Supreme Court of the United States in nullifying the Congressional legislation passed by the so-called Radical Republicans in behalf of the blacks. Much of this judicial action came, of course, in the period from 1877-1896, culminating in the famous Plessy v. Ferguson decision which enunciated the doctrine of separate but equal as constitutional under the XIV Amendment, a fateful decision not re-examined or reversed until 1954.

NOTES--PART I

1. W. A. Low, "The Freedmen's Bureau in the Border States," Radicalism, Racism, and Party Realignment, The Border States During Reconstruction, ed., Richard O. Curry, (Baltimore: The Johns Hopkins Press, 1969), pp. 245-264.

2. Thomas E. Miller, Speech delivered in the South Carolina Constitutional Convention of 1890, cited in Sketches of Negro Life and History in South Carolina, by Asa H. Gordon (Industrial College, Georgia, 1929), pp. 67-68.

3. Kenneth M. Stampp, The Era of Reconstruction, 1865-1877, (New York: Alfred A. Knopf, 1965), pp. 79-80.

4. Writings of Abraham Lincoln, Constitutional ed., Vol. VII, p. 362ff., cited in Documents of American History, edited by Henry Steele Commager, (New York: Appleton-Century-Crofts, Inc., 1949), p. 448.

5. Monroe N. Work, Negro Yearbook, 1919, (Tuskegee, Alabama, The Negro Yearbook Publishing Co., 1919), p. 190.

6. Ibid., p. 191.

7. Ibid., p. 191.

8. Ibid., p. 193.

9. Ibid., p. 193.

10. Loren Miller, The Petitioners, The Story of the Supreme Court of the United States and the Negro, (New York: Pantheon Books, 1966).

PART II

SURVIVING EMERGENT SEGREGATION: 1877-1896

INTRODUCTION

During the period from 1877 through 1896, the black population continued to struggle, not only for survival, but also in order to enjoy the opportunities, advantages and rewards of living as did other American citizens. However, their fortunes continued to plummet against the onslaught of what C. Vann Woodward has called "the strange career of Jim Crow." Policies and programs designed during congressional reconstruction to enhance their general welfare lost weighty support in all branches of the Federal government, executive, legislative and judicial. Consequently, survival depended on black people's ability to adapt themselves to the variant programs and policies of the several states which seemed determined to isolate, alienate, segregate, subordinate, or otherwise diminish their civic and social stature in the body politic.

Of special import was the sequence of events which followed the withdrawal of Federal troops from the former rebellious states of the Confederacy, an action which not only permitted but encouraged the employment of terror and violence, intending to intimidate those blacks sufficiently bold and capable of making a way for themselves in the mainstream of American society. It was evident that the military occupation must come to its inevitable end. But, its demise came much too soon to prevent or delay the erosion of the civil rights and liberties embodied in the Constitutional Amendments and legislative enactments passed by the Reconstruction congresses to aid the black population and set its members on the road to full participation in American society. For the constructions and interpretations placed upon these amendments and the legislation by the Federal judiciary, particularly by the Supreme Court of the United States, tended to nullify the intent and to obstruct the implementation of programs and policies meaningful to the black population. As the law became inoperative and ineffectual as an agency for social change, not one of the chief executives during this period provided the necessary moral vigor in national leadership to challenge the racism which quickly became institutionalized. The power of the state governments to establish invidious social, political and economic controls in contravention of constitutional rights expanded as the power of the Federal government was relinquished to them. Segregation became as potent a force in American life and behavior as slavery had been. Legislation was said to be ineffectual against the mandates of morality. The culmination came with the 1896 decision of the Supreme Court in Plessy v. Ferguson, when the Court proclaimed the constitutionality of the separate but equal doctrine.

Nevertheless, blacks survived, struggled and, despite the handicaps of limited skills, resources and means, managed to cope with the basically hostile national situation by planting in their respective local communities the seeds of mutual aid, which sometimes fell upon fertile soil and bore fruit. It was as if the blacks had a resilience which summoned forth unheralded potential for advancement. The optimism which basically sustains the American values of freedom and equality was never abandoned. There was despair, but there was also the promise of a better future to be won and shared.

Black efforts at survival, limited by legal circumscription, resulted in the contagious desire to emigrate. Some blacks emigrated north and west, away from the locale of slavery and peonage, to settle both individually and in colonies, in those communities which seemed to offer new hope and relief from despair. We shall see that, in some cases, these new settlements attempted to establish communities restricted to members of their own ethnic group--that is, all-black towns or all-black sections of larger towns. But most blacks took up residence among whites, until prejudice and discriminatory behavior relegated them to a segregated, isolated and alienated lifestyle, forcing them to band together ethnically and to organize institutions of self-help and mutual aid.

In other words, welfare enterprises among blacks were undertaken as a result of multiple stimuli, originating both within and without the group in response to whatever peculiarities were present in the social situation which prevailed within the local communities in which they happened to reside. There were the general needs to provide for the young and the aged who were lacking in the resources and supports of stable family living; for the unemployable; for the infirm and the sick; and, finally, for those who became subject to the physical and social devastation of accidental or personal crisis. In all of the communities, whether all-black, segregated or integrated, the slow process of building viable social welfare institutions to insure the basic necessities of survival and to provide minimal personal and social security began to emerge under the impetus of brilliant and creative leadership assumed by individuals whose energies could not be inhibited, blocked, suppressed, submerged or intimidated by whatever oppressive social forces or agencies were arrayed against them. New leaders often emerged, often with different tactics and strategies, such as Booker T. Washington and W. E. B. DuBois, who readily come to mind; and Maggie L. Walker and R. L. Smith who do not. Their courageous and bold actions, however, paved the way for the resurgence yet to come, after what Rayford Logan called the nadir.

COLONIZATION

One response, not necessarily a major one, was reminiscent of the antebellum scene; that is, the consideration of colonization outside the United States as a possible alternative for the mass of black people. For some it was viewed as the only solution which would afford full freedom, justice, equality and dignity. Early espoused by Martin Delaney, the standard bearer of this epoch became the distinguished Bishop of the African Methodist Episcopal Church,

Henry McNeal Turner.

Turner visited Africa three times, organizing church conferences in Sierra Leone and in Liberia. He believed that the race should ultimately return to Africa, no doubt disillusioned with American politics because of the treatment he and other black legislators received in the general assembly of Georgia. "Two races of people living in the same country under the same institutions, and subject to the same laws with no social contact", he declared "is an anomaly and productive only of evil results."[1*] In 1896, he concluded that "the Negroid race has been free long enough now to begin to think for himself and plan for better conditions that he can claim to in this country or ever will. There is no manhood future in the United States for the Negro."[2] But attempts at this kind of colonization were not conspicuously successful, owing to the ravages of endemic and epidemic diseases, such as smallpox and malaria; the inadequacy of financial resources; and the inability of creolized American blacks to adapt themselves to a situation, physical and social, which had become alien to them, despite their African descent. In retrospect, such activities as advocated by Delaney and Turner seem to have made more of an impact upon the African than American blacks. The African Methodist Episcopal Church, for example, came to be highly regarded in Africa as a result of its missionary services and organizational skills. Not only Africa, but other locales outside the continental United States such as Mexico, were also considered to have the potential for black colonization.

Document 1

Excerpt of speech delivered by Henry McNeal Turner, 1896, reprinted in Africa and the American Negro, edited by J. W. E. Bowen, (Atlanta, Georgia, 1896), pp. 195-98.

I believe that the Negroid race has been free long enough now to begin to think for himself and plan for better conditions than he can lay claim to in this country or ever will. There is no manhood future in the United States for the Negro. He may eke out an existence for generations to come, but he can never be a man--full, symmetrical and undwarfed. Upon this point I know thousands who

*Footnotes to Part II begin on page 174.

make pretensions to scholarship, white and colored, will differ and may charge me with folly, while I in turn pity their ignorance of history and political and civil sociology.... The colored man who will stand up and in one breath say that the Negroid race does not want social equality and in the next predict a great future in the face of all the proscription of which the colored man is the victim, is either an ignoramus, or is an advocate of the perpetual servility and degradation of his race variety. I know as Senator Morgan (of Alabama) says, and as every white man in the land will say, that the whites will not grant social equality to the Negroid race, nor am I certain that God wants them to do it.

And as such, I believe that two or three millions of us should return to the land of our ancestors, and establish our own nation, civilization, laws and customs, styles of manufacture, and not only give the world like other race varieties, the benefit of our individuality, but build up social conditions peculiarly our own, and cease to be grumblers, chronic complainers and a menace to the white man's country, or the country he claims and is bound to dominate....

It is idle talk to speak of a colored man not being a success in skilled labor or fine arts. What the black man needs is a country and surroundings in harmony with his color and with respect for his manhood. Upon this point I would delight to dwell longer if I had time. Thousands of white people in this country are ever and anon advising the colored people to keep out of politics, but they do not advise themselves. If the Negro is a man in keeping with other men, why should he be less concerned about politics than any one else? Strange, too, that a number of would-be colored leaders are ignorant and debased enough to proclaim the same foolish jargon. For the Negro to stay out of politics is to level himself with a horse or a cow, which is no politician, and the Negro who does it proclaims his inability to take part in political affairs. If the Negro is to be a man, full and complete, he must take part in everything that belongs to manhood. If he omits a single duty, responsibility or privilege, to that extent he is limited and incomplete.

J. Fred Rippy speaks to the activities of a few who migrated to Mexico in 1895 under a joint effort of private enterprise and the Federal Government.

Document 2*

J. Fred Rippy, "A Negro Colonization Project in Mexico, 1895," Journal of Negro History, 1921, Vol. VI, pp. 67-68.

The project ... had no official element motivating it, however. It was merely a private enterprise conducted for the profit of a Mexican land company and a member of the Negro race; and not un-

*Reprinted by permission of the publisher.

til the scheme had failed did the United States government take a hand. On December 11, 1894, H. Ellis, a Negro, entered into a contract with the Agricultural, Industrial, and Colonization Company of Tlahualilo, Limited," for the transportation from the United States by February 15, 1895, of one hundred colored families between the ages of twelve and fifty. The company obligated itself to pay the passage of the colonists provided it did not exceed $20, and after they were established upon the land, to furnish them agricultural implements, stock, seed, and housing quarters, as well as $6 monthly during the first three months, and thereafter a sum later to be agreed upon. Each family was to be given sixty acres for cultivation, forty for cotton, fifteen for corn, and five for a garden. The company was to receive 40% of the yield of cotton and corn, the colonists 50%, and Ellis 10%. The colonists were to have two years in which to pay their passage; but, of course, the money advanced for sustenance was to be paid from the first crop, except in the event of an extremely lean year. The entire produce of the garden was to go to the Negroes. Stores were to be established in the colony, the colonists were to have their cotton ginned at the gins of the company at the rate of $1.50 per bale, and the company was to be given preference on all the produce sold. The contract was to endure for a period of five years.

Ellis set about immediately to fulfill his agreement. Going among the Negroes of Alabama and Georgia, he issued a rather extravagant circular representing his proposition as presenting the "greatest opportunity ever offered to the colored people of the United States to go to Mexico, ... the country of 'God and Liberty.'" He declared that the land of his company would easily produce a bale of cotton and from fifty to seventy-five bushels of corn per acre; spoke of irrigation facilities which made them independent of the rain, of "fine game, such as deer, bear, duck, and wild geese, and all manner of small game, as well as opossum," and of schools and churches to be constructed; and sought especially to impress upon their minds the fact that "the great Republic of Mexico extends to all of its citizens the same treatment--equal rights to all, special privileges to none."

ESTABLISHMENT OF ALL-BLACK TOWNS

As we have seen, the concept of a black utopia existed prior to the Civil War, when it required the emigration and aggregation of free blacks for it to come into existence. Black communities also emerged as a result of emancipation, notably in the Port Royal, South Carolina and Davis Bend, Mississippi areas. The latter gave way to the founding of Mound Bayou, which has persisted into the present, under the leadership, organizational talents and skills of a former slave of Jefferson Davis, Isaiah T. Montgomery.

Document 3*

Stanley Cisby Arthur, biographical sketch of Isaiah T. Montgomery, The Item, (New Orleans), September 25, 1921, reprinted in The Journal of Negro History Vol. VIII, January, 1923, pp. 87-91.

One of the most interesting figures at the meeting of the secretaries of the Federal Farm Loan Association, was an aged negro, "Uncle" Isaiah T. Montgomery, of Mound Bayou City, Bolivar County, Mississippi. "Uncle" Isaiah is not only one of the wealthiest farmers in his district, but he founded the town of Mound Bayou, which is composed exclusively of colored people, who run the stores, the banks, the post office, the schools and the peace offices, but "Uncle" Isaiah was a former slave and a body servant of Jefferson Davis, president of the Confederacy.

Black of face, with white hair and a white chin beard "Uncle" Isaiah looks exactly the part of the regulation stage "Uncle" of the old regime. He looks every bit of his 74 years but his mind is exceedingly bright and he recounted the happenings of over half a century with the utmost clarity of speech and showed many evidences of his education, which he says he gave himself. When he took recourse to a piece of paper and a pen to estimate the ginnage of his community, he set down words and figures with Spencerian exactness. His handwriting was truly a revelation to the interviewer.

"I was born on Hurricane plantation, in Warren county, Mississippi, in 1847, and my father and I were owned by Joseph E. Davis, brother of Jefferson Davis. The plantation owned by the late president of the Confederacy adjoined the Hurricane, and was called Brierfield plantation," said the aged colored man and former slave who is now a prosperous banker in the town he founded. "I was about nine years old when I first remember Jefferson Davis real well. I was working in my master's office when his brother came back from Congress and I was told to meet the steamboat Natchez in a row boat and get Mr. Jeff.

"When the Natchez blew her whistle as she came around a bend of the river I rowed out and Mr. Jeff got in my boat with his grips and things and I took him to shore and toted all his things into the 'White Room' where Mr. Jeff staid for a considerable spell. While there I was his personal attendant, I blacked his shoes, kept his room in order, held his horse for him and other little things that a servant like I was was supposed to do. On one of his trips down the river on the Natchez (Mr. Jeff and Captain Tom P. Leathers, the historic commander of that boat, were close friends), he brought his wife and daughter, who was afterwards Mrs. Hayes, and they all were very kind to me because I was Mr. Jeff's personal servant all the time they were at the Hurricane.

"When the war between the states came I staid on the Joseph

*Reprinted by permission of the publisher.

Davis plantation all during the fighting. In '62 or '63, anyway, after the battle of Corinth, the Yankees commenced overrunning the South and Mr. Joe, took all his stock and colored people to Jackson, and later on to Alabama. He had me return to the plantation with my mother and act as sort of caretakers and we were there when Admiral Porter's Mississippi squadron made its way up the river. It seems sometime before a gunboat, the Indianola, had been sunk in the river, just off the Hurricane plantation and folks in the neighborhood had dismantled her.

"When Admiral Porter came up the river he stopped at the plantation so as to look at the wreck and see if her guns could be found. But they had been thrown overboard and had gone down in the quicksand. The Admiral asked me if I wanted to go with him as cabin boy. I said yes, and ran to get my mammy's consent which was given. This was in April of '63 and a few months later I was with the Admiral in the siege of Vicksburg and later the battle of Grand Gulf. Soon afterwards I got a sickness from drinking Red River water and when I was sent back to Hurricane I found my parents had gone to Cincinnati and when I got word of this to Admiral Porter he secured transportation there for me.

"When the war was over Mr. Joe Davis got in touch with my father and had him come back to Hurricane plantation and after we got there he made a proposition that we could buy the two plantations, Hurricane, that Mr. Joe owned, and Brierfield, of 4,000 acres, that Mr. Jeff Davis owned. While he could not sell to colored people under the existing laws, through a court action by which my father Benjamin T. Montgomery, and my brother William T. and myself agreed to pay $300,000 for the combined properties, they were turned over to us and we were to pay six per cent a year on the whole until it was paid off.

"Our first year working the plantation resulted in almost disaster as we suffered from an overflow and when the first payment came around we were only able to pay $6,000. When we sent this to Mr. Joe Davis with our excuses he sent us back a canceled note for the rest of the $18,000. The Davis brothers, were gentlemen, sir. Well, we kept the plantation going for thirteen years and in that time we ranked as third in the production of cotton in Warren county. While we were growing cotton I became very well acquainted with Captain John W. Cannon, the commander of the famous steamboat the Robert E. Lee. He and Captain Tom Leathers, the commander of the Natchez, were always having some sort of fight or another and I saw the famous race between the two when they actually settled the matter for good and all.

"The death of Mr. Joe Davis and taking over of his properties by his heirs lost us our holdings and I became interested in the Yazoo Delta. I heard that the Y. & M. V. was asking colored people to come in and open up the country and after going over the situation I decided to select Mound Bayou for the seat of my future operations. This place was selected because between Big and Little Mound Bayous there was an old Indian mound. This was in 1887 and it certainly was a wild territory, it had rich land but it was thickly grown over with oak and ash and gum, and acres and acres of cane. Well, I plundered around here and induced other colored folks to settle there. I founded Mound Bayou Settlement--the railroad folks wanted to name it Montgomery, a few years ago but I made the original name stick.

"Building up our community was slow work. All the colored folks bought their places on 10-year contracts and it was hard work for some of them in the face of a few crop failures, overflows, boll weevil and other set-backs but we succeeded. Mound Bayou Settlement is now a town of a little over 1,000 population and there are about 2,500 in the country nearby. The town is of wholly colored population and we have three big churches, one costing $25,000, another costing $15,000, and another $10,000. There are several other less pretentious places of worship, as well.

"We have two big mercantile establishments. The largest being the one I founded and known as the Mercantile Co-operative Company which now has a $20,000 stock. We also have the Mound Bayou State Bank, with $10,000 capital, a $3,000 surplus, with resources between $150,000 and $200,000. I am a member of the board of directors and we make a great many loans to our colored people to see they get out their crops, and being in the staple cotton belt, we make most of it on this crop.

"We have just completed a consolidated school house, 95 feet square, three stories high, with 16 large class rooms. It cost us $100,000 which was raised by a local bond issue. We have a seven to eight months' term and employ an agricultural expert, co-operating under the Smith-Lever national fund and a very fine domestic science class.

"The town has a mayor and a board of aldermen, all office holders being colored folks, and the present mayor, B. H. Green, was the first man born in the settlement. I was mayor for over four years, being the first to hold office, resigning it to hold the office of receiver of public monies at Jackson, Miss.

"We have four gins that can handle over 5,000 bales and our people now feel that the upward trend of the cotton price will make for further prosperous times."

EMIGRATION TO NORTH AND WEST

The withdrawal of Federal troops from the former states of the Confederacy and the emergence of terror and violence directed against powerless blacks gave rise to a powerful impulse to emigrate in the year 1879. The following documents relate to the social conditions and behaviors which stimulated this great mass movement.

Document 4

Letters from Ministers Encouraging Migration to Kansas, Christian Recorder, February 27, 1873, p. 2.

Bro. Tanner--In looking over the Christian Recorder of the 30th., ult., I noticed an article, "Come West." I was very much interested in the article, and this morning I called to see the general Agent of the A. T. & Pacific Railroad, and I can but agree with Bro. Henderson, that this is the most desirable place that immigrants can strike; especially colored, coming from the place mentioned (Georgia). 1st. This is the State made famous for its death struggle for freedom in the days of John Brown, through the scenes of much blood during the war (or late unpleasantness as the rebs used to call it) from which it derived the name of bleeding Kansas; yet it was the land of rest to the weary slaves as they travelled through Missouri and Arkansas swamps to reach the borders of free Kansas.

Now I can say of her that she is one of the best States for farming there is in the Union, greater inducements offered to immigrants than any other State; there is stone coal in abundance, millions of acres of land to be had at your own price in the Arkansas Valley in the Southern part of the State, there is some of the best land of the Mississippi river, good to raise anything you want on it. In different parts of this State the farmers have burned corn in place of wood and coal. This seems rather strange you may say but it is the truth. 2nd. There is greater advantages here also for the education of your children, than in any other State West of the Mississippi. In every District, Township, in every County there are schools; colored children share the same schools, except in cities of the first and second class, and before many days, that law allowing separate schools in said cities will be repealed. And now, Mr. Editor let me say to those friends as I did Bro. Henderson, "They need not think to live here without working." This is a new country and it must be improved. But I am not afraid of idleness on the part of my people as I understand they want to work, but those tyrants of Democracy and Rebellion will not allow them a chance. Remember the admonition of our late friend, Horace Greeley "Go West." Come on my friends and we will try and assist you in finding homes. I will send you, Bro. Tanner, a paper with a complete account of the land that you may be able to give them a better account than I am able, or have the time to give. I am now in the midst of a revival again.

Come on, come on, come on.

B. F. Watson

Topeka, Kansas, Box 214

"Come West," by Rev. T. W. Henderson

Dear Mr. Editor:

I have read in different papers that a Convention of colored men would soon be held in the State of Georgia, to discuss the propriety of emigrating. The idea, I think is a capital one, and it is to be regretted that it has not been acted upon before. It is well known to all, that none of the Southern States can well afford to loose any of their laborers; yet, if the land-holders and those that need laborers, refuse to see them protected in the exercise of their rights, and in the enjoyment of life and liberty, then those laborers are to be justified in leaving those lords, to reap the consequences of their own folly; while they seek more congenial homes elsewhere.

Having lived in Kansas for five years, and being pretty well acquainted with the advantages offered to new settlers, I thought that through your columns, I would make known to those that are not already informed, a few important facts. Kansas is truly an inviting field to the energetic emigrant. She has thrown wide her doors to all, and invites men, women and children from every clime and of every race to come and settle on her rich and fertile lands.

How Land May Be Obtained

First, there is yet much land subject to pre-emption.

Second, there are many broad acres that may be taken under the Homestead act.

Third, much good and cheap land may be bought on long credit of any of the many Rail-road companies of the state.

To large companies, the first or second way of obtaining land is the best; but to individuals that prefer homes near thriving towns and good markets, the better plan is to purchase Rail-road land, the ruling price of which is from three to ten dollars per acre. I need not add, that the usual plan adopted by emigrants is to send a trusty agent out ahead to arrange for them before they come. This should never be neglected, as an agent may obtain many advantages not to be obtained after all have arrived.

A fatal mistake, which I would guard our people against, is one frequently made by emigrants. I have seen many on their road back to the State from whence they came, discouraged and disgusted. Being inquisitive I found that the sum and substance of the trouble was they had come here thinking that a living could be had without working for it. Friends, don't come with any such expectation; the law of nature and of God is here as elsewhere--By the sweat of his brow, man must obtain his bread.

The soil in most parts of Kansas is rich, and consequently very productive; and only needs thrifty men to make the very best farms. But I have written my three pages.

A Committee of the Senate of the 46th Congress was selected to hear testimony from blacks concerning their removal from the Southern states. This selection records the testimony of an articulate and intelligent black leader, J. M. Brown.

Document 5

Report and Testimony of the Select Committee of the United States Senate to Investigate the Causes of the Removal of the Negroes from the Southern States to the Northern States. Senate Report No. 693, Part 2, 46th Cong., 2nd Sess. (Washington, D. C., United States Printing Office, 1880), pp. 360-363.

A number of the colored people have settled in Wabaunsee County; two sections of forty acres each have been settled up with colored families; and two more sections will be settled in a short time. We settled them there last May. We gave them a couple of teams and some farming utensils, and supported them for two or three months; since then they have been able to take care of themselves. Some of them have since died of lung troubles. Three hundred dollars has taken care of the colored people that our society has had to aid this winter. We built barracks for them--buildings put up in a cheap manner, like soldiers' barracks; and there the little children, and the women, and the men who were too old to work, remained, while the others went out to work. A considerable number of colored families have been settled on the Indian reservation on the Neosho River. There is an Indian reservation there, a large body of land, twenty miles square, owned by the Kaw Indians; the uplands sell for a dollar and a quarter an acre; the bottom lands are higher in price. They have mostly all been able to make their own living, except a few sent out lately. They have, so far as we can hear, given general satisfaction. Wherever we have sent them, there has been a large demand for more of the same class. They have been a very good class of colored people. Out of the whole twenty-five thousand, I have seen but two who seemed to be drunk. Only one has been arrested on charge of stealing, and he was proven clear; this can be shown by the records of the city of Topeka. The care of all these colored people has never cost the city of Topeka twenty-five cents; the society has looked after them. They have proven themselves willing to work, and their work has given general satisfaction; their work is in demand. The farmers are taking them, and they are being sent for to work in the coal mines of Iowa, Illinois, and Colorado. Friends now in Illinois offer to take fifty thousand of them into that State; that offer was made only last week. In Kansas we have now as many as we ought to have of the poor class, whether white or black. But persons having even a little money can do well there. They can buy land on the Indian reservation at a dollar and a quarter an acre; or they can secure railroad land at from three to five dollars per acre. If you pay cash down, the railroad companies will knock off one third; if you take it on six years' time, they will knock off one fifth; if you take it on eleven years' time, they will charge only full price, and you can pay one fifth down and seven per cent interest on the rest till you can pay it. Some farmers there rent their land--the same to a colored man as to a white man, on the same terms--the tenant giving one-third of the crop where he furnishes everything; where the white owner furnishes everything, he gives the colored man one-half the crop. Wages range from ten to eighteen dollars a month, according to the nature of the work and the need of hands.

Q. What proportion of the twenty-five thousand are now unemployed and in barracks waiting for employment?--A. I left Topeka last Thursday, a week ago yesterday; we had then on hand about three hundred, the most of whom had come in within the preceding ten days. Some families had come in, one or more members of which were sick; they had to stay there until they had recovered. There are about three hundred there under our charge; there were some in the city who were not under our charge.

Q. Were there any other points in Kansas where emigrants gathered?--A. Yes, sir; there have come into the southern part of Kansas, from Texas and places down that way, between two thousand and two thousand five hundred.

Q. Do you include these in the total, the twenty-five thousand that you mentioned?--A. No, sir; those twenty-five thousand that I referred to were those who had passed through the hands of our society there in Topeka. But those that came into the southern part of Kansas were looked after by our branch societies. We have a branch society at Parsons, Kansas, and one at Fort Scott, and one at Independence. They can get into Kansas by a nearer route, that way; some of them walked, some came in wagons; and some in cars, if they have the money. The majority of them have about money enough to get there. They find employment among the farmers. They are going to make an attempt, in the southern part of Kansas, at raising cotton this spring.

Q. Have you conversed with many of these people who have passed through your hands, with reference to the causes of their leaving the South?--A. Yes, sir; I have conversed with a great many of them. I have taken special pains to inquire upon that point. I have lectured to them in the public halls there to as many as five hundred at a time. I have asked them to state, in the presence of other people, what was the cause of their leaving the South. They generally gave in answer three causes. They said there was no security for life, liberty, or property. This is about what they claim.

Q. Did they state facts upon which they base that claim?--A. They say that since the war, and for the last few years especially--since 1875, I suppose--hundreds of colored men have been killed in the State of Mississippi, and probably in some other parts of the South, in riots and private broils, or have been shot down by white men, but that they never saw a white man hung or sent to the penitentiary in the State of Mississippi for killing a colored man;

I know that I have never heard of one. The records of the State courts will show whether such is the fact or not, but they say no white man has ever been hung or sent to the penitentiary for killing a colored man, to their knowing. They have seen the men that allowed these riots, and were the instigators of them, murderers of colored men, going at large unpunished; they say they can see that every day. They are hardly ever indicted; if they are ever tried it is in reality a mock trial; they are taken before the magistrate's court, where they give a bond of five hundred dollars. All offenses are bondable in Mississippi, I understand. The case is continued from time to time until finally it is thrown out of court, so there is no punishment for anything that a white man may do to a colored man; but if a white man and a colored man get into a private quarrel, and the colored man shoots the white man, he will be mobbed or hung. There is no security whatever for the life of a colored man; every colored man's life is at the tender mercies of the lowest white man in the community. If a white man and a colored man get into a fuss, and the colored man happens to whip the white man, he has got to go or he will be murdered. If a colored man is working at a place, and a white man owing him or for any other reason wants to get him out of the way, the white man can get him mobbed in a few hours; his life must pay the penalty. They claim that the white community are all leagued together against the colored men; whether this is true or not I do not know; I am giving you what they say to me when I ask them why they have left the South. As for liberty, they claim to have laws in Mississippi, Alabama, Louisiana, and other states, the same for white men as for colored men. They claim that there is no discrimination under the laws between white and black. The trouble is there is discrimination in the execution of the laws; if a colored man comes before court in a case with a white man the white man will get the best of it. They charge high prices for the land they rent. In the Mississippi Valley, when I was there, they charged ten dollars an acre. The planter demands ten dollars an acre rent; if he don't take ten dollars rent he takes so much lint cotton, equivalent to it. This rent must be paid first, out of the crop; next in order comes the merchant's lien, owing for supplies furnished; this is arranged so as to take up all that has been raised on the place. If the tenant has raised enough to cover it and something to spare. Just before picking-time comes, the merchant sends men around from place to place to see how the crop is getting along; how many bales will probably be made. By this means the merchant knows how large to make his bill. He lets the colored man come and buy a few things, run up an account, charging four or five prices for everything. For instance, he will charge twenty to twenty-five cents a pound for sugar, for which you or any white man would pay eight or nine cents; or twenty-five cents a pound for bacon for which you would have to pay six or seven cents. I have seen some of their bills in Kansas; in fact, I had before seen them many times in the South. If the colored man refuses to pay the bill, which, as I have said, is always made large enough to cover the value of the entire crop, after paying the rent, the merchant comes into court and sues him. The white man brings his itemized account into court; the colored man has no account, and of course he is beaten in the suit, and the cost is thrown onto him. They stand against him, if he cannot pay it. And colored men soon learn that it is better to pay any account, however unjust, than to refuse, for he stands no possible chance of getting justice before the law.

Another thing; the colored people are anxious to educate their children. Some few schools are kept, in some parts of the South, for three or four months in the year; but the white men claim the right to employ inferior teachers, who do very little toward educating the colored children; they are of no particular benefit to the children.

The colored men are anxious to accumulate property. You can buy land in most of the Southern States, but there is a great deal of trouble in the South in regard to titles of land. A great many planters were killed during the war, and for that and other reasons the titles to lands are very complicated. Colored men do not know much about titles; they have no means of determining whether the title to a piece of land is good, legal or not. They will buy land on time and go to work to improve it, and after working hard for some years, along comes somebody else and lays claim to it, and the colored man loses it; so they are afraid to buy lands for themselves.

For these reasons the colored men in the South have very little confidence in the white men, and the white men have very little confidence in the colored men. This is the feeling; the colored men claim that there is no chance in the world for them to better their condition in the South; so, as a last resort, they have determined to come north.

Another thing, in regard to the way they are treated in boats or railroad cars when traveling. A man or a woman may be ever so well educated or well behaved--may have been educated at the best college in the land--but in traveling that woman must be put into a colored car on the railroad; must go into the smoking car, no matter how much whisky or tobacco there may be there, or how sick it may make her; I know something about that myself. Or if she is traveling on a steamer she must be put up in the texas with the roughest class of men. Education amounts to nothing, good behavior counts for nothing, even money cannot buy a colored man or woman decent treatment and the comforts that white people claim and can obtain; and this is the case all over the South. The colored people have become tired of submitting to these things, and have made up their minds that if there is any place on American soil where they can be free, to go there.

Q. Do they complain of any denial of their political rights and privileges?--A. They do; they claim that it is impossible to get either a fair vote or a fair count. In some counties the colored men are allowed to vote. But if they vote, the colored vote is counted out, unless certain white men that the white men like very well are running for office; then, sometimes, they will allow a fair count. But in many counties, in most places in the South, no matter how large the Republican majority might rightfully be, there is no chance of a fair count, so that he would be declared elected. So that now no Republican is willing to run the risk of making the canvass--of risking his life for the certainty of being counted out if he should be elected by ever so large a majority. Another thing: white men do not like this sort of thing any better than colored men do. So a great many Southern white Republicans are leaving the South. When they are gone the colored men do not understand affairs, and do not know what the result will be. Some of them think that slavery is to be re-established. I do not think so, but a great many of the colored people do. They fear that this thing will go on until finally their liberties will be taken away, if they remain in the South. So they think it best to get away in time.

Q. They feel, when they are denied their rights as voters, or cheated out of them, that they have no means of protecting themselves?--A. No means of protecting themselves whatever. And the white men are all armed, and if any riots are started, the colored men always get the worst of it. They cannot get any help from the government, or from anywhere. They feel uneasy about their condition in every way, and especially their vote. If there is anything they want to exercise freely, it is the right to vote as they please, as American citizens; and that right they say, is denied them in the South.

Q. Do they complain of personal violence--of outrages committed upon them personally?--A. Yes, sir; many of them bring statements of whipping and murdering. Some colored men have been called to their doors and shot; others were taken in the night, or in the daytime, and whipped. I have heard of a great many such cases occurring in almost all parts of the States. But the fact is, I had so much of this before this exodus began that it was no new thing to me, and so I have paid no particular attention to it. Never thinking of being called for a witness, and never desiring to be one, I paid very little attention to what these emigrants have said on that point, so that I cannot now state particulars as to names, places, dates, &c.

Q. Did any of them say anything about resistance on the part of the white people to their coming away?--A. Yes, sir; the white people at first resisted their leaving, especially along the river; they tried to keep the boats from taking them. But at present there seems to be a little different state of feeling; in most sections the white men do not try to stop their coming by force; they say, if you will go, you can go. But the leading colored men who are there, and who are trying to get others to leave--their lives are in danger. There was E. Handy, who came up last summer on an excursion trip. When he went back South he told the colored people that the best thing they could do was to leave there and come North. They made preparations to kill him, in order to intimidate others....

Document 6*

Glen Schwendemann, "St. Louis and the Exodus of 1879," Journal of Negro History, Vol. 46, 1931. pp. 32-46.

A visitor to the St. Louis waterfront in the early morning hours of March 16, 1879, would have witnessed one of the most unusual sights ever seen in that colorful and everchanging part of the city. The scene about to be enacted was, in fact, so significant that reporters for two St. Louis newspapers, the Globe-Democrat and Missouri Republican, had roused themselves from their slumbers to be present. By four o'clock around a dozen persons had congregated on the levee at the foot of Pine Street, and with these two newsmen stood shivering in the falling snow awaiting the arrival of the steamer Grand Tower, expected momentarily from the South. Aboard the river boat, as telegraphic dispatches had previously announced, were nearly six hundred "Exodusters," a few of the many thousands of freedmen who had suddenly begun to desert the plantations along the river in Mississippi and Louisiana to find new homes in the "Promised Land" of Kansas.

To the Globe-Democrat reporter, at least the drama about to unfold was not new. Just five days previously, on March 11, he had interviewed some of the 280 men, women and children who had arrived on the steamer Colorado, the first major group of the immigrants to reach the city. How well he recalled that first boatload! At nine o'clock in the evening he had observed their pitiful condition as they huddled among the piles of freight in the darkness of the levee. The newsman, curious as to the cause of this sudden and unprecendented transfer of colored people, had sought out W. H. Whitesides, the "spokesman" for the group, who proved to be a willing and able informant. Whitesides, an intelligent Negro of about forty years of age, immediately launched into a recital of the many abuses inflicted upon his people by the southern economic system and the white residents of the region. But at the moment, he was particularly inflamed by the way the Negroes on the Colorado had been "duped." The entire group, according to Whitesides, had come northward firmly believing they would be furnished free transportation to Kansas where farms, implements, and subsistence awaited all who succeeded in making an appearance. All of this was to come from a benevolent government which had remembered the colored man at last. . . .

When the newcomers began to realize how greatly they had been misled, however, the Caanan (sic) toward which they had so joyously set their faces a few days earlier suddenly seemed far removed. Dejected, disillusioned and stranded in a strange and seemingly indifferent city they had resigned themselves to their fate and prepared to face events of the new day on the "hard side of unsympathetic skidpiles," or on the dirty floor of the Memphis wharfboat.

The dawn, however, had revealed no improvement in the

*Reprinted by permission of the publisher.

newcomers' condition, and when the Globe-Democrat reporter returned to the levee the following morning, he found the migrants scattered along the waterfront warming themselves at several bonfires, all without food or the means to obtain it. It was this juncture, when hope seemed to have fled from before them, that the colored residents of the city had come to their rescue. The first of the local Negroes to become concerned was Charleton H. Tandy, who had received word of their arrival and destitution and hastened immediately to the waterfront. By working throughout the day, Tandy succeeded in finding deserted houses and wharfboats in which to quarter the migrants temporarily.

While busily engaged on behalf of his new charges, Tandy received assurance from a former secretary of the Mullanphy Emigrant Relief Board that the Negroes were entitled to some aid from that organization. The fund had been established years before under the provisions of the will of Bryan Mullanphy of St. Louis to provide financial assistance for needy settlers moving to western lands. Although the Board received the idea of aiding the migrants with "great coolness," $100 was finally contributed to the newcomers' relief after Tandy made an impassioned plea on behalf of his suffering people. Before a final policy was established regarding relief for the Negroes, however, the Board had instructed the president to consult with the mayor to determine the course of action to be taken by the city administration....

Meanwhile, on March 14, Charleton H. Tandy had issued a call to the Negroes of St. Louis to assemble in a mass meeting, time and place to be designated, to arrange for the "temporary relief" of the newcomers. With the city already sheltering between 300 and 500 migrants, who had arrived on the Colorado and other vessels, and from 500 to 600 more expected within two days on the Grand Tower, this action was wise. The news from the South was more alarming. At an unidentified landing in Louisiana, around 500 colored people were awaiting transportation, while for 100 miles north and south of Vicksburg, an estimated 5,000 Negroes were reportedly on the river banks prepared for departure....

The arrival of the Grand Tower increased the number of migrants in St. Louis to between 700 and 800. The care of this enlarging host of people, a task assumed by the colored residents of the city, irrevocably committed them to a greatly expanded program of relief. The first step, of course, was to provide shelter for the newcomers. A small number were lodged at Union Hall at 1015 Christy Avenue, but the majority were quartered in St. Paul's Chapel (AME) and the Eighth Street Colored Baptist Church, the former welcoming around forty and the latter receiving about 200. The faithful of both churches brought food and other necessities and the migrants were made as comfortable as possible....

In response to Charleton H. Tandy's call of March 14, the colored people of St. Louis met at St. Paul's Chapel on March 17. The meeting under the chairmanship of Tandy, immediately proceeded to the business at hand. A resolution committee, whose report was readily accepted by those present, recommended the appointment of a committee of fifteen to give "careful and correct consideration" to the problem of providing aid to the migrants who had become "stalled" in the city. A finance committee was also created and empowered to receive all donations made on behalf of the newcomers.

On the following afternoon, March 18, the Committee of Fifteen met again at St. Paul's and selected the Reverend John Turner, pastor of the host church, chairman of the group, and Charles Starkes, head of the finance committee. The group was expanded to twenty-five and committees to handle the various phases of the groups' work were created. The transportation committee began its labors immediately by arranging with the Missouri River Packet Company to transport a load of the freedmen to Wyandotte, Kansas, on Saturday, March 22. The committee's decision to send the migrants on to their destination was a wise move, for transportation costs would ultimately prove less burdensome than the continued and unrealistic relief of so many dependents.

... Between March 16, when the churches were opened to the travelers, and March 20, the three congregations had spent $800, and the Eighth Street Baptists alone had provided 2,500 meals and 300 suits of clothing. Unfortunately, complete reports of relief work in the other two churches are not available, but one must presume their sacrifices were comparable. While the results of the labors of the colored citizens were truly remarkable, it was clear that the Negroes of the city would need much help from the white residents of St. Louis and throughout the country if relief work was to remain at its present rate. The Negroes might continue to provide used clothing, and to feed the migrants from their not over-stocked larders, but it would prove impossible to find sufficient funds to send their charges on to the Promised Land....

However laudable its objectives, Turner's new society succeeded in bringing the Committee of Twenty-five under a cloud of suspicion and ultimately caused its replacement. To give the committee more strength and stability the Twenty-five organized again on April 22 as the Colored Refugee Relief Board and placed the Reverend Moses Dickson at its head. The Reverend John Turner, took over the job of treasurer after Charles Starkes had left the post in protest. On May 6, no doubt to help quiet the public criticism directed at the group, the board held a mass meeting in the Union Hall to report on the work of the old Committee of Twenty-five and its successor since March 18, when the group commenced its labors. From that date to May 3, the Board had issued 50,500 meals valued at $5,050, of which a "large part" had been donated by the colored people of the city. Around 13,500 pieces of clothing, valued at $3,377, had been given to the Negroes, four-fifths of which came from friends of the race in the eastern states. Between March 14 and May 3, approximately 5,169 men, women and children had been aided by the Board. Of this number 5,004 had been shipped to Kansas, leaving only a handful remaining in the city.

Between March 17, the date of the first mass meeting, and May 3, the committee had received $4,705.36 from all sources, and paid out $4,527.08 for expenses. From citizens of St. Louis the committee had collected $1,201.25. The remainder had been donated by eastern humanitarians, the bulk of which sum undoubtedly came from the solicitations of Charleton H. Tandy, who reportedly collected $2,000 in a tour of the East in April. The average number of migrants arriving in St. Louis during the four weeks preceeding May 3 was 150, and the average expenses for the same period amount to $787.50.

With the rendering of this report, the Colored Refugee Relief Board had concluded the period of its greatest service, and in the future the management of its affairs would fall more and more into the hands of well-known and highly respected white men....

More regrettable, however, was the political aspect that was now manifesting itself in the migration. The first indication of this new development came early in April when a group of leading Republican politicians organized the National Emigration Aid Society with its headquarters in Washington, D. C. The temper of the group was indicated by the fact that most of them were Senators and Representatives who had a long history of anti-slavery sentiments or had been participants in the reconstruction congresses....

The forces thus set in motion by the creation of the new society in Washington soon reached St. Louis....

Thus, in the Negroes' flight from bondage, as throughout their short but strife-torn period of freedom, they again found themselves the "pawn" of the major political parties to be rewarded or rejected, used or misused, as the two antagonists felt their own interests might best be served....

This document speaks to the fact that distress was so great that English charitable organizations became interested in their problems. The following debate calls for the Congress to enact legislation to permit the clothing donated by the English societies to be granted duty-free passage into the United States.

Document 7

Debate on Relief to Exodusters. Proceedings and Debates of the 46th Congress, 2nd Session. Congressional Record - Senate. February 20, 1880. pp. 1041-1042.

Relief of Colored Emigrants

Mr. MORRILL. I have the unanimous consent of the members of the Committee on Finance who are present to report back without amendment the bill (H. R. No. 3288) for the relief of colored emigrants, which was referred to that Committee, and I ask the Senate to consider it at this time.

The bill was read, as follows:

Be it enacted, &c. , That all clothing and other articles, being charitable contributions or the avails of charitable contributions, imported in good faith for the relief or aid of colored persons who may have emigrated from their homes to other States, and not for sale, and all such articles imported and now in bond, shall be admitted free of duty under such regulations as the Secretary of the Treasury may prescribe: Provided, That such articles shall be delivered only to State or municipal corporations, or to some society or institution established for charitable purposes: And provided further, That the importers or consignees of such articles shall give such security as the Secretary of the Treasury may prescribe for the payment of lawful duties on such articles, should any of them be sold or used contrary to the provisions and intent of this act. This act shall take effect from its passage, and remain in force until February 1, 1881.

Passed the House of Representatives February 10, 1880

Attest: George M. Adams, Clerk.

The PRESIDING OFFICER. Is there objection to taking up the bill?

Mr. PENDLETON. I object to it.

Mr. VOORHEES. I object.

Mr. THURMAN. May I inquire how the bill just read comes up? I hope that bill will not be passed just now.

Mr. VOORHEES. It cannot be passed now.

Mr. THURMAN. If the people who live abroad interfere with the migration of persons from one State to another in the United States, or, as this bill has it, the migration of colored people from one state to another, I should like to have that matter very fairly and fully considered before the American people. There was migration to my State when every man carried his life in his hands, because he did not know but what an Indian would seek to take his scalp.

Mr. WITHERS. Let me suggest that objection has been made and the bill has gone over.

Mr. CONKLING. Mr. President, my application in this behalf was made because I have at this moment in my hand a telegraphic dispatch from a charitable and prominent citizen of the city of New York stating that thirty packages of clothing for Kansas refugees, given by friends in England and brought here free, have been received. He then refers to this bill which has passed the House, and asks whether it cannot be expedited on its passage here.

That is the bill and that is the occasion of which the honorable Senator from Ohio the senior Senator (Mr. Thurman) has felt moved to make the observations which have fallen from him. I trust he will take no offense and ascribe no unkindness to me if in reply I say thus much. Charitable persons in England, moved by a sense of pity for the starving and the poor have sent at their own cost to us a quantity of clothing to cover and shelter them. The Senator from Ohio objects to even considering a proposition to allow this charity to reach its destination; and he does that in the same Chamber in which by unanimous consent we have very recently adopted a joint resolution to send across the sea to the starving people of Ireland contributions given by the charity of our own people. So that here stand the two facts and the two spectacles in contrast with each other, that charitable people in Great Britain moved by charity send to a class of our people who are suffering clothing and raiment, and send this charity, to men born here, and the Senator refuses to allow the Senate to even consider the question whether we will permit the reception and application of this clothing. Our citizens, in the midst of considerable need of our own, send food and send raiment to the suffering people of other lands and I think no member of any body, no official, has been found in England to object to receiving and applying what we have sent there.

It seems to me, Mr. President, very hard that this should be so. I almost think if the honorable Senator from Ohio would reflect upon it he would scarcely feel moved to refuse to consider whether he will allow to perish and go for naught these contributions lying on the wharf in the city of New York or whether he will allow them to be sent on, not at his expense, not at the expense of the government, but at the cost of the charitable people who chose to forward them, for the use of those people for whom they were designed.

Mr. BRUCE rose.

Mr. EDMUNDS. What is the pending question, Mr. President?

The PRESIDING OFFICER. There is no question.

Mr. BRUCE. Mr. President---

The PRESIDING OFFICER. By unanimous consent the Senator from New York was permitted to make the remarks which he has made. The Senator from Mississippi now addresses the Chair.

Mr. BRUCE. It is not my purpose to discuss this question. I have studiously avoided giving expression to any views on this floor touching the movement of colored people from the South, and I have hoped no occasion would arise for me to engage in that discussion. I shall not do so now.

It seems to me that the only question involved now is whether or not we will relieve suffering humanity; whether we will allow these people who are in Kansas--whether they have left their homes for cause or without cause, wisely or unwisely, is a matter of no importance, so far as this question is concerned--to die by hundreds, rather than permit a charity which the English people have sent here to pass through the custom-house free of duty. That is all. Money is being collected in this country by thousands of dollars to be sent across the seas to relieve the suffering people of Ireland. It is right--.

Mr. FERRY. Hundreds of thousands

Mr. BRUCE. Yes, hundreds of thousands. I am glad to say I have been one of the persons who have contributed. Nobody up to this moment I believe has objected to this money being sent; and, if I mistake not, two or three days ago, a joint resolution was introduced, and on the next day reported and passed without a dissenting vote, authorizing the Secretary of the Navy to fit up a ship and use that ship to carry provisions and clothing to those suffering people.

Now, I do not believe that the Senator from Indiana (Mr. Voorhees) desires to be understood as opposing a movement simply to relieve these suffering people. It is not now a question of how they came there or why they went there; it is not a question whether they ought to have gone there or not; but they are there and they are in distress, and it seems to me that the honorable Senator from Indiana (Mr. Voorhees) whom I know well and favorably, does not intend to antagonize this bill because he may not believe, as many of us may not believe, that these people should have originally gone to that State.

In the name of the hundreds of colored people now starving in Kansas I appeal to the Senate to pass the pending measure, that they may receive the immediate benefits of this charity.

***

The PRESIDING OFFICER. The bill goes on the Calendar.

Mr. WITHERS. I move that the Senate adjourn.

The motion was agreed to; and (at four o'clock and forty-two minutes p. m.) the Senate adjourned.

Benjamin "Pops" Singleton was one of the great grass-roots leaders of the emigration movement. In this excerpt from his testimony, he explains his point of view that economic factors were the basic reasons in the decision to emigrate.

Document 8

Excerpt from Testimony of Benjamin Singleton. Report of the Select Committee of the Senate. Senate Report 693, 46th Congress, 2nd Session, 1880, Part 3, pp. 380-383.

What made you help in the migration? Well, my people, for the want of land--we needed land for our children--and their disadvantages that caused my heart to grieve and sorrow; pity for my race, sir, that was coming down instead of going up--that caused me to go to work for them.... Right emphatically, I tell you today, I woke up the millions right through me! The great God of Glory has worked in me. I have had open interviews with the living spirit of God for my people; and we are going to leave the South. We are going to leave it if there ain't an alteration and signs of a change.

What do you mean by a change? Well, I am not going to stand bulldozing and half pay and all those things.... I am the whole cause of the Kansas migration!... Allow me to say to you that confidence is perished and faded away; they have been lied to every year.... My plan is for them to leave the country and learn the South a lesson.... We don't want to leave the South, and just as soon as we have confidence in the South, I am going to be an instrument in the hands of God to persuade every man to go back, because that is the best country.

WELFARE INTERESTS OF THE BLACK CHURCH

The following excerpts from Dr. Lindsay's dissertation discusses the continued significance of the role of the black church in promoting the welfare of blacks.

Document 9

Monroe N. Work, "The Negro Church and the Negro Community," Southern Workman, XXVII, 37 (August, 1908), pp. 428-29. Cited in Inabel B. Lindsay, "The Participation of Negroes in the Establishment of Welfare Services, 1865-1900," with special reference to the District of Columbia, Maryland and Virginia, 1952. pp. 123-130.

... the church as an organization has greatly affected the Negro's social life. For the first twenty years of freedom, the church was in close touch with the people's social and economic life, and it contributed in no small way to the race's progress.... For many years after freedom, the church building was the only place for public meetings that the people had. It was their social center. Here were discussed all those questions and problems that were concerned with their welfare. The pastor was the most important and influential person in the community. He was often the only person who was able to read or who possessed any knowledge of the outside world. The people consulted him on all matters, both spiritual and temporal. His opinions and judgements, were generally accepted as final. The development of the Negro church may be roughly divided into three periods. The first period was the fifteen or more years immediately following emancipation. This was a period of congregation forming and church organization ... during this time ... in the south, church buildings were erected.... These three periods have produced special types of ministers. The minister of the first period was a leader along all lines....

EMERGENCE OF MULTIPLE FUNCTION SOCIAL WELFARE AGENCIES IN THE BLACK COMMUNITY

Other black leaders, responding to the deteriorating conditions, chose to utilize their own resources, human and material, in rural and urban areas, toward self-elevation and race uplifting. They organized and expanded mutual aid associations designed to ensure social and economic security for their people. Persons exemplifying such acts were Maggie Walker of Richmond, Virginia, and R. L. Smith of Colorada County, Texas.

Document 10*

L. H. Hammond, "A Woman Banker," In the Vanguard of a Race, New York: Friendship Press, 1922.

On a corner just a block from Broad Street, in Richmond, Virginia, stands a handsome three-story building of brick and stone which bears a tablet with the legend, "St. Luke's Penny Savings Bank. Established 1902." This is said to be the first bank in the country founded by a woman, and it is still one of the very few that have a woman president--the only bank founded or run by a colored woman.

St. Luke's Bank started with $25,000 of paid-up capital. This was afterwards increased to $50,000; and it has a surplus of $25,000 more. It has paid its stockholders a five per cent dividend steadily, regardless of panics and hard times; and once, during a severe money stringency, when the white banks of Richmond were unable to extend further loans to the city, this colored woman banker lent the city $100,000 in cash to carry on the public schools for both the white and black races.

How did the daughter of a colored laundress and one-time slave come to start a bank and guide it to success through twenty-one years filled with other important work? Something went before it, of course, not merely unusual ability, which she plainly has, but long, hard, faithful work in helping the poorer members of her race to win through in times of adversity and to get on their feet.

*Reprinted by permission of the publisher.

Mrs. Maggie L. Walker was born in Richmond. Her mother was Elizabeth Mitchell--a woman born a slave and unable to make a living for herself and her little girl except at the washtub. But what she could do, she did well, and her own lack of opportunity fixed in her the determination that her child should have a chance. What this determination cost the mother in toil and sacrifice one may not know,--washing was not a lucrative profession in those days in the South. But mother and daughter took their hardships cheerfully, and the girl did her best to lighten her mother's load so far as she could. When she was eighteen, she graduated from high school, and that fall became a teacher in one of the public schools. From that time to the present, one of her main purposes in life has been to make life easier for the mother to whose sacrifices she owes her first start toward better things....

There was a little benefit society in Richmond--one of probably a dozen or two such. They are pathetically popular among Negroes, to whom sickness is a catastrophe such as only the poorest people can fully comprehend. This particular society was the Independent Order of St. Luke. It collected small weekly dues from its members, of whom at that time it had a thousand. If they fell ill, it paid them a certain sum weekly. If they died, a death benefit was paid which provided for the funeral expenses, thus saving the family from what is often, among the very poor, a crushing burden of debt.

Mrs. Walker was offered the secretaryship of this society at the munificent salary of eight dollars a month. She was to collect dues, verify cases of illness and of death, keep the books, and pay out all sums due.

She accepted the opportunity at once. The Order might be a small one--for an Order, but looking after a thousand members did seem a job to keep one busy, and it certainly helped the people it reached. As soon as she had the work at her fingers' ends, however, she began reaching out. If the Order helped a thousand, why shouldn't it help twenty thousand--fifty--a hundred thousand? Why should it confine itself to giving help in trouble? Why couldn't it train people to help themselves in time of health to save, invest, to win their way to economic independence? Why couldn't it get hold of the children and teach them thrift, build up self-control and forethought in their careless little souls, and start them on the path to success before they should form habits of self-indulgence and waste? Why it could do all that! And it should, and it would. So it has done and still does today.

There are now a hundred thousand members of the Order in twenty-one states, seventy-five thousand of whom have held their membership long enough to be entitled to benefits if they become ill or die. Five dollars a week is paid in case of sickness; and from one hundred to five hundred dollars, according to the amount of dues paid, in case of death. There is over $70,000 cash in the emergency fund--a fund that didn't exist when Mrs. Walker took charge.

A hundred and forty field workers are employed, and forty-five clerks are in the home office. The assets of the Order amount to $360,000. A handsome office building has been put up at 900-904 St. James Street, Richmond, costing $100,000. It provides ample office space for the work of the Order, a large auditorium, a number of rooms for club and lodge meetings, a large supply department where the badges, regalia, account books, and so forth, of the Order are manufactured and sent out, and a complete printing establishment with two linotype machines. Here the St. Luke's Herald, another of Mrs. Walker's enterprises, is printed and goes out to its big constituency. It gives full reports of the Order's business, stories of members, both children and adults, who are getting ahead financially or doing anything else worthwhile, suggestions for meetings, and sound teaching in regard to health, thrift, morals, and education. It goes to city and country, to educated and ignorant. To scores of thousands of unprivileged Negroes it is giving inspiration and a horizon.

It was because of all this rapidly extending work that Mrs. Walker felt the need of a bank. In 1902 she started one and built a home for it a few blocks away from the headquarters building. In 1920 this bank had nearly six thousand depositors and resources of over half a million dollars....

But Mrs. Walker's social service work is enough for a story in itself. Through her club affiliations, she became deeply interested in Mrs. Barrett's school at Peake. She organized in Richmond a Council of Women with fourteen hundred members, which did yeoman service in raising the first five thousand dollars to buy the farm at Peake and has ever since given liberally to all the needs of the school. Mrs. Walker is one of the colored members of the school's bi-racial board of trust. As a result of this work for Peake came the community work in Richmond.

> The white women of Richmond began it [she said]. You know what some of them have done here--women who stand at the top socially and who are leaders in the church and the club life of the city and state. They had done fine community work for white people, and at length they went to our preachers and asked them to invite their leading women to a conference. As a result, we began some forms of community work. Then a white philanthropist who gave the white women a house for a working girls' home said that if we colored women would show our interest in social work among our people by raising a thousand dollars for it, he would give us the use of a large house, and if we made good, he would deed it to a board of white and colored women for colored work.
>
> You know we had to make good after that. We raised the thousand dollars, and we kept right on. The house has been deeded now to our bi-racial board. The white women don't work for us,--they work with us; and they've

> helped us to connect up with every charitable organization in the city. We have four paid workers, and the Community House is just such a center of influence as we have needed all these years.

In this article the Farmers' Improvement Society of Texas is discussed by R. L. Smith, its Grand President.

Document 11

R. L. Smith, "An Uplifting Negro Cooperative Society," World's Work, 16 (June, 1908), pp. 10462-10466.

In the summer of 1889 I read a very brief article in the Youth's Companion descriptive of the work of the village improvement societies in Litchfield, Conn., and South Framingham, Mass. It came as an inspiration. "For," said I, "if these people, representing the highest type of American civilization with generations of culture behind them, have any need for special work along aesthetic lines, how much more necessary is a work of this kind among Negroes, who lack any hereditary tendency to efforts of this sort!" At that time I was a teacher in a rural school in Colorado County, Texas. The village where I lived was nine miles from the nearest railroad station, a hamlet of some two or three hundred people, called Oakland, on the Southern Pacific Railway....

In December, 1889, after talking the matter over with a few good men and securing their approval, at the close of a fervent appeal to the people in a general mass-meeting at which almost the entire Negro population of the place was present, I organized the Village Improvement Society of Oakland, Texas. I tried in this meeting to show them that the time had come when we must wipe out, in so far as we could, the ear-marks of the race from the civic landscape: dilapidated dwellings, broken window-panes stuffed with pillows and rags, unkempt yards, and front fences made of barbed wire loosely strung on crazy posts. These front fences were utilized on wash days as clotheslines, and regularly, once-a-week, tattered garments and rags emphasized the lack of order and of thrift that obtained among their owners. I wrote out a constitution which bound the members to do everything in their power to improve the conditions of their homes and the appearance of the village.

Monthly meetings were held, and during the winter and spring a good beginning was made. Front fences were straightened, some yards planted with roses, common flowers, and arbor-vitae, and much improvement was made by transplanting wild flowers from the prairies and planting trees in the streets. The streets were also leveled. Altogether a fair start was made.

The Hindrance of Poverty

We had not yet begun on the improvement of our homes because we lacked the money, and we all felt that if the crops of 1890 were good there would be a general step in that direction. All that summer I felt that the future was big with hope and that the transformation soon to be effected would make our little village a prettier and better place to live in. During the fall I was constantly urging our members to fix up their cabins, add more rooms, and carry out the pledges that they made when they joined the association. But when all the cotton was sold there remained very little in anyone's pockets to spend on improvements. This failure led me to inquire into the causes of the general poverty, and I found it in the method that prevailed among farmers, then and now, of carrying on their business. The credit or mortgage system absorbed the entire crop, and a man was considered quite fortunate if he "came out even" at the end of the year. Most of our people carried on their farming in this way and it is a wonder to me that they managed to pay for the lots that they had bought and the cabins that they had erected upon them. I saw readily that so long as they operated under the credit system no "village improvement" was possible and that what the Negro farmers of Texas and of the South really needed was not, at this stage, a Village Improvement Society. So, calling a meeting, I revised the constitution, inserting clauses aiming to abolish the credit system by raising or purchasing for cash all necessary supplies, and to encourage in all ways an intelligent interest in farming and an economical and efficient conduct of that and all other business.

The bane of the Negro farmers of the South is the credit system. Belonging to a race altogether unused to business methods and not at all acquainted with market prices, their exploitation was a simple matter. I had to find a better system of getting supplies than by running an account. Our first cooperative efforts were exceedingly simple. They were confined to getting our members to purchase at wholesale the supplies that they needed, in so far as their means would allow.

Cooperation Instead of Credit

Some by economy had succeeded in saving a few dollars, and at a meeting called for that purpose we made up a fund, taxing each head of a family twenty-five cents for railroad fare, and two of us went down to Houston, our nearest wholesale centre, to spend about a hundred dollars. This was the era of cheap prices and the amount of flour and sugar, coffee and beans, soda, baking powder, and other articles that we bought for a hundred dollars was the greatest object lesson in money-saving that the Negroes of that community ever had. Many of them had raised enough meat and corn to suffice them for the year, and the purchase of such other articles as I have named above made them almost independent.

To illustrate the difference between the credit system and the cooperative plan above mentioned, my brother-in-law had a jug holding two gallons of molasses which he sent up regularly to the village store to be filled. This cost him at that time seventy cents a gallon. Under the cooperative system he had the jug filled with the identical molasses for forty cents, to which five cents per gallon should be added for freight.

Later, in Austin, I bought about two hundred pounds of sugar for six dollars and sixty-five cents. Sugar was remarkably cheap that year and, never having heard of any sugar at such a price, I emptied my trunk and filled it and got home by the friendly aid of train porters and baggage men along the route, though at one change a trail of white betrayed the contents. I had to own up, but it was regarded as a good joke. When I got home, just for curiosity, I went up to one of the stores and asked the price of sugar. "Credit or cash?" was the query. "On credit," I replied. "Fourteen pounds for a dollar," was the answer, at which price my six dollars and sixty-five cents would have bought ninety-one and one-tenth pounds instead of two hundred. I began to realize that practically the Negro race had merely exchanged one form of slavery for another so far as the acquisition of wealth was concerned, and I had found that wealth honestly earned and wisely expended was as absolutely essential to the elevation of a race as were schoolhouses and churches.

The Woman's Barnyard Auxiliary

Then, too, another source of income overlooked by my people appealed to me as worth the effort to develop. It was the egg, poultry, and butter industry and, knowing that the men were indifferent to such little things as eggs and a few chickens or a pound or two of butter, I got up a special organization of women and named it the Woman's Barnyard Auxiliary of the Farmers' Improvement Society of Texas. Thus organized and encouraged, some of the women made enough money to run their homes.

With these changes and by constant encouragement we are in a fair way to realize our hopes of village improvement, for the good work has gone on in full swing. In six years the external aspect of Freedmantown was changed. A church was built at a cost of a thousand dollars when both lumber and labor were cheaper by far than they are at present. A two-story schoolhouse was erected, then as now the best rural school building in the county. The shanties gave way to three, four and five-roomed painted houses with neat yards enclosed with palings. Inside of them, neatness was the order; the children were better educated and the demand for teachers from our community was far greater than the supply.

All this had an interesting effect upon the white people. In the summer of 1895 the Republican convention of Colorado County nominated me as their candidate for the legislature. I made a canvass, addressing people of both races, and much to my surprise was elected. Since it was entirely in the power of the white people to defeat me, the county having a majority of white voters, and since many white people were kind enough to say that a man who felt such an interest in upbuilding his own people, should be approved in some way by the whites, I felt that the race problem was solved sure enough. I accepted invitations to address my people in many different communities and began extending the work of the society.

The First Assembly

In 1896 I called the first delegated assembly of the movement. I had to be very careful in giving this annual meeting a name, for the masses of my race in Texas are divided into two camps, religiously speaking--Methodists and Baptists--and they used to be jealous of each other. If I called this annual gathering a conference, this term, having a Methodist savor, might frighten away the Baptists; and by the same token, if called a convention the Methodists might look on the whole thing as a trap. So I borrowed boldly from the Episcopal Church, and called the meeting an Annual Convocation. This allayed all suspicion, and settled for all time any distrust that might hinder the work.

At our first meeting we adopted a form of report which gave us the information we needed as to the actual progress made by our members on the things that brought us together as an organization.

We adapted the nomenclature and forms of fraternal organizations to our use, and issued degrees to those who followed the rules of the society.

These degrees were twelve in number, and they indicated the progress that the member had made in ridding himself of debt and making progress in civilization.

The first degree was conferred upon the member who succeeded in "running" himself three months without opening an account. The second upon the member running himself six months; the third nine months, and the fourth twelve months; the fifth was conferred upon members who maintained themselves the entire year, and had a surplus of twenty-five dollars; the sixth the same with a surplus of a hundred dollars; the seventh the same with a surplus of one hundred and fifty dollars; the eighth with a surplus of two hundred dollars; and so on up to the twelfth degree, which was called the Grand Patriarch degree and entitled its possessor to membership in the annual convocation without election, thereby creating a permanent delegateship of successful members who had worked out their own salvation and were actually fitted for leadership by growth in the essentials of civilization.

The first four degrees were grouped together under the head of "Coming Degrees" which simply meant that their possessors were on the road to independence and would "get there" some day if they kept on. The next four were grouped under the general head of the "P. L. Degrees," by which is meant "Possible and Probable Landowners," the way being clearly opened to securing homes if desired.

After the first convocation at which a branch was represented, no member was eligible to be a delegate unless he had passed up a degree.

By these simple means and the adaptation of the lodge system, with which the race is familiar, a lever was secured that made the plan workable and at the same time gave to the movement the fraternal spirit absolutely essential as a means of getting hold of the people.

As I have stated before, I have been encouraged in this work by my white neighbors and the press of my state. When suddenly elevated to represent my county in the 24th legislature, the Houston Post, the leading Democratic paper of South Texas, was kind enough to say this of me:

Oakland, Texas, November 14.--Professor R. L. Smith, the recently elected representative of Colorado County to the next legislature, is a colored man and is one of the two Negroes elected to so honorable a position in Texas. It would be hard for the colored people of Texas to find a member of their race better qualified to influence legislation in their behalf than the present representative. Born in South Carolina in 1861, largely by his own efforts he has secured an education second, perhaps, to no man of his color in the state, and as an instructor, his reputation is deservedly high all over the state.

At home he has the confidence and respect of all classes, irrespective of race, being a man of broad and liberal views, of great self-respect and agreeable address. He came to this state in 1885 and has resided continuously at Oakland. Here he has completely transformed the character of the Negro settlement, and today it is doubtful if in the whole state there is a more valuable class to the population of any town than these. Here are thrifty, enterprising, law-abiding, intelligent and moral Negores--Negroes who are the possessors of homes and public buildings, and to no man is more credit due than to Professor Smith who has ever held himself in readiness with his time, talent, and money to keep abreast with the strides of civilization, prosperity and modern progress. It is hoped now that opportunity is given him that work of this kind will be undertaken by others.

In the next election I was reelected by a majority twice as great as before and I naturally felt that the increased majority and endorsement of my legislative career was due to my efforts to better the condition of my race, as well as to the earnest, thoughtful, and prayerful consideration which I gave to all the problems arising in the legislature.

Later, our society began to get hold of the people en masse, largely through annual fairs, the seat of these gatherings being Columbus, the county seat of Colorado County.

We had none but the finest and most practical speakers and all denominational and political subjects were barred. Dr. Booker Washington, Bishop Grant, Mr. H. T. Kealing, a gifted speaker and writer, are representative of the men we invited to address us, and such colored men, together with the able array of white speakers, always at our disposal, made these meetings memorable and exceedingly useful.

Influence of Booker Washington

Before our first annual convention I went to Tuskegee and came into contact with Dr. Booker Washington and saw what a master of men he was in his rude parliament, the Negro Farmers' Conference. He was very kind and sympathetic; he had the keenest eye for shams and considered nothing worth hearing in the conference unless it was both practical and helpful. It was the most picturesque assembly I had ever seen. There was the native Negro wit, absolutely unapproachable by any other race. Then there was the pathos--those submerged types, fresh from slavery, blindly struggling into the dim beginnings of something better in their lives, guided by the wise, patient, masterly hand of the great leader. As I recall, they were led to tell how they got their forty acres, how they added a month to their exceedingly short school terms, how they raised hogs. They were asked about the moral character of their teachers and ministers, about loafing on Saturdays in town, about going to courthouses to see trials in which they were neither defendants, witnesses, nor even remotely interested. The masterpieces were the stories of those steady-going, level-headed fellows that had bought their farms, improved them, raised good stock, and were educating their children. These were the pillars of Booker Washington's church for the masses. He was an uncompromising and relentless enemy to the one-room log cabin.

Founding an Agricultural College

It was after this first meeting in 1897 that I resolved that the thing our Farmers' Improvement Society should do for the farming Negro of Texas was to emphasize the training of our youth in agricultural schools, and to meet the needs of the race in Texas we needed about twenty of them.

These schools should be practical rather than scientific, and should be normal agricultural institutions. That is, a good deal of the teaching should be by observing good methods and seeing actual results accomplished.

It was a long wait from the time of forming this purpose and the passage of the resolution committing the membership to this course, to the actual founding of our first school.

We did not grow strong enough to attempt it until 1906, when we had accumulated about twelve hundred dollars. This was spent for fifty-eight acres of very poor land in Fannin County, Texas. Twenty dollars per acre for poor land seems fabulous but, while the tract we bought was sandy, it was in the midst of the famous black lands of North Texas and this was before the cotton boll weevil had invaded that country and good land was selling at from forty to one hundred dollars per acre.

The purpose of this agricultural college is threefold: first: to give the student a practical training in correct methods of farming; second: to give him a good, well-trained mind by pursuing a fair course of instruction at least as far advanced as the high school; third: to train him up to true family life where habits of order, system, and thoroughness prevail.

The family life of the Negro needs reconstruction. Even where there is no taint of moral looseness, there is lack of order and perhaps of fixed purpose. To be neat and careful, to be orderly and systematic, to be patient and persistent, these are more valuable than to be able to extract a cube root or to demonstrate propositions in geometry. We do not have, therefore, and will not have, large and imposing buildings, but small ones in which students are grouped in families under the immediate eye and care of the best teachers that we can get. The practices that should be in every home we insist upon these in school homes. Systems, order, industry and consideration for the rights and preferences of the other members of the family. Whenever I visit our humble school, situated four miles from the town of Ladonia, my heart swells with joy to see the influence that this training has exerted upon the children of the freedman.

The progress of the movement may be gaged by the report of the Grand Secretary summarizing the reports made by branches at the Twelfth Annual Convocation held at Marlin, Texas, October 3, 4, and 5, 1907.

The number of organized groups	475
Number of members	9,256
Number of acres owned by members	71,439
Value of the same at $15 per acre	$1,071,585
Value of cattle, horses, mules, etc., owned by members	$275,000
Value of improvements made October, 1906 to October, 1907	$58,148

The amount spent in cooperation was more than fifty thousand dollars.

The Negro problem so far as the Negro himself is concerned is to teach him <u>how to live</u>; how to take hold of the things that are about him and <u>use them</u>, so that, in that which makes for better citizenship, tomorrow will find him more advanced than to-day. It is that he may take the soil and the sunshine, the rain and the snow, fair weather and foul, the great institutions upon which civilization rests--the family, the church, and the science of government--and turn them to his own account, beginning with whatever he finds at hand--the axe, the hoe, the plow, the tool of the mechanic, the pot, the scrubbing brush, as well as the pen and the sword, and work out for himself a place in the best thought and life of the republic.

This the Farmers' Improvement Society is trying to do.

It is a school for those simpler virtues of hard and well directed industry, for economy and thrift, for foresight, for cooperation, the mighty tool of weaklings, for the home, its founding, its beautifying, and its highest use.

It has done very little, but its aims are those upon which the hope of the Negro's future rests.

Others will carry it on to a larger success.

EMERGENCE OF SINGLE-FUNCTION SOCIAL WELFARE AGENCIES IN THE BLACK COMMUNITY

Many institutions were established by single individuals to fulfill a specific function only, such as the development and maintenance of an orphanage. However, some of these institutions eventually came to extend more than one service. As is illustrated in one of the following documents, one organization began by extending aid during adverse times but, later, began to assist its members during good times as well.

Document 12a

E. R. Carter, "Mrs. Carrie Steele Logan," The Black Side, Atlanta, Georgia, 1894, pp. 35-37.

This noble, Christian woman is a native of Georgia, and in this State was reared She was a slave till, through divine providence, that great benefactor, Abraham Lincoln, set her free. While a slave she learned to read and write, the acquisition of which she has always found indispensable to her. For more than twenty years she has been in public work, and her contact with the world has been a complete education of itself. Being, for a long while, a stewardess at the depot in this city, this good woman had daily experiences of the sufferings and wants of her people.

Daily she saw hungry, half-clad, ignorant children wandering about the streets, being tossed hither and thither by the rude winds of adversity; waifs drifting down the stream of destruction! Children barefooted and crying for bread, seeking, in vain, places to lay their tired heads!

These sad sights touched the heart of Mrs. Steele, and moved to pity, she resolved to do something for the children of her race. By her industry and economy she had some time previously purchased a valuable lot on Wheat Street, and upon it built a handsome cottage. She now began to think how she could better the condition of the children of her people. A divine inspiration came to her, and she grasped it eagerly; it was that she might erect a place of retreat for these little ones.

She began this arduous work by writing a short account of her life, which she placed before the public for sale. Her little book took well, and she realized an acceptable profit from it. This was the first step in the great undertaking of her life.

She then solicited aid in other ways, and to her requests many kind hearts of both races responded, and she was soon able to begin the erection of the Orphanage, which now stands a lasting monument of the great work done by this good woman.

This building is three stories in height, built of brick with a stone foundation, and well adapted to its usages. Within its walls Mrs. Logan has gathered around her fifty heretofore friendless and homeless little ones, who, at the time of their coming, were mostly ignorant and uncouth, but now are tidy, trained and being taught to read, etc.

These are taught, first of all, to pray. The older ones are being taught domestic work, in all its parts, and fancy work. The boys do farm work. All attend school, which is provided for them at the Home.

They have Sunday-school every Sunday, and even the little ones of four years can repeat chapters in the Bible.

The campus is spacious and most beautiful.

The Orphanage was erected at a cost of five thousand dollars, all of which was raised through the efforts of Mrs. Logan.

She is deeply interested and wrapped up in her work, which she claims is the greatest joy of her life.

Since this noble woman has done so much for humanity, all should lend a helping hand to push forward the grand and glorious work.

Mrs. Logan has done work which will tell in years to come. She has placed the stepping stones for the betterment of the race, by striving to save the boys and girls. They are the ones to be shielded from dangers and temptations. Save O, save the children! God's choicest blessings rest upon him who works to this end.

Just after resigning her place at the depot, she married Mr. Logan, of New York, a Christian gentleman, a man of sterling worth. Their ideas are mutual, both having at heart the elevation of the race; both laboring to the same end. In Mrs. Logan he possesses a treasure rare; in him she finds all which could be desired in any one.

This Home is non-denominational; it is free to all homeless, friendless children of the city of Atlanta. It was dedicated June 20, 1892.

Long after the founder shall have gone to her final rest this structure will still tower heavenward, and may the good work done within its limits make her memory imperishable, her name immortal.

Document 12b

Petition of Carrie Steele, et al., to the Superior Court of Fulton County, Georgia to establish a home for "indigent colored orphan children," October 12, 1888.

The petition of Carrie Steele, Sidney Roah, J. G. Gains, and J. R. Steele, respectfully showeth;

That they together with their associates desire to be incorporated under the name of "The Carrie Steele Orphan Home," for the purpose of establishing a home for indigent colored orphan children, to be located in said State and County, where such children may be cared for and educated, and taught to sew, cook, etc., that they may be prepared to earn an honest living and have instilled into their minds while young sound principles of integrity and industry.

Said institution shall be undenominational, and will accommodate all colored orphan children without regard to their religious faith.

Being an elementary institution and not formed for profit will have no capital stock; but desires to be authorized to receive such donations and in such quantities money and property both real and personal, as may be given it, and to avail itself of the statute exempting such property as it may acquire which is necessary to carry out its purposes, from taxation.

The management of the affairs of such institution shall be confided to a board of directors composed of not less than three nor more than thirteen, to be selected in such manner and upon such terms as may be agreed upon between interested, and it shall be the duty of said board of directors in addition to supervising and controlling the business of the institution to appoint such officers, teachers, etc., as may be deemed necessary, and to prescribe their respective duties and salaries.

Petitioners further pray that they be authorized to do such other and further acts as are incident to or will conduce to the accomplishment of the general purposes herein contained not inconsistent with the laws of the State.

And your petitioners will ever pray, etc.

Petitioners Atty.

The foregoing petition being read and considered it is ordered, adjudged and decreed, the Judge of the Atlanta Circuit being disqualified, that Carrie Steele, J. G. Gains and J. R. Steele be and the same are hereby declared to be a body politic and corporate under the name and style of the "Carrie Steele Orphan Home," with full power to establish a home for colored orphan children, where they may be protected and educated and given practicle (sic) training as cooks, housemaids, etc. To receive donations from any and all sources in such quantities money, and property, both real and personal, as from time to time may be given to it, and to acquire such real estate exempt from taxation as is necessary for its purposes, To make by-laws, To select directors, to manage the affairs of the institution, and to appoint such officers, etc., as shall be deemed expedient and to do such other and further acts as will conduce to the success of the institution not incompatible with the laws of Georgia.

This done in open Court this the 12th day of October Anno Domini, 1888.

Richard W. Clark
Judge

Document 13

E. R. Carter, "The Good Samaritan Order," The Black Side, Atlanta, Georgia, 1894, pp. 25, 27.

The order of the Independent Order of Good Samaritans and Daughters of Samaria was introduced into the State by the organization of Crystal Fount Lodge, No. 1, in Atlanta, Georgia, on Friday night, July 9, 1875, by Rev. W. G. Strong, of Mobile, Ala., under the jurisdiction of the R. W. E. D., Grand Lodge, No. 1, of Brooklyn, New York.

The secret of the marvelous financial and numerical success of this lodge is due to the fact that its treasury has always been open to all charitable objects, suffering humanity, and the poor inebriate. It contributed to the yellow fever sufferers in Savannah, Ga., in 1876, to the afflicted in Memphis, Tenn., 1875, during the great cholera epidemic that carried off so many souls; in this and other ways caring for the poor, sick, afflicted, dead, the lodge has disbursed upwards of $26,000....

Document 14

E. R. Carter, "Rev. N. J. Jones, Founder of the Colored Men's Protective Association--Able Baptist Minister," The Black Side, Atlanta, Georgia, 1894, pp. 38-42.

Rev. N. J. Jones the subject of this sketch was born in Nashville, Nash county, North Carolina, in the year 1844, and when six years of age was brought to Pike county, Georgia, at which time he was the property of a Mr. Milton Riggins. In 1862, when but eighteen years old, he was, for his thrift, aptness and integrity, appointed driver and foreman over a large and prosperous plantation, which was managed chiefly through his directions.

He also worked at the blacksmith trade, and was considered a skilled and first-class workman in that line. When emancipation was declared, he was still the property of the same man, and when all of the slaves had gone, he remained with his former owner, Mr. Riggins. Mr. Jones was a great favorite with him, and until this day he highly respects him.

He came to Atlanta in the year 1866, and the following year was converted and joined the Friendship Baptist Church, under the venerable Rev. Frank Quarles....

Along with the other noteworthy events of his life, might be mentioned the formation of the Colored Men's Protective Association, an organization which is known far and near, and is looked upon as being one of the best societies among the race. This large and flourishing institution was projected and founded by this good man in the year 1886. After careful study and consideration of the poor class of the race, he devised a means to bring them in closer connection with that class which was more able to help them. Thus he called a council of good men to whom he stated his object; which was, that he desired to establish an order or union which would take care of and help those who were unable to help themselves. Accordingly, he, with the council, set to work, and soon the good results of their hard toil manifested themselves. Of course they did not have smooth sailing. There was much opposition; but the harder seemed the struggle, the more vigorous grew these combatants, for they felt they were fighting for the good of humanity. Rev. Jones finally succeeded in gathering together a large mass of people from different points in the State, and with the committee of the following gentlemen, himself being chosen chairman of said committee, applied to the superior court of Fulton county for a charter. Committee, N. J. Jones, Chairman; A. Blalock, A. Payne, H. C. Davis, A. B. H. Lowry.

December 17, 1886, the charter was received for a term of twenty years. During the same year Rev. Jones was elected President of the Association. During the year 1887 the order had increased in number to one thousand, and soon after to eighteen hundred.

Great and good have been the results of this order, and all due to the noble-hearted, unselfish Rev. N. J. Jones. Sick members receive the best attention, the poor are cared for and the dead decently buried. This good work is not confined to Atlanta, the society has State rights, and, as a consequence, several branch lodges are doing creditable work, and be it said to the honor and credit of Rev. N. J. Jones, that under his leadership the prosperity of the lodge has been great and rapid. As expression of the confidence placed in him, he has been made president every year since its organization, and this without opposition. He is the acknowledged leader and chief commander, and is backed by a number of intelligent citizens. It is an established fact that the Colored Men's Protective Association of Atlanta has done more to lift up fallen humanity than any other organization in the city.

Its doors are open to all with no respect to persons; the rich, the poor, the cast down, may enter and receive protection, all that is needed being a reformation on the part of those who have been or are cast down.

Those who are received must take most solemnly the pledge which strictly requires good morals, decency and uprightness of character, and so soon as one violates this pledge he is excommunicated. So rapid has been the growth of this order that the wise president saw the need of enlarging its borders, thus giving access to a broader field of labor. Accordingly, he called a convention to meet at Atlanta, October, 1890. In that grand assembly were many distinguished business men from many cities of the State. In addition to widening the field of work and establishing better laws, the president's object was to organize a grand lodge for the State.

Document 15

E. R. Carter, "I. O. of O. F. St. James Lodge No. 1455," The Black Side, Atlanta, Georgia, 1894, pp. 50-52.

In the year 1870, January 20, Mr. Augustus Thompson met upon the streets of Atlanta one Mr. James Lowndes, of Louisville, Ky., who had only a day previous come to Atlanta. Mr. Thompson was recognized by Mr. Lowndes by the likeness he bore to his brother who resided at Louisville, and who was a friend and acquaintance of Mr. Lowndes. A conversation arose, during which Mr. Lowndes asked Mr. Thompson if the people of Atlanta had an Odd Fellows Lodge here. Receiving a reply in the negative, he said to him that he (Mr. L.) could tell him how to organize such. The proposition was accepted, and they proceeded forthwith to discuss matters relative to it. The Lodge could be organized with twenty-five good men. Accordingly Mr. Thompson set about in search of this number. He first succeeded in gathering together six or seven good men, and on the following Sunday they met in a basement on corner Pulliam and Rawson streets, belonging to E. E. Rawson. After arranging preliminary matters, they dispersed, each promising to bring some one to the next meeting. The following week they organized with the desired number--twenty-five--among which number were some of the best citizens, such as Revs. J. A. Wood, J. A. Carey and Brothers J. D. Render, A. Thompson, and others. Their next action was to write to Philadelphia to Mr. James Netum, General Secretary of Committee of Management, who forwarded the application to England. The charter was delayed for twelve months, thus it was some time before the body could be fully organized. But during this time the members cared for their sick and buried their dead, while waiting for their charter.

Finally a letter from them fell into the hands of D. B. Bowser, who had been installed as General Secretary of Committee of Management in the place of the deceased Mr. James Netum. He wrote the body telling them so soon as their charter arrived from England he would so inform them.

In the meantime, after they had been started a period of about ten months, Rev. F. J. Peck, hearing of the movement on foot and being an ex-member from Boston, Mass., also started up a lodge and named it the Star of the South. January, 1871, the charter and books arrived, and immediately arrangements were perfected for D. B. Bowser, of Philadelphia to come to Atlanta to set up the lodge. He came by the members paying him $3.00 per day, from the time he left Philadelphia till his return to that city, and also his traveling expenses, board, and one gallon of beer per day. March 5, 1871, he reached Atlanta, and during the same day set up the St. James Lodge No. 1455, one hundred members strong.

The St. James agreed to let Mr. Bowser set up the Star of the South Lodge if it would agree to pay half of the expenses, which they did. The officers installed in St. James Lodge No. 1455 were as follows: Augustus Thompson, Noble Father; James Lowndes, Noble Grand; Rev. J. A. Wood, Vice-Grand; L. S. Smith, P. S.

The Star of the South No. 1456, with sixty members and Vine Ware (now deceased) as Noble Father, was also set up.

Under the St. James Lodge a lodge was organized at Marietta, Ga., with thirty-four members. Also one at Dalton, Ga., with forty or more members. Then one at Augusta, Ga.

Thus it is seen from the start, the St. James No. 1455 began to work, and is still burying her dead, caring for her sick, and at this time, taking care of an old brother who has been blind for ten years; all of this time giving him from $10 to $12 per month. This Lodge has done great work. It has a lot which cost the members $3,350, and a four-story brick building costing over $11,000, making a total of $14,356. The Lodge is still growing and has a very large membership.

Document 16

E. R. Carter, "The Colored Protective Association," The Black Side, Atlanta, Georgia, 1894, pp. 55-57.

In this thrifty, rushing nineteenth century, when invention and enterprise are lending much in aiding the human family in rising to the high mark of that civilization which characterizes all thoroughgoing industrious people, the negro has not shown in the least that he is wanting on any of these lines. He has organized banking systems, building and loan associations, institutions of learning, and corporations of such nature as do aid the people in acquiring wealth in many ways which enable them to have some income outside their daily labor.

The Colored Men's Protective Association, which is the subject of this sketch, is one of those enterprises which render many a poor man, washerwoman and mechanic's condition in time of sickness or disability less burdensome than it otherwise would have been without the existence of such an enterprise.

This benevolent enterprise was organized in Shiloh African Methodist Episcopal Church, Atlanta, Ga., August 24, 1888, by Lodge No. 1, with Robert Farmer as its President and Robert Collier as Secretary, having at the time of the organization forty-two members. Since the date of its organization the membership has grown to be 1,068. They have as a financial basis $1,633.25. They have paid out as sick benefits $842.75, and for burying the dead of the Association $275.00; for other expenses and charitable purposes $40.90. The object of this enterprise is not simply to administer to the wants of their members and to protect them in the many disadvantages that they may be called to undergo in these lines, but to stand by their fellow-men at all times and in any case of emergency or danger; and further, to help their fellow-citizen of the "Black Side" in building up business establishments, to induce the people of the race to patronize the men of their race that are in business; and further, to aid the unfortunate in obtaining his legal rights at this time.

The Colored Men's Protective Association has been instrumental in doing grand service to its race. Since their organization they have held their meetings in buildings owned by colored men; first, for some time in the Shiloh African Methodist Episcopal Church; then in the River's Hall, and now in the Shell Opera House, a splendid three-story building.

EMERGENCE OF BLACK LABOR ORGANIZATIONS

As it was generally recognized that, in an increasingly segregated society, much of the efforts for survival would have to depend on blacks themselves, institutional arrangements mirrored an awareness of real social consciousness which benefited the total group. This notion seems to be in contradiction to the perspective of white proponents of social welfare, judging welfare activities according to their welfare functions and ignoring their latent functions as foci of group identity and ladders of social mobility.[3] One of the two additional areas which influenced the lives of blacks during this period was that of the incipient development of black labor organizations.

Several black leaders, such as Frederick Douglass, Henry McNeal Turner, and Thomas Fortune, recognized the need for black workers to form organizations to protect their means of livelihood and, consistently raised these issues at the yearly meetings of Negro convention movements. The most active of black leaders was Isaac Myers, who founded the successful Chesapeake Marine Railroad and Drydock Company in Baltimore, Maryland in 1865, which, ultimately, declined in 1877 because of the technological shift from wood to steel in building ships. Myers was elected President of the first State Labor convention of black laborers at the Douglass Institute in Baltimore on July 19, 1869, and following this there were several additional state and national meetings primarily addressing themselves to resolutions for organizational development and united action. However, separate unionization did not prove fully effective at this time. Eventually, the Knights of Labor, a secret order until 1881 when it was open to all workers, became the most successful effort in labor organization, and by 1877 it counted four hundred all-black locals totalling 90,000 to 95,000 members.

This document, excerpted in a letter in an 1886 edition of an important labor journal of the day, speaks to the inability of the Knights of Labor to function as an organizational vehicle for black workers.

Document 17

Excerpt from letter in John Swinton's papers of November 28, 1886 in "The Organization of Negroes in the Knights of Labor," Journal of Negro History, XXXVI (July, 1952): p. 252. Cited in "The Black Worker and the Trade Union Movement, 1865-1900," by Patrick O'Leary, unpublished M. S. W. thesis, Atlanta University School of Social Work, 1974, pp. 19-20.

I am a colored man. I had a letter sent me from Georgia by a colored man asking if colored men would be recognized in the Knights of Labor, and I have similar questions from others in my race, both in New York and Brooklyn. My answer is yes and I especially refer to the case of the colored delegate to Richmond from D. A. 49. I myself belong to a local that is wholly composed of white men, with two exceptions, and I hold a very high position of trust in it. I was elected junior delegate to the D. A. and there is no office in the organization that I could not be elected to.

I will say to my people, Help the cause of labor. I would

furthermore say to colored men, Organize. I also appeal to you to support Henry George and the K. of L. You will never gain anything from the Republican Party.... You are a man. Let us break this race prejudice which capital takes. Let us put our shoulder to the wheel as men and victory is ours....

The white and colored mechanics and laborers of the city are working in great harmony as K. of L. This is a grand scale. The organization of the K. of L. has done this much for the South when everything else had failed, the bond of poverty united the white and colored mechanic and laborer.

The 1886 National Colored Press Association encouraged blacks to join unions and specifically endorsed the Knights of Labor. T. Thomas Fortune, a well known black leader of the late 1880's and early 90's supported the Knights of Labor in the late 1880's in the following manner: "The hour is approaching when the labor classes of our country, ... will recognize that they have a common cause, a common humanity and a common enemy; and that, therefore, if they would triumph over wrong.... They must be united."[4]

The second area influencing black life during this period was in the educational arena, the significant development being the recognition of the need to move beyond an emphasis on elementary education toward the development of higher educational institutions which would better prepare a more informed citizenry to deal more effectively with problems facing it. This was the period of the expanding activities of such educational institutions as Howard University, Fisk University, Tuskegee Institute, Hampton Institute, and Atlanta University to name only a few.

W. E. BURGHARDT DUBOIS: SOCIAL SCIENCE IN THE SERVICE OF SOCIAL WELFARE

In the last decade of the nineteenth century black colleges initiated the scientific study of the problems of the black population. By 1895 both Hampton Institute and Tuskegee Institute sponsored conferences concerned with the study of the rural black population. At the annual meeting of the Board of Trustees, Atlanta University, July 1, 1895, its president, Horace Bumstead, proposed that the University sponsor a "systematic and thorough investigation of the conditions of living among the Negro population of cities". It was planned that this investigation was to be undertaken with the cooperation of the graduates of the University, and, that its findings were to be presented at a conference held on the occasion of the 1896. Approved by the Trustees and executed by its graduates, according to the guidelines prepared by a young trustee from Boston, George Bradford, the initial investigation became the first of the Atlanta University Publications, Mortality Among Negroes in Cities, 1896. A second Study and conference (Social and Physical Condition of Negroes in Cities) was held the next year. These studies constitute the first social science research undertaken by a black university, and may also be the first empirical research studies in the urban sociology of the Negro to be undertaken.

About the same time, W. E. Burghardt DuBois, a young Harvard Ph. D with a year of post-doctorate study in Berlin, began an investigation of the condition of the Negro population living in the Seventh Ward of the City of Philadelphia. The resulting work, The Philadelphia Negro, has gained deserved recognition as the first sociological study of a black (if not any other) community in the United States, owing to the elegance of its design and the expertise with which its research was executed.

A budding scholar with high ambitions, DuBois proposed a plan for comprehensive program of research in an 1897 essay, "The Study of the Negro Problems." In it he noted that actual work had already been inaugurated at Atlanta University. The major universities would not sponsor the scientific study of American blacks, so DuBois went to Atlanta University in December, 1897 as Professor of History and Economics, with the special task of developing sociological studies. DuBois, whose research on The Philadelphia Negro should be balanced with his complementary work The Negroes of Farmville, Virginia: A Social Study, widened the scope of the Atlanta University studies and conferences and in 1898 assumed editorship of the Atlanta University Publications with its third edition, entitled Some Efforts of American Negroes for Their Own Social Betterment, which stands as perhaps the first explicitly scientific excursion into the field of social welfare.

Document 18*

W. E. Burghardt DuBois, "The Study of the Negro Problem," Publications of the American Academy of Political and Social Science, No. 219, pp. 230-237. (An address to the Academy, November 19, 1897.)

It is my purpose in this paper to discuss certain considerations concerning the study of the social problems affecting American Negroes; first, as to the historical development of these problems; then as to the necessity for their careful systematic study at the present time; thirdly, as to the results of scientific study of the Negro up to this time; fourthly, as to the scope and method which future scientific inquiry should take, and, lastly, regarding the agencies by which this work can best be carried out.

Development of the Negro Problems

A social problem is the failure of an organized social group to realize its group ideals, through the inability to adapt a certain desired line of action to given conditions of life. If, for instance, a government founded on universal manhood suffrage has a portion of its population so ignorant as to be unable to vote intelligently, such ignorance becomes a menacing social problem. The impossibility of economic and social development in a community where a large per cent of the population refuse to abide by the social rules of order makes a problem of crime and lawlessness. Prostitution becomes a social problem when the demands of luxurious home life conflict with marriage customs.

Thus a social problem is ever a relation between conditions and action, and as conditions and actions vary and change from group to group from time to time and from place to place, so social problems change, develop and grow. Consequently, though we ordinarily speak of the Negro problem as though it were one unchanged question, students must recognize the obvious facts that this problem, like others, has had a long historical development, has changed with the growth and evolution of the nation; moreover, that it is not one problem, but rather a plexus of social problems, some new, some old, some simple, some complex; and these problems have their one bond of unity in the act that they group themselves about those Africans whom two centuries of slave-trading brought into the land.

Now first we should study the Negro problems in order to distinguish between the different and distinct problems affecting this race. Nothing makes intelligent discussion of the Negro's position so fruitless as the repeated failure to discriminate between the dif-

*Reprinted by permission of the publisher.

ferent questions that concern him. If a Negro discusses the question, he is apt to discuss simply the problem of race prejudice; if a Southern white man writes on the subject he is apt to discuss problems of ignorance, crime and social degradation; and yet each calls the problem he discusses the Negro problem, leaving in the dark background the really crucial question as to the relative importance of the many problems involved. Before we can begin to study the Negro intelligently, we must realize definitely that not only is he affected by all the varying social forces that act on any nation at his stage of advancement, but that in addition to these there is reacting upon him the mighty power of a peculiar and unusual social environment which affects to some extent every other social force.

In the second place we should seek to know and measure carefully all the forces and conditions that go to make up these different problems, to trace the historical development of these conditions, and discover as far as possible the probable trend of further development. Without doubt this would be difficult work, and it can with much truth be objected that we cannot ascertain, by the methods of sociological research known to us, all such facts thoroughly and accurately. To this objection it is only necessary to answer that however difficult it may be to know all about the Negro, it is certain that we can know vastly more than we do, and that we can have our knowledge in more systematic and intelligible form. As things are, our opinions upon the Negro are more matters of faith than of knowledge. Every schoolboy is ready to discuss the matter, and there are few men that have not settled convictions. Such a situation is dangerous. Whenever any nation allows impulse, whim or hasty conjecture to usurp the place of conscious, normative, intelligent action, it is in grave danger. The sole aim of any society is to settle its problems in accordance with its highest ideals, and the only rational method of accomplishing this is to study those problems in the light of the best scientific research.

Finally, the American Negro deserves study for the great end of advancing the cause of science in general. No such opportunity to watch and measure the history and development of a great race of men ever presented itself to the scholars of a modern nation. If they miss this opportunity--if they do the work in a slip-shod, unsystematic manner--if they dally with the truth to humor the whims of the day, they do far more than hurt the good name of the American people; they hurt the cause of scientific truth the world over, they voluntarily decrease human knowledge of a universe of which we are ignorant enough, and they degrade the high end of truth-seeking in a day when they need more and more to dwell upon its sanctity.

Document 19

W. E. Burghardt DuBois, The Philadelphia Negro, A Social Study. Publications of the University of Pennsylvania. Series in Political Economy and Public Law, No. 14, (Philadelphia, University of Pennsylvania, 1899), pp. 1-2.

1. General Aim. This study seeks to present the results of an inquiry undertaken by the University of Pennsylvania into the condition of the forty thousand or more people of Negro blood now living in the city of Philadelphia. This inquiry extended over a period of fifteen months and sought to ascertain something of the geographical distribution of this race, their occupations and daily life, their homes, their organizations, and, above all, their relation to their million white fellow-citizens. The final design of the work is to lay before the public such a body of information as may be a safe guide for all efforts toward the solution of the many Negro problems of a great American city.

2. The Method of Inquiry. The investigation began August the first, 1896, and, saving two months, continued until December the thirty-first, 1897. The work commenced with a house-to-house canvass of the Seventh Ward. This long narrow ward, extending from South Seventh Street to the Schuylkill River and from Spruce Street to South street, is an historic centre of Negro population, and contains to-day a fifth of all the Negroes in this city. It was therefore thought best to make an intensive study of conditions in this district and afterwards to supplement and correct this information by general observation and inquiry in other parts of the city.

Six schedules were used among the nine thousand Negroes of this ward; a family schedule with the usual questions as to the number of members their age and sex, their conjugal condition and birthplace, their ability to read and write, their occupation and earnings, etc.; an individual schedule with questions as to the number of rooms, the rent, the lodgers, the conveniences, etc.; a street schedule to collect data as to the various small streets and alleys, and an institution schedule for organizations and institutions; finally a slight variation of the individual schedule was used for house-servants living at their places of employment.

This study of the central district of Negro settlement furnished a key to the situation in the city; in the other wards therefore a general survey was taken to note any striking differences of condition, to ascertain the general distribution of these people, and to collect information and statistics as to organizations, property, crime, and pauperism, political activity, and the like. This general inquiry, while it lacked precise methods of measurement in most cases, served nevertheless to correct the errors and illustrate the meaning of the statistical material obtained in the house-to-house canvass.

Throughout the study such official statistics and historical matter as seemed reliable were used and experienced persons, both white and colored, were freely consulted.

3. The Credibility of the Results. The best available methods of sociological research are at present so liable to inaccuracies that the careful student discloses the results of individual research with diffidence; he knows that they are liable to error from the seemingly ineradicable faults of the statistical method, to even greater

error from the methods of general observation, and, above all, he must ever tremble lest some personal bias, some moral conviction or some unconscious trend of thought due to previous training, has to a degree distorted the picture in his view. Convictions on all great matters of human interest one must have to a greater or less degree, and they will enter to some extent into the most cold-blooded scientific research as a disturbing factor.

Nevertheless here are social problems before us demanding careful study, questions awaiting satisfactory answers. We must study, we must investigate, we must attempt to solve; and the utmost that the world can demand is, not lack of human interest and moral convictions, but rather the heart-quality of fairness, and an earnest desire for the truth despite its possible unpleasantness.

In a house-to-house investigation there are, outside the attitude of the investigator, many sources, of error: misapprehension, vagueness, and forgetfulness, and deliberate deception on the part of the persons questioned, greatly vitiate the value of the answers; on the other hand, conclusions formed by the best trained and most conscientious students on the basis of general observation and inquiry are really inductions from but a few of the multitudinous facts of social life, and these may easily fall far short of being essential or typical.

Despite all drawbacks and difficulties, however, the main results of the inquiry seem credible. They agree, to a large extent, with general public opinion, and in other respects they seem either logically explicable or in accord with historical precedents. They are therefore presented to the public, not as complete and without error, but as possessing on the whole enough reliable matter to serve as the scientific basis for further study, and of practical reform.

Document 20

"Results of the Investigation" Some Efforts of American Negroes for Their Own Social Betterment. Edited by W. E. Burghardt DuBois. The Atlanta University Publications, No. 3, 1898, pp. 4-5.

1. Scope of the Inquiry. The aim of this study is to make a tentative inquiry into the organized life of American Negroes. It is often asked What is the Negro doing to help himself after a quarter century of outside aid? The main answers to this question hitherto have naturally recorded individual efforts in education, the accumulation of property and the establishment of homes. The real test, however, of the advance of any group of people in civilization is the extent to which they are able to organize and systematize their efforts for the common weal; and the highest expression of organized life is the organization for purely benevolent and reformatory purposes. An inquiry then into the organizations of American Negroes which have the social betterment of the mass of the race for their object, would be an instructive measure of their advance in civiliza-

tion. To be of the highest value such an investigation should be exhaustive, covering the whole country, and recording all species of effort. Funds were not available for such an inquiry. The method followed therefore was to choose nine Southern cities of varying size and to have selected in them such organizations of Negroes as were engaged in benevolent and reformatory work. The cities from which returns were obtained were: Washington, D. C., Petersburg, Va., Augusta, Ga., Atlanta, Ga., Mobile, Ala., Bowling Green, Ky., Clarksville, Tenn., Fort Smith, Ark., and Galveston, Tex. Graduates of Atlanta University, Fisk University, Howard University, the Meharry Medical College, and other Negro institutions cooperated in gathering the information desired.

No attempt was made to catalogue all charitable and reformatory efforts but rather to illustrate the character of the work being done by typical examples. In one case, Petersburg, Va., nearly all efforts of all kinds were reported in order to illustrate the full activity of one group. The report for one large city, Washington, was pretty full although not exhaustive. In all of the other localities only selected organizations were reported. The returns being for the most part direct and reduced to a basis of actual figures seem to be reliable.

2. General Character of the Organizations. It is natural that to-day the bulk of organized efforts of Negroes in any direction should centre in the Church. The Negro Church is the only social institution of the Negroes which started in the African forest and survived slavery; under the leadership of the priest and medicine man, afterward of the Christian pastor, the church preserved in itself the remnants of African tribal life and became after emancipation the centre of Negro social life. So that to-day the Negro population of the United States is virtually divided into Church congregations, which are the real units of the race life. It is natural therefore that charitable and rescue work among Negroes should first be found in the churches and reach there its greatest development. Of the 236 efforts and institutions reported in this inquiry, seventy-nine are churches.

Next in importance to churches come the Negro secret societies. When the mystery and rites of African fetishism faded into the simpler worship of the Methodists and Baptists, the secret societies rose especially among the Free Negroes as a substitute for the primitive love of mystery. Practical insurance and benevolence, always a feature of such societies, were then cultivated. Of the organizations reported, ninety-two were secret societies--some, branches or imitations of great white societies, some original Negro inventions.

Both the above organizations have efforts for social betterment as activities secondary to some other main object. There are, however, many Negro organizations whose sole object is to aid and reform. First among these come the beneficial societies. Like the burial societies among the serfs of the Middle Ages, there arose early in the Nineteenth century among Free Negroes and slaves, organizations which did a simple accident and life insurance business, charging small weekly premiums. These beneficial organizations have spread until to-day there are many thousands of them in the United States. They are mutual benefit associations and are usually connected with churches. Of such societies twenty-six are returned in this report.

Coming now to more purely benevolent efforts we have reported twenty-one organizations and institutions of various sorts which represent distinctly the efforts of the better class of Negroes to rescue and uplift the unfortunate and vicious. Finally, we have a few instances of co-operative business effort reported which typify the economic efforts of the weak to find strength in unity....

8. General Summary. We have reviewed in detail the efforts for social betterment of the following organizations:

Churches	79
Secret Societies	92
Benevolent Societies	26
Insurance Societies	3
Cooperative Societies*	15
Benevolent Organizations	21
Total Organizations	236

(*Two partially reported are not counted here.)

This we must remember represents only a part of the benevolent and reformatory activity of Negroes in a few cities of the South. It includes many of the more important enterprises, but not all even of them. It gives a rough, incomplete and yet fairly characteristic picture of what the freedmen's sons are doing to better their social condition.

The first point of interest we have in this picture is a scientific one. No more interesting example of the growth of organizations within a group could be adduced. Here in a half-century, or at most a century, we have epitomized that intricate specialization of the different human activities and that adaptation of the thoughts and actions of men to the thoughts and actions about them, which we call advance in civilization. The process here has been hastened, the environment has had unusual features, the action of the group unusual hindrances; and yet we catch here a faint idea of what human progress really means, and how infinitely complicated its methods are. Compared with modern civilized groups the organization of action among American Negroes is extremely simple. So much so that most persons not acquainted with the matter regard them as one vast unorganized homogeneous mass. And yet there are among them 23,000 churches, with unusually wide activities, and spending annually at least $10,000,000. There are thousands of secret societies, with their insurance and social features, large numbers of beneficial societies with their economic and benevolent cooperation;

there is the slowly expanding seed of cooperative business effort seeking to systematize and economize the earnings and expenditures of millions of dollars. Finally, there are the slowly evolving organs by which the group seeks to stop and minimize the anti-social deeds and accidents of its members. This is a picture of all human striving--unusually simple, with local and social peculiarities, but strikingly human and worth further study and attention.

Again, we have a scientific interest in the kinds of organs with which this group is seeking to accomplish certain ends. Nowhere can the persistence of human institutions be better exemplified. Men seldom invent new ways of social advance, they rather exchange and adapt old ways to new conditions. The communism of the African forests with its political and religious leadership is a living, breathing reality on American soil to-day, even after 250 years of violent change--strangely altered, to be sure, and shorn of many peculiarities.

The African clan life of blood relatives became the clan life of the plantation; the religious leader became the head of the religious activity of the slaves, and of whatever other group action was left; monogamy without legal sanction was little more than thinly veiled polygamy. Then came emancipation, and the church resumed more of the functions of the old tribal life, while the minister added political and economic functions to his religious duties. Next the church itself began to differentiate organizations for different functions; economic and cooperative action became the business of the beneficial society and secret society; and benevolence, of special associations and institutions; finally, cooperative business and insurance sprang from the beneficial societies. How curious a chapter is this of the adaptation of social methods and ways of thinking to the environment of real life.

The second point of interest in this study lies in the light these facts few and scattered as they are, may throw on the solution of the Negro problems. Here we must first notice that the race prejudice of whites acts so as to isolate this group and to throw upon it the responsibility of evolving its own methods and organs of civilization. The problem of cooperation among the members of the group becomes then the central serious problem. And cooperation is peculiarly hard for a nation of slaves. Moreover, this process under the present circumstances has to be artificially quickened. We want the Negro to advance toward civilization much more quickly than would be the case if he were otherwise situated. This quickened process itself gives rise to new problems. There then lies the reason and excuse for outside aid. The nation helps the Negro not simply to recompence the injustice long done him, but rather to make it possible for him to accomplish more quickly a work which usually takes centuries. Nor is it impossible to give such aid effectively. Modern civilization is continually trying it in the case of its slums and rabble, and has had some marked success.

It is however, a delicate process, in which the chances of

error in two ways are about equal. The group may be helped so much that it will cease to help itself; or it may be helped so little or so injudiciously that its best efforts will leave it unprogressive and discouraged. For this reason the first step, before aid is given, should be a thorough study and knowledge of the situation. One guide here is the initiative of the Negroes themselves. If they are found striving in new directions, as to-day toward asylums, homes and hospitals, this is a pretty fair indication of a social want, and judicious aid to such enterprise can be applied usually with gratifying results. On the other hand, there will always be fields for aid to anticipate future wants and efforts, which only trained thinkers and observers can foresee.

At present even the few efforts of Negroes toward benevolent enterprise are highly gratifying and deserving of active aid and encouragement. The pressing need of the coming decade will be organized work or rescue and reformation among Negroes--benevolence in its broadest and best sense, and not as pure alms-giving. For the establishment of such work the great hindrance among Negroes themselves is their poverty, even among the better classes. If the economic condition of the best classes of Negroes were better then relief work could be broadened.

The question, therefore, resolves itself into a call for more light on the economic condition of the Negro, and to this subject the Atlanta Conference of the next few years will devote their energies.

In this document Frederick Howard Wines expresses the opinion of the white leadership in social welfare of that period, and perhaps, also the opinion of that leadership toward the role of blacks in the American social system.

Document 21

Letter to Second Annual Atlanta University Conference from Frederick Howard Wines, editor of the Charities Review, published in Social and Physical Conditions of Negro Life. The Atlanta University Publications, No. 2, 1897, pp. 71-72.

I am very much obliged for your invitation to attend the second conference with reference to the condition of the colored population in the cities of the United States. I regret that my official duties will not permit my absence from home at the date of this meeting. My word to the conference is simply this: that if the Negro race is ever to be elevated in the social scale, as I believe that it will be, it can only be by self-culture and self-control. Help from the outside will go but a little way. The Negro must realize his manhood and his responsibilities as a man and citizen, and meet them, if he wishes to survive in the struggle for existence. It is absolutely essential that he should receive not only a literary education, but manual training; and that he should cultivate in himself the virtues of industry, thrift, chastity, honesty and temperance. When he learns to respect himself, his women, the rights of others, and especially the rights of property; to meet the reasonable expectations of his employers, and to fulfill his contracts both in letter and in spirit, he will command the respect of the world, and his advancement will be both sure and rapid. If race prejudice on the part of the white people towards the colored is to be deplored, so also is race prejudice on the part of the colored people towards the white. The two races must live in peace and harmony, or the weaker race will inevitably go to the wall.

THE ROLE OF WOMEN

As in prior historical periods black women, individually and in groups, responded ably and significantly in confronting problematic situations facing blacks. Locally or nationally, their primary emphasis was on utilizing varied techniques toward self-improvement of racial conditions.

The following document describes the typically insightful response of a brave black woman, Ida Wells Barnett, at times singly, at times with others, as a newspaper editor and lecturer she exposed the vicious aspects of the social system, such as the crime of lynching.

Document 22

Ida Wells Barnett, A Red Record, (Chicago: Donahue and Henneberry, 1895), pp. 8-15.

Ida B. Wells Barnett (1862-1931) was born in Holly Springs, Mississippi, the eldest child of slave parents. She was educated at Rust College. When she was fifteen years old, her parents and a brother died in a yellow fever epidemic. She concealed her age, secured a position teaching school, and became the support and substitute parent for her five surviving brothers and sisters. In 1884 she moved to Memphis, Tennessee, where she worked as a schoolteacher and continued her education by attending classes at Fisk University. During this time she began to write articles for black newspapers under the pen name "Iola." In retribution for her exposure of the inadequate school facilities for black children, she was fired from her job in 1891. She then began a full-time career in journalism and soon became one of the two owners of the Memphis Free Speech.

Her hard hitting columns were marked by race pride and urgent appeals to black resistance against discrimination. In 1892, three black men, all personally known to her, were lynched in Memphis. Ida Wells charged in her paper that the motives for the lynching were purely economic--all three men having been successful in business. She also urged the black population of Memphis to emigrate to the West.

This case became a turning point in her life. While she was on a business trip in the East, the offices of her paper were destroyed and her life was threatened if she were to return. She then began her one-woman crusade against lynching--lecturing, writing and organizing. Her approach was hard-hitting: she gathered the facts, using the services of detectives, Pinkerton agents or informants, then exposed them to all who would hear her, laying bare the politics and economics of lynching. Her contention was that lynching was an integral part of the system of racial oppression, and that the motives for lynching usually had little to do with crime, but were either economic or political. She dared to bring out into the open what was the most taboo subject of all in Victorian America--the habitual sexual abuse of black women by white men and the myth that the only sexual contact between white women and black men must be based on rape.

Ida Wells toured Great Britain in 1893 and again in 1894. Her public speeches aroused British liberals against American lynching and led to the formation of a British Anti-Lynching Society. Her agitation in Britain aroused a great deal of displeasure and unfavorable comment in the American press and engendered a public controversy between Ida B. Wells and Frances Willard, the national President of the Women's Christian Temperance Union. Miss Willard was visiting in Britain at the same time as Miss Wells and the latter was repeatedly asked whether white reformers such as Miss Willard not only had not spoken out against lynchings, but had returned from a Southern tour as an apologist of the white Southern attitude on the race question, an action for which the Negro press had universally condemned her. Stung by this charge, Miss Willard gave a published interview, disputing these facts. In the course of the interview she repeated the very apologetic statements for which Miss Wells had chided her. The incident is significant because Frances Willard was a lifelong abolitionist, suffragist and ardent reformer and had enormous influence over hundreds of thousands of women. She was, as Ida Wells acidly commented, "no better or worse than the great bulk of white Americans on the Negro question." Still, possibly as the result of this public debate, Frances Willard's name appeared as one of the subscribers of the British Anti-Lynching Society.

On her return to America, Ida B. Wells continued her solitary campaign against lynchings by pamphleteering and lecturing on the subject. She later became chairman of the Anti-Lynching Bureau of the National Afro-American Council. The work of black club women and later the NAACP on this issue is a direct outgrowth of Ida B. Wells' persistent muckraking journalism, exposes, lectures and organizations.

She was also a very important force in the growth of the women's club movement. She helped to organize the first black women's club in Chicago, which took her name and over which she presided. She kept in close touch with the leading club women in the country. In 1895, she married Ferdinand Lee Barnett, a prominent attorney in Chicago, and, although announcing her retirement, managed and edited The Conservator, a newspaper her husband had founded. "My duties as editor, as president of the Ida B. Wells Woman's Club, and as speaker in many white women's clubs in and around Chicago kept me pretty busy. But I was not too busy to find time to give birth to a male child the following March 25, 1896. Four months later she attended the first convention of the National Association of Colored Women, bringing along her baby boy and a nurse. A few months later she undertook a speaking tour all over the state on behalf of the Republican Party, again taking her nursing baby along.

In 1908, she organized the Negro Fellowship League and became its President. The organization maintained a settlement house in the slums and was instrumental in organizing militant action around various local racial issues. It was distinguished by its close ties to the poor and working class community which it served. Mrs. Barnett also was a founding member of the NAACP, but later withdrew from activity in the organization because she advocated more militantly race-conscious leadership. All her life she was critical of and in conflict with Negro leaders who accommodated themselves to whites, although at various times in her career she worked well with some whites, such as Jane Addams and Municipal Court Judge Harry Olsen. The latter appointed her Adult Probation Officer, the first woman in Chicago to hold this job.

Ida Wells Barnett was active in politics and always saw woman suffrage as an instrument for achieving the emancipation of black people. She founded the first black women's political club, the Alpha Suffrage Club of Chicago which mobilized the women's vote in the 1914 mayoralty elections. During the years when she devoted most of her time to raising her four children, she played a leading role in mobilizing protest action in the wake of the post-World War I lynchings and race riots. On several occasions she was the first and only Black on the scene right after the violence and on fact-finding commissions. Her persistent militancy and courage gave her a position of undisputed leadership in her own community and prominence on a national level.

In addition to her journalistic work and anti-lynching pamphlets, Ida B. Wells wrote an autobiography.

In her dissertation, The Participation of Negroes in the Establishment of Welfare Services, 1865-1900, Inabel Lindsay describes well the activities and welfare services initiated by the black women's club movement. Of special interest were the activities of Mrs. Josephine St. Pierre Ruffin, founder of the New Era Women's Club of Boston, and later organizer of the first National Conference of

Negro Women of America in Boston in July, 1895. As an indication of organizational responses of women to national and regional needs, we cite a letter in which Mrs. Ruffin supports apparent efforts of some Southern white women to help establish welfare programs for black children in Georgia.

Document 23

Josephine St. Pierre Ruffin, "An Open Letter to the Educational League of Georgia," Appendix C, in The Participation of Negroes in the Establishment of Welfare Services, 1865-1900, Inabel B. Lindsay. Unpublished Ph. D dissertation, University of Pittsburgh, 1952, pp. 222-225.

Ladies of the Georgia Educational League:

The telegram which you sent to Governor Northern to read to his audience, informing the people of the North of your willingness to undertake the moral training of the colored children of Georgia, merits more than a passing notice. It is the first time, we believe, in the history of the South where a body of representative Southern white women have shown such interest in the moral welfare of the children of their former slaves as to be willing to undertake to make them more worthy the duties and responsibilities of citizenship. True, there have been individual cases where courageous women have felt their moral responsibility, and have nobly met it, but one of the saddest things about the sad condition of affairs in the South has been the utter indifference which Southern women, who were guarded with unheard of fidelity during the war, have manifested to the mental and moral welfare of the children of their faithful slaves, who, in the language of Henry Grady, placed a black mass of loyalty between them and dishonor. This was a rare opportunity for you to have shown your gratitude to your slaves and your interest in their future welfare.

The children would have grown up in utter ignorance had not the North sent thousands of her noblest daughters to the South on this mission of heroic love and mercy; and it is worthy of remark of those fair daughters of the North, that, often eating with Negroes, and in the earlier days sleeping in their humble cabins, and always surrounded by thousands of them, there is not one recorded instance where one has been the victim of violence or insult. If because of the bitterness of your feelings, of your deep poverty at the close of the war, conditions were such that you could not do this work yourselves, you might have given a Christian's welcome to the women who came a thousand miles to do the work, that, in all gratitude and obligation belonged to you,--but instead, these women were often persecuted, always they have been ruthlessly ostracized, even until this day; often they were lonely, often longed for a word of sympathy, often craved association with their own race, but for thirty years they have been treated by the Christian white women of the South,--simply because they were doing your work,--the work committed to you by your Savior, when he said, "Inasmuch as you did it to one of the least of these my brethren, you did it unto me,"--with a contempt that would serve to justify a suspicion that instead of being the most cultured women, the purest, bravest, missionaries in America, they were outcasts and lepers.

But at least a change has come. And so you have "decided to take up the work of moral and industrial training of the Negroes," as you "have been doing this work among the whites with splendid results." This is one of the most hopeful stars that have shot through the skies of the Southern sky. What untold blessing might not the educated Christian women of the South prove to the Negro groping blindly in the mass of the swamps and the bogs of prejudice for a way out of servitude, oppression, ignorance and immorality!

The leading women of Georgia should not ask Northern charity to do what they certainly must have the means for making a beginning of themselves. If your heart is really in this work--and make not question--the very best way for you to atone for your negligence in the past is to make a start yourselves. Surely if the conditions are as serious as you represent them to be, your husbands, who are men of large means, who are able to run great expositions and big peace celebrations, will be willing to provide you with the means to protect your virtue and that of your daughters by the moral training you propose to give in the kindergartens.

There is much you might do without the contribution of a dollar from any pocket, Northern or Southern. On every plantation there are scores, if not hundreds, of little colored children who could be gathered about you on a Sabbath afternoon and given many helpful inspiring lessons in moral and good conduct.

It is a good augury of better days, let us hope, when the intelligent, broad-minded women of Georgia, spurning the incendiary advice of that human firebrand who could lynch a thousand Negroes a month, are willing to join in this great altruistic movement of the age and endeavor to lift up the degraded and ignorant, rather than to exterminate them. Your proposition implies that they may be uplifted and further imports a tacit confession that if you had done your duty to them at the close of the war, which both gratitude and prudence should have prompted you to do, you would not now be confronted with a condition which you feel it necessary to check, in obedience to the great first law of nature--self-protection. If you enter upon this work you will doubtless be criticized by a class of your own people who think you are lowering your own dignity, but the South has suffered too much already from that kind of false pride to let it longer keep her recreant to the spirit of the age.

If, when you have entered upon it, you need the cooperation either by advice or other assistance, of the colored women of the North, we beg to assure you that they will not be lacking--until then, the earnest hope goes out that you will bravely face and sternly conquer your former prejudices and quickly undertake this missionary work which belongs to you.

SEGREGATION ENSHRINED

There was great ambivalence in this period on the part even of those whites who had been most often in the vanguard of movements concerned with the welfare of blacks, especially when their activities were open to a charge of promoting blacks to a plane of social equality. As an example, we note the letter of Congressman Benjamin F. Butler, once famous as the general who declared refugee blacks "contraband of war". According to him, for example, blacks need not be accorded rights of service in public taverns because he thinks they should not drink. Although he supported, in general, the purposes of the Civil Rights Acts of 1875, his reaction, as expressed in the following document, seems similar to Senator Everett Dirksen's contention in the debates on Civil Rights Bills proposed in the later 1950's and early 1960's: that guaranteeing public accommodations to blacks would interfere with the operation of "boarding houses." Spurious moral or social objections obscure basic fears that the admission of blacks to public accommodations or the extension of common social courtesies and amenities threaten in some fashion, not only the privileges of whites, but also the social progress of blacks. Thus, equity and justice were not yet free commodities accessible to blacks in the American social system.

The development of an industrial, urban society leads to increased social ills, which in turn generate the need for organized ways of coping with them. This period witnessed the organization and development of the State Boards of Charities and of the National Conference of Charities and Corrections, beginning in 1879. Similar notions regarding equity and justice appear in the thinking of those interested in the development of social welfare programs for blacks and looking at the annual proceedings of the latter, the general treatment accorded to blacks by it tended to follow customary national thought and policy. Southern thinking dominated national programs. The problems of the South, for example, had to be handled by the South, which of course meant, however benevolently, handling them in an essentially racist manner. In the proceedings are to be found one or two articles having reference to nursing homes, homes for the aged or orphanages. But a few articles refer to the condition of peonage and the nefarious practice of convict leasing. However, no writings offered any real solutions to the general trend of white social thinking, which seemed to wish the problems away, or to the predictions of white sociologists that blacks would die out as a viable population in the first decade of the twentieth century.

Document 24

Letter of Congressman Benjamin F. Butler to Robert Harben, Jr., Cincinnati, Ohio, Washington, D. C., March 8, 1875.

Washington, March 8, 1875

Sir:

I have the pleasure to acknowledge receipt of your's of the 14th containing expressions of appreciation of my efforts on behalf of the Civil Rights Bill, for which accept my thanks.

You further ask, "Will you be kind enough to inform me if colored men are entitled to the privileges of saloons and barber shops under its provisions?"

To this I answered: I understand by "saloons" you may mean drinking saloons, and I am happy today that the Civil Rights Bill does not give any right to a colored man to go to a drinking saloon without the leave of the proprietor, and I am very glad that it does not. I am willing to concede, as a friend of the colored race, that the white race may have at least this superior privilege to the colored man, that they can drink in bar rooms and saloons, and I never shall do anything to interfere with the exercise of that high and distinctive privilege. I would not advocate a bill which should give that right to the colored man. If I were to vote for any bill on the subject at all, it would be for one to keep the colored man out of the drinking saloons; and I hope no barkeeper will ever let a colored man have a glass of liquor at any bar open for drinking. Indeed, I would be glad, whenever a colored man should go into a drinking saloon for the purpose of drinking at the bar, if somebody would at once take him and put him out, doing him as little injury as possible. He would do the colored man no greater kindness.

As to the other branch of your question in reference to barber shops. Let me say that the trade of a barber like that is like any other trade to be carried on by the man who is engaged in it at his own will and pleasure, and the Civil Rights Bill has nothing to do with its exercise. A barber has the right to shave whom he pleases, as much as a jeweler has a right to repair a watch for whom he pleases or a blacksmith to shoe such colored horse as he pleases. In other words, these are not public employments but private businesses, in which the law does not interfere.

From time immemorial all men have had equal rights at the

common law in places of public amusement, in public conveyances, and in inns for or licensed taverns, because all such business was for the public under special privileges granted by the government. The theater and like public amusements were licensed by the public authorities and were protected by the police. The public conveyances used the king's highway. The public inn had the special privilege of a lien or claim upon the baggage or other property of any traveler using it for his keep; and if any man was refused while behaving himself well and paying his fare, a seat in any place of public amusement or carriage by public conveyance or shelter in a public inn, he had in common law a right of action against the party so refusing. The Civil Rights Bill not only confirms these rights of all citizens to the colored man in consideration of the prejudices against him and an attempt in certain parts of the country to interfere with the exercise of those common law rights, and has enacted a penalty as a means of enforcing the right in his behalf in consideration of a helpless and dependent condition. The Civil Rights Bill has not altered the colored man's right at all from what it was before by the common law applicable to nearly every state in the union. It had only given him a greater power to enforce that right to meet the exigency of combined efforts to deprive colored citizens of it; and all ideas that the Civil Rights Bill allow the colored man to force himself into any man's shop or into any man's private home or into any eating house, boarding house, or establishment other than those I have named is simply an exhibition of ignorance as well as in some cases, of insufferable prejudice and malignity. And while I would sustain any black man in firmly and properly insisting upon his rights under the Civil Rights Bill which were his at common law, as they were the right of every citizen, yet I should oppose to the utmost of my power any attempt on the part of the colored man to use the Civil Rights Bill as a pretense to interfere with the private business of private parties. It is beneath the dignity of any colored man to do so, and all acts such as shutting him out from drinking saloons may be well left to the ignorant and generally vicious men who keep them as a badge of their superiority to the colored races.

I have the honor to be
very respectfully
your obedient servant
Benjamin F. Butler

Robert Harben, Jr.
Cincinnatti, Ohio

The following brief prepared by lawyers and social scientists for the challenge in the Supreme Court of the separate but equal doctrine in October, 1953, is an excellent review of the legal and political events which contributed to the rise and diffusion of Jim Crow, i. e., segregation laws. These laws effectively circumscribed the exercise of political power by blacks, sanctioned denial of due process and equal protection of the laws and placed difficulties in the way of economic advancement as well. By the end of the nineteenth century segregation was fact of national policy and, DuBois could state, that the problem of the twentieth century is the problem of the color line.

Document 25

Charles L. Black, et al., Brief for Appellants.... in the Supreme Court of the United States, October Term, 1953. New York Supreme Printing Company, Inc., 1953, pp. 50, 56-65.

Viewed in the light of history the separate but equal doctrine has been an instrumentality of defiant nullification of the Fourteenth Amendment.

This history of segregation laws reveal that their main purpose was to organize the community upon the basis of a superior white and an inferior Negro caste. These laws were conceived in a belief in the inherent inferiority of Negroes, a concept taken from slavery. Inevitably, segregation in its operation and effect has meant inequality consistent only with the belief that the people segregated are inferior and not worthy, or capable, of enjoying the facilities set apart for the dominant group.

Segregation originated as a part of an effort to build a social order in which the Negro would be placed in a status close as possible to that he had held before the Civil War. The separate but equal doctrine furnished a base from which those who sought to nullify the Thirteenth, Fourteenth and Fifteenth Amendments were permitted to operate in relative security. While this must have been apparent at the end of the last century, the doctrine has become beclouded with so much fiction that it becomes important to consider the matter in historical context to restore a proper view of its meaning and import.

C. The Compromise of 1877 and the Abandonment of Reconstruction

The return to power of the southern irreconcilables was finally made possible by rapproachment between northern and southern economic interests culminating in the compromise of 1877. In the North, control of the Republican Party passed to those who believed that the protection and expansion of their economic power could best be served by political conciliation of the southern irreconcilables, rather than by unswerving insistence upon human equality and the rights guaranteed by the post war Amendments. In the 1870's those forces that held fast to the notion of the Negro's preordained inferiority returned to power in state after state, and it is significant that one of the first measures adopted was to require segregated schools on a permanent basis in disregard of the Fourteenth Amendment.

In 1877, out of the exigencies of a close and contested election, came a bargain between the Republican Party and the southern leaders of the Democratic Party which assured President Hayes' election, led to the withdrawal of federal troops from the non-redeemed states and left the South free to solve the Negro problem without apparent fear of federal intervention. This agreement preserved the pragmatic and material ends of Reconstruction at the expense of the enforcement of not only the Fourteenth Amendment but the Fifteenth Amendment as well. For it brought in its wake peonage and disfranchisement as well as segregation and other denials of equal protection. Although there is grave danger in oversimplification of the complexities of history, on reflection it seems clear that more profoundly than constitutional amendments and wordy statutes, the Compromise of 1877 shaped the future of four million freedmen and their progeny for generations to come. For the road to freedom and equality, which had seemed sure and open in 1868, was now to be securely blocked and barred by a maze of restrictions and limitations proclaimed as essential to a way of life.

D. Consequences of the 1877 Compromise

Once the South was left to its own devices, the militant irreconcilables quickly seized or consolidated power. Laws and practices designed to achieve rigid segregation and the disfranchisement of the Negro came on increasing numbers and harshness.

The policies of the southern states was to destroy the political power of the Negro so that he could never seriously challenge the order that was being established. By the poll tax, the Grandfather Clause, the white primary, gerrymandering, the complicated election procedures, and by unabated intimidation and threats of violence, the Negro was stripped of effective political participation.

The final blow to the political respectability of the Negro came with disfranchisement in the final decade of the Nineteenth Century and the early years of the present century when the discriminatory provisions were written into the state constitutions. That problem the Court dealt with during the next forty years from Guinn v. United States, 238 U.S. 347 to Terry v. Adams, 345 U.S. 461.

A movement to repeal the Fourteenth and Fifteenth Amendments shows the extremity to which the irreconcilables were willing to go to make certain that the Negro remained in an inferior position. At the Mississippi Constitutional Convention of 1890, a special committee studied the matter and concluded that "the white people only are capable of conducting and maintaining the government" and that the Negro race, "even if its people were educated, being wholly unequal to such responsibility," should be excluded from the franchise. It, therefore, resolved that the "true and only efficient remedy for the great and important difficulties" that would ensue from Negro participation lay in the "repeal of the Fifteenth Amendment ... whereby such restrictions and limitations may be put upon the Negro suffrage as may be necessary and proper for the maintenance of good and stable government...."

A delegate to the Virginia Constitutional Convention of 1901-1902 submitted a resolution calling for a repeal of the Fifteenth Amendment because it is wrong, "in that it proceeds on the theory that the two races are equally competent of free government." Senator Edward Carmack of Tennessee gave notice in 1903 that he would bring in a bill to repeal the Amendments. The movement, though unsuccessful, clearly illustrates the temper of the white South.

Having consigned the Negro to a permanently inferior caste status, racist spokesmen, with unabashed boldness, set forth views regarding the Negro's unassimilability and uneducability even more pernicious than those held by the old South. Ben Tillman, the leader of South Carolina, declared that a Negro should not have the same treatment as a white man, "for the simple reason that God Almighty made him colored and did not make him white." He lamented the end of slavery which reversed the process of improving the Negro and "inoculated him with the virus of equality." These views were expressed many times in the disfranchisement conventions toward the end of the century. Nor were the politicians alone in the uttering of such views about the Negro. Drawing on the theory of evolution as expressed by Darwin and the theory of progress developed by Spencer, persons of scholarly pretension speeded the work of justifying an inferior status for the Negro. Alfred H. Stone, having the reputation of a widely respected scholar in Mississippi, declared that the "Negro was an inferior type of man with predominantly African customs and character traits whom no amount of education or improvement of environmental conditions would ever elevate to as high a scale in the human species as the white man." As late as 1910, E. H. Randle in his Characteristics of the Southern Negro declared that "the first important thing to remember in judging the Negro was that his mental capacity was inferior to that of the white man."

Such was the real philosophy behind the late 19th Century segregation laws--an essential part of the whole racist complex. Controlling economic and political interests in the South were convinced that the Negro's subjugation was essential to their survival, and the Court in Plessy v. Ferguson had ruled that such subjugation through public authority was sanctioned by the Constitution. This is the overriding vice of Plessy v. Ferguson. For without the sanction of Plessy v. Ferguson, archaic and provincial notions of racial superiority could not have injured and disfigured an entire region for so long a time. The full force and effect of the protection afforded by the Fourteenth Amendment was effectively blunted by the vigorous efforts of the proponents of the concept that the Negro was inferior. This nullification was effectuated in all aspects of Negro life in the South, particularly in the field of education, by the exercise of state power.

As the invention of the cotton gin stilled the voices of Southern Abolitionists, Plessy v. Ferguson chilled the development in the South of opinion conducive to the acceptance of Negroes on the basis of equality because those of the white South desiring to afford Negroes the equalitarian status which the Civil War Amendments had hoped to achieve were barred by state law from acting in accordance with their beliefs. In this connection, it is significant that the Populist movement flourished for a short period during the 1890's and threatened to take over political control of the South through a coalition of the poor Negro and poor white farmers. This movement was completely smashed and since Plessy v. Ferguson no similar phenomenon has taken hold.

Without the "constitutional" sanction which Plessy v. Ferguson affords, racial segregation could not have become entrenched in the South, and individuals and local communities would have been free to maintain public school systems in conformity with the underlying purposes of the Fourteenth Amendment, by providing education without racial distinctions. The doctrine of Plessy v. Ferguson was essential to the successful maintenance of a racial caste system in the United States. Efforts toward the elimination of race discrimination are jeopardized as long as the separate but equal doctrine endures. But for this doctrine we could more confidently assert that ours is a democratic society based upon a belief in individual equality.

E. Nullification of the Rights Guaranteed by the Fourteenth Amendment and the Reestablishment of the Negro's Pre-Civil War Inferior Status Fully Realized.

Before the end of the century, even without repeal of the Fourteenth and Fifteenth Amendments, those forces committed to a perpetuation of the slave concept of the Negro had realized their goal. They had defied the federal government, threatened the white defenders of equal rights, had used intimidation and violence against the Negro and had effectively smashed a political movement designed to unite the Negro and the poor whites. Provisions requiring segregated schools were written into state constitutions and statutes. Negroes had been driven from participation in political affairs, and a veritable maze of Jim Crow laws had been erected to "keep the Negro in his place" (of inferiority), all with impunity. There was no longer any need to pretend either that Negroes were getting an education equal to the whites or were entitled to it.

In the Constitutional Convention of Virginia, 1901-1902, Senator Carter Glass, in explaining a resolution requiring that state funds be used to maintain primary schools for four months, before being used for establishment of higher grades, explained that "white people of the black sections of Virginia should be permitted to tax themselves, and after a certain point had been passed which would safeguard the poorer classes of those communities, divert that fund to the exclusive use of white children ..."

Senator Vardaman thought it was folly to make such pretenses. In Mississippi there were too many people to educate and not enough money to go around, he felt. The state, he insisted, should not spend as much on the education of Negroes as it was doing. "There is no use multiplying words about it," he said in 1899, "the negro will not be permitted to rise above the station he now fills." Money spent on his education was, therefore, a "positive unkindness" to him. "It simply renders him unfit for the work which the white man has prescribed and which he will be forced to perform." Vardaman's scholarly compatriot, Dunbar Rowland, seconded these views in 1902, when he said that "thoughtful men in the South were beginning to lose faith in the power of education which had been hitherto given to uplift the negro," and to complain of the burden thus placed upon the people of the South in their poverty.

The views of Tillman, Vardaman, Stone, Rowland, Glass and others were largely a justification for what had been done by the time they uttered them. The South had succeeded in setting up the machinery by which it was hoped to retain the Negro in an inferior status. Through separate, inferior schools, through an elaborate system of humiliating Jim Crow, and through effective disfranchisement of the Negro, the exclusive enjoyment of first-class citizenship had now become the sole possession of white persons.

And, finally, the Negro was effectively restored to an inferior position through laws and through practices, now dignified as "customs and tradition." Moreover, this relationship--of an inferior Negro and superior white status--established through laws, practice, custom and tradition, was even more rigidly enforced than in the ante-bellum era. As one historian has aptly stated:

> Whether by state law or local law, or by the more pervasive coercion of sovereign white opinion, 'the Negro's place' was gradually defined--in the courts, schools, and libraries, in parks, theaters, hotels, and residential districts, in hospitals, insane asylums--everywhere including on sidewalks and in cemeteries. When complete, the new codes of White Supremacy were vastly more complex than the ante-bellum slave codes or the Black Codes of 1865-1866, and, if anything, they were stronger and more rigidly enforced.

This is the historic background against which the validity of the separate but equal doctrine must be tested. History reveals it as a part of an overriding purpose to defeat the aims of the Thirteenth, Fourteenth and Fifteenth Amendments. Segragation was designed to insure inequality--to discriminate on account of race and color--and the separate but equal doctrine accommodated the Constitution to that purpose.

NOTES--PART II

1. In Afro-American Encyclopedia, edited by James T. Haley, (Nashville, Tennessee, Haley and Florida, 1896), pp. 35-59.

2. Speech reprinted in _Africa and the American Negro_, edited by J. W. E. Bowen, (Atlanta, Georgia, 1896), pp. 195-98.

3. James Leiby, "Social Work and Social History," _Social Service Review_, September, 1969, p. 314.

4. Patrick O'Leary, "The Black Worker and the Trade Union Movement, 1865-1900," unpublished M. S. , Atlanta University School of Social Work, 1974, p. 20.

PART III

RENEWAL AND RESURGENCE: 1895-1915

INTRODUCTION

A year prior to the Plessy v. Ferguson decision of the United States Supreme Court, Booker T. Washington, Principal of Tuskegee Institute, was invited to address the Atlanta Cotton States and International Exposition. In his speech Washington uttered remarks which stirred up great controversy among blacks and which had great import for the future of social welfare programs for the black population of his day.

It was not Mr. Washington's intention to be controversial; but, rather, to offer a formula for uniting blacks and whites in cooperative efforts to accomplish the broad objectives which they held in common. His appeal was almost unanimously approved by whites, because he did not attack the enforced racial segregation which developed from the discriminatory application of justice in the county courthouses and the discriminatory legislation enacted in the statehouse. However, his speech divided the black community, alienating many prominent blacks who dubbed the speech, at best, a compromise and, at worst, a sellout.

Mr. Washington was certainly correct to admonish blacks to help each other and to urge whites to vigorously aid and assist them, in his words--"to cast down your buckets where you are." But, his advice to blacks became most controversial when he urged them to regard as their highest priority the development of their economic rather than their political potential. In giving this advice, Washington ceded to whites, by default, all of those advantages, and opportunities, and powers which accrue to a group that vigorously and aggressively pursues its own legitimate political aims and objectives. Eight months earlier Washington had said:

> The wisest among my race understand that the agitation of questions of social equality is the extremest folly, and that progress in the enjoyment of all the privileges that will come to us must be the result of severe and constant struggle rather than of artificial forcing. No race that has anything to contribute to the markets of the world is long in any degree ostracized. It is important and right that all privileges of the law be ours, but it is vastly more important that we be prepared for the exercises of these privileges. . . . 1*

This statement gave considerable more sanction and support to the legalization of segregation, which by the construction placed on Plessy v. Ferguson by the Supreme Court, was to become the national policy, the law of the land. The general import of the Washington position was that the "severe and constant struggle" of blacks must proceed without the support and protection of the law at all levels, community, state and national. And, at the Exposition: "If the civil and political rights of both races be equal one cannot be inferior to the other civilly and politically. If one race be inferior to the other socially, the Constitution of the United States cannot put them on the same plane."[2] No wonder that whites such as Clark Howell, editor of the Atlanta Constitution, characterized the remarks of Washington as

> . . . one of the most notable speeches, both as to character and as to the warmth of its reception, ever delivered to a Southern audience. The address was a revelation. The whole speech is a platform upon which blacks and whites can stand with full justice to each other.[3]

Upon reflection many blacks agreed with neither Booker T. Washington nor with Clark Howell. They saw clearly that there would be no justice without a black exercise of the ballot. A month or so later another black, the Reverend J. W. E. Bowen, Ph. D, D.D. , Professor of Historical Theology in the Gammon Theological Seminary in Atlanta, also addressed the Atlanta Exposition on its

*Footnotes to Part III begin on page 280.

Negro Day, October 21, 1895. He did not directly attack Booker T. Washington, but the tone and temper of his remarks were quite different. The so-called Negro problem, he stressed, is a human problem, and one which

> ... assumes a different name in different parts of the world.... In California it is the problem of the Chinese, in the great middle west it is the Scandinavian and other foreign struggles; in the north, central and eastern states, it is the Irish and Italian problem, while overreaching all of these is the problem of the battle for bread, and in the south it is the Negro problem. It is therefore no sign of breadth of vision to declare that there is only one great problem in the United States and that one is the Negro problem. These problems will require centuries of persistent effort that they may be solved upon the ethical and equitable basis of the New Testament teachings. In dealing with all of these the principles of equality and of brotherhood should obtain.[4]

Dr. Bowen voiced the aspirations of the "New Negro" who, given equality of opportunity, "will think off his chains and have both hands free to help you build this country and make a grand destiny of himself."[5] For aspiring blacks there was greater hope and vision offered in the remarks of Bowen than in those of Washington, the key difference being that Bowen's approach called for the exercise of intelligent social action by blacks in their own self-interest and in the interest of building a viable black community.

Unnoticed by whites, Dr. Bowen's speech reflected at this time the emergence of a body of social thought initiated, formulated and activated by a group of young, well-educated and highly articulate black leaders, who had no intention of abdicating or deferring the exercise of political responsibility to whites. They resisted this tendency and disclosed to the world as best they could in the press and in conventions the sordid devices used by whites to disfranchise blacks and to reduce them to the condition of a powerless proletariat.

Despite the encroachment of patterns of segregation and practices of racial discrimination, despite the terrorism and violence of race riots and lynchings, despite all circumscriptions of the options and choices available to an aspiring black population, a new leadership trained in the colleges of both the North and South had risen. These new leaders displayed their initiative, their creativity and innovative potential 1) by devising and pioneering the recruitment and training of a cadre of blacks competent to staff the kinds of social welfare organizations necessary to assist the increasing numbers of blacks who fled the farms or the cities; and 2) by organizing group activities primarily designed to contribute to the development of the black community. These organizations, varying in social structure from relatively amorphous social movements to highly formal voluntary associations, constitute a legacy which looms large in the structure of social welfare today, including and advancing beyond the settlement house type of institution established by whites to ease the adjustment and assimilation of the immigrant Europeans to the great urban centers of the nation. Rather, the activities of institution-building were planned and formulated with reference to the whole community. In other words, they pioneered, with great distinction, community development on a comprehensive scale and of particular note were the efforts of George Edmund Haynes, Lugenia Hope, Hugh Proctor and Garrie Moore.

Some engaged in the organization of social movements, enlisting and educating others in the broad issues of racial discrimination which made a mockery of American claims to justice and equality of opportunity for all. DuBois, and others of similar mind, pioneered the Niagara Movement, making possible the creation of an interracial social protest organization, the National Association for the Advancement of Colored People. Others attacked the problems of blacks on a local community level, organizing institutions for the care of the young, the poor, the uneducated and the handicapped, with the primary responsibility placed upon blacks themselves, with the assistance of philanthropic whites. They recognized, also, the need for professionally trained leadership to develop these institutions to their highest potential, an effort which in this period was to find fruition in some of the black colleges.

There were, of course, notable individuals who, despite great obstacles, still pursued those approaches previously proposed as solutions for the problems of blacks: migration culminating in either the colonization of territories overseas or the formation of the all-black community at home. These options, however, proved unattractive to the majority of blacks. Individuals and families moved slowly and surely into the urban centers of the North and Midwest, where they faced the dual problems of finding the social and ecological niches which would allow them the greatest opportunity for survival and successful enterprise in communities no less basically racist than the rural communities from which they fled. It was in these communities that the challenge was greatest. For "the severe and constant struggle" to which Booker T. Washington made reference required the organization and development of strong, viable social institutions which embraced the total community. To do this work DuBois envisioned the mobilization of the "best" of the race, of a "Talented Tenth" of the black population. The new leadership was never able to achieve this objective; but, that leadership provided the base from which, in future years, professionally trained blacks became available to staff the institutions created to service the needs and aspirations of the black community. This period (1895-1915) generated the great institutions of social service and social welfare which flourished in the next period (1916-1929).

BUILDING ALL-BLACK COMMUNITIES BY MIGRATION AND COLONIZATION

Previously we have seen how racism encouraged blacks to separate from whites in two ways. The first way was the migration of individuals and families to previously unoccupied domestic territory. The intention was to form completely new all-black towns and communities wherein blacks assumed full responsibility for the conduct of their own economic, political and social welfare, subject of course to the higher jurisdictions of state and nation. The second way was that of emigration to territory overseas, usually in Africa, but sometimes to the Caribbean or Latin America. Neither option could be exercised without the risk of failure on either economic or other grounds but, in either case, white racism generated additional difficulties.

In the following document we see the opposition by racist whites 1) to the development of the all-black towns (especially those in eastern Oklahoma), and 2) to the development of such settlements as territorial bases for the development of black political power. Frustrated in these ambitions, some blacks embraced the utopian vision of Alfred Charles Sam and joined him in emigration to the Gold Coast.

Document 1*

William E. Bittle and Gilbert L. Geis, "Alfred Charles Sam and an African Return, A Case Study in Negro Despair," Phylon, XXIII, (1962), pp. 178-194.

In the pre-dawn grayness of August 21, 1914, the British merchant vessel Liberia cleared the port of Galveston and steamed off into the Gulf of Mexico, en route to the Gold Coast Colony, British West Africa. On board were sixty American Negroes, their jubilance somewhat restrained by their apprehensions, but intent, nonetheless, upon resettling in a location where life might be easier for them and where political and social equality would be their right. They were returning, they believed, to their own people and a better existence than they had found in the New World.

The leader of the group was Alfred Charles Sam, an implausible, "low, brown man" who had spent the past year recruiting emigrants from back-country cotton farms in eastern Oklahoma. Slow-speaking and with a convincingly ungrammatical accent, Sam claimed to be an Ashanti chief born in the interior of the Gold Coast and ruling, at one time, over a town in West Akim. His followers, feverish to believe him, called him "Chief."

Left behind as the Liberia labored slowly away from her berthing in the Bolivar Roads were some five hundred persons, part of two remnant groups of Sam's followers who could not make the African trip this first time. These people, standing on the dock and waving their farewells, tried not to show their disappointment in having been left, but resolved to return to their tent city on the outskirts of Galveston and ready themselves for the return of the Liberia and their eventual emancipation.

The other body of Sam's faithful were breaking camp at "South Gold Coast," a pathetic and sordid settlement at Weleetka, Oklahoma, where for eight months they had collected, awaiting news of the departure for Africa. Though Chief Sam had repeatedly warned his followers not to dispose of their lands and possessions prematurely, many had, in their anticipation of the exodus, disregarded his warning and had ultimately found themselves expatriates in the Weleetka camps, destitute for the most part, and with the fleeting symbol of the Liberia the only one upon which to pin their

*Reprinted by permission of the publisher.

hopes.

Persons other than Sam's followers also noted with no little interest the sailing of the ship. From his diplomatic post in Washington, Sir Arthur Cecil Spring-Rice, Britain's ambassador to the United States, had continually attempted to abort the colonization project. To Spring-Rice, his own government now threatened with disastrous involvement in the European crisis, the Sam affair could not have been more trivial. Yet the possibility of a large Negro exodus from the United States to a British colony posed an embarrassing prospect for the ambassador, and he moved to stem the migration.

From the Gold Coast, too, came an expression of concern over the project. The Governor of that colony urged, on several occasions, that "every effort should be made to prevent the continuance of Sam's operations in the United States ... for were he to succeed in inducing a number of American Negroes to attempt colonization in the Gold Coast his victims would be foredoomed to disappointment.

The warning was prophetic, but it had little deterrent effect....

The exodus began, then, early on a warm August morning. The Liberia carried its sixty passengers to anticipated freedom in what they, in their frightened phantasies, had defined as their ancestral home.

The movement failed. When the Liberia finally did return to the United States two years later, she was on the end of a towline, and she no longer belonged to Sam and the African pioneers....

Although African returns infrequently dot American history, none of those preceding the Sam exodus had been Negro conceived and Negro implemented throughout. Both before and after the Civil War, the African continent had appeared a reasonable place to send manumitted slaves. But such schemes depended less upon Negro receptiveness to an African return than upon the expediencies adopted by a nation somewhat embarrassed by its slavery, but unwilling to live with its onetime chattel on equal social and political terms. The freedman, indeed, was often the most articulate opponent of African colonization, and even the respectable backers of the American Colonization Society met with Northern Negro protests in their attempts to colonize the Republic of Liberia.

Until 1914, the American Negro had lacked not only a champion with whom he could successfully identify and in terms of whom the Negro population could be put into direct and intimate touch with Africa, but, more important, he lacked the appropriate emotional and attitudinal climate necessary for emigration.

It is to this general climate that one must turn to explicate not only the genesis of the movement, but its largely unpredicted success. For the attitudes which the Negroes involved in the exodus shared with one another provided both impelling motives and irrefutable rationales for an African return.

Despite the fact that Sam's followers were drawn from a number of states, including Kansas, Texas, Arkansas, and even Massachusetts, it was from Oklahoma that the bulk of the emigrants came. It is for this reason, then, that the present discussion will center around the Negro milieu in Oklahoma.

Eastern Oklahoma had early received a relatively large Negro component, both from migration into the area and from the residual Negroes who had earlier come as slaves with members of the Five Civilized Tribes. The component swelled in the years prior to statehood, when a number of all-Negro communities were founded in the state.

In the first days of these all-Negro towns, little difficulty was encountered with the whites. They were relieved, it seems evident, at the voluntary maintenance of residential segregation, a pattern which had functioned for so long in the Deep South. Further, land was sufficiently abundant that the Negroes posed no immediate threat to white economic success. Previous to statehood, too, elections were entirely local, each town electing officials to manage its affairs, so that a large Negro element in any part of an area could be dismissed as a political non-sequitur, posing, after all, no danger to white political supremacy in the all-white towns.

The Negroes moved into the all-Negro communities from other states in response both to new and available land and the hope of finding economic and social equality on this ambiguous frontier. For the Negro family resettling in Oklahoma, a town like Boley (the largest and most dominant of the Negro communities) constituted an exclusively operated Negro entity, physically independent of white communities and, at least superficially, unconnected with the economic matrix of the white areas. The all-Negro town was not interpreted by the Negro as a ghetto, but rather as a racial experiment, a manifest example of Negro self-fulfillment.

The early Negro immigrants into Okfuskee County (in which Boley is located) were principally laborers. Though many of these men had come to work on the railroads with embryonic ideas of remaining, they were essentially rootless. As the area boomed, though, ever-increasing numbers of Negroes moved in with their families, and townsite promoters, some free-lancing for an easily made dollar, others designated by the railroad, established the all-Negro towns and sold land to all comers. In time, these enclaves became well enough established to attract middle-class professionals from the Deep South and the border states. These people, vocationally frustrated in their previous homes, trooped to Oklahoma in the hope of making use of their special skills and training in a context of unrestricted opportunity without the familiar prejudices of superordinate whites.

The later migrants, recruited with vigor from the South, were principally farmers, individuals who had been lured to Oklahoma by brochures and the elegant blandishments of the Negro press at Boley.

The development of the self-fulfillment ethos in the Negro towns was largely the result of the middle-class professionals, though, with grim irony, they suffered least in the disillusionment which ultimately beset the Negroes. It was especially true for the professional that the articulation of a "great opportunity" motto was most important, since the Negro farmers were already finding their own self-fulfillment in the sheer ownership of land.

With the constant reiteration of the self-fulfillment goal in the press, and with the reinforcement of this goal by the prestigeful and economically centripetal middle-class, the farm population ultimately interiorized the ethic and conceived themselves in their current occupancy of the land as evidence of great success for their race.

Race relations in general were somewhat indefinite in this area. Negro-white contacts were minimal, and the whites tended even to find something a little amusing in the development of all-Negro enclaves. In addition, there was the "frontier" context in which there was a sharp situational difference from the plantation South. The traditionally backward economic status of the South was relieved, and the whites could well afford to allow the Negro a new freedom, one which he could not have afforded to grant before.

In the context of the new freedom, the Negro communities flourished and gained notably in size. Five years later after the founding of Boley, the vicinity immediately surrounding the town had nearly five thousand Negroes in residence. The same phenomenal growth, but to a proportionately smaller degree, was experienced by the other Negro towns.

It was not really until the first election that the whites began to realize slowly what Negro numerical dominance in this almost artificially democractic environment might mean. In 1906, when the State Constitutional Convention was held, the Boley vote numbered nearly 300. The white towns, of which there were three immediately surrounding Boley, cast 875 votes. But these votes were split almost evenly between the Republican and the Democrat delegates, and the Boley vote, almost a solid bloc against the Democrats, threw the election to the Republicans. The whites did not tarry, recognizing the Convention vote as but an insignificant rehearsal of what was to come. When the first local election after statehood was held in Okfuskee County, the Negroes captured the Republican County Convention with no difficulty, named two Negroes to the slate as county commissioners, and, to the absolute dismay of the whites, proceeded to elect this slate at the September election. The whites moved rapidly, and the County Election Board declared the returns from the Negro precincts invalid. Though the case underwent almost immediate litigation, a series of maneuvers pushed it through the higher courts until at last the State Supreme Court upheld the action of the Election Board. From the point of view of the Negroes, the clearly immoral act of the Election Board had now received official sanction, and the character of race relations in the county now underwent a drastic, definitional change. To the Negroes, the Supreme Court decision was essentially irrelevant, since it was reached at the end of the terms of office which their duly elected commissioners would have held. The important fact had been the summary dismissal of the Negro vote, for clearly this pointed the extent to which the whites were prepared to go in their disenfranchisement of the Negroes. The evasively worded decision of the Supreme Court some two years after litigation began simply reiterated in more awesome form the white affirmation that Negro dreams of equality, to say nothing of control, were vapid.

Election after election, the Negroes were defeated. Gerrymandering, cavilling objections to the Republican slate (which remained for some time the Negro-Republican slate), and outright threats of physical violence to the person of the Negro who attempted to exercise his franchise were all employed as tactics. The very symbol of equality which the Negroes had demanded in their increasingly unfeasible empire now became an anathema. With the vote, the Negroes came into open conflict with white interests; without it, they regressed to the positions they had held in the South. Finally, in 1910, the people of Oklahoma settled the problem in another way by approving a constitutional amendment which effectively removed the Negro from the political scene on the basis of his ancestry. The disenfranchisement was complete.

Shortly after the enactment of the "grandfather clause," the whites in Okfuskee and adjoining counties, having now had the Negro defined as politically non-existent, attempted to render him physically non-existent as well. Little by little, through unashamed threats Negro farmers were displaced by whites, and Farmers' Commercial Clubs enlisted members who signed oaths in which they bound themselves not to employ Negro labor. The patent object of the organizations was to choke off Negro emigration into the county and to encourage Negro exodus from it. Though many Negroes resisted the persuadings of the Clubs (violence was constitutionally outlawed to their membership), others felt greater discomfort by their persistence. Unlike the townspeople, well-insulated in their strongholds, the farmers had no place of retreat, and it was with them that the whites had the greatest vis-a-vis contact.

By 1913, a brutal lynching had taken place in the county, again punctuating the growing feeling that the Negro would not be tolerated on any but the most subordinate of grounds.

The falling price of cotton contributed additional hardships to the Negro communities, and many farmers lost their holdings altogether. Totally unable to withhold their crops for a day of higher prices, they moved quietly away to the urban centers of the state. Many left Oklahoma altogether, for it was now becoming as infamous for its race contacts as the South.

Into this fertile context in which the Okfuskee Negroes were pathetically casting about for a new solution to their problems walked Alfred Charles Sam. Full of vision of a mass exodus from what had now become a land of mockery, and with the apparent support of His Majesty's Government, Sam was a potent figure indeed.

Sam had been raised in a small town in the interior of the Gold Coast. During his youth he attended the Basel Mission Society School at Kibi, and there had come into contact with European traditions. As a young man, Sam was occupied in several rubber exporting ventures, and it was during this period that he conceived his idea of establishing an exclusively Negro trading company that would traffic in goods between the United States and his African homeland.

In 1911, he came to the United States for the first time, and formed here a corporation in terms of which he could effect his plan. Taking its name from the land of his birth, the Akim Trading Company flourished briefly, transporting tropical products to New York. In early 1913, however, and for reasons compelling to Sam, he chose to short-circuit the New York offices of the company, and independently drew up contracts with several London fruit merchants. When the Gold Coast-New York trade fell off, Sam was called for an accounting before his board of directors. In a fashion which later became typical of him, he was unable to give a clear accounting of his actions, and he was hastily impeached by an angry board and dropped entirely from the company.

Unconcerned with this setback, Sam promptly formed a new company, and unembarrassedly called it the Akim Trading Company, Ltd. He incorporated it for one million dollars, splitting the stock into forty thousand shares. In his prospectus, he not only provided for trade between the Gold Coast and the United States, but "in foreign countries as shall from time to time be found necessary and convenient." He also proposed to found a "college of agriculture and industry in all the trades of manufacturing and agriculture . . . (and to) construct hotels, restaurants, bath houses, theaters, and other places of amusement.

The real and most immediate purpose of the company, however, was to sell stock. Sam had earlier corresponded with a number of leading Negroes in Oklahoma, and had been invited to visit Okfuskee County and describe the opportunities which Africa offered. Sam arrived in the state May 11, 1913, with a plan which was marvelously simple.

The principal business of the company was to conduct trade. But since the ships to be used (and yet to be acquired) would be large, it would be possible to transport a limited number of colonists to the Gold Coast on each voyage. These people would be established on lands for which Sam had previously arranged and would promote colonies, designed both as havens for American Negroes and as centers of instruction for Africans. Since the company would soon be engaged in a highly lucrative trade, the cost of transportation for the colonists would be small. Sam decided that the purchaser of any one share of stock would be entitled to a trip to Africa for himself and his dependents. Food for the voyage would be provided on board for a slight additional fee.

Sam's personal contacts in the state were supplemented by clubs, formed under the aegis of P. J. Liddell, a "professor" from Boley who came ultimately to be the executive secretary of the African group. The clubs were organized throughout the state, intent upon spreading the word of the African return, and selling, incidentally, Sam's stock.

Sam himself met personally with large groups of people during the remainder of the year. His appeal was extraordinary, and there was no denying its durability. With each encounter he attracted more people to the movement, and his activities soon spilled over into Kansas, Texas and Arkansas....

The movement, meanwhile, grew by leaps and bounds. Despite Sam's periodical warnings to his followers that they should maintain their farms until the affairs of the movement were better formalized, and despite his awareness that ten ships the size of the Curityba could not carry his now five thousand stockholders to Africa, many of the colonists, eager to be done with Oklahoma, sold their possessions and cheerily established themselves in tent-cities at Weleetka. During the late fall of 1913, the "Gold Coast Camps" were quite pleasant. Freed from the routine agriculture duties which had annually characterized their lives, they interacted socially with one another and talked about their future in Africa.

As winter came on, however, the camps became centers of despair. Food and clothing were short, and the majority of the colonists had invested all their excess capital in the movement. Waleetka, a small town, afforded no opportunities for employment and starvation seemed to be imminent.

Sam's plan at the moment was to outfit the Curityba, which he had lately renamed the Liberia, in New York and then to sail to Galveston, where he would pick up the waiting colonists. But delays and financial insolvency had slowed the outfitting of the vessel, and the date for her departure from the East Coast changed almost weekly.

Finally, on January 30, the Liberia moved into the harbor at Saltpond after five months at sea. The landing was the fulfillment of every hope for the passengers, and one of them, writing home, likened it to the return to Canaan of the Israelites.

Though the Gold Coast natives welcomed the Negroes with open arms and open houses, the British Colonial Government felt somewhat differently. While the ship had been at sea, the Governor had summarily caused legislation to be enacted which imposed a hundred and twenty-five dollar per capita tax on each colonist who landed in the Colony. Such a sum was to be held by the proper authorities against the return of the colonist in the event of his destitution on the Gold Coast. Already crippled financially, this last sum was almost impossible for the colonists to raise. But Sam finally produced the amount and the colonists were permitted ashore.

Sensing the difficulty, and having had vague communications with one of the pioneers, a friend back in Oklahoma petitioned the American State Department for relief of the now stranded victims of Sam's scheme. But the State Department, acknowledging the condition of the emigrants, remarked that it had no funds available for such repatriation.

The British, still determined to do what they could to prevent additional ingresses of American Negroes, turned their attention to the Liberia. The government had forbidden the sale of coal to the ship and had, thereby, effectively stranded it at a point between Saltpond and Annamabou. The colonists were permitted to move on and off the vessel at will, though many of them preferred makeshift accommodations at Saltpond.

The crew of the ship, unpaid from the beginning of the voyage, finally brought charges against Sam, and, as he fled, the government seized the vessel and sold it, reimbursing the claimants. The crew finally made their way home as distressed seamen, though the equally distressed passengers languished in Africa.

Although black migration to California did not peak until after World War II, there was always a small but steady movement of blacks thereto. This culminated in the formation of several all-black communities, among which the most notable was that at Allensworth, California. In concluding her discussion of this community, Delilah Beasley comments: "There are many districts in California where there are well organized Negro settlements, namely: Furlong Tract and Albia, but Allensworth is the only one governed by Negroes, and it is destined to become a real city." But, this was not to be.

Document 2*

Delilah L. Beasley, The Negro Trail Blazers of California, Los Angeles, California, 1919, pp. 154-57 (reprinted by Greenwood Press, a division of Williamhouse-Regency, Inc.).

Allensworth, California, is a settlement of colored citizens located south of Hanford in Tulare County. It was founded by the

*Reprinted by permission of the publisher.

late Colonel Allensworth, who, together with a number of other colored gentlemen, in 1908 organized the California Colony and Home-Promotion Association. It was officered as follows: President, Colonel Allensworth (retired) chaplain of the Twenty-fourth Infantry of the United States Army; secretary, Professor W. A. Payne, formerly principal of Grant County colored school of West Virginia. The remaining members of the company were: Dr. W. H. Peck, J. W. Palmer, a Nevada miner, and Harry Mitchel. The company received its state corporation papers in 1908 and immediately began to find a suitable location for a tract of land for colonization. Mr. Oscar Overr was one of a committee of five gentlemen sent out to look over the present tract with regard to colonizing the same. Mr. Overr was so impressed with it that he purchased twelve acres immediately, but soon sold his holdings for a handsome margin, which enabled him to make another purchase of twenty acres. From this beginning has grown the prosperous town of Allensworth, California, which is destined to be one of the greatest Negro cities in the United States.

The company of colored gentlemen who had made it possible for this colony, almost immediately placed the land on the market. They met with encouragement, colored citizens not only purchasing, but locating and building good homes. They were not only settlers, but pioneers in spirit and deeds, willing to toil and hustle for development.

The rapid settlement of the colony necessitated the establishment of a school for the colored children of the colony. Through the county superintendent of schools, a Mr. Walker, of Visalia, in 1910 they secured a county school for the colony of Allensworth, California, and a school house was built. The following are the names of the members of the first school board of the colony of Allensworth, California: President, Mrs. Allensworth; Secretary, Mrs. Oscar Overr, and Mr. W. Hall, member of the board.

In 1912, Allensworth was made a voting precinct school district, and in 1914, a judicial district, covering an area of thirty-three square miles. The school is a regular County school, the district being known as Allensworth school district, and ample funds are furnished to carry on the work. A state fund of $550 for every teacher employed, also a County fund of $120 per average attendance, and, when occasion demands, there is available a district or special fund. The work of Allensworth school, which has been equipped with all modern apparatus for school work, including a good piano, is on a par with that of any other district school in the State of California. The building is so arranged that it can be thrown into an assembly room. It is truly the Allensworth social center. Services are conducted there on Sabbath, while a stage with two dressing rooms make it possible to hold entertainment in it. When the school was first established, through the influence of Mr. O. Overr the Pacific Farming Company donated enough lumber to build the school-house, the Alpaugh school district supplying the money for its teacher. To the surprise of this district the colony selected a colored teacher, Mr. William A. Payne. Later, when the school warranted, another teacher was appointed in the person of Miss Whiting from Berkeley. The rapid growth of the colony soon made it necessary to erect a large school building to accommodate the children of school age. The colony having been declared a school, voting and judicial district by the County Board of Supervisors in 1914, the citizens of Allensworth voted bonds to the amount of $5,000 for a new school-house and furnishings. Upon the completion of the building, Mrs. Allensworth donated the old building for a library. She remodeled it and dedicated it to the memory of her mother, Mary Dickinson, and the building is now known as "The Mary Dickinson Memorial Library" and reading room of Allensworth, California....

While hundreds of race men all over the State are anxious about employment, Allensworth citizens are given all they can do. Were there a larger population they could secure many contracts. Their steadiness, honesty and integrity make them much sought after in Tulare and adjoining counties. Not only are they given ordinary employment, but they have secured valuable contracts, to-wit:

George Johnson, carpenter, has built many excellent homes in the vicinity, and was given the contract to build the school-house in the colony; Travis & Hedges, plasterers, keep in their employ continually four men, and at present are completing the building of a forty-room hotel at Corcoran, doing the brick work and plastering; John Morris is a well driller and a driver of traction engines. He has continuous employment on large ranches; John Heitzig, a wealthy farmer, continually employs a force of Negro workmen; W. H. Dodson, formerly of Oakland, is manager of several acres and is king of the poultry business in that district; W. H. Wells constructed more than $6,000 worth of irrigation ditches for the Pacific Farming Company; Oscar Overr is general manager of the Lambert-Detwiler interests and has a force of men continually under his supervision. A number of others find profitable employment in harvesting grain and sugar beets and in the gathering of fruits. Elmer Carter, a young man of business foresight, readily seized the opportunity to open a livery barn in Allensworth. He has a number of excellent horses, good-looking vehicles and a good barn to keep them in, and he takes care of the rapidly-growing traffic between Allensworth and vicinity.

Mr. Zebedee H. Hinsman conducts a general merchandising store. He has thoroughly prepared himself by studying and graduating from the National Co-operative Realty Company of Washington, D. C. He was appointed notary public for Tulare County by ex-Governor Hiram Johnson, and is the Allensworth agent for the Home Insurance Company of New York. Mr. Hindsman places the value of his stock in the general merchandise store at $7,000. He also conducts a coal and feed yard and owns four town lots. Mr. G. P. Black, coming from Cleveland, Ohio, owns twenty acres of land, ten of which he has planted in alfalfa and eight in grain which averages about twenty-five bushels to the acre. He also has raised twenty-nine turkeys from two turkey hens and has three cows, a beautiful span of horses, a modern home and a charming wife.

Mr. Hedges, coming from Cleveland, Ohio, owns a modern cement house and has a chicken ranch with every modern improvement. It is not only the most sanitary the writer has ever visited, but is a gem in its uniqueness. Mr. Hedges does cement work and is also a member of the Allensworth Water Company. Mr. Powell, coming from Pueblo, Colorado, has ten acres in grain. He has a son who graduated from the high school of Alpaugh, California.

Mr. Anderson Bird, formerly a member of the Twenty-fifth Infantry, U. S. Army, Company D, having been retired, moved his family to the town of Allensworth and purchased five acres of land. He is a very successful raiser of sugar beets. Mr. George Archer, coming from Logan County, Kansas, owns five acres on which he cultivates sugar beets and which yield three tons to the acre. He also owns a larger number of chickens and pigs and a modern home. Mr. John and Mrs. Vena Ashby were among the first inhabitants of the colony, coming from Pueblo, Colorado. He is employed as section boss on the Santa Fe Railroad, and is also a member of the Allensworth Water Company. Sergeant James Grimes, from the Twenty-fourth Infantry (retired), U. S. Army, owns eleven and a half acres. Mr. Wallace Towne came from New York City because of poor health, never expecting to regain it. After a residence of three years in the colony of Allensworth he has fully regained his health and owns and manages a forty-acre ranch. He has planted one-half in wheat and the remainder in barley and hay. He has sold as high as one hundred and fifty sacks of wheat from twenty acres, at two dollars a sack. He owns six horses, eight cows, four heifers, four pigs, and one hundred and fifty broilers, thirty-five hens (he usually keeps two hundred hens), one hundred young ducks and four old ducks. Previous to coming to Allensworth he married Miss Annie Wanter, of Washington, D. C., who is truly a helpmate, so cheerful, kind and helpful to all in the colony. Mr. Towne is actively engaged in every movement for the interest of the colony and is a prominent citizen of the County.

THE EMERGENCE OF NEW LEADERSHIP FOR SOCIAL MOVEMENTS

Perhaps the most controversial speech ever made by an American Negro was the address of Booker T. Washington to the Atlanta Exposition on September 18, 1895. The prominent educator called for blacks to exercise self-help and mutual aid with the approval and assistance of likeminded, or at least sympathetic, whites. Washington, however, appended a qualifying utterance which not only denied the desire of blacks for social intimacy with whites but, more importantly, in the opinion of his critics, abdicated to whites the exercise of political rights and action. Although his appeal was received most favorably by many prominent whites and, ironically, helped to catapult Washington himself into a situation in which he could make political decisions affecting the lives of other blacks, Washington's speech and his subsequent actions were to alienate the emerging Negro intelligentsia. The Reverend J. W. E. Bowen subtly repudiated Washington on the same forum a month later, and DuBois, William Monroe Trotter, the Grimké brothers and many others opposed him also. Compared to the thought and actions of these men, the Washington approach to social welfare seems naive.

Document 3

Booker T. Washington, "The Atlanta Exposition Address," Up From Slavery, An Autobiography, (New York: A. L. Burt Company, 1900), pp. 219-20.

A ship lost at sea for many days suddenly sighted a friendly vessel. From the mast of the unfortunate vessel was seen a signal, "Water, water; we die of thirst!" The answer from the friendly vessel at once came back, "Cast down your bucket where you are." A second time the signal, "Water, water; send us water!" ran up from the distressed vessel, and was answered, "Cast down your bucket where you are." The captain of the distressed vessel, at last heeding the injunction, cast down his bucket, and it came up full of fresh, sparkling water from the mouth of the Amazon River. To those of my race who depend upon bettering their condition in a foreign land or who underestimate the importance of cultivating friendly relations with the Southern white man, who is their next-door neighbor, I would say: "Cast down your bucket where you are"--cast it down in making friends in every manly way of the people of all races by whom we are surrounded.

Cast it down in agriculture, mechanics, in commerce, in domestic service, and in the professions ... Our greatest danger is that in the great leap from slavery to freedom we may overlook the fact that the masses of us are to live by the production of our hands, and fail to keep in mind that we shall prosper in proportions as we learn to dignify and glorify common labour and put brains and skill into the common occupations of life; shall prosper in proportion as we learn to draw the line between the superficial and the substantial, the ornamental gewgaws of life and the useful. No race can prosper until it learns that there is as much dignity in tilling a field as in writing a poem. It is at the bottom of life that we must begin, and not at the top. Nor should we permit our grievances to overshadow our opportunities.

To those of the white race who look to the incoming of those of foreign birth and strange tongue and habits for the prosperity of the South, were I permitted I would repeat what I say to my own race, "Cast down your bucket where you are...." Casting down your bucket among my people, helping and encouraging them, as you are doing on these grounds and to education of head, hand, and heart, you will find that they will buy your surplus land, make blossom the waste places in your fields, and run your factories ... we shall stand by you with a devotion that no foreigner can approach, ready to lay down our lives, if need be, in defense of yours, interlacing our industrial, commercial, civil and religious life with yours in a way that shall make the interests of both races one. In all things that are purely social we can be as separate as the fingers, yet one as the hand in all things essential to mutual progress.

In a subtle answer to the speech of Booker T. Washington, delivered a month later at the Atlanta Exposition, the Reverend Dr. Bowen appeals to "American sentiment, who is the King, for equality of opportunity in all matters that effect the welfare of the state." Particularly, he refers to that equality of opportunity which would place "the education of the Negro on a par with that of the white man." Anticipating the phrase to be used some thirty-odd years later in the Harlem Renaissance, he challenges America to take notice of the emergence of the "New Negro," and to receive the "New Negro" into the body politic of American society. Dr. Bowen, like Dr. DuBois, and other young and well-educated blacks, resisted any restrictions placed upon their opportunity to acquire an education, expecting to use their intellect to formulate plans for intelligent social action beneficial to other blacks.

Document 4

J. W. E. Bowen, An Appeal to the King, (The Address Delivered on Negro Day in the Atlanta Exposition, October 21, 1895), Atlanta, Georgia, n.d., 8 pp.

Our ears have become familiar to the so-called race problem which has been popularly interpreted to mean the Negro race problem. A truer and larger conception of the subject would speak of the human race problem, instead of the narrower Negro race problem. This great problem assumes different names in different parts of the world. We have nihilism in Russia, socialism in Germany, communism in France, socialism and the submerged tenth in England, while in the United States it is as multiform in its elements as the nation is composite in its blood physiognomy. In California it is the problem of the Chinese, in the great middle west it is the Scandinavian and other foreign struggles: in the north, central and eastern states it is the Irish and Italian problem, while overreaching all of these is the problem of the battle for bread, and in the south it is the Negro problem. It is, therefore, no sign of breadth of vision to declare that there is only one great problem in the United States and that one is the Negro problem. These problems will require centuries of persistent effort that they may be solved upon the ethical and equitable basis of the New Testament teachings. In dealing with all of these the principles of equality and of brotherhood should obtain. It is a basal and sociological truth, that other things being equal, like treatment and like opportunities produce like results, the breadth and quality of which will depend upon native power and inherent ability. What is the condition of the development of the noblest type among men? There can be but one answer to this question, namely, equality of opportunity. The largest struggle of human society is to obtain this concrete reality of civil justice. Under it, each will produce according to his ability for the good of mankind, and that good will not be a passive uniformity cast into the stereotyped mold of racial capacity, but will be complex in its essentials and divinely human in its cast....

When it is asserted that he must be a worker, all sensible Negroes answer yea and amen? A worker in clay wrenching from nature her hidden stores; a worker in wood, iron, brass, steel and glass turning the world into an habitation fit for the Gods; a worker in the subtile elements of nature in obedience to the original command to subdue and conquer it; a worker in the realm of mind contributing to the thought products of mankind, thereby vindicating for himself a birthright to the citizenship of the republic of thought; a statesman in church and the state; a publicist and a political economist; in short, he must be a man among men, not so much a Black man but a MAN though black. And for the attainment of all the possibilities of his rich, unexplored African nature of docility and tractability; of enthusiasm and perseverance with his burning African fervor, there must be measured to him as well as to the white man three feet to make a yard. Such an equality of opportunity not only establishes an equality of responsibility, but must be reached before human society shall prosper under the normal laws of true development. The Negro does not shrink nor ask to be exempted from the working of the latter half of this statement, namely, equality of responsibility; but simply prays to the American sentiment, who is the King, for equality of opportunity in all matters that effect the welfare of the state. In all matters relating to the security of the homes of the people and the institutions of the republic, we say to the king that the story of our past fealty is the best answer we can make touching our future devotion and interest. It is on record for us, written by one of the greatest of democratic presidents, Andrew Jackson, that we may be actuated by lofty purposes as seen in the noble defense made by Negro soldiers of the city of New Orleans in the second British war. It is on record for us that in all of the social upheavals between capital and labor the Negro has never been found with fire brand in hand. We point with pride to our loving and lucid history that we are humane as well as human.

Before asking now what is the Negro's place in American

civilization, a larger question comes into notice that effects all men, namely, what is the place of any branch or family of the human race in the sum total of humanity? The man who attempts to answer this question will risk his wit. The Negro's place will be what he makes for himself, just as the place of every people is what that people makes for itself, and he will be no exception to the rule. The method whereby he shall make that place us under consideration. One class contends that he must make it by staying in the three "R's" and they are specially at pains in ridiculing the higher education of the Negro's, even for leaders in church or state. Yea, he must learn the three "R's;" he must master the king's English and then he must plume his pinions of thought for a flight with Copernicus, Keppler and Herschel; he must sharpen his logic for a walk with Plato, Emanuel Kant and Herbert Spencer; he must clarify his vision for investigations with Virchow, Huxley and Gray; he must be able to deal in the abtruse questions of law as do Gladstone, Judge Story and Judge Speer; he must fortify himself to divide rightly the Word as do Cannon Farrar, Bishop Foster, Bishop Haygood, Dr. John Hall and Dr. H. L. Wayland. In short, the education of the Negro must be on par with the education of the white man. It must begin in the kindergarten as that of the white child and end in the university as that of the white man. Anything short of this thorough preparation for all of the stages of life for the Negro would be unfair to a large part of humanity. We ask that nothing be done that would spoil his nature or masculate his personality, but let everything be done that would fit him to fill every situation in life that man may fill from the blacksmith and hod carrier to the statesman and philosopher. And if such preparation require a knowledge of the old blue black spelling book or of Aristotle's logic; a knowledge of the plow or the trip hammer of the spade or of the driving wheel; or of simple addition or integral calculus; or the first reader or Kant's "Critique," simple justice and common sense require that he be acquainted with whatever shall fit him to fill his station in life. Does this mean that the Negro be turned into a white man? Is he to be so educated that he will cease to be what God meant that he should be? Nay! verily, for any education that makes a people dissatisfied with their racial personality is a farce and a reproach....

... The Negro's present days of infancy and of small beginnings are no criterion to measure his future by. The depths from which he has come and the obstacles surrounding him must be remembered when expressing judgment of him; and when superficial writers on the other side of the water, as well as on this side, declare that the Negro can never assimilate a high civilization nor approach the present attainments of the Anglo-Saxons, they discover an immaturity of thought worthy of the schoolboy's effort. This proves that the social problems of any country are to be learned only by long years of contact and of unprejudiced study. A railroad observation in sociology may make fascinating reading, but it lacks the elements of endurance and accuracy and cannot command the respectful notice of more than novelistic readers for one decade. To understand the rapid strides that the Negro has taken one must know the pit from which he was digged, and the rock from which he was hewn. The cold facts of his present standing press out in bold relief with the distinctness of a mosaic and declare that there is a wealth unmeasured in that hidden mine. The first step has been taken and if the south and the north will measure to him an equality of opportunity there will come as the result splendid achievements for society. He longs to have a full chance; he longs to do nobly.

Finally, oh king! a new Negro has come upon the stage of action. As you enter the main entrance of the Negro building you will observe the statue of a Negro with broken manacles upon his wrists. This statue was born in the fruitful brain of a Negro, Mr. Hill of Washington. His frame is muscular and powerful; his eye is fixed upon his broken but hanging chain; his brow is knit in deep thought. This is the new Negro. What is he doing? He is thinking! And by the power of thought he will think off those chains and have both hands free to help you to build this country and make a grand destiny of himself. In generous affection for our native soil, in fealty to our institutions and in a universal love for all men, his spirit is that of his fathers made over. Being to the manor born, he cannot be alienated in sentiment and patriotic devotion to the institutions of the south and the whole country. It must be, remembered however, that this Negro has had born in him the consciousness of a racial personality under the blaze of a new civilization. With this new birth of the soul, he longs to have an opportunity to grow. With this new birth of the soul, he longs for an opportunity to grow into the proportions of a new and diviner manhood that shall take its place in the ranks of one common humanity. This Negro, when educated in all of the disciplines of civilization and thoroughly trained in the arts of civil and moral life, cannot fail to be an invaluable help to our American life. It is his deepest desire to rise and work manfully and he is willing to bide his time until the American white man shall have that element conquer in him which always conquers, namely, the love of fair play. Having been so generously treated by our southern friends in this exposition, we shall go forth to prove to them that, in the development of the south and in the protection of our institutions, we are at heart one with them. And in the classic words of Edmund Burke before his constituents in Bristol, England, we pray: "Applaud us when we run; console us when we fall; cheer us when we recover; but let us pass on, for God's sake, let us pass on."

The cumulative effects of racism, expressed in the economic and political disabilities laid upon blacks, reinforced by terrorism and violence as expressed in lynchings and rioting, triggered the realization that a national organization which would take effective action in behalf of the civil rights of blacks was sorely needed. These documents report the holding of the two conferences collectively known as the Niagara Movement, both called into being by Dr. W. E. B. DuBois, who became the General Secretary. Although significant in its own right, the Niagara Movement was especially so because, eventually, most of its leadership was attracted into the newly-formed civil rights organization, the National Association for the Advancement of Colored People, a more broadly based organization with an interracial membership.

Document 5

"The Niagara Movement," (Editorial), The Voice of the Negro, Vol. II, No. 8, August, 1905.

The Niagara Movement

A remarkable conference of colored men was held at Fort Erie, Ontario, on the 11th, 12th, and 13th of July. The conference was called by Dr. W. E. B. DuBois, Professor of Sociology and Economics in Atlanta University, and was attended by some of the strongest colored men of the United States. The conference was called for the purpose of beginning organized, determined, aggressive action to oppose certain underhanded methods of strangling honest criticism, manipulating public opinion and centralizing political power by means of improper and corrupt use of money and influence; to organize thoroughly the intelligent and honest Negroes throughout the United States for the purpose of insisting on manhood rights, industrial opportunity, and to encourage independent men and newspapers. The time was ripe for such a conference and the men who responded to the call were earnest. In the next issue of the Voice we shall give a more detailed account of the conference. In addition to our account, we shall publish an article from the pen of Dr. DuBois giving the objects of the conference. We shall also publish the address of the conference to the country, which address we regard as quite the strongest declaration of principles any Negro convention has given to the country in fully a half century. The conference called itself "The Niagara Movement," and elected Dr. DuBois as its General Secretary.

Document 6

W. E. B. DuBois, "The Niagara Movement," The Voice of the Negro, Vol. II, No. 9, September, 1905, pp. 619-622.

The Niagara Movement

What is the Niagara Movement? The Niagara Movement is an organization composed at present of fifty-four men resident in eighteen states of the United States. These men having common aspirations have banded together into an organization. This organization was perfected at a meeting held at Buffalo, N. Y., July 11, 12 and 13, 1905, and was called "The Niagara Movement." The present membership, which of course we hope to enlarge as we find others of like thought and ideal, consists of ministers, lawyers, editors, business men and teachers. The honor of founding the organization belongs to F. L. McGhee, who first suggested it; C. C. Bentley, who planned the method of organization and W. M. Trotter, who put the backbone into the platform.

The organization is extremely simple and is designed for effective work. Its officers are a general secretary and treasurer, a series of state secretaries and a number of secretaries of specific committees. Its membership in each State constitutes the State organization under the State secretary.

Why this organization is needed. The first exclamation of any one hearing of this new movement will naturally be: "Another!" Why, we may legitimately be asked, should men attempt another organization after the failures of the past? We answer soberly but earnestly, "For that very reason." Failure to organize Negro-Americans for specific objects in the past makes it all the more imperative that we should keep trying until we succeed. Today we have no organization devoted to the general interests of the African race in America. The Afro-American Council, while still in existence, has done practically nothing for three years, and is today, so far as effective membership and work is concerned, little more than a name. For specific objects we have two organizations, the New England Suffrage League and the Negro Business League. There is, therefore, without the slightest doubt room for a larger national organization. What now is needed for the success of such an organization? If the lessons of the past are read aright there is demanded:

1. Simplicity of organization.
2. Definiteness of aim.

The country is too large, the race too scattered and the rank and file too unused to organized effort to attempt to impose a vast machine-like organization upon a wavering, uncertain constituency. This has been the mistakes of several efforts at united work among us. Effective organization must be simple--a banding together of men on lines essentially as simple as those of a village debating club. What is the essential thing in such organization. Manifestly, it is like-mindedness. Agreement in the object to be worked for, or in other words, definiteness of aim.

Among ten million people enduring the stress under which we are striving there must of necessity be great and far-reaching differences of opinions. It is idle, even nonsensical, to suppose that a people just beginning self-mastery and self-guidance should be able from the start to be in perfect accord as to the wisdom or expediency of certain policies. And some universal agreement is impossible. The best step is for those who agree to unite for the realization of those things on which they have reached agreement. This is what the Niagara Movement has done. It has simply organized and its members agree as to certain great ideals and lines of policy. Such people as are in agreement with them it invites to co-operation and membership. Other persons it seeks to convert to its way of thinking; it respects their opinion, but believes thoroughly in its own. This the world teaches us is the way of progress.

What the Niagara Movement proposes to do. What now are the principles upon which the membership of the Niagara Movement are agreed? As set forth briefly in the constitution, they are as follows:

(a) Freedom of speech and criticism.
(b) An unfettered and unsubsidized press.
(c) Manhood suffrage.
(d) The abolition of all caste distinctions based simply on race and color.
(e) The recognition of the principle of human brotherhood as a practical present creed.
(f) The recognition of the highest and best training as the monopoly of no class or race.
(g) A belief in the dignity of labor.
(h) United effort to realize these ideals under wise and courageous leadership.

All these things we believe are a great and instant importance; there has been a determined effort in this country to stop free expression of opinion among black men; money has been and is being distributed in considerable sums to influence the attitude of certain Negro papers; the principles of democratic government are losing ground and caste distinctions are growing in all directions. Human brotherhood is spoken of today with a smile and a sneer; effort is being made to curtail the educational opportunities of the colored children; and while much is said about money-making not enough is said about efficient, self-sacrificing toil of head and hand. Are not all these things worth striving for? The Niagara Movement proposes to gain these ends. All this is very well, answers the objector, but the ideals are impossible of realization. We can never gain our freedom in this land. To which we reply: We certainly cannot unless we try. If we expect to gain our rights by nerveless acquiescence in wrong, then we expect to do what no other nation ever did. What must we do then? We must complain. Yes, plain, blunt complaint, ceaseless agitation, unfailing exposure of dishonesty and wrong--this is the ancient, unerring way to liberty, and we must follow it. I know the ears of the American people have become very sensitive to Negro complaints of late and profess to dislike whining. Let that worry none. No nation on earth ever complained and whined so much as this nation has, and we propose to follow the example. Next we propose to work. These are the things that we as black men must try to do:

To press the matter of stopping the curtailment of our political rights.
To urge Negroes to vote intelligently and effectively.
To push the matter of civil rights.
To organize business co-operation.
To build school houses and increase the interest in education.

To open up a new avenue of employment and strengthen our hold on the old.
To distribute tracts and information in regard to the laws of health.
To bring Negroes and labor unions into mutual understanding.
To study Negro history.
To increase the circulation of honest, unsubsidized newspapers and periodicals.
To attack crime among us by all civilized agencies. In fact to do all in our power by word or deed to increase the efficiency of our race, the enjoyment of its manhood, rights, and the performance of its just duties.

This is a large program. It cannot be realized in a short time. But something can be done and we are going to do something. It is interesting to see how the platform and program has been received by the country. In not a single instance has the justice of our demands been denied. The Law Register of Chicago acknowledges openly that "the student of legal and political history is aware that every right secured by men either individually or as a nation has been won only after asserting the right and sometimes fighting for it. And when a people begin to voice their demand for a right and keep it up, they ultimately obtain the right as a rule." The Mail and Express says that this idea is "that upon which the American white man has founded his success,"--all this but--and then have come the excuses: The Outlook thinks that "A child should use other language." It is all right for the white men say the Mail and Express, but black men--well they had better "work". Complaint has a horrible and almost a treasonable sound to the Tribune while the Chicago Record-Herald of course makes the inevitable discovery of "Social Equality." Is not this significant? Is justice in the world to be finally and definitely enough to protest, or shall the sneer of the Outlook and its kind be proven true that out of ten millions there are only a baker's dozen who will follow these fifty Negro-Americans and dare to stand up and be counted as demanding every single right that belongs to free American citizens? This is the critical time, Black men of America; the staggering days of Emancipation, of childhood are gone.

God give us men! A time like this demands
Strong minds, great hearts, true faith, and ready hands;
Men whom just office does not kill;
Men whom the spoils of office cannot buy;
Men who possess opinions and a will;
Men who have honor, men who will not lie;
Men who can stand before a demagogue,
And damn his treacherous flatterers without winking.
Tall men, sun-crowned, who live above the fog
In public duty and private thinking.
For when the rabble, with their thumb worn creeds,
Their large professions and their little deeds,

Mingle in selfish strife--lo, Freedom weeps,
Wrong rules the land, and waiting Justice sleeps.

Document 7

J. Max Barber, "The Niagara Movement at Harper's Ferry," The Voice of the Negro, Vol. III, No. 10, October, 1906, pp. 402-412.

Heretofore we have given the history and aims of the Niagara Movement. Thinking that this issue of the magazine might fall into the hands of some person who does not know about the movement and fearing lest some of those who have heard about it either a vague or an erroneous idea of its aims and purposes, I shall give briefly my interpretation of the Niagara Movement.

The work of this movement for the first year has now passed into history. The men who belong to and sympathize with the Movement feel that they have cause for fervent gratulations. They say that the Negro's awakening is a great fact in the Nation's history and they claim credit for the breaking of this spell of apathy. Opposition was expected from the very day of the inauguration of this Movement. There are honest and dishonest opposers both white and black. The great body of Southern white people are bound to oppose us. The atmosphere in this section is charged with preconceived theories of racial inequality. In the South the time of reason is not yet. There are some colored people who doubt the wisdom of such fearless agitation at this time. In their breasts they want what we want but they differ honestly with us as to methods of procedure. There is a class of whites who believe with this class of colored people. They have our highest welfare at heart but they shrink from the consequences of our agitation. Then there is a class of black men who are paid to deprecate agitation and complaint, to counsel acquiesence in all kinds of abuses, to misquote history to show that the eschewing of politics by a race bodes good, and to put a quietus on our ambitions for equality. Paid? Yes, paid in dollars and newspaper notoriety, in the opportunity to hobnob with those high in authority and in the allotment of spheres of influence. Lastly there is that class of Northern hypocrites like Lyman Abbott, who indulge in fine sneers, senseless sophistries, subtle-phrase-mongering against us merely because we embarrass the nation by insisting that she enforce her own laws. But from whatever source comes the opposition, the Niagara Movement is here and is here to stay. In the years to come it will undoubtedly become a great civic and political power in this country.

Four things stand out as principal events at the Harpers Ferry meeting. They were the recapitulation of the history of the movement and the work accomplished during the first year of its existence, the celebration of John Brown's one hundredth anniversary, the enlarging of the scope of the Movement and the beginning of certain definite and aggressive work against class legislation.

The summarization of the work of the year showed that the organization had directed its energies towards two objects: first, it has thrown itself forward as the exponent of high ideals, of all that is noble and high and holy in a people, and second it has worked for equal opportunity for the races. When I say that the Niagara Movement has stiffened the backbone of the Negro race, I am aware of the fact that the principles of the Movement have reached but a few, comparatively speaking, of the masses of our people. But the Movement marks the beginning of a new epoch. It is the tiny piece of leaven which we expect to leaven the whole lump. Ideas travel with amazing rapidity and gather accelerated force as they go. We have reached the leaders of the people and depend upon them to reach the masses. Still we will never be satisfied until every black man in this country knows that he is not tethered to some kind of sub-human super-animal world, but that he is a man and as such belongs to strive for and demand all the duties and privileges of a full-fledged man. The underlying facts of society warrant us in saying that when that day comes the Negro will be treated as a man. He cannot feel that he is a man without improving his environments, and this done, he will never be content to merely hold the towel at the white man's toilet.

As to definite and tangible work accomplished, we shall refer to some of the principal reports of states committees. In many of the states, Niagara Movement men worked in conjunction with suffrage leagues, protective leagues and health societies. That but shows the fluidity of the Movement. It was organized not to get credit and name, not for merely posturing and phrase-mongering, but for work. Wherever the Movement in a state or town has been too weak to work alone or could help to advance the cause of justice by cooperation with other organizations or men, it has done so. We know that schismatic action and disruption of strength are synonymous and we are not hankering after mere fulsome flattery.

It is hard to tell which state organization--that of Illinois or that of Massachusetts--did more work last year. Both states did good work. Dr. Charles E. Bentley as Secretary of the Illinois branch of the Movement gave a very interesting report of the work in his state. The first constructive work of the Illinois State organization was the securing of the appointment of a colored man on the new charter committee for the city of Chicago. This appointment was secured from Mayor Dunne after the colored people had been turned down by a Republican governor and legislature. Certain newspapers in Chicago were calling upon the charter convention to separate the races in the public schools. Dr. Bentley and his associates managed to secure the appointment of three men as the Education Committee whose views they knew. A Committee from the I. B. Niagara Movement has secured from the Education Committee the assurance that a law will be incorporated in the charter prohibiting the separation or segregation of the races in the public schools. It was interesting to see how the N. M. managed the "Clansman" in Chicago. When Dixon went to Chicago with his new play he met very little notice. The Niagara Movement was responsible therefor.

The opinions of the Chicago colored people varied all the way from bomb-throwing to injunctions. Jane Addams of the Hull House was consulted. She sympathized with the colored people and called a conference of all the prominent dramatic critics of Chicago. The conference decided to take no notice of the play. All of the dramatic critics of Chicago pledged themselves to abide the decision of the conference. "The Clansman" went to Chicago, stayed seven weeks and left without a line of advertisement save that it paid for and a few unfriendly literary criticisms of one or two papers. They called it an aesthetic blemish and desired to be done with it. The Illinois men also did effective work against the Warner Amendment to the Rate Bill. When Chicago abolished her justice shops and police courts and instead established municipal courts, Niagara Movement men succeeded in having one of her number appointed as one of the judges.

The Massachusetts men have been very active in their state. Their two great fighters were against the Warner Amendment to the rate bill and against the appropriation of money by the Massachusetts legislature to the Jamestown Exposition, unless Virginia should stipulate that all citizens of Massachusetts regardless of color should receive the same treatment on the Exposition grounds. The Massachusetts men probably deserve the credit for the death of the Warner Amendment. They did not quite succeed in their fight on Jamestown Jimcrowism but they fought right nobly.

In Maryland Secretary Waller worked with the Maryland State Suffrage League and aided materially in overwhelming Gorman's disfranchisement propaganda. There were good reports from Waller of Brooklyn, Mitchell of Philadelphia, and Gunner of Newport, R. I. McGhee of Minnesota, told of an interstate conference in the west and some definite work in St. Paul. The reports of all the Committees showed that the men were working.

The most interesting session of the whole four days at Harpers Ferry was John Brown's Day. The day opened with a pilgrimage at six o'clock to the Old John Brown Fort, which is not in the village of Harpers Ferry, but about a mile from the town. It was placed here when it was returned from the World's Fair some years ago. At the Fort Richard T. Greener, Ex-Consul to Vladivostok, gave some personal recollections of Brown. In the afternoon two great speeches were made, one by General Secretary W. E. B. DuBois, and the other by Rev. Reverdy C. Ransom of Boston. The concensus of the competent pronounced Dr. DuBois' address the most remarkable analysis of the history of American slavery and of John Brown's relation thereto that has been delivered publicly in many a year. The address was profound and scholarly and claimed the intellectual admiration of the entire Convention. Mr. Ransom followed in the most eloquent address the writer has ever listened to. He spoke on "The Spirit of John Brown," and before he was through speaking everybody in the house must have felt that John Brown's spirit was with us. Men and women who had attended the New England anti-slavery meetings fifty years ago said that they had witnessed nothing like the enthusiasm in that meeting since the dark days of slavery. Women wept, men shouted and waved hats and handkerchiefs and everybody was moved. Mr. Ransom's address will be found in another column of the magazine. John Brown could not have imagined as he looked through the barred windows of his dungeon that some day such a remarkable tribute would be paid to him on the very ground where he made his gallant stand. But the old Puritan is not one of the vanishing figures of history.

On the stage behind Mr. Ransom sat Louis Douglass, son of Frederick Douglass, Richard T. Greener, who has personal recollections of John Brown and Mrs. Evans, mother of Bruce Evans of Washington, mother-in-law of Mr. Daniel Murray of the Library of Congress, sister to Sheridan Leary who was killed October 19th, 1859, fighting with Brown at Harpers Ferry, and aunt to John Copeland who was in the raid and was hanged at Charlestown. Mrs. Evans was asked to say a word. In a voice made slender by age she told of the bravery, the love for freedom and the self-sacrifice of her kinsmen in dying as they died for the race. Of her brother she said his enemies paid him the tribute of saying that he was a very brave man. The whole audience hung with bated breath upon every word uttered by Mrs. Evans and what she said made a great impression. John Brown Day was full of inspiration; it were worth a trip across the continent to have been there.

A trip to old Charleston the next day gave the Movement an opportunity to see the jail where John Brown was incarcerated, the court house where he was tried, spot where he was hanged. Souvenirs from all of these places were gathered.

The Niagara Movement will gradually enlarge its work from time to time in order to meet the demands of the hour. This year several new departments were added, but probably the most notable was the Women's Department. Hereafter women will be admitted to full membership on an equal footing with the men. There are now the Legal, Suffrage, Civil Rights, Army and Navy, Suppression of Crime, Health, Educational, Press, Pan-African, Women's, Junior, Art, Economic and Religious Departments.

Definite work will be done this year against Jimcrowism and disfranchisement. The movement will not try to cover the whole country in rash haste but hopes to secure two or three significant court decisions. As stated above Niagara men are glad to and will work in conjunction with any organization or anybody who is honestly seeking to uproot these evils. What we want to do is to dislocate meanness and injustice.

In this organ of the Niagara Movement, W. E. B. DuBois announces the formation of the National Association for the Advancement of Colored People: its objectives, the methods it expects to employ, the honorary committee of one hundred citizens and the officers of the Association. In the same issue of Horizon, under an article entitled "Our Grievances," DuBois states that "as the most complete and clearly reasoned formulation of our grievances, we reprint a portion of the call of the National Independent Political League for a convention to meet at Atlantic City, August 4th and 5th." It is a vigorous and inspiring document of protest against the disfranchisement of blacks, the completion of which is charged to President William Howard Taft.

Document 8*

W. E. Burghardt DuBois, "The National Association for the Advancement of Colored People," The Horizon, Vol. VI, No. 2, July, 1910, pp. 1-2.

On the one hundredth anniversary of Abraham Lincoln's birth there was issued in New York City a call to conference. This call was signed by Jane Addams, William Lloyd Garrison, Jenkin Lloyd Jones, Brand Whitlock, Charles Edward Russell, Mary W. Ovington, William English Walling and others. The manifesto said: "Is this not a fitting time for the Nation to contemplate the condition of its Colored citizens?"

As a result of this call two conferences have been held in New York City: in May, 1909 and 1910. These conferences were earnest quiet talks with a few public meetings at which speakers of national prominence expressed themselves in no uncertain terms.

The result was the formation of the National Association for the Advancement of Colored People.

The object of this organization is to arouse and organize public opinion among American citizens to the present unjust treatment of Colored citizens and to the danger of such treatment to the democratic and religious ideals of the land.

The methods of work employed by this organization will be simple and direct, and will consist in the main of:

a. Getting reliable information.
b. Placing such information at the disposal of the public.
c. Publishing tracts, pamphlets and a monthly periodical.
d. Maintaining a legal bureau in connection with the Constitution League.
e. Endeavoring to increase co-operation in the efforts of the Colored people and their friends in all directions.
f. Holding conferences and public meetings and maintaining a

*Reprinted by permission.

lecture bureau.

The Association is organized as follows: At its head stands an honorary committee of one hundred citizens....

The Association occupies a suite of offices at 20 Vesey Street, New York, in the building of New York Evening Post.

In other words we have at last organized and started a business organization, housed in the metropolis of the Nation and devoted to the solution of the Negro problem in accordance with the best ideas of modern philanthropy and democracy. Back of the organization stand men of thought, heart and wealth--all we need now is your help and co-operation....

Our Grievances

Those who read any considerable number of race papers, and indeed those who do not, must be impressed by the widespread dissatisfaction, even resentment, that is manifest and is being expressed concerning the present conditions and tendencies in political affairs, which, in this country, comprehend or involve all affairs.

Much of the complaining, particularly from the heretofore knuckle-close writers, turns on a narrow, but not a wholly un-important, ground; that of office-holding.

As the most complete and clearly reasoned formulation of our grievances, we reprint a portion of the call of the National Independent Political League for a convention to meet at Atlantic City, August 4th and 5th. This national convention of Colored citizens is called under what grave conditions touching the object of this organization, the supreme aim of which is to maintain and secure for all Colored Americans the same rights and privileges of citizenship as are enjoyed by the other citizens of these United States of America?

In the Southern States 95 per cent of the nine million Colored citizens of the United States are deprived of the exercise of the ballot, the fundamental right under our system of government, without which there is for citizens neither protection nor freedom. This rape of the ballot is consummated in plain violation of the national constitution which forbids denial of the right to vote because of race or color. The executive head of the federal government within sixteen months officially admitted this disfranchisement in inaugural address and palliated the violation of the federal constitution instead of declaring his purpose to enforce the law in obedience to the oath he had just solemnly taken. President Wm. H. Taft even intimated the legality of those devices for nullifying the 15th Amendment by State laws which are as much worse than fraudulent practices as law is stronger than custom. The Legislative branch of the federal government, specifically clothed with power to enforce the suffrage articles of the constitution, has viewed with apathy and inaction their flagrant violation save when actively condoing (sic) it by seating congressmen elected under the violation as against centestants (sic) entitled to seats if the federal law had been obeyed in their districts in the South. The judicial branch has dodged the issue in all cases brought involving Southern disfranchisement laws, thus by persistent refusal of relief strengthening the nullification and emboldening the nullifiers of the supreme law of the land.

But what train of evils were let loose upon Colored Americans with disfranchisement! In the Southern States unequal and oppressive laws have destroyed all their civil rights, excluding them from public places of business, of accommodation, or resort, even public parks and public libraries, barring from State quasi-public and public schools, forcing them into separate and inferior schools, fastening upon them the public ignomy and caste stigma of segregation in public travel, casting them even into peonage. They are under the tyranny of taxation without representation. Left in that hopeless and helpless condition of citizens without voice as to law-maker, law-enforcer, or law interpreter, they are not only the victims of injustice in the courts, but, denied all trial by court or jury, are the prey of the fiendish white mob, until now the almost daily lynching of human beings has disgraced our country before the civilized world.

Inevitably this race persecution infects the North. Color prejudice is on the increase. Discrimination based on color in civil rights and in economic opportunities is gaining ground. Jim crow cars have reached the borders of the national capital, twice color disfranchisement has raised its horrid head above Mason and Dixon's line, while bloody race riots and barbarous lynchings have reached up to Illinois, even to the home of the martyred Lincoln.

Most harmful and portentous of all in this crusade of race hate and color prejudice is the action, under the present administration, of the federal government itself. For the first time in the United States a President has officially proclaimed color a political disability. By his declaration that he would not appoint colored citizens to office where white citizens objected, he completed Southern disfranchisement. It is colored soldiers who are the victims when for the first time a battalion is discharged wholesale and without trial because of an alleged affray with civilian, and the new departure, aggravated by the failure to establish individual guilt after trial, is boldly continued. That unique degredation [sic] of free citizens, segregation and nationalized by a federal commission, while the federal court in support declares the right of even an interstate railroad to segregate colored passengers.

Unless one-eighth of the citizens of the United States are to be reduced to political serfdom, unless our Republic is to abandon democracy for the caste of color, this present trend must be resolutely opposed. Graver crisis in a Republic could hardly be.

THE RURAL SCENE

The majority of blacks in the South continued to live in rural areas, and their struggle for survival was challenged by many efforts to restrict their attempts toward social mobility. Two particularly nefarious practices that were rampant throughout the South were 1) peonage and 2) convict leasing.

Not the least among their many problems was the lack of opportunity to sell their labor in a free market. The actions of state and county governments, particularly in post-Reconstruction days, were supportive of efforts of private white planters and farmers to reintroduce slavery under the guise of peonage.

The following document comments on the decision made by the United States Supreme Court, March 13, 1905, in the case of Clyatt v. United States regarding what constitutes involuntary servitude, or peonage. According to Loren Miller:

> Peonage, permissible under the Spanish law and widespread in New Mexico was just a cut above slavery: the state compelled the workman to serve the landowner or employer to whom he had become indebted. After ratification of the Thirteenth Amendment Congress passed sweeping legislation nullifying all state laws protecting peonage and punishing all individuals who attempted its practice. The validity of such legislation insofar as it purported to punish individuals reached the Court in 1905, in the case of Clyatt v. United States.[6]
>
> ... Whatever its other shortcomings, the case settled the issue that congressional legislation punishing individuals for holding others in a state of peonage was valid. No man could compel another to work out a debt.[7]

Document 9

"The Peonage Law Upheld," The Voice of the Negro, Vol. 2, No. 4, April, 1905, pp. 222-223.

On the 13th of March, the United States Supreme Court handed down a decision which has a more or less vital bearing upon agricultural conditions in the South. Samuel L. Clyatt, a white man of Georgia, had been tried and convicted by the Circuit Court of Appeals of the Fifth Circuit of the State of holding two colored men in involuntary servitude. Clyatt appealed the case to the United States Supreme Court. The case was argued before the Court by some of

Georgia's best lawyers. Clyatt set up the contention that the peonage legislation was unconstitutional and that even if it were constitutional, it could not apply in his case. He claimed that the definition for peonage would not cover his case inasmuch as he had never "returned" these men to involuntary servitude. He had simply caused the arrest of Gordon and Ridley for larceny on warrants issued by a Georgia magistrate, and when he brought them to Georgia, he requested them to work out a debt. The Court held that there was no evidence introduced to sustain the charge that these men had been held in a state of peonage. However, it held that the peonage legislation is constitutional and it could apply to individuals as well as corporations or states. It seems perfectly clear to us that Clyatt had violated the statute under which he was tried, for he had caused to be arrested two men who owed him debts. To leave him without paying these debts he considered larceny, and so he had brought them back to his place to compel them to work out these debts. The men did the work under stress. They would have settled the debts otherwise or not settled them at all. This is holding men in involuntary servitude and Clyatt should suffer the penalty of the law. But in these days, when the United States Supreme Court interprets anything pertaining to the Negro so that it will not be considered a slap in the face of Southern sentiment, we could hardly expect much better. Probably we should be thankful that the Court sustained the validity of the peonage statutes at all. It ought to be mentioned that Justice Harlan dissented from the opinion of the Court, saying that there was sufficient evidence to make a case against Clyatt.

Despite continued racist practices, there was evidence of organized ways to meet some of the needs of black people. In this essay Miss Rossa B. Cooley, who eventually succeeded to the leadership of the Penn Industrial Institute, St. Helena Island, reports the progress in rural community development on the Sea Islands, the site of the first governmental program in social welfare. In this area the leadership provided by missionary and other sympathetic whites was of the greatest importance, involving the kinds of cooperation and social relations envisioned by Booker T. Washington. Aloof from the conflict engendered by competition with whites in cities, this black population, overwhelmingly the majority, had a modest success. It will be seen, however, that eventually the children of this community were unable to resist the lure of the big city. (See Clyde V. Kiser, Sea Island to City, A study of St. Helena Islanders in Harlem and Other Urban Centers, New York: Columbia University Press, 1932.)

Document 10*

Rossa B. Cooley, "The Regeneration of Colored Population in the Rural South," Proceedings of the National Conference of Charities and Corrections, 38th Session, Boston, 1911. (Fort Wayne, Indiana, the Fort Wayne Printing Company, 1911), pp. 107-110.

There could be no more hopeful subject than that upon which I have been asked to speak and while I come to you from a Sea Island off our South Carolina Coast, I come from the midst of a rural population of over 6,000 Negro people among whom are only some 50 white. As a worker among these Sea Island Negroes I can speak of their regeneration--but on the whole problem, that is, the regeneration of the Negro population of the rural South,--I can speak only as a student and observer.

Those of us who have lived in the South during the last fifteen to twenty years have watched with interest an increasing tendency toward cooperation among the educators.

When Anna T. Jeanes left her fortune to be used for the betterment of the small Negro rural schools, a step was taken for the advancement of the entire rural South. In large sections of the South the children have a term of from one to four months school. As would naturally follow, the buildings are quite inadequate for their purpose; dreary and poorly maintained. The children often learn in spite of the conditions, rather than because of them. This would all seem hopeless had there not been a new note struck and did we not know that the better things are coming and that they are coming to every out-of-the-way corner of our rural districts.

The Jeanes Board is studying the present situation and schools are changing and whole communities are changing.

What is being done in Henrico County, Virginia, can be done in every county of the South, and at no far distant day we shall see a change in our present inadequate country schools. A young Negro woman has been appointed under the auspices of the Jeanes Rural School Fund as Supervisor of the Negro schools of Henrico County. In each of the schools she has organized School Leagues, introduced industrial work and helped the school teacher. Twenty-three schools are thus brought into a closer organization, school terms are lengthened and the buildings kept in good repair, as well as being made more attractive. Other Supervising Industrial teachers are being sent out by this Board and in every case the community is uplifted and education is made more real.

In all our Southern States, except two, supervisors of rural schools are now appointed. This is indeed a step forward. It is natural perhaps that this attention should be given to the white

*Reprinted by permission of the National Conference on Social Welfare.

schools, in many cases fully as bad and in some cases worse than the Negro, but there is every reason to believe that before very long the Negro schools will be as carefully supervised. Already in Virginia there is a Supervisor of the Negro Rural Schools, Mr. Jackson Davis, a Virginian of the white race, an educator of high rank, and his success will go far toward making the people in other States realize the necessity of there being such an officer appointed.

In all of this awakening, and it is indeed an awakening in the real sense, the work among the farmers through the farm demonstrators organized by Dr. Seaman A. Knapp, is of greatest importance. Beginning with one acre, prepared, fertilized, planted and cultivated according to the instructions of an experienced farmer; the farmers in the South have been aroused; they have been educated by the results, made enthusiastic and given a new courage. What this means in a discouraged or indifferent community of farmers must be felt rather than described.

On St. Helena Island there is a Negro community of about 6,000 among whom would be found some 50 white people. This island must be reached in an open boat from Beaufort on Port Royal Island where is the nearest railroad station, a half hour's row and a drive of six miles over Ladies Island brings you to St. Helena and here you find what might be called a thoroughly Negro Rural Community. The isolation of the people, the difficulties of mingling with people of the white race, has resulted in their retaining the real characteristics of the Negro people in a greater degree, perhaps, than anywhere else in our country.

As you drive along the white oyster shell road you will meet the Negroes who greet you courteously. You will find yourself among a very polite people and if you live among them you will find them a grateful people. There is the desire to do what they can and as in Africa the gift of the egg to the guest is common; so on St. Helena eggs are urged upon us.

These Negroes are a religious people. This is true generally of the Negro race, but our people are more realistic and there is a greater earnestness in their religion. As one of the old men said in the Praise House: "God done gib de white folks a heap of things, but He ain't forgotten we, cause He gib we religion and we have a right to show it out to all the world. De Buckra (white people) deys got de knowing of de whys and de hows of religion, but dey ain't neber got de feel ob it yet."

All day Sunday is usually spent in church going. The Island children are taught to pray in the silence at "Day Clean" (sunrise) turning toward the East because there is the dawn of the new day.

The language of the people is filled with odd words and expressions due doubtless to their isolation. Here are some of their expressions: "The fever am still very rapid." "I tell ooner (you) de years walk along fast." "Water do be most becoming now, and if he cold ain't follow him, de crops sure be glad." "Ain't yo got no shoes keener to the mout." "Some white folks are so feeling able." "It has a rising of the ground."

Probably 98 per cent of the people are farmers, raising a bare living on land that is equal to giving rich results. They are land owners and among them you find the self respect that is always found among very proud people who own their homesteads. The whites have been friendly to them, and there has been little race friction.

If we had gone out into the cotton fields less than 50 years ago we would have found the people naked to the waist, men and women, working from "day clean," sunrise, till sunset. There were 61 plantations and the large majority were field hands who had no civilizing contact with white people. They talked a strange dialect, keeping many of their African words. Their religion was most crude, for the terms of the Christian religion which they imitated were but little understood. Their homes were but mere sleeping places, cheerless and comfortless one-room cabins, with bunks built in for beds. A log brought from the nearby woods served for chairs. The iron pot in which they cooked their meals was their only cooking utensils and oyster shells, worn smooth in the service, served as spoons.

Now in these same fields are the Negroes, descendants of those I have just described. But the people I have just left on that Sea Island are self-respecting farmers. Their homes have 2, 3 or 4 rooms, and some have 2 stories. Most of them are whitewashed and painted, a sure sign of progress in the rural South.

How has this change come about? There have been two forces at work. When the Union Army was victorious, the whites fled to the mainland and the Island was soon after put in charge of Northern white men who were to direct the Negroes until they could buy land. The plantations were sold off in small holdings of about 10 acres and they were bought by Negroes who have proudly held on to the land and in many cases added to the acreage.

Some missionary teachers went down with the soldiers and plantation directors, and two of them, Miss Towne and Miss Murray found Penn School.[8] They went down to show these people who had been left entirely without leaders, how to help themselves. They did heroic service and to them much of the credit is due for changing these people from the half naked ignorant workers in the field to self-respecting land holders and home owners.

Another circumstance combined to help in this work of uplifting a people. The merchant who happened to go to that Island became a friend of the people and urged them to keep out of debt, so the mortgage crop system which has so terrible a grip on some parts of the South did not get so firm a hold on our people.

Farming methods are very primitive and uninteresting. Is it any wonder that the young people want to leave the rural districts and go to the cities? They hear of the high wages and easier work; they know nothing of the expenses of living and you know the history of the large majority. One of the young men of our Farmers' Conference who had been asked to study the physical condition of the young people of one population who had gone to the city, said in his report: "In round figures I may say 1-3 comes back to visit; dey is solid; 1-3 comes back sick, dey is wrapped up in disease such as consumption--dey is damaged; and 1-3 comes back all ready for de graveyard, no good to nobody."

The school founded in 1862 became an industrial school in 1904, organized under a board of trustees of which Dr. H. B. Frissell of Hampton Institute is chairman.

We have to be more than a school. We must be a center for education and inspiration for the people along all lines. The school is built on the farm. We have our class rooms and our shops, where they can take off their own shoes and learn how to mend them, also where they can learn how to make African baskets like those brought over by their ancestors from Africa. The girls have lessons in housekeeping which are needed to be applied to their own homes. In our Extension Work, the farmer goes from the school farm to the outside farm. Last year we began with 6 men who were willing to take a half acre and plant it exactly according to his instructions. A Negro minister raised 54 bushels to the acre where in previous years he had only raised 16 bushels. This year 63 men are doing that kind of work on their own land, and some of them are on the nearby islands. Our farmer goes to these different farms and gives instructions, and others are getting instruction from the Negro farmers. The indirect influence is greater than I can tell you. The school teachers come into our school for their inspiration once a month with all their school children to hold a temperance meeting. We have an audience of 600 to 800 school children and through them we fight drunkeness. That organization has been existing 40 years.

In all of this work the home and the farm must be the basis. The Negroes are needed in the rural South. Experiments with immigrant labor show that the Negro is the best worker for those conditions and if we make the conditions favorable, the young Negro will stay in the country.

Typical of the conferences held to deal with the problems of the rural black population were those of Hampton and Tuskegee Institutes. For example, 238 persons attended the Hampton Negro Conference in 1912 to discuss several subjects, including "amusement and recreation in relation to the efficiency of everyday life."

Document 11*

W. E. Burghardt DuBois. "Play for Negroes," The Survey, (August 17, 1912), Vol. XXVIII, No. 20, pp. 641-642.

Something of the spirit which informs the movement of Negro betterment in 1912 was shown at the recent meeting of the Hampton Conference, by the enthusiasm with which the leaders of the race in agriculture, the ministry, business and social work discussed the subject of amusement and recreation in relation to the efficiency of every-day life. Negro ministers who had gone on record as opposed to all forms of dancing and who had vigorously insisted that the Negro of the present needed to buckle down to hard work and sober thought, were finally won over to the cause of furnishing young colored people with legitimate and health-giving amusements.

Mrs. G. W. Cook, of Washington, D. C., outlined the growth of the play movement. She emphasized the importance of adapting play to the child's "play ages"--the dramatic stage, the self-assertive or "big Injun" stage, and, finally, the critical period of adolescence. She advocated story telling, as well as the reading and reciting of poetry, as part of the play life of children. To meet the problem of keeping the country child on the land and in sympathy with the life of those about him, Mrs. Cook declared that teachers would do well to take their "big Injuns" and show them the great advantages of country over city life by playing ball with them and indulging in various kinds of outdoor life to forestall the hankering for the city. She urged, too, the instilling in the child of a sense of responsibility toward work and life. The reports of seventeen colored teachers who are at work in eighteen counties in Virginia, under the direction of Hampton Institute, trying to secure the more complete co-operation of parents, ministers and teachers in improving school life, showed them to be carrying on school demonstration work aimed to give new life and fresh hope to neglected country districts.

Jackson Davis, supervisor of the rural elementary schools of Virginia, gave a summary of the industrial supervisors' work in Virginia, showing that work was carried on in eighteen counties, where there are 469 Negro schools with an average term of six months. In these schools over $6,200 has been spent on new buildings this year. There are in these counties 348 improvement leagues, and the Negroes in these counties gave in cash $13,744.16 for buildings, improvements, lengthening school terms, and industrial materials. One hundred and two schools have introduced individual drinking cups.

Prof. J. M. Gandy, executive secretary of the Negro Organization Society of Virginia, declared that today 32,228 Negroes, or 67 per cent of the 48,114 Negro farm operators, controlling 2,238,000 acres, own and operate their farms in Virginia. While the Negroes

*Reprinted by permission.

are not getting on an average as much produce per acre as the white farmers, Professor Gandy believes that with improved methods of soil cultivation the hard working Negroes of Virginia will soon be able to make a much better living on the farm. He summed up the real needs of Negro rural life as follows: reinforcement of the idea of keeping colored youth on the farm, of buying and improving land, of producing better crops and farm animals, of building better school houses, and of improving home life.

M. W. Reddick, principal of Americus Institute, Americus, Ga., described his method of raising money for Negro education among Negroes themselves. His school was organized in October, 1897, with the avowed object of teaching the colored people how to give for the improvement of their own race. It is owned by an association of seventy Baptist churches. The first year $154 was raised for education. Some of those who at that time gave one dollar are now contributing from fifty to one hundred dollars. The annual receipts have gone up to almost eight thousand dollars. By the publication of his accounts, Mr. Reddick has secured the cooperation of white and colored organizations as well as church workers.

George E. Haynes, of the social science department of Fisk University and director of the National League of Urban Conditions among Negroes, New York, gave the following as causes of the movement of colored people to the city: the divorce of the Negro from the soil; the growth of commercial and industrial centers; legislation affecting urban conditions; the relations of tenant and landlord; the influence of employment runners in the South; exaggerated stories of success in the city. In his opinion, the remedy lies "on the land," in farming and pointing out to rural Negroes the disadvantages and dangers of city life and "in town," in helping the Negro to adjust himself to his new environment.

Study of the 238 registration cards shows a distribution by states as follows: from Virginia, 173 delegates; North Carolina, 27; Kentucky, 4; South Carolina, 8; District of Columbia, 5; Maryland, 4; Georgia, 6; Tennessee, 2; Indiana, 2; Florida, 2; 1 each from Oklahoma, Connecticut, Mississippi, Delaware and Alabama. Occupations were represented as follows: teaching, 138; homemaking, 25; missionary work, 2; club workers, 4; ministers, 25; farmers, 15; dressmakers, 6. Practically all who attended the Hampton Negro Conference have been engaged in some form of professional or volunteer community work.

SURVEYING CONDITIONS FIFTY YEARS AFTER EMANCIPATION

The Survey was one of the few instances of white social welfare publications which addressed itself to reporting the problems of blacks. The documents cited below both appeared in the February

1, 1913, issue of The Survey, celebrating the fiftieth anniversary of the Emancipation Proclamation.

In the first, George E. Haynes explores the bases upon which there may be better social adjustment in the next fifty years than there had been in the previous fifty. He proposes conferences between blacks and whites in their local communities, and says that "each community with a Negro population needs a conscious plan and program. The two races must map them out together if success is to follow." In the second document W. E. Burghardt DuBois assesses the trends and developments, advances and disabilities of blacks since the Emancipation.

Document 12*

George E. Haynes, "The Basis of Race Adjustment," The Survey, February 1, 1913, pp. 569-570.

It is an axiom that justice is the basis of social order. It follows that it must be at the foundation in the adjustment of relations between nationalities and races. This idea of justice is broader than civic privileges, for it includes economic and social justice. It means that every individual should have an opportunity for physical, mental and moral development to the limit of his capacity. It waives the question of superiority and inferiority of individuals or races and vouchsafes to all the chance for self-realization. It means equal opportunity.

In the Negro's relation to the white people of America permanent progress can be made only by the increase of this type of justice. Equal chance for the Negro to get work; to hold work, to develop his capacity for work; equal protection of life and property; equal opportunity to educate his children to the limit of their varied capacity and to provide such a home for his family as his taste dictates and his purse allows; equal opportunity in sharing political responsibilities and of responding to the duties of citizenship, conditioned by character only, are fundamental conditions without which permanent adjustment cannot be made.

Another factor, which must grow stronger, is mutual confidence and sympathy between black and white citizens. Alfred H. Stone in his Studies in the American Race Problem points out the apprehension of white people about the Negro which grows out of "the association of ideas" of past experiences, especially during the reconstruction period. Although probably not arising from the same experience, there is apprehension in the Negro mind due to

*Reprinted by permission.

"association of ideas" which colors his view of the present attitude of white people toward him. To bring about amicable adjustment this apprehension of both races must be displaced by a mutual trust, which will expect only help the one from the other in their efforts for self-realization.

For centuries the Negro has been habitually sympathetic and unresentful. Prof. John W. Work of Fisk University, who for twenty years has gathered, set to score, studied and sung the Negro folk songs, says that in the nearly 500 he has collected not a rhythm or sentence of hatred, malice or revenge has been found. Probably every other passion of the human heart has been expressed in these songs. Most of these compositions are the sorrow songs of slavery. If this could come out of Egypt, nothing is improbable in the promised land of mutual sympathy between manly men.

Justice, confidence and sympathy must find community expression in co-operation. Competition, which tends to eliminate the weak, is not more fundamental than co-operation, which calls upon the strong to help the weak to attain strength. In fact, such just and sympathetic consideration is the purchase price exacted of the strength of the strong. But the Negro has valuable elements of strength to offer to American civilization. Music in the soul, meekness of spirit and wonder at the mysterious world are inner qualities of strength, though not reckoned by birth and banks and battleships.

In art, in literature, in music, in oratory, in education, in reform, in industry and in business, co-operation will bring rich rewards to both races.

But ideal principles must have practical application to foster adjustment between the two peoples in America. A long stride toward securing economic justice can be made by the labor unions extending a welcome to the Negro. Their interests are bound up with the industrial freedom of the Negro today as surely as the welfare of the free workingmen before the war was affected by slave labor. Civic justice will gain great headway when the Negro shares in its administration according to his capacity. A police force and judiciary in which he can have no part, regardless of his attainments, produce lukewarm loyalty; and political life from which color alone excludes him ties a millstone about the neck of democracy.

Newspapers are probably the greatest single agency for dispelling apprehension and developing mutual confidence. The periodicals and magazines come in for their share of influence. If in some way both the white and Negro papers could be induced to present the good qualities, attitudes and actions, past and present, of the races toward each other, the wisest prophet could not predict the impulse to progress which would follow.

When the more thoughtful elements of the white people and the Negroes in each community begin to confer together about their common problems, substantial advancement will have been made in race adjustment. Each community with a Negro population needs a conscious plan and program. The two races must map them out together if success is to follow.

Justice, equal opportunity, mutual confidence, sympathy and co-operation in developing the weak by the aid of the strong should bring us nearer to complete race adjustment during the next half-century than that to which we have attained at this jubilee year of emancipation.

Document 13*

W. E. Burghardt DuBois, "Social Effects of Emancipation," The Survey, February 1, 1913, pp. 570-573.

In endeavoring to sum up the results of emancipating the Negro slaves in the United States fifty years ago, it will be natural to note the material and educational advances the colored people have made; the evidences of group consciousness among them; their present legal and political status and the outlook for social reform.

In 1863 there were about 5,000,000 persons of Negro descent in the United States. Of these 4,000,000 and more were just being released from slavery. These slaves could be bought and sold, could move from place to place only with permission, were forbidden to learn to read or write, legally could never hold property or marry. Ninety per cent were totally illiterate and only one adult in six was a nominal Christian. Until 1863 the total slave population had been steadily increasing, and the South was passing laws to enslave free Negroes. The three-quarters of a million free Negroes had been equally divided between the North and South. Those in the South were a wretched, broken-spirited lot for the most part and slaves in all but name. Here and there in cities there were a few among them who were prosperous mechanics and property holders to a small extent.

The 250,000 Negroes of the North were the leaven and had been making for nearly a century a struggle for survival. They aided in the anti-slavery movement, had a few newspapers, and had produced leaders like Frederick Douglass and Harriet Tubman. They had planned and carried through a systematic migration to Canada where several prosperous settlements sprang up. They started schools in a number of cities and founded the catering business in Philadelphia. They had held several general conventions appealing for justice. For the most part these appeals fell on deaf ears, although Garrison Sumner, Phillips, Harriet Beecher Stowe and John Brown had come to their aid.

Nevertheless, up to the time of the opening of the war, the

*Reprinted by permission.

Negroes in the North were forced to live in the worst slums and alleys, were either excluded entirely from the public schools or furnished cheap and poor substitutes, and in 300 years only twenty colored men had received a college education. Except in parts of New England and partially in New York, the Negro was disfranchised and largely without civil rights. Indeed, the Fugitive Slave Law of 1850 made personal freedom difficult, and in 1857 the Supreme Court had declared that Negroes were not citizens, and that they had always been considered as having no "rights which the white man was bound to respect."

Then came the war, which was not started with the idea of liberating the slaves, but which soon showed the North that freedom for the Negro was not only a logical conclusion of the war, but the only possible physical conclusion. Two hundred thousand black men were drafted in the army and the whole slave support to the Confederacy was threatened with withdrawal. Insurrection was in the air and the emancipation of the slaves was needed to save the Union. Such, then was the situation in 1863.

Fifty years later, in 1913, there are in the United States 10,250,000 persons of Negro descent, an increase of 105 per cent. Legal slavery has been abolished, leaving, however, vestiges in debt peonage and the convict lease system. The freedmen and their sons have "earned a living as free men; shared the responsibilities of government; developed the internal organization of their race, and aspired to spiritual self-expression."

Economic Progress

The Negro was freed as a penniless, landless, naked, ignorant laborer. Very few Negroes owned property in the South; a larger number owned property in the North; but 90 per cent of the race in the South were field hands, servants of the lowest class. Today 50 per cent are farm laborers and servants, and over one-half of these are working as efficient modern workmen under wage contract. Above these, to use the figures of 1900, there are 750,000 farmers, 70,000 teamsters, 55,000 railway hands, 36,000 miners, 33,000 sawmill employes, 28,000 porters, 21,000 teachers, 21,000 carpenters, 20,000 barbers, 20,000 nurses, 15,000 clergymen, 14,000 masons, 13,000 dressmakers and seamstresses, 10,000 engineers and firemen, 2,500 physicians, and, above all, 200,000 mistresses of independent homes, and 2,000,000 children in school.

Fifty years ago the overwhelming mass of these people were not only penniless, but were themselves assessed as real estate. By 1875 the Negroes probably had gotten hold of something between 2,000,000 and 4,000,000 acres of land through their bounties as soldiers and the low price of land on account of the war. By 1910 this had increased to about 18,000,000 acres.

In 1890 Negroes owned 120,738 farms; in 1900 they owned 187,799; in 1910 they owned about 220,000. Thus, over 25 per cent of the Negro farmers owned their own farms, and the increase of farm owners between 1890 and 1910 has been over 83 per cent. The value of land and buildings owned by Negroes in the South was in 1910 $272,992,238. This is an increase of nearly 90 per cent in a single decade. This does not include land owned by Negro farmers but rented out. On a basis of the value of farm property in 1900, a committee of the American Economic Association estimated the value of Negro wealth in the United States at $300,000,000. On the same basis we can estimate the total Negro wealth today at $570,-000,000.

The Negro and Organization

Today the Negro is a recognized part of the American government; he holds 9,000 offices in the executive service of the nation, besides furnishing four regiments in the army and a large number of sailors. In the state and municipal civil service he holds at least 10,000 other offices, and he furnishes 500,000 of the votes which rule the Union.

In these same years the Negro has relearned the lost art of organization. Slavery was the absolute denial of initiative and responsibility. Today Negroes have 35,000 church edifices, worth $56,000,000, and controlling nearly 4,000,000 members. They raise themselves $7,500,000 a year for these churches.

There are 200 private schools and colleges managed and almost entirely supported by Negroes, and other public and private Negro schools have received in forty years $45,000,000 of Negro money in taxes and donations. Five millions a year are raised by Negro secret and beneficial societies, which hold at least $6,000,000 in real estate.

Above and beyond this material growth has gone the spiritual uplift of a great human race. From contempt and amusement they have passed to the pity and perplexity of their neighbors, while within their own souls they have arisen from apathy and timid complaint to open protest and more and more manly self-assertion. Where nine-tenths of them could not read or write in 1859, today two-thirds can; they have 200 papers and periodicals, and their voice and expression are compelling attention.

Already the poems of Dunbar and Braithwaite, the essays of Miller and Grimké, the music of Rosamond Johnson and the painting of Tanner are the property of the nation and the world. Instead of being led and defended by others, as in the past, they are gaining their own leaders, their own voices, their own ideals. Self-realization is thus coming slowly but surely to another of the world's great races, and Negroes are today girding themselves to fight in the van of progress, not simply for their own rights as men, but for the ideals of the greater world in which they live--the emancipation of women, universal peace, democratic government, the socialization of wealth, and human brotherhood.

This, then, is the transformation of the Negro in America in fifty years; from slavery to freedom, from 5,000,000 to 10,250,000, from denial of citizenship to enfranchisement, from being owned chattels to ownership of $570,000,000 in property, from unorganized irresponsibility to organized group life, from being spoken for to speaking, from contemptuous forgetfulness on the part of their neighbors to uneasy fear and dawning respect, and from inarticulate complaint to self-expression and dawning consciousness of manhood.

Legal Disabilities

Notwithstanding this creditable showing the present situation has dark and threatening aspects. First, we have in the United States the distinct growth of a caste system. It has been adjudged in many states a misdemeanor to call a white man a Negro; it has been adjudged in many states that a person having the slightest degree of Negro blood is a "Negro"; intermarriage of Negroes and whites is prohibited in twenty-six states even if the persons are living as man and wife; travel is interfered with by separating whites and Negroes in the South and it has been decided that Negroes do not have to be given absolutely "equal" accomodations; colored and white people are separated in the South on street cars, in waiting rooms, on many elevators, on steamboats, etc. In practice Negroes are liable to discrimination in hotels, restaurants, saloons, soda fountains, theaters, cemeteries, insane asylums and in the militia. This is forbidden by many northern states, but the law is difficult to enforce. Church organizations either refuse Negro members entirely, as in the case of most white churches of the South, or put them in an allied organization or in separate congregations. Separate school systems are compulsory in the South and allowed in a few northern cities, as Indianapolis.

In the courts, Negroes are not legally discriminated against, but an extra-legal system has arisen in the South, to a less extent in the border states and to some extent in the North, which tries and punishes the Negro criminal on an entirely different basis from the white criminal. The result is that the number of long-term Negro convicts is extraordinary. In the South it is unusual to send a white man to the penitentiary or to capital punishment, or to punish a white woman under any circumstances. The penitentiaries, therefore, are filled with Negroes, and are among the worst penal institutions in the world. They are, most of them, run for profit under the convict lease system. There are very few reformatories for colored children, and their conviction, therefore, means the manufacture of confirmed criminals. There is a widespread tendency, which shows no decided reduction, to murder by mob violence Negroes accused of crime. Since 1885, 2,584 such murders have taken place. Only 25 per cent of those lynched have been even accused of crimes against women, and in most of these accusations the offense alleged was not criminal.

Since 1890 five and a half million Negroes, over half of whom can read and write and who own fully $300,000,000 worth of property, have been practically deprived of all voice in their own government. The restrictions by which this has been accomplished are eight in number: 1. Illiteracy: the voter must be able to read and write. 2. Property: the voter must own a certain amount of property. 3. Poll tax: the voter must have paid his poll tax for the present year or for a series of years. 4. Employment: the voter must have regular employment. 5. Army service: soldiers in the Civil War and certain other wars, or their descendants, may vote. 6. Reputation: persons of good reputation who understand the duties of a citizen may vote. 7. "Grandfather" clause: persons who could vote before the freedmen were enfranchised or descendants of such persons may vote. 8. Understanding clause: persons may vote who understand some selected clause of the constitution and can explain it to the satisfaction of the registration official.

If these laws were impartially administered the result would be bad enough; but they are deliberately, openly and avowedly administered so as to admit any white man, however, ignorant, to the polls and to exclude any colored man however intelligent.

To illustrate the immediate effect of these disfranchising laws, the following statistical tables are given:

Louisiana

		White	Negro
1900	Population	729,612	650,804
1900	Males 21 years or over	178,595	147,348
	Literate	146,219	57,086
	Illiterate	32,376	90,262
1908	Registered voters	152,135	1,743

Lowndes County, Alabama

		White	Negro
1900	Males 21 years or over	1,138	6,455
	Illiterate	81	4,667
	Literate	1,057	1,788
1902	Registered Voters	1,097	39
1906	Registered Voters	1,142	52

Under a strict educational qualification the literate Negroes of Lowndes County could outvote all the whites, literate and illiterate, yet only fifty-two are given the franchise!

Social Reform and Educational Opportunities

The result of all this has been to retard public education and social reform among colored people except that which can be carried on in private institutions or by voluntary taxation.

In the North they share somewhat in the general results of social reform work. There is, however, in this field a great deal of discrimination. Social settlements often exclude them--the "Lincoln" settlement, for instance, in Boston; fresh air funds sometimes make no provision for them; day nurseries discriminate; and even where they are not actually discriminated against, they are not made to feel welcome. On the other hand, they have their full share, heaped up and running over, of all the disabilities due to city congestion and municipal misrule. So too they are common sufferers with the rest of the South, in the general backwardness of the southern states in education, in public health regulation, in inadequate provision for the insane, the feebleminded and the delinquent. They are sufferers without the power to vote for change.

The colored people through their women's clubs are bearing almost the whole burden of their own internal social reform. They have one hundred old folks homes and orphanages, about 40 hospitals (some of which have partial public support), at least 500 private cemeteries, and a large number of charitable organizations of various kinds.

Not only has the general enrollment and attendance of Negro children in the rural schools of the lower South and to a large extent of the city schools been at a standstill in the last ten years and in many cases actually decreased but many of the school authorities have shown by their acts and in a few cases expressed declaration that it was their policy to eliminate the Negro schools as far as possible.

There is a distinct endeavor to curtail the facilities of education which the Negroes already possess. This can be seen in the persistent campaigns carried on in the North and directed toward the North which say in effect, that the Negroes' education as carried on by northern philanthropists has been a mistake, that it is an interference with the local conditions in the South, and that the stream of benevolence ought to be stopped. There is no doubt but that this argument has had tremendous influence upon the benevolent public.

Again, there has been a continual effort to curtail Negro education by reducing the number of grades in the Negro public schools. Macon and Augusta, Ga., and New Orleans, La., are typical in this connection. The lack of public high schools for Negroes is one of the greatest drawbacks of the southern school system.

At the same time the Negroes are helping to pay for the education of the whites, in the sense that public monies which Negroes pay in indirect taxation or which are endowments from past generations are diverted entirely to white schools. A southern city school superintendent gives this table:

	Virginia 1907	N. Carolina 1908	Georgia 1907
Total cost of schools	$3,308,086.00	$2,958,160.00	$2,850,211.00
Cost of Negro schools	489,228.00	402,658.00	506,170.00
Per cent of total cost going to Negro schools	14.7	13.6	17.7
Per cent of Negroes in population	35.7	33.3	46.7
Negroes proportion of direct and indirect taxation and of endowments	$507,305.00	429,197.00	647,852.54

On the whole, the, it may be said that the efforts of the Negroes since emancipation have been very promising and beyond what could be reasonably expected; that, on the other hand, the caste system which attempts to exclude Negroes from the benefit of the general social and political organization of a great modern state is strong and growing both North and South, and is not only a hindrance to Negro-Americans but a serious menace to American democracy.

THE URBAN SCENE

The great influx of black people into the large Northern cities did not alleviate any of the social needs that were not met in the South; rather, further need was created, including that of helping blacks "to live in town." The following documents record the varied responses with which these new social conditions were met. However, the overwhelming concern remains with the total community.

In this document DuBois points with pride to the accomplishments of the Negroes of Durham and Durham County, North Carolina. He sees these economic accomplishments developing not only by black initiative, but with the encouragement of enlightened white philanthropy, led by professors of Trinity College (later to be named Duke University).

Document 14

W. E. Burghardt DuBois, "The Upbuilding of Black Durham," World's Work, Vol. 23, January, 1912, pp. 334-338.

Durham, N. C., is a place which the world instinctly associates with tobacco. It has, however, other claims to notice, not only as the scene of Johnston's surrender at the end of the Civil War but particularly today as the seat of Trinity College, a notable institution.

It is, however, because of another aspect of its life that this article is written: namely, its solution of the race problem. There is in this small city a group of five thousand or more colored people, whose social and economic development is perhaps more striking than that of any similar group in the nation.

The Negroes of Durham County pay taxes on about half million dollars' worth of property or an average of nearly $500 a family, and this property has more than doubled in value in the last ten years.

A cursory glance at the colored people of Durham would discover little to differentiate them from their fellows in dozens of similar Southern towns. They work as laborers and servants, washerwomen and janitors. A second glance might show that they were well represented in the building trades and it would arouse interest to see 500 colored girls at work as spinners in one of the big hosiery mills.

The chief interest of any visitor who stayed long enough to notice, would, however, centre in the unusual inner organization of this group of men, women and children. It is a new "group economy" that characterizes the rise of the Negro American--the closed circle of social intercourse, teaching and preaching, buying and selling, employing and hiring, and even manufacturing, which, because it is confined chiefly to Negroes, escapes the notice of the white world.

In all colored groups one may notice something of this cooperation in church, school, and grocery store. But in Durham, the development has surpassed most other groups and become of economic importance to the whole town.

There are, for instance, among the colored people of the town fifteen grocery stores, eight barber shops, seven meat and fish dealers, two drug stores, a shoe store, a haberdashery, and an undertaking establishment. These stores carry stocks averaging (save in the case of the smaller groceries) from $2,000 to $8,000 in value.

This differs only in degree from a number of towns; but black Durham has in addition to this developed five manufacturing establishments which turn out mattresses, hosiery, brick, iron articles, and dressed lumber. These enterprises represent an investment of more than $50,000. Beyond this the colored people have a number of financial enterprises among which are a building and loan association, a real estate company, a bank, and three industrial insurance companies. The cooperative bonds of the group are completed in social lines by a couple of dozen professional men, twenty school teachers, and twenty churches.

All this shows an unusual economic development and leads to four questions: (1) How far are these enterprises effective working businesses? (2) How did they originate? (3) What has been the attitude of the whites? (4) What does this development mean?

The first thing I saw in black Durham was its new training school--four neat white buildings suddenly set on the sides of a ravine, where a summer Chautauqua for colored teachers was being held. The whole thing had been built in four months by colored contractors after plans made by a colored architect, out of lumber from the colored planing mill and iron work largely from the colored foundry. Those of its two hundred and fifty students who boarded at the school, slept on mattresses from the colored factory and listened to colored instructors from New York, Florida, Georgia, Virginia, Pennsylvania, New Jersey, and North Carolina. All this was the partially realized dream of one colored man, James E. Shepard. He formerly worked as secretary for a great Christian organization, but dissatisfied at a peculiarly un-Christian drawing of the color line, he determined to erect at Durham a kind of training school for ministers and social workers which would be "different."

One morning there came out to the school a sharp-eyed brown man of thirty, C. C. Spaulding, who manages the largest Negro industrial insurance company in the world. At his own expense he took the whole school to town in carriages to "show them what colored people were doing in Durham."

Naturally he took them first to the home of his company--"The North Carolina Mutual and Provident Association," an institution which is now twelve years old. One has a right to view industrial insurance with some suspicion and the Insurance Commissioner of South Carolina made last year a fifteen days thorough examination of this enterprise. Then he wrote: "I cannot but feel that if all other companies are put on the same basis as yours, that it will mean a great deal to industrial insurance in North and South Carolina, and especially a great benefit to the Negro race."

The company's business has increased from less than a thousand dollars in 1899 to an income of a quarter of a million in 1910. It has 200,000 members, has paid a half million dollars in benefits, and owns its office buildings in three cities.

Not only is the society thus prosperous at present but, it is making a careful effort to avoid the rocks upon which the great colored order of "True Reformers" split, by placing its business on an approved scientific basis. It is installing a new card bookkeeping system, it is beginning to construct morbidity and mortality records, and its manager is a moving spirit of the Federated Insurance League for colored societies which meets annually at Hampton, Va.

The Durham office building of this company is neat and light. Down stairs in the rented portion we visited the men's furnishing store which seemed a business-like establishment and carried a considerable stock of goods. The shoe store was newer and looked more experimental; the drug store was small and pretty.

From here we went to the hosiery mill and the planing mill. The hosiery mill was to me of singular interest. Three years ago I met the manager C. C. Amey. He was then teaching school, but he had much unsatisfied mechanical genius. The white hosiery mills in Durham were succeeding and one of them employed colored hands. Amey asked for permission here to learn to manage the intricate machines, but was refused. Finally, however, the manufacturers of the machines told him that they would teach him if he came to Philadelphia. He went and learned. A company was formed and thirteen knitting and ribbing machines at seventy dollars apiece were installed, with a capacity of sixty dozen men's socks a day. At present the sales are rapid and satisfactory, and already machines are ordered to double the present output; a dyeing department and factory building are planned for the near future.

The brick yard and planing mill are part of the general economic organization of the town. R. B. Fitzgerald, a Northern-born Negro, has long furnished brick for a large portion of the state and can turn out 30,000 bricks a day.

To finance these Negro businesses, which are said to handle a million and a half dollars a year, a small banking institution has been started. The "Mechanics' and Farmers' Bank" looks small and experimental and owes its existence to rather lenient banking laws. It has a paid-in capital of $11,000 and it has $17,000 deposited by 500 different persons.

A careful examination of the origin of this Durham development shows that in a peculiar way it is due to a combination of training, business capacity, and character. The men who built 200 enterprises are unusual, not because the enterprises in themselves are so remarkable, but because their establishment met peculiar difficulties. To-day the white man who would go into insurance or haberdashery or hosiery making gathers his capital from rich men and hires expert managers who know these businesses. The Negro gathers capital by pennies from people unused to investing; he has no experts whom he may hire and small chance to train experts; and he must literally grope for success through repeated failure.

Three men began the economic building of black Durham: a minister with college training, a physician with professional training, and a barber who saved his money. These three called to their aid a bright hustling young graduate of the public schools, and with these four, representing vision, knowledge, thrift, and efficiency, the development began. The college man planned the insurance society, but it took the young hustler to put it through. The barber put his savings into the young business man's hands, the physician gave his time and general intelligence. Others were drawn in--the brickmaker, several teachers, a few college-bred men, and a number of mechanics. As the group began to make money, it expanded and reached out. None of the men are rich--the richest has an income of about $25,000 a year from business investments and eighty tenements; the others of the inner group are making from $5,000 to $15,000--a very modest reward as such rewards go in America.

Quite a number of the colored people have built themselves pretty and well-equipped homes--perhaps fourteen of these homes cost from $2,500 to $10,000; they are rebuilding their churches on a scale almost luxurious, and they are deeply interested in their new training school. There is no evidence of luxury--a horse and carriage, and the sending of children off to school is almost the only sign of more than ordinary expenditure.

If, now, we were considering a single group, geographically isolated, this story might end here. But never forget that Durham is in the South and that around these 5,000 Negroes are twice as many whites who own most of the property, dominate the political life exclusively, and form the main current of social life. What now has been the attitude of these people toward Negroes? In the case of a notable few it has been sincerely sympathetic and helpful, and in the case of a majority of the whites it has not been hostile. Of the two attitudes, great as has undoubtedly been the value of the active friendship of the Duke family, General Julian S. Carr, and others, I consider the greatest factor in Durham's development to have been the disposition of the mass of ordinary white citizens of Durham to say: "Hands off--give them a chance--don't interfere." As the editor of the local daily put it in a well deserved rebuke to former Governor Glenn of North Carolina: "If the Negro is going down, for God's sake let it be because of his own fault, and not because we are pushing him."

Active benevolence can, of course, do much in a community, and in Durham it has given the Negroes a hospital. The late Mr. Washington Duke conceived the idea of building a monument to ex-slaves on the Trinity College campus. This the colored people succeeded in transmuting to the founding of a hospital. The Duke family gave nearly $20,000 for building and equipping the building and the Negroes give largely to its support. Besides this, some white men have helped the Negroes by advice, as, for instance, in the intricacies of banking; and they have contributed to the new training school. Not only have Southern philanthropists thus helped, but they have allowed the Negroes to administer these gifts themselves.

The hospital, for instance, is not simply for Negroes, but is conducted by them; and the training school is under a colored corps of teachers.

But all this aid is as nothing beside that more general spirit which allows a black contractor to bid on equal terms with a white, which affords fair police protection and reasonable justice in court, which grants substantial courtesy and consideration on the street and in the press, and which in general says: "Hands off, don't hinder, let them grow." It is precisely the opposite spirit in places like Atlanta, which makes the way of the black man there so hard, despite individual friends.

A Southern community is thus seen to have it in its power to choose its Negro inhabitants. If it is afraid of ambition and enterprise on the part of black folk if it believes that "education spoils a nigger," then it will get the shiftless, happy-go-lucky semi-criminal black man, and the ambitious and enterprising ones will either sink or migrate. On the other hand, many honest Southerners fear to encourage the pushing, enterprising Negro Durham has not feared. It has distinctly encouraged the best type of black man by active aid and passive tolerance.

What accounts for this? I may be over-emphasizing facts, but I think not, when I answer in a word: Trinity College. The influence of a Southern institution of learning of high ideals; with a president and professors who have dared to speak out for justice toward black men; with a quarterly journal, the learning and catholicism of which is well known--this has made white Durham willing to see black Durham rise without organizing mobs or secret societies to "keep the niggers down."

To be sure, the future still has its problems, for the significance of the rise of a group of black people to the Durham height and higher, means not a disappearance but, in some respect, an accentuation of the race problem.

But let the future lay its own ghosts; to-day there is a singular group in Durham where a black man may get up in the morning from a mattress made by black men, in a house which a black man built out of lumber which black men cut and planed; he may put on a suit which he bought at a colored haberdashery and socks knit at a colored mill; he may cook victuals from a colored grocery on a stove which black men fashioned; he may earn his living working for colored men, be sick in a colored hospital, and buried from a colored church; and the Negro insurance society will pay his widow enough to keep his children in a colored school. This is surely progress.

R. R. Wright, Jr. founded the Trinity Mission Settlement in Chicago "in the dreariest part of the black belt" (West 18th Street between Clark and State Streets). Later, Wright became both the first black to take the Ph. D. degree in sociology from the University of Pennsylvania and also a Bishop in the African Methodist Episcopal Church. These were notable achievements of one of the most able of the "New Negroes."

Document 15

Fannie B. Williams, "Growth of Social Settlement Idea," The New York Age, August 5, 1905, p. 6.

The social settlement idea of seeking out and helping the masses has at last reached down and out in search of the socially neglected people of the Negro race. Only recently has it occurred to the social workers that those who speak a foreign tongue and belong to the "submerged tenth" are not the only ones in need of guidance, protection and encouragement.

A big northern city is a trying place for a plantation Negro who has escaped from Arkansas, Mississippi or elsewhere in the rural South. He finds himself segregated in the most unsanitary and forbidden parts of the city. Race prejudice compels the virtuous and vicious to live in close proximity. There is no such thing as escaping the "black belt" for those who deserve a better habitation. What is worse still, the "black belt" is not only black, it is also the neglected spot in the city. Things are allowed to go from bad to worse with no hope of relief.

In other parts of the city where the poor and the ignorant are compelled to live, there is always some effort being made for social improvement. There is always some mission, some visiting nurse, evangel of mercy, some student of sociology, or some effort and somebody to bring a ray of light and promise into these nooks and corners that are darkened by poverty and misfortunes of all kinds. Not so with our "black belts." Here we have stagnation and worse. The best of us are poor and have nothing to divide, either of time, money or heart. We are apt to excuse ourselves with the plea that the black man's misfortunes and sins are the white man's burden and business. We have not had time or heart to cultivate a sense of responsibility for the life of the neglected amongst us. We have not yet become strong enough to ask ourselves the question, "Am I my brother's keeper?" The great social sin of the day is that thousands are lost who might be saved, if we but know how, and possessed the will, to save them.

But a new spirit is rising within us. There are signs of an out-reaching of heart and hand in quest of new duties. A sense of civic responsibility begins to manifest itself, with a generosity of proffered service that is both interesting and significant. What is being done in New York, in Newark, New Jersey, in the slum districts of Washington, D. C., and finally in Chicago is most encouraging. The fact that this new work in the neglected quarters of our large cities is inspired and carried on, in the main, by college men and women of fine culture and careful training for the work, is perhaps the best assurance that it is not merely a fad, but is something that is striking its roots down into the very heart of our civic life.

In Chicago what is known as the Trinity Mission Settlement is an interesting example of this new movement in behalf of the neglected colored people. Trinity Mission is located down in the dreariest part of the "black belt." It is on West 18th Street between Clark and State Streets. In this district there is not a single agency of social redemption. It is a region given over to all forms of social degradation. It is in this environment that the Trinity Mission Settlement is creating a place for itself.

The founder or warden of this centre of helpfulness is a young man who is a B. A. graduate of Chicago University and took a special course of study in the Berlin University, Germany. His name is R. R. Wright, Jr., of Georgia, a son of Prof. R. R. Wright, one of the most prominent and successful educators in the South. When Mr. Wright graduated, flattering offers came to him from all parts of the South to teach in the different schools and colleges. I know of no Negro scholar, fresh from university honors, who has been so much sought after as a teacher and leader. Yet he has had the courage resolutely to turn away from all such offers and adhere to his original purpose.

While a student at the Chicago University, he made a careful study of the conditions of colored people. He saw here the possibilities of a work that other men saw "but passed by, on the other side." But he had seen the "vision splendid," and it took hold of him with such firmness that the work became of supreme importance to him. He clearly saw that unless something was done to save the city Negro from city vices, race prejudice would increase to an alarming extent in the North, and belief in the utter unfitness of the Negro for citizenship would justify all sorts of injustice and restrictions.

I do not know of a finer example of self-sacrifice among our cultured young men than that of Mr. Wright. He has already realized in many positive and painful ways, that hard work, no money and a denial of all social pleasures must be his portion, perhaps for a long time but he does not hesitate.

Such considerations on the part of this capable young man are of great importance in its influence and effect upon others. It has in it the quality of prophecy. Mr. Wright, I am pleased to record, is beginning to receive substantial encouragement. He has a three-story building, in which he has already a kindergarten, day nursery, reading room, sewing school, and apartments for working girls. The Federated Woman's Club, under the leadership of Mrs. I. A. Davis, have offered their assistance to Mr. Wright. He is also receiving much substantial aid from men and women of wealth, who understand the value of this kind of service to the forgotten and neglected. This movement is fortunate not only in having a university man at its head, but also in the fact that he is a young man of unaffected manners, gentle bearing and strong sympathies. Though a preacher by profession, he is wholly without cant and unusually tolerant and liberal in his religious beliefs.

I believe it is not too much to prophecy that if Mr. Wright is permitted to develop and carry out his plans, he is destined to be one of the marked men of the near future.

In the case of this young evangelist of good work, we have an interesting example of the value of a good inheritance. The law of heredity would have been tricked if there had been a less worthy son of a noble father. R. R. Wright, the father, is now in the city and an eager student of the new methods of saving men and women from the blight of a city's plague spots, as they are being worked out by his son. The elder Wright seems both surprised and entranced by the "Pauline" zeal of the younger Wright. Worthy father! worthy son! It is not always so, but when it is, human nature is exalted and the world is always better for their living....

The Kindergarten Association for Colored Children, documented in its fifth year of service, moved from 41st Street to 60th Street on the West Side of New York, because the latter area of the city was in more urgent need of its services. Applications for admission to the kindergarten came from both races and their growing number required the addition of an afternoon session. A public meeting in behalf of the kindergarten was held in Madison Square Garden, and it is interesting to note that Booker T. Washington presided and Dr. W. E. B. DuBois spoke.

Document 16

Fifth Annual Report of the Free Kindergarten Association for Colored Children, November 1, 1900, New York City, New York.

The Fifth Annual Report of the Free Kindergarten Association for Colored Children comes to its patrons from new quarters. A Kindergarten having been established in the Public School on the block in West 41st Street, we realized that our Kindergarten was no longer needed in that neighborhood, and therefore sought and found a location where the demand for such work as we are endeavoring to accomplish was most urgent.

By the advice of Mr. Jacob Riis we have carried our work into West 60th Street, recognized as one of the worst and poorest colored settlements in the city. The neighborhood was thoroughly canvassed in advance by Miss Annie Strathern, who found a great many colored families sorely in need of the humanizing influence of a Kindergarten.

The apartments selected were put in excellent order, made

cheerful and attractive and on Monday, April 2nd, the Kindergarten opened with a register of 16 pupils which had increased by the end of the month to 27.

The teachers find that they have to deal with a different class of children from those previously taught. A great lack of home training is apparent among them, and they have been accustomed to spend their time mostly on the streets. They know no other authority save that of fear, and are governed by blows and hard usage. In view of these facts, it is the aim of the teachers to counteract the evil by making the acquaintance of the mothers.

The neighborhood where our Kindergarten is situated was one of the scenes of the riots of last summer; and it is such a particularly poor one that many of the children are prevented from coming to school by the want of decent clothing. The Association furnishes them with garments as far as possible, but the demand is greater than the supply. We find that the little ones come to us hungry and a light luncheon of crackers and milk is given to them at eleven o'clock.

The satisfactory results obtained thus far by the new Kindergarten, are largely due to the efforts and energy of Mrs. James M. Walton who has supervised the work, and aided and directed the teachers.

The Mothers' Meetings are still continued with the most beneficial effects. So interested have the fathers and mothers become in the school that they often stop here, on their way to work, to listen for a few moments, to some of the early exercises.

We had so many applications from both colored and white children that we were able, through the generosity of Mrs. C. B. Hackley, to try the experiment of having an afternoon school also; but the hours being unfavorable for the purpose, those sessions have been discontinued, and we now propose, if we can meet with the proper encouragement, to organize afternoon classes or clubs among the older girls.

The closing exercises of both the morning and afternoon schools were held Friday, June 29th, with 80 parents and children present each time.

By the end of the term the interest among the families in the neighborhood had grown to such an extent that the register was 40; and now, since the re-opening on Monday, September 10th, there are 60 pupils enrolled. The school is already crowded and more applications than we can receive are coming to us every day.

The most noteworthy event connected with the history of the new Kindergarten was the large and successful public meeting held Tuesday, April 3rd, at Madison Square Garden Concert Hall.

Through the enthusiastic efforts and under the able management of the President, Mrs. James Herbert Morse, an audience representing much of the finest intellect and philanthropy of the city filled the hall on that evening. Booker T. Washington presided and the meeting was addressed by Miss Maria L. Baldwin, Supt. of the Agassiz School, Cambridge, Mass., and Prof. W. E. Burghardt DuBois, of Atlanta University; Mr. Henry T. Burleigh gave musical selections. Thus the race to be benefited by the meeting was ably represented.

The next afternoon Mr. and Mrs. Henry Villard gave a reception at their home, to the speakers and Mr. Burleigh. It was at this reception that Booker T. Washington said to Mrs. Morse:

> I have never seen the best representatives of the two races brought together as they were at your meeting last night and as they are here, to-day. In my opinion that is the way to accomplish the most good. If you bring those representatives together, you discover that the object for which you have been toiling for years is suddenly attained.

It is evident that there is a pressing need for philanthropic work, in the neighborhood where our Kindergarten is situated, but without sufficient funds our new enterprise cannot be successfully continued, and the field of labor broadened to meet the necessities of the occasion as they may arise. We therefore sincerely trust that our patrons, who have so generously aided us in the past, may renew their efforts in our behalf, with the assurance that the money expended will yield tenfold its value in the uplifting of needy humanity.

H. Cordelia Ray,
Secretary

The heightened concentration of blacks in urban centers led to a concern for helping blacks "learn to live in town." However, unwilling to place such assistance in the hands of "inefficient, and inexperienced enthusiasts," Dr. George E. Haynes, recognized the need for professional training for blacks engaged in social welfare and social work. He reports the establishment of a department of Social Science and Social Work at Fisk University to accomplish these three objectives: 1) the preliminary instruction and training of Negro students in the colleges of the South; 2) the selection of promising students for further training in New York and other cities; and 3) to provide opportunities for these trained social workers to practice their skills for the social betterment of the black population. This goes beyond the social laboratory and conference procedures established by Dr. DuBois at Atlanta University, where it was considered desirable that each college graduate have knowledge of social conditions and be stimulated to engage in efforts toward social betterment as an integral part of the liberal arts degree program. Here Haynes proposes the attainment of professional training and competence at both undergraduate and graduate levels of study.

Document 17*

George E. Haynes, "Cooperation with Colleges in Securing and Training Negro Social Workers for Urban Centers," Proceedings of the National Conference of Charities and Correction, Boston, 1911, (Fort Wayne, Indiana, Fort Wayne Printing Co., 1911), pp. 384-387.

While my paper discusses a plan for uniting the Negro college, a professional school and social work among Negroes in urban centers, it has a grain of suggestion which may be generally applied in schooling and training white students for social work.

It is only necessary to remind you of the fact that there is a growing concentration of Negroes in urban centers, and a primary concern for the Negro is to learn to live in town.

This urban situation, like other great human problems is fundamentally one of efficient men and women who are thoroughly trained to the special service in which they are engaged. The conditions affecting Negroes in cities can best be improved by those of their own race whose latent capacity has had superior training directed toward social service.

The youth in Negro colleges furnish the key to the situation, for those less thoroughly trained will not be able to grapple successfully with such serious conditions. Several Schools of Philanthropy are open to Negro students, but these institutions are out of the reach of nearly all of these. Several Negro colleges have offered courses in Economics and Sociology but in nearly every case they have been scarcely more than class room discussions, often remotely relating to conditions among Negroes. So it is safe to say that, until we started last year, there had been no definite training for social work offered anywhere for Negro students and no arrangements existed to connect them when prepared with the serious conditions among our people in cities. For those who are working to remedy conditions in cities are not connected with a source or supply of capable recruits for social work.

Without delaying longer, some of us made a beginning to secure and train Negro college youth for Social work and to relate the Negro college to urban communities. The plan as started has three prongs. First, the preparatory instruction and training in the Negro

*Reprinted by permission of the National Conference on Social Welfare.

college; second, the selecting of promising students and providing them with the opportunities for further professional study and practical experience among their own people in cities; and third, the organization of social betterment work in the cities where these trained people may use their ability for social uplift.

First, the preparatory instruction and training of the students should be given in Negro colleges of the South because it should begin during college years of enthusiasm, and because it should be brought to bear upon large groups of select, capable, enthusiastic Negro youth such as gather at these colleges. In this way prospective social workers may be found. Again, the preparation should begin in the Negro college, because the city conditions among the Negroes demands minds and characters which have been moulded by a broad course of education.

Besides, some training for understanding the conditions surrounding my people should be put within the reach of all Negro college students. The problem of social uplift is so great that, in addition to expert social workers, all Negro ministers, doctors, lawyers, teachers and others should have the benefit of instruction in scientific methods and the new social point of view. Finally and emphatically, the Negro colleges themselves need to be vitally articulated with the conditions and needs of the Negroes in the communities where these colleges are located. This will help the people and the students and show both the true aim of colleges.

With this in view, we have established at Fisk University, Nashville, Tenn., a department of Social Science and Social Work. In order to give a thorough preparation for social and religious workers, courses are given in industrial history, economic theory, sociology, economic and labor problems and methods of social work. In the senior year lectures are given on special problems relating to Negroes. During the past school year lectures were given by experts from several cities on the religious problems among Negroes in cities; delinquents and probation problems; special problems of Negro women in cities; of Negro children; and on Principles of Belief. Running through half of the Junior year and all of the senior year is a course in the History of the Negro in America and the Negro problem. This furnishes historical perspective and knowledge of the present condition of the Negro in America as seen from the points of view of various writers.

During the last semester of the Senior year, the students are required to give ten hours per week to methods of statistics and social investigations, and actual field work among the conditions of the colored people of Nashville. Thus we aim to bring the university into closer relation to our people in that city.

And this is just a beginning. We shall not confine our efforts to the students and graduates of Fisk University, but in a similar way we contemplate a general co-operation of Negro colleges for the betterment of the urban population of our people. However, Fisk

University has its strategic location in the South, by the way it looms up in the center of Negroes themselves, by its standing among colleges of the country and by its tradition and sentiment for social service, is pre-empting the place for the inception and development of such a movement.

Second, I turn to the selection of students of promise for Social Work and their further training in New York and other cities. A number of the leading white and colored citizens of New York, who have to meet these urban problems, have organized the Committee on Urban Conditions Among Negroes. This Committee has three main purposes. First, to bring about co-operation among the existing agencies and also among Negroes in urban centers, to find out where additional work is needed and where existing work involves duplication; second, to make provisions for discovered needs or to attempt otherwise to remedy the situation, and third, to secure and train Negro social workers.

To carry out the last named purpose, promising graduates of Fisk University and other colleges, who wish to make social work a career calling, will be given an opportunity under the auspices of this Committee to get experience in such social work and to pursue under further study as the social betterment efforts and educational facilities in New York and other cities afford.

We have a field secretary in New York, who devotes his entire time to the Committee's work, and one of his special functions is to plan for the further training of these prospective social workers. This year we have selected from two colleges, one graduate each. Our only means in securing them was a lack of funds. These young people will be provided with fellowships that will afford opportunity to study at the New York School of Philanthropy and Columbia University.

The third part of the plan is the relation of these trained people to social betterment efforts in the cities. This is both cause and effect of the first two parts. In New York and other cities there is a persistent demand on the part of those doing and supporting social work and a crying need among my people, that the many agencies for betterment shall be standardized and co-ordinated, and that efficient workers be secured and put in charge. We have begun to meet this need and demand. Last year, our Committee laid out the following five year program of work for New York City:

(1) Registration and co-operation of existing social agencies; (2) Co-operation of agencies at work for the improvement of the community at large; (3) Improvement of housing and neighborhood conditions; (4) Development of employment agencies and facilities; (5) Development of thrift agencies and co-operative business enterprises; (6) Provision of amusement and recreation facilities; (7) Improvement in the relation of the Negro church and other religious institutions to the social conditions; (8) Co-operation with other cities in exchange methods and in securing and training social workers.

Our resources have been very limited, but we have gathered and placed on file for reference, a reliable set of reports on eighteen of the existing agencies; in co-operation with the National League for the Protection of Colored Women, we made a preliminary survey of the largest Negro district in Manhattan. This resulted in a movement of the colored residents themselves for such improvements on better police protection and wholesome recreation and amusement facilities. We have under supervision arrangements for a model boy's camp and for co-operation of all Negro fresh-air agencies. Committees are appointed looking toward the union with us of two or three other important organizations to act as a general clearing house for the city. Workers in several other cities have signified their desire to join the movement.

Let me sum up this brief and fragmentary account of our plan; the urban concentration of Negroes demands a large number of trained Negro social workers. The usual way of securing and training them is to get any one who is available and to put him in charge of social work with the expectation that he will know by intuition and learn from failures to understand what are our most serious social conditions.

Now, if there is any one fact well known, it is that the Negro's situation cannot be helped by inefficient and inexperienced enthusiasts. Our Committee goes back to the years of youth, the years of college enthusiasm for service, picks out the people of promise, insures them a good foundation training and practical experience before entrusting such serious work into their hands.

The plan is feasible; our first year has succeeded beyond our hopes. It is meeting a need of the Negro college youth, and it is meeting the demand of those who have often lamented the lack of competent Negro workers. It is a new departure in the training of social workers, because it not only definitely links the training of the professional school for social workers with educational institutions of college rank, but also links the institutions and the students with a practical working committee, whose officers are to supervise the training of prospective social workers.

We believe firmly that, with financial support and co-operation, we shall give equipment and inspiration for social uplift to a number of capable Negro men and women; that we shall point the way for Negro colleges to articulate themselves with the increasing urban life; that we shall raise the standard and increase the efficiency of social betterment work among the urban Negro population of the country, and that we shall suggest some methods of connecting college youth with the social problems which confront the Nation.

The next document contains several important statements: the circumstances governing the founding of the National League on Urban Conditions Among Negroes, later known as the National Urban League (co-founders: Dr. George E. Haynes and Eugene Kinckle Jones); the announcement of the initial development of social work education in black colleges, beginning with Fisk University, Howard University and Paine College; the award of fellowships for the education of professional social workers; and the actual employment of a professional social worker in Atlanta. The reference is to Garry Moore, who served both Morehouse College as an Instructor and the Neighborhood Union as its first probation officer.

Document 18a*

Bulletin of National League on Urban Conditions Among Negroes, Report 1912-1913, Announcement 1913-1914, "Foreword," Vol. III, No. 2, November, 1913, pp. 5-8.

The migration of Negroes to the cities, as a part of the general movement of population to the cities, is a fact of common observation. A careful study of the causes of this migration has shown conclusively that fundamentally they are economic and social, resulting in a large permanent Negro urban population.

The census of 1910 showed that more than one-fourth of the Negro population is located in urban centers (places of 2,500 or more); 39 cities have ten thousand or more Negroes; and 12 cities have more than forty thousand Negroes each; five of these are Northern cities and seven Southern cities. Negroes constitute one-fourth or more of the total population in each of 27 principal cities, and in four of these cities they make up more than half.

In every city where the Negro population has reached a considerable proportion, it is largely collected into distinct neighborhoods, thus making more acute the problems growing out of their change from rural to urban life.

To help counteract this migration to the cities and to make efforts for improving the serious social conditions growing up among the Negroes in the cities, the National League on Urban Conditions Among Negroes was formed.

The National League on Urban Conditions Among Negroes is in a sense a new organization, for it came into existence on October 16, 1911. The constituent parts out of which it developed are, however, much older, for it is a union--organized to secure co-operation, efficiency and united action--of three organizations working among Negroes, namely: the Committee for Improving the Industrial Conditions of Negroes in New York, the National League for the

*Reprinted by permission of the National Urban League.

Protection of Colored Women and the Committee on Urban Conditions Among Negroes. The National League on Urban Conditions Among Negroes is now incorporated under the Membership Corporations Law of the State of New York.

The National League for the Protection of Colored Women was organized in 1906, as the outcome of an investigation of employment agencies in several Northern cities which revealed abuses connected with the emigration of Negro women from the South. The League sought to check this emigration, and to direct those who did emigrate to proper lodgings, assist them in finding suitable employment and wholesome recreation. The League also maintained workers at Norfolk, Philadelphia and Baltimore, who met travelers on incoming boats and trains. The Protective League has now consolidated with the other organizations, and its work, with some new developments, is carried on as a standing committee of the National League on Urban Conditions Among Negroes, which committee is known as the Committee for the Protection of Women.

The Committee for Improving the Industrial Conditions of Negroes in New York was organized in 1907. It grew out of a general recognition of the serious industrial and economic handicap under which the Negro labors, not only by reason of race discrimination, but also by reason of lack of industrial training and efficiency.

This Committee has become an integral part of the incorporated National League and continues its work as a standing committee under the name, Committee for Improving Industrial Conditions.

The Committee on Urban Conditions Among Negroes was established in October, 1910, by representatives from many institutions and organizations and advocates of many points of view, with the following purposes:

1. The study of social and economic conditions among Negroes in cities with a view to securing co-operation among all agencies seeking to better conditions among Negroes.

2. The development of other agencies if necessary.

3. The training of Negro social workers.

The national features of this committee work were taken over by the League upon its organization in 1911. The local parts of this work are being carried on by a standing committee of the National League under the name of the Committee on General Welfare.

The objects of all the united organizations have been included in the purposes of the National League which are stated as follows:

1. To bring about co-ordination and co-operation among existing agencies and organizations for improving the in-

dustrial, economic, social and spiritual condition of Negroes and to develop other agencies and organizations, where necessary.

2. To secure and train Negro social workers.

3. To make studies of the industrial, economic, social and spiritual conditions among Negroes.

4. To promote, encourage, assist and engage in any and all kinds of work for improving the industrial, economic, social and spiritual conditions among Negroes.

All members of the three united organizations became members of the consolidated body. These members elect an Executive Board of thirty Directors, ten being elected every year to serve three years. This Executive Board has power to elect its officers, who are ex-officio officers of the National League, to appoint standing committees which conduct the various parts of the League's work, to establish branches and to enter into agreements of affiliation with other bodies, to elect members of the organization and to appropriate funds for the purposes of the League.

Document 18b

"Results of the 1912-1913 Program," Bulletin of National League on Urban Conditions Among Negroes, Vol. III, No. 2, November, 1913, pp. 10-11.

The Further Development of Educational Work along Social Lines in Co-operation with Fisk University and Other Negro Colleges.

1. At Fisk University the courses in Economics, Sociology, Negro History and Social Investigation and the lectures by experts in Social Work from various cities have been conducted as planned. In addition, a special course on the Negro problem has been added. In another forward step the University has entered upon a plan of co-operation with the Women's Missionary Council of the M. E. Church, South, and the Methodist Training School of the same church, in conducting a social settlement, known as Bethlehem House, the seniors of the University to be used as community workers of the Settlement.

2. A worker, trained by the League last year in New York City, has begun work in Atlanta, Ga., as instructor at Morehouse College (formerly Atlanta Baptist College), and is engaged in carrying out the plans for Social Science education and for practical efforts which has been undertaken by a local organization.

3. Agreements of affiliation have been completed with Paine College, Augusta, Ga., and Howard University, Washington, D. C. Paine College has begun extension work in the City, and courses of

training for a social ministry and Christian workers. Howard University has had good courses in Economics and Sociology for several years, and now plans some practical work in the City in co-operation with the National League.

4. A student from Howard University and one from Virginia Union University have been selected as "fellows" to take the League training in New York City during 1913-1914. This training includes courses at the New York School of Philanthropy and Columbia University, and field work under the direction of the National League.

THE ATLANTA EXPERIENCE: A CASE STUDY

These documents provide a case study of social welfare developments in a large Southern city beset by the problems of race riots, lynchings, neglect and deprivation. Of particular interest is the creation, development and implementation of the Institutional Church, in this particular instance, the life of Atlanta's First Congregational Church.

Document 19*

Henry Hugh Proctor, Between Black and White, (Boston: Pilgrim Press, 1914), pp. 91-129.

The Lure of the New South

On the day of my graduation Professor Stevens, who later visited my church in Atlanta, came to me and said: "You are now prepared to fill any pulpit in the land." I appreciated his kind expression. But my heart was in the Southland, and I was happy to respond to the call of the First Congregational Church in Atlanta immediately upon my graduation, where I had the privilege of serving as minister for a quarter of a century. I reached Atlanta on Memorial Day, and began work in this central city of the new South at the most inspiring time of the year in the beautiful Southland.

The South is the most unique part of our country. With its rare climate, remarkable fertility, romantic history, and baffling racial atmosphere, it holds a fascination no other part of our country does. But its greatest charm for me at the time was that it was the chief home of the people of whom I was a part, and I longed to go back and help them. It was, therefore, with peculiar pleasure that I turned my face toward the South when I had finished my study at Yale. I went from New England to the South, to put into prac-

*Reprinted by permission.

tice some of the things I had been nurturing in my heart all my lifetime.

In the sense that Paris is France, London, England, and New York America, so is Atlanta the South. Atlanta is a unique city sitting on more hills than ancient Rome. It is too near the stars for a flood, being a thousand feet above the level of the sea. It has one of the most ideal climates of any city in the United States. It is the commercial center of the Southeast. There she sits like a goddess, with one hand on the coffers of the East and the other on the products of the South. Every great business house in the country has a sub-office in Atlanta, so that the city has more sky-scrapers than any other city of its size in the world. And I have sometimes said that Atlanta is the biggest city of its size in America!

Atlanta has more colleges for colored youth than any other city in the world. On one hill stands Atlanta University, founded by the Congregationalists; on another Atlanta Baptist College, a school for young men; on another Spelman Seminary, a Baptist school for girls (named for Mrs. Rockefeller); on another Clark University, founded by the Methodists; on another Gammon Theological Seminary, a theological school endowed by the Methodists with a million dollars; and on still another Morris Brown College, founded by the African Methodists (a monument to self-help and sacrifice). The encircling hills of Atlanta are crowned with colleges for colored youth like bon-fires of living light. And these very hills were once occupied by contending armies, for Atlanta is built on a battlefield. It was here that Sherman broke the backbone of the rebellion. It was in this city that Sherman gave his famous definition of war. It was here that the famous march to the sea began.

In the very heart of this city, within a block of where the first shell of the battle of Atlanta struck, killing a little child, is located the First Congregational Church of Atlanta. This church was organized one year before I was born. Its first ministers came from New England, and were graduates of Yale. They organized the Storrs School, the first school in Georgia for colored people, and in this school the church was born. This church in turn became the mother of Atlanta University. This may account for the fact that so large a proportion of its members are imbued with the spirit of education.

It was to this church, housed in a little brick structure on the corner, that I was called. The membership was composed of some of the finest people in Atlanta. The only fault I found with them was that there were not enough of them. I preached on quality plus quantity, and the one hundred members grew into a thousand. In its growth the quality was preserved.

This church had some remarkable characteristics. In it was organized the first temperance society in Georgia, and its members were required to sign a pledge of total abstinence for admission. It thus became the forerunner of prohibition in Georgia, the South, and the nation. From the beginning the spirit of thrift was instilled in its members, and today two-thirds of them own their own homes; some of these are among the most beautiful and commodious in the city. Industry was one of the things instilled in the early day, and today you cannot find the name of a loafer on the church roll. As a matter of fact, just being a member of that church is sufficient as a credential for employment. Great stress was laid on putting religion into character, so that in all the history of the church only one man was ever sent to the state prison, and not a single one was ever accused of the unspeakable crime against womanhood. The death rate in the church was lower than that among the white population by one-third. Of the thousand members of the church not one was illiterate.

In this church was organized the National Convention of Congregational Workers Among Colored People by Dr. George W. Henderson, professor at Straight University, New Orleans, Louisiana, and myself, through the inspiration of the Young People's Congress, which brought together young colored people from all parts of the country. The purpose of this convention was to bring together for mutual helpfulness the workers in church and school in the Congregational churches of the colored people. The first meeting of the organization was held in Atlanta, the next in New Orleans, and the third in Memphis, meeting once in two years. This organization has grown year by year until it is the most hopeful thing among the colored Congregational churches in the United States.

It was while attending the meeting of this convention at Memphis that tidings came to me of the breaking out of the Atlanta Riot, Saturday, Sept. 22, 1906. It can be easily imagined how distressing was the news when it is recalled that not only were my church people there, but also my children left in the care of a friend. The papers contained increasingly unfavorable reports of conditions, and we hastened home, only to find the city in two hostile camps, with the blood of both races undried on the streets of the city. Fortunately our children were safe, although rioters came into the church yard and looked into the windows of the church, while my children looked out through the shutters of the parsonage near by. Although many were killed and wounded, not a member of my church was hurt. But my heart went out beyond the members of my parish, and I endeavored to console all I could.

While on this errand of mercy a surprising call came to me from a lawyer in the city. His name was Charles T. Hopkins, a native born Southerner trained in an Eastern institution. We bared our hearts on the situation, and felt that something must be done and that we were the ones to do it. A plan was agreed upon, and he called in two white men and I called in two colored men. These six agreed, and a still larger number were called in, making twenty on each side. Through these two bodies working together peace was restored. It was found that both working together could do things that neither group could do alone. This was the beginning of the movement for interracial cooperation in the South. Other cities adopted the plan, and now there is a permanent organization working on this line with headquarters in Atlanta and New York. Without doubt this is the key to the solution of the problem of the races not only in the South, but also in the North, and in all the world where white and colored races meet in large numbers.

My efforts in this line were not without much misunderstanding and actual danger. Some among my own people felt that I was giving away their case by seeking cooperation with the whites. Others thought that because I had openly denounced the conditions productive of riots that I had therefore produced the riot. Only a week before the riot I had spoken before the city council, saying that unless they closed the dives of the city blood would run in the streets. In response to my plea the city council passed an ordinance closing the dives, but it was too late; the poison was in the blood. Through misrepresentation in the press false rumors were started, and on Saturday night the crowds that poured in from surrounding towns for a frolic were stampeded into the bloody riot that followed and upset the city for a week.

During the upset conditions that followed, my name was much in the mouths of the people because of the part I took in attempting to promote peace. One evening near dusk a colored man came to my front porch with a bludgeon in his hand, and called for me. Fortunately, my wife met him at the door, and when that good woman looked him in the eyes he tucked his head and ran. I was in the little parlor within a few feet of him, but did not know of the nature of his errand until after he had gone.

Not long after, another queer character came to see me. Again, my wife let him in. She informed me of his presence, but said she did not like his looks. But I went right in to see him, and I met a typical Georgia Cracker. His hair was long and dishevelled, his elbows protruded through his sleeves, and he made a formidable appearance. As I entered he quickly rose from his chair, and took me by both my hands, saying, "My dear brother, I have followed your course in the matter of the riot. I sympathize with you. I love your people, and I have come to pray with you." We fell on our knees and prayed together. I have heard the great metropolitan preachers pray, but no prayer ever touched my heart like the prayer of this plain man from the backwoods of Georgia. I never saw him before, and I have never seen him since. His going and coming were like that of Elijah.

But after the storm came the calm, and we looked up and saw the rainbow covering the shoulder of the dying storm. In that hour God gave me a message for my people. It was only natural that they should want to leave. I tried to assure them that out of this would come a better Atlanta, that now was the time to settle down and build anew. That voice was heeded, for few left the city. Some of those who did leave came back later. The breaches were healed, the work of cooperation between the better elements of both races progressed, and it was unanimous opinion that the city was better afterwards than before.

But in order to make this appeal effective I had to introduce some tangible evidence to my people that the good will of them was genuine. In that hour a vision came to me. For ten years I had sat on my porch near the church and seen the people of my race go by the church down to the dive, into the prison, up to the gallows. I asked myself why it was that the people passed by my church and went to the dive. The answer was simple. My church was locked and barred and dark, while the dive was wide open, illuminated, and attractive. Then I said: "God helping me, I will open my church and make it as attractive as the dive."

To do this required money. My people were not rich and had many obligations. In response to my appeal they subscribed ten thousand dollars. Colored people of other denominations subscribed two and a half thousand dollars. I made an appeal to the white people for a similar amount and they gave twice as much, thus demonstrating their good will. I then turned to the people of the North on the ground that this was a national question, and that this was a good way to promote interracial good will. My appeal made in many churches throughout the North was generously responded to, and the funds came to make real the vision I had seen. Of the realization of this vision I will speak more fully later.

One who rendered invaluable service in the work I undertook was Booker T. Washington. I first met him when he came to Atlanta to deliver the speech at the Cotton States Exposition that made him famous. I sat beside his wife as he leaped into fame. Afterwards he frequently came to my church to speak, and was often a guest in my home. I had the privilege annually of securing large audiences for him to speak to in our city auditorium. In turn he was of much help to my cause. It was through him that the Ogden party came to our church one Sunday on their way to Tuskegee, and made our church the center of the city for the day. This gave me an introduction to some of the leading people in the North, and greatly helped me in securing funds for my larger work. Mr. Washington was also generous in giving me the names of influential people, and he presented me once before the Twentieth Century Club of Boston. I found his name a key North and South. I once called upon Mr. Carnegie in New York to give a portion to my organ fund, and he asked me whom I had to recommend me, and I told him I had letters from ex-President Roosevelt, President Taft, Senator Smith, and Booker T. Washington. He said that if I had the recommendation of Mr. Washington I did not need the others. I left off the names of the others, and I got my request.

As is well known, there are two wings to the colored race, the radical and the conservative. The more radical is headed by Dr. W. E. B. DuBois, and the conservative by Dr. Washington. I was in school with Mr. DuBois and I have worked most harmoniously with Mr. Washington. I was a friend to both, and I believe there is much good in the positions of both. But there need be no conflict. They are the right and left wings of a great movement. Just as a bird must have both wings for successful flight, so must any movement have the radical and conservative wings. I can recall when Dr. Washington and Dr. DuBois worked together harmoniously. Many a time have they come to my house, sometimes in the night, and we have conferred together on plans that were afterwards consummated. The same position I took then I take now. If there is any one thing my people need it is that broadness of spirit which the radical and conservative elements may work together unitedly for the advancement of the race as a whole. This spirit of cooperation, not only between the various wings of the race but also between white and black, was perhaps the chief contribution the First Church of Atlanta made to social betterment during the quarter of a century of my pastorate.

The Bells of Atlanta

I once overheard a hot-blooded young white Southerner say that the race question would be settled at the point of the bayonet and by the shedding of blood. The question will be settled by sword and blood, but it will be by the sword of the spirit and the blood of the Lamb. My invariable answer to the oft-asked question as to whether there will be a race war in the South is in the negative. I base this opinion on the overlooked fact that both races in the South are religious. Our white people are religious; they keep the Sabbath, they go to church, and they read their Bibles. In fact they form the very backbone of American orthodoxy. We colored people are nothing if not religious. We have a genius for religion, and it is not too much to say that we are the most religious people in the world.

When I first went to Niagara I saw a beautiful body of water going over a precipice a mile wide. It was a magnificent sight, but power was going to waste. When I went there again some shrewd Yankee had hitched those falls to a dynamo, by which they made enough electricity to light up the whole region for many miles around. There runs in the South a magnificent stream of religion, to which both races contribute, but too much of it is going to waste. The religion of the South is sentimental rather than practical, individual rather than social. Hitch up the religion of the South to its great unsolved problem, and a new day will come to that section.

That was the vision that come to me in the midst of my ministry in the South, and we endeavored to hitch up the First Church of Atlanta to the great problem of the South. The first step in this direction was to secure a church building adapted for the purpose. The result was the structure that now stands in the heart of the city. I saw this building rise from the foundation to the capstone, and much of my life is built into its very walls. There is a basement, containing Sunday-School facilities, a library and a reading room, a gymnasium, a kitchen, a shower bath, the engine room, and lavatories. On the main floor is an auditorium with a seating capacity of one thousand. Here are also the office of the church and the study of the pastor. On the third floor are a gallery and a ladies' parlor. In this industrial temple we dedicated the pulpit and the parlor, the auditorium and the organ, the dumb-bell and the needle, the skillet and the tub, to the glory of God and the redemption of a race.

Hard by the church stood the parsonage, next to which was the home for colored working girls. This was the first home in the world opened by any church for colored girls. The colored girl is the most unprotected woman in the world, and it was an inspiring occasion when the home was opened for service to this needy group. This was the best equipped church plant for colored people anywhere in the world, and is conservatively estimated to be worth $250,000.

At the time it was opened it met in each of its facilities a special need. There was no Y. M. C. A. for colored young men in the city, and ours was the only gymnasium in the city for that group. There was no Y. W. C. A. in the city, and our home for young colored women was the only one of its kind in Atlanta. There was an employment bureau, and in this we served the people of both races in the city. A water fountain outside the church (breaking the color line) was the first water fountain opened in the city. Our trouble bureau was a clinic for all sorts of ills. Our prison mission served the man at the very bottom. Our Music Festival brought the best musical talent of the race to the city, and attracted great audiences of both races. As a matter of fact, we found that music was a great solvent of racial antipathies, just as David found it a solvent for personal antagonism with Saul.

These facilities were at the disposal of all, Monday as well as Sunday, night as well as day. We served all without regard to denominational or racial affiliation. It was in the real sense of a church of the people. Its purpose was to serve man in his three-fold nature, body, mind and spirit. It will be remembered that the great founder of the church went about teaching, the ministry to the mind; preaching, the ministry to the spirit; and healing, the ministry of the body. I predict that when the church catches up with Jesus she will again exert her old-time power, not in the old way, but in a new and better way. It will do better than merely save men's souls; it will save the whole man, body, mind and soul. Save the body alone, and you have a Jack Johnson; save the mind alone, and you have a Robert Ingersoll; save the soul alone, and you have an Uncle Tom; but save the body, mind, and soul, and you have an Apostle Paul--a Jesus Christ!

Naturally such a church with such a program began to attract attention. It was doing things. Visitors came from all parts of the world. Among these were many newspaper writers. Dr. Abbott, of the Outlook, came, and because of its Circles of Ten, an original form of church work, called it the best organized church in the South. Bruce Barton spent a Sunday with us, and after studying the work of the church in the Atlanta Riot called it "The Church That Saved a

City," in a brilliant article published in The Congregationalist and Christian World. One of the shrewdest observers that visited us was Russell Conwell, who after looking through the building examined the doorstep, to see how it was worn, and it passed the test.

But we were honored with the presence of two men who had sat in the presidential chair at Washington. The first was Mr. Taft, who just before his inauguration visited the South, and in coming to Atlanta was shown our church by his millionaire host as one of the sights of the city. He and I were photographed together on the front steps of the church, and the photograph was sent throughout the country. As he stood there the choir sang in his honor the Negro melody, "Let Us Cheer the Weary Traveler." I revisited my old church some time ago, and was greatly delighted that they sang this selection for me. It became our custom to sing this melody for those visitors we wanted especially to honor. We were greatly impressed with the big-heartedness of Mr. Taft as he went about in the building patting little children on the head.

The other was Mr. Roosevelt, who came to us just after his return from Africa. I shall never forget the first question he asked as he entered the church radiating enthusiasm. After he had signed his name in big bold hand on the church register, he turned upon me sharply and said: "Mr. Proctor, what is an institutional church?" I had supposed that he knew everything. "Come with me, Mr. Roosevelt," I replied, "and I will show you." First I took him to the reading room, and on the table among other periodicals was the Outlook--"Theodore Roosevelt, Contributing Editor." "You understand that, Mr. Roosevelt," I said. "Delighted," he replied. Then I took him to the gymnasium, with its dumb-bells, riding-horse, etc. "You understand that," I said. "Bully, bully!" he exclaimed. Then I took him into the kitchen, named in honor of my mother, and he inquired if we could make real cooks there. When I told him we could, he expressed very great satisfaction. Then I took him to the men's room of the church, named in his honor, and in which hung a picture of himself, above which was poised a big stick. This pleased him greatly, and he chuckled delightedly. When he came into the main auditorium, where he was greeted by a great audience, he made a notable address. Among other things, he said that he hailed the day when churches like this were opened, churches that served all the people. Later, when I saw him in New York City, he presented me to Father John, telling him how he was impressed with the First Church of Atlanta.

Of course, other churches began to do the same thing. Imitation is the sincerest form of flattery. One of the most notable instances of this is the St. John's Church, Springfield, Mass., which, under the inspiring leadership of Dr. W. N. DeBerry, has improved on the original conception by our church. Another instance is that of the Tabernacle Baptist Church of Augusta, of which the late Rev. C. T. Walker was builder. Another church was built on this plan in Harlem, the largest Negro city in the world. The present condition of the colored people demands this type of church for their full development.

Document 20*

Merlissie R. Middleton, "Residential Distribution of Members of an Urban Church," (Unpublished Master of Arts Thesis, Atlanta University, 1953), pp. 10-11.

... Out of the race riot also grew the Atlanta Inter-racial Committee that has had as its purpose the seeking of a better understanding between the races.

The National Medical Association, now recognized as one of America's outstanding professional and learned societies had its beginning among Atlanta medics and under the inspiration and leadership of First Church.

The first public library for the use of Negroes of Atlanta was started at First Church.

The first organized program of social service for Negro people in Atlanta was that of First Church.

The National Convention of Congregational Workers for colored people had its origin in First Church under the leadership of its first Negro pastor.

The pastors of First Church have traditionally been civic and welfare leaders. Pastors of First Church have served on the following: Board of Directors and Executive Committee, Atlanta Branch National Association for the Advancement of Colored People; Executive Committee of the Atlanta Urban League; the Board of Management for the Butler Street Y. M. C. A., Atlanta; Advisory Committee, Fulton and Dekalb County Child Welfare Association; Board of Directors, Carrie Steele Logan Home for Orphans; Troop Committee of Troops 90 and 140, Atlanta Council Boy Scouts of America; Board of Directors and Executive Committee Atlanta Civic and Political League; Negro State Planning Committee; State Inter-racial Commission; State Advisory Committee Federal Forum, and Atlanta Vocational Guidance Council.

Document 21†

David A. Russell, Jr., "The Institutional Church in Transition: A Study of First Congregational Church of Atlanta, Georgia," (Unpublished Master of Arts Thesis, Atlanta University, 1971), pp. 30-32, 35-42.

The History of First Congregational Church

The history of First Congregational Church may be divided into two periods: the period 1867-1894 and the period 1894 to the

*Reprinted by permission of the author.

†Reprinted by permission of the author.

present. A look at the events which took place during these two periods may prove to be helpful in understanding First Congregational Church as an institutional church in transition.

The First Historical Period: (1867-1894)

Following the signing of the Emancipation Proclamation by President Abraham Lincoln in 1864, three young theological students in the Yale University Divinity School decided that they would devote their lives to the spiritual and educational development of the Freedmen. Two of these young men, the Rev. Erastus Cravath, later founder of Fisk University, and the Rev. Edmund Asa Ware, the founder of Atlanta University, enlisted in the service of the American Missionary Association and went South where they began their work. These young men along with the Rev. Cyrus W. Francis, an American Missionary Association spokesman, traveled throughout the state of Georgia in an effort to recruit Freedmen for what was to be known as the new "Open Door," an educational center in Atlanta, Georgia.

The recruitment process involved women as follows:

> 'Key Mothers' were selected from the more populous sections to come to the city. They were to canvass the homes as they were established and find boarding homes for the many expected pupils--some to be sent by their families, others (sic) to come unattached.

Freedmen migrated from all over the state to the City of Atlanta. Here the American Missionary Association had organized a primary and secondary school for Freedmen and their children.

> This school, the Storrs School, situated on the northern side of Houston Street near the corner of Piedmont Avenue was a social service center for the ever-growing community. Its chapel became a focal point for religious-minded patrons. They looked forward eagerly to the 'Worship Service' conducted by the New England missionaries. Ere long they expressed a desire for a church of their own in which their children could be trained to that type of reverence and quiet dignity in worship.

On May 22, 1867, a committee of persons affiliated with the school voted to organize a Congregational Church. The following Sunday, May 25, 1867, was the date of the First Congregational Church service to be held in the City of Atlanta, Georgia. Services were held in the chapel of the Storrs School, conducted by the Rev. Erastus Cravath, then secretary of the American Missionary Association.

First Church was presided over subsequently by pastors recommended by the American Missionary Association. These men had been trained in the leading colleges and divinity schools of New England. Most of them were graduates of Yale University. The following are names of each pastor presiding during the initial period: the Rev. Frederick Ayer, the Rev. Cyrus W. Francis, the Rev. Simon S. Ashley, the Rev. Charles W. Hawley, the Rev. Evart E. Kent and the Rev. Samuel H. Robinson. The first church edifice was erected during the pastorate of the Rev. Ashley on the corner of Houston and Piedmont Streets. The first parsonage was built during the ministry of the Rev. Evart Kent. The construction of both the church and the parsonage was financed by the American Missionary Association.

The Second Historical Period: (1894-1968)

In 1894, the second historical period began. The Rev. Henry H. Proctor, a graduate of Fisk University and a student of Yale Divinity School, became the first Negro pastor. It was at this time that the church became independent of the American Missionary Association. However, it served as a beneficiary of that organization for some time.

Under the leadership of Dr. Proctor, First Church is reported to have become the largest and most progressive Negro Congregational Church in the nation....

Community Building

Services rendered by First Congregational Church to the Atlanta community may be classified into three categories: (1) religious endeavor, (2) social welfare, and (3) cultural promotion.

Religious Endeavor

First Congregational Church has sponsored a vast number of projects designed to enhance the religious life of the community. According to Mrs. K. R. Adams, the historian of First Church, the church conducted three missions in different sections of the city during the First Period. The missions were used for conducting Bible classes in which the scriptures were taught to the general public.

From 1894 to 1920 First Congregational Church conducted five missions known as "Afternoon Sunday Schools" throughout the city; namely, the Betsy Woods Mission at 123 Cain Street; the Irwin Street Mission on the corner of Irwin and Hogue Streets; the Carrie Steele-Pitts Orphanage on East Fair Street; and the Prison Mission (Vespers) for inmates of the Federal Prison at Fulton County Tower.

Furthermore, Mrs. Adams reports that First Church sponsored a number of other religious projects in the community. An annual Vacation Bible School was organized and conducted by the church and a weekly pastor's column was printed in the Atlanta Daily World. The church continues to maintain an annual Vacation Bible

School in the summer but the pastor's weekly column in the Atlanta Daily World has been discontinued. Instead the church began a thirty-minute radio broadcast of the morning service on Radio Station WERD on Sunday afternoons from 2:30 to 3:00 p.m.

Another broadcast called "I've Got A Question" featuring young people on Saturday afternoons was started on that same radio station under the management of a former student assistant to the pastor. Both of these broadcasts were recently discontinued and the writer has been informed by the pastor that the church is looking for another radio station with which to continue its radio ministry.

Social Welfare

As mentioned earlier First Congregational Church has exhibited the characteristics of an institutional church, as defined by McConnell, from time to time. As early as 1873 health centers were conducted in three districts of the city by the church. The first was located in the vicinity of the church on Houston Street, the second was situated in a wagon yard on Decatur Street, and the third was in South Atlanta.

First Church was also instrumental in the founding of the Carrie Steele-Pitts Home for orphans. The present director of the home, herself a member of First Church, informs the author that many of the early founders of the home were members of First Church. Another member reports that the church rendered financial support to the home during those early years. At present the Carrie Steele-Pitts Home for orphans is a private institution but many members of the church, including the pastor, serve on the board of trustees.

First Church played a significant role in the reconstruction of the Negro Community following Atlanta's race riot of 1906. Bruce Barton describes that riot as follows:

> Enough destruction was achieved to leave its eternal mark upon the glory of the city and to plunge a portion of the population, at least into complete despair. There were 51,902 Negroes in Atlanta, over one-third of all the people in the city.
>
> ... After two or three days the terror died on the street, but it raged still in the hearts of the people. And particularly of that first class of colored folk, who had come out of the country to make their homes in Atlanta and to acquire money to educate their children and be credit to their kind. 'We shall have to move,' they said one to another, repeating it over like frightened children. 'There will be no opportunity for us in Atlanta from now on; the disease is checked, but there remains the wound, ugly, glaring, a bitter reminder forever that we are set behind the veil, that we may go thus far and no farther.

> Whatever we have gathered together here that cannot go must be sacrificed, for we must seek out a new city where there is no scar.'
>
> So the comment ran, and all over the city--that is, the colored city of 51,902 with which the story deals--men began trembling to gather their goods about them preparatory to flight. For a few hours a whole city of 51,902 souls hung in the balance. One day it was there, prosperous, contented, aspiring; and the next day it shuddered on the brink of oblivion.

Of First Church's role in the restoration of the city's Negro community, Barton comments as follows:

> But between those two days there moved in and through Atlanta the great towering figure of Henry H. Proctor of the First Congregational Church, colored, in Atlanta, graduate of Yale, successor to two white preachers and a figure in the city as unmistakable and as unavoidable as Piedmont Hotel or Union Depot. To one stricken businessman after another he went with this message: 'Now is no time to think of leaving Atlanta. This riot gives us our opportunity. It is over. The city is forever sobered by it. Out of it will come a better understanding between races and a glorious progress for us. This is our appointed time if we can show ourselves worthy of it.' 'What do you mean worthy of it?' they questioned. And he answered them:
>
> 'Now's our chance to show them the stuff we're made of--that we're real men, not grown-up children as they want to believe us. Let's show them the men we are. Let's begin by erecting a church as has never been erected by colored men before, an institutional church embodying all that is modern and approved in church work. Let that be our answer to the riot; and let's begin now.'
>
> So there arose out of the havoc of the riot this monument to the courage and manhood of a people, a voice still but by no means small, following the earthquake and the fire. It is hardly too much to say that the City of Atlanta--the colored city of 51,902 souls found itself in the building of that church. Fixing its vision and determination on that, eager to show to the white city the substance of the soul, it forgot terror, forgot all the thoughts of desertion and stood fast. It is the only church I know that has the right to claim for itself that it saved a city.

In 1908 Dr. Proctor erected the present structure of First Church located at Houston and Courtland Streets in what is now downtown Atlanta. During his pastorate the church organized an Institutional Department which served the Negro people of Atlanta during that time. In 1917 Dr. Proctor went to New Haven, Connecticut, and solicited the help of Ralph J. Miner, a wealthy friend of his, who before his death included First Church in his will. Of this matter Mrs. Adams provides the following note:

> Dr. Proctor went north and found friends to aid. Ralph J. Miner of New Haven, Connecticut, and his wife, became the most substantial donors during his lifetime. By his will the department received $1100.00 yearly. The church supplied many volunteers to assist the two paid workers. Miss Nellie Watts, a social worker, of the membership, was paid by the Phelps-Stokes Fund, N. Y. Rev. Fletcher Bryant was financed by The Social Service Commission of Congregational Churches of the United States. The Cooking School and the Working Girls' Home paid the teacher and the matron respectively.

With the financial aid provided by the Ralph J. Miner estate the church operated an employment bureau, a business school, a kindergarten, public water facility, a playground and secretarial service for illiterate soldiers at Camp Gordon during World War I.

The employment bureau was successfully instrumental in helping people coming into Atlanta to find jobs in the city. Its clientele is said to have included white as well as Negro persons seeking employment. At the request of Mrs. Proctor, the wife of the pastor, the Remington Typewriter Establishment in Atlanta agreed to furnish typewriters for business classes at the church. Mrs. Proctor, who had been trained in business at Fisk University, conducted business classes in typing and shorthand.

The library of the church was supplied with books donated by Congregational churches in the northern states. It was situated in what is now the primary Church School room of the church. The gymnasium was housed in the rear of the basement and the working girls' home and cooking school were located next door to the church. In front of the church on the Houston Street side were a drinking fountain for passersby and a trough for horses.

It is also reported that on Saturdays two young ladies from the church would go to Camp Gordon where they served as secretaries for illiterate soldiers stationed there. These young ladies also operated a postal service at the camp. All of these projects comprised what was called the Ralph J. Miner Institute, named after the church's late friend and donor, Ralph J. Miner of New Haven, Connecticut.

In 1920 the church discontinued its institutional ministry as such due to the advent of the Urban League and other civic agencies. With the close of the Ralph J. Miner Institute, the money that had financed the department was forfeited. However, it is understood that by 1921, 4,200 persons were still using the curtailed institutional facilities.

In regard to the membership of First Church, Barton makes the following declaration:

> Many city churches I have seen whose pastors could name over to me prominent and wealthy men among their members, or the husbands of their members. But I do not know where else there is a church that seems so thoroughly to have permeated the life of the city--as has the First Congregational Church (sic) in Atlanta. For a whole day I went back and forth in its city and up and down in it. The largest Negro printing establishment is owned by one of its members and the only Negro newspaper is edited by him. The oldest drug store in the city, the one singled out by the government to be a sub-postal station, is presided over by one of the Church's staunch supporters. I talked with a church trustee, a grocer who in his forty years and more of active business life gathered a clientele more largely white than colored and accumulated a fortune of more than 40,000 (sic) dollars. Stationery stores, tailoring establishments, theaters, meat markets, photograph galleries--it seems to me as we passed among them that everyone of particular merit bore upon its face the name of a member of First Church.... In three cases the principals were members of the church and teachers in the Sunday School; and half of all the teachers that I saw, it seemed to be they were connected in one way or the other with the life of the church as well.

The first scout troop for Negro boys in the city was organized at First Church. In 1910 members of the church made petition for a charter for a troop. However, it was not until 1931 when Rev. William J. Faulkner, the third Negro pastor of the church, went to the proper authorities and strongly pled for the charter was it granted. In 1934 the troop received a 100% standard rating. "The troop won every honor in Scouting and the scout-master the highest award in Scouting." says Mrs. Adams. However, for some unexplained reason scouting was later discontinued at First Church, and now the church is without a scout troop.

First Church also played a vital part in the organization of Metropolitan Atlanta Association For The Blind. During the pastorate of Dr. Proctor the church accommodated the classes of the association until they were able to get a building of their own. First Church contributes financially to the organization and Dr. McEwen, the present pastor, is a deacon for the association.

First Congregational Church has figured prominently on both local and national levels. The Atlanta Interracial Commission was organized in First Church under the leadership of Dr. Proctor and Dr. Plato Durham, pastor of the First Presbyterian Church of the city. Pastors of First Congregational Church have traditionally been civic and welfare leaders....

Cultural Promotion

As mentioned above First Church has sponsored programs of cultural entertainment for the city. Artists of both local and national fame have been featured in the concerts and festivals of those early years. Among the artists featured by the church were Joseph R. Douglass, violinist; Richard B. Harrison, dramatic reader; Mme. Azalia Hackley, soprano; William Bush, organist and Adrienne Herndon who along with Truman K. Gibson was featured in the play "Everyman." This was the first play given in the new building, thus pioneering the black theater in the city.

Looking in retrospect Mrs. Adams writes:

> Memorable, in the minds of Atlantans and many adjacent smalltown lovers of good music, are the 1909-1912 Music Festivals. While visiting his Alma Mater, Fisk University, Dr. Proctor noticed a tenor voice of exceptional quality. Quick as a wink the City Auditorium, still under construction in Atlanta, flashed in his mind: 'A city-wide Music Festival; Star this tenor; Have an inter-denominational choir'--The Music Festivals were born.
>
> Roland Hayes, that golden-voiced tenor made his debut thru (sic) First Congregational Church in 1909. It was the first public concert staged in the City Auditorium.

The church sponsored other music festivals which featured such nationally acclaimed artists as Madam Lillian Evanti, soprano, Washington, D. C.; Hazel Harrison, pianist; "Anita Fetti," (Mme. Brown) soprano, Chicago, Ill.; Harry T. Burleigh, baritone-composer; and the "Creole Nightingale," Mrs. J. C. Olden, soprano, New Orleans, Louisiana.

Dr. DuBois' interest and studies influenced the founding of the Gate City Free Kindergarten Association by Atlanta women in 1905. The following shows that the thoughts of DuBois and J. W. E. Bowen bore fruition in direct action beneficial to the needs and problems of urban blacks.

Document 22*

Louie D. Shivery, "The History of the Gate City Free Kindergarten Association," The History of Organized Social Work Among Atlanta Negroes, 1890-1935, (Unpublished Master of Arts Thesis, Department of Sociology, Atlanta University, 1936), pp. 4-11.

History. As a result of papers read and findings of the At-

*Reprinted by permission.

lanta University Conferences 1896, 1898, and 1905, on "Mortality Among Negroes in Cities," "Social and Physical Conditions of Negroes in Cities," and "Methods and Results of Ten Years' Study of the American Negro," the Gate City Free Kindergartens were established.

Some twelve years before 1897, there was a model Jones' Kindergarten, under the care of Miss Amy Chadwick. It had to be discontinued for want of means. Although this movement had been started, it was not considered because it was the plan of the conference to discuss only such reforms as were immediately practical and would be dependent only on local cooperation and support.

Survey. The results of the 1896, and 1897 conferences revealed a definite demand for Day Nurseries and Kindergartens for Negro Children of pre-school age whose mothers were away at work all day, leaving their children with neighbors or neglected to run the streets. One paper revealed that a child left with neighbors developed typhoid and died almost before the mother knew it was sick.

The following extracts from the 1897 conference will give the reader something of an idea of the deplorable condition of neglected Negro children of pre-school age at this time.

> With all the ardor of an anxious mother, I repeat that day homes or Kindergartens are a glaring need, an absolute necessity if the masses are to be raised.

Another plea was made for "Day Nurseries." The following is an extract:

> Among the important questions of today is the need of day nurseries in cities and towns where children of parents who, by force of circumstances, are obliged to earn a living by working in service, may receive a good and wholesome influence during that period of life when impressions are easily made and character readily molded, either for good or bad.

Commenting upon the plight of the Negro child who was left alone while the mother went to work, the report states:

> It is a daily experience to find a child of tender years left to tend the baby with but a scant meal of meat and bread, while the widowed mother is out at work, who returns at night tired and exhausted to feed and care for the children. Such a state of constant activity exhausts her vital force and she dies at an early age leaving little children in the hands of chance, to be brought up among the weeds of vice and sin. If there had been a day nursery with good conscientious persons at its head, in which these children have had their physical, mental and moral natures properly cared for at a small cost to the mother, they would have

> developed into characters with sufficient magnitude to lift humanity to a higher plane, instead of degrading it; and the mother who would no doubt have lived out her three score years and ten.

Again it was brought out in the conference that the records of mortality of Negroes of Atlanta showed one third of the deaths occurred among children; and that a large number of boys, almost babies, were to be found loitering and making mischief in the alleys, and some had drifted into the chain gangs.

The papers read at the conference went on record as stating:

> We need an institution where mothers who are obliged to be away from home in order that they may earn an honest living may leave their children and have the satisfaction of knowing that their little minds are lifted above the miry slough and prepared to shun the pitfalls that have been the destruction of many a young life born to usefulness.

After the 1897 conference, the appeal was so urgent, and the cases to pathetic, the director of the Conference, Dr. W. E. B. DuBois, lately from Harvard where he had known Mr. George Bradford of Boston, discussed this phase of the conference with the sister of the late Edward Twitchell Ware, Miss Gertrude Ware of Atlanta University, with a view to organizing some such work.

The Gate City Free Kindergarten Association, 1905

Gate City Kindergarten Organized as a Direct Result of Tenth Atlanta Conference, 1905. In 1905 at the Atlanta University Conference on the study of Negro life, it was shown by the studies made during the ten previous years, that one of the great needs among Negroes was for day nurseries or free kindergartens for children whose mothers were compelled to be away from home all day at work. The real need was for day nurseries, but on account of the lack of money to support them, it was felt that care during part of the day in free kindergartens would be better than no care; and so the Gate City Free Kindergarten Association was organized with Mrs. Gertrude Bunce as president. Others who were connected with the Organization at that time were: Mrs. David T. Howard, Mrs. J. W. E. Bowen, Mrs. George Burch, Mrs. A. Graves, Mrs. John Hope and Mr. and Mrs. A. F. Herndon and others, besides a large number of associate members. In the autumn of 1905, two kindergartens were opened in two of the sections of Atlanta, where the need seemed greatest. Later, two more were opened and a fifth one was started in 1908. The first kindergarten was given the use of a mission on Cain Street, a congested district, and was paid for by the First Congregational Church of which Rev. H. H. Proctor was pastor. Miss Amy Chadwick gave rent and fuel for a kindergarten in the Leonard Street Children's Home. For still another of the kindergartens, Mrs. Raoul gave a house at very low rental. Later she sold the house to the Association at a very reasonable figure and a committee of women of the Inter-racial Commission gave substantial help in the purchase of the property. One teacher's salary and the milk for one kindergarten was paid by the late Mr. A. F. Herndon, who early took a deep interest in the work, and who subsequently gave and put into condition a house in White's Alley--a congested section--where one kindergarten was located. This house was named the Herndon Day Nursery. After a number of years, the location became morally and physically threatening to the safety of the children, so that it seemed advisable to secure another location. At a short distance, another piece of property was secured and the nursery was removed to its present location on Stonewall Street, Southeast, and retained the name of the Herndon Day Nursery. These five free kindergartens were continued and maintained until the organization of the Atlanta Community Chest, the work being financed by a multitude of efforts and solicited contributions. When the Community Chest was organized, the long-felt need of day nurseries was partially met and these five free kindergartens became two day nurseries including kindergartens. This work has continued for thirty years without any cessation. The most important factor in the development of the work has been the deep unselfish interest of the women who formed the Association and who have been willing to do everything in their power to meet the great need of Negro children of working mothers in Atlanta. These women went to work and work unceasingly until Kindergartens in five separate wards of Atlanta were established, operating at an annual cost of $1,200, not including food and clothes which were donated above the $1,200, this being spent for teachers' salaries, and rental of houses in which to operate the Kindergartens.

Miss Ola Perry was an Atlanta University graduate, who interested Mrs. Raoul in the work. The property was bought later for $1,800, $300.00 down payment and the balance $25.00 a month at 6%. One Hundred and Fifty Dollars of the initial payment was made by the Inter-racial Committee.

Other Sources of Income for Support of the Kindergartens. To maintain this kindergarten, for several years Proctor & Gamble gave five boxes of ivory soap annually. This soap was used in the kindergarten and nursery department and sold to members of the Association. Another method of raising funds was through working circles throughout the city. These circles raised money by various objects. From Bazaars held at Thanksgiving time, lasting as long as a week, when every circle was responsible for a day, one day of which a turkey dinner was served. Money was made by sales in items of fancy work, aprons, etc., canned fruit, cakes and whatever could be begged. The association realized as much as $250.00 at a Bazaar. From track meets sponsored by colleges, and participated in by the children of the public school, $100.00 gate receipts were cleared. Food and cake sales brought at times $50.00. April sales brought $50.00, and one time the women realized as much as $100.00 from the sale of aprons. Sales of papers, magazines and tin foil brought as much as $50.00. A baby contest brought $50.00. Intercollegiate contest brought $100. Post-season baseball games realized as much as $25.00. Sale of soap wrappers, soap powder wrappers, saved and collected from housewives, and baking powder coupons brought $25.00. On Tag Day $100.00 was raised. Lawn parties and Egg Hunts netted $10.00. Donations from individuals, and collections from churches aided. Friendship Baptist Church always gave from $25.00 to $50.00 annually. Candy sales and rummage sales also came in to swell the funds of the Association. Members paid $1.00 a month dues for several years; those unable to pay $1.00 paid Fifty Cents a month. Clothes were donated every year by the Local Needle Work Guild, a group of white women, for the needy children who were naked as often as hungry. Gifts of clothes and food were given by many individuals. For many years, Mr. Cleveland Dodge gave $100.00 a year in memory of his sister, Miss Grace Dodge. For many years, the Southern Manchester Committee Sunday School sent $10.00 annually. Mr. Heman Perry, founder of the Standard Life Insurance Company, the first Negro straight Life Insurance Company, gave $40.00 a month as rent for the Kindergarten set-up on Piedmont Avenue, 4th ward; after the success and funds of the Rock Street Kindergarten warranted the establishment of another, where Day Nursery No. 2 was opened. Mr. Perry also put sanitary plumbing into the house for the Association, free of charge.

Teachers, rentals, food, clothing, school equipment, fuel, labor and other expenses cost enormously. Funds were raised from personal contributions and from various projects, but for ten years they never had any sum of money in view on which they could count.

Morehouse College, Atlanta University, Public School Officials, teachers and pupils cooperated in aiding these Negro women, who assumed such tremendous financial obligations every year without any funds, appropriations or visible incomes. It was all done through charity, yet they stuck to the job. Not a cent was paid for salaries, except for Kindergarten teachers, and that the most meager. Hours, days, weeks were given freely. For 19 years people of Atlanta were appealed to for money, food, fuel and equipment. Projects that taxed the body, soul and mind were undertaken to raise funds. The help and cooperation of the city, the public schools, and the colleges were sought as well as the assistance of churches; that shelter, food and care might be given to children whose parents had to work and could not care for them during the day; that the underprivileged might start on life's journey of good citizenship unhandicapped, with a love of the beautiful and just sense of proportion of life's mental horizon; that mothers might be enabled to work more efficiently, by being relieved of anxiety, because the nursery had cared for their children during the day. Thus, nurseries aided in building the health and character of these underprivileged children, and sheltered them from the influence of "curbstone education."

How the Expansion of the Work into Five Free Kindergartens Resulted From These Efforts. When Kindergartens were maintained, only one paid worker was employed for each kindergarten. At first there was only one. Then as soon as the Association could see its way to raise the money for another teacher, another was opened in another ward of the city, and so on until there were five, located in five different sections of the city.

The teacher's salary was the main expense, because the rent for a place in which to operate the Kindergarten was paid in this way: Rent for Kindergarten No. 1 was paid by the First Congregational Church; Rent for Kindergarten No. 2 by Mr. A. F. Herndon; Rent for No. 3 by Miss Amy Chadwick; Rent for No. 4 by the Presbyterian Mission; and Rent for No. 5 was practically paid by Mrs. Mary Raoul. Of course, this rent was not in cash. Kindergartens were held in buildings owned by the parties named. And the expense increased in proportion to the increase of the number of Kindergartens for the reason given; hence these courageous women faced a Herculean task each year which would have discouraged the practical business expert.

Nineteen Successful Years. The approximate expenditures for the nineteen years before the Association's Kindergartens were taken into the Chest, was $190,283.89, including clothes, foods, fuels, and equipment, which, if estimated by the appropriations for these items for a year by the Atlanta Community Chest, would approximate this amount.

It cost $1,200 a year to maintain the five free kindergartens. All of the money was raised in the ways that have been mentioned. In time, Miss Chadwick took over the kindergarten which the association had rented in her Chadwick home and the Presbyterian Mission did the same for the one which was on Richardson Street, operated in its mission.

High Points of the Organization. It entered the Atlanta Community Chest in 1924.

The Community Chest Said of the Gate City Free Kindergarten Association in 1924:

> Nineteen years ago the people of Atlanta were asked to give money to provide shelter and protection for the poor and needy little children whose parents could not care for them during the day. The struggle of those early years was pitiful, and until the Community Chest was created, the support of this work was meager.
>
> A. F. Herndon's gift of the Herndon Day Nursery at 44½ Dover Street put the Association on a solid basis. Before the Chest support became available, the struggle was great to finance this one day nursery.

This document, a digest of the Master of Arts Thesis of Louie D. Shivery, relates the history of the organization and the growth of a model experiment and experience pioneering a community development approach to social work and social welfare, the Neighborhood Union. Launched in 1908 by dedicated black women of Atlanta, Georgia, under the leadership of Mrs. John Hope (wife of the president of Morehouse College), this organization was staffed for three years by non-professional volunteer workers, emerging without precedent and surviving for a twenty year period, "as the sole agency of social reform in the Negro community." Finally, in 1928 more specialized agencies staffed by professionals took over its principal functions.

Mrs. Shivery, who graduated from Atlanta University in 1903, served as a public school teacher for thirty-eight years, and as secretary of the Neighborhood Union from 1910 to 1930. The article is not reproduced in its entirety, but the service of the Neighborhood Union continued far beyond the period under immediate examination. Inasmuch as the needs of the blacks required the mobilization of the total resources of the community, it is seen that the Neighborhood Union pioneered a concept in social welfare and a mode of organization far advanced over the settlement house pattern developed in Northern cities to assimilate the European immigrant.

Document 23*

Louie D. Shivery, "The Neighborhood Union, A Survey of the Beginnings of Social Welfare Movements Among Negroes in Atlanta," The History of Organized Social Work Among Atlanta Negroes, 1890-1935, (Unpublished Master of Arts Thesis, Dept. of Sociology, Atlanta Univ., 1936).

Social work among Negroes was begun in Atlanta by the founding of the Carrie Steele Orphanage in 1890 through the efforts of a former slave, Carrie Steele, who was employed as a laborer at the Atlanta Union Depot. The work of the orphanage was eventually taken over by the city and a graduate of Atlanta University, Mrs. Howard W. Pitts, still stands as its head. A second effort was the Leonard Street Orphan's Home, conducted by an Englishwoman, Miss Amy Chadwick, from 1890 to 1936. The property was bought by Atlanta University and now houses the Spelman College Nursery School. A third effort grew directly out of the Atlanta University Conferences and was the Gate City Free Kindergarten Association, started by Gertrude Ware in 1905. This was carried on as a private institution for many years but finally was taken over by the Gate

*Reprinted by permission.

City Day Nursery Association, supported by the Community Chest. This brings us to the series of efforts undertaken by the Neighborhood Union.

The Neighborhood Union was an organization founded in 1908 by a group of women led by Mrs. John Hope. The occasion for organization was an incident: a woman in the neighborhood, who seldom spoke to anybody, was missing from her accustomed place on her porch. The neighbors instituted an investigation, and found her dying alone in the house. A meeting of the neighbors was called and an organization effected which had this motto: "And Thy Neighbor As Thyself."

The colored West Side of Atlanta furnished an unusually fitting birthplace for the growth and development of any kind of community project, for it is built around Atlanta University, Spelman and Morehouse Colleges. This has been true for more than fifty years. The death of this lonely woman aroused the necessary community consciousness and the Neighborhood Union was founded.

In this first meeting, it was decided that each family in the neighborhood should be known. The women present were assigned to districts. A house-to-house visit was made in each district. The results gained from these contacts revealed an astounding need for better and more highly integrated home life.

The Union investigated conditions, tabulated facts, and analyzed the data. From the first survey which the women made there was a house-to-house visitation and from Mrs. Hattie R. Watson's survey of a hundred families around Morehouse College, the social problems of the West Side were disclosed and the data revealed: that the foremost of these evils were unsanitary conditions, poor housing, lack of recreation, family disorganization and delinquency.

The study also disclosed the fact that streets were badly in need of improvement with insufficient lights. There was little sewerage, the water supply consisted mostly of surface wells. Crime, delinquency, houses of ill repute, neighborhood disturbances and evil influences to which young boys and girls were exposed, were the findings to which the Union turned its immediate attention and which served as a basis for its organization.

The remedial work began by the organization of a health clinic in 1908. The Union bought a piece of property on Lee Street, where the Atlanta University School of Social Work now stands. Here were conducted health classes, clinics, home economic classes, boys' and girls' activities, mothers' meetings, citizenship groups, lecture courses and literary societies.

As finally adopted the plan of the Neighborhood Union was to divide a section of the city one-half a mile square in the vicinity of Morehouse College, into twelve areas with committees appointed for each of these districts to conduct a house-to-house campaign for the promotion of a practical knowledge of domestic science, and the observance of the elementary laws of health.

The Neighborhood Union in 1908 and 1910, through its various zones, eventually planned to reach every section of Atlanta in a movement to educate Negro parents. It attempted to show them how easy it would be to provide an hour or more every day for wholesome recreation for their children. The zone workers or leaders demonstrated various games on vacant lots, in backyards and indoors, to show parents the value and necessity of such activities.

Various methods of raising money and furnishing group entertainment were adopted. There was an "Intercollegiate Track Meet" put on in 1909 in connection with supervised playgrounds operated on Morehouse College campus. In addition, especially directed playgrounds with days for boys and days for girls were set up in 1910.

In 1911, the Union secured a charter and set in motion a program so effective that eventually the city turned over to it most of the social work of Atlanta among Negroes. The organization was taxed to the limit to carry out its objectives. The family welfare program was heavy. Sickness, deaths, births, insanity, want, unemployment, truancy, and related problems kept the women busy. Recreation was provided by the annual track meet and new classes in folk dances. Activities for raising funds to buy a center were numerous. By 1911, five neighborhoods had been organized, each representing densely populated Negro settlements. The women had concentrated their efforts and set up these communities as the need for such work was brought to their attention by those who had become acquainted with what was being done by the organization located on the West Side.

The West Side was neglected section of the city. Fair Street was a slum, full of holes, mud and debris. Areas named "Beaver's Slide," White's Alley, Peters Street, and Roach Street terrified even children because of fights, brawls, gambling and killings that were all too frequent occurrences there. Beckwith Street, (where the Atlanta University president's home now stands) was full of hill and holes, mud and rocks, with no pavements. The city used it as a dump for rubbish. As late as 1914 automobiles and wagons could not go through. Chestnut Street, flanking this section, was partly developed first by whites, later by graduates of Atlanta University, Spelman and Morehouse, who built homes on the street to live near the colleges. But there were no water mains, and residents had to appeal to the City Council to stop the burning of garbage in the area because of the resultant stench and smoke. Behind Atlanta University on the north was a similar section, known as "Vine City" or "Mechanicsville" where slums, dumps, hovels, crime and want prevailed. Directly behind this section, going north, was another section known as "Lightning" where the city permitted houses of ill repute. On the other side of Atlanta, going south, was "Summerhill," a Negro settlement in which many Negroes owned small pieces of unimproved property and where the same neglect as to lights, water, sewerage, pavements and housing prevailed.

The work of these women established the need for a probation and juvenile officer for Negro work. Through the auxiliary of eleven representative men in the Union they secured the appointment of Garrie Moore for this work. In 1912, he was elected by them as director. Mr. Moore, a graduate of the New York School of Social Work and a professor of sociology in Morehouse College, was the first boys' worker ever appointed for work among Negro boys by the YMCA in the United States, and the first juvenile officer for colored delinquents in Atlanta. He was a man of fine spirit, and an excellent organizer and leader.

The work of the Neighborhood Union was also actively assisted by Professor J. A. Bigham, who was, at the time, conducting the Atlanta University Conferences and making a special study of Negro crime. He cooperated with the Union, especially in the matter of securing paroles for Negro adult prisoners.

The work of the Neighborhood Union for the first three years was practically the same and the history of 1912 is but a continuation and expansion of these activities. In an effort to improve sanitation, lighting, sewerage, health, housing and streets, it petitioned again to the City Council and the Board of Health. It continued to push its regular program of family welfare, education, cultural meetings and clubs with no let-up. However, there were high points in the year 1912 not to be forgotten.

By this time the plan of the Neighborhood Union had been worked out and tested and was so effective that eventually it was adopted by other cities and organizations. It provided for an official staff of eight, consisting of a president, three vice-presidents, a treasurer and three secretaries. There were forty-two persons on the board of directors and fourteen persons in charge of the various districts.

As has been stated before, the plan of the Neighborhood Union has been in constant demand since the organization of the Union. Three times in its history it has been revised to meet the needs. In 1908, it was designed to serve a single neighborhood, the West Side, in the First Ward of Atlanta. A second time, in 1911, it was revised to include five sections of Atlanta: the First Ward, Fourth Ward, South Atlanta, Pittsburg, and Vine City or Mechanicsville. A third time, in 1915, it was revised to include all neighborhoods of the city of Atlanta, for use by the Anti-Tuberculosis Association, at which time the city was divided into sixteen zones.

Steps were next taken to locate places suitable for the operating program of the organization and a request was made to Superintendent William M. Slaton for the use of public school buildings for meetings and other activities. The request was granted in part and for the first time in the history of Atlanta, public school buildings were used for civic meetings. There were five sections organized, but only three schools were granted. These were Roach Street in the West Side district, Storrs Street in Fourth Ward, and Pittsburg School in the southwest section.

The most important thing done in 1913 was the survey of the Atlanta public schools. A group of women headed by the Neighborhood Union was organized to investigate school conditions. It was called the Women's Social Improvement Committee. It consisted of one hundred leading colored women of Atlanta. Their efforts called forth the aid of some white women who joined the fight for better schools. The meetings lasted through the summer, and were held at the Butler Street "Y". Every Councilman was interviewed; every member of the Board of Education was visited personally by a representative of the committee; the white "Lady Board of Visitors" of the Board of Education was visited, and some of them visited the meetings of the colored women. White ministers were appealed to; pictures of the school conditions, and a survey of schools gave facts which the committee carried directly to the public. The matter was at last brought before the City Council. It resulted in much comment from the Council and from the press. The Atlanta Constitution carried a long editorial on the subject.

The tabulation of facts showed that the seating capacity in Negro schools in 1913 and 1914 was 4,102, but there were 6,163 children enrolled, and there were 4,122 pupils affected by double sessions. Much of the retardation and failure to make grades had been repeatedly attributed to these double sessions. Despite this revelation no immediate results for the Negro public schools followed.

On June 11, 1914, the organization took steps to purchase a piece of Spelman Seminary property at 41 Leonard Street, Southwest, for a community center. The center was opened on Leonard Street in 1914, with a paid trained social worker, Miss Carrie Dukes Cole, and operated successfully as a community center until 1926 when the Fair Street Clinic was dedicated....

The following editorial is from the Atlanta Constitution, February, 1911, and is representative of the attitude of the white press toward the organizational efforts of Negro women. Although praise is given to their achievements, its prevailing tone is paternalistic and condescending. One of the greatest social welfare experiments of the day is characteristically interpreted only as an effort by blacks to approximate the "superior civilization" of whites. The editorial entitled "Treating Negro Problem at Basis,"[10] is as follows:

An organization sought to be chartered by fifty or more representative negro women of Atlanta under the title, the "Neighborhood Union," deserves more than passing attention from the students of the negro problem in its fundamental aspects.

The organization, headed by Lugenia Hope, wife of the president of Atlanta Baptist College, has already been at work for sometime in that section of the city bounded by Ashby, Chapel and Beckwith Streets and Greensferry Avenue.

Having demonstrated the feasibility of the principle upon which they operated, the intention now is to find a central body which shall gradually create similar unions in every negro neighborhood in the city.

The primary purposes of the organization are to elevate moral, social, intellectual and spiritual standards in each neighborhood; to lead mothers to better care of infants, cleaner and more sanitary care of the premises; to campaign everywhere against vice and disease, by appealing to individual members of the home, to organize classes for tuition in cooking, sewing and general housework.

The program gets at the very basis of the negro problem, wherever located. It is by the purity, virility and aspiration of the home that the white race has achieved and safeguarded its civilization. The same influences must be directed against the problems of disease, vice, crime, and inefficiency, if the negro race is ever to solve its own problems.

It is to be hoped progress will be made in these directions by this new organization, which is not of a commercial nature. The Constitution has many times pointed out, co-operation from the superior race is called for in the degree that the white man is inevitably affected by the progress or retrogression of the negro.

The documents cited below are from Mrs. Shivery's master of arts thesis and supplement the text of her article in Phylon, reproduced in part above.

Document 24*

Louie D. Shivery, "The History of Organized Social Work Among Atlanta Negroes, 1890-1935," (Unpublished Master of Arts Thesis, Department of Sociology, Atlanta University, 1936). Appendix No. 2: Survey, Sociological Department, Morehouse College, Directed by Professor Watson, pp. 431-436. Appendix No. 3: "The Constitution of the Neighborhood Union," pp. 437-439. Appendix No. 4: "Charter of the Neighborhood Union," pp. 441-444. Appendix No. 6: "Plan of Organization," pp. 447-451. Appendix No. 7: "Aims of the Neighborhood Union," p. 452. "Initial Procedures of the Neighborhood Union Founders," pp. 46-54.

*Reprinted by permission.

Appendix No. 2

... This effort included sixty-three homes which are located on 20 different streets. These homes are occupied by four hundred and sixty-nine people. The actual home life of these people, such as sleeping, cooking, eating and congregating is confined largely to three hundred and fifteen rooms. Based on this estimate there are seven and four-tenths persons for each five rooms or one and five-tenths persons to each room. The above figures are averages and might mislead one into believing that the actual living conditions of these people are more ideal than is actually the fact. In reality the greater number of these houses had from two to seven rooms, which of course tends to show that there are some over-crowded conditions. Fifty-six of these houses might be listed as private homes and seven as lodgings. Sixty-two of them face front streets and one faces an alley. The provisions according to families was as follows: Forty-nine houses contained one family each, 12 housed two families and 1 three families. On a whole the families were small--twenty-one of them had only one child. From a standpoint of physical appearance the majority of these houses were in a rather poor condition internally--while on the other hand the external condition of about half of them is good. Most of these people are renters and live in what is known as "Negro Rent Property."

Slightly more than half of these homes are poorly kept. Some extenuating circumstances, however, are to be noted--for instance the majority of the women work away from home. However, some of those who remain at home give an impression of not having a domestic interest, while some others are interested in housekeeping but just do not know about the kind of mechanics that makes for an appreciated home life.

Only five of these houses had cellars and these were used for storage and were well-kept. A look at the backyards leaves one under the impression that fences are built for the purpose of hiding a multitude of faults, for our investigation reveals that the majority of the backyards are only fairly or poorly kept. More than half of the front yards were well kept and only five were really in poor condition. Of the sixty-three homes in this study ten did not have front yards.

The roads in front of forty-seven of these houses are paved but in twelve instances the conditions of these roadways is bad. The sidewalks in front of forty-nine are paved but in only twenty-eight instances could the condition of these be called good. The remaining sidewalks and streets are not paved and are in poor condition. It is probable that the good paving is due largely to the result of an effort on the part of the city in very recent years to better physical conditions in neighborhoods essentially negroid in population.

The general appearance of the neighborhoods surrounding the homes subjected to specific study is from fair to bad--the weight of evidence being in favor of fair. At least eight of the streets involved are integral parts of the best neighborhoods of the first and seventh wards.

The moral status, judging from the general external appearance of the several communities and their inhabitants is fair. Of course external appearances can not be used as barometers of moral status but might give some evidence of existence of conditions undesirable.

While the home conditions do not reveal a dangerous amount of overcrowded living conditions--there is enough suggested by the figures in the body of this study to warrant some attention from the executive of the organization.

The large number of homes that were occupied by only one family tended to show that the general economic status is slightly above the average type of Negroes who attend free clinics. The fact that there were twenty-one families with just one child strengthens the above statement. These figures suggest some further phases of investigation that might be profitable to the organization, namely: (1) Is the financial condition of these families of such nature as to justify their attendance at a free clinic; (2) Are these families practicing birth control for any purpose, for instance, to raise the standards of their living, because they want more freedom, by force of poverty, etc. ?

The poor internal and good external appearance of the larger number of these houses leads one to feel that probably it takes home ownership to create home pride--on the other hand the good external condition of such a large per cent of this group of homes may be indicative of a growing liberality on the part of landowners whose livelihood is drawn from "Negro Rent Property."

The community welfare worker does more of an effective job when her community contacts are used for a basis of diagnosing the internal condition of home-making and its resultant effect on the mental reactions of her clients--then uses this information for a guide in prescribing the right therapeutics.

The investigators determined that the poor conditions of backyards was due largely to the fact that parents force children to play in the yard and allowed them to mess up things generally. This is probably true, but upon second thought the comparison of front and backyards might promote the thought that there is a definite effort to put the "best foot forward." In many instances the inner conditions of the homes revealed that the front rooms were well-kept while the remainder of the house was badly arranged.

Exhibit I shows the questionnaire used in the Survey:

Housing Survey

Street Morehouse College Ward 1 Date March 8, 1928

House Brick

No. Rooms 46 No. Families Students of college standing one child, age 7, 2 in family

College Dormitory Facing Front

Total No. Persons 88

Physical Appearance, Internally:

The mother in this family is away in college leaving a two room apartment to the father and small child, about age 8. The two rooms and bath are rather systematically arranged in order that the father may be able to find things when he puts them down. Furniture is good but dusting is needed. The front room is quite full of toys, etc., the playthings of Albert who is kept most of the time in the house. Ten pictures and many books are in evidence. The general appearance of the two rooms is neat with the touch of a man's crude housekeeping. Meals are served in a common dining room which eliminates cooking, etc.

Is house well kept, why?

Small-simplicity. There is no external appearance because the building is rather new and well kept by the college; plenty of light; that is, the windows are large and well placed.

Cellar: Describe general condition. If used for sleeping quarters or other purposes, explain use in full. Describe condition of yards: Back?

The basement of the building is used for the college dining room seating some 300 students. The backyard is ill kept due to the fact of outsiders spilling solids over the yard.

Front?

The two rooms face the campus and are on the northwest corner of the building. Building faces north, campus usually pretty well kept.

Streets: Paved? Yes Sidewalk: Paved? Yes

Condition of Streets and Sidewalks: Most of the streets nearby are paved and the sidewalks covered with bricks which are uncomfortable for walking.

Describe appearance of houses in neighborhood:

Well kept as to repair and paint.

What is your opinion of moral status of neighborhood?

Because of the location, the influence of the college shows itself. The general housing and alley conditions are average or above most districts of the city. No dance halls or pool room or vice makers are nearby.

Why did you form this opinion?

I believe the neighborhood is above average due to the fact that I have lived here 8 years and watched it grow and noticed the attitude of the people towards the college and the feeling of quiet and respectable well kept homes and the college allows the children to play on the athletic field, which prevents the bad gangs that are common in all neighborhoods.

A. Walter Childs 38"
Investigator

Appendix No. 3

The Constitution of the Neighborhood Union: We, the women living in the section bounded by Ashby Avenue, Walnut and Roach, Greensferry South, and Beckwith North, agree to organize ourselves into an association to be known as the "Neighborhood Union." The neighborhood should be divided into districts. The Object, shall be to become better acquainted with one another and to improve the neighborhood in every way possible.

Qualification for Membership: Its membership shall consist of any worthy family residing within said boundary.

Officers: The officers shall be President, Vice President, Secretary, Assistant Secretary, Treasurer and Chairman of Board of Directors. The President shall preside over organization and shall be ex-officer over all members. The Vice President shall preside in absence of the President. The Secretary's duty shall be to keep an accurate record of all meetings and attend to the correspondence. The Assistant Secretary shall serve in the absence of the Secretary and keep enrollment of committee, circles, families, address, number of children and notify members when necessary. The Treasurer must be custodian of the money of the Union and keep a record of all incoming and outgoing money and get receipt of all expenditures, and report at each monthly meeting of Board. The Chairman shall preside at all meetings of Board of Directors and shall be responsible for success of same.

Board: There shall be a Board of managers consisting of president, vice president, secretary, assistant secretary, treasurer and chairman of the Board, together with directors of each district. The directors shall be appointed by the President.

Duty of Directors in Charge: It shall be the duty of the Directors in charge of districts, to visit and become acquainted with each family in her district and organize the women and children into circles, and be at their work and play. It shall be their duty to make a report of the general condition of the district at each business meeting. The members of the Board shall be elected by said body.

Election: The annual election shall occur on the second Thursday of July each year.

By-Laws of the Parent Neighborhood:

1. Seven shall constitute a quorum.
2. Fees--There shall be a membership fee of 10¢ per month for all families residing in Neighborhood Union.
3. The second Thursday in each month is the Board meeting. The fourth Friday of each month is the Union meeting.
4. Any member who fails to meet three successive meetings without a lawful excuse shall pay a fine of twenty-five cents.

Amendments: Five persons shall constitute a quorum.

Appendix No. 6

Plan of Organization

The Neighborhood was divided into districts. A leader was appointed to go from house to house and acquaint the neighbor and get the cooperation of every house. But soon other neighborhoods were requesting organization. Consequently a plan was made to embrace practically the entire colored population. The following plan was adopted for the city. The portions of the city inhabited by colored people were divided into 16 zones. Each zone was again divided according to its size and location into neighborhoods. Finally the neighborhoods were divided into districts. From each district a leader endorsed by the residents in the district, was selected by the organizer of the movement. The director of the district had a book in which were such facts as would acquaint her with the economic and social status of each family. The directors of the district elected one of their number president, who with her co-workers constituting a board of directors, directed the work of the whole neighborhood. There was a zone chairman elected by the neighborhood presidents, whose duty it was to organize neighborhoods and receive the reports of the neighborhood work. The city organization was placed under the direction of a Board of Managers composed of Neighborhood presidents, zone chairmen, and department heads, who organized and initiated such activities as recreation, health and sanitation, and child welfare, etc....

Program

The program of the Union is entrusted to a number of departmen heads who organize certain activities and devise methods for carrying out the program. The department of recreation helps each neighborhood to organize playgrounds. In fact, the first playground in the city was established on Morehouse College campus under the Neighborhood Union. The City provided school grounds later.

The literary department provides literature, especially by Negroes, and programs for the neighborhoods. It is natural that the department of music should be popular. For the neighborhood about the college, concerts have been held at the college. Negro music has been the central theme of these concerts. The Department of Health and Sanitation has exerted a tremendous influence on the health of the colored community. It has staged lectures on health, conducted classes in sanitation and forced the stores which supply Negro families to clean up. Lectures on health and demonstrations were held in every colored public school. Demonstrations of methods for caring for the sick were carried to the churches and even from street to street. In a clean-up campaign 40,000 colored people were reached. Child welfare is a special department. Clinics first held in the Neighborhood House inspired the creation of clinics in other sections of the city.

The religious life of the neighborhood, which has been the basis of Negro community life, is placed under the Department of Churches. This department secures the cooperation of the churches and sees that the unaffiliated residents are directed to the church of their choice.

Community entertainments have been provided in the form of block carnivals when the houses have been the centers of different attractions. It is also a rule of the Union that ten persons in any neighborhood can be provided with instruction in any subject or art they desire. At present there are many girls who reflect their instruction in dressmaking in the style of their clothes.

Although a neighborhood house has been maintained in one neighborhood, it is not necessary for the success of the program as it aims to improve the home.

Appendix No. 7

Aims of the Neighborhood Union

1. To unite for their advancement the people of each section of the city into an organization, which shall be a branch of the Neighborhood Union; and to effect similar Neighborhood Unions in other cities.

2. To develop a spirit of helpfulness among the neighbors and to cooperate with one another in their respective neighborhoods for the best interest of the community, city, and race.

3. To provide playgrounds, clubs, good literature, and Neighborhood centers for the moral, physical and intellectual development of the young.

4. To establish lecture courses, classes, and clubs for adults, for the purpose of encouraging habits of cleanliness and industry, promoting child welfare, and of bringing about culture and efficiency in general homemaking.

5. To improve the sanitation of homes and streets, and to bring to the attention of the city the needs of lights and of other im-

provements.

6. To abolish slums and houses of immorality, to investigate dance halls, pool rooms, and vaudeville shows; and generally to cooperate with city officials in suppressing vice and crime.

7. To cooperate with the Associated Charities and the Juvenile Court.

8. To make surveys of small communities showing the operation of factors and forces at work therein; and, at intervals, to take a census of the neighborhoods in Atlanta showing the status of each family and individual therein as well as to prepare maps of the sections inhabited by Negroes.

9. To bring about a better understanding between the races.

"Initial Procedures..."

Evils of Poor Housing Conditions. Among the problems on which the women worked very hard were HOUSES. A law had been passed and whereas before, whenever a contagious disease had caused death, the house had to be fumigated by the City Health Department, this was no longer done. This, it was found from the survey, was a source of much sickness. They took houses, which were suspected, and traced them back through several years until they found that someone had died in that house with a contagious disease. Sometimes it was smallpox, again it was typhoid, and in a few instances, diptheria (sic). From this they knew that the house had never been rid of the disease germs.

Procedure Followed by Women in Planning Their Program-Women Make First Survey. Immediately after this thing happened (the death of the lone woman, as before described), the women felt that the thing to do was to get acquainted with their next door neighbors so that it could not happen again. They felt that the future was in the children so their aim was to help the children. This is the way they did it:

They made a house-to-house canvass of the community. They went to every house, inquiring for children, telling people that they wanted to get the children together so that they could teach them how to play and how to sew, cook, clean and beautify the house, clean the yards and plant flowers; to teach them pretty stories and encourage them to learn to love to read so that they would not want to play in the streets always. There wasn't a person who turned them down. All were anxious to send their children and those who did not have children wished they had so that they could send them, or they helped other mothers to get their children to them.

When they were making their house-to-house visitation, they were selecting their key women for the first meeting of the organization while they were planning to get acquainted so that they might assist one another in case of need, and plan to help the children.

After selecting the key women, they were invited to come to a meeting which was called at the home of Mrs. Hope on Morehouse campus. At this meeting, they talked over the situation and decided what they wanted to do. They elected officers and divided the neighborhood into districts and a woman living inside the district was appointed Director, whose duty it was to know everyone in the district, every child, and what to expect of every one and how to meet the problems. This Director was also to make a survey of her district.

Results of the Early Surveys. The Union investigated conditions, tabulated the facts, and analyzed the date (sic), which resulted in these findings: from the first survey which the women made there was a house-to-house visitation and from Mr. Watson's survey of a hundred families around Morehouse College, the social problems of the West Side were disclosed and the data revealed that the foremost of these evils were--poor health; unsanitary conditions, poor housing, lack of recreation, family disorganization, and delinquency which is one of the direct resultants of bad housing conditions and which had been one of the Negro's gravest handicaps in Atlanta. The study also disclosed the fact that streets were badly in need of improvement, insufficient lights, which tends to breed crime, there were little or no sewerage facilities, and the water supply consisted mostly of surface wells. Crime, delinquency, houses of ill repute, neighborhood disturbances and evil influences to which young boys and girls were exposed were the findings to which the Union turned its immediate attention and which served as a basis for their organization at this period. Among other findings were delapidated schools with insufficient accommodations for the Negro school population. The research investigation of the Atlanta community also disclosed that the municipal authorities of Atlanta had not assumed the responsibility for their citizens not only Negroes but white as well. The Neighborhood Union was destined to demonstrate to Atlanta and to the nation at large that it was an agency of social policies capable of rendering service among and for Negroes over an area which embraced municipal and federal areas.

They Improvise a Simple Questionnaire. In their tablets, they made some leading questions. These they undertook to get answered. The questionnaire was somewhat crude and not so scientific as some later types, but it served the purpose, and sufficient facts were gathered from which summary a program was worked out for the betterment of the community and the child. Some of the questions asked were: Names of both parents, address, renting or taxpayer, No. of rooms, No. of males, No. of females, No. of children, No. of children of school age, ages of children, No. of children in school, No. of children out of school of school age, if they were employed and how, occupations of mother, of father, if parents worked out, who is left in the home with the children. What kind of water, whether wells, cistern; what kind of toilets, privy or watercloset; to what church they belonged; what was the condition of the house and premises in which they lived; what was the conditions of the streets, lights and pavement; what were the health conditions in the home; conditions of the flues of the fireplaces for fire hazards, and health; if they owned and kept in their yards, horses, cows, pigs, or other cattle? Had they paid their poll tax; and to what lodge or organization they belonged. The interesting thing about this was that each director had to bring a complete survey of her district to every meeting.

When the questionnaire was summarized, the findings were discouraging; but they furnished a basis on which to work. The most amazing of these were open wells flat on the ground into which the children might fall; also were sources of disease, such as typhoid, and there was a great amount of typhoid in this city at that time, before the Neighborhood Union started; surface toilets were plentiful, unscreened and the scavenger charts only came around sometimes in a month; there was little sewerage; garbage was seldom emptied as frequent as once a month and it was never covered. Many epidemics of various kinds often broke out before the Neighborhood Union started its health program among the Negroes in this section.

Housing Conditions Found Detrimental to Both Life and Health. As to housing conditions, it was found that there were no laws for regulating the placement of the houses built to rent to the Negro. Houses at that time of the poorer sections of the West side were set as if they had been dropped out of an airplane. Often the front door of one house faced the backyard and the privy of the other house was in the front door. Too often the kitchen door opened into the door of the outhouse. Flies and germs bred and sickness followed. Real estate men could not be induced to correct these evils, nor would they reduce the rent. It mattered not how houses for Negroes were thrown up. A few years later the Union made a big fight on these conditions and got some correction for the evils, but in these early days the task of the Directors was centered on those things the people could do for themselves. Before leaving the findings, two other matters should be mentioned. The launderesses, and there were many, often were confronted with conditions conducive not only to poor health, but they could not get their work done because of it. The chimneys of many of the poorer dwellings had no bricks at the back of the fireplace. Hence, the smoke came out so terribly that the women were made sick and did not know the cause, and the clothes were so smoked, that often they lost their work. Children had no playgrounds or health centers.

A Survey. From the very beginning the Neighborhood had expert assistance from the Sociological Departments of the local colleges and the first scientific study was made for the organization in 1908.

Mr. Watson's Survey of Sixty-three Homes. This treatise was the result of a study made by the Sociological Students of Mr. Watson at Morehouse College at the request of the Neighborhood Union.

A study of the documents of the Neighborhood Union reveals

that from the very start their policy was the child's welfare, the future citizen rather than the adult; preventive measures rather than remedial and the results of their first house-to-house visitation and their earliest formal survey was so comprehensive in its scope that it reveals many needs covering varied aspects of community problems. Again, from the beginning, their policy was to find the need and fill it until an agency better fitted to carry it on took it over. For example, they established and fostered playgrounds until the city took them over. Thus, the Plan and Program continued to grow as demands arose. We have tried to show the organization Program and Plan of the Neighborhood Union, which occupied in a large way, the greater part of the time lying between the year of its organization, 1908, and the thirteen years, but its organization by no means consumed every hour of its time.

Contacts with the National Association of Colored Women. As early as August, 1908, we read in the minutes that the organization planned to send the picture of the organization to the National Association of Colored Women.

By-Laws Were Submitted July 23, 1908. The Committee on By-Laws reported on July 23rd, read laws submitted. Again in August, the records show that the By-Laws Committee was heard from.

Meeting Place. At first the women went from house to house, chiefly at the home of the president. Then the work expanded to such an extent, especially the health program, that they were forced to rent a center, in which to hold the clinic. This could not be very well conducted in a private home.

The Neighborhood Union's first Health Clinic was organized in 1908. It has continued to operate such clinics and at present is putting a great deal of its interest in pre-school children.

First Clinic in Atlanta for Negroes. For a small sum an old brick building located at the corner of West Fair and Mildred Streets was obtained. It was then that the first case-finding clinic was held--October 14, 1908. This building was sold after a short period--so in order to forestall the disrupting influence of a constant moving, plans were made looking forward to purchasing a permanent house. Quoting from the records, we read:

> As a result of these first activities and the findings of the Survey by Prof. Watson and his students, October 14, 1908, a clinic was established in connection with the Health Program of the Neighborhood Union in which children were given treatment by the leading Physicians of the Medical Association with the trained nurses cooperating. This was the first clinic to be held for Negro children in the city of Atlanta, and continued until the Neighborhood Union entered the Community Chest Organization.

> August 19, the first Health Program was conducted at the regular meeting at the residence of the president. The subject, 'Discussion on Tuberculosis' was led by the president. Thus we see health topics, especially tuberculosis were discussed at the very beginning of the organization.

In studying the activities later, we will find that the Health Program of the Neighborhood Union became nation-wide, and was destined to bring signal honors to the city of Atlanta. Not only that, but it will be found from a search of the records, that the Plan was not the least factor in the health sponsoring activities, for through it, the Federal Government was able to be assisted in rehabilitation of the Flood victims whose health had been impaired by that great deluge.

Immediate Need for a Center. The work grew so rapidly, that the organization was pressed from the beginning for a place in which to meet. The clinic had taken on wide scope; the health classes for mothers had grown; the clubs for boys and girls were increasing in size; hence steps were taken to find a place suitable for a center and make-shift was found in which an open house was held, and which was sold from under them almost before they were well located in it.

There was a great desire to organize classes in sewing, cooking, home nursing, handicraft, and the like. Where could such classes be held and who could instruct them? The lack of a center hindered this.

The various club members opened their homes to these classes and became volunteer instructors. Morehouse College loaned a section of its campus and these women became playground supervisors. Here was developed overnight a group of untrained but conscientious social workers. The playground met with such an appreciative response that it was decided to emphasize this phase of work. Club work was also curtailed.

Investigation of Food Dealers. There was another problem which the Union attacked in 1908--The white grocers would offer sales. Most of such businesses in the section were conducted by whites. It would be advertised that on a certain day certain articles as sugar, flour, rice, etc., would be sold at greatly reduced prices. The people would crowd in for this profit to find that they had been cheated. They found that the flour sack had been opened and some of the flour removed, which made the sack weigh less. On the other hand, rocks and other heavy articles were put into sacks....

NOTES--PART III

1. Booker T. Washington, Up From Slavery, An Autobiography, (New York: A. L. Burt and Company, 1900), p. 219.

2. Ibid.

3. Ibid.

4. J. W. E. Bowen, "An Appeal to the King." Address delivered on Negro Day in the Atlanta Exposition, October 21, 1895, Atlanta, Georgia, 8 pp.

5. Ibid.

6. Loren Miller, The Petitioners, the Story of the Supreme Court of the United States and the Negro, (New York: Pantheon Books, 1966), p. 190.

7. Ibid., p. 191.

8. Named for William Penn, that early apostle of freedom.

9. Louie D. Shivery, "The History of Organized Social Work Among Atlanta Negroes, 1890-1935," (Unpublished Masters Thesis, Department of Sociology, Atlanta University, 1936).

10. Editorial, Atlanta Constitution, February, 1911.

PART IV

THE GREAT MIGRATION AND ITS CONSEQUENCES: 1915-1930

INTRODUCTION

The period from 1915 to 1930 has tremendous significance for blacks. It further defines the nature of black social movements; problematic welfare situations extend from local to national proportions; and, particular practices, designed to circumvent the continuance of white-imposed barriers, were institutionalized. And, constructive, organized ways to upgrade and enhance the overall quality of living were developed as well. During this period over a million blacks migrated to urban centers, north and south, attracted primarily by the opportunity for economic advancement. As pointed out by Monroe N. Work in 1919, this migration differed from those previous to it in the following ways: it was directed geographically to the north as distinguished from the west; and, lacking in both charismatic and bureaucractic leadership, it was basically a migration of individuals.

> Whereas the Thirteenth Amendment granted physical emancipation, the conditions brought about by the World War made for the economic emancipation of the Negro, in that he found for the first time opportunities to go practically anywhere in the United States and find employment along a great many lines... 1*

The migration had, of course, both economic and social causes:

> The chief economic causes of the migration were (1) the

---

*Footnotes to Part IV begin on page 464.

> 1914-1915 labor depression in the south and the accompanying cotton price demoralization which came as a result of the World War, for cotton was the foundation of a large part of the economic activity of the south, so far as it related to the Negro; (2) the ravages of the cotton boll weevil in the summer of 1915-1916 over considerable sections of Louisiana, Mississippi, Alabama, Georgia, and Florida and the threat for 1917 to ravage the crop of a large area of the whole South. Thus unsettled farming conditions greatly affected the situation as it related to the Negro tenant farmer; (3) unusual floods over large sections of Alabama, Mississippi, Georgia, and Florida, which in conjunction with the boll weevil, demoralized farming conditions; (4) the generally low wages which had always obtained the South; (5) increase in the cost of living with an accompanying tendency to decrease rather than to increase wages. Low wages was the reason most often given as the economic cause for migrating; (6) the great shortage of labor in the North.
>
> From the standpoint of the migrants themselves, the chief social causes were (1) failure of the law to give physical protection and thus prevent lynching; (2) the treatment accorded Negroes in the courts, such as imposing heavy fines for trivial causes and misdemeanors; (3) the mistreatment of Negroes by officers of the law especially constables and policemen; (4) the lack of legal protection and legal redress against insults to Negro women and for wrongs perpetrated against them. In no state of the South can a Negro woman get a verdict or in most instances enter a suit against a white man for seduction; nor where a white man is concerned is the law of consent made to apply to a Negro girl; (5) the "Jim Crow Car" (separate coach law) compelling all classes of Negroes to ride in one compartment of a railway coach, and denying to them the privilege of sleeping and dining cars; (6) the disenfranchisement laws. (7) The generally neglected conditions of the Negro sections of towns to sanitation, improved streets and street lights; (8) the lack of adequate school facilities; (9) the insulting attitude and treatment accorded Negro patrons in many stores.[2]

The first set of documents presented are from an assemblage of letters written by blacks, who themselves participated in the early phases of the migration, 1916-1918, and who relate therein their personal experiences.

Earlier documents illustrated the kinds of black self-help responses which resulted in the establishment of all-black towns as independent economic and political communities. It now became apparent that these aspirations would prove illusory. The largest of these communities, Boley, Oklahoma, never attracted appreciably more than 3,000 inhabitants, as compared with the hundreds of thousands of migrants who streamed into the large cities of St. Louis, Chicago, Philadelphia, and New York. As previously suggested, these towns were inaccessible to blacks politically, because control of the machinery of the county and state governments remained a monopoly in the hands of white politicians. In contrast, as we shall see, the increased concentration of the black population in the large urban areas led, on the one hand, to the development of bases for political action in the black neighborhood; and, on the other hand, to the kind of political sophistication and power that resulted in the election of black officials to represent the wishes of the black population. Oscar Depriest's election in 1915 as alderman of southside Chicago signaled a breakthrough into municipal politics, eventually to be completed by his election to the Congress of the United States as a member of the House of Representatives in 1928. Thus was ended the 28-year period during which no black sat in the halls of Congress, and the door was opened for blacks to regain some political influence on the national level.

In the past, the possibilities of overseas migration, particularly to Africa, were viewed as viable options open to blacks, given adequate financing, organization, and administration. Encouraged by W. E. B. DuBois and his associates, middle-class blacks embraced the ideology of Pan-Africanism, but at this time they did not contemplate large-scale colonization of Africa, being concerned only with organizing blacks to overthrow colonial rule. Colonization, as a viable solution for coping with the problems of the black masses, was to lie dormant for years to come, particularly after the demise of the one great movement directed toward this objective by Marcus Garvey. A West Indian immigrant and a charismatic leader, Garvey did attempt to organize a large-scale colonization project known as the Universal Negro Improvement Association, or UNIA. This movement floundered, however, through mismanagement, and it failed to accomplish its announced objectives: to provide a homeland for blacks in Africa and a means to migrate there. It heightened black self-consciousness, however, and left an ideological heritage of black pride and black nationalism never wholly submerged.

By ruling out the all-black community and overseas migration and colonization as viable problem-solving options for the black masses, the problems of the social welfare of blacks became problems of adaptation to the various ecological, political and social environments encountered within the borders of the United States. Problems arising from the exigencies of the rural scene remained; but, those problems which were generated by urban migration and its consequences were augmented and accelerated. Specifically, the problems of employment, housing, health, education, voting and political action, and the administration of both civil and criminal justice became more pronounced and exacerbated and, in turn, provoked the need to develop reliable social welfare practices and services. The black community within the metropolis was viewed as socially disorganized, if not pathological.

The extent to which some blacks were able to rise above the social obstacles placed in their path was used as a criterion to evaluate the "progress of integration" of the American black into the body politic. Such evaluations were usually negative. The black victims were blamed for the lack of initiative, on the one hand, and the lack of know-how and organizational skills, on the other. It was soon to be apparent with the onset of the Great Depression, however, that solutions to these problems required organized ways for coping with them, not only on the local but also on the national level.

This awareness, sensed by most blacks, came to whites slowly, and it tended to generate the kinds of interracial, cooperative efforts which were not only necessary for survival but also for sustaining themselves in instances where all-black organizations failed. Integration, then, emerged as the goal of the "New Negro." Examples of its institutionalization are the N. A. A. C. P., the National Urban League, and the Commission on Interracial Cooperation. While many all-black organizations, such as the black church, the fraternal organizations, and the National Association of Colored Women continued to expand their social service endeavors, nonetheless, interracial enterprises ultimately prove to be durable also, to have sustaining power and lasting value. This seems to be because they fit in with and support the value structure of the nation and do not basically, rhetorically or politically oppose it. It is ironic, however, that in the economic field, and especially in labor unionization, where integration is presumably an American birthright, institutionalized racism limits the participation of Negroes to a minimum and allows blacks to exercise leadership only in those areas where the bulk of the laborers are black (as, for example, among the railroad industry in the case of the Brotherhood of Sleeping Car Porters, and in the government in the case of the National Alliance of Postal Employees). The massive reception of blacks into the labor movement comes only after organization in the 1930's of the Congress of Industrial Organization (CIO).

The economic, political and social potential offered the blacks by the migration, the stimulation of war industries, and service in the armed forces was negated by the failure of the national leadership to accept and implement integration as a national policy. Rather, the nation's government chose only to include blacks and to respond to their special needs as the conduct of the war intensified and expanded, virtually forcing the government's attention and intervention. The armed forces, however, remained segregated; its black leadership was denied promotion, as in the celebrated case of Colonel Charles Young. The increased participation of blacks, however, did require the government to develop supplemental and subsidiary services to provide for black social welfare, as in the activities of the American Red Cross and the National Y. M. C. A. and Y. W. C. A. The cessation of hostilities, however, did not advance the aspirations of blacks who, as did others, had made sacrifices in the national cause and interest. As veterans returned to the cities and to their rural communities, they were met with a rash of violence: race riots, lynchings, and the usual miscarriages of justice to which many had previously been subjected.

Despite the convergence and concomitance of all the above-mentioned elements in the post-war national situation, which would seem to have doomed forever the aspirations and energies of the beleaguered blacks, they retained their creativity and vitality and developed ideologies, practices and policies for meeting their most urgent needs. They became aware of the necessity to rationally and scientifically define problems, and then to develop the kinds of professional educational institutions to prepare the new leadership that was required.

THE URBAN MIGRATION

In this section are presented documents which emphasize the migration of blacks to urban areas, both south and north, in quest of economic opportunity, improved social services and civil rights.

Document 1*

"Letters of Negro Migrants of 1916-1918," Journal of Negro History, Vol. IV, (July, 1919): pp. 290-291, 300-301, 333, 337-338. "Additional Letters of Negro Migrants of 1916-1918," Journal of Negro History, Vol. IV, (October, 1919), pp. 413, 432-433, 439-439.

The exodus of the Negroes during the World War, the most significant event in our recent internal history, may be profitably studied by reading the letters of the various migrants. The investigator has been fortunate in finding letters from Negroes of all conditions in almost all parts of the South and these letters are based on almost every topic of concern to humanity. These documents will serve as a guide in getting at the motive dominant in the minds of these refugees and at the real situation during the upheaval. As a whole, these letters throw much light on all phases of Negro life and, in setting forth the causes of unrest in the South, portray the character of the whites with whom the blacks have had to do.

These letters are of further value for information concerning the Negroes in the North. From these reliable sources the student can learn where the Negroes settled, what they engaged in, and how they have readjusted themselves in a new situation. Here may be seen the effects of the loss resulting from the absence of immigrants from Europe, the conflict of the laboring elements, the evidences of racial troubles and the menance of mob rule.

Letters Asking for Information About the North

Galveston, Texas,
this 24th day of May, 1917.

*Reprinted by permission of the publisher.

Sir: Please inform me of a situation. please ans. if fill out or not so I will no. answer at once.

Mobile, Ala., June 11, 1917.

Dear Sir: Will you please send me the name of the society in Chicago that cares for colored emigrants who come north seeking employment sometime ago I saw the name of this society in the defender but of late it does not appear in the paper so I kindly as you please try and get the name of this society and send the same to me at this city.

Pine Bluff, Ark., 4/23-17.

Mr. R. S. Abbott

Kine frind: I am riting you asting you to see if you can get me a job with some of the ship bilders I am a carpenter & can Do most iny thing so if you can get me a job pleas rite me at once.

Atlanta, Ga.

To the Urban Committy--

Dear Sir: I am comming north and have read advice in the Chicago Defender and I would be very much obliged to you if you would direct me to some firm that is in need of brick layers for that is my Professical trade and can do any class of work and if I can't get Brick Work now I will consider any other good job as I want to come right away I have 3 in fambly and I have no objection to work in other small towns I will be very glad to hear from you right away as I have never been north and advice will be excepted yours truly and friend of the race.

Hattiesburg, Miss., 12/4/16.

Hon. John T. Clark, Sec. National League on Urban Conditions, New York City, N.Y.

Sir: I am writing you on matters pertaining to work and desirable locations for industrious and trust worthy laborers. Me for myself and a good member of Friends especially thousand of our people are moving from this section of whom all can be largely depended upon for good service, for the past 15 years I have been engaged in insurance work of which I am at the head of one now, And have a large host of people at my command. I have....

Letters About the Great Northern Drive of 1917

Pensacola, Fla., 4-21-17

Sir: You will please give us the names of firms where we can secure employment. Also please explain the Great Northern Drive for May 15th. We will come by the thousands. Some of us like farm work. The colored people will leave if you will assist them.

New Orleans, La., April 25, 1917.

Dear Sir: Would you kindely advise me of a good place where I can get a good job out in some of the small places from Chicago about 50 or 60 miles. I am expecting to leave the south about the 15th of May will bring my family later on. Answer soon.

Jacksonville, Fla., May 2, 1917.

Dear Sir: I am writing you a few lines seacking information about some work as I was read a Chicago Defender i saw where labarers wanted very much I am a labarer now have not no work here to do i am married man have one child and would like for yo to give me work to do anything I am well expereinced in ware house and foundry and if there any way for you to fearnish me a transportation to come at once do i can go so i can make my family a desen living you will please let me know and if you would help a poor need man i am willing to come any time if I had the money i would pay my own way but i realy ain got it so i am asking you to please do this for me i am realy in need if you can do a poor negro any good please do this for me.

Sherman, Ga., Nov. 28, 1916.

Dear Sir: This letter comes to ask for all infirmations concern emplyoment in you connection in the warmest climate. Now I am in a family of (11) eleven more or less boys and girls (men and women) mixed sizes who want to go north as soon as arrangements can be made and employment given places for shelter and so en (etc) now this are farming people they were raised on the farm and are good farm hands I of course have some experence and qualefication as a coman school teacher and hotel waiter and along few other lines...

Letters Stating That Wages Received Are Not Satisfactory

Brookhaven, Miss., April 24, 1917.

Gents: The cane growers of Louisiana have stopped the exodus from New Orleans, claiming shortage of labor which will result in a sugar famine.

Now these laborers thus employed receive only 85 cents a day and the high cost of living makes it a serious question to live.

There is a great meny race people around here who desires to come north but have waited rather late to avoid car fare, which they have not got ...

Nashville, Tenn., April 22, 1917.

Sir: I am in Nashville and I have a job but is not satisfied with the money that I am getting for my work and I ask of you to please give me a good job working any place I am a expirence fire man and all so some expirence in engineer and please answer soon and let me know what you can find for me to do.

Alexandria, La., June 6, 1917.

Dear Sirs: I am writeing to you all asking a favor of you all. I am a girl of seventeen. School has just closed I have been going to school for nine months and I now feel like I aught to go to work. And I would like very very well for you all to please forward me to a good job. but there isnt a thing here for me to do, the wages here is from a dollar and a half a week. What could I earn Nothing. I have a mother and father and my father do all he can for me but it is so hard. A child with any respect about her self or his self wouldnt like to see there mother and father work so hard and earn nothing I feel it my duty to help ...

Letters About Better Educational Facilities

Anniston, Ala., April 23, 1917.

Dear Sir: Please gave me some infamation about coming north i can do any kind of work from a truck gardin to farming i would like to leave here and i cant make no money to leave i ust make enought to live one please let me here from you at once i want to get where i can put my children in schol.

Dear Sir: I saw your add in the Chicago Defender for laborers. I am a young man and want to finish school. I want you to look out for me a job on the place working morning and evening. I would like to get a job in some private family so I could continue taking my piano lesson I can do anything around the house but drive and can even learn that. Send me the name of the best High school in Chicago. How is the Wendell Phillips College. I have finish the grammar school. I cannot come before the middle of June.

New Orleans, La., 5/5x17

... I have been living here in New Orleans only seven years I formerly live in the country but owing to bad conditions of schools for my children I sold my property and moved here I didnt think there was any justice in my paying school taxes and had no fit school to send by children to. I have been employed here as night watchman for the last four years and are still working at it but my wajes are so small the high cost of living leaves very little for traveling expenses but never the less I have a boy sixteen years old as soon as school closes I will take him north with me hoping to find work for him and I during vacation. You will see me soon. Thanking you kindly.

Letters About the Treatment of Negroes in the South

Macon, Ga., April 1, 1917.

Dear Sir: I am writing you for information I want to come north east but I have not sufficient funds and I am writing you to see if there is any way that you can help me by giving me the names of some of the firms that will send me a transportation as we are down here where we have to be shot down here like rabbits for every little orfence as I seen an orcurince hapen down here this after noon when three depties from the shrief office an one Negro spotter come out and found some of our raice mens in a crap game and it makes me want to leave the south worse than I ever did when such things hapen right at my door. Hopeing to have a reply soon and will close a stamp from the same.

Sanford, Fla., 5/12/17

Dear Sir: The winter is about over and I still have a desire to seek for myself a section of this country where I can poserably better my condishion in as much as beaing asshured some protection as a good citizen under the Stars and Stripes so kind sir I am here asking you agin if you know directly or indirectly of any opening that you could direct me to where I can make a reasonable livelyhood kindly inform me. Why I write you agin is because it appears to me from your headings that your concern ar making some opening for the (col) from the south and agin I do not cear to live here in a simple way if poserable I would like to be shure of an imployment before I leave Kindley do what ever good you can for me.

From the closing session of the Southern Sociological Congress, Ashville, North Carolina, are taken the following comments by George Edmund Haynes and Hugh H. Proctor.

Document 2

"Negro Migration as the South Sees It," The Survey, (August 11, 1917), p. 428.

The sessions of the closing day of the Southern Sociological Congress, held at Asheville, were on race relations and emphasized the newly developed problem of Negro migration. The sense of a number of speakers on the subject was that Negro migration was not a new thing; that probably no more than 250,000 Negroes have gone North in the last year (in spite of prevalent reports of much greater figures); that migration in large part is caused by high wages in the North, with ill treatment of the Negroes a varying factor in different parts of the South, and that the movement is to be stopped, not by repression, but by cooperation between colored and white people to ensure opportunity and treatment for the Negroes.

A Number of colored speakers expressed the feeling of their people.

The present migration is simply an acceleration of the movement of the last thirty years, according to Prof. George E. Haynes of Fisk University, Nashville, Tenn.

> The largest exodus has been from the places where there have been the poorest economic conditions and the greatest race friction. One Negro who moved North said to me, 'There's been so much killing of Negroes around here I didn't know when my turn might come.' The colored and white people must get together and talk frankly and act honestly in common.

Another colored speaker, the Rev. H. H. Proctor, of Atlanta, Ga., said:

> This is the most unique movement in history. The colored race, known as the race which is led, has broken

away from its leaders. This movement has all the earmarks of spontaneity. There are a number of contributing causes, but the basic fact is that Negroes are seeking men's wages and men's treatment. They have been restless at living under a double standard not only of conduct and character, one code for white and one for black, but also of wages, while unfortunately, expenses have increased on a single standard, that of the white man.

The colored man carries in his heart a deep and abiding sense of mistreatment. He resents segregation, disfranchisement, 'Jim Crowism.' He wants a sense of physical safety. He wants to be left alone, to be safe in a democratic community.

The highest good of the colored people lies right here in the South. We can stop this movement northward by giving them a square deal. If the leading white folks and the leading colored folks can get together, this can be done.

In this article, Dr. George E. Haynes, one of the more careful students of the Migration, discusses its effects on the life of the family and the community in the northern urban environment. Stressing the search for self-development and self-determination, he indicates a need for integration of their individual selves into the life of the community.

Document 3*

George E. Haynes, "Negro Migration, Its Effects on Family and Community Life in the North," Opportunity, Vol. 2, No. 22, October, 1924, pp. 303-304.

Types of Migrants

The types of migrants are interesting. In 1916 and 1917, the earlier years of the present migration, the majority of the newcomers were men--particularly detached men--either men without families or men who would not venture to bring their families with them into an unknown country. Included among them were a great many younger men, with the "floaters" and ne'er do wells, who had been easily attracted away from southern towns and cities by the stories of easy work at high wages and by free transportation offered promiscuously by labor agents and railroad companies. A second class was made up of a large number of single women, detached from their families, who came because of the large opportunities for remunerative work, particularly in domestic service.

These gradually were accompanied and followed by the third type, the substantial laboring man of unskilled or semi-skilled abilities. For the most part these men either brought their families, soon married, or sent for their families as soon as they could find remunerative employment. Fourth, with parts of such families as fathers and sons had left behind came a great many broken families--widows with children, attracted by the opportunities for an education for the children in public schools and wages in domestic service. There came also the aged relatives of the wage earning men and women of families. As those in the larger southern cities and towns moved on to the North, others moved in from the hamlets and rural districts to fill their places and to swell the proportions. Thus much of the movement was by successive stages.

Beginning about 1919 those who had come in the two or three years preceding had gained a substantial economic footing and knowledge of being able to stand the climate and other living conditions. Consequently a general assurance spread throughout cities, towns and rural districts of the South. Frequently whole families or neighborhoods, sometimes with previous arrangements for employment in some of the industrial communities, migrated in a group. A few cases have been recorded of whole church congregations bringing their pastors with them.

As the type described above settled, they furnished a field for the small tradesmen and the professional class who either came along with the crowd or followed closely after. In many cases, of course, the more enterprising wage earners, finding themselves in the midst of a large Negro population with considerable wages to spend, ventured into business. Along with this host of mixed humanity, there came a vicious and criminal element. It is the testimony, however, of social workers, railroad officials, law officers and other observers, that to an unusual degree these people are law-abiding, unoffending folk who are seeking larger opportunities in a new environment.

Effects of Migration on Negroes

The foregoing facts lead the way to our consideration of effects on families and communities in the North.

Some of the outstanding effects of migration on the average Negro family are better standards of food and clothing due to higher wages. The children have better school buildings with teaching equipment and higher paid, better trained teachers. The permanent effects on health and mortality can only be surmised. Statistics of the births and deaths are as yet meager but they seem to indicate trends toward improvement. A survey made by Forrester B. Washington, under the auspices of the Interracial Committee of Toledo, Ohio, showed a Negro death rate for 1922 of 15.2 per cent as compared with the general death rate of 11.7 per cent--a difference of 3.5 per cent; but in 1912, before the 200 per cent increase of Negro population due to migration, the Negro death rate was 20.5 per cent while the general death rate was 13.8 per cent--a difference of 6.7 per cent. In Cincinnati, the Negro death rate was 34.9 per cent for the decade 1902-1912 and declined to 27.4 per cent for the decade 1913-1923. Dr. Dublin, of the Metropolitan Life Insurance Company, states that in nearly two million Negro industrial policyholders, including men, women and children, the "mortality rate was 17.5 per 1000" in 1911 and 14.5 in 1923, a decrease of more than one-sixth; death from tuberculosis, "the outstanding cause of death among colored people," was 41 per cent less in 1923 than in 1911 ... "Nothing indicates so well the general health condition of a race as the incidence of tuberculosis and nothing reflects so well an improvement in its mode of life as does a big drop in the tuberculosis death rate.... The improvement in typhoid fever is especially noteworthy," declining 77.5 per cent between 1911 and 1923. There has been a "marked increase in the number of colored policyholders" in Illinois and Michigan, mainly concentrated in Chicago and Detroit.

In most northern cities the housing condition shows a majority of the Negro families coming North are grievously overcrowded and in practically all of the cities the rents for them have been far in excess of those for residents who are residing at the same time in similar localities. A survey made by the Federation of Churches of Buffalo in 1922 disclosed the fact that about 75 per cent of the colored families occupied a section of that city which contained the poorest houses, some of which had formerly been condemned as not habitable. A similar survey made by the Federated Churches of Cleveland showed that while a substantial part of the colored people have secured good houses, inadequate and unsanitary conditions still exist in one of the principal Negro communities of the city.

In Philadelphia, the Philadelphia Housing Association found in a recent survey that only 10.5 per cent of the houses occupied by Negro families were equipped for sanitation, convenience and comfort, while 28.6 per cent of the houses occupied by whites were so equipped. There was no room overcrowding, however. In New York, Pittsburg, Chicago and other cities, while there are many good houses, the majority of the people are overcrowded in houses lacking in facilities for sanitation, convenience and comfort. A striking development of their settlement has been their effort to improve their housing condition. This is evinced in their increased striving to purchase the homes they occupy. In the survey of Toledo, previously referred to, about 27.6 per cent of the families investigated owned or were purchasing their homes, nearly half of these having their homes free and clear. In 1910, in thirteen northern cities and two boroughs of New York City, from ten to over twenty-five per cent of Negro families owned or were buying the houses they occupied, and in seven additional cities and two boroughs of New York, from four to ten per cent owned or were buying the houses they occupied. During the past ten years there has been a great eagerness of Negro migrants to buy houses and in some cities real estate manipulators have forced many to buy or move. We may conclude then that in northern cities from ten to twenty-five per cent of the Negro families own or are buying their homes.

Negroes believe that the Negro community in the North, although considerably segregated, has advantages over their former homes in the South, such as theatres, public libraries, parks, playgrounds, museums and non-"Jim Crow" railroad and street cars. Negroes are taking part more and more in the civic and political affairs of the community. Newspapers and magazines, especially Negro newspapers and magazines, are being read as never before. Negro newspapers and magazines with the largest circulation are published in Chicago and New York. The headquarters of nearly every one of the Negro betterment organizations are now in northern cities and many of the general officers of the Negro churches have moved North. Small Negro business enterprises are increasing rapidly. A study of "The Negro at Work in New York," in 1910, before the present migration, listed about 475 enterprises in Manhattan; in 1921, a similar survey showed at least 584 such business enterprises in the Harlem district alone--a larger number than in the three Negro neighborhoods of Manhattan in 1910. General observations in Philadelphia, Chicago, Detroit and Cleveland give a similar impression of increase.

Effects on Negro Church

What has been the effect of migration on the Negro church, which we saw was the most influential institution in Negro life in the South? In the northern cities it has increased greatly in membership, although many small mushroom store-front churches have sprung up and often become a hindrance to progress. There have developed some strong organizations in every one of these cities. Their great need is better trained leadership. In a few cities Negro congregations have bought or built institutional plants and are employing trained social workers. Abyssinia Baptist Church, St. Philip's P. E. Church, Williams Institutional C. M. E. Church, and Mother Zion A. M. E. Church in New York City; St. John's Congregational in Springfield, Mass; Mount Zion Congregational Church and St. John's A. M. E. Church in Cleveland; Olivet Baptist Church and two community churches in Chicago; and Sharpe Street M. E. Church in Baltimore, are prophecies of great community service and show the possibilities.

I realize the serious shortcomings of the church in community service and I respect the opinion of many social workers who think that the church is not able to function with technical efficiency in case work. Yet I am moved to maintain that the Negro church is by far the most substantial institution we have for reaching the Negro rank and file with our social programs. Trying to look at the matter without bias, it seems to me that many of our efforts have not carried over to the masses of the Negro people because we have not sold our social programs through the Negro churches which have already a hold upon the thousands who had developed the churches for more than a hundred years and now find them their social agency. If we get our plans accepted in the programs of those churches, much of our efforts would not need to go into building social service programs and trying to force Negroes into them. It is true that there are great obstacles in the way of getting scientific technique in this field. There are other dangers involved. There are baffling difficulties of leadership and restricted vision. These Negro church organizations, however, have a willingness and zeal for service which has brought results wherever skilled social workers have been able to link them up to the scientific methods and directions needed.

These Negro migrants are a part of a great body of American citizens who are permeated with a deep community and group consciousness and who have shown their ability for team work with other racial and national groups in America by unselfish cooperation on their part in communities, North and South.... These people, seeking opportunity for self-development and self-determination, have moved by thousands to the North. If we help them to integrate their lives into the community and to make their contributions to the common life as the years come and go, there will grow increasingly in America, our America, a realization of that democracy which is to be in "the land of the free and the home of the brave."

Excerpted from an earlier article by Haynes, the following is a discussion of housing conditions as they were encountered by migrants in some major cities.

Document 4*

George Edmund Haynes, "Negroes Move North. II. Their Arrival in the North," The Survey, January 4, 1919, pp. 459-460.

A Glimpse at the Housing Conditions and Recreation Slum housing has been the main outstanding evil which has confronted the newcomers to northern centers. From Chicago, Cincinnati, Cleveland, Columbus, Pittsburg, Philadelphia, Newark and a score of lesser cities comes the information that migrants are being crowded into basements, shanties, fire bunks and othertypes of houses unfit for human habitation. In most cases high rentals have been charged for these inferior houses. In Pittsburg "almost 98 per cent of the people investigated lived either in rooming houses or in tenements containing more than three families.... In many instances, houses in which these rooms were located are dilapidated dwellings with the paper torn off, the plaster sagging from the board lath, the windows broken, the ceiling low and damp, and the whole room dark, stuffy and unsanitary." Although the rents charged in a railroad camp near Pittsburg were very low, about 5 cents per night, still there was serious overcrowding in the box cars used as bunk houses and in the two-story wooden houses. Of 157 families in Pittsburg, 49 per cent lived in one room each, 21 per cent in two-room apartments each and only 30 per cent in three or more rooms each.

*Reprinted by permission.

In Chicago, "the housing problem is urgent," says the housing report ... "It is impossible to do much else short of the construction of apartments for families and for single persons." In Cincinnati, James H. Robinson, of the Negro Welfare Committee, said in October, 1917, "The houses available are few and poor at best ... while the tendency to charge the Negro higher rents than anyone else is almost universal.... The Joint Housing Committee, after widely advertising its efforts to find better houses for colored people, finds itself confronted with far more applications for houses than it can supply." The admirable model houses built before the migration in Cincinnati on a large, liberal scale by J. G. Schmidlapp are an example of one of the ways to meet such a situation.

In Philadelphia, the Whittier Center Housing Company, in cooperation with the Octavia Hill Association, built in 1916, seven two-family houses for newcomers on a plan similar to the Schmidlapp apartments in Cincinnati. In Detroit probably one of the most acute situations prevails because the city had an unusual increase in the white population at the same time that the Negro migrants were arriving. Many of the houses into which Negroes were crowded are nothing more than dilapidated shacks, usually without baths and inside toilets. Some of the apartments and rented rooms were so crowded that one observer wittily remarked that the occupant of a room was often forced to "stand in the middle of the bed to dress." Successful efforts were made by the local Urban League in opening some first-class apartment houses that had been previously built.

In Newark, N. J., one of the daily papers last November began a series of articles with the following headlines:

> Wretched Homes for Negroes
> One Feature of Housing Lack
> Majority of Newcomers from South are Declared to Be Living in Quarters Unfitted for Human Habitations, Though Anxious to Pay for Better Ones.

This newspaper cited numbers of cases and presented a series of photographs. The health department of the city was aroused to make a special investigation. The chief health officer was reported as saying that some of the owners of the old houses had been called to task and had cleaned up and made repairs, and that the Board of Health had consented to further occupancy after the most needed repairs had been made. "But," he is reported to have added,

> what is the use? I suppose these houses are as bad as they were months ago. That is the trouble with these old shacks. The filth is in the walls and in the floors, and no amount of surface renovation will give a complete sanitary cure. The only sure way is to pull them down, and this is what ought to be done. But I do not see how we can take such action at the present time.... From a practical viewpoint, these houses must remain open because of housing congestion. Considered simply from the health

viewpoint, they could not be razed too quickly....

In this next excerpt, Jesse O. Thomas of the National Urban League is concerned not with the economic, but the social and fraternal problems of the migrant. He suggests a program which includes recreational opportunity for the underprivileged.

Document 5*

Jesse O. Thomas, "A Social Program to Help the Migrant," Opportunity, March, 1924, pp. 72-73.

... Most of the influences that make it difficult for the migrant to become quickly assimilated in his new environment are those of poor educational advantages and early training; economic inefficiency; lack of contact with elevating personalities; difficulties in securing adequate housing accomodations; and disposition to cling to the customs and habits of their old environment.

While these people have little or no difficulty in becoming absorbed in the economic life of their new environment, they do experience much difficulty in becoming adjusted in the social and fraternal life of the urban communities and industrial centers....

A program adequately providing recreational opportunity for the migrant as well as for other safeguards, health and well being, together with educational advantages and industrial and economic efficiency would require more of what is being regarded as community organization than has been attempted in any large measure in any of our cities thus far. Social workers must develop community organization in their sections, to the point where a majority of the people of fortunate circumstances will concern themselves more directly with the welfare of the under-privileged. This to a large extent will require the changing of the mental attitude of the more fortunate members of our society group toward the social needs of the man farthest down....

There is a sufficient number of intelligent young men and women in every city to constitute or organize recreational influence if they were sufficiently interested. Each high school could have a recreational center largely directed by the young people in the high school. College students in college towns could be a wonderful factor in making possible recreational programs. Each church could have a recreational committee, just as a Stewardess Board of a Board of Deacons, to provide entertainment at the church--not for the purpose of raising money for foreign missions, but for the purpose of providing recreation for the young people. A vocational councillor should be located at every large center where hundreds

*Reprinted by permission of the National Urban League.

of children migrate from the South, to help them determine their adaptability or their compatibility. And then all of the national organizations with branches in local communities should federate and concentrate on certain phases of community development. Community centers on a large scale, supported by the business men of the community should provide capable supervisors, and the churches should pool together their finances and employ nurses....

Large industrial and manufacturing concerns and business enterprises, as well as private individuals who employ these migrants and profit by their toil, must be induced to recognize efforts on behalf of their social well being as an investment in the industrial and economic efficiency.

Where the employee eats and sleeps and spends his leisure hours must be of as much concern to the employing interest as to where he works, and to the business man as to where he spends his money.

THE ALL-BLACK COMMUNITY

Edgar Iles, a participant observer, extols life in the all-black community of Boley, Oklahoma, which had little appeal for the mass of blacks. He comments, however, that such communities born of racial pride, in the midst of a racist society, often stagnate and succumb to social isolation. As we shall see, urban blacks developed racial pride and consciousness unaided by the powerful stimuli of the Garvey movement and the "New Negro" concept of the intelligentsia of the Harlem Renaissance. Such stimuli directed black energies toward achieving integration into the mainstream of American society.

Document 6*

R. Edgar Iles, "Boley (An Exclusively Negro Town in Oklahoma)," Opportunity, III, August, 1925, pp. 231-235.

... The towns themselves are an evidence of a race consciousness and of the development of one aspect of race pride in the midst of an unconquerable prejudice--the process in this case leads on to deliberate isolation from the dominating group....

The town is laboring under one rather peculiar disadvantage--with a population of about 3500 Boley has been scattered over an expanse of territory large enough for a town with a population of

*Reprinted by permission of the National Urban League.

10,000. This has worked an economic hardship upon the municipality in that it has made lights, water, pavements and sewers cost more than three times as much as it should cost a town of that size.

The problem of self government offers an interesting study. Some of the citizens of this village never knew what suffrage was until they went there from various sections of the South. Being free for the first time to exercise their suffrage, they have carried it beyond its usual province. One of the Baptist churches, by virtue of its large membership, is always certain of a successful candidate in political campaigns. Every office to be filled in larger towns of the state claims the interest of Boley's politicians. Elections and campaigns are always spirited. Boley's weekly news journal has its pages almost completely monopolized by office-seekers and campaign managers. Near the close of the campaigns, political mass meetings are held, at which time opposing candidates discuss the life history of each other to the prospective voters, sometimes almost coming to blows.

The two major political parties--Republican and Democratic--are strongly represented. Needless to say, this situation gave rise to a more intense political struggle than Boley had ever witnessed. To most of the Negroes from the South, Democrat and race prejudice are synonymous terms. He reasons thus: The South is practically a solid Democractic machine, and it is in this section that the Negro received the most brutal and unjust treatment. Therefore, any Negro who allies himself with the Democratic party simply approves the way in which southern whites treat Negroes. To many of them it is sacrilegious for a Negro to vote a Democratic ticket. This, of course, is used by the Republicans for propaganda in their campaigns. The presence and activity of Negro Democrats in Boley may be accounted for by the fact that the county in which Boley is located is primarily Democratic, and some of the Negro lawyers, who are also leaders, have found it advantageous to ally themselves with the dominant political party for the return in privileges to them in their practice in the county courts. This has led, however, to certain peculiar practices, an example of which is given. Before a person is allowed to vote in Oklahoma he must present a registration certificate at the polls. Boley maintains its own voting precincts for local, state and national elections. Since the county is Democratic, Negroes have been placed in charge of the elections and the registration of voters. This gives one faction an advantage in the political control of the town. In order to maintain such control, a large number of those who would vote a Republican ticket have been totally disfranchised. As the disfranchised agreed to register as Democrats, they were given their suffrage.

The results of such political strife might be easily inferred. Several cases of ambushing have been traced indirectly to political differences between opposing parties. The disfranchised group carried their case to the Federal Court in November, 1924; and the judge ordered those in charge to cause all Negroes to be registered. The ultimate result of such a move was a near riot between white people of the county and Negroes of the town.

Boley, like towns generally where political interests eclipse the interest of the citizens, has some faulty sides to its administration. But, on the whole, the reasonably fair way in which these Negroes handle their affairs tells without a question that Negroes are capable of self-government. Bond issues are passed for civic improvement; and the revenue is utilized with an efficiency that is commendable.

The economic life of the town is another point of interest. Almost the entire support of Boley is by the farmlife surrounding the village. As was mentioned above, nearly all of the farmers around Boley for a radius of five or six miles are Negroes. The staple crop is cotton. This means that there are years when the farmers do not have any money to spend, due to the uncertainty of cotton crops. The farmers, for the most part, being of the dependent class, must seek credit from the merchants until their crops are made. Whenever there is a failure in the cotton crops, the merchants, who are almost wholly dependent upon the farmer for an income, operate at a loss. From 1920 to 1924 most of the mercantile establishments struggled between economic life and death because of successive failures of crops. The fact that these proprietors have been able to keep their businesses alive is argument sufficient that the business ability of the Negro should no longer be a question.

Occupational opportunities, aside from farming, are not numerous. Only a negligible number may find employment there. The municipal pay-roll contains the names of the town marshall, a few street workers, and five or six employees of the electric light and power company. The city judge and the city clerk receive a small salary for their services, not intended to compensate them fully....

Beyond question, the most interesting aspect of Boley is its social situation. The population of the town is, in the language of Dr. Edward Cary Hayes, "a personal group." The fact that the social instincts operate very effectively in a personal group may account for the fact that there has never been much crime among this group of Negroes who have access to almost absolute freedom of living.

It was stated in the outset that the one thing that led to the establishment of Boley was the desire for territorial isolation. Around this situation, these Negroes have built a strong body of ideas and sentiments concerning the dominant white group which is not over-favorable. The writer has in his possession a copy of a song that was composed by an early citizen of Boley and which embodies the spirit of the group. This piece of music is "Respectfully dedicated to Hon. T. M. Haynes (solver of race problems.)" Some of the words of the song are: "Be courageous, brother, and forget the past--the great and mighty problem of the race has been solved at last. Boley is the salvation of the Negro race." These words are not offered for the music they contain, but for the spirit of the race that they embody.

There is, really, an over-developed pride of race. This has lead to uncomfortable fears and suspicions that white people envy the success of Boley and that secret plans are laid to destroy it. This idea has in turn reinforced their defense attitude.

White people are allowed to own property in this town. They are allowed to come there for trading purposes, and may stay over night, but that must be the extent of their visit in the village. Whenever it becomes necessary for a white person to remain over night, he does so with great anxiety unless he is familiar with the situation. The writer recalls an incident when a white salesman who had finished his business for the day with Negro merchants, asked a Negro youth if there was a hotel for white people in the town. The lad replied with a great deal of sarcasm, "We don't practice segregation here. If you want to stay here over night, you'll have to stay where everybody else stays. There's a hotel on the corner over there, one block east and a half block south is another, either one of them will accommodate you."

The institutional life of the town is fairly well developed. Like most Negro communities, Boley is over-churched. This means poor ministry, and consequently, a lifeless religious environment. There are approximately 13 churches in the town, which is another way of saying that the membership of the various churches is too small for efficient church-life. The failure of the church to keep pace with modern Christian movements has resulted in the almost complete desertion of the church by the young people.

Like most small towns, Boley tends to commercialize its amusements. The social engineers of the town seem to have lost sight of the relation between plenty and wholesome amusements for young people and a normal social life. There is a movie theater which is operated once a week; but the majority of the pictures shown are of the Wild West type, underworld pictures, and thrilling serial shows. As it might be expected, many colored productions are featured.

Aside from the picture shows a highly commercialized baseball team is maintained; however, this is a sport of the summer months only.

The most fruitful professional field appears to be that of law. The pride of race so highly developed there gives both the criminal lawyer and the civil lawyer many clients among his own race group. What is true of the law profession is also true of the field of medicine. At least seven practicing physicians are trying to thrive on this meager population. With few exceptions, these men of professions adhere very closely to the ethics of their professions.

As was stated at the outset, there is no pretense of an exhaustive report of the many aspects of this little Negro town in the West; nor has all been said of the phases mentioned that might be said. The attempt has been merely to present a sufficient amount of representative and rounded information concerning life in such a settlement, for students of social psychology of race and of human behavior generally, to utilize the information in the interpretation of similar or related social situations.

The project of exclusively Negro towns does undoubtedly offer an outlet for repressions and wounded race pride; for the independent development of institutions and the acquirement of a certain amount of wealth. Along with these, however, go other factors that are negative and dangerous. The isolation from the main currents of progress registers in a certain retardation; it also tends to build up a rigidly hostile defense attitude toward the traditional oppressor which does not always contribute to the inter-racial peace.

COLONIZATION: "THE BACK-TO-AFRICA" MOVEMENT OF MARCUS GARVEY

Some attention must be given to Marcus Garvey (1887-1940), not because he offered a program of social welfare for blacks which was relevant to conventional conceptions of social welfare in his day, but precisely because he did not. At a time when urban migration had concentrated more and more of the black population in the metropolis, Garvey advocated that blacks remove themselves entirely from the American scene by emigration and colonization. A massive social movement, the Universal Negro Improvement Association, was to assume under his direction the leadership and responsibility of removing American blacks to Africa.

This movement materialized and launched a bold appeal to the masses, raising the racial consciousness of blacks perhaps to heights never before attained. The irony of his ideology was that it shared some aspects of racism in its concept of racial purity and superiority similar to that of the newly reconstituted Ku Klux Klan, which enthusiastically endorsed that aspect of Garvey's program which called for racial separation and removal of blacks to an African homeland. Because this association was apparent to members of the black intelligentsia of the day, Garvey's program was opposed by officials of such organizations as the N. A. A. C. P. and the National Urban League, to mention but two.

The following document states the aims and objectives of the Universal Negro Improvement Association, as stated by its leader, Marcus Garvey.

Document 7*

"Aims and Objects of Movement for Solution of Negro Problem," in Philosophy and Opinions of Marcus Garvey, or Africa for the Africans, compiled by Amy Jacques Garvey, with a new introduction by E. U. Essien Udom, 2 volumes in one, 2nd edition, Vol. II, 1923. pp. 37-38.

Generally the public is kept misinformed of the truth surrounding new movements of reform. Very seldom, if ever, reformers get the truth told about them and their movements. Because of this natural attitude, the Universal Negro Improvement Association has been greatly handicapped in its work, causing thereby one of the most liberal and helpful human movements of the twentieth century to be held up to ridicule by those who take pride in poking fun at anything not already successfully established.

The white man of America has become the natural leader of the world. He, because of his exalted position, is called upon to help all human efforts. From nations to individuals the appeal is made to him for aid in all things affecting humanity, so, naturally, there can be no great mass movement or change without first acquainting the leader on whose sympathy and advice the world moves.

It is because of this, and more so because of a desire to be Christian friends with the white race, why I explain the aims and objects of the Universal Negro Improvement Association.

The Universal Negro Improvement Association is an organization among Negroes that is seeking to improve the condition of the race, with the view of establishing a nation in Africa where Negroes will be given the opportunity to develop by themselves, without creating the hatred and animosity that now exist in countries of the white race through Negroes rivaling them for the highest and best positions in government, politics, society and industry. The organization believes in the rights of all men, yellow, white and black. To us, the white race has a right to the peaceful possession and occupation of countries of its own and in like manner the yellow and black races have their rights. It is only by an honest and liberal consideration of such rights can the world be blessed with the peace that is sought by Christian teachers and leaders.

The Spiritual Brotherhood of Man

The following preamble to the constitution of the organization

*Reprinted by permission.

speaks for itself:

> The Universal Negro Improvement Association and African Communities' League is a social, friendly, humanitarian, charitable, educational, institutional, constructive, and expansive society, and is founded by persons, desiring to the utmost to work for the general uplift of the Negro peoples of the world. And the members pledge themselves to do all in their power to conserve the rights of their noble race and to respect the rights of all mankind, believing always in the Brotherhood of Man and the Fatherhood of God. The motto of the organization is: One God! One Aim! One Destiny! Therefore, let justice be done to all mankind, realizing that if the strong oppresses the weak confusion and discontent will ever mark the path of man, but with love, faith and charity toward all the reign of peace and plenty will be heralded into the world and the generation of men shall be called Blessed.

The declared objects of the association are:

> To establish a Universal Confraternity among the race; to promote the spirit of pride and love; to reclaim the fallen; to administer to and assist the needy; to assist in civilizing the backward tribes of Africa; to assist in the development of Independent Negro Nations and Communities; to establish a central nation for the race; to establish Commissaries or Agencies in the principal countries and cities of the world for the representation of all Negroes; to promote a conscientious Spiritual worship among the native tribes of Africa; to establish Universities, Colleges, Academies and Schools for the racial education and culture of the people; to work for better conditions among Negroes everywhere.

Supplying a Long Felt Want

The organization of the Universal Negro Improvement Association has supplied among Negroes a long-felt want. Hitherto the other Negro movements in America, with the exception of the Tuskegee effort of Booker T. Washington, sought to teach the Negro to aspire to social equality with the whites, meaning thereby the right to inter-marry and fraternize in every social way. This has been the source of much trouble and still some Negro organizations continue to preach this dangerous "race destroying doctrine" added to a program of political agitation and aggression. The Universal Negro Improvement Association on the other hand believes in and teaches the pride and purity of race. We believe that the white race should uphold its racial pride and perpetuate itself, and that the black race should do likewise. We believe that there is room enough in the world for the various race groups to grow and develop by themselves without seeking to destroy the Creator's plan by the constant introduction of mongrel types.

The unfortunate condition of slavery, as imposed upon the Negro, and which caused the mongrelization of the race, should not be legalized and continued now to the harm and detriment of both races.

This is a judicious and prophetic assessment of the movement led by Marcus Garvey, written by the distinguished sociologist, E. Franklin Frazier, who was, at the time, the Director of the Atlanta School of Social Work.

Document 8*

E. Franklin Frazier, "The Garvey Movement," Opportunity, Vol. IV, November, 1926, pp. 346-348.

Garvey, himself, could not have planned a more strategic climax to his career in America than his imprisonment in Atlanta. The technical legal reason for his incarceration is obscured by the halo that shines about the head of the martyr. There is a sort of justice in this; for if the government were to punish all those who use the mails to defraud, it would round up those energetic business men who food the mails with promises to give eternal youth and beauty to aging fat matrons, to make Carusos and Galli Curcis of members of church choirs, and to make master minds of morons. Garvey's promises were modest in comparison. And, indeed, what does one ship, more or less, matter in an imaginary fleet of merchantmen?

There are aspects of the Garvey Movement that can not be treated in this cavalier manner. It is those aspects we propose to set forth here. The writer recalls that when he was a child one could still hear Negroes express the hope that some Moses would appear among them and lead them to a promised land of freedom and equality. He has lived to see such hopes displaced by more prosaic and less fanciful efforts towards social betterment. When Booker T. Washington first appeared on the scene he was hailed as a Moses. This was chiefly an echo of the white man's appraisal and soon died down when the Negro heard a message of patient industry, unsweetened by any prospect of a glorious future. What has distinguished the Garvey Movement is its appeal to the masses. While Negroes have found a degree of self-magnification in fraternal orders and the church, these organizations have not given the support to their ego-consciousness that whites find in the Kiwanis and especially the Klan. Garvey re-introduced the idea of a Moses, who was incarnate in himself and with his masterly technic for dealing with crowds, he welded Negroes into a mass movement.

Before considering Garvey and his work, something should

*Reprinted by permission of the National Urban League.

be said of the people he had to work with. The social status of the Negro in America should make them fertile soil for a mass movement to spring up in. They are repressed and shut out from all serious participation in American life. Not only does the Negro intellectual feel this repression, but the average Negro, like all mediocre people whose personalities must be supported by empty fictions, must find something to give meaning to his life and worth to his personality. One has simply to note how the superficial matter of color raises the most insignificant white man in the South to a place of paramount importance, in order to appreciate how much support a fiction gives one's personality. Yet American Negroes have been relatively free from mass movements. This fact should not be regarded as a further testimony to the Negro's reputation for a policy of expediency in his present situation. There have been other factors to take the place of mass movements.

Many American Negroes have belittled the Garvey Movement on the ground that he is a West Indian and has attracted only the support of West Indians. But this very fact made it possible for him to contribute a new phase to the life of the American Negro. The West Indian Negroes have been ruled by a small white minority. In Jamaica, the Negro population has often revolted and some recognition has been given to the mulattoes. This was responsible for Garvey's attempt, when he first came to this country, to incite the blacks against those of mixed blood. He soon found that there was no such easily discernable social cleavage recognized by the whites in this country. Yet his attempt to draw such a line has not failed to leave its effect. The fact that the West Indian has not been dominated by a white majority is probably responsible for a more secular way of life. The Garvey Movement would find the same response among the Negroes of the South as among the West Indians were it not for the dominating position of the preacher, whose peculiar position is symtomatic [sic] of an otherwordly outlook among the masse. Even in the face of this situation foreign Negroes have successfully converted hard-shelled Baptists to the Movement in spite of the opposition of their ministers. This secular influence in the life of the Negro attains its true significance when viewed in relation to the part that preparation for death plays in the life of the black masses.

The Garvey Movement afforded an asylum, as all mass movements, for those who were dissatisfied with life for many reasons, which could in this case be attributed to their status as Negroes. Although most of his followers were ignorant, we find among them intellectuals who had not found the places in the world that their education entitled them to. Instead of blaming themselves,--and they were not always individually responsible--they took refuge in the belief that in an autonomous black Africa they would find their proper places. The black rabble that could not see its own poverty, ignorance, and weakness vented its hatred upon obscure "traitors" and "enemies," who generally turned out to be Negro intellectuals who had achieved some distinction in American life. There is good reason to believe that Garvey constantly directed the animosity of his followers against the intellectuals because of his own lack of formal education.

We have noted how the Garvey Movement turned the Negro's attention to this world. This was accomplished not only by promising the Negro a paradise in the future in Africa; but through the invention of social distinctions and honors, the Negro was made somebody in his present environment. The humblest follower was one of the "Fellowmen of the Negro Race," while the more distinguished supporters were "Knights" and "Sirs." The women were organized into the Black Cross Nurses and the men into the Great African Army. "A uniformed member of a Negro lodge paled in significance beside a soldier of the Army of Africa. A Negro might be a porter during the day, taking his orders from white men, but he was an officer in the Black Army when it assembled at night in Liberty Hall. Many a Negro went about his work singing in his heart that he was a member of the great army marching to 'heights of achievements.'" Yet these extravagant claims were based upon the deep but unexpressed conviction in the minds of most Negroes that the white man has set certain limits to their rise in this country.

In his half acknowledged antagonism towards Negro preachers and the soporific religion they served the masses, Garvey did not ignore its powerful influence. In fact he endeavored to fuse the religious experience of the Negro with his own program. The symbolism associated with Christmas was made the sign of the birth of a Negro nation among the nations of the earth; while Easter became the symbol of a resurrected race. Nor did he overlook the opportunity to make his position appear similar to that of Jesus. According to him, his own people, especially the recognized Negro leaders, had incited the American authorities against him just as the Jews had incited the Roman authorities against Jesus. In this connection the idea of gaining a lost paradise appears as it does in most mass movements. The "Redemption of Africa" became the battle cry. To his followers he trumpeted: "No one knows when the hour of Africa's redemption cometh. It is in the wind. It is coming one day like a storm. It will be here. When that day comes, all Africa will stand together."

The messianic element in this movement is not altogether lacking, although it does not stand out prominently. When Garvey entered the prison in Atlanta, besides commending his wife to the care of his followers, he spoke of the possibility of his death as only a messiah would speak. Under the caption, "If I Die in Atlanta," he bade his followers: "Look for me in the whirlwind or the storm, look for me all around you, for, with God's grace, I shall come and bring with me the countless millions of black slaves who have died in America and the West Indies and the millions in Africa to aid you in the fight for liberty, freedom and life."

By this promise Garvey raised himself above mortals and made himself the Redeemer of the Black World.

Many people are at a loss to understand how Garvey was able to attract supporters to a scheme which was manifestly infeasible and has been discredited by continued exposes of corruption and bickering within the organization. But such tests of reasonableness can not be applied to schemes that attract crowds. Crowds, it has been said, never learn by experience. The reason is clear, for the crowd satisfies its vanity and longings in the beliefs it cherishes. Not only because of their longing for something to give meaning to their lives, but because of the scepticism (sic) about them, Negroes do not find the satisfaction that their fathers found in the promise of heavenly abode to compensate for the woes of this world. They therefore offer a fine field for charlatans and fakirs of every description. This Movement has attracted many such men who give the black crowds the escape they are seeking. The work carried on by the National Association for the Advancement of Colored People, which has been the subject of so many attacks by Garvey, has never attracted the crowd because it does not give the crowd an opportunity to show off in colors, parades, and self-glorification. The Association appeals to intelligent persons who are trying to attain tangible goals through cooperation. The same could be said of the Urban League. Dean Kelly Miller, it is said, once made the shrewd observation that the Negro pays for what he wants and begs for what he needs. This applies here as elsewhere. Those who support the Movement pay for it because it gives them what they want--the identification with something that makes them feel like somebody among white people who have said they were nobody.

Before concluding this brief interpretive sketch, we must add a few observations. Doubtless the World War with its shibboleths and stirrings of subject minorities offered a volume of suggestion that facilitated the Garvey Movement. Another factor that helped the Movement was the urbanization of the Negro that took place about the time. It is in the cities that mass movements are initiated. When the Negro lived in a rural environment he was not subject to mass suggestion except at the camp meeting and revival.

One of the picturesque phases of the Movement has been the glorification of blackness which has been made an attribute of the celestial hierarchy. To most observers this last fact has been simply a source of merriment. But Garvey showed a knowledge of social psychology when he invoked a black god to guide the destiny of the Negro. The God of Israel served the same purpose. Those whites who said they would rather go to hell than to a heaven presided over by a black god, show what relation the average man's god must bear to him. The intellectual can laugh, if he will; but let him not forget the pragmatic value of such a symbol among the type of people Garvey was dealing with.

The question is often asked, "Is Garvey sincere?" The same question might be asked of the McGee brothers of the Kentucky Revival and of evangelists in general. Although Garvey's appeal has been more permanent, his methods have been in many respects those of the evangelist. Just because evangelists as a rule are well fed and free from material wants, it would be uncritical to put them all down as common swindlers. Likewise, with the evidence we have, we can not classify Garvey as such. He has failed to deal realistically with life as most so-called cranks, but he has initiated a mass movement among Negroes because it appealed to something that is in every crowd-minded man.

THE CONCEPT AND CONSCIOUSNESS OF THE "NEW NEGRO"

The concepts of race pride and black consciousness proved to be broader in scope and content than as used and applied in the Garvey Movement. They permeate the total life styles and perspectives of all black Americans on matters of economic, social, political and cultural affairs; and they are a significant factor in the ways that blacks define problems, create and initiate organized ways to alleviate problems, and resolve conflict situations.

We have noted the appearance of the "New Negro" concept as early as the end of the nineteenth century. It becomes increasingly stressed in this period to the point where, as a concept, it has tended to define the age. In an article by the editors of The Messenger, Chandler Owen and A. Philip Randolph, the concept is defined and examined with respect to its implications, aims, and methodology in its economic, political and social dimensions. In the article by Alain Locke, Professor of Philosophy, Howard University, however, are set forth its humanistic and aesthetic implications and its meaning for creative artists and intellectuals.

Document 9a*

Editorial: "The New Negro: What Is He?" The Messenger, August, 1920, pp. 73-74.

Our title was the subject of an editorial in the New York Age which formed the basis of an extensive symposium. Most of the replies, however, have been vague and nebulous. The Messenger, therefore, undertakes to supply the New York Age and the general public with a definite and clear portrayal of the New Negro.

It is well nigh axiomatic that the most accurate test of what

*Reprinted by permission.

a man or institution or a movement is, is first, what its aims are; second, what its methods are, or how it expects to achieve its aims; and third, its general relations to current movements.

Now, what are the aims of the New Negro? The answer to this question will fall under three general heads, namely, political, economic and social.

In politics, the New Negro, unlike the Old Negro, cannot be lulled into a false sense of security with political spoils and patronage. A job is not the price of his vote. He will not continue to accept political promisory notes from a political debtor, who has already had the power, but who has refused to satisfy the political obligations. The New Negro demands political equality. He recognizes the necessity of selective as well as elective representation. He realizes that so long as the Negro votes for the Republican or Democratic party, he will have only the right and privilege to elect but not to select his representatives. And he who selects the representatives controls the representative. The New Negro stands for universal suffrage.

A word about the economic aims of the New Negro. Here, as a worker, he demands the full product of his toil. His immediate aim is more wages, shorter hours and better working conditions. As a consumer, he seeks to buy in the market, commodities at the lowest price.

The social aims of the New Negro are decidedly different from those of the Old Negro. Here he stands for absolute and unequivocal "social equality." He realizes that there cannot be any qualified equality. He insists that a society which is based upon justice can only be a society composed of social equals. He insists upon identity of social treatment. With respect to intermarriage, he maintains that it is the only logical, sound and correct aim for the Negro to entertain. He realizes that the acceptance of laws against intermarriage is tantemount to the acceptance of the stigma of inferiority. Besides, laws against intermarriage expose Negro women to sexual exploitation, and deprive their offspring, by white men, of the right to inherit the property of their father. Statistics show that there are nearly four million mulattoes in America as a result of miscegenation.

So much then for the aims of the New Negro. A word now about his methods. It is with respect to methods that the essential difference between the New Negro and the Old Negro relates.

First, the methods by which the New Negro expects to realize his political aims are radical. He would repudiate and discard both of the old parties--Republican and Democratic. His knowledge of political science enables him to see that a political organization must have an economic foundation. A party whose money comes from working people, must and will represent working people. Now, everybody concedes that the Negro is essentially a worker. There are no big capitalists among them. There are a few petit bourgeoisie, but the process of money concentration is destined to weed them out and drop them down into the ranks of the working class. In fact, the interests of all Negroes are tied up with the workers. Therefore, the Negro should support a working class political party. He is a fool or insane, who opposes his best interests by supporting his enemy. As workers, Negroes have nothing in common with their employers. The Negro wants high wages: the employer wants to pay low wages. The Negro wants to work short hours; the employer wants to work him long hours. Since this is true, it follows as a logical corollary that the Negro should not support the party of the employing class. Now, it is a question of fact that the Republican and Democratic parties are parties of the employing or capitalist class.

On the economic field, the New Negro advocates that the Negro join the labor unions. Wherever white unions discriminate against the Negro worker, then the only sensible thing to do is to form independent unions to fight both the white capitalists for more wages and shorter hours, on the one hand, and white labor unions for justice, on the other. It is folly for the Negro to fight labor organization because some white unions ignorantly ignore or oppose him. It is about as logical and wise as to repudiate and condemn writing on the ground that it is used by some crooks for forgery. As a consumer, he would organize cooperative societies to reduce the high cost of living.

The social methods are: education and physical action in self defense. That education must constitute the basis of all action, is beyond the realm of question. And to fight back in self defense, should be accepted as a matter of course. No one who will not fight to protect his life is fit to live. Self defense is recognized as a legitimate weapon in all civilized countries. Yet the Old Crowd Negroes have counseled the doctrine of non-resistance.

As to current movements, the Negro would accept, praise and support that which his enemies reject, condemn and oppose. He is tolerant. He would restore free speech, a free press and freedom of assemblage. He would release Debs. He would recognize the right of Russia to self-determination. He is opposed to the Treaty and the League of Nations. Yet, he rejects Lodge's reservations. He knows that neither will help the people. As to Negro leaders, his object is to destroy them all and build up new ones.

Finally, the new Negro arrived upon the scene at the time of all other forward, progressive groups and movements--after the great world war. He is the product of the same world wide forces that have brought into being the great liberal and radical movements that are now seizing the reins of political, economic and social power in all of the civilized countries of the world.

His presence is inevitable in these times of economic chaos, political upheaval and social distress. Yes, there is a New Negro.

And it is he who will pilot the Negro through this terrible hour of storm and stress.

Document 9b*

Alain Locke, "The New Negro," Survey Graphic, Vol. LIII, 1924-25, pp. 631-634.

In the last decade something beyond the watch and guard of statistics has happened in the life of the American Negro and the three norms who have traditionally presided over the Negro problem have a changeling in their laps. The Sociologist, The Philanthropist, the Race-leader are not unaware of the New Negro, but they are at a loss to account for him. He simply cannot be swathed in their formulae. For the younger generation is vibrant with a new psychology; the new spirit is awake in the masses, and under the very eyes of the professional observers is transforming what has been a perennial problem into the progressive phases of contemporary Negro life.

Could such a metamorphosis have taken place as suddenly as it has appeared to? The answer is no; not because the New Negro is not here, but because the Old Negro had long become more of a myth than a man. The Old Negro, we must remember, was a creature of moral debate and historical controversy. His has been a stock figure perpetuated as an historical fiction partly in innocent sentimentalism, partly in deliberate reactionism. The Negro himself has contributed his share to this through a sort of protective social mimicry forced upon him by the adverse circumstances of dependence. So for generations in the mind of America, the Negro has been more of a formula than a human being--a something to be argued about, condemned or defended, to be "kept down," or "in his place," or "helped up," to be worried with or worried over, harassed or patronized, a social bogey or a social burden. The thinking Negro even has been induced to share this same general attitude, to focus his attention on controversial issues, to see himself in the distorted perspective of a social problem. His shadow, so to speak, has been more real to him than his personality. Through having had to appeal from the unjust stereotypes of his oppressors and traducers to those of his liberators, friends, and benefactors he has subscribed to the traditional positions from which his case has been viewed. Little true social or self-understanding has or could come from such a situation.

But while the minds of most of us, black and white, have been burrowed in the trenches of the Civil War and Reconstruction, the actual march of development has simply flanked these positions, necessitating a sudden reorientation of self. We have not been watching in the right direction; the North and South on a sectional axis, we have not noticed the East till the sun has us blinking.

*Reprinted by permission.

Recall how suddenly the Negro spirituals revealed themselves; suppressed for generations under the stereotypes of Wesleyan hymn harmony, secretive, half-ashamed, until the outrage of being natural brought them out--and behold, there was folk-music. Similarly the mind of the Negro seems suddenly to have slipped from under the tyranny of social intimidation and to be shaking off the psychology of education and implied inferiority. By shedding the old paralysis of the Negro problem we are achieving something like a spiritual emancipation. Until recently, lacking self-understanding, we have been almost as much of a problem to ourselves as we still are to others. But the decade that found us with a problem has left us with only a task. The multitude perhaps feels as yet only a strange relief and a new vague urge, but the thinking few know that in the reaction the vital inner grip of prejudice has been broken.

With this renewed self-respect and self-dependence, the life of the Negro community is bound to enter a new dynamic phase, the buoyancy from within compensating for whatever pressure there may be of conditions from without. The migrant masses, shifting from countryside to city, hurdle several generations of experience at a leap, but more important, the same thing happens spiritually in the life-attitudes and self-expression of the Young Negro, in his poetry, his art, his education and his new outlook, with the additional advantage, of course, of the poise and greater certainty of knowing what it is all about. From this comes the promise and warrant of a new leadership. As one of them has discerningly put it:

We have tomorrow
Bright before us
Like a flame

Yesterday, a night-gone thing
A sun-down name.

And Dawn today
Broad arch above the road we came.
We march!

This is what, even more than any "most creditable record of fifty years of freedom," requires that the Negro of today be seen through other than the dusty spectacles of past controversy. The day of "aunties," "uncles," and "mammies" is equally gone. Uncle Tom and Sambo have passed on, and even the "Colonel" and "George" play barnstorm roles from which they escape with relief when the public spotlight is off. The popular melodrama has about played itself out, and it is time to scrap the fictions, garret the bogeys and settle down to a realistic facing of facts.

First we must observe some of the changes which since the traditional lines of opinion were drawn have rendered these quite obsolete. A main change has been, of course, that shifting of the Negro population which has made the Negro problem no longer exclusively or even predominantly Southern. Why should our minds remain sectionalized, when the problem itself no longer is? Then the trend of migration has not only been toward the North and the Central Midwest, but city-ward and to the great centers of industry--

the problems of adjustment are new, practical, local and not peculiarly racial. Rather they are an integral part of the large industrial and social problems of our present-day democracy. And finally, with the Negro rapidly in process of class differentiation, if it ever was warrantable to regard and treat the Negro en masse it is becoming with every day less possible, more unjust and more ridiculous.

The Negro too, for his part, has idols of the tribe to smash. If on the one hand the white man has erred in making the Negro appear to be that which would excuse or extenuate his treatment of him, the Negro, in turn, has too often unnecessarily excused himself because of the way he has been treated. The intelligent Negro of today is resolved not to make discrimination an extenuation for his shortcomings in performance, individual or collective; he is trying to hold himself at par, neither inflated by sentimental allowances nor depreciated by current social discounts. For this he must know himself and be known for precisely what he is, and for that reason he welcomes the new scientific rather than the old sentimental interest. Sentimental interest in the Negro has ebbed. We used to lament this as the falling off of our friends; now we rejoice and pray to be delivered both from self-pity and condescension. The mind of each racial group has had a bitter weaning, apathy or hatred on one side matching disillusionment or resentment on the other; but they face each other today with the possibility at least of entirely new mutual attitudes.

It does not follow that if the Negro were better known, he would be better liked or better treated. But mutual understanding is basic for any subsequent cooperation and adjustment. The effort toward this will at least have the effect of remedying in large part what has been the most unsatisfactory feature of our present stage of race relationships in America, namely the fact that the more intelligent and representative elements of the two race groups have at so many points got quite out of vital touch with one another.

The fiction is that the life of the races is separate, and increasingly so. The fact is that they have touched too closely at the unfavorable and too lightly at the favorable levels.

While inter-racial councils have sprung up in the South, drawing on forward elements of both races, in the Northern cities manual laborers may brush elbows in their everyday work, but the community and business leaders have experienced no such interplay or far too little of it. These segments must achieve contact or the race situation in America becomes desperate. Fortunately this is happening. There is a growing realization that in social effort the cooperative basis must supplant long-distance philanthropy, and that the only safeguard for mass relations in the future must be provided in the carefully maintained contacts of the enlightened minorities of both race groups. In the intellectual realm a renewed and keen curiosity is replacing the recent apathy; the Negro is being carefully studied, not just talked about and discussed. In the art and letters, instead of being wholly caricatured, he is seriously being portrayed and painted.

To all of this the New Negro is keenly responsive as an augury of a new democracy in American culture. He is contributing his share to the new social understanding. But the desire to be understood would never in itself have been sufficient to have opened so completely the protectively closed portals of the thinking Negro's mind. There is still too much possibility of being snubbed or patronized for that. It was rather the necessity for fuller, truer, self-expression, the realization of the unwisdom of allowing social discrimination to segregate him mentally, and a counter-attitude to cramp and fetter his own living--and so the "spite-wall" that the intellectuals built over the "color line" has happily been taken down. Much of this reopening of intellectual contacts has centered in New York and has been richly fruitful not merely in the enlarging of personal experience but in the definite enrichment of American art and letters and in the clarifying of our common vision of the social tasks ahead...

Each generation, however, will have its creed and that of the present is the belief in the efficacy of collective effort in race cooperation. This deep feeling of race is at present the mainspring of Negro life. It seems to be the outcome of the reaction to proscription and prejudice; an attempt, barely successful on the whole, to convert a defensive into an offensive position, a handicap into an incentive. It is radical in tone, but not in purpose and only the most stupid terms of opposition, misunderstanding or persecution could make it otherwise. Of course, the thinking Negro has shifted little toward the left with the world-trend, and there is an increasing group who affiliate with radical and liberal movements. But fundamentally for the present the Negro is radical on race matters, conservative on others, in other words, a "forced radical," a social protestant rather than a genuine radical. Yet under further pressure and injustice iconoclastic thought and motives will inevitably increase. Harlem's quixotic radicalisms call for their ounce of democracy today lest tomorrow they be beyond cure.

The Negro mind reaches out as yet to nothing but American wants, American ideas. But this forced attempt to build an Americanism on race values is a unique social experiment and its ultimate success is impossible except through the fullest sharing of American culture and institutions. There should be no delusion about this. American nerves in seconds unstrung with race hysteria are often fed the opiate that the trend of Negro advance is wholly separatist, and that the effect of its operation will be to encyst the Negro as a benign foreign body in the body politic. This cannot be--even if it were desirable. The radicalism of the Negro shows no limitation or reservation with respect to American life; it is only a constructive effort to build the obstructions in the stream of his progress into an efficient dam of social energy and power. Democracy itself is obstructed and stagnated to the extent that any of its channels are closed. Indeed they cannot be selectively closed. So the choice is between one way for the Negro and another way for the rest, but between American institutions frustrated on the one hand and American ideals progressively fulfilled and realized on the other ...

Fortunately there are constructive channels opening out into which the balked social feelings of the American Negro can flow freely.

Without them there would be much more pressure and danger than there is. These compensating interests are racial but in a new and enlarged way. One is the consciousness of acting as the advance-guard of the African peoples in their contact with the Twentieth Century civilization; the other, the sense of a mission of rehabilitating the race in world esteem from that loss of prestige for which the fate and conditions of slavery have so largely been responsible. Harlem, as we shall see, is the center of both these movements; she is the home of the Negro's "Zionism." The pulse of the Negro world has begun to beat in Harlem. A Negro newspaper carrying news material in English, French and Spanish, gathered from all quarters of America, the West Indies and Africa has maintained itself in Harlem for over five years. Two important magazines, both edited from New York, maintain their news and circulation consistently on a cosmopolitan scale. Under American auspices and backing, three pan-African congresses have been held abroad for the discussion of common interests, colonial questions and the future cooperative development of Africa. In terms of the race question as a world problem, the Negro mind has leapt, so to speak, upon the parapets of prejudice and extended its cramped horizons. In so doing it has linked up with the growing group consciousness of the dark-peoples and is gradually learning their common interests. As one of our writers has recently put it: "It is imperative that we understand the white world in its relations to the non-white world." As with the Jew, persecution is making the Negro international.

As a world phenomenon this wider race consciousness is a different thing from the much asserted rising tide of color. Its inevitable causes are not of our making. The consequences are not necessarily damaging to the best interests of civilization. Whether it actually brings into being new Armadas of conflict or argosies of cultural exchange and enlightenment can only be decided by the attitude of the dominant races in an era of critical change. With the American Negro his new internationalism is primarily an effort to recapture contact with the scattered peoples of African derivation. Garveyism may be a transient, if spectacular, phenomenon, but the possible role of the American Negro in the future development of Africa is one of the most constructive and universally helpful missions that any modern people can lay claim to.

Constructive participation in such causes cannot help giving the Negro valuable group incentives, as well as increased prestige at home and abroad. Our greatest rehabilitation may possibly come through such channels, but for the present, more immediate hope rests in the revaluation by white and black alike of the Negro in terms of his artistic endowments and cultural contributions, past and prospective. It must be increasingly recognized that the Negro has already made very substantial contributions, not only in his folk-art, music especially, which has always found appreciation, but in larger, though humbler and less acknowledged ways. For generations the Negro has been the peasant matrix of that section of America which has most undervalued him, and here he has contributed not only materially in labor and in social patience, but spiritually as well. The South has unconsciously absorbed the gift of his folk-temperament. In less than half a generation it will be easier to recognize this, but the fact remains that a leaven of humor, sentiment, imagination and tropic nonchalance has gone into the making of the South from a humble, unacknowledged source. A second crop of the Negro's gifts promises still more largely. He now becomes a conscious contributor and lays aside the status of a beneficiary and ward for that of a collaborator and participant in American Civilization. The great social gain in this is the releasing of our talented group from the arid fields of controversy and debate to the productive fields of creative expression. The especially cultural recognition they win should in turn prove the key to that revaluation of the Negro which must precede or accompany any considerable further betterment of race relationships. But whatever the general effect, the present generation will have added the motives of self-expression and spiritual development to the old and still unfinished task of making material headway and progress. No one who understandingly faces the situation with its substantial accomplishment or views the new scene with its still more abundant promise can be entirely without hope. And certainly, if in our lifetime the Negro should not be able to celebrate his full initiation into American democracy, he can at least, on the warrant of these things, celebrate the attainment of a significant and satisfying new phase of group development, and with it a spiritual Coming of Age.

PROBLEMS REQUIRING NATIONAL ATTENTION

Many problems of American blacks were national in scope. They did not yield to a multiplicity of small scale local ad hoc undertakings, laudable as many of them were in aims, objectives and accomplishments. One problem of overriding national import was that of controlling the violence directed against blacks. Lynching of individuals happened mainly in the rural areas, whereas rioting against groups and neighborhoods occurred primarily in the larger centers of population.

The anti-lynching campaign occupied the time and efforts of many, but the N. A. A. C. P. and, especially, the organizations of Colored Women, made it their particular interest. In 1921 the N.

A. A. C. P. persuaded Representative Dyer to introduce an anti-lynching bill in the House of Representatives and lobbied for many years for its passage. Although it was passed in the House, the anti-lynching bill never passed in the Senate.

a. Lynching and the Anti-Lynching Campaign

The following probably is a draft of a protest made to high officials of the United States Government. Such petitions had little impact, as there was no possibility of imposing political sanctions against the government officials who ignored them. However, it is a valuable example of popular concern and outrage. Document 10b is a cautionary note refuting the concept that lynching was subject to inevitable decline.

Document 10a*

Anti-Lynching Petition, Atlanta, Georgia, March 1, 1918. Neighborhood Union Collection Papers. Trevor Arnett Library, Atlanta University, Atlanta, Georgia.

Atlanta, Georgia
March 1, 1918

To the President, the Cabinet, the Congress of the United States, the Governors and the Legislatures of the Several States of the United States of America:

During the past three decades nearly three thousand American colored men, women and children have suffered butchery and death in almost every conceivable form at the hands of the lynchers of America. Last year alone the number thus murdered was two hundred twenty-two. The reported causes for such appalling brutality run the gamut from alleged violation of the honor of white women to disputing the word of white men. The fact however that only about five per cent of these murders are reputed to have been inflicted upon accused violators of womanhood, argues almost conclusively that the desire to protect womanhood is almost negligible among the so-called causes of lynchings.

We accordingly regard lynchings as worse than Prussianism which we are at war to destroy. Lynching is not a cure for crime, either imaginary or real. It decreases faith in the boasted justice of our so-called democratic institutions. It widens the frightful chasm of unfriendly and suspicious feeling between the races and positively foments the spirits of antipathy and resentment. We are accused of concealing criminals. Who has concealed the many crimi-

*Reprinted by permission of Atlanta University.

nals that have mercilessly murdered these three thousand defenseless men, women and children of our race? That these murderers frequently ply their trade in broad daylight and in plain view of the entire citizenry even, does not facilitate their punishment or detection. Within less than one year one state alone has tortured and burned at the stake three colored men without even the semblance of a trial or an effort to apprehend and punish the murderers. In the last instance an entire helpless colored population was marched around the fire, amid fumes of a burning human being and put on notice that as that black man was suffering they too should fear to suffer. Thus the defiant lynching giant strides on apace. While we are sacrificing the best blood of our sons upon our nation's altar to help destroy Prussianism beyond the seas, we call upon you to use your high offices to destroy the lynching institutions at our doors.

We are the one group of American people, than whom there is none more loyal, which is marked out for discrimination, humiliation, and abuse. In great patriotic and humanitarian movements, in public carriers, in federal service, the treatment accorded us is humiliating, dehumanizing and reprehensible in the extreme. This persistent and unreasonable practice is but a thrust at the colored man's self-respect--the object being not merely to separate the races but to impress us with the idea of supposed natural inferiority. Such demoralizing discrimination is not only a violation of the fundamental rights of citizens of the United States, but the persistent segregation of any element of our country's population into a separate and distinct group on the sole basis of color is creating a condition under which this nation cannot long endure.

When we reflect upon these brutalities and indignities we remember they are due to the fact that in almost every southern state we have systematically, by law or chicanery, been deprived of the right of that very manhood suffrage which genuine democracy would guarantee to every citizen in the republic. This propaganda of filching from colored Americans the ballot is but a supreme effort to re-enslave us and to force our assent to, and our impotence against, any legislation of our opponents. To this policy the black man does not, cannot and will not agree. Of it, our intolerance is cumulative. Against it, we shall exert our righteous efforts until not only every eligible black man but every eligible black woman shall be wielding the ballot proudly in defense of our liberties and our homes.

We are appealing to you neither as vassals nor as inferiors. Bull Run and Appomattox fixed our status in this nation. We are free men. We are sovereign American citizens--freemen who have purchased with our own blood on every battle field from Bunker Hill to Carrizal full rights and immunities such as are freely granted others but systematically refused us.

We are writing to you, gentlemen, that you may give us the assurance and guarantee which every American citizen ought to have without reference to color. We are loyal and will remain so, but we are not blind. We cannot help seeing that white soldiers who massacred our black brothers and sisters in East St. Louis have gone scot free. We cannot help seeing that our black brothers who massacred white citizens in Houston have paid the most ignominous penalty that can come in this country to a man in uniform. Do not these undemocratic conditions, these inhumanities, these brutalities and savageries provoke the Rulers of the nation to speak out of their long sphinxlike silence and utter a voice of hope, a word of promise for the black man? Do the rulers of the nation also hate us, and will they, Pilate-like, forever give their assent to the crucifixion of the bodies, minds and souls of those in whom there has been found nothing worthy of the death we are dying, save that we are black. May not your silence be construed as tacit approval or active tolerance of these things? What think you will be the effect on the morale of black men in the trenches when they reflect that they are fighting on foreign fields in behalf of their nation for those very rights and privileges which they themselves are denied at home?

We appeal to you in the name of democracy!

We appeal to you in the name of our American citizenship!

We appeal to you in the name of God, and,

We will be heard!

Document 10b*

An editorial, "Lynchings Increase," Opportunity, Vol. IV, No. 47, November, 1926, pp. 336-337.

In 1924 there were 16 lynchings. Last year there were 18. To the tenth month of this year there have been 25. Lynchings, quite obviously and disturbingly, are again on the increase. The temper of mobs shows change. Once they were the reckless, infuriated stampede of men out to avenge with punishments more terrible than the law provided, although death is but death. The last reported lynchings of three Negroes in Aiken, South Carolina, reveal the difference. They were not lynched for rape or alleged rape; nor had they need to fear that the law would not be satisfied, for they took their victim out of court. Not even the excuse of mere savage impetuosity could be urged, for they planned their steps and their defense before they executed their crime. They did it, so far as it is at present apparent, simply because they knew no punishment would follow. And none did.

An approach to the mystery of the urge to lynching is possible in the cause of the decline from 35 in 1923 to 16 in 1924 and 18 in 1925. Surely one or two years cannot make such sharp differences in human nature and instincts. One fact is offered as a suggestion. Those lean years were by chance filled with the hot discussion of penalties and Federal laws--the Dyer Bill. One of the strongest arguments offered against legislation was the fact that lynchings were

*Reprinted by permission of the National Urban League.

already declining because of the imminence of law was that they would cease to decline when this imminence disappeared.

The defeat of legislative proposals temporarily deflected the point of interest and the lynching record moves to its old level. It is a reasonable speculation that the pressure of interest in Congressional action on this crime re-applied will force the record back to 16 again, and actual legislation will stamp it out entirely.

b. Race Riots

Document 11*

Reports of Race Riots. The Negro Year Book, 1918-1919, edited by Monroe N. Work, Tuskegee Institute, Alabama, 1919, p. 50.

The East St. Louis Riots

From May 27-30 and from July 1-3, 1917, there were race riots in East St. Louis, Illinois. The general causes of these riots were importation of Negro laborers from the South; objection of Labor Unions to this importation and also to the use of Negroes as "strike breakers." This serious situation was supplemented by very bad civic and political conditions. The reports were that, in the May riot one Negro was killed and a large number of both white and Negroes were injured. Hundreds of Negroes were driven from the city.

> The second riot was precipitated on the night of July 1 by an automobile load of 'joy riders' passing through a Negro section of the city and firing promiscuously into houses. Immediately following the 'joy riders,' came an automobile load of policemen and detectives, whom the Negroes mistook for the 'joy riders' and fired upon them, killing one and wounding another. The estimates of the number of persons killed in the July riot ranged from forty to two hundred and fifty. A congressional report of the riot said: 'It is not possible to give accurately the number of dead. At least thirty-nine Negroes and eight white people were killed out right, and hundreds of Negroes were wounded and maimed.' 'The bodies of the dead Negroes,' testified an eye witness, 'were thrown into a morgue like so many dead hogs.' There were three hundred and twelve buildings and forty-four railroad freight cars and their contents destroyed by fire.

The horror and atrocities of the East St. Louis riots were exceeded by few massacres or riots anywhere in the world. The congressional report further said: "Your Committee cannot go into all the harrowing details of how the Negroes--men, women and chil-

*Reprinted by permission.

dren--were killed and burned during the riot, but there were so many flagrantly cruel cases that a bare recital of the facts concerning some of them will be given."

The Houston Riot

On August 23, 1917, there was a riot at Houston, Texas. A battalion of the Twenty-fourth Infantry (colored) of the United States Army had been stationed at Houston to assist in preparing Camp Logan for the concentration of soldiers for the war in Europe. The riot grew out of friction between the city police and the Negro soldiers, especially the Negro military police.

In this document William M. Tuttle enclosed a letter, written one month after the Chicago riot, by Stanley R. Norvell, a black war veteran, to Victor F. Lawson, editor and publisher of the Chicago Daily News.

Document 12*

Stanley R. Norvell and William M. Tuttle, Jr., "Views of a Negro During 'The Red Summer' of 1919," Journal of Negro History, Vol. LI, July, 1966, pp. 209-218.

On the torrid afternoon of Sunday, July 27, 1919, white and Negro swimmers collided in savage combat on a South Side Chicago beach and thus ignited a long and fearfully anticipated race war. Sparked by this conflict, during which a Negro youth drowned, the interracial friction which for over two years had been smoldering in Chicago exploded in furious rioting.

The rioting raged for five days. Day and night white toughs assaulted isolated Negroes, and Negro mobsters beat white peddlers and merchants in the "black belt." As rumors of atrocities circulated through the city, members of both races craved vengeance. White gunmen in automobiles sped through the Negro district shooting indiscriminately as they passed, and Negro snipers fired back. Roaming mobs shot, beat, and stabbed to death their victims. The undermanned police force was an ineffectual deterrent to the waves of violence which soon overflowed the environs of the "black belt" and flooded the North and West Sides and the Loop, Chicago's downtown business district. Only six regiments of state militiamen and a cooling rain finally quenched the passions of the rioters, and even then sporadic outbursts punctuated the atmosphere for another week.

During the riot police officers fatally wounded seven Negroes, and vicious mobs and lone gunmen brutally murdered 16 Negroes and 15 whites. Well over 500 Chicagoans sustained injuries. This bloodshed inflicted an ineradicable scar on the city's reputation and

---

it outraged the sensibilities of numerous Americans.

Chicago, however, was not the only scene of racial violence that summer. In the five-and-one-half months from April 14 to October 1, 1919, race riots bloodied the streets of 22 cities and towns throughout the country. In addition, 74 Negroes were lynched. James Weldon Johnson called this rash of racial violence in 1919 "the Red Summer."

The causes of "the Red Summer" were several. In a nation motivated in great measure at this time by prejudice and intolerance --as evidenced by the xanophobia of the Red Scare--Negroes were highly susceptible objects of aggression. They possessed appropriate stimulus characteristics: that is they were visibly distinct, their behavior was ostensibly strange or alien, and the white populace had long been antipathetic to them. Interracial competition was keen in the labor market and, in northern metropolises like Chicago where Negroes had migrated by the thousands during World War I, in the political arena as well. Due to a hiatus in residential construction during the war, adequate housing was at a premium; countless bombs ripped apart Negro homes in predominantly white neighborhoods in attempts to drive Negroes back to their black ghettos. In 1919, furthermore, acute interracial conflict was mounting due to the widespread white determination to reaffirm the Negroes' prewar aspirations for a larger share in democracy. During "the Red Summer" these various motivations coalesced and racial violence erupted on a massive scale throughout the country.

Less than one month after the Chicago riot, Stanley B. Norvell, a Negro war veteran residing in Chicago wrote a letter to Victor F. Lawson, editor and publisher of the Chicago Daily News. This letter is moving evidence that in 1919 a Negro with new needs and goals had emerged in the United States. As an upshot of the race's abundant contributions to the Allied victory--as soldiers, industrial workers, and purchasers of Liberty Bonds--Negroes were imbued both with pride in their race and a fierce determination to possess the rights pledged to all Americans by the Constitution. They felt they had earned the enjoyment of these guarantees. The "New Negro" was resolved also to defend militantly his life, liberty, and property against the aggressions of the white man. Norvell's letter mirrors what numerous Negroes were thinking in 1919, and it provides valuable insights into that turbulent summer of racial violence.

***

My dear Mr. Lawson:

As the cause of the Negro in America is one that is nearer and dearer to my heart than any other, it has become an obsession with me, and for that reason I am taking the liberty of inflicting upon you this unsolicited treatise on the subject. It is my fond hope that these unlettered lines--which are intended to throw a little light upon the controversy from the dark side--may be of some little service to you and your worthy commission, as data....

I take it that the object of this commission is to obtain by investigation and by conference the cause or causes of the friction between the two races that started the molecules of race hatred into such violent motion as to cause the heterogenous mixture to boil over in the recent riots.

Few white men know the cause, for the simple reason that few white men know the Negro as an entity. On the other hand, I daresay that almost any Negro that you might meet on the street could tell you the cause, if he would, for it is doubtful--aye, very doubtful--if he would tell you, because Negroes have become highly suspicious of white men, even such white men as they deem their friends ordinarily. The Negro has always been and is now largely a menial dependent upon the white man's generosity and charity for his livelihood, and for this reason he has become an expert cajoler of the white man and a veritable artist at appearing to be that which he is not. To resort to the vernacular "conning" the white man has become his profession, his stock in trade. Take for example the Negro in Chicago--and Chicago is fairly representative--sixty per cent of the male Negro population is engaged in menial and servile occupations such as hotel waiters, dining car waiters, sleeping car porters, barbershop porters, billiard room attendants, etc., where "tips" form the greater part of their renumeration. Thirty per cent are laborers and artisans, skilled and unskilled, governmental and municipal employees; while the remaining ten per cent are business and professional men.

Unfortunately it is always by the larger class--the menial, servitor and flunkey class--that the race is judged. Even at that, we would not object to being judged by this class of our race, if those who did the judging had a thorough knowledge of the individuals who make up this class. Unfortunately they have not this knowledge nor can they get it except through the instrumentality of just such a commission as that to which you gentlemen have been assigned. The white man of America knows just about as much about the mental and moral calibre, the home life and social activities of this class of colored citizens as he does about the same things concerning the inhabitants of the thus far unexplored planet of Mars. If any white man were to be asked what he thought of George the porter on the Golden State Limited; or of James the waiter on the Twentieth Century diner; of Shorty who gives him his billiard cue at Mussey's; or of Snowball who polishes his boots at the Palmer House; or of that old gray-haired relic of by-gone days ... who withholds his hat and menaces him with a long-handled whisk broom until he capitulates with a nickel; I say were you to ask any white man concerning these dusky servitors he would tell you that he was either honest or dishonest, that he was either industrious or lazy, that he was smart or stupid as the case might be. He will discuss him in a general superficial sort of way and if you press him further you will be surprised to know that in spite of his years of acquaintance with the subject he knows absolutely nothing about intellect, ability ambition(,) the home life and environment of one with whom he has come into daily contact for years. He is just a "nigger" and he takes him for granted, as a matter of course....

In hotels, barber shops and billiard rooms where the patrons come in regularly, Sambo has a chance to get well acquainted with them ... He knows just what each one's business is and where it is located. He knows just where each one lives and in what circumstances.... He knows just how much each one is going to give him. There are some that never give him anything but still he likes them immensely because they treat him with kindness and consideration. There are some who tip him most liberally whom he despises because they are always making some aspersion about his race or because they always want him to clown and demean himself in order to get their money ... He knows that if he says, "Yassay, Boss," and grins that you will vote him a "good nigger" and give him something; but were he to say, "Very good, Sir," you would not only give him anything but would probably take a dislike to him and consider him supercillious ...

I can walk down the "Boul Mich" and be surveyed by the most critical of Sherlock Holmes's and I will wager that none of them can accurately deduce what I am or what I represent. They cannot tell whether I am well off or hard up; whether I am educated or illiterate; whether I am a northerner or a southerner; whether I am a native born Negro or a foreigner; whether I live among beautiful surroundings or in the squalor of the "black belt." I defy the shrewdest of your pseudo detectives to know whether I am a reputable citizen or whether I am a newly arrived crook. They cannot tell by looking at me what my income is.... The point is that I am only an ordinary, average Negro and that the white man is constantly making the mistake of discounting us too cheaply. He should wake up to the fact that brain is not peculiar to any race or nationality but is merely a matter of development.

This in a measure explains how the American white man knows less about the American Negro than the latter does about the former ....

The further causes of the apparent increased friction between the two races, in my opinion is due to the gradual, and inevitable evolution--metamorphosis, if you please--of the Negro. The Negro has also progressed in knowledge by his study of the white man, while the while [sic] man blinded by either his prejudice or by his indifference has failed to study the Negro judiciously, and as a consequence, he knows no more about him than he did fifty years ago and still continues to judge him and to formulate opinions about him by his erstwhile standards. Today we have with us a new Negro. A brand new Negro, if you please. What opportunities have you better class white people for getting into and observing the homes of the better class of colored people (?) Yet the duties of the colored man in his menial capacities gives him an insight of your home life. As a suggestion, if I may be permitted to make one, I suggest that the white members of this commission make it their business to try to obtain an opportunity through some of the colored members of the commission to visit the homes of some of our better class people. You will find that "Uncle Tom" that charming old figure of literature contemporary with the war of rebellion is quite dead now and that his prototypes are almost as extinct as is the great auk, the dodo bird, old Dobbin and the chaise, and the man who refused to shave until William Jennings Bryan was elected. You will have committed an unpardonable faux pas if you should happen to call any eminently respectable old colored lady "mammy" or "auntie," and yet there still remain many misguided and well-intentioned folks of the white race who still persist in so doing. This was all brought about by education.... When a young colored boy of Chicago goes through the eight grades of grammar school and wins the cherished Victor F. Lawson diploma; then through a four year high school course and wins a university scholarship; and then goes to college and wins a degree.... and is highly popular and well received among his fellow classmates, it is a very difficult thing for him to get it into his head that he is inferior to anybody that has no more knowledge, ability nor money than himself. Regardless of what the eminent sociologists may say, and the fiery and usually groundless claims of the southern negrophile (negrophobe) to the contrary notwithstanding, there is no amount of logic, nor philosophy, nor ethnology, nor anthropology, nor sociology that can convince him to his own satisfaction that he is not the possessor of all the lesser and major attributes that go to make up a good citizen by all of the standards which our republican conventions hold near and dear.

Take the late war for example, and consider the effect that it has had upon the Negro, by and large. I believe that the mental attitude of the Negro that went to war is comparable in a certain degree to the mental attitude of most of the Negroes throughout the country; so far as the awakenings are concerned. The Negro of this country has gone through the same evolution that the white man has, in his own way; and in a large percentage of the total, that way is not far removed from the way the white man's mind thought out the matter or is thinking it out, especially the soldier mind. The Negro of our country ... the Negro of the mass I mean, is comparable in his awakening and in his manner of thought after that awakening, to these white boys who went to war. The white soldiers --being young--had but little thought of anything but their immediate concerns, and the Negro, until lately, had but little thought of anything but his immediate concerns--being segregated. How I loathe that word.

Since the war the Negro has been jolted into thinking by circumstances.... (Negroes) have learned that there were treaties and boundaries and Leagues of Nations and mandatories, and Balkan states, and a dismembered Poland, a ravished Belgium, a stricken France, a soviet Russia and a republic in Ireland and so on, and they have ... for the first time in their lives taken a peep of their own volition and purely because they wanted to know, into the workings of governmental things of those other countries, and have tried to reason out the possible real cause of all of this bloodshed and woe and misery along such international, allied and foreign government and other vague lines.

Now then, this has logically--and we are nebulously logical, despite what the southern white says about us--brought us round to a sort of realization of how our government was made and is conducted. I venture to claim that any average Negro of some education, if closely questioned, and the questions were put to him in simple understandable form, will tell you that he finally has come to know that he counts as a part of his government, that he is a unit in it. It took a world war to get that idea into general Negro acceptance, but it is there now. Centuries of the dictum, which heretofore not many of us disputed, that, "This was a white man's country and that we were destined to always be hewers of wood and carriers of water," was set aside by circumstances and conditions and reactions and reflexes and direct contacts of this war. Negroes were pulled out of their ordinary pursuits all over the country and called upon to do things that they had to do because there was nobody at hand to do them, and those circumstances induced an awakening that must inevitably continue for all time.

The five hundred thousand Negroes who were sent overseas to serve their country were brought into contacts that widened both their perceptions and their perspectives, broadened them, gave them new angles on life, on government, and on what both mean. They are now new men and world men, if you please....

What the Negro wants and what the Negro will not be satisfied with until he gets is that treatment and that recognition that accords him not one jot or tittle less than that which any other citizen of the United States is satisfied with. He has become tired of equal rights. He wants the same rights. He is tired of equal accommodations. He wants (the) same accommodations. He is tired of equal opportunity. He wants the same opportunity. He must and will have industrial, commercial, civil and political equality. America has already given him these inalienable rights, but she has not always seen to it that he has received them. America must see that the Negro is not deprived of any right that she has given him otherwise the gift is bare, and in view of her recent international exploits she will stand in grave danger of losing her national integrity in the eyes of Europe and she will be forced to admit to her European adversaries that her constitution is but a scrap of paper.

Social equality--that ancient skeleton in the closet of the southern negrophile (negrophobe), whose bones are always brought out and rattled ominously whenever the Negro question is discussed--is in no way a factor in the solution of the problem, but is a condition that will quite naturally exist when the problem is eventually solved--just a little prior to the millenium. Leastwise considering the unsettled condition of the world at large, the white man of this country has a great deal more to be sensibly alarmed about than the coming of social equality. Looking into the future I can see more ominous clouds on the horizon of this country's destiny than the coming of social equality.

When the Negro ponders the situation--and now he is beginning to seriously do that--it is with a feeling of poignant resentment that he sees his alleged inferiority constantly and blatantly advertised at every hand, by the press, the pulpit, the stage and by the glaring and hideous sign-boards of segregation. Try to imagine, if you can, the feelings of a Negro army officer, who clothed in the full panoply of his profession and wearing the decorations for valor of three governments is forced to the indignity of a jim-crow car and who is refused a seat in a theatre and a bed in a hotel. Think of the feelings of a colored officer, who after having been graduated from West Point and having worked up step by step to the rank of colonel to be retired on account of blood pressure--and other pressure--in order that he might not automatically succeed to the rank of general officer. Try to imagine the smouldering hatred within the breast of an overseas veteran who is set upon and mercilessly beaten by a gang of young hoodlums simply because he is colored. Think of the feelings in the hearts of boys and girls of my race who are clean, intelligent and industrious who apply for positions only to meet with the polite reply that, "We don't hire niggers," Think how it must feel to pass at the top of the list and get notice of appointment to some nice civil service position that is paid for out of the taxes of the commonwealth, and upon reporting to assume the duties thereof, to be told that there has been a mistake made in the appointment.

When you think of these things, and consider them seriously it is easy to see the underlying, contributory causes of the friction that led up to the recent racial troubles. It is a well known fact that civilization is but a veneer which lightly covers the surface of mankind; that if slightly scratched, with the right kind of tool, a man will turn into a bloodthirsty savage in the twinkling of an eye. The overt act that is alleged to have started the recent conflagration, would not have in itself been sufficient to have ignited and exploded such vials of wrath had not the structure of society been long soaked in the inflammable gasolene of smouldering resentment.

As soon as the white man is willing to inform himself about the true status of the Negro as he finds him today, and is willing to take off the goggles of race prejudice and to study the Negro with the naked eye of fairness, and to treat him with justice and equity, he will come to the conclusion that the Negro has "arrived" and then voila, you have the solution to the problem.

We ask not charity but justice. We no longer want perquisites but wages, salary and commissions. Much has been said anent the white man's burden. We admit to having been a burden. But in the natural order of things the infant soon ceases to be a burden and eventually grows up to be a crutch for the arm that once carried him. We feel that now we are able to take our first, feeble diffident steps, and we implore the white man to set his burden down and let us try to walk. Put us in your counting rooms, your factories and in your banks. The young people who went to school with us and who learned the three R's from the same black-board as ourselves will surely not object to working with us after we have graduated. If they do, it will only be because they are not yet accustomed to the new conditions. That is nothing. People soon become accustomed to new things and things that seem at first preposterous soon become commonplace. We have surely proven by years of unrequited toil and by constant and unfaltering loyalty and fealty that we are worthy of the justice that we ask. For God's sake give it to us!

Stanley B. Norvell
William M. Tuttle, Jr.

Arlington, Va.

Below, Dr. Haynes attempts to explain the sociological factors that generate race riots, namely, "the lack of friendly contact between the races in the local community, the sensational newspaper publicity and the changes in the feelings and thoughts of Negroes are paramount factors in race riots. They relate themselves," he writes, "to the fourth and last factor--our country's new relation to oppressed and liberated peoples.... For the sake of her world leadership, as well as for the liberty of her own citizens, our country must insure opportunity, justice and full protection of the law to every citizen, black or white. Action is imperative." Although Dr. Haynes does not mention explicitly the Chicago riot of July 27th, his article, dated August 9, 1919, is most timely for its sociological analysis.

Document 13*

George E. Haynes, "Race Riots in Relation to Democracy," The Survey, August 9, 1919, pp. 697-699.

The conditions in the local community, the change in the mind of the Negro, and America's new relation to oppressed and liberated peoples give the recent race riots a serious importance to our democracy. Our democracy must be safe at home, or we shall be humiliated in our efforts for democracy abroad. We have overthrown the despotism of the few. Let us beware lest we be overcome by the tyranny of the many.

Race riots grow out of complex conditions which may be [ ]

*Reprinted by permission.

and remedied. Sensational newspaper publicity about matters of Negroes, unpunished lawless acts of white persons against Negroes, misunderstandings, fears and suspicions of the two races that live almost in two separate worlds are all [ ] of racial antagonism and conflict. Careful examination of these factors is of imperative importance to every thoughtful American.

Briefly considering the conditions in the local community, one finds the growing town and city Negro populations segregated into districts and neighborhoods. In such districts, Negroes are neglected in public schools, public sanitation and health, fire and police protection and other public facilities. Often the red light element of the white world is crowded among or near them. Many Negroes feel that by methods of competition, fair or unfair, they have been kept out of the most desirable jobs and economic advantages. They believe that much of the antipathy towards them has its origin here.

New York has its segregated Harlem and Columbus Hill districts, Washington has its northwest and southwest areas (the scene of many of the recent race riots), Chicago has its State Street, Atlanta its Auburn Avenue and its West End. When the United States Supreme Court declared segregation ordinances void, real estate understandings and gentlemen's agreements remained valid. These restrictions on property rights of Negroes are not always confined to residential districts but often to business properties as well.

The Lack of Contact

Besides the separation into neighborhoods, an increasing number of Negroes have little or no occasion for business or professional dealings with white people. With the additional separation in churches, schools, railways, street-cars and other public places, even hospitals and cemeteries, there is developing a racial cleavage from the cradle to the grave. This cleavage leaves little or no personal contact for the growth of mutual understanding and mutual good-will. Without sufficient contacts for knowledge to the contrary, popular opinion of white people classifies the law-abiding, thrifty, industrious and intelligent Negroes indiscriminately with the lawless and the undesirable. The entire race is popularly charged with the criminal acts of the individual Negro. Thus misunderstanding, fears, suspicions, prejudices are lighted. They smolder. A crime or a street fight occurs, and the slumbering racial feelings on both sides burst into flames.

This lack of contact has increased with the years. Older residents of Washington and Chicago tell you of the growing racial antagonism with the growth of separation. Only a few weeks before the riots in both cities, some leading people of Washington were discussing the fact that in former years the white and colored representatives of various philanthropic and community agencies were accustomed to meet more frequently than now for the exchange of views and plans on matters of community interest. The holding of such meetings has grown more difficult and less frequent.

The situation is a good seed-bed for the sensational newspaper publicity about Negro criminals. Several Negroes within as many months may commit or be accused of crimes in a community. The newspapers play upon these with flaring headlines and minute descriptions suggestive of racial turpitude and criminal tendencies. Some newspapers have been known to manufacture suggestive news. During the Washington riots, one newspaper went so far as to give the announcement of the time and place for the rendevous of men in the service for a "clean-up that will cause events" of the preceding days "to pale into insignificance."

It is common knowledge that nearly every one of the serious city race riots in the last ten years was preceded by a period of sensational newspaper publicity. Thousands of peaceable, law-abiding, Negro citizens of sterling character in city after city had life, limb and property destroyed or put in jeopardy partly because of the excitement aroused by sensational newspaper publicity. Further, events that have transpired, while they may not be different from those happening among other defenseless classes, serve to make Negroes doubt that the law will be impartially enforced for them. For the last four months the repeated bombing of Negro homes with little or no apprehension of the perpetrators was reported from Chicago. Negroes claim that sometimes abuses and injuries by officers of the law are passed without much redress. They point out that lynchings have continued for a generation in spite of much protest. One of the leading Negro newspapers said recently: "The failure of authorities to enforce the law has created a feeling of distrust and resentment on the part of American Negroes which should not be a source of surprise to those who reason from cause to effect. This state of mind is not confined to Washington." The discussion and anxiety about these things are ever present and are changing the Negro's attitude. He says his safety demands that he protect himself and his home.

Let us look, then, at the change in the condition and mind of the Negro. The war has wrought many changes in his condition. About half a million able-bodied wage-earners moved from the South to the North. The entire body of wage-earners who make up nearly three-fourths of the total Negro population, because of war labor demands moved into better grades of employment, into higher wages, or both. About 400,000 of the picked men of the race were drafted into the army, had its discipline, shared in its sacrifices for liberty and in its glories. (In the army, Negroes testify, however, that they tasted race prejudice, both at home and abroad.) They felt the thrill of giving and serving to win the war. From the field-hands of Georgia and Mississippi to the business and professional men and women of Washington, Chicago, Philadelphia and New York, they gave and served by labor, by saving food, by buying bonds and thrift stamps, by contributions to the Red Cross and to other causes to win the war and to make the world safe for democracy.

The changes in occupations and wages brought more of the material satisfactions of life and spurred the desire for higher standards of living. The migration to the North showed both those who went and those who did not go that liberty allowed a man to move more freely from place to place. It taught them that their change of residence need not be attended with loss of the opportunity to make a living or with danger of suffering from the climate or from strangeness in a strange land. The writer has just read scores of letters of migrants published in the Journal of Negro History. The outstanding desire expressed in those letters is to know whether or not a living may be secured in the new home and the dangers of the new climate escaped.

This new understanding of the meaning of liberty has been driven deep into the consciousness of the masses of Negroes. The thinking and feeling of the Negroes themselves, therefore, when in contact with the white community, has assumed a new aspect. The new experiences in the migration, in the war services and in the new economic opportunities have developed a new Negro. It is not to be denied that in shuffling off the coil of servility, the Negro will pass through a transition period of awkwardness to achieve civility. This calls for sympathetic understanding and guidance, not scolding and censure; for all kinds of education; for poised, respected Negro leadership; for community contacts and cooperation; for opportunities, not restrictions. Withal, there is need of reckoning with the opinions of this new Negro, who is doing some thinking and speaking for himself.

A New Leadership

Negro opinion and activity for adjustment of their relationship to white people may be classified into three groups. The first may be described as the revolutionary and radical Socialist group now in the first stages of development. There is considerable testimony that this is being fostered by revolutionary white Socialists and out-and-out Bolsheviks. The second group is made up of those who say, "Fight! fight! fight!" for the full-fledged rights and privileges of American citizenship. The third group has stood for citizenship rights and opportunities no less than the second group. This third group differs from the second, however, in the methods and policies to which it adheres as the means of securing its ends. It believes in conciliatory, cooperative agreements, in awaiting times and seasons, in fitting actions to circumstances to achieve the ends desired.

But the trend of events in the past four or five years has been favorable to the fighting methods and the militant policy. The rank and file of the Negroes have been hearing of wars and rumors of wars. They have seen the rights and liberties of oppressed peoples vindicated by the arbitrament of war. Many Negroes, therefore, seem to be gradually leaning toward the aggressive, militant policies and methods of adjustment. A growing class or race consciousness has made them more mindful of their own situation. They are less patient and less conciliatory.

The lack of friendly contact between the races in the local

community, the sensational newspaper publicity and the changes in the feelings and thoughts of Negroes are paramount factors in race riots. They relate themselves to the fourth and last factor--our country's new relation to oppressed and liberated peoples. The mid-European peoples recently liberated from the oppressor's yoke are now starting with faltering feet upon the path of democracy. They are looking to us for examples of group adjustment no less than for cash and cargoes. We have made our humanitarian efforts that nations and peoples, great and small, may have the same attitude toward each other that we wish our own people to have among themselves.

As one of the great world powers, we are already face to face with the problem of dealing with the darker peoples of Asia, Africa, Central and South America. The treatment of the darker peoples within our borders is our best and most effective answer to the questions of the darker peoples that lie beyond our borders. An Abyssinian high commission is on a visit to this country and has seen the President. In an interview with the members of the commission, the writer was especially impressed with their deep concern and many inquiries about the treatment accorded to Negroes in America. Thousands of aliens are now leaving this country and scattering to their native lands in all parts of Europe. A lover of his country may well be anxious about the opinion these people may spread concerning the safety of American democracy. For the sake of her world leadership, as well as for the liberty of her own citizens, our country must insure opportunity, justice and full protection of the law to every citizen, black or white. Action is imperative.

In a concluding paragraph, one may refer to suggestions previously made in articles in the Survey, the Review of Reviews and other journals. Cooperative committees of white and Negro citizens, both under private and under governmental auspices, have demonstrated the utility of such contracts for mutual understanding, good-will and cooperative action. At the present time efforts to secure newspaper publicity of helpful events and the worthy activities of Negroes will change attitudes. It has been done in more than one community. Public-spirited citizens may well counsel with officers of the law about its impartial enforcement. Lynchings and lynchers must feel the strong arm of the law. Democracy in America and democracy abroad wait upon our action.

c. Welfare Problems

In addition to the problems of lynching and race riots, there were a complex set of urban social problems which required the attention of welfare specialists and which were to demand national attention and redress. In the following document, Monroe N. Work summarizes and discusses these problems as they claimed national attention in 1924. It was not until much later, however, that the

Congress agreed that these problems required the instrumentality of the Federal Government to assist in their solution.

Document 14*

Monroe N. Work, "Problems of Negro Urban Welfare," The Southern Workman, January, 1924, pp. 10-16.

In the past thirty years the rural population of the country increased by 11,166,804 persons. During this same period, however, the urban population was increasing by 31,594,253 persons. In other words, for each person added to the rural, three were added to the urban population of the country.

Although the majority of the Negroes in the North live in cities, it is not true that the greater proportion of the Negro city population of the whole country is in the North. On the contrary, there are, in the cities of the South, twice as many Negroes as there are in the cities of the North. The greater number of cities with large Negro population is in the South. Of the 53 cities in the country with Negro populations of 10,000 or more, 17 are in what the Census designates as the North and West, and 36 are in what the Census designates as the South. Continuing this contrast it is found that there are, in the North and West, 10 cities with 20,000 or more Negroes and in the South, 17 such cities. There are in the North 4 cities--New York, Chicago, Philadelphia, and St. Louis--which have in their populations 50,000 or more Negroes. In the South there are 7 cities which have in their populations 50,000 or more Negroes. These are Atlanta, Baltimore, Birmingham, Memphis, New Orleans, Richmond, and Washington. From these facts it would appear that the problems of Negro urban welfare are of as great importance to the South as to the North. The custom, however, is to consider Negro city problems as relating to the North and Negro rural problems as relating to the South.

When the Negro population is considered it is found that in the past thirty years the number in cities has had an increase of over two million. The Negro urban population of the United States is now, in round numbers, about 3,500,000, and even more when towns and villages of less than 2500 inhabitants are included; that is, one-third of the Negroes of the United States are now living in villages, towns and cities.

The larger part of the increase in Negro urban population has been due to migration. In the past five years some 500,000 Negroes have moved from rural districts into the towns and cities. A large proportion, therefore, of the Negro population live under urban conditions. It is this more or less sudden change in the living conditions that contribute to the many problems of Negro urban

*Reprinted by permission.

welfare with which we are now confronted.

It has been well said that all problems of race are after all only human problems. This is especially true with reference to problems of urban welfare which relate to the Negro. These are, in the main, no different from the problems of welfare which relate to any urban people. What are the many problems with which modern welfare work is attempting to deal? They come chiefly under the following heads: family life, housing, health, sanitation, religious life, employment, poverty, and crime. To these might also be added the problem of recreation, and the even more general problem of education. In the purely rural community unaffected by city life, the problems just enumerated are either much less acute or unknown.

Let us take the matter of the family. In a country district the tendency is for the family to be much more of a unit than it is in a city. All the members of the Negro family in the country, especially on a plantation, are generally engaged in the same sort of occupation. Planters endeavor to have tenant families with a large number of children, in order that the advantage of the labor all the family may be used. I am not minimizing the disadvantages that come to a rural family, but simply pointing out some of the forces which tend to keep it together.

When the rural family migrates to the city new forces begin to operate. The tendency is for the various members of the family to engage in different kinds of occupations. Each is probably working for a different employer. This tends toward the disintegration of the family. There are other disintegrating forces which might also be mentioned. I wish to speak of one more, and that is divorce.

In the recent years there has been a considerable increase in the number of divorces among Negroes. In 1890 the number among Negroes in the Southern States was reported by the Census to have been 13,252. In 1910, twenty years later, the number was reported as being 44,505, an increase of over 230 per cent. It is very seldom that we hear of divorce cases among either whites or blacks in the rural districts. It may in general be said that the problem of divorce is largely a city one.

The housing problem is another of the problems which particularly concerns the family upon which its stability depends. There is, for rural Negroes, a housing problem. It consists mainly in the need for better conditions of dwellings, with larger rooms and more reference to comfort and architectural beauty. In the country it is generally true that there is no house rent, as such. In the city, house rent must be paid. It is noteworthy that of those who suffer from rent profiteering, Negroes suffer most. It is they who are usually compelled to pay the highest rents and forced to dwell in the worst habitations.

Negroes in cities have two kinds of housing problems. One of these relate to a properly constructed house, provided with modern sanitary conveniences. A very large part of the housing problem in Southern cities is of this nature. It is well to call attention just here to the fact that a large part of the Negro urban population in the South is living in cities under what are, to a large extent, country conditions; that is, although living in towns, they are not provided with the conveniences of cities, particularly water, light, and general sanitation. It is usually the case in every Southern city that on the outskirts of the town, just beyond the zones for water, light and other city conveniences, there is a fringe of Negro tenant houses built often on the gun-barrel plan, without any reference whatever to the laws of health or sanitation.

The other kind of housing problem that has to do with the dwellings of city Negroes, relates to those dwellings which are within sanitary areas. These, very often in Southern cities, and almost generally in all Northern cities, are comfortably constructed and have light, water and other sanitary conveniences. The rent, however, is generally so high that it is necessary to take in boarders to pay it. The housing problem among Negroes is further aggravated by the restricted areas in which, to a large extent, they are compelled to live.

Another problem very closely connected with family life is that of health. A normal family life is one of the main factors upon which health depends. Any city people who have a normal family life and are able to live under good sanitary conditions will generally enjoy good health. There are several reasons why the mortality rate of the Negro is high. The most important of these in my opinion, are the result of the conditions under which Negroes are compelled to live. It is generally true that people in the country have better health and a lower mortality rate than people living in cities.

Let us note the crime problem. It also is more or less the result of urban conditions. It is very generally true that the crime rate is higher in cities than in the country. This is particularly true with reference to Negroes. There are a number of factors which tend to increase their crime rate.

Let me draw here a distinction between crime rate and actual criminality. The crime rate is usually determined, in police statistics, by the number of arrests; in jail statistics, by the number of persons who have been placed in jail. It is true, however, in the case of police statistics, that a great many of the persons arrested are innocent of any crime and are eventually turned loose. This is also true of many persons up and the crime rate is determined, all of these persons are reckoned in the rate, and by implication are returned as criminals.

There is a common practice with reference to crime in the rural districts to which I wish to call attention. There it very often happens that if a Negro commits a crime which is not against a white person, he will most likely be protected, especially if he is on a large plantation. A great many of the abuses which have grown up in rural districts with reference to peonage have come about as a result of this practice of protection in the rural districts and of not inflicting direct punishment for crime. The plantation system is more or less a patriarchal form of government; that is to say, the owner of the plantation, both in slavery and later, looked after and assumed responsibility for all of the individuals on the plantation. This fact must be taken into account in order to understand more fully the problem of crime.

When the Negro comes into the city there is no one to assume responsibility for him. He must look out for himself. If he is arrested, it very often happens that he gets word to the owner of the plantation from which he came, and the owner comes into the city, pays his fine, takes him back, and places him too often in a state of peonage. Account should also be taken of the fact that in the city the migrant enjoys, in a certain way, freedom which he did not have in the country, and as a result commits acts which in the country would not be taken into account, but for which in the city he is arrested and committed to prison. The conditions under which Negroes are compelled to live in the cities also tend to increase crime. For this reason it is important that welfare work should endeavor to reduce the crime rate by improving the general living conditions of the people.

Let us next consider the problem of poverty. In general this is unknown among Negroes in the rural districts of the South. In the country there is usually someone to look after those who are needy or unfortunate in other ways. There is also something that every individual can do for which he can at least get food and a place to stay. When this individual, however, comes into the city, the situation is very different. The food that is eaten must be bought by some one, the clothes and shelter must be paid for. The tendency of city life is toward individualism; that is, toward the breaking down of the family life so that each individual is compelled to look out for himself. If he becomes incapacitated for work, if he is unable to find employment, or for other reasons is unable to provide the necessities of life, he becomes an object of charity. The general result is that we find the tendency is for poverty to increase among urban Negroes. I understand that there are now a great many more cases of charity work among Negroes than there were twenty years ago.

The religious problem is another very important factor which one has to consider in order to get the deeper significance of the change from rural to urban life. The country church is generally the center of life for the community. In the rural districts the Negro church has practically no competition. The whole social life centers in it. In the city the church has to compete with a great many other attractions. Important among these are the moving picture shows, the theaters, the dance halls, and the pool and billiard rooms. The result is that the church has less control over the city Negro than over the rural Negro, or perhaps it would be more correct to say that the social life of the urban Negro centers much less in the church than the social life of the rural Negro. This is a serious problem that the urban Negro church has to meet.

Negro churches could learn a lesson from the work of the Catholic church among immigrant populations. A Catholic church, located in a district of foreigners, in a great city of the North, is usually very different in its activities from the Catholic church located in a district where the population is more or less of native stock. The difference is that the church located in a district where the population is more or less native, does not attempt to become the center of social life for all the activities of the people. In contrast, in some of the districts composed entirely of foreigners, the Catholic church does attempt to become the center of all community activities and to minister to all the needs of the people.

One of the most important problems of urban welfare is that of employment. This is especially true with reference to the effect upon the general social life of the large population which has recently come from rural districts into urban centers. Work on a plantation does not train an individual for city life or city work. There is a difference in the length of hours and the rate of speed at which one works. There is also a difference in the wages paid and in requirements as to punctuality; that is, getting to work at a particular time and remaining on the job for a specified length of time. Probably the greatest difference, however, between employment in the city and employment in the country is that, in general, in the country, the job hunts the man, whereas in the city the man has to go out and hunt the job. Upon the thousands of migrants who have recently come into city conditions, the effect of having to hunt jobs instead of having jobs hunt them is profound. What this means is that when in the country they generally were not placed upon their own resources. In the city, on the other hand, they are to a large extent forced to depend upon their own initiative.

Another city problem is that of recreation. This is bound up with religious and family life, in fact, with the whole social life of the urban group. In the country the question of recreation does not present so serious a problem as it does in the city, for the reason that there is not as large a number of people in a given area who have some leisure time. In the city there is always the question of what to do with leisure time. In the country there is, in general, not the question of what to do with leisure time, for usually after work comes sleep, and after sleep comes work. In the city, however, with shorter working hours, the people have leisure time on their hands. There is also the fact that a great number of people during their leisure time are coming into contact with each other.

The question of the proper use of one's leisure time on Sunday and holidays is also important. The problem of recreation does not consist so much in the lack of opportunity for recreation as in the matter of providing adequate recreation of a wholesome sort. Negroes are placed under a greater handicap with reference to wholesome recreation than are the whites in Southern cities. It is very generally true that Negroes have no part in the recreational facilities provided at public expense; they are shut out as a rule from public parks and playgrounds, and also from the public libraries. Because of these facts the question of recreation from a welfare standpoint becomes a most important one; it needs the most serious attention and effort to be adequately handled.

In all of the problems of welfare which I have discussed, there centers the general problem of education. The individual coming from the country into the city has to receive some education in the ways of city life. This education may be bad and lead to depravity and crime. On the other hand, it may be good and assist the individual to a larger, fuller, and more useful life. It is a part of the work of welfare agencies to provide means so that the individual coming from the country into the city may receive education of a good rather than of a bad sort.

Another phase of education in cities has to do with the providing of public-school facilities. Practically every city in the land is faced with this problem. In the cities, however, which have separate schools for the races, it is especially acute with respect to Negroes. There are a number of funds and foundations which help to improve school conditions for Negroes, such as the Slater Fund, the Jeanes Fund, the Rosenwald Building Fund, and the General Education Board. The work of these boards, however, in improving public schools is confined almost entirely to the improvement of schools in purely country districts. The problem of school improvement for Negroes in cities and towns is not receiving the attention that it should. No program of welfare work among Negroes should omit the very important problem of the improvement of educational facilities.

This discussion, I trust, will lead to an appreciation of the tremendous cost of life, health, and of morals which the movement from rural to urban centers is entailing. Over against these losses we are of course able to place a great many gains. There is a distinct advantage in having a large number of Negroes living in urban centers. It is here that group leadership is developed. It will probably be true that for a great many years to come the bulk of Negroes will continue to live in rural districts. It is a distinct advantage, nevertheless, to have a large part of them living in cities. It enables Negroes to diversify their occupations, and to have all of the activities--industrial, personal, professional and trading--that tend to make a normal and well-rounded group.

The real question, after all, as I have tried to indicate, is not so much the cost of the change from rural to urban life as it is how this cost can be reduced. The real function of the increasing number of welfare workers among urban Negroes, it appears, is to assist in helping reduce this cost by indicating the ways in which the problems of employment, family life, crime, poverty, health, sanitation, recreation and education can be handled so that the general welfare of the Negroes will be promoted in the best way.

d. Health Problems

The problem of the survival of the Negro was early associated with the problem of his health. Many white observers prophesied a decline in the population of the Negro due to the deteriorating condition of his health. Eugene Kinckle Jones, in his article read to the National Conference of Social Work in 1923, relates the problems of Negro health to the overall problems of learning to live in an urban environment. He also relates some of the history of black efforts to improve health, the delivery of health services, and the conditions which make for improved health.

T. J. Woofter, discussing the health problem in relation to the rural scene, points out the fact that the health problems of both blacks and whites are interrelated and that the improvement in the health conditions of the one is beneficial, also, for the health conditions of the other.

Document 15a*

Eugene Kinckle Jones, "The Negro's Struggle for Health," Proceedings of the National Conference of Social Work, 50th Annual Session, Washington, D. C., May 16-23, 1923. pp. 68-72.

Strange as it may seem, this subject partakes very much of the idea of the Negro's struggle to regain health. Research into the condition of the Negro's health in Africa and in slavery presents a most interesting picture. Travelers in Africa have noted, prior to the advent of the white man in numbers, the almost total absence of certain diseases to which the Negro in America is addicted in larger proportion than the whites. This is especially true of tuberculosis and the venereal diseases which directly or indirectly have taken such a great toll of Negro lives.

In the slave regime in America it was to the advantage of the masters to keep their slaves in good health. Regular inspection of the slaves, clean quarters, good, wholesome food, enforced regulation of habits, and the like were on the best plantations and in city homes insisted upon in order that the slaves might be in the best of physical condition and thus be able to render the largest possible amount of service. At the close of the Civil War, therefore, we find a group of Negroes living principally in the South, rural in the main, possessed of relatively good health, and prepared with a good physical background to begin a life of freedom and to

*Reprinted by permission of the National Conference on Social Welfare.

take up the intricate and difficult problems of the new civilization.

For a period of nearly sixty years, the Negroes though free in name have struggled against great odds. Negroes have been the last group to get the benefit of better health movements, yet in analyzing the Negro's health condition, one must take into account the Negro's remarkable powers of orientation, whether of the flesh or of the spirit. Self-preservation as the first law of nature asserts itself in most adjustments which this race makes. This law is seen in the struggle of the Negro group in cities to acquire better living quarters. In many large cities persons have misunderstood the motive behind the effort of members of this race to purchase or rent houses formerly occupied by whites. They have been accused of seeking "social equality" and "association with the whites" when it has been only some unconscious impulse which has prompted the Negroes, in their endeavor to survive or prolong life, to seek living quarters in that section of the city where garbage and refuse are regularly collected, where sanitary inspection is assured, where streets are paved and cleaned, where proper drainage is possible, and where the physical condition of the property is kept up to standard.

It would be natural to suppose that Negroes, as descendants of a tropical race, would be constituted, by nature, especially to withstand the ravages of the diseases which are peculiar to temperate zone races. Just as north Europeans have with difficulty acclimated themselves to preserve good health in torrid-zone regions, so would it be safe to assume that Negroes would find difficulty in meeting the health requirements of a temperate zone climate. Some writers have gone so far as to say that the laws of natural selection have been operative, and the weaker of the Negro group have been the first to feel the effects of the attacks of those diseases which have become less destructive to white men, not only through the increased knowledge of methods to combat these diseases, but through the operation of the law of natural selection. That the disproportion death rate of Negroes, however, has been due to environmental forces rather than constitutional weakness, is evident, as certainly it would not be possible for a race either to deteriorate or make a complete change for the better within a period of ten years. Even if the law of natural selection were in operation, one could not observe constitutional changes in a whole group within a period of more generations than are recorded within the life span of our longest lived individual.

There are two sets of facts resulting from widely separated sources which when put together seem to have tremendous significance. Dr. Alfred Hess of New York City, who has devoted several years to the study of rickets and has conducted a number of successful experiments in the control of this disease, estimates that 90 per cent of the Negro children of New York suffer from rickets in infancy. This disease seems to have an unusual incidence among colored children and is the result of poorly controlled environment; specifically, inadequate exposure to sunlight and insufficient nourishment, both characteristic deficiencies of city life. The "bowed legs" and "knocked knees" which are the result of retarded development of the bone tissue of the body, while not in themselves conspicuous in adult life, have a most serious effect upon the bone tissue in more vital parts of the body. Narrow chests and lower muscle tone are some of the most serious aftermaths of rickets. These in turn result in diminished breathing capacity and render those children affected susceptible to respiratory diseases, especially bronchitis, pneumonia and tuberculosis. On the other hand, the report of the surgeon general's office on army recruits shows that although Negroes registered superior physical proportions in practically all the measurements, they had a narrower chest circumference and showed a greater susceptibility to respiratory diseases. It is perhaps not too far fetched to suggest a possible connection between rickets in infancy and susceptibility to respiratory diseases in adult life.

The struggle of the Negro for health has indeed been an effort to learn "how to live in the city." The death rate of Negroes in rural sections is about the same as that of the neighboring whites in the same section. As has been indicated, the Negro has in the past fared poorly when he has settled in cities. The Metropolitan Life Insurance Company has, however, increased its Negro policyholders to more than 1,800,000 or about one-sixth of all the Negroes living in the United States. Its experience with these Negro policyholders shows that there has been a reduction of 22 per cent in their death rate during the eleven years between 1911 and 1922. This has been due, principally, to a reduction in the deaths of children under fifteen years of age, at which age period the proportion of Negro deaths is highest in comparison with whites, and also to the reduction of the proportion of deaths from pulmonary diseases. The Negro death rate in 1920 for the registration area was 18.4 per thousand. The white death rate for the whole country was 17.1 per thousand. Thus it would seem that the Negro is less than twenty years behind the white people of America in his struggle for a longer life.

The continuous migration of Negroes to the North since the Civil War, and the great influx of the past ten years which is still in progress, is beginning to challenge the prediction of many that the Negro could not survive the rigors of northern winters and the competition of northern industrial life. In considering the 12.5 per cent reduction in the mortality rate of colored people living in the registration area of the United States between 1910 and 1920, it is interesting to learn that the death rate among colored people in New York City during that period declined 24.3 per cent. Between 1910 and 1921 the death rate among Negroes of Philadelphia declined 41.2 per cent. The rate was 15.7 per thousand in 1921. Between 1910 and 1920 the Negro death rate in Chicago declined 17 per cent.

The army records for the world-war show that Negroes had a larger percentage of men accepted for the army from those drafted than was the case with the whites; also that after they were registered, a larger percentage of Negro registrants were admitted for full military service. If we assume that in some sections of the country injustice was shown the Negro and a larger percentage of Negroes than whites were inducted into service as a result of physical examinations by the draft boards, the fact that a smaller percentage of Negroes were rejected after they had been inducted into service would indicate that the first figures were not far amiss.

I have presented vital statistics from various points and given facts concerning the Negro's general physical condition to show conclusively that the Negro has actually improved in health and is capable of improving further. It is just as interesting to study some of the causes of this change. Most of the improvement that has come about in Negro health has been the result of the Negro population seeking an adjustment to the requirements of their environments that they might survive. The forces that have been created by organized effort to improve the living conditions among whites have been tardy of approach to the Negro population. Of course, some of the work of city health departments and of private organizations has had effect on the Negro group, yet but little definite conscious effort has been made to reach the Negro population with health programs until a decade ago. The past twelve years, however, have seen a remarkable change in this situation.

In the first place, Negroes have, both through their own personal efforts and through the efforts of active placement organizations, found better jobs for Negroes, paying more wages and affording them advancement while at work. This has tended to create a greater degree of satisfaction and hope in the minds of the masses of Negroes, and just as is always the case when wages increase, general mortality and especially infant mortality, among the group has decreased. A smaller percentage of colored mothers in our large cities are now working from day-to-day to supplement the meager family income. In 1915 when an investigation was made of infant mortality among the Negroes in New York City, it was discovered that in one section of the city where the largest percentage of mothers worked and where the families had the smallest incomes and the largest percentage of lodgers and therefore more overcrowding, infant mortality was 314 per thousand, while in the entire city for the colored people it was 202 per thousand, and for the whites, 96 per thousand. A campaign of improvement was organized in which social welfare agencies, the health department, employment placement bureaus, public schools, and in fact all agencies that touch the life of the family were brought into active cooperation to handle effectively this unfortunate situation. The Negro infant mortality rate for the city was reduced in two years' time from 202 per thousand to 173 per thousand, or a reduction of 19 points. In 1919 the infant mortality among Negroes in New York was 151 per thousand births. In 1920 the infant mortality among Negroes in that district in New York City where the rate was 314 per thousand had been reduced to a point lower than the infant mortality of the whites in the same district.

These figures for New York in themselves tell a complete story when one compares them with the Negro infant mortality of

1890 in Richmond, when it was recorded as 529.8 per thousand; in Charleston, when it was recorded as 461.7 per thousand; in New Orleans, when it was rated as 430.2 per thousand. In this connection, I might add that the infant mortality among whites in New Orleans in 1890 was 269.4 per thousand; in Charleston 200.4 per thousand; in Richmond 186.9; far in excess of the infant mortality among Negroes in New York at the present time.

Possibly the most effective educational movement for improving health among Negroes generally has been the National Negro Health Week which was started in 1914 by Booker T. Washington through the National Negro Business League at the suggestion of the Virginia Organization Society, which immediately received the co-operation of the National Urban League and, subsequently, the active aid of the surgeon general's office, state boards of health, and other national organizations. These agencies each year early in the spring conduct a week's campaign of health education followed up in as many places as possible by continuous health propaganda throughout the year.

One of the notable organizations performing this continued health service is the American Social Hygiene Association, which has a department which has given especial attention to sex education among Negroes. In connection with this reference to the effort to reduce venereal disease, it is proper to mention again the absence of venereal diseases among Negroes on their advent to this country. Possibly one of the most unfortunate incidents in connection with the Negro's contact with the whites was the transmission, from the whites, of the curse of venereal diseases to the Negroes. The Young Men's Christian Association and the Young Women's Christian Association have also conducted helpful health programs. At the formation of the Community Service, Incorporated, Negroes were considered, and now there are more than 400 committees throughout the country engaged in providing leisure-time activities for the colored population. This of course has had and is still having a very excellent effect on the health conditions among Negroes, as recreation which affords fresh air and wholesome exercise is recognized as an aid to health. Through these educational campaigns, both of a health and of an economic nature, Negroes have been induced to save their money, to purchase their own homes, and to invest in housing projects. One out of every four Negro families in the United States today owns its own home. This of course tends to regulate the home life of the family with good results in improving health.

In the United States there are now among the Negroes 6,000 physicians, 3,000 trained nurses, 150 hospitals and sanatoriums; 100 national or state sick-benefit societies, with many hundreds of locals, and 500 social-service workers engaged in active service among the colored people. Fifteen years ago there were probably no trained colored social workers. There is a Negro physician now for every 1,700 of Negro population. Twenty-five years ago, not only were there few colored physicians, but it was claimed that Negroes had no faith in colored physicians and would not call in even a white physician except in cases which threatened to be fatal.

The Negro's struggle for health might be considered an effort of the race to survive. And yet in the mind of each individual it is simply an effort on his part to live as long as possible and to contribute as much as possible economically as well as spiritually to the world.

With the educational facilities being extended throughout the South, with the migration of Negroes from the South to the North still in progress, bringing more Negroes within the zone of better living conditions, with Negro leaders increasing in their appreciation of the value of public-health education, and with the whole standard of living of Negroes being raised to a higher level, there is sufficient reason to expect a continued improvement in the health of the race. This will result not necessarily in any increase in the percentage of increase decennially in the Negro population, but certainly in a steady increase in the population due, if not to more births, certainly to a much greater percentage reduction in deaths than in births.

Document 15b*

T. J. Woofter, Jr., "Organization of Rural Negroes for Public Health," Proceedings of the National Conference of Social Work, 50th Annual Session, Washington, D. C., May 16-23, 1923, pp. 72-75.

The South will never be wholly healthy or wholly efficient until greater stress is laid on the health of the Negro. As the southern states gain admission into the United States vital statistics registration area the evidence accumulates proving the fact that the health of the whole southeastern and much of the southwestern section of the United States is conditioned by the health of Negroes.

There are nine million Negroes in this section, most of them rural Negroes. In addition, the contacts between the races are such that the health of the white people is dependent upon that of their colored neighbors. The food is cooked, the clothes washed, and many of the children nursed by colored people. A diseased colored community therefore, of necessity, means a diseased white community. But this works both ways, the health of the colored people is just as dependent upon the health of the white people. The dependence is mutual, and for this reason public-health work in the South must be teamwork between the two races. No other procedure will succeed. This phase of southern health problems is self-evident, and should be well understood. It has not, however, been sufficiently emphasized in the past.

As a general rule the same diseases affect the colored and

*Reprinted by permission of the National Conference on Social Welfare.

the white communities, but the colored people have their peculiar health problems which require special emphasis in health work. They suffer more from tuberculosis. In Georgia there were more than twice as many deaths from this scourge among the colored people as among whites. A very high infant mortality rate accounts for the death of between 10 and 15 per cent of the babies before they reach their first birthday. Valuable lives of young mothers are unduly sacrificed in child birth. Chronic diseases, such as heart disease, Brights disease, and cerebral hemorrhage cause relatively very many more deaths among colored people than among white. The general death rate of colored people is 60 per cent higher than that of white people.

But there is a brighter side to the picture. Colored health is improvable and is rapidly improving. Based on their experience and careful record of 1,500,000 policy-holders, Dr. Dublin, of the Metropolitan Life Insurance Company, in a recent very optimistic report, announces a striking improvement in Negro health during the past ten years. That this improvement is not an accidental thing and really reflects a thoroughgoing change in the mortality situation is indicated by the fact that the death rate has declined in every age period of life, and mortality from a diversity of conditions has been lessened. Among the very young children the death rate has dropped more than one-half. Tuberculosis mortality has decreased from 418 per 100,000 to 244 or 42 per cent. Deaths from typhoid and malaria, which especially affect the rural districts, declined 75 per cent. In spite of the influenza epidemics deaths from pneumonia have declined 26 per cent. Improvement along so many and diverse lines is most hopeful and indicates beyond a shadow of a doubt that the colored people have awakened to the importance of the health problem in their affairs. They have actually determined to profit by the opportunity to reduce the unnecessary loss of life from which they have suffered.

If, to this determination and increased activity on the part of colored people, there can be added more organizations whose programs whole-heartedly provide for public-health work in the colored community, much progress can be made in the coming two or three decades.

The difficulties may as well be faced first, however. These are two: the ignorance of the mass of Negroes, especially rural Negroes, and the lack of organizations for spreading the health message.

The traveler in the rural south is impressed with the poverty of the community life in many areas. Where the land is held in large plantations, tenant houses are scattered, villages relatively few, and communication poor. The only rural institutions are the church and the school, and these are scattered, poorly equipped, and hampered by reason of their shifting constituency. Fifty per cent of the tenants live on farms only a year and then move elsewhere. They are pilgrims, merely sojourning a while and having little or no interest in their community or its institutions and leaders. As weak as these institutions are, however, they are the starting point of any program which would reach out and be effective in the country districts. By ignoring them, too many of our county organizations have become units functioning only in the principal town and lacking in constituency and influence in the villages and open country. The colored preachers and the colored teachers are the natural advisers and counselors of their people, even more so than white preachers and teachers are of white people, because their leadership is not divided with other classes as is white leadership.

Very little has been done so far to increase the interest of rural preachers in public health, but some distinct progress is being made with the teachers. The Anna T. Jeanes Foundation, in co-operation with the state and county school authorities, maintains supervising teachers in 250 southern counties. These teachers travel throughout the county aiding all rural teachers with their problems and bringing up the standards of the country school as much as possible. Within the past few years these teachers have been very useful in attacking the school health problems and through the school the health problems of the community. This is a big field, however, and one in which much remains to be done. Entirely too many communities provide carefully for the medical inspection of white school children and ignore the black school children. So far as epidemics are concerned, such a policy defeats itself, for an epidemic among the colored children will rapidly spread to the white schools and undo the work there. Any effort to reach the colored population with health programs must take into account these colored leaders--the preachers, the teachers, and the farm and home demonstration agents.

Next in importance to the colored leader is the southern employer. The living conditions on many tenant farms are such that hygiene and sanitation are strangers. It has been said of some of the houses that the school children can return home and study geology through the floor, botany through the sides, and astronomy through the roof. Our landlords need to be impressed with the actual cash value of a healthy labor supply. It is estimated that 450,000 colored people in the South are seriously ill all the time and 225,000 colored people die annually. If half of the sickness and death from preventable causes were eliminated, the saving in earnings alone would amount to about $150,000,000. Much aid has been given to landlords by governmental agencies interested in better pigs, better mules, and better chickens, but, as yet, comparatively little has been done to help the farmer have better labor. Within the past few years the farm and home demonstration agents have passed from a purely agricultural program to one which lays more stress upon farm health and sanitation. These are the strategic people for reaching the landlord. Only comparatively few colored farm and home demonstration agents are now employed, but those who are on the job are demonstrating their worth in reaching their own people and influencing the sentiment of the employer.

These then are the elements in the community upon which to

build: the present health organizations, the colored leaders, the farm and home demonstration agents, and the employers. The proper person to focus all these efforts effectively is the colored county nurse--not someone to do bedside nursing, but someone who can organize parents and teachers to follow up medical inspection of school children, organize neighbors to do the house- nursing work, organize midwives into instruction groups, and interest the doctors in clinics, especially venereal-disease clinics.

Many counties are now ripe for the services of such a worker if part of the funds could be supplied by an outside source for beginning the experiment. For every one of the 250 supervising teachers now at work there should be a county nurse on the job. Here is a big field of public health work ripe for harvest. There is great need for the interest and financial support of foundations for Negro health operating as the foundations now in the field of stimulating Negro education. These foundations supply aid to states in maintaining county supervisors and strategic schools. There is nothing whatever to correspond to these agencies in the field of public health.

Colored nurses, although working under established health agencies, will need aid in enlisting the interest and organizing the forces of the community. In order that this may be accomplished, an advisory body of white and colored citizens should be formed. The personnel of this body should represent the county and voluntary health organizations, the white employers, the educational boards, the farm demonstration forces, and the colored leaders. This board will provide the real teamwork which is so essential. In many counties such an advisory board may be found already existing in the county interracial committee. Eight hundred of these county committees have been organized by the Commission on Interracial Co-operation. The primary object of these groups is to promote good will between the races, but they feel that good will is promoted best by working together for the good of the community. In a few places these committees are already backing health projects and through their co-operation during the past three years National Health Week has been more widely observed than ever before.

ORGANIZATIONAL RESPONSES TO PROBLEMS OF NATIONAL IMPORT

We have seen that the stimulus of poverty and the promise of improved economic opportunity impelled the black population to seek its fortune in the industries and associated service occupations located in the urban areas, particularly those of the North. We have seen that the exigencies of a segregated social system, which denied basic social justice, stimulated the need for governmental intervention, reluctantly yielded by presidents, congresses and courts, to provide blacks with both due process and the equal protection of the laws. We have seen that the constraints of institutional racism operating in a cultural environment which promised, but did not fulfill, equality of opportunity rallied blacks to effect a unity based upon racial pride and racial consciousness, and a determination to persevere and overcome these constraints. Thus, in the post-World War I period, the black population continued to exhibit its resilience. In response to urgent social needs it created appropriate organizational structures, where none previously existed. And, it perfected, or at least improved, existing organizational structures specifically designed to cope with the exigencies of the new urban environment.

Specifically, the N. A. A. C. P. and the National Urban League are representative of those organizational structures which recognized a need to focus national attention on the kinds of problems for which they were invented to cope. The N. A. A. C. P., for example, continued to develop and expand its capacity to provide protection for the civil rights of the black population. Similarly, the National Urban League assumed leadership in developing the kinds of social welfare activities most appropriate in assisting blacks to adapt to their new urban environment, especially regarding the requirements of industrial employment.

Beyond these organizations of broad scope, it became apparent that there was a need to incorporate blacks into labor unions in order to provide for collective bargaining and to afford other protections generally available only to white workers. As we have seen above, there was also the need to develop health programs and services and specific agencies as well to cater to the needs of orphaned and dependent children, the handicapped, the young and the aged. All of these things were undertaken. Some were organizational responses which originated as self-help ventures by blacks for blacks; some of them, on the other hand, originated as cooperative ventures involving relations with whites, both philanthropic and professional.

a. Labor

Employment is a central problem necessary for basic biological and social survival. It was especially urgent for migrants into the cities, for they were recruited by industrial firms to supply needed manpower created by shortages in the labor supply due to the demands of World War I. During the war the black worker was well received and proved to be an excellent worker. However, when the war ended and the problem arose of protecting their interest in their jobs, their relationship to the labor unions which evolved to provide, among other things, job protection and better working conditions, became crucial. The organized labor unions, for the most part members of the American Federation of Labor, in many cases protected the jobs of white workers by setting qualifications and standards for membership which excluded black workers. Furthermore, the jobs of A. F. of L. workers were for the most part jobs for skilled workers, and therefore did not meet the needs of the black workers who were denied the apprenticeship training and the other opportunities provided for acquiring industrial skills. The only recourse seemed to be the development of separate unions in those occupations where there existed the sufficient numerical strength and the leadership with organizational skills. Cases in point are the organization of the Brotherhood of Sleeping Car Porters and the Colored Actors Union.

In this article Haynes exposes the differences between immigrant labor of Europeans and the unskilled black migrants from the agricultural South. He argues for more attention to the development of the Negro labor corps.

Document 16*

George E. Haynes, "The Negro Laborer and the Immigrant," The Survey, May 14, 1921, pp. 209-210.

The principal factor in immigration, although obscured by discussion, is that of labor. The principal element in the so-called "Negro question" is that of labor, although frequently overlooked. These two groups of workers--the Negroes and the immigrants--have entered industry at the bottom and have really become competitors in the unskilled and the semi-skilled labor market of the North.

*Reprinted by permission.

So long as northern industry had access to the surplus population of European countries before the great war, the southern Negro who migrated North found himself largely limited in domestic and personal service, for even the truck farmers of New Jersey and the tobacco growers of Connecticut looked across the Atlantic for their "help." When, however, the great war shut off the immigrant tide and called many of the foreign-born home for army service, northern railroads, mines, steel-mills, founderies, packing houses and other basic industries soon found it necessary to have their agents searching the South for Negro workers. These came in response by the thousands. Pennsylvania in 1919 probably had more Negroes in industrial work than Alabama; Ohio industrial plants that year probably could have mustered more Negroes than those of Virginia. Pittsburgh steel mills in some cases took on the complexion of those of Birmingham and some section gangs of the Pennsylvania Railroad looked for a time like those of the Southern.

With the signing of the Armistice, and with the resumption of immigrant passage from Europe, questions of the relation of these two groups of workers and their relations to employers naturally arose. Two such questions may reasonably be considered here as pertinent elements of present practical labor policies: First, will the immigrants come in such numbers that they will supply the northern demand when industry again approaches "normalcy?" Second, what will be the effect upon the place in industry of the thousands of Negroes who entered northern industry during the war and since then, directly or indirectly, upon the great body of the Negro worker of the nation?

The first question concerning the probable future supply of immigrant labor can be discussed only in the light of past experience. The average net gain in population of the United States from immigration, according to figures in the January issue of The Nation's Business, for the five years preceding the great war was about six hundred thousand; it exceeded that figure on only four occasions in the whole history of immigration and exceeded 800,000 only three times, and the record smashing years prior to the war would yield an average of something less than a half million." Moreover of the immigrants who came over before 1914, 3 out of 20 were skilled workers and 11 out of 20 were unskilled workers; in 1919 less than 5 out of 20 were unskilled workers. These figures have important significance for labor.

To these facts may be added the probable decrease of immigration from Poland and from Russia for some years to come, the slowing down of immigration from Greece, the French efforts to attract Italian emigrants and the labor treaty of Italy with Brazil to control the settlement of Italians in the South American Republic. The limitation of accommodations for steerage passengers during the next five years has often been spoken of as a natural hindrance to very excessive traveling. Thousands of the diseased and maimed as a result of the war will be excluded under our immigration laws even with secure passage to our shores. Furthermore, we shall probably have a revision of our immigration laws during our next Congress. Whatever may be the restrictions of the laws and the results of their administration; whatever be the effects of the emigration policies of European governments, we may reasonably expect industry from now on to be more largely dependent upon its home labor supply. It is not all prophecy, indeed, that there will hardly be any "immigrant hordes" to flood the northern labor market for some years to come, if at all.

We may even ignore or discount the reports and statements so frequently published during the past two years about the thousands of aliens who were returning or about to return to their native lands with large sums saved from high war wages. We may calculate our "net balance" of incoming foreigners this year and the years just ahead of us on any set of facts we may reasonably use. We shall still be led a long way from predicting such a supply of European immigration as will create surplus laborers in the American market once our industry and agriculture again swing into their normal strides.

The recovery and expansion of industry and agriculture in the United States in the coming years is another phase of the first question. Floating the $100,000,000 foreign banking corporation; expansion of our foreign trade; development of our ocean transportation; President Harding's recent announcement that his administration will foster our merchant marine to support our foreign commerce, and the information available about the enlarged plans of many national and international industrial and commercial enterprises are all indicative of the coming demand for brain and brawn of every calibre and from every source.

When one considers the question of the effects of a limited supply of immigrant labor in the face of the expansion of industry and commerce upon the Negro workers throughout the whole country, there is a temptation to go far afield into racial factors which play upon the Negro in his labor relations. It is well here, however, if only for the sake of clarity to hew close to the labor line.

The Negro will maintain a hold upon Northern industry based upon his ability to fill the demands for production in such ways as to leave a profit for his employer and the lowest price for the consumer.

From all available, accurate data the Negro achieved a new position in the calculations of industrial managers, North and South, during the war. Eighty-seven out of every 100 Negroes ten years of age and over were wage earners in 1910. The Negro speaks English. He is 100 per cent American in feeling and ideas as shown by his sacrifices in every war from that on Boston Common where the Negro Crispus Attucks, fell, down to the fields of France where thousands paid the supreme price of loyalty to the flag. No "Americanization" is needed for him except to see that he is accorded the opportunities, rights and privileges of an American citizen.

Some facts recently published by the Department of Labor in a study, the Negro at Work during the World War and during Reconstruction, give firm ground for the view that on the whole the Negro has made good during the war in many of the basic industries such as iron and steel, shipbuilding, slaughtering and meat packing. The Negro worker shared very largely in war production. More than twenty-four thousand Negro men were employed in the shipyards under the supervision of the Emergency Fleet Corporation. The packing houses of Chicago increased the percentage of their Negro labor from two- to five-fold during the three years preceding 1919 and at last accounts the percentage of Negroes among their total employes was near the higher levels.

The recorded opinions of the large majority of thirty-eight superintendents and managers of large industrial plants were that Negro workers showed ambition for advancement when encouraged by the opportunity; that in work where materials were handled there was little or no difference in the loss of materials due to defective workmanship; that, as a rule, it took about the same amount of time for breaking in new white workers as for new Negro workers. The consensus of opinion of these employers of more than one hundred thousand white workers and more than seven thousand Negro workers, mainly in unskilled and semi-skilled work, after their experience with both races was that, all things considered, Negro workers had been nearly as satisfactory as white workers on the same jobs and operations, and that in some cases the testimony showed that they had been more satisfactory.

The test of comparative average earnings per week and of comparative average number of hours worked per week in twenty-three plants in six basic industries showed that Negro workers not only held their own but in some operations surpassed white workers in the same plants. During the war times Negro unskilled workers were largely employed in war industries in twelve southern states and fourteen northern states. Only twenty-three firms out of a total of 292 of these firms that employed Negroes reported less than 50 per cent war work.

It is true that the Negro is not yet accustomed to the rigid routine of the modern industrial plant. He still suffers from the slipshod habits and uncertain ways of the slave plantation, the tenant farm and the small-town activities. The encouraging thing, however, is the rapidity with which he learns new customs and methods of work and the happy, easy [way] he has of adapting himself quickly to new conditions.

The preceding facts relate to Negro men. Negro women workers have made quite as good a record. Visits made by special agents of the Women's Bureau of the Department of Labor, to selected establishments in 1918-1919 and in 1920 show this to be true. In

1919 visits were made to 152 establishments employing 21,547 Negro women. The largest number were employed in tobacco plants, textile and clothing factories, laundries, hardware and glassware establishments and in office work.

In 1920, about two years after the Armistice, a second round of visits was made to 150 selected plants employing more than 11,000 Negro women. These were engaged mainly in the same types of industry as those visited nearly two years before, although the same plants were not always included and others were substituted. The large number of Negro women still employed during the present clump indicates that they have given sufficient satisfaction to keep a foothold in industry even when unemployment is wide-spread.

The significance of the place the Negro woman has secured in industry in relation to immigration and the future of the race in industrial labor may be illustrated by the clothing trade in New York where so many foreign-born women are employed. Ten years ago a careful survey made by the writer in that city revealed hardly a Negro woman in such factories except occasionally on other than trade operations. Today, literally hundreds, if not thousands, are employed and in many factories without restrictions on the operations they may perform.

The Negro has been heretofore the largest undeveloped part of the home labor supply. Northern employers have learned his value during the experience of the past six years. The labor shortage in many parts of the South following the Negro migration to the North has led to the increase of wages to new levels, has opened the minds of employers to the possibilities of Negro development and is enlisting them in behalf of Negro education, justice in the courts and protection in the enjoyment of community opportunities.

With the probable limitations on the immigrant labor supply and the demonstrations the Negro has made of his capacity to serve industry, there seems to be reasonable ground for believing that industrial managers, North and South, will make large demands upon the Negro labor source when normal production is the order of the day and the present depression is a matter of history. Already employers and their organizations are giving more attention than heretofore to the possibilities of training and development for these workers. A new day has dawned for the Negro wage-earner and a new labor recruit has entered the door of American industry.

In this paper T. Arnold Hill, then Executive Secretary of the Chicago Urban League, reviews the position of the Negro vis-a-vis the structure of organized labor.

Document 17*

T. Arnold Hill, "Recent Developments in the Problem of Negro Labor," Proceedings of the National Conference of Social Work, 48th Annual Session, Milwaukee, Wisconsin, June 22-29, 1921, (Chicago: University of Chicago Press, 1921), pp. 321-325.

Until 1915 developments in the problem of Negro labor were indiscernable. From the landing of the first slaves in 1619 until the outbreak of the world war, Negroes labored principally at farming and domestic service. In 1910 three-fourths of the gainfully employed Negro population was confined to these two occupations. In the South where 78 per cent lived in rural districts, 62 per cent of those gainfully occupied were agriculturists; while in the North, with two-fifths of its Negro population of southern birth, 60 per cent were engaged in domestic and personal service. The Negro's one labor problem has been that of combatting industrial handicaps both North and South. In the South, slavery, peonage, robbery, through a corrupt commissary system, and pilfering of crops, land and wages; and in the North, a decisive exclusion from little except jobs as porters, janitors, waiters and domestics, and a well-oiled system of poor wages and separation from benefits of organized laborers--such was the Negro's industrial horizon when the labor conditions of the war gave him his first real opportunity in mechanical and industrial pursuits. Such an inheritance for the North when, pressed for workers and cramped with unfilled war orders, she called four or five hundred thousand Negroes to industries untried by them before! The Negro's exodus from the South and oppression marks his first real industrial development. It is not possible to discuss here all the problems involved in this transition. In the wake of his transference from the South to the North, problems of capital and labor, employer and white employee, wages, hours, shop requirements, housing transportation--these and many more have been issues in his assimilation to his new environment.

We are to confine our remarks to some of the outstanding developments since the migration. The significant development is that certain anticipated difficulties did not develop. It was expected that discord and, in fact, open clashes between white and colored labor working in the same plants would of necessity occur. Surprisingly few instances of open hostility have been reported. Demands for separate conveniences and segregated compartments for the purpose of keeping the races apart were yielded to in a comparatively small number of cases.

When the migration began, it was conjectured and accepted that epidemics would be generated in every city to which newcomers from the South would go. Exciting prophecies of the physical inability of Negroes to withstand the rigors of northern climate could be heard on every hand. Cities were to be visited with epidemics of pneumonia and tuberculosis. There was to be no end to small

*Reprinted by permission of the National Conference on Social Welfare.

pox. Crime waves would sweep the North and bread lines were to be numerous. It is interesting to note that while in 1919 and 1920 there were epidemics of pneumonia and influenza, they were neither brought about nor accentuated by the presence of Negroes, in fact, the death rate among colored people during these epidemics was exceedingly small; and in no city has an alarming increase in morbidity or mortality ratios been discerned. In fact, in Detroit, the death rate has actually declined five or six points.

It is of course, too soon to say whether Negro labor has satisfied every demand. It would be unreasonable to expect such development in six years after an experience such as we have indicated for three hundred years. And, too, what a difference between the passionless cotton fields of Mississippi and Georgia and the engaging and uninterrupted existence of Pittsburgh, Philadelphia, Detroit, and Chicago! Yet, Negroes actually "made good." Of course their turnover was high; in the beginning they were not punctual; they had difficulty conforming to northern frugality; in certain classes of work they did better, and in other classes, worse than whites; they jumped from job to job when no incentive or promotion was promised. In short, there were many inequalities, but when these are brushed aside there still remains the frequently acknowledged fact that Negroes rendered satisfactory service and made gratifying progress in their new fields of labor.

But success was not instantaneous. Churches, clubs, agencies, and individuals united in a campaign of education. Placards and letters containing advice to newcomers were distributed. Pastors preached about efficiency, orderliness, and citizenship. Counsel and warnings of every conceivable description followed the new workers into the shop where noon meetings were conducted, as well as into the home where talks with wives and neighborhood meetings were held frequently. There is still the problem of trade training. In the North, Negro boys and girls have not heretofore taken advantage of technical courses. Heretofore they have not been able to get jobs as mechanics and machinists and have, therefore, never acquired in the North the habit of attending trade schools. It is hoped that progress in this direction will be realized as opportunities for skilled workers appear.

Relationship between unionists and Negroes, each of whom looked upon the other with mutual suspicion and fear, was regarded as one of the most serious potentialities of the whole movement. The American Federation of Labor has all along affirmed the right of Negroes to organize, but protests from autonomous internationals and locals have made the federation's avowals mere perfunctory expressions of good intentions. In 1920, at the fortieth annual convention of the federation, held in Montreal, Canada, a resolution was passed that "where international unions refuse to admit colored workers to membership, the American Federation of Labor will be authorized to organize them under charters of the American Federation of Labor."

The attitude of the American Federation of Labor has been reflected in decisions and policies of most of the internationals. In fact, out of 110 national and international unions affiliated with the federation, only 8 have constitutional provisions barring Negroes. During the steel strike, Negroes were organized in the same local with whites. At the stockyards, the Butcher Workmen's Union has for the past four or five years made overtures to Negroes. When the riots occurred in 1919 in Chicago, the police authorities, fearing a revival of attacks, would not permit Negro workers to go out of the districts in which large numbers of them lived. This kept practically all of them out of the stockyards. The Chicago Federation of Labor sought the governor, the mayor and the chief of police to say that, so far as conflict within the yards was concerned, organized labor guaranteed that no trouble would come to Negro workers if the police were withdrawn and the situation left to union workers. Notwithstanding the fact that practically every Negro worker was kept out of the yards for ten days or more, it should be said to the credit of the packers as well as the credit of organized labor that Negro workers, men and women, were allowed to return unmolested to their old jobs. Packers and unionists did all within their power to restore and maintain order.

The significant point in this development is that it indicates that organized labor has begun to recognize the Negro as an industrial factor in the North. Wherever colored workers are employed in large numbers, the unions involved will seek their membership. They may dislike to have them employed; but once they are, the tendency is to admit them to membership. Organized labor constructed on purely personal lines, realizes that the Negro must be recognized. Since there is a disposition on the part of manufacturers to use Negro labor, labor leaders see the advisability of organizing colored workers as a means of protection and strengthening their own forces.

Notwithstanding the favorable attitude of the American Federation of Labor and its internationals, four of the six nationals and internationals not affiliated with the American Federation of Labor have constitutional provisions which exclude Negroes from their membership. These are the four railroad brotherhoods. The other two, the Amalgamated Clothing Workers of America and the Industrial Workers of the World, admit Negroes to membership. As a protest against the discriminating practices of the railway brotherhood and certain internationals of the American Federation of Labor, there has arisen a strong and successfully managed national of colored railway men. Chicago is the headquarters of this association. Editors of a radical New York magazine formed an association for the purpose of encouraging Negroes to unionize and a former organizer of the American Federation of Labor is vigorously pushing a national of colored unionists. The fear is that whites and blacks organized in separate unaffiliated bodies will, sooner or later, be on opposite sides of some important issue which ought to affect all alike. This would be unfortunate now when progress toward unionizing Negroes is being made with certain tendencies toward permanency. Negro leaders are still unagreed as to whether to encourage or impede unionizing of Negroes. They remember unfortunate experiences with unions and distrust their invitation to extend privileges to members of the colored working fraternity. While little practical progress has been achieved, we note with relief a more friendly feeling on the part of white workers organized and unorganized--a feeling which will make improbable widespread discord such as was anticipated.

Of recent months the problem of industry for all has been that of unemployment. The practical and human question is how did Negroes fare during the winter of unemployment just passed. Chicago increased its Negro population from 44,000 in 1900 to 110,000 in 1920. How did the new increment of 148 per cent manage when work became scarce and factories shut down? Unemployment among Negroes has been a problem. Negroes, the last to be hired, were, because of an industrial practice which gives preference to seniority in service, the first to be discharged. Moreover, because of their newness and consequent inadaptability to all varying conditions, numbers were failures and put on the toboggan as soon as depression set in. Others were poor workers and, of course, a way was found for their dismissal. Chicago at one time had approximately 20,000 colored people out of work. Many of these were roomers, for Chicago's population before the exodus was 30 per cent lodgers. Soon they found themselves on the streets of Chicago with no place to go. But their exodus from below the Mason-Dixon line, though occasioned by the opportunity to labor in the North had other and far reaching causes. Negroes would have left the South long ago if they could have found work, and they would not have left in 1915 in such large numbers for work, had not intolerable conditions in the South urged them on. Thus, though unemployment faced them in the North, they turned their backs on the South, refused transportation home, and openly avowed their preference for streets and alleys rather than return to friends and family in their native habitat. In Chicago, hundreds were found sleeping in doorways, halls, and poolrooms. Police stations, no longer able to accommodate them, turned them back into the street. Manufacturers and railroads brought them to Chicago but now offered them no aid.

But, strange as it might appear, unemployment did not deter their entrance into Chicago. The Chicago Urban League sent articles to southern Negro papers, advising about the hard times and urging that for the present no more Negroes come to Chicago. But this was of no avail; they came just the same. One young fellow who had been in Chicago three days was asked why he came. "To try to get work," he said. "Did you not know there was no work in Chicago?" "Yes," he said, "I also know that there is no work in Mississippi and I had rather be out of work in Chicago than out of work in Mississippi." Another who had been in town over night only said, "There is no use staying in Georgia. All of my last year's crop is still in the barn. Why stay down there and raise more, when I cannot sell what I harvested last year."

Alarmed by the increase in unemployment, the Chicago Urban

League organized ministers, social agencies, and club women into a special committee which undertook the feeding and sleeping of unemployed Negroes, but not until public and private agencies had refused aid. Mostly single men were cared for by this committee, for the United Charities found itself unable to provide for them. Churches prepared and served meals for awhile, at their own expense and from a fund given to the league by the colored citizens for this purpose. Some clubs furnished lodging, and others, unable to feed or sleep, gave money.

In order to avoid duplication and to weed out undesirables, the Urban League was allowed to receive and record the meals and beds of all persons who were thus helped. Exception to this rule was permitted church members who could go to their pastor and receive aid without clearance. Donations of meats and vegetables in generous quantities were given daily by the packers, and a large baking company gave bread. Local merchants assisted. Colored people gave liberally and proceeds from entertainments were put into the common fund.

During the six months from January 1 to June 23, 41,074 meals were furnished and for 16,902 separate times men were given shelter. The extent of unemployment is seen from the fact that only 631 men were placed during this entire field of six months. Prior to this the league placed 1,200 a month, or twice as many monthly as were placed in six months during the period of unemployment.

Women returned to domestic service from the factories and their placements were double those of the men for the same period.

It should be borne in mind that the Salvation Army, the Young Men's Christian Association Hotel, the Dawes Hotel, the Christian Industrial League, and some other Institutions which run lodging houses, deny Negro men the privilege of sleeping in them.

In commenting upon the work for the unemployed, the president of the United Charities wrote the Urban League thus: "As the report showed such excellent work being done by the Urban League in organizing the activities of the various agencies on the South Side, the directors of the United Charities requested me to write to you expressing their thanks and commendation for the excellent and efficient services which the Urban League has been rendering during the past few months."

But the significant development in this matter of unemployment is the fact that Negroes have retained their ratio in all the large factories and industries now opened. If the plants suspended operations, or curtailed force, of course the Negro suffered along with others. Except in the case of a few small shops, no replacement of Negroes by whites is noted. In fact, the Negro has not only kept his own job but the jobs of others who would be glad to get them now when choice of occupation is no longer possible.

The answer to the often asked query "Will Negroes retain their gains in industry?" is found in their retention now when idle white labor is seeking jobs on every hand. If colored workers who occupied positions that were vacated by whites during the war can retain these places now, when many of these same white workers are looking for employment, it is fair to assume that they have made very definite progress toward permanency in industry. Of course, immigration will be a factor, but the exact effect of foreign workers on Negro labor is debatable. It will depend upon whether the immigrant comes to remain or to make money and acquire American experience with which to build up Europe; whether he brings with him anarchistic tendencies; or whether, tired of drudgery and wastage of war, he comes not for work but for ease and contentment. The advance made by the southern Negro laborers has exceeded expectations. Employers acknowledge their satisfaction and are still hiring them.

A. Philip Randolph in this excerpt discusses the organization and problems of organizing a black labor union, giving an inside perspective.

Document 18a*

A. Philip Randolph, "The Truth About the Brotherhood of Sleeping Car Porters," The Messenger, February, 1926, pp. 37-38, 61.

When Organized

The Brotherhood of Sleeping Car Porters was organized August 25, 1925, New York City, New York.

Who Organized It?

As a result of a speech by the writer at the Pullman Porter's Athletic Association on organization, the porters of New York were aroused. Immediately thereafter Mr. W. H. Des Verney interviewed the writer on the matter of organizing the porters. He called a meeting at his home at which Messrs Roy Lancaster, at the time, recently discharged, A. L. Totten and the writer, attended.

Why Organized

1. To get a living wage.

2. Pay for preparatory time.

3. Conductor's pay for conductor's work.

4 Pay for delayed arrivals.

*Reprinted by permission of the author.

5. Doubling is injurious to the health of the porter. Doubling means leaving for a point immediately the porter arrives off a run, however long. It throws a regular porter out of line and he earns less.

6. Sleep....

7. Extra porters are not paid if they report for duty and there is no line for them to be sent out on. This is obviously unfair. Extra porters who are required to report at the yard for duty should be paid whether they are sent out or not. They are required to report regularly or be put off the list.

8. Regular porters who miss their line as a result of having doubled out, are not paid during the time they are lying around waiting to catch their line. This is unjust. They should be paid for this time spent waiting for their line, since they were thrown out of line accommodating the Company ...

9. Porters are required to buy the polish and equipment for shining the passengers' shoes. If he does not shine their shoes, he is given 15 or 30 days on the street, and, if he shines them and requests pay for same, he is penalized. Polish and equipment should be supplied by the Company.

10. Porters should receive adequate rest before they are required to double out. They should not be required to double out during their lay-overs, except where necessity [] very pressing. At present, a porter running from St. Louis to Chicago to New York, is often required to double right out to Boston or to some other point, before he sees his family, gets anything to eat, freshen up himself or change his clothes. During rush periods such as holidays, he is given bad hot coffee and buns. This is palpably against the health of the porter.

11. Maids don't receive the same lay-overs as porters. Having the same runs, they are entitled to the same lay-overs.

12. Whenever a porter is compelled to report for investigation, he does so on his own time. Facilities should be provided that a minimum of time is lost, since the lay-overs of the porters are their rest periods and the time for attending to their personal business.

13. Deadheading....

14. That the porters be not subjected to threats, intimidations and reprisals because of their membership in a labor union.
    (a) The Company has fired porters because of activities in the interest of the union. It has compelled porters to vote for the Company union by threatening to withhold

their pay checks or to withhold giving them their sign-out slip, that is, hold them off their runs. It has put inexperienced and untrained Filipinos on the club cars in order to frighten the porters away from their union. This is in violation of the seniority rule which the Company pledged to uphold in the agreement with the porters in the last wage conference, 1923. A club car is considered preferential service and supposed to go only to men of long service, efficiency and responsibility. But the company overrode this rule and placed Filipinos on the club cars over the protest and request of Negro porters who have given probably thirty of their best years in the service.

(b) Under the Transportation Act, enacted by Congress in 1920, any group of workers on the railroads were invested with a right to organize and present their grievances to the Railroad Labor Board, machinery was set up under the said act to handle the workers' grievances. Thus the Pullman Company is violating a Federal statute in opposing the men to organize.

(c) In the Employee Representation Plan of the Company, a clause specifically states that the company will not discriminate against a porter or maid because of his or her membership in a fraternal society or union. This is Article 6 and Section F. Still has done everything to prevent the men from organizing from hiring Filipinos to hiring Mr. Perry W. Howard, Negro Special Assistant to the United States Attorney General.

The editors of the Methodist Federation of Social Service provide an information sheet relative to the organization of the Brotherhood of Sleeping Car Porters for its membership. This is an example of an effort by a church related group to provide a basis for interracial understand.

Document 18b*

"The Brotherhood of Sleeping Car Porters," The Social Service Bulletin of the Methodist Federation for Social Services, XVII, (April 1, 1927), Reprinted in The Messenger.

Introductory

Porters Organize. In the summer of 1925 the dissatisfaction of Pullman porters with working conditions and with the company union as a means of bettering them had reached an acute stage. They therefore organized themselves into the Brotherhood of Sleeping Car Porters and formulated a series of demands. Within a year

*Reprinted by permission.

they had a national labor union (headquarters, 2311 Seventh Ave., New York City) with groups in Chicago, St. Paul and Minneapolis, Omaha, Kansas City, St. Louis, Denver, Portland, Seattle, Los Angeles, Oakland, New Orleans, Washington, Boston, Detroit and Buffalo, and other termini for porters, and with groups working secretly among the porters in other centers.

Endorsement. It has the endorsement of the American Federation of Labor, the Railroad Brotherhoods, leading negro organizations such as the National Association for the Advancement of Colored People, National Urban League, Negro Elks, and of prominent attorneys. In New York a citizen's committee of 100 is supporting the organization and leading negro clergy have issued a statement in its favor.

Opposition. The Pullman Company is actively opposing the union. It added to its payroll as spokesman against the union, the prominent negro leader, Perry Howard, who is on the payroll of the U. S. Department of Justice as special assistant to the Attorney-General. A company representative states emphatically that the Pullman Company has done more than any other agency for the negro in this country. A. Phillip Randolph, editor of the Messenger and general organizer of the Brotherhood, is in his estimation, "socialistic" and "Atheistic," an organizer for the union is an undesirable character, porters who join the union are "disloyal." The Brotherhood complains of the dismissal of union porters, new releases in papers across the country warning against joining the union, subsidies to negro papers in the form of company advertisements, employment of spies, suppression of information about the strength of union meetings.

An Issue. Shall the company union or the Brotherhood represent the men before the Railroad Mediation Board? This board, provided for by the Watson-Parker law, states that 'representatives for the purposes of this act shall be designated by the respective parties in such a manner as may be provided in their corporate organization or unincorporated association, or by other means of collective action, without interference, influence or coercion exercised by either party over the self-organization or designation of representatives by the other.' The company claims that 85% of the 12,000 porters and maids have by secret ballot endorsed the Employee Representation Plan. The Brotherhood claims a membership of nearly 7,000 of whom 900 have been enrolled since Dec. 1st. The board is just now investigating these claims.

A Porter Survey. Employing the technical help of the Labor Bureau, Inc., the Brotherhood has made a comprehensive study of its own situation, drawing upon government documents and well known statistical studies, and obtaining first hand information from a questionnaire and case studies. The following data are drawn largely from that report.

Nature of Porters' Service

Part of Pullman Service. Since 1867, the Pullman Company has sold service to the travelling public. That service does not include transportation which is provided by the railroad companies; the Pullman Company undertakes to provide comforts. The porter's service is a major element in this comfort, so recognized by the company. "Without the efficient help given by its loyal employees," said President Carry to the stockholders in 1925, "the Pullman Company could not have made the splendid record it did."

Duties. Pullman instructions list 217 matters to which the porter must give continuous attention--rules pertaining to care of bedding, berths, baggage, guarding of cars, care of cars, ventilation, heating and lighting, etc. , matters of great importance to the traveller.

They Must Be Negroes. Company policy calls for employment of negro porters and maids. Negroes are recruited from the south. The Company Benefit Association, by its constitution, restricts membership to negro male persons and a declared object is to render service "attractive to the best elements of the negro race." Yet the porters' occupation is a blind alley job with no chance of promotion, as representatives of the company have admitted in government hearings. And the chance for a raise in wages is extremely limited --$3 after two years in the service, $3 more after five years, a slightly larger increase after 15 years, in all a range of about $10.

Concerning Porters' Wages

Present Minimum. The minimum wage of porters is $72.50 a month and is based on a mileage system by which porters must cover 11,000 miles or complete about 400 hours of road service during a month before they receive overtime pay. This overtime is on the basis of 60 cents for every 100 miles in excess of 11,000 miles. "Doubling out," the term used for an immediate run after one trip is completed, without a rest period, is paid for at the same rate, as are also delays after the first hour, on the basis of 30 miles an hour. Averages compiled from a questionnaire returned by 673 regular porters and 104 extra porters showed a monthly mileage of 10,402.8 that is less than the 11,000 miles on which overtime is based. The average wage was $78.11. Tips which averaged $58.15 a month increased this wage, but occupational expense brought the total down to about $97.43 a month.

Porters and American Living Standards. The porters put their average net income of $97.43 a month--about $1,100 a year--over against estimates of living costs of different categories of working men's families in the United States made by the Federal Bureau of Labor Statistics, the National Industrial Conference Board, the New York and Philadelphia Bureaus of Municipal Research, the National War Labor Board of Estimate and other agencies. These brought up to 1926 by well known statistical methods range from about $1,460 to $2,500. Concerning their wages the Brotherhood concludes that "measured by every test which they may be submitted ... they are below the average maintenance expenditures which are actually made by families throughout the United States; they are below the standards which have been set by reputable agencies of all kinds of laborers, for 'workers' and for clerical workers; for the 'subsistence' of an unskilled laborer and for the achievement of a minimum of health and decency for any worker; for the maintenance of the actually small family of the average porter or for the maintenance of the standard 'census' family" (man, wife and three minor children).

Porters' Wages, Past and Present. The Pullman Company has emphasized the percentage increase of porters' wages--the 1926 wages are 163% higher than those of 1913. The Brotherhood points out that the increase was from so low an original wage--$20 in 1897, $27.50 from 1911 to 1913--that it is still totally inadequate, especially as living costs have risen so tremendously that they have left purchasing power far behind--the $540 additional annual wage represents only about $170 in added purchasing power.

Movement of Comparative Wages. Finally the Brotherhood quotes figures which show that the porters' wages lag behind those of other workers. Between 1897 and 1924, wage earners in transportation increased their average earnings from $544 to $1,572 (with somewhat higher levels from 1920 to 1923). The porters' average gain in the same period was from $240 to $793. Between 1915 and 1926 conductors' wages went from $70 to $150 a month ($155 in 1920 and 1921). Porters' wages in the same period went from $27.50 to $72.50--a higher percentage raise, yet the conductors were all the time faring better.

Tipping

The porters' wage is augmented by tips. The company uses this as an excuse for keeping wages low.

Union Emphasis. The Brotherhood claims that the tipping system affects the porter's working condition adversely in many ways. It recognizes that the evil is not peculiar to its work but argues that the prevalence of an evil is no justification for its existence. (Other grievances are considered below under Brotherhood demands.)

Economic Aspects. The average tip revealed by the questionnaire and substantiated from other sources was $58.15 a month or, subtracting the $33.82 paid out in occupational expenses, a net increase to wages of $24.33 a month. But averages do not tell the whole story. Tips vary with runs and seasons and types of patronage, resulting in inequalities, uncertainty of income and speculative risks. Thus, 376 porters reported tips of less than $50 a month, 245 reported more than that amount. Five porters earned less than $15 a month on tips, while two earned more than $200. Moreover, the tipping system has again and again blocked the porters' efforts for shorter runs and for a shorter basic month, the company arguing that the porter himself could not afford reforms which would prevent him from "following tips to their destination."

Social Aspects. "The porter is a negro. The tipping system ... creates a peculiar relation between the tipper and the man tipped. On the one hand ... a sensation of power and patronage and on the other ... a possibility of obsequiousness and dependence. But when to this we add the fact that the man tipping is usually white ... while the man tipped belongs to a race that is even now struggling to a recognized social status, we aggravate all the inherent social evils of the tipping system."

The Company Saves. The company's monthly wage bill for porters is approximately $811,200, the approximate income to the porters from tips $703,200, saving the company (assuming that to get porters if the system were abolished it would have to raise the wages to cover present tips), about $700,000 a month, or nearly $9,000,000 a year. Moreover, indirect savings are made by the company in that it bases wage rates of extra porters and pensions to superannuated porters on the regular wage, not the wage plus tips; and on that basis it limits stock sold to employees. The Brotherhood raises the pertinent question, Who gets tipped, the porters or the company? (Are we who ride responsible?)

Welfare Work

Over against porters' grievances must be put the various types of welfare work which the company maintains for its employees, and its provision for selling them stock.

The Benefit Association. The Pullman Porters' Benefit Association provides that porters who affiliate with it pay an annual assessment of $28 if they are less than 45 years of age and $32 if older. In return the Association cares for members in time of sickness, incapacity or death. The company maintains a close relationship with this organization, dominating its policy and contributing to payment of expenses.

Pensions. The company grants a pension equivalent to 1%, of the annual salary during the past 10 years of service, multiplied by the years of service, amounting to an average of about $18 a month to porters who have given twenty years or more of consecutive service and have reached seventy years of age.

Other Provisions. The company has also established various educational courses, bands, entertainments and field days and an employee magazine, the Pullman News, all of which it claims have a beneficial effect upon the workers, contributing to *esprit de corps*.

Stock Distribution. In February, 1926, a company announcement stated that stock would be sold to employees at reduced quotations on an installment plan. Each employee is entitled to purchase one share per year for each $500 of his annual salary. Present wage rates make it possible for a porter to purchase but one share in a year.

Jackson's article is an example of union organization in a situation in which blacks were organized to cope with the exigencies of work on the circuit of the Theatre Owners Book Association, "the corporate body that controls employment in the majority of theatres presenting Negro acts."

Document 19*

J. A. Jackson, "Colored Actors' Union," The Messenger, (September, 1925): pp. 362-363.

There is an Iowa town, one of many, in which the spirit of Unionism is a very important factor. Everything seems to be organized there. A Negro novelty act happened to "close" with a summer carnival outfit in the town; and upon application to a local vaudeville theatre for an engagement, the team was told that they might work if they were "Union". The manager, a white man, of course, had determined upon this reply as an easy way to avoid a more direct refusal. To his consternation, he was handed a card inscribed COLORED ACTORS UNION. Though he had admitted that the organization was one of which he had never heard, he capitulated, and the act worked a pleasant week's engagement in the local theatre.

The incident occurred early in 1924, when the Colored Actor's Union was indeed new to everybody. To-day its unique red label may be seen on trunks in theatres and hotels in almost any city in the land. It is not only on paper. It is a virile, aggressive and thrifty group of hard pressed actors who work in vaudeville, musical comedy, tabloids, with circuses on carnivals, and in churches, halls, and schools. They are determined to find more pleasure and greater profit in their chosen profession than has heretofore prevailed. There is plenty of evidence that the determination is real....

The Union officials have done wonders with the small funds at their command toward relieving its members of the different forms of distress incident to their calling. A sick member was brought from Jacksonville, Fla., to his home in Washington; a group that suffered the loss of wardrobe and scenery in a St. Louis fire were very promptly re-equipped so that they resumed work with little loss of time. The Union has assisted in defraying the funeral expenses of several members, has provided flowers for the funeral of others; and has loaned money to widows of its members pending the adjustment of insurance claims for death benefits. Insurance for every member is a hoped for feature of the near future.

The records of the secretary's office reveal that the need of transportation for stranded performers is an oft-met situation. A minstrel performer was moved from Syracuse to Washington; a tab-

*Reprinted by permission.

loid company of a dozen performers was brought from St. Louis to Washington Headquarters. Another came in from Kansas City. An act was sent from Buffalo to New York, and a stranded chorister was sent from Elmira, N. Y., to Philadelphia. These transportation advances are in the nature of loans to be repaid so that others may in turn be helped should the need arise.

Several performer-producers have been advanced funds with which to equip miniature companies with scenery and wardrobe. So far these advances have been repaid with reasonable promptitude. Without the Union assistance, the performer helped would not have been able to have become a producer on his own account.

b. The National Association for the Advancement of Colored People.

The N. A. A. C. P. was organized in 1910. Among its chief functions were the protection of the civil rights guaranteed by the Fourteenth Amendment: due process and equal protection of the law. In the twenties the N. A. A. C. P. vigorously waged an anti-lynching campaign. It was most effective perhaps in the taking of test cases to the courts in protection of civil rights. In Nixon v. Herndon, the N. A. A. C. P. asked the Supreme Court to declare unconstitutional the white primary in Texas.

Document 20

Nixon v. Herndon, et al., 273 U. S. October Term, 1926. Error to the United States District Court for the Western District of Texas. No. 117. Argued January 4, 1927.--Decided March 7, 1927. Cases Argued and Decided in the Supreme Court of the United States, Book 71, Lawyers' Ed., Rochester, N. Y.: Lawyers Co-operative, 1928, pp. 536-541.

1. An action for damages may be maintained against judges of election for unlawfully denying to a qualified voter the right to vote at a state primary election. P. 540.

2. A state statute (Texas, 1923, Art. 3093a) barring negroes from participation in Democratic party primary elections held in the State for the nomination of candidates for senator and representatives in Congress, and state and other offices, violates the Fourteenth Amendment. P. 540.

Reversed.

Error to a judgment of the District Court which dismissed an action for damages brought by a negro against judges of election in Texas, based on their refusal to permit the plaintiff to vote at a primary election.

Messrs. Fred C. Knollenberg and A. B. Spingarn, with whom Messrs. Louis Marshall, Moorfield Storey, James A. Cobb, and Robert J. Channell were on the briefs, for Nixon.

The primary was a public election under the Constitution and laws of the State. Section 8 Art. 5 of that Constitution provides that the District Court shall have original jurisdiction of contested elections. This provision has been held by the courts of Texas to confer upon the District Court jurisdiction over contested primary elections.

Casting a ballot in a primary election established and regulated by state law is an act of voting within the meaning of the Fifteenth Amendment to the federal Constitution, and the immunity against discrimination on account of race or color which is guaranteed by said Amendment protects the plaintiff in his right to vote in such primary, where the only obstacle interposed is that he is a Negro....

When the negro, by virtue of the Fifteenth Amendment, acquired immunity from discrimination in voting on account of his race and color, he thereby acquired the right and privilege as a free man to exercise, to the same extent as a white man, his untrammeled choice in the selection of parties or candidates; and when the legislature of a State, solely because of his race and color, undertakes by law to exclude him from any party, or deny him the same latitude in registering his preference as a member of any party of his choice that it allows to white members of such party, it thereby abridges his right to vote under the Amendment, and denies him the equal protection of the law guaranteed by the Fourteenth Amendment....

No appearance for defendants in error.

Messrs. Claude Pollard, Attorney General of Texas, and D. A. Simmons, First Assistant Attorney General, filed a brief for the State of Texas, by special leave of Court.

Argument for the State of Texas

The nominating primary of a political party is not an election in which everyone may vote.

There are many organized groups of persons, voluntary in character, in the several States of the Union. In many of these the election of officers and the purposes and objects of the organization depend upon the votes of the individual members. Some of these are maintained for charitable purposes, some for the support of religious worship, some for the diffusion of knowledge and the extension of education, some for the promotion of peace, and some for the advancement of political ideas. It clearly appears, therefore, that the right to vote referred to in constitutions, and elections mentioned therein, do not include within their scope all elections and all voting by persons in the United States. The act of the legislature of Texas and the nominating primary in which the vote of plaintiff in error was refused, dealt with voting within a designated political party, which is but the instrumentality of a group of individuals for the furtherance of their own political ideas.

It must be remembered that "nominating primaries" were unknown at the time of the adoption of the Constitution of the United States and of the Constitution of Texas in 1876. The nominating primary, like its predecessors, the nominating convention and the caucus, is not the "election." Nomination is distinct from election and has been so differentiated from the beginning of our government.

The question of parties and their regulation is a political one rather than legal. The District Court of the United States has no jurisdiction in a case of this character. Political questions are not within its province....

Because the Democratic party holds a nominating primary, can it be contended that outsiders can be forced upon the party over its expressed dissent? If the party should abandon the primary and go back to the convention or the caucus system, could it be consistently maintained that the courts could force upon the convention or upon the caucus, the plaintiff in error, if the membership of the party, the convention or the caucus were restricted against negroes? We contend that a nominating primary is purely a political matter and outsiders denied participation by the party councils cannot demand a redress at the hands of the courts....

Chandler v. Neff, 298 Fed. 515, disposed of a case almost identical with this one, and holds with the Supreme Court of Texas that a primary of a political party is not an election, and the right of a citizen to vote therein is not within protection of the Fourteenth and Fifteenth Amendments to the Constitution of the United States. Nor is this doctrine limited to Texas....

Mr. Justice Holmes delivered the opinion of the Court.

This is an action against the Judges of Elections for refusing to permit the plaintiff to vote at a primary election in Texas. It lays the damages at five thousand dollars. The petition alleges that the plaintiff is a negro, a citizen of the United States and of Texas and a resident of El Paso, and in every way qualified to vote, as set forth in detail, except that the statute to be mentioned interferes with his right; that on July 26, 1924, a primary election was held at El Paso for nomination of candidates for a senator and representatives in Congress and State and other offices, upon the Democratic ticket; that the plaintiff being a member of the Democractic party, sought to vote but was denied the right by defendants; that the denial was based upon a statute of Texas enacted in May, 1923, and designated Article 3093a, by the words of which "in no event shall a negro be eligible to participate in a Democractic party primary election held in the State of Texas," &c., and that this statute is contrary to the Fourteenth and Fifteenth Amendments to the Constitution of the United States. The defendants moved to dismiss upon the ground that the subject matter of the suit was political and not within the jurisdiction of the Court and that no violation of the Amendments was shown. The suit was dismissed and a writ of error was taken directly to this Court. Here no argument was made on behalf of the defendants but a brief was allowed to be filed by the Attorney General of the State.

The objection that the subject matter of the suit is political is little more than a play upon words. Of course the petition concerns political action but it alleges and seeks to recover for private damage. That private damage may be caused by such political action and may be recovered for in a suit at law hardly has been doubted for over two hundred years.... If the defendants' conduct was a wrong to the plaintiff the same reasons that allow a recovery for denying the plaintiff a vote at a final election allow it for denying a vote at the primary election that may determine the final result.

The important question is whether the statute can be sustained. But although we state it as a question the answer does not seem to us open to a doubt. We find it unnecessary to consider the Fifteenth Amendment, because it seems to us hard to imagine a more direct and obvious infringement of the Fourteenth. That Amendment, while it applies to all, was passed, as we know, with a special intent to protect the blacks from discrimination against them.... That Amendment "not only gave citizenship and the privileges of citizenship to persons of color, but it denied to any State the power to withhold from them the equal protection of the laws.... What is this but declaring that the law in the States shall be the same for the black as for the white; that all persons, whether colored or white, shall stand equal before the laws of the States, and, in regard to the colored race, for whose protection the amendment was primarily designed, that no discrimination shall be made against them by law because of their color?" Quoted from the last case in Buchanan v. Warley, 245 U. S. 60, 77.... The statute of Texas in the teeth of the prohibitions referred to assumes to forbid negroes to take part in a primary election the importance of which we have indicated, discriminating against them by the distinction of color alone. States may do a good deal of classifying that it is difficult to believe rational, but there are limits, and it is too clear for extended argument that color cannot be made the basis of a statutory classification affecting the right set up in this case.

Judgment Reversed.

c. The Commission on Interracial Cooperation.

This document relates to the organization of the Commission on Interracial Cooperation in the South. It reads as follows:

Document 21a

"Interracial Group," Ms. Neighborhood Union Papers, 1918.

Trevor Arnett Library, Atlanta University Library.

Founded 1918 at close of World War--Cause Negro Soldiers associating with French women, there was fear that they would want to do the same thing here in America.

Ku Klux organized on Stone Mountain. This Interracial group was organized to offset this.

Original group--
Negro
Dr. Bryant, Jesse Thomas, John Hope, Dr. Singleton, J. W. Wilkes, W. Woods, Mrs. John Hope, Mr. John Hope, et al.

White
Durham, Ashby Jones, Alexander, Eagan.

In this excerpt on the life of John Hope, Will W. Alexander recounts the formation of the Commission on Interracial Cooperation, to which he refers as the Interracial Commission, and the role of John Hope, President of Atlanta University, who served many years as its chairman.

Document 21b*

Will W. Alexander, "Phylon Profile, XI: John Hope," Reprinted from Phylon, Atlanta University, First Quarter, 1947, pp. 4-13.

I recall little that was done or said at a student conference at Gammon Seminary in Atlanta back in 1911 except that there I first saw President Hope. He was then forty-three years old and had been President of Morehouse College for five years. He was a man of average height, erect, who moved with ease. I was struck first with the light complexion and fair hair in one who was classed as colored. My greater interest, however, was in his finely chiseled, intelligent face, his well-modulated voice, and disciplined speech. I realized that he would have been outstanding among any group of men. By a stranger he might have been mistaken for a great artist, actor, or a surgeon. There was something about him that, at first sight, might have created the impression of austerity or aloofness. However, one could not doubt that here was an unusual person.

He had no prominent place as a speaker on the program. He listened with interest, and when he occasionally took part in the discussion, his remarks were brief--with an entire absence of oratory--

*Reprinted by permission of the publisher.

but his words illuminating, and the members of the conference were visibly impressed. I had never known, up to that time, that such a person could, or did, exist in what I vaguely knew as the Negro world that lay across the tracks.

I had grown up in a middle-class Methodist tradition that went back to Bishop Francis Asbury. A relative had been the first Methodist missionary to China from the South after the Civil War. From its beginning, Vanderbilt University, where I was then a student, had contacts with the Far East. Distinguished Chinese, Japanese, and Korean alumni came to the campus from time to time and were well known to the students. I had classmates from these countries. I left the Gammon conference puzzled by Dr. Hope. Afterwards, I was to learn that even my teachers at the University were unaware of the existence of such men as President Hope, or the things which he represented.

After graduation, I soon discovered that the work of a Methodist minister, for which I had prepared at Vanderbilt, was a disappointment. World War I offered an opportunity to leave the ministry quietly and without unpleasantness. I became attached to the National War Work Council, with headquarters in Atlanta, giving my time to civilian welfare activities in the nearly forty military training establishments in the southeastern states. This experience enabled me to see a new aspect of southern life, particularly through contacts I had with large numbers of Negroes being trained in these camps. Gradually my work was increasingly concerned with their problems and later, as well, with the problems of civilian Negro communities in relation to the war.

Soon after American soldiers reached Europe, President Hope went to France to work among Negro troops and remained there for the duration of the war. After the armistice, he returned to Atlanta. Hearing of my interest in Negroes, he came to my office soon after this. This was our second meeting. We talked for most of the afternoon. I was impressed by the recital of his experiences with the troops overseas, his observations about the French, and his hopes for America. I became so engrossed in the conversation that when President Hope rose to go, I accompanied him down the elevator, and into the street, continuing the conversation until he boarded the street car.

From that day, until his death, there was hardly a day when we were both in the city that I did not talk to him directly or at least by phone. I was to be associated with new developments that were to take place at Atlanta University, and he, with my work in the Interracial Commission, although at that time neither of us had any intimation of this. In fact, the Interracial Commission had its beginning, in part, in these conversations.

The Commission was organized in 1919. Its membership was interracial and the white members were southerners who were concerned in one way or another with Negro education, or who had shown a personal interest in race relations--for the most part, educators and church people. The Negro members were prominent southern Negroes of that period. The Commission was committed to cooperation between white and colored people in the solution of community problems and to changing attitudes on both sides from antagonism to good will. This may sound very indefinite and perhaps to some very timid in view of the things that are happening today. The white members of the Commission were, on the whole, persons without wealth or official standing. They had no creed or final program for the solution of the race problem. They did, however, challenge with considerable courage, specific abuses such as lynching and peonage, attempted to improve the attitude of the press, and to enlist the cooperation of the churches, colleges, and local groups throughout the South. Perhaps the change that took place in the attitudes of the white people who worked with the Commission was more significant than the specific things which it attempted to accomlish.

To this, President Hope made a weighty contribution. He gave the Commission priority on his busy schedule. He was almost always at the meetings where there was much talk. In important discussions, he usually had something pertinent to say. These talks were practical, constructive and inspired the confidence and challenged the faith of the group. His delivery was quiet and restrained his words simple and direct. There was, however, persuasiveness, and he came to have an increasing influence with the members of the Commission. This was due, in part, to the fact that he obviously believed in the sincerity of the people composing the Commission.

President Hope's influence with this group grew year by year until, in a very few years, he was spontaneously and unanimously elected chairman of the Commission. It had been something new in the South for white people to sit down to confer with Negroes and to work <u>with</u> them rather than <u>for</u> them. It was revolutionary, in a quiet way, when southern whites voted for a Negro to lead them and felt honored to follow him. The election of President Hope as chairman marked an advance in the growth of the organization and set a new landmark in race relations in the South. This was to him no empty honor. He gave much time and thought to the work--and we all grew under his guidance. Since then, I have known that, even in the South, white people would follow a Negro if he had real leadership. President Hope demonstrated that. The <u>man</u> was more important than his race.

As chairman of the Commission, he represented it on many important occasions. He spoke extemporaneously, never with oratorical effect. There was a moving quality, almost mystical, about this man's quiet, chaste, conversational speeches. At an important conference of students at the University of North Carolina, there were speakers of national importance on a three-day program. President Hope spoke at the noon hour in the chapel packed with students and visitors. He seemed to see only the students. He did not plead the case of "My People." He spoke to the group as specially privileged young Americans and what that privilege entailed. He was saying only what he had said many times to Morehouse men in the quiet of their own chapel. He did not have two speeches, one for white and another for colored. As he spoke, a hush came over the audience. At the end of about thirty minutes the students moved quietly, and almost reverently, out of the building. Dr. Howard Odum has said many times since that this was one of the most impressive addresses ever delivered at Carolina.

Soon after World War I, the president of Atlanta University was retiring. The philanthropic foundations were convinced that the time had come to expand the Negro educational opportunities in Atlanta. They felt that it could not be done through the multiplicity of inadequately financed, competing, undergraduate institutions which then existed. The situation seemed to offer an opportunity to reorganize, unify, and refinance the whole effort. The vacancy in the presidency of Atlanta University seemed the place to launch such a movement. Where to begin was not apparent. As a member of the Atlanta University Board, I was feeling pressure to do something about this before another president was elected. I had not the slightest idea of how to begin and so expressed myself to Clark Foreman one cold day on the street in Washington. Without a moment's hesitation he said, "Elect Dr. John Hope president of Atlanta University, as well as Morehouse, and he can work it out." I believed at once that he was right. I went, within an hour, to James Weldon Johnson with the idea. He was a member of the board and an outstanding alumnus of Atlanta University. Without hesitation, he committed himself to the idea. It was agreed that he would begin a quiet canvass of Atlanta board members and key alumni. I was to see if President Hope would accept the post.

There had been a long time rivalry and sometimes feeling between the two colleges. President Hope recognized that this might stand in the way of our plans. It was probable that some Atlanta alumni would fear loss of prestige for their own alma mater. In spite of this, President Hope was willing to accept, if elected. It was agreed that Atlanta University should become the graduate school with the undergraduate colleges affiliated and cooperating in a unified university system. There was little time to think about the details beyond this central idea. Atlanta University had to have a president. Prolonged delay meant public discussion and controversy and probable defeat. On the other hand, there was danger of resentment and a charge of steamrolling if we acted too quickly. James Weldon Johnson was so convinced of the soundness of the idea that he was willing to act first and convince the public afterwards. The Atlanta board met in a few weeks and voted to make the University a graduate school affiliated with the undergraduate colleges and elected Dr. Hope as president.

The new president took over the general idea, as well as considerable opposition from certain quarters. But the idea seemed so sensible and President Hope was of such standing as a man and as an educator that the opposition did not gain momentum.

President Hope was confronted with the necessity of developing the idea and of promptly finding large sums of money for carrying it forward. Here began the crowning work of his life. There were two institutions in America of the general pattern contemplated: Claremont College in California and Toronto University in Canada. He promptly studied both of these in detail and brought to the board a clear conception of the plan for the new Atlanta University.

His leadership was an inspiration to the board. Mr. Dean Sage, the board chairman, was a man of large affairs. He recognized that Dr. Hope was talking in terms that would appeal to men of vision. Mr. Sage's chairmanship of the board, which up to that time had been somewhat of a routine matter, became to him under President Hope's leadership an interesting adventure. I have never seen a more resourceful devoted chairman than he grew to be. President Hope had rare skill in dealing with his board. He did not dominate them, but he always led them. Out of his own well-disciplined enthusiasm, he was able to impart genuine enthusiasm to others. He never brought to the board any half-baked ideas. He was meticulously careful about details. His orderly mind never seemed more apparent than in presenting plans to his board. Service on the board under him became a great pleasure to all of us, free from bickering, pettiness, and personal self-seeking.

With the growth of the plans and the enthusiasm of the board, funds began to pour in. We were hardly aware of how they were secured. Mr. Sage had important contacts. He and Dr. Hope visited and talked with people who had money, and they caught enthusiasm. President Hope was no expert in making "contacts." He was not skilled in pushing in to see important, busy people. He never slapped backs. First and always he was a reserved, well-mannered gentleman. He had an idea and believed in it profoundly and that proved to be the best way to get money. There was much in common between President Hope and William Rainey Harper of Chicago in raising money.

President Hope had, all of his life, worked with inadequate funds. The generous contributions for the new buildings were something new. For once he did not have to skimp and improvise. The architect, James Gamble Rogers, had built the distinguished new buildings at Yale and other American universities. He found in President Hope a rare understanding and appreciation of architectual planning. They became friends and worked together as fellow artists in outlining one of the most dignified and beautiful academic plants among American colleges. These buildings seem to me to have a quality superior to those at Yale. They were the work of a great architect and a sensitive, imaginative client.

As I look at the campus now, I am sure that Mr. Rogers gave form to President Hope's inspiration and vision. In such a situation an able architect can do his best work. Great architecture is primarily a thing of the spirit. President Hope's spirit is embodied in the physical plant of Atlanta University as definitely as it is in the men who were his students in the old Morehouse days.

***

If one could use a single word that would characterize him, it would probably be some form of the word excellent; his clothes were of the best material and design; he enjoyed a superior automobile; he appreciated good food; he honored careful, painstaking work. Only the best in the theater, music, and painting interested him. He shrank from that which was shoddy and cheap, as he did filth and cruelty. He lived for--and by--excellence.

His greatness as a person has grown upon me since he left us. I often wonder just what had made him what he was. Occasionally he spoke of stimulating experiences as a boy: his mother; a Negro woman who taught him; a white man of education and culture who had loaned him books and had given him encouragement. It had been a great experience to go from Augusta to Worcester Academy in Massachusetts where there were freedom and great teachers. Brown University had been another satisfying experience and his life-long contacts with Brown, and Brown friends, meant much to him. The whole adventure of the common man in building America stirred his imagination, and in spite of slowness and inconsistencies, he felt that American life at its best was the finest thing humanity had ever striven to work out.

Segregation never looked shabbier and more indefensible than when applied to him. Superficial people often wondered why President Hope had not "passed" when he left Brown University. He did pass, in the only real way it could be done, by refusing to be confined within the narrow limits of the segregated society where he happened to work. He rose completely above racial, regional, and even national boundaries and lived as a free spirit in fellowship with the best minds of his time--and of all times.

d. Roles and Activities of Black Women

As a part of the northern migration, of course, women were also involved. Many of the first wave of migrants were especially recruited to work in domestic service. A part of the interest of the National Urban League was to provide protection for and prevent the exploitation of these black women, as the Association for the Protection of Colored Women was one of the agencies who coalesced to form the League.

Frances A. Kellor, then General Director of the Inter-Municipal Committee on Household Research of New York, reports the circumstances of the recruitment of black women as domestics and the need for an agency, such as hers, to provide for the protection of their industrial needs.

Document 22

Frances A. Kellor, "Assisted Emigration from the South," Charities, Vol. 15, October 7, 1905, pp. 11-14.

Scene, at the Old Dominion dock, New York:

> "What foh yo dun ask me whar am I going? I'se going to work for a lady in Sufhamton."
>
> "Have you any money or do you know the way?"
>
> "Dis yare ticket taks me and I doan need no help. Dis yere Sufhamton is right here in dis Noo York."

Such interviews take place, often many times a day, at the wharves, and stations, during the season when large numbers of Negro women are brought North to take positions in households, summer hotels, and the like. Many, many women arrive, thinking they are to remain in New York, when their only offer of employment is in some far away place. Others come thinking their steamship ticket will take them to their destination, and have made no provision for street-car fare or baggage transportation; still others, expecting their employers to meet them. Some come with one address, when in many instances the friends or relatives have removed, while in many others the addresses represent unsafe places for women to go. My readers would scarcely believe me if I were to give the percentage of the four hundred women directed and helped this summer, who took the long journey from Georgia, the Carolinas, or Virginia without one cent of money, who look upon New York as the haven of all good things, and who believed that they would be able to reach their destination by a five minutes' walk.

We hear it said that the Negroes are "wild to come Norf." In a sense this is true, but the great class of laborers--the household, hotel, and boarding-house workers--who are most in need of protection, cannot come without assistance, and many who have scarcely dreamed of the North have this assistance placed before them as a temptation. What is this assistance, which directly and indirectly is responsible for a large percentage of women who comes North? It comes from three sources: 1--Friends and relatives who write them to come, but often fail to meet them. 2--Northern employers who deal directly with Southern employment agents or work through friends who urge Negro women to come North. These are for the most part honest employers, but many fail to provide more than the actual transportation, so that the hapless employees often are without money for food on the journey, and have no resources if the employer fails to meet them or decides she does not want them. 3--The employment agents who bring them North under promises of good employment, high wages, and other extravagant representations. This article deals with the industrial causes and must be limited to the influences of the last two.

So great is the demand for general houseworkers and so small the supply, that Northern housewives are willing to let unknown, unseen, untrained and unvouched-for workers enter their homes. At the same time many of these same employers are expecting to receive a skilled, energetic, willing worker. In the first place, the training of the Negro worker in the southern home, so radically different from the northern, does not adequately fit her for her duties in the North. In the second place, many small deceptions are practiced. The agent whom she patronizes sends North not only incompetent workers, but many women who are old, weak, or otherwise unable to compete under the industrial conditions of New York, or any other northern city. But not only this. Misrepresentations are made as to the kind and amount of work, the wages to be paid, and many girls are en route to some little suburban place as dull as their own town, when they think they are to stay in the glare of the city which has been the main inducement. What is the result in many cases? Some refuse to take the places offered. One girl came on the promise of a nurse's position only to be offered general housework. Another came with the expectation of being a lady's maid, and found the position was on a farm and part of the work was milking cows! Others take the places, but are dismissed because of incompetency, etc. A result is that the cities thus get a group of unemployed who are strangers often without resources, and who must find other employment, or drift into immorality, for there are always sharks watching women who are placed in such helpless conditions. The picture thus drawn representing many women each year, is not a belief, it is not an estimate; it is a practical problem, which those working among Negroes are endeavoring to meet. Without question there are many good places open to household workers, but so long as they are brought North by a selfish, irresponsible employer class, which is comfortably ignorant of, or has no conscience about, methods which rob and mislead the girls on the way to their homes, and even lead them astray, just so long will the housekeepers find them a "shiftless, ungrateful lot," unfitted for their positions. There is no doubt that the Negro is the main American source of supply for general houseworkers, and will be available when housewives give their support to methods which will bring them North under safe conditions, and uncorrupted by these employment agents as to wages, truth telling, capacity, morality and honesty. To-day not more than one-half ever reach the households in which they are intending to work.

The Combination System North and South

A combination system of northern and southern employment agencies, which has such a power for good, too often at present uses methods of robbery and fraud, unrestrained by any federal or state laws, or by a public opinion awake to their methods. There is no question but that many of these agents render good service and that without them the dearth of houseworkers would be much greater; but at present little or no protection is afforded women by the agents whose property they become. The southern states, especially Virginia and Georgia, are honey-combed with the slick agents of these employment bureaus, who not only gather the workers from the fields and very dooryards of their southern mistresses, but resort even to brass bands to get them into line so they can be talked into going north. Without money often, some with their little belongings done up in pillow cases, or carpet sacks, many gaudily and poorly dressed, with no other friend than the agent--they come to be shipped.

When they reach the agencies at Savannah, Norfolk and other ports, three things--good wages, easy work (really nothing to do), and good times, are promised to them. To them, going to Philadelphia or to New York seems like going to Heaven, where the streets will be paved with gold, and all will be music and flowers! While these visions are still bright, they sign an innocent looking contract. This contract binds the employment agency to pay their fare. In return, they agree to work one or two months without pay after they arrive. They further agree that their baggage shall be taken to the northern employment agency to which they are going; also that if they cannot redeem it at the end of two months it goes by default to the employment agent. Most of them never read this contract, nor is it explained to them. This is all the southern agency does--gathers the women up, gets the contract signed, pays the fare and puts them aboard the boat with but one address. Many of them are told that their steamship tickets include meals, and find this is not true, and being without money, endure the entire journey without food.

The Newcomer, the Shark and the Agency Runner

The steamships dock at the New York and Philadelphia ports. Scores of eager Negro women pour forth, and they find, what? Not the promised golden land, but ugly docks looking out to an unknown country, and, instead of friendly faces, agency runners and sharks. Their baggage, the property of the agent, goes to the agency, and they, also the property of the agent, follow to a lodging-house which he runs in connection with the agency, or which some friend of his runs. There they wait until a position is offered. If they have money, often no places are offered until their small fund is spent for board; if they have not, they are in danger of yielding to the easy, evil life held out for them.

The woman who has left her happy-go-lucky, cheerful life in the South, a splendid cook, a good servant, perhaps, faces an entirely new condition in the North, for the northern home is like an unexplored country in its appointments and methods. Be it said to the credit of some agencies that they do bring many Negro women North with the intention of sending them to honest homes to work. But the woman who proves inefficient; or who will not take the position offered; or who cannot meet the conditions of the northern home; or who has come on promises of twice the wages which she can earn and insists that she must have them; or who has come on the promise of one thing and is offered another--these the agent turns loose upon the city, perhaps to find their way into hospitals, almshouses, and prisons.

But there are agencies--many of them--that never intend to send women to honest places. When the newcomers are safely in the agency lodging-house, the runners or "friends" of the agency show them the "sights of the town," usually ending up with concert halls; and after such evenings the Negro woman may have lost her chance for honest work. A few days of sight-seeing, during which time she lodges at the agency, and she finds that she owes not only her fare, but from $17 to $20, for she learns in New York that this sum is the price for her transportation and agent's commission--almost four times the regular fare, which is $5. In some agencies she cannot even open her trunk without permission from the agent, and she must work two months without pay. To whom can she turn? The agent tells her she may leave her trunk without charge, taking only the little she needs, until she sees if she will like the place. At the end of two months, she calls for her trunk and finds fifty cents a week or month is the charge for storage. She has earned no money during those weeks, because of the terms of her contract with the agent; so she forfeits all her possessions. There is cunning in this arrangement! By keeping the girl's baggage and permitting her to use it at the agency the agent holds her indefinitely in his power. He always knows where she is, he places her when she is out of work, or takes her away from one employer for another; he even compels her to give names and addresses of her southern friends, so that he may write to them to come North using her name as an inducement.

Associations for the Protection of Negro Women Organized

The cities of New York and Philadelphia contain some eighty Negro agencies, and of this number about forty are bringing up southern Negro women under these conditions. There are also some dozen white agencies which bring them under no better conditions, and with no better intentions. The first remedy lies in compelling these agencies to adopt better methods of protection, or in driving the hopelessly unscrupulous ones out of business.

At the time of these investigations, there existed no organization primarily interested in the industrial problems of Negro women. For this reason the Inter-Municipal Committee on Household Research has been the means of organizing associations for the protection of Negro women in Philadelphia and New York. These organizations include both Negroes and whites. They first placed at the docks women agents who have directed more than four hundred and fifty women during the summer. These will be visited this fall in their new places of employment, the desire being to maintain a friendly interest in them. Penniless women have been taken to destinations; lost addresses have been found; the sick have been cared for and lodgings found for others; addresses of disreputable houses, which many green southern Negroes have held, have been investigated and the women induced to go elsewhere; in a few instances girls have been rescued from disreputable agency sharks and disorderly places, sometimes with the necessary aid of the authorities. One of the methods is for expressmen to get the baggage of these poor women at the docks, and then insist on the girls going to their address in order to reclaim the things.

The question is not only one of rescue, but to provide lodging and work. In Philadelphia an attractive new home has been opened at 714 South Seventeenth Street, where such women may stay while waiting for work. In New York no new home has been found necessary, for use has been made of the Colored Mission, the Young Women's Christian Association, in Brooklyn, the White Rose Home and others. The finding of employment has been entrusted to the agent, or to the employment agencies which maintain the standard required by the association but as soon as endowments can be secured these associations mean to start their own employment agencies so that they can exert a more permanent influence upon the women who are strangers in the cities.

Besides the direct rescue and industrial work, these associations are undertaking co-operative and educational work. To make the protection of migrating Negro women effective, there must be a system including Baltimore, Washington, Richmond, and Savannah, so that women going from one city to another can be sent through, and communication established among the cities. The associations therefore are concentrating their winter's work upon such organizations in these cities, endeavoring to bring about systematic methods of finding work for Negro women by existing organizations and a start is being made to secure protective legislation so much needed in the states from which the women are sent north.

Educational work has been taken up in connection with Hampton Institute and with various pastors and churches. Large numbers of circulars describing the conditions have been distributed through the southern states; ministers are preaching upon it; and efforts are being made to safeguard the girls before leaving. To give the women before coming the knowledge necessary for them to take care of themselves, to guide them at the stations, to send them to and provide safe lodgings, to find them work, or to send them back if they cannot compete under the industrial conditions in the North, this is the pressing, practical work of these associations. They have cared for four hundred and fifty women this summer at a per capita cost of about eighty cents.

Apart from the specific needs of unskilled migrant female labor, black women created, or continued, various organizations, collectively feeling the need to organize to deal with a broad range of welfare problems on a national scale. These women, for the most part of superior educational advantage, often educators or professional women themselves, worked assiduously in their local communities in the interest of promoting the social welfare of blacks. We have often noted, for example, the work of Mrs. Lugenia Hope in the Neighborhood Union, Atlanta, and her counterpart is found in many other cities. Outstanding women in education were also prominent in national women's club work. Mary McLeod Bethune and Charlotte Hawkins Brown, both founders of educational institutions, assumed leadership in this generation over programs activated in previous generations by women such as Lucy Laney. In many cases, these women, and others less illustrious, were the wives of prominent professional men, such as Elizabeth Ross Haynes, wife of George Edmund Haynes, who was the first secretary for colored work on the national board of the Y. W. C. A.; Mrs. Addie W. Hunton, also important in Y. W. C. A. affairs, was the wife of W. A. Hunton, the first International Secretary of the Y. M. C. A. for Colored Men. Many of these women had been classmates, educated in the colleges of the South; they tended to know each other socially as well as professionally. They organized the Greek Letter sororities and the National Council of Negro Women, and all the multiplicity of clubs which did social welfare work on local and state as well as national levels.

In the excerpts of this chapter of Emmett J. Scott's history of black participation in World War I, Alice Dunbar Nelson reports on the activities of black women in organizations such as the Y. W. C. A., the American Red Cross, and the Colored Nurses Association.

Document 23*

Alice Dunbar Nelson, "Negro Women in War Work," Chapter XXVII, The American Negro in the World War, by Emmett J. Scott. Published by Author, 1919, pp. 376-392.

The problem of the woman of the Negro race was a peculiar one. Was she to do her work independently of the women of the other race, or was she to merge herself into their organizations?

*Reprinted by permission.

There were separate regiments for Negro soldiers; should there be separate organizations for relief work among Negro women? If she joined relief organizations, such as the Red Cross Society, and worked with them, would she be assured that her handiwork would reach black hands on the other side of the world, or should she be great-hearted and give her service, simply for the sake of giving, not caring who was to be benefited? Could she be sure that when she offered her services she would be understood as desiring to be a help, and not wishing to be an associate? As is usually the case when any problem presents itself to the nation at large, the Negro faces a double problem should he essay a solution--the great issue and the lesser problem of racial adjustment to that issue.

However, the women of the race cut the Gordian knot with magnificent simplicity. They offered their services and gave them freely, in whatsoever form was most pleasing to the local organizations of white women. They accepted without a murmur the place assigned them in the ranks. They placed the national need before the local prejudice; they put great-heartedness and pure patriotism above the ancient creed of racial antagonism. For pure, unalloyed unselfishness of the highest order, the conduct of the Negro women of the United States during the world war stands out in splendid relief, a lesson to the entire world of what womanhood of the best type really means.

Colored Women and the Red Cross

At the very beginning of the war, the first organization to which the women of the country naturally turned was the Red Cross Society. It was to be expected that the colored woman, preeminently the best nurse in the world, would necessarily turn to the Red Cross Society as a field in which to exercise her peculiar gifts. Red Cross branches were organized in practically every community in the country. Yet it is extremely difficult to tell just what the contribution of the colored woman has been to this organization. We are told that, "The American Red Cross during the war enlisted workers without regard to creed or color and no separate records were maintained of the work of any particular Auxiliary. We know that some eight million women worked for the Red Cross in one way or another during the war, but we have no figures indicating how many of them were colored."

In the Northern cities the colored women merged their identity in their Red Cross work with the white women, that is, in some northern cities. In others, and in the South, they formed independent units, auxiliaries to the local branches presided over by the women of the other race. These auxiliaries sent hundreds of thousands of knitted garments to the front, maintained restaurants, did canteen service where they could; sent men from the local draft boards to the camps with comfort kits; in short, did all that could be done--all that they were allowed to do.

But the story of the colored woman and the Red Cross is not

altogether a pleasant one. Unfortunately, her activities in this direction were considerably curtailed in many localities. There were whole sections of the country in which she was denied the privilege of doing canteen service. There were other sections in which canteen service was so managed as to be canteen service in name only. Local conditions, racial antipathies, ancient prejudices militated sadly against her usefulness in this work. To the everlasting and eternal credit of the colored woman be it said that, in spite of what might have been absolute deterrents, she persisted in her service and was not downcast in the face of difficulties.

The best part of the whole situation lies in the fact that in the local organizations of the Red Cross the Negro woman was the beneficiary. The Home Nursing classes and the classes in Dietetics not only served to strengthen the morale of the women engaged therein, but raised the tone of every community in which they were organized. This was shown during the influenza epidemic of 1918, when a panic-stricken nation called upon its volunteer nurses of every race and color, and the women of the Red Cross were ready in response and in training.

Theodore Roosevelt has said, "All of us who give service and stand ready for sacrifice, are the torch-bearers. We run with the torches until we fall, content if we can then pass them to the hands of other runners." If that be the case, the gray chapter of the colored nurses in overseas service is a golden one. Early in 1918 the Government issued a call for nurses. The need was great overseas; it was greater at home. Colored women since the inception of the war had felt keenly their exclusion from overseas service. The need for them was acute; their willingness to go was complete; the only thing that was wanted was authoritative sanction. In June, 1918, it was officially announced that the Secretary of War had authorized the calling of colored nurses in the national service. It was an act that did more complete justice to our people, in enfranchising our women for this noble service than any other of the war. All colored nurses who had been registered by the American Red Cross Society were thus given the right to render service to their own race in the army. Colored nurses were assigned to the base hospitals at Camp Funston, Kansas; Camp Grant, Rockford, Illinois; Camp Dodge, Des Moines, Iowa; Camp Taylor, Louisville, Kentucky; Camp Sherman, Chillicothe, Ohio, and Camp Dix, Wrightstown, New Jersey. At these camps a total of about 38,000 colored troops were located.

The Service of Colored Nurses

Colored people throughout the country felt deep satisfaction over this authorization of the enrollment of colored nurses at the base hospitals and camps. Hundreds of competent colored nurses had registered their names for many months with the Nursing Division of the American Red Cross, in the hope of finally securing positions where their skill and experience could be utilized to proper advantage. These last were particularly gratified over the happy turn of affairs. At the convention of the National Association of Colored Graduate Nurses held at St. Louis, Missouri, a formal message of appreciation was sent to the War Department, the American Red Cross Society, and other agencies that had been instrumental in pushing their claims.

Mrs. Adah B. Thomas, R. N., president of the National Association of Graduate Nurses, attached to the staff of the Lincoln Hospital and Home in New York City, gave a typical expression of the sentiment of the colored nurses and the colored people generally with reference to the admission of colored women to this branch of service. Indianapolis, Indiana, sent a contingent for active service at once. Elizabeth Miller of Meharry College, Nashville, Tennessee, answered the Government call and was assigned to duty at a nitrate plant in Alabama.

These were but sporadic instances indicating the instant response to the long-waited call to service. Unfortunately, before any considerable change in existing circumstances surrounding this branch of service could be made, the Armistice was signed and history will never know what the colored woman might have done on the battlefields of France as a Red Cross Nurse. Rumor, more or less authentic, states that over 300 nurses were on the battlefields, though their complexion disguised their racial identity.

Young Women's Christian Association

Of the remedial agencies at work for the relief of humanity, and the shouldering of responsibility for the health, morals, and happiness of those also working for the relief of humanity, the Young Women's Christian Association in its operation among the colored girls, women, and men stands out pre-eminently. The reason for this is not hard to seek--the qualities of personality in the leader of this work among colored women, Miss Eva D. Bowles.

At the time the country faced the possibility of war, the National Board of the Young Women's Christian Association was confronted with the great responsibility of helping to safeguard the moral life of women and girls as affected by war conditions. Request came from the United States War Department Commission on Training Camp Activities and from the Young Men's Christian Association, for women workers to undertake work among girls in communities adjacent to army and navy training camps. Hence the formation of the War Work Council. It was organized in June, 1917, with a membership of 100, its function to help meet the special needs of girls and young women in all countries affected by the war. Allied with this was the Junior War Work Council, and the Patriotic League. The extension of these activities among colored girls and women was simultaneous, and one of the brightest chapters in the story of women in the war is the one which records how this work measured up to the responsibilities laid upon it.

The War Work Council of the Young Women's Christian Association, recognizing the loyalty and the need of the colored women and girls of the country, devoted $400,000 of its 1918 budget to the work among the colored girls. When it was organized there was one colored National Secretary and sixteen associations or communities, with nine paid workers. The great demand for a better morale among girls of the country soon raised that number to twelve National workers, three field supervisors, and forty-two centers, with sixty-three paid workers.

There were opened up in the various camps fifteen hostess houses with complete staffs of colored women. These houses served a splendid purpose. When the War Department planned the great training camps it may not have remembered the women of the country in the stress of making up the army of men, or it may have thought that if it said that there were to be no women in the camps, there would be none. But every woman knows that as long as there is a path to the camps, that path the women will follow; be it on foot, by boat, in cars, trains, trolleys, motor cars, or on horseback; and if there be no trail, the women will blaze one. They must see if their men are ill, or living, and how they are living. If they are ill, they must get to them; if homesick, they must cheer them; if they are leaving for overseas, they must say goodby to them. And if there are none of their own, they must be charitable enough to extend their good-will to the lonely and heart-hungry of others.

Hence the birth of the Hostess House idea, a bit of home in the camps, a place of rest and refreshment for the women folks belonging to the soldiers; a sheltering chaperonage for the too enthusiastic girl; a dainty supplement to the stern face of the camp-life of the soldiers; an information bureau for women and soldiers alike; a clearing-house for the social activities which included the men in camps and their women visitors.

As the colored troops came into the camps in large numbers, there was an urgent appeal to meet the needs of their women. The first house to be opened was at Camp Upton, when the "Buffaloes" (367th) were being made into the crack regiment that it afterward became; Mrs. Hannah C. Smith, the pioneer among the Hostess House leaders, going there to take charge in the early part of November, 1917. Only great enthusiasm and faith in the value of the work to be done could have brought about the results which Mrs. Smith achieved at Camp Upton at this time. The temporary headquarters for the hostess house were in a barracks with few conveniences and almost no possibilities. Mrs. Smith, with her co-worker, Mrs. Norcomb, soon made the place as homelike as possible. This was the beginning of the Hostess House work for colored women.

In no great while Hostess Houses in seven of the large camps were in operation and others soon followed. In some camps, where there was a definite surety, work was begun in the barracks. From many Southern camps came the request for the immediate erection of houses on an insufficient plan, but these plans were rejected. Finally, in the natural progress that came, the houses were erected, and used the same as other Hostess Houses. The relationship of the staff to the whole staff of the camp developed into an ideal, and all groups working under the general tutelage of the Young Women's Christian Association understood each other and had a better appreciation of mutual problems by working together.

The Y. W. C. A. and War Industries

As the war progressed, our colored girls were taken into almost every phase of the industrial field. It was then recognized early in the work that the success of the movement depended largely upon the correct interpretation of the colored girl to her employer and her white co-worker, and of a fair, just attitude of the white worker toward the colored girl. The war opened up many avenues of employment and service to the colored girls that had not hitherto been her privilege to accept, principally in the industrial field, and with the opening up of these new lines of work, new problems were developed; consequently there came a demand for women to go into localities where factories were located, to make investigations as to working conditions, housing and recreational facilities; to create a better understanding between the employer and employee, and to assist in the opening up of new opportunities for work. As a result of this, an industrial worker was placed at such vital points as Detroit, St. Louis, Louisville, East St. Louis, Nitro, West Virginia; Penniman, Virginia, and Philadelphia, with one appointed for Baltimore, and an acute situation in Washington cared for.

Not only was there need for the care and protection of the girl in the factory, but equally as much so for those in more social communities. This led to the development of club and recreational centers especially in cities near which camps were located. To-day, these centers reach from New York to Los Angeles, California, and from St. Paul, Minnesota to San Antonio, Texas. These clubs and recreational centers are also an important feature in industrial communities.

Splendid Colored Women Workers

Not only in groups, but as individuals, the women felt the call of this great and important work, and responded from every walk of life. There were many offers of volunteer service, and Miss Mary Cromwell, of Washington, D. C., was one of those to offer. She spent the summer at Camp Dix as a volunteer information and emergency hostess, and completed her two months of observation and service, feeling that there was an imperative need for the workers to be able to differentiate between types of people and to deal with each type scientifically as well as sympathetically; to know enough about such things as Home Service, War Risk Insurance, Protective Agencies, and Allotments, to answer any question that might be asked.

Miss Cromwell was well fitted both by training and experience for her work. As an undergraduate at Ann Arbor, she spent her summers in New York doing special investigations for the Charity Organization Society. After graduating, she became a teacher in the Dunbar High School of Washington, and there she became interested in the Washington alleys, and opened a settlement in one of the most congested districts. Later, she received her "master's degree" from the University of Pennsylvania for special research work in psychology.

The arduous task of directing the work of the Industrial Section of the War Work Council was given over to Miss Mary E. Jackson, as Special Industrial Worker among Colored Women for the War Work Council. She was appointed in December, 1917. Prior to that time, Miss Jackson did statistical work in the Labor Department of the State of Rhode Island.

Associated with Miss Bowles in this War Work Council of Colored Women as heads of departments in addition to Miss Mary E. Jackson, were Miss Crystal Bird, girls' worker; Mrs. Vivian W. Stokes, who at one time was associated with the National Urban League and assisted in making a survey of New York City in connection with the Urban League of New York (Mrs. Stokes' work in connection with the Room Registry work has already been mentioned); Mrs. Lucy B. Richmond, special worker for town and country; Miss Mabel S. Brady, recruiting secretary in the Personnel Bureau; Miss Juliette Dericotte, special student worker; Mrs. Cordelia A. Winn, formerly a teacher in the public schools of Columbus, Ohio; Mrs. Ethel J. Kindle, special office worker. Miss Josephine V. Pinyon was appointed a special war worker in August, 1917. She is a graduate of Cornell University, a former teacher, and a student Y. W. C. A. secretary from 1912 to 1916.

The field workers were Mrs. Adele Ruffin, South Atlantic Field, appointed in October, 1917. Mrs. Ruffin was a teacher for some years at Kittrell College, and then secretary of the Y. W. C. A. branch at Richmond, Virginia. Miss May Belcher had charge of the South Central field and Miss Maria L. Wilder of the Southwestern field. Miss Elizabeth Carter was loaned to the Association work by the Board of Education of New Bedford, Massachusetts, where she is the only colored teacher in the city. She is chairman of the Northeastern Federation of Colored Women's Clubs, and former president of the National Association of Colored Women's Clubs. She was placed in charge of the center in Washington, D. C.

Aside from these, there was a small army of club and recreation workers, Hostess House workers, industrial workers, and supervisors. Throughout the trying ordeal of directing the work of these assistants, and meeting the huge problems presented to the council, Miss Bowles remained perhaps the most effective and achieving, and at the same time, noiseless worker among the colored women in this country.

Women's Division, Council of National Defense

The Council of National Defense made the best organized attempt at mobilizing the colored women of all the war organizations. In most Northern states it was felt that separate organizations were superfluous, yet, on the other hand, in many cases it was agreed that the work could be best served by distinct units. There were many ramifications to the work of the Council of Defense; registration of women, the weighing and measuring of babies, the establishment of milk stations, health and recreation centers, supervision of women in industry, correlation with other war organizations. Different states excelled in different phases of the work. In the establishment of Child Welfare and the conservation of infancy Alabama seems to be the banner state, the best work emanating from Tuskegee, where the examination of infants was under the care of Mrs. J. W. Whitaker. At Birmingham, Alabama, Mrs. H. C. Davenport had charge of the activities of the Council and was particularly successful in the establishment of Community houses at two great industrial centers, Acipco and Bessemer. In the first community, where the managers of the plant had established a model village with community house and all forms of Community life, the entire program of the Council of Defense was carried through, conservation of children, attention to health and recreation, with a very strong emphasis on food conservation. In the latter instance, a Community house established in the heart of the village of Bessemer concentrated on child welfare, food conservation, and war gardens.

Service in Various States

Two women in Florida stand out as doing yeoman service under the work of the Women's Committee of the Council of Defense. Mrs. Mary McLeod Bethune, who at Daytona, where her splendid school is situated, pushed forward the work of the Emergency Circle, Negro War Relief, and Miss Eartha White, the State Chairman of the Colored Woman's Section of the Council of Defense. Under her direction, Florida was organized into excellent working units, with a particular concentration on a Mutual Protection League for Working Girls, who had taken up the unfamiliar work of elevator girls, bell girls in hotels, and chauffeurs. From this it was not far to a Union of Girls in Domestic Service, a by-product of war conditions that might well be continued in every city and hamlet of the country.

In Colorado, the women formed themselves into a Negro Women's Auxiliary War Council, a Negro Women's League for Service, and a Red Cross Auxiliary, all apparently working under the general management of the Council of Defense. In Georgia, the president of the Georgia State Federation of Colored Women's Clubs, Mrs. Alice Dugged Carey of Atlanta, reported organizations in Tallapoosa County, a community canning center in Bremen, Coweta, and Cobb Counties, with other organizations in every important city. The Illinois women, organized into a Committee on Colored Women, worked in cooperation with the Urban League for training Negro Women.

Delaware did not have a separate organization of the Council of Defense, but the race was represented on the State Committee, and through them work was carried on. Mrs. Blanche W. Stubbs, president of the City Federation of Christian Workers, represented the women, and through her efforts the usual classes in food conservation were established at the Thomas Garrett Settlement, while a baby-weighing station was established, and a public nurse appointed.

The work in Indiana was carried on by a separate division, largely directed by the State President of Colored Women's Clubs, Mrs. Gertrude B. Hill. Kentucky, with no special woman's division, specialized on the protection of girls. The best work done in Louisiana was in the conservation of children through the weighing and measuring of babies, and in the effective registration of the women and the conservation of food.

Maryland did some splendid and effective work under the direction of Miss Ida Cummings, the State Chairman of the Colored Women's Committee. Practically every phase of the inclusive program mapped out by the Council of Defense was carried through and a public-speaking class at the Bowie Summer School was most successful. Mississippi was organized by Miss Sallie Green, of Sardis, into eleven sections, corresponding with a similar organization among the white women, with good work done in child conservation at Jackson. Mrs. Victoria Clay Haley saw to it that Missouri did effective work. Colored women in North Carolina merged their war activities into one, and were most successful in training camp activities, the War Camp Community Service maintaining an interesting work at Charlotte. In Portland, Oregon, the Rosebud Study Club, as was the case with so many clubs, turned its attention to knitting and a practical study of food conservation. In Columbia, South Carolina, the Phyllis Wheatly Club opened a community center to be used as a clearing-house for war activities, welcoming all organizations to work within its walls--Y. W. C. A. , Red Cross, War Camp Community Service, and Council of Defense.

In Tennessee, Mrs. Cora Burke, of Knoxville, had a successful work; registration of nurses was particularly complete. The colored women of Nashville had a tag day to raise funds for their Branch Council of National Defense. Virginia concentrated on food conservation and the Children's Year, with most successful war gardens. A Colored Woman's Volunteer League was organized at Newark, New Jersey, as a branch of the Mayor's committee, of the Woman's Committee of the Council of National Defense, Mrs. Amorel Cook, president. This league established a canteen and specialized on making soldiers feel at home.

War Problems of Living

The problems of living, made by the war, which were solved sometimes in whole, sometimes in part by the Woman's Committee of National Defense, were many and various. For instance there was the shifting of the percentage of women in the rural population particularly in the South, the same condition which was met in the North in industrial plants. The employment of women in the cotton fields was as great a problem in its way as the mass of girlhood in the Northern mills. This employment of the women could not but react upon the child, with a consequent lowering of child vitality and raising of infant mortality. It was this condition which the Council of Defense tried to meet, and to forestall the inevitable problems of reconstruction. Hence the establishment of stations where babies were weighed, measured, tested, and placed under weekly supervision with competent nurses in charge. Perhaps the various units did not always accomplish this end, but it was an ideal worth striving for.

"The Lure of the Khaki"

One of the fundamental problems of the War--no new one but suddenly aggravated by the abnormal atmosphere and excitement accompanying the presence of large numbers of soldiers--was that of the relationship of the young girl and the soldier. What has been called "the lure of the khaki" is but an expression on the part of the girl of her admiration for the spirit of the men who are willing to give their lives, if need be, in the defense of their country. How to win this feeling into the right channels was one of the problems of the women in the war. It was met by two organizations, the Young Women's Christian Association, of which we have spoken, and the War Camp Community Service. It was the duty of the latter organization to recreate home ties for enlisted men in cities adjacent to training camps.

It was in providing this home atmosphere that the War Camp Community Service was most successful. Entertainment was developed for the colored soldiers; concessions let for poolrooms, picture shows, canteens and cafeterias in connection with the work. But where the War Camp Community Service was most successful was in the chaperoned dances, given at the clubrooms. Here "the lure of the khaki" might find conventional self-expression. The largest of the Negro Community Service Clubs were in Des Moines, Iowa; Battle Creek, Michigan; Louisville, Kentucky; Chillicothe, Ohio; Charlotte, North Carolina; Petersburg and Newport News, Virginia; Washington, D. C.; Baltimore, Maryland; Atlanta, Georgia; Montgomery, Alabama; and Columbia, South Carolina.

This working together for a common purpose is resulting in building up a new community consciousness among our own people and in turning our thoughts to community projects of a permanent nature....

The Circle for Negro War Relief

Time and time again it was borne upon the inner consciousness of the women of the race that though the various organizations for war relief were doing all tnat was humanly possible for the soldiers of both races, they were inadequate for all the needs of the Negro soldier and his family. There were avenues open for more extensive relief; there were places as yet untouched by any organization; there were programs of direct War Relief and Constructive Relief work which needed to be carried out and some separate organization for this work was an imperative necessity. So the Circle of Negro War Relief came into existence in November, 1917. The leading spirit in this movement was Mrs. Emily Bigelow Hapgood, the president, and associated around her were the best minds of the country, white and colored. The Circle was incorporated, and dedicated itself to the purpose of promoting the welfare of Negro soldiers and their dependent families as they might be affected by the emergencies of war.

The success of this Circle was immediate and phenomenal. Within a few months, sixty "units" were formed, extending from New York to Utah, to the far South, throughout the East, and middle West. Each unit dedicated itself in its particular locality to the relief of some vital need either in the Community or in some nearby camp. For instance Ambulance Unit of N. Y. gave a two-thousand dollar ambulance to Camp Upton. Unit No. 29 in St. Helena, South Carolina, not only did the usual war knitting and letter writing, but during the influenza epidemic formed itself into a health committee in cooperation with the Red Cross.

It would be difficult to give a complete report of the work of all the units. It forms a voluminous mass of interesting and illuminating statistics. The activities of the Circle ranged from the making of comfort kits to the furnishing of chewing gum to the soldiers; from the supplying of victrolas and records to the introduction of Theodore Roosevelt, Irvin Cobb and Needham Roberts at Carnegie Hall; from the giving of Christmas trees in Harlem to Southern dinners for the home-sick boys in Augusta, Georgia; from contributions of air-cushions from Altoona, Pennsylvania, to the issuing of educational pamphlets on the subject of the Negro soldier.

The Circle of Negro War Relief and the Crispus Attucks Circle organized in Philadelphia in March, 1918, constituted the nearest approach to a Red Cross or other organization of this character through which the colored people cooperated during the war. The Crispus Attucks Circle did for Philadelphia what the Circle of Negro War Relief did for New York. Its name fitly commemorated the first Negro who gave up his life to help make "the world safe for democracy." The one great project to which it directed all its energies was the attempted establishment in Philadelphia of a base hospital for Negro soldiers, in which Negro physicians and Negro nurses should care for their own.

It may be objected and is frequently a source of controversy that separate hospitals are non-essential. Idle and fallacious reasoning! They are needed in some places as schools, churches and social organizations are needed. A moot question, not to be thrashed out here; merely a remark in passing that the Crispus Attucks Circle saw a need, a vital need, and aimed to fill it. Certainly if every individual in the world saw the vital need in his own particular home circle or community and met that need with joyous service, there would be no more wars. This is what the women of the race have done since April 1917.

As the Circle of Negro War Relief radiated its influence from New York City and the Crispus Attucks Circle concentrated its efforts in Philadelphia, so all over the United States various independent and private organizations for the relief of the soldier came into being. The Soldiers' Comfort Unit of the War Service Center opened headquarters on Massachusetts Avenue, Boston. It was one of hundreds of similar organizations made up of women who instinctively got together to work for the great cause, and who, with a small beginning, found themselves a part of a big work with possibilities only limited by the ability to meet them. In February, 1918, Mrs. H. C. Lewis called together a small group of women who in a week's time supplied an urgent need for knitted garments at Newport News. From this beginning, made with a dozen women, the unit grew into an organization of a hundred and seventy-seven women and eventually connected itself with the Circle of Negro War Relief.

In the first days the work was almost exclusively for the comfort of soldiers, but before many months had passed the scope of the organization had widened to a place of entertainment for the soldiers, visits to hospitals, visits to the nearby camp--Devins, with home-made pies and cakes; liberty sings on Sunday afternoons; lectures on social hygiene and special educational lectures; cooperation with "Company L" auxiliary, and with the Red Cross....

After a year of work the Soldiers' Comfort Unit found itself facing a still larger field, the returning of soldiers coming from scenes of horror and devastation with problems and needs. Like all of the war organizations of the women of the race, they found their work had only just begun.

Woman's Auxiliary of the 15th Regiment

In the early days of the old Fifteenth New York Regiment, when colored men were volunteering as members of the military organization which was to become the first New York State Guard composed of colored men, it occurred to a thoughtful woman of the race, a New Yorker by birth, that earnest colored women banded together could be a potent factor in the life of the regiment.

The idea was carried out, and the Woman's Auxiliary, Fifteenth Regiment, was organized May 2, 1917, with one hundred members. It received its credentials from Colonel William Hayward, May 9. The first definite work undertaken was the investigation of the cases of men whose dependents claimed exemption for them. This was an important factor in the perfect recruiting of the regiment and won commendation from the commanding officer and his official staff.

It is the exclusive privilege of the colored people to adopt the slogan, "No Color Line." It would seem a strange commentary on the magnanimity of the American people to note that those who are the first to adopt the policy of no discrimination are the ones against whom that discrimination is most often practiced. We have noted how in every instance where organizations of colored women have been formed for War Relief there is a definite policy of "No Color Line." Now and then the fact was proclaimed publicly in sign or in motto, as in Boston and by the Josephine Gray Colored Lady Knitters of Detroit, Michigan, who "knitted for all American soldiers regardless of race, color or nationality."

Colored Women in the Loan Drives

But not only in the definite work of relief, in knitting, sewing, care of dependents of soldiers or in the more spectacular forms of war work were the women engaged. The raising of the sinews of war was a problem which the United States faced. Every man, woman and child in the country needed to be taxed to the utmost. How to make the giving a pleasing privilege rather than a doleful duty devolved upon the women of the country. Five Liberty Loan Drives, six Red Cross drives, the constant Thrift Stamp Drive, and a tremendous United War Camp Drive, wherein uncountable billions were spoken of airily, staggered the average mind both in prospect and retrospect. But Americans learned to think in big figures. Every one got the habit of saving; and the purse-strings of America were permanently opened for the relief of the needs of the nation and to aid needy people overseas.

This reaction on the national conscience is of inestimable value. Charity will never again be the perfunctory thing that it was before the Great War. Penury in giving will be frowned down upon as immoral. And this quickening of the national conscience, this loosening of the national purse, is due in no small measure to the fervor and zeal with which the women of the nation threw themselves into the campaigns for filling the war coffers.

As was to be expected, the colored women were foremost in all the financial campaigns. The National Association of Colored Women organized at the very beginning of the war to cooperate in every way with the Woman's Council of Defense. Mrs. Philip North Moore, President of the National Council of Women, says, "No women worked harder than the women of the National Association of Colored Women."

Mrs. Mary B. Talbert, President of the National Association of Colored Women, which has a membership of a hundred thousand, is authority for the statement that in the Third Liberty Loan the colored women of the United States raised about five million dollars. Savannah, Georgia, alone raised a quarter of a million dollars. Poor colored women in a tobacco factory of Norfolk, Virginia, subscribed ninety-one thousand dollars. Macon, Georgia, subscribed about twenty thousand.

The National War Savings Committee appointed colored women to conduct campaigns for the War Savings Committee. One of the most notable of these appointments by the Secretary of the Treasury was that of Mrs. Laura Brown, of Pittsburg. She maintained an office from which whirlwind campaigns emanated, and set a standard of efficiency of organization not easily equaled.

War Work Among Negro Children

One of the most effective ways of reaching the people of any community is through the children. Hence the work of the colored teachers in reaching the race through the children under their care, has been in the highest degree effectual. Throughout the South, in the middle Atlantic states in which there is a separate school system, in the Middle West, and in the Southwest; in public schools, in endowed institutions, in colleges--in short wherever colored teachers are employed to teach colored children, there was a constant and beneficial influence being exerted in the entire race through its children. This influence made for loyalty, patriotism unquestioning and devoted; and particularly did this influence raise the quota of the race's contribution to the National war chest. Colored schools taught by colored teachers sent in every community a pro rata to the Thrift Stamp, Red Cross, United War Campaign, and Liberty Loans in considerable excess of the natural percentage. It would have been easy to have failed just here with the children; it was difficult in many communities to overcome the natural obstacles. But they were overcome. The amounts raised in all National drives through the colored women teachers working with their children, are a monumental credit to the women of the race.

e. Roles and Activities of Black Men

In addition to the National Urban League there were other areas of social welfare activities in which black men assumed leadership roles. Emmett J. Scott reviews some of the contributions of these men and their agencies during World War I.

Document 24*

Emmett J. Scott, "Social Welfare Agencies," Chapter XXVIII, The American Negro in the World War, Published by Author, 1919, pp. 398-408.

(Important Welfare Work of the Young Men's Christian Association and Other Organized Bodies--Negro Secretaries of the Y.M.C.A.--the Problem of Illiteracy in the Camps--The Social Secretaries--Results of Education--The Y.W.C.A. Hostess Houses--The Knights of Columbus--Caring For Returned Soldiers.)

*Reprinted by permission.

Prior to the outbreak of the war it was a well-established fact that the Young Men's Christian Association, the Young Women's Christian Association, the Red Cross, and other organized bodies primarily concerned with the welfare of people in general, had figured so largely in the life of the young men prior to their call to arms that something should be done to enable these agencies to throw around them the same influences under which they came when at home. One of the first efforts, therefore, to provide for the social betterment of the men under arms was to connect these movements officially with the Government, that they might function efficiently in caring for the soldiers at the front. It was observed that the social welfare organizations could adapt themselves as successfully to the needs of men in times of war as in times of peace. At the beginning of the war the War Work Council declared that the same thing done for white men would be done for colored men when in the various cantonments, and while it has been difficult to carry out this letter of the law, for many reasons too tedious to be mentioned, Dr. J. E. Moorland, the Senior Secretary of the Young Men's Christian Association in charge of colored men's work, believes that the Negro has come more nearly to receiving a square deal in this instance than in anything else in the history of the country.

When the unusual appeal was made to the American people, adequate funds were raised to finance the work of the welfare organizations. Nearer to the end of hostilities, however, when a more systematic effort for financing all of these social organizations had to be made, the Government provided that all such agencies should be absorbed by the seven recognized groups, and a national drive for $170,000,000 was made by these organizations, resulting in raising the desired amount. They were therefore at an early period in a position to construct successful machinery for the training of social workers to supply these needs throughout the camps in this country and among the soldiers overseas. While it must be admitted that it was impossible to choose upon such short notice persons who met in every way the requirements for this unusual task, the personnel of the Young Men's Christian Association staff so far as the colored workers were concerned were of a high class.

At the head of this staff, to select and equip for this unusual service the numerous secretaries needed in the camps and cantonments, was Dr. J. E. Moorland, Senior Secretary of the Young Men's Christian Association. Associated with him was Mr. Robert B. DeFrantz, visiting secretary of the Des Moines camp, and formerly engaged in the work at Kansas City, Missouri. There were also the placement secretaries, Mr. William J. Faulkner and Mr. Max Yergan, who after his return from Africa, assisted in recruiting men; Professor Charles H. Wesley of Howard University doing similar work. J. Francis Gregory and George L. Johnson, two specialists in religious work, were later added. The former directed his efforts toward the religious life of the men in the camps, while the latter, a noted tenor, rendered valuable service in his singing.

Negro Secretaries of the Y. M. C. A.

At the beginning of the War Work Council it was decided to send Negro secretaries to care for troops of their own race. There were fifty-five centers or groups in Army camps with Association privileges, served by two hundred and sixty-eight secretaries in the home camps and forty-nine secretaries serving overseas. The grand total of all colored secretaries was three hundred and thirty-one. The buildings in which these secretaries worked were twenty-five "E" type and National Guard buildings. The other centers were housed in barracks, mess halls and tents.

"This work, too," according to Dr. J. E. Moorland, its moving spirit, "was not a haphazard one. It had a definite purpose, promoted by carefully selected specialists. To be more explicit, it is well to describe a staff organization which is responsible for the work in a building. It is composed of a building secretary, who is the executive; a religious work secretary, who has charge of the religious activities, including personal work among the soldiers, Bible class and religious meetings; an educational secretary, who promotes lectures and educational classes, and uses whatever means he may have at hand to encourage intellectual development; a physical secretary, who has charge of athletics and various activities for the physical welfare of the soldiers, works in the closest relationship with the military officers and is often made responsible for all the physical activities in the camp; a social secretary, who promotes the social activities, including entertainment, "stunts" and moving pictures; a business secretary, who keeps close tab on the sale of stamps, postcards, and such supplies as may be handled by the Association, and is held responsible for the proper accounting of finances. In every case these secretaries were thoroughly investigated before being appointed and were required to be members of evangelical churches in good standing, and men capable of commanding the respect of the soldiers with whom they work.

The Problem of Illiteracy

"The large number of illiterates who were brought into the various camps of the country brought with them a tremendous problem. Many of them could not sign the payroll. Some of them did not know the right from the left hand, and not a few were not sure about their names. The Association was able to solve this problem by teaching thousands of men to read and write their names. "Some men after having learned to write their names," says Dr. Moorland, "have actually shouted for joy over the new-found power which at last had released them from the shackles of an oppressive ignorance. Speakers of both races have inspired the men and enlarged their vision. Many men with a better educational equipment have increased their talents by sober thinking along with purposeful programs of reading.

"The religion of the soldiers was not neglected. Hundreds of Bible classes were conducted and religious meetings with purpose were largely attended. The best of both races have been able to give encouragement and helpful messages to the men, many of whom have had their faith strengthened; many others for the first time in their lives accepted the Christian faith. The effort was to give a religious program adapted to the lives of the men and enable them to go overseas and come back fit to look mother, wife, sister, and sweetheart in the face and not be ashamed.

"The emphasis, however, was placed upon life, and speakers were requested to avoid emphasizing death. Although the training in the army camps is physical development to a very marked degree, it was soon learned that there must be a recreational side. The physical director had to meet this need to prevent men from becoming sullen and morose. Baseball games were staged. These proved to be as essential in the matter of self-defense as lectures and private talks on health and the protection of the body against the ravages of every form of vice."

Work of the Social Secretaries

The social secretaries rendered no less a service than the other workers. In providing programs for the entertainment of the men, in presenting interesting moving pictures, in utilizing the talent of various communities near the camps for the needs of the men in camps, they accomplished a task which in the past had seemed impossible. The social secretary, moreover, enabled these men to entertain themselves. The Selective Draft brought together men of all grades, from the most illiterate to the highly trained university graduate, messing together side by side daily. Men who had lived in the atmosphere of vice and those who had been trained in the best Christian homes were thrown together in a common cause, wearing the same uniform, obeying the same orders. In this great mass the social secretary discovered remarkable talent, which was able to provide entertainment for the soldiers in the camps and at certain times for the people outside the camps.

According to Dr. Moorland, the letters of appreciation received from many soldiers for the service rendered by these faithful secretaries sound like a new edition of the Acts of the Apostles. "Not only in France are our men serving. We also have secretaries in East Africa, working with natives and British troops, and their story is that of pioneers laying foundations as Christian statesmen for the building of future manhood in that great continent; for they are serving men representing tribes from all parts of the continent of Africa, and these men are learning what unselfish service means as well as, in many cases, learning to read and write in the little evening schools provided for them."

There were thirty-nine official directors, giving their entire attention to directing recreational activities and thirty secretaries who served as song leaders. There were six or more secretaries, physical and social directors, however, to do recreational work and direct singing. It has been estimated that two million men attended these various centers for Negro soldiers every month; that there were two hundred lectures with an attendance of eighty a month; ten thousand scriptures circulated every month; nine thousand personal interviews; seven thousand Christian decisions; eleven thousand war roll singers; one hundred and twenty-five thousand taking part in physical activities; five hundred motion picture exhibitions with an attendance of three hundred thousand; 1,250,000 letters written, and $110,000 worth of money orders sold.

Important Results of Education

Out of such unusual efforts to educate, in fact to remake, the enlisted man, came important results. The Negro soldier was brought, so to speak, from a sequestered vale into the broad light of modern times, where various agencies which have constituted a leverage in the elevation of men gave him during these few months more opportunity for mental improvement than he had experienced during the other part of his life. Thousands of men were not only taught to read and write, but also formed the habit of reading good books, which in a short time showed results in the appreciation of higher ideals and in giving them a more intelligent attitude toward life. These agencies, too, operating among the whites and the blacks equally deficient in education during their early careers, tended to promote better relationship between the races and as a result to produce a higher class of men.

The record of these secretaries was highly commendable. First among those to attain recognition was Dr. Geo. W. Cabaniss, of Washington, D. C., known for a long time as the dean of the colored secretaries, a man who had much to do with making possible the camp for the training of the colored officers at Fort Des Moines; and who after the camp had been provided went into the service with them to serve these young men as a Y. M. C. A. secretary. Returning home after they were commissioned, Dr. Cabaniss abandoned his lucrative practice in the city of Washington and went to Camp Meade to serve as a secretary at one of the Y. M. C. A. huts. Being a Christian gentleman, Dr. Cabaniss was especially anxious to look after the morals of the young men, and in the end he was glad to report that the habits in general of the men who came under his supervision were of a very high order, and they exhibited evidences of being men who would make good at the front. Among those who won distinction in reaching men may also be mentioned Matthew W. Bullock, William Stevenson, and J. C. Wright.

Distinguished Service of Supervisors

Some mention should be made also of those men of color who although Y. M. C. A. workers went to France for supervision, to render a larger service than that of the average social worker. Among them were Mr. Max Yergan, President John Hope of Morehouse College, and Dr. H. H. Proctor of the First Congregational Church, Atlanta, Georgia. Mr. Max Yergan had already rendered distinguished service as an earnest worker among the British troops of color in Africa. His work in France, like that of President Hope, was largely that of a field secretary to consider cases of friction, discipline, and general difficulty and to administer affairs which could not be attended to by the staff on this side of the Atlantic. It was only late in the war that Dr. Proctor answered the call to engage in this same work. These gentlemen, in manifesting a spirit of sacrifice and interest in the welfare of the men at the front, not only exhibited examples worthy of emulation, but rendered the race and the country a distinguished service.

The Y. W. C. A. Hostess Houses

The work had not gone forward very far when the peculiar need for a plan by which the wives and daughters of the enlisted men might visit them at camp necessitated the bringing in of women as Y. W. C. A. workers. It was accordingly provided that each of these camps, wherever practicable, should have hostess houses, to be placed in charge of a woman of honor. The hostess house was a means of communication between the enlisted men and their relatives. Here the sweetheart came to say goodbye to her loved one, the wife to see her husband for the last time, and the mother to bid her son farewell. The Y. W. C. A. maintained a colored hostess house in every camp where there were colored soldiers, the plan being the same as that for the white soldiers. The official report states that these houses "are not only hospitality centers, but also demonstrations to visitors of the best ways of entertaining and of serving food. Many men and women are here first brought in contact with high yet simple standards of social intercourse. Each house is a training center for new colored social workers."

The heads of these houses are among the best known women of the race, many of whom have been doing social work of a high type among their people for years. The need for such women, of course, was experienced abroad, but there was much objection to the sending of women of color to the front, just as there had been in the case of barring them from the Red Cross Units. In the course of time, however, this prejudice was overcome and it was possible to send a number of women of color to serve in the hostess houses in France. The first of these to sail was Mrs. Helen Noble Curtis of New York, the widow of the late James L. Curtis, Minister Resident of the United States to Liberia. For a number of years she had been a member of the committee of management of the colored women's branch of the Y. W. C. A. As she had been in France and had learned to speak the language thoroughly, she was much desired for this work.

The appointment of Mrs. Curtis proved to be such a success that another colored secretary was sent over in the following month. This was Mrs. Addie W. Hunton of Brooklyn, New York, widow of the late William A. Hunton, the first International Secretary of the Y. M. C. A. for colored men in America. She is an educated woman of excellent standing and had for a number of years been a moving spirit in Y. W. C. A. work. She had also traveled in Europe, studied at the University of Strasburg, and formed certain connections which enabled her to render the race invaluable service abroad. Mrs. Hunton was soon followed by Miss Kathryn M. Johnson, and later by twelve of more women of the same high character.

Tributes to Y. M. C. A. Workers

"The colored Y. M. C. A. workers here in France," said Ralph W. Tyler,

> working under handicaps, and limited, as to numbers, in proportion to the number of white Y. M. C. A. workers, and considering the proportionate number of colored soldiers in France, have been paid a high tribute by Colonel (now General) W. F. Creary. Writing to Wm. Stevenson, Colored Y. M. C. A. secretary of Hut No. 2, General Creary said:
>
> 'I have seen the workings of your huts along the line, from the front line trenches to the base ports, and have been a personal recipient of the comforts afforded by them on many occasions.
>
> 'I have always been impressed by the zeal with which the secretaries, and others, have prosecuted their work, with untiring energy, and with their valor and bravery, for the work at the front cannot be done except by real red-blooded men.
>
> 'I have been particularly interested in the activities of your huts, devoted exclusively to the interests of colored soldiers since my assumption of the command of this camp, and I congratulate you on the progress you have made, and are making now.
>
> 'Besides the splendid athletic, social and canteen service offered by yourself and your assistants, I have been much impressed by your activities in the educational departments, and have been much pleased to see many of OUR Colored soldiers who have had but few advantages of early education, availing themselves of the advantages offered by you for the acquirement of knowledge of the elementary branches of education.
>
> 'Your thrift department is the means of many of OUR men saving their money and purchasing money orders to send back home, thereby placing their money where it should be.'
>
> Thus far, my only regret is that there were not more colored Y. M. C. A. workers over here to enlarge and spread the splendid work being done by Mrs. Curtis, Mrs. Hunton and Miss Johnson. The right sort of women, fine, big-hearted, devoted colored women, have such a refining influence in camps such as this, and the colored Y. M. C. A. secretaries themselves are anxious for them, and feel that women sent over by the Y. M. C. A., would further

> tend to make camp life for these soldiers ideal, and render easier the disciplinary work of the army.

Early in April, 1919, some ten or twelve additional well-educated, solid, substantial women were selected and sent to France to work among colored soldiers and to supply the need mentioned by Mr. Tyler.

The Knights of Columbus

Another organization was of much service in making Negro soldiers comfortable at the front. This was the Knights of Columbus, a Catholic society, which has to its credit that, unlike the other social welfare organizations operating in the war, it never drew the color line. It provided separate huts for Negroes at some of the camps when special requests to this effect were received. These were recreational buildings, provided with home surroundings for the preparation of which no pains were spared. Such arrangements were made at Camp Meade, Camp Dodge, Camp Funston, Fort Riley, Camp Taylor. As an evidence of the general liberality of the management of the war work conducted by the Knights of Columbus, no better testimony can be given than that by Joseph J. Canavan in a report to the Kansas Plain Dealer.

> Under the system as it now has been working out [says he], the Negro soldier needs no other countersign than his khaki uniform to gain for him every advantage offered by the Knights' service. True there are places both in this country and abroad where the Knights of Columbus have erected special huts for the use of the Negro soldiers, but where that has been done it has been at the express request of the Negro soldiers themselves, who in numerous instances have expressed a preference for a building of their own where they may enjoy their own pleasure in their own way and be assured of meeting their own friends when and where and under circumstances they desired. Similarly the other day [says he], when there were six Negro soldiers in training at Port Jervis, New York, on their way to Goshen, New York, whence they were to start upon their journey to a training camp, it was a group of Knights of Columbus' secretaries who met them and supplied them with cigarettes and tobacco.

It happened, however, that the six Negroes did not take a train for Port Jervis. Instead the Knights loaded them into automobiles and drove them across the pretty hilly country to their point of departure for the camps. There were only six men in that draft consignment, but the Knights would have been as hearty and as generous if there had been 600. There have been innumerable instances where a larger number of men have been cared for and had their wants provided for by the Knights, as the men themselves have testified.

f. The Black Church in Social Service

As we have seen in the "Institutional Church" pioneered in Atlanta by the Reverend Hugh H. Proctor, some black churches offered many social welfare services, and many of the larger denominations set up their own agencies to deal with problems of race relations and/or social service within the denomination. This was the case in the North as well as in the South. The following two documents are descriptive of church involvement in social services. The article of George E. Haynes treats this subject comprehensively. The article by the Reverend A. Clayton Powell reports the activities of his own church, the famed Abyssinia Baptist Church of Harlem in New York City.

Document 25*

George E. Haynes, "The Church and the Negro Spirit," Survey-Graphic, 1925.

The last Sunday of September, 1924, was a dramatic day in Harlem. The Salem Methodist Episcopal Church, a congregation of Negroes, took possession of the church building, parish house and parsonage of the Metropolitan Methodist Episcopal Church, a body of white communicants. The white congregation had assembled in large numbers for the last service they were to hold in their accustomed place of worship. Just a few blocks away there was an unusual attendance of the Negro congregation at the building--two converted apartment houses with the partition walls removed--they had used for fourteen years, beginning with the days when the church was a mission. At a designated hour, the Negro congregation marched quietly and in an orderly manner out of their old structure and up Seventh Avenue toward the Metropolitan Methodist Episcopal church house. The doors of the Metropolitan Church opened wide; the white pastor and his people arose to receive the Negro pastor and his people. There were Negro and white visitors from their common denomination to witness and participate in this historic event. The Negro pastor and the president of his board of trustees were welcomed to the pulpit by the white pastor and the president of his board. After appropriate songs and addresses, the keys of the church property were presented by the white trustees of the outgoing congregation to the Negro trustees of the incoming congregation. The benediction was pronounced amid expressions of joy and fellowship not unmixed with tears.

The taking over of church by Negroes is a frequent occur-

*Reprinted by permission.

rence in Harlem, as it is in the other rapidly growing Negro centers in the cities of the North. About eight years ago the Metropolitan Baptist Church bought from a white congregation an imposing stone building at Seventh Avenue and 128th Street and moved into it. Three years ago the Williams Institutional Church of the Colored Methodist Episcopal denomination purchased an excellent plant--once a flourishing Jewish synagogue--in 130th Street.

Such a transfer of white church property not infrequently accompanies a shifting of population. Within the past three years the Negro population of Harlem has pushed forward as the white population has moved westward across Eighth Avenue to St. Nicholas Park and up beyond 145th Street almost to the boundary of 125th Street, between Eighth and Lenox Avenues. During that time the fine building of a Swedish congregation west of Eighth Avenue has been taken over by a body of Negro Congregationalists, the Grace Congregational Church of Harlem. The imposing structure of a Lutheran Church at Edgecombe Avenue and 140th Street has been bought and occupied by the Calvary Independent Methodist Church. According to a recent announcement, the Mt. Olive Baptist Church, one of the oldest and largest Negro congregations in the city, after worshipping for many years in a church house in 53rd Street, has purchased for $450,000 the beautiful Adventist Temple, built of white Indiana limestone, at 120th Street.

Quite as interesting as these acquisitions of existing edifices has been the success of Negro congregations in erecting new church structures in the face of the high cost of land and building construction in Manhattan. About fifteen years ago St. Phillip's Protestant Episcopal Church sold its property in the Pennsylvania Station zone for a large sum and used a part of the proceeds to erect, under the supervision of a Negro architect, an attractive and very serviceable brick church building and parish house on lots extending from 133rd to 134th Streets. The Abyssinian Baptist Church sold its property in 40th Street and built, on 138th Street, a church building and community house at a cost of about $325,000. In plan and program, like many of the churches named here it is a thing of beauty and an instrument of service. "Mother Zion" Church, of the African Methodist Episcopal Zion connection, found about twenty years ago that its constituency was becoming too far removed from its location in Bleecker Street. A fine structure therefore was erected in 86th Street where its leaders thought a Negro neighborhood would develop, but the subway opened up and carried Negroes further north. About twelve years ago "Mother Zion" moved again and erected a building in 136th Street. To accommodate its growing institutional activities a new addition to the structure is now completed on a plot which runs through to 137th Street. In a triangle near 138th Street, St. Mark's Methodist Episcopal Church, now in the mid-town district, is erecting an institutional structure to cost a half million dollars.

In the purchase of buildings from white congregations and in the erection of new structures, the development in Negro church equipment in New York is typical of what has happened on smaller scale in such cities as Baltimore, Chicago, Cleveland, Saint Louis. Also in a few small cities churches have made commendable efforts to meet the growing demands of these people. In Saint Louis during the observance of Race Relations Sunday this winter delegations from white congregations that had sold their structures to Negro congregations returned for services on that day to their former churches to worship with the present occupants. St. John's Congregational Church in Springfield, Mass., Bethel African Methodist Episcopal Church of Chicago, the Sharp Street Methodist Church of Baltimore, Olivet Baptist Church in Chicago, "the largest Protestant church in the world," with nearly 11,000 members, and the Second Baptist Church of Detroit are outstanding examples of a broad and vigorous institutional service.

The Negro church is at once the most resourceful and the most characteristic organized force in the life of the Negroes of the Northern cities as it was in the Southern communities from which they come. Some of its main problems may be summarized in a four-fold statement:

1. To provide adequate buildings and other physical equipment for attracting and serving the rapidly increasing populations.
2. To give fellowship to newcomers who have been connected with the church of the same faith and order in their former homes.
3. To have adequate personnel and organization for rendering social service in the housing, health, recreational and other needs of a large proportion of the masses in the community.
4. To meet with understanding and wisdom the increasing throng of intelligent people, who know little of serfdom, and who feel the urge of their vigorous years in the turmoil of the city.

We have spoken of typical solutions of the first of these; let us now consider the others.

So recently have men of all races come to dwell in cities that their churches often have the organization and equipment typical of the small town and rural district. This is especially the case with the Negro church because only in the past sixty years have its constituents been moving with the population stream from the rural districts to urban centers. Only within the last twenty years have the numbers assumed large proportions in most of the communities that have grown up around the industrial plants of the Northern cities. As Negroes moved North they have brought their church with them. Individuals and groups, mainly of Baptist and Methodists, have transferred their relationships from the little churches of their Southern communities to the "watchcare" or to full membership of churches of the "same faith and order" in Northern communities. In a few cases whole congregations from Southern communities have moved North together and brought their pastors with them. In other cases Negro churches in Northern cities, which before the heavy migration of the last ten years had small struggling congregations, have increased their membership to large numbers and have become powerful in resources. Many of them have able ministers who, like the physicians, lawyers, editors, and business men who followed in the wake of the wage-earners, have come from the South to answer the Northern call.

Back in the Southern communities the little rural church, conspicuous for its bell tower, rests among the trees beside the road. It is the natural meeting place of the people once or twice a month when the non-resident minister comes to preach, and when the weather does not make the roads unfit for travel. Often the people come as far as ten or fifteen miles. Frequently they bring baskets of food and remain all day. Between the enthusiastic and extended services and amid the social amenities of meal time, they exchange the gossip of the countryside, the wisdom and experience of the cropping season, and the prospects, hopes and fears of the future.

In the typical Southern town or small city one or two churches of each of the more popular denominations, particularly of Baptists and the four principal Methodist denominations, have a resident minister. The church building is better built than those of the churches in the open country and the services are held usually every Sunday with Sunday School for the children. The church enters considerably, too, into the leisure time and recreational life of the people by an occasional sociable or picnic, stereopticon exhibition, and, on rare occasions, a traveling moving picture show. Around the church revolve the interests of family life. The churches in the larger cities such as Atlanta, Memphis, Louisville or Richmond, in architectual design, physical facilities, and personnel compare reasonably with other favorable phases of Negro life. In Norfolk one of the leading Baptist churches, under the guidance of a young college trained man, has a community program including extension classes for boys and girls, day nursery, playground and other social features.

From these communities of the South--rural districts, towns and cities--thousands of Negroes have moved to Northern cities. With the rapid increase of colored populations in the Northern cities, church facilities have not been adequate either in seating space for the assembly of worshippers, in arrangements for religious education, still in its infancy among white groups, or in sufficient personnel to give the service of social ministry to the thousands that come. For example, in 1920 the estimated seating capacity of Negro churches in Greater New York was about 14,000. In 1924 with the increase that has been made by taking over additional churches from white congregations and the erection of commodious buildings, the estimated seating capacity of twenty-seven Negro churches and sixteen missions in Harlem alone is about 21,000. There are thirteen churches with estimated seating capacity from 500 to 2,500 each; the others range from 200 to 400.

The thirst of the people for the cooling water brooks of religion is shown in the way they crowd the buildings that are available. Examples are many. The seats of the large auditorium of the Abyssinian Baptist Church are filled when the hour of service arrives and often standing room is at a premium. St. Philip's Protestant Episcopal Church, with a service of high church type, is often crowded to the doors on Sunday morning. Mother Zion African Methodist Episcopal Church and Metropolitan Baptist Church often have larger numbers than they can comfortably seat. Frequently some of these churches have overflow services.

Besides the large self-supporting congregations with well-appointed buildings, there are nearly a score of "house-front" and "mission" churches. The "mission" churches are those that receive a part of their support from denominational missionary or extension societies which are stirred to action by the teeming unchurched masses of the district. These societies subsidize salaries of ministers, assist in the purchase of buildings or in other ways help to extend their denominational effort to evangelize and serve the people of the region. The "house-front" churches are started usually when some individual who has felt the call to the ministry has gathered about himself a little flock, or when several persons join together and ask a minister to lead them. The purchase of an equity in a private house is usually made. The double parlors on the first floors serve as a residence for the minister or for other tenants.

The organization, support and operation of Negro churches have become increasingly independent of white people. Negroes have thus had valuable experience and group training in standing upon their own legs and in going forward to achieve ends mapped out by themselves. The Negro churches are almost exclusively racial both in their membership and in their administration. Even congregations that belong to denominations made up of a majority of white communicants, such as the Protestant Episcopal, Methodist Episcopal and the Congregational Churches, are for all practical purposes autonomous, exercising great independence in government and being controlled only to a nominal extent by the general organization.

In no place, perhaps, is the independent, voluntary character of the Negro church better illustrated than in Harlem. One of the strongest Baptist churches in this area has been developed during the past fifteen years under the guidance of a minister of striking power, who once remarked that "a leader is a fellow who has some followers." In about ten years his preaching and work have enlarged a handful of members into a host. With money largely raised by themselves, they moved from a dingy brick basement to one of Harlem's best stone church edifices. St. Philip's Protestant Episcopal Church is widely known for its financial resources; it purchased, more than ten years ago, a number of apartment houses in 135th Street. Three of these churches have parish houses, three others have institutional equipment, and two others that are soon to come into the district have announced their plans for developing work along these lines....

Document 26*

A. Clayton Powell, "The Church in Social Work," Opportunity, January 14, 1923, p. 15.

The church must enlarge its religious activities if it is to retain the respect and support of intelligent men. Christianity is more than preaching, praying, singing and giving; it is all of these but a great deal more. The purpose of the Christianity of Jesus as revealed in the New Testament is to supply man's social as well as spiritual needs. The church is being called upon to give the world a Christianity of deeds as well as a Christianity of creeds. Very few people ask any more "What the church believes?" but "What the church is doing for the amelioration of the condition of mankind?" The majority of people care very little about church doctrines. They are looking for a translation of the spirit of Jesus Christ in the everyday life of his professed followers. The church will never draw and hold the masses by essays on faith, but by showing her faith by her works.

The church has not discharged its obligations when it has hired a man to stand up twice one day in seven, and piously ram the Bible down the throats of the people. It must go into the highways and hedges during the week caring for the sick, the wounded, the distressed and all that are needy and then on Sunday they will hear us and believe us when we tell them of "Jesus, the Mighty to save."

The Abyssinian Baptist Church of New York City is planning to carry out this larger program of applied Christianity. A $300,000 Church and Community House is being erected in Harlem, the most densely populated Negro Center in the world. This Church will be kind of an intellectual go-between for the public schools and the higher institutions of learning. Thousands of Negroes are coming to Northern cities each year who are too old to be reached by the public schools and too poorly informed to enter universities. This large group has in it tremendous undeveloped possibilities. Thru the classes in English, Reading Circles and Lecture Courses that will be provided, there will be not only a vision of the great world in which we live, but a means by which they may helpfully relate themselves to a movement for world betterment.

The church should be the social center of the community in which it is located. Man seeks the fellowship of other human beings, as surely as water seeks its level. If he cannot find the fellowship he craves with good men he will find it with bad ones. The majority of people who go to disreputable places do not go because they desire to do wrong, but for fellowship. The Church should cease criticizing and abusing people for spending their evenings in questionable places until it has given them a place to socialize in a wholesome environment. The Church which will grip and hold men in the future will be the Church that vitally relates itself to every problem of the masses. This does not mean that emphasis will be shifted from man's spiritual to his social needs. It is the paramount duty of the Church to Christianize the social order. The Church therefore, which undertakes to carry out a large social program must be more spiritual than the one which deals simply in emotional religion. The world has gone wild like an uncaged beast of the jungle and there seems to be no power in science, politics, diplomacy, or economics to gird it. Only the social reign of God can bring order out of man's social confusion.

g. Specific Practices of Social Welfare Agencies

The following paragraph by George E. Haynes explains the kinds of activities undertaken by single and coordinated agencies during this period:

> In Wichita, Kansas; in Kansas City, Mo.: St. Louis, Chicago, Toledo, Cincinnati, Brooklyn and other cities, the white and Negro social workers and the white and Negro church leaders have begun inter-racial committees through Urban Leagues and Y. M. and Y. W. C. A. cooperative community planning which has achieved results and promises larger things for the future. Perhaps the most fully worked out and best piece of social engineering in race relations in a northern community has developed during the past six years in Cincinnati, Ohio, in the inter-racial work of the Council of Social Agencies, with James H. Robinson as executive secretary. They have coordinated the Negro churches, fraternal bodies, women's clubs, Y. M. C. A. and Y. W. C. A. with the white social agencies and organizations. The Negro population increased from about 20,000 to 35,000 in ten years, largely during the 1916-18 migration. These people have been integrated into the city's life through their leaders and organizations to an extent which hardly seemed workable ten years ago. In Philadelphia the Armstrong Association, with Forrester B. Washington as secretary, has successfully started somewhat similar plans and policies. Other cities, with the cooperation of Urban Leagues, are beginning such policies.[3]

The following documents illustrate Haynes' observations.

Document 27a

Report of the Negro Civic Welfare Committee of the Council of Social Agencies (Cincinnati, Ohio), February, 1921.

Introduction

The Removal of the Office

On the 31st of January our administrative office was removed from the Ninth Street Y. M. C. A. to the Social Agencies' building 25 East Ninth Street.

From this office we are doing the administrative end of the work and placing greater stress on the problems of co-ordination, leaving the assistant secretary and the field workers in our West End office at the Y. M. C. A. The advantages are at once apparent. Many agencies are in the Social Agencies' building and this has made it convenient to confer with them. Many opportunities to function which we missed before come to us now.

Section I.

Lodging Bureau

The opening of a central lodging bureau for homeless men by the Council of Social Agencies has placed responsibilities on the Negro Civic Welfare Committee, as a large number of the unemployed are colored. Contributions made by our organization follow:

1. We arranged for suitable quarters for the men in the basement of the Ninth Street Y. M. C. A. with the hearty co-operation of the organization.
2. We arranged for bedding and equipment from the Central Purchase Committee.
3. Found a suitable place for the men to eat and made the necessary arrangements. The place is 508 W. Fifth Street.
4. We have kept workers at the Bureau ever since the week it was established. In order not to interfere seriously with the regular work, we have used every member of our staff. From February 10th to March 5th, they put in 276 hours, the equivalent of 23 days of 12 hours each, at the Lodging Bureau.
5. We found some jobs at the institutions which the men could do. This has been a help to the institutions and has enabled some of the men to earn what they have received.

Industrial Welfare for Women and Girls

The world war called the colored woman into industry in numbers unprecedented. There had been little in her previous experience to fit her for the new responsibility--the tedious processes, the necessity of speed, promptness and accuracy and the problem of working together incident to factory life.

Obviously, on some one devolved the duty to help the worker to make good for the sake of herself and her country and to protect her many interests which were at stake.

Our industrial welfare worker has created friendly contacts with 23 plants and firms employing over 800 colored women. To these she goes and gives friendly advice on punctuality, regularity, efficiency, thrift, and tries to develop in them the proper attitude toward their work. She advises with the employer on the many problems which arise. Her assistance has been welcomed by both employer and employees.

During the month of February she has established contacts with 2 other plants employing respectively 25 and 96 women. During the recent period of unemployment, many women have applied for work. During the past week this situation has begun to show signs of relief.

The Y. W. C. A. has agreed to take over this piece of work with the worker after the thirty-first of May.

Child Placement

The child placement secretary, who has been working half time in our office and half time with the Committee on Child Care, has held thirty-two conferences this month resulting in two placements in foster homes, eight in boarding homes and the listing of three for adoption.

On June 1st, her full time will be given to the Committee on Child Care under which agency she will be interested in three phases of child placement-boarding homes, adoption and institutional placement. The adoption will be done in the name of the New Orphan Asylum for Colored Youth, if agreeable to that agency.

The Associated Charities agrees to do the family case work in the homes from which children are taken, the committee on Child Care will investigate the homes in which the children are placed and both agree to co-ordinate with the Negro Civic Welfare Committee.

Recreation

The recreational program reaches regularly each week 45 groups of people with occasional larger public meetings. The total attendance at these meetings from September 1st to February 1st exceeded 26,000. In February 172 meetings, classes and events were held with a total attendance of 7560.

The attendance at our Madisonville center has doubled with the use of the local school buildings which was accorded our groups this month. New groups interested in dramatics have held meetings this month at the Douglass School, Union Baptist Church and the Y. W. C. A.

Eight community sings have been held, three church choirs assisted and band and orchestra rehearsals conducted while the Lockland Glee Club made its initial appearance before a large and appreciative audience. Our athletic teams continue to win.

These activities are filling the lives of young people with

something that interests them, giving vigorous exercise to their bodies and minds. Talent and leadership are being discovered, developed and guided into useful channels. Many of the formerly neglected communities have been truly made glad by the coming of our workers.

These recreational activities are being followed up by a citizenship program. It is planned that this will be intensified and the audiences may hear from our representatives white and colored speakers messages on health, thrift, education, the home and other phases of citizenship, its opportunities and responsibilities. We plan to extend to the various social agencies, opportunity to present their programs to these audiences.

The Community Service League has agreed to carry on this recreational program after the thirty-first of May and to co-ordinate through our agency.

Section II.

Day Nursery

Some interesting conferences have been held on day nursery work. These committee meetings were 4 in number. The movement had its origin when Rev. Wm. H. Tilford of the Freedmen's work of the Cincinnati Presbytery came to our office with a plan.

A committee of 10 people representing as many interests was called into a conference with the executive committee of our organization on the day nursery situation.

In summary that committee found no recognized day nursery for colored children in Cincinnati. It makes the general estimate that $4972 would provide well for a unit of 25 children and initial expenditure; that a larger unit would reduce the overhead and the initial cost would be confined to the first year.

The findings were reported to the Director of the Council of Social Agencies and the Superintendent of Public Schools. The use of the Stowe and Douglass Schools would be ideal, if granted.

The meetings were interesting and a large amount of co-operation was in evidence. Worthy of special mention is the work done by the teachers of Stowe and Douglass schools and Stowe Colony. At these schools 43 teachers made inquiries among their pupils about unattended and pre-school age children left at home during the day. 187 of these were reported. Teachers received their blanks in the morning and were ready to make their reports in the afternoon.

Board Meetings

One general board meeting and two executive committee meetings have been held during the past month. This does not include the 4 meetings of the day nursery at which the committee members were present. At these meetings the budget was drawn up and approved by the committee. After the distribution of our workers to various agencies we had a request of $7270. The Central Budget Committee cut this request by $400, leaving a budget of $6880.

Presenting and Representing the Work

By way of illustration, the Executive Secretary has this month held 76 conferences and interviews, and the work has been recognized in calling the Executive to serve on a number of important committees, the Mayor's committee on unemployment, Central Budget Committee, Clean-up Committee at the Chamber of Commerce and Committee on Factory Contracts. The work has been represented at 20 committee meetings held by other agencies and there have been 12 committee meetings under our own agency.

A number of addresses have been given. On the 3rd, the work was presented before a group in Covington, Ky., on the 14th, an address was delivered at Washington Terrace where one of the women's clubs is making a special study of our work. During the budget committee meetings the work was presented to the committee with a very favorable response. Our workers have been going into the field each day and evening doing their work and presenting their special programs to special groups.

Conferences and Letters Arranging for the Co-ordinating Program

During the past month we have made a definite effort to bring into full force our co-ordinating program, and to make official the status of our organization as the co-ordinating agency for the colored work. On the morning of February 11th, we had a conference with executives of agencies doing colored work. Fourteen persons were present. At this time we traced the development of our organization and mentioned the direct service activities which we proposed to transfer to other agencies, leaving ourselves the problem of co-ordinating the whole. The plan was unanimously approved, and it was stated that letters would be sent to the executives and each would be asked to place the matter officially before his board. Accordingly we have made arrangements to transfer by June 1st, our recreational work to Community Service, child placement to Boarding Homes, industrial welfare for women and girls to the Y. W. C. A. and homes registry to the Better Housing League. This involves the transfer of the workers also; and in the transfer, one more organization will be enabled to give more attention to the colored work by taking one of our workers. I refer to the Ohio Humane Society. This will leave in our co-ordinating office a staff of three persons.

The letters have been sent to the various agencies as promised, and to date 4 have written a general approval of the co-ordinating relationship. Among the points placed before them were: (1) Representation on our board; (2) Copy of monthly report on the colored work; (3) Attendance of workers at a conference of workers; (4) Specific suggestions touching the need of each agency which will mean a fuller development of the work in the colored field.

In bringing to pass these events we believe we have established a clear relationship and a permanent status for the Negro Civic Welfare Committee, a federation (within the Council of Social Agencies) of those forces colored and white in Cincinnati interested in the welfare of the Negro. I believe its possibilities are immense.

Respectfully,

Signed: Jas. H. Robinson
Executive Secretary

In their book, Blacks in the City, Guichard Parris and Lester Brooks detail the history of the National Urban League. The document by Eugene Kinckle Jones is but a summary of the accomplishments of the League for one calendar year alone.[4]

Document 27b*

Eugene Kinckle Jones, "Building a Larger Life," (A Report of the Accomplishments of the National Urban League for the Year 1922), Opportunity, Vol. I, (March, 1923), pp. 19-21.

The year 1922 opened with country-wide unemployment due to the general business depression. Philanthropic organizations were facing financial deficits and an increased demand for services. Although the National Urban League felt that the previous year had been its most productive period of service, it looked forward with some concern to its next year's plans as it had just closed the year with a deficit of $3,500. We come to the close of the year 1922 with a full record of service--all debts paid; the largest income recorded during any previous year--the largest surplus yet held and the prospects brighter than ever before.

It is well to begin this report of the year's accomplishments with a reminder that the underlying cause of the League's existence is the misunderstanding that has existed between the races in America. The sufferings that Negroes have undergone are probably due more to that than to any other one cause. Any excess in the difficulties attending social problems among Negroes over those faced by white people in America can be traced to misunderstanding and the main purpose of the Urban League is to remove the cause of this misunderstanding which is possible only through the development of harmonious relations between the races by getting the best elements of the two races to work together. It is now possible in almost every city in the United States--north or south--where social work is undertaken, to form joint committees of white and colored people to attack the social problems of Negroes and of the community at large. It is increasingly becoming possible to get Negroes themselves on the community welfare committees in cities where Negroes live in large numbers.

The advantage of the Urban League's program of race cooperation has been that the local organization formed by the League adopts a social welfare plan of work which requires the constant oversight and review of the Board of Directors. Thus, in addition to the occasional getting together of white and colored people to discuss points of difference and to adjust the misunderstanding between the racial groups, representatives of the two races have an opportunity to discuss actual service in behalf of the masses of Negro people who have been denied a chance to become normal human beings or to make of themselves the best possible members of society.

The national program of the Urban League during the past year has been as follows:

1. The organization of new communities for the development of social service activities--this through the formation of Urban Leagues or thru aiding or stimulating in the establishment of welfare activities for Negroes under some other name;

2. Investigation or research into social conditions that obtain among Negroes as basis for some constructive social service for the purpose of publicity that would tend to acquaint the people with the actual facts as to Negro life. This matter of giving facts concerning Negroes to the public is, we feel, one of the most important tasks to be performed. There are many false opinions concerning alleged deficiencies of the Negro which need to be corrected;

3. The providing of opportunities to colored social workers to obtain training in order that more persons may be available to carry out the League's program as it is extended;

4. The education of the colored public in the possibilities of social service programs through the publication of a journal and the lecture platform, conferences and personal interviews with leading Negroes;

5. Extension of social service to Negroes thru persuading general social service organizations to include Negroes in their programs of work--in many instances inducing them to add Negro social workers to their personnel that Negroes may have a share in performing the duties which bring to them better social conditions.

The following are a number of accomplishments of the League under these headings:

Organization. New movements have been established in Canton, Ohio, Joplin, Mo., Columbia, Mo., Tampa, Florida, and ground work for organizations has been laid in Baltimore, Md., Hartford, Conn., St. Paul, Minn., and Tulsa, Oklahoma. An inter-racial committee which was established in the preceding year in Buffalo to meet the emergency unemployment situation completed its work and the movement is now on foot to organize an Urban League in Buffalo using the members of the former inter-racial committee as a nucleus. Buffalo is experiencing a considerable increase in the Negro population and by spring it is expected that more than 5,000 additional Negro workers and their families will add considerably to the already increasing colored population there.

Visits have been made to Birmingham, Ala., Jacksonville, Fla., and Albany, Ga., where a re-organization plan is in operation and in Indianapolis where a conference of colored and white people was held to consider plans for the proper development of a community-wide program in that city.

Department of Research and Investigations. The Department of Research and Investigations of the League has completed a survey of the Negroes of Hartford, Conn. This report covers the school life, industrial activities, housing, crime and recreation. In fact, it is a complete study of nearly 65 per cent of the total Negro population of that community. This report is now in the hands of a committee of white and colored citizens in Hartford who are considering the recommendations as a basis for a constructive social service program for Negroes in Hartford.

An industrial survey of the Negroes of Baltimore was made and the complete report will be presented to a similar committee in Baltimore early in 1923. A summary of the figures shows that this investigation covered 51,106 men, of which 6,525 were colored in 175 plants and was endorsed by the Mayor of the city and the Board of Trade.

This Department maintains a clipping bureau and files for assembling data of all kinds having a bearing on Negro life. From this material, information has been supplied for lectures, articles and discussion on the Negro for students, professors and lecturers on social work. The League is gradually building up an invaluable library and file of information just for this purpose.

Training Workers. At the close of the school year 1921-22, two persons who are in training at Schools of Social Work--one at the New York School of Social Work and the other at the Carnegie School of Technology at Pittsburgh--completed their year of training and entered into social work. One is Family Case Worker in Minneapolis and the other is with the Y.W.C.A.

At the beginning of the fall term, 1922--the League placed two "Fellows" in training at the New York School of Social Work and one at the School of Technology, Pittsburgh, Pa. In addition, the League has furnished living expenses in New York for two young college graduates who gained experience working from the League's headquarters in New York City and who subsequently accepted positions--one with the New York Urban League and the other with the National Urban League. The League has served as a placement agency for social workers who have been sent to local Leagues and to other organizations.

In Milwaukee, Toledo, Cleveland, Springfield (Mass.), Tampa, St. Louis and Baltimore, the League has placed workers. This, of course, is in addition to workers placed by local Urban Leagues either in their own cities or with other local social agencies.

Conference and Publicity. Lectures have been delivered by League representatives at many important national conferences as well as at churches, colleges, and meetings of local service organizations.

The Annual Conference of the League was held in Pittsburgh, Pa., October 17th to 20th, with representatives from most of the 40 cities in which the League has branches as well as representatives from several of the national and many local social service agencies. There was a good representation of interested white persons present who entered heartily into the general discussion of social service problems as well as the subject of co-operation between the races which was given an important place. An inventory of the League's work throughout the country was made and prospects for the future were discussed. All present agreed that it was a most important conference and will prove the most far-reaching of the League's seven annual conferences.

Efforts have been made to put the Negro in a favorable light before the public in articles which have appeared in such prominent magazines as the "Current History" magazine, published by the New York Times Publishing Company--the "Missionary Review of the World," "The World Tomorrow." Our files show that a considerable number of daily papers from many sections of the country have carried articles dealing with the League's program and its ideals.

A special effort has been made this year to apprise Negro leaders of the importance of social service programs among colored people. The Extension Secretary of the League has not only had numerous personal interviews with leading colored people in such cities as Chicago, Columbus, Pittsburgh, Providence and Newport, R.I., and other New Jersey towns, Philadelphia, Charleston, W. Va., Richmond, Norfolk and Portsmouth, Va., Galveston and Houston and other Texas towns, St. Louis and Kansas City but he has addressed large audiences of colored people in churches and at conventions in many of these cities,--all of this to popularize the work of the League and to show to the people who are most helped, the benefit that may be derived from the expansion of the program of the League.

During the year five issues of the League's Bulletin were published and just before the year ended, the January, 1923, issue of "Opportunity"--"a Journal of Negro life" appeared. This magazine presents monthly scientific discussions of facts about the Negro. It will serve as a guide to those who wish to attack the problems among Negroes with a full knowledge of the conditions they face and with the most up-to-date philosophy of their life and hopes. This will correct the unreasonable myths and opinions entertained about the Negro. Already evidence is in hand of the good impression this first number has made. This magazine is published by the Department of Research and Investigation as the official organ of the National Urban League.

Extension of Social Service to Negroes. The League is co-operating with the National Child Welfare Association in distributing its health panels for the education of Negro children. The secretaries of the local organizations of the League act as representatives of the National Child Welfare Association at conferences and local meetings.

The League is distributing 500 copies of the Directory of Social Resources in the United States for the Red Cross Society for which it has rendered other service such as recommending workers and assisting in the handling of difficult family cases. The League co-operates annually with a number of social agencies in the active part in securing more definite consideration by the National Conference of Social Work of social problems in America as they affect Negroes. The League is endorsed by the National Information Bureau.

The work of the Locals consisted of the conduct of settlement houses; employment bureaus--both for juveniles and adults; getting contracts for Negro contractors; placing personnel workers in industrial plants to raise the efficiency of Negro workers and to reduce labor turnover as well as to enlarge the number of opportunities for Negro workers to advance on the job; the organization of health campaigns--some of which were maintained throughout the year providing milk stations for babies, pre-natal clinics, district nursing service and fresh air activities for children and convalescent care for women; working girls' homes; boys clubs; home economics work in connection with families that need assistance in arranging budgets and preparing nutritious food; work with children in juvenile courts often involving the operation of Big Brother and Big Sister movements. In one city, in the far south, for the first time in years through the League's activities, women prisoners were removed from regular work,--sweeping the city streets. In another, colored matrons were placed in police stations; Travelers' Aid Workers were maintained in busy railroad terminals in several cities as a result of the League's initiative.

In eight cities the Urban League secretaries were placed on Mayor's Unemployment Committees and in another city a survey was made of Negro business places as a basis for the establishment of a Negro Board of Trade.

Cost. The Expenses of the National headquarters in 1921 were

$29,398; in 1922 the national organization raised $44,626. In 1923 the budget is $65,320. In 1910, $2,500 was spent in the whole Urban League movement. In 1920 the amount was $185,000. In 1921 it was $220,000. In 1922 it exceeded $250,000.

As evidence of the confidence of the contributing public in the League's work, 76% of those who contributed $5.00 and over to the League during 1921 renewed their contribution and 80% of those contributing $10.00 and over renewed their contribution for 1922.

Plans. The League's plans during 1923 to continue its work along the lines indicated by the activities last year. It hopes to bring its local activities up to a higher standard and to organize work in additional cities--north and south. In the case of the northern communities, this will be especially necessary and helpful in view of the probable large migration of Negroes to the North to fill the industrial gap occasioned by restricted immigration to our shores. Already, in most of the large industrial cities of the North, any Negro who wishes employment can find a job and in many communities industrial agents are bringing in colored workers from the South in increasing numbers.

We plan to specialize in the industrial field, placing on our staff a national industrial secretary whose principal duties will be as follows:

1. To standardize and coordinate the local employment agencies of the League so that exchange of information and more regular correspondence between them can assure applicants for work more efficient and helpful service and employers of labor a more efficient group of employees;

2. To work directly with large industrial plants both in cities where the League is established and in communities removed from such centers to procure larger opportunity for work and for advancement on the job for Negro workers and to stimulate Negro workers to a fresh determination to "make good on the job" so that their future in industry may be assured.

3. To work with organized labor to the end that Negroes employed in the trades represented by the unions may be given an opportunity to affiliate with organized labor on equal terms.

SOCIAL WORK EDUCATION FOR PROFESSIONAL PRACTICE

The foundation for the professional training of blacks as social workers administering to the social welfare concerns of the urban black community were laid in the previous historical period,

1896-1915. We recall that the scientific study of the Negro problems began with the publication in 1889 of The Philadelphia Negro, by W. E. B. DuBois, Professor of Economics and History, Atlanta University, and is recognized even today as a major work of empirical sociological research. Such study was further nurtured and cultivated by the Atlanta University Conferences and the resulting series of Atlanta University Publications. Most of the research was done by undergraduate students in black colleges who used the city and urban environment as a sociological laboratory. Among the latter were, of course, the students of DuBois, his associates and successors at Atlanta University, and of his colleagues, like Matthew W. Bullock, Professor of Social Sciences, Atlanta Baptist (later Morehouse) College. Bullock required his students to affiliate themselves with and to volunteer their services to social agencies administering to the needs of the urban black community. His outstanding student, perhaps, was Garry Ward Moore, who succeeded him at Morehouse College, and who continued this tradition of instruction.

The extension of this concept to embrace the need for professional training in social work is properly credited to Dr. George Edmund Haynes. He was the first black to have professional training in both research (Columbia University) and social work (New York School of Philanthropy). As founder of the National League on Urban Conditions Among Negroes, and as Professor of Social Sciences, Fisk University, he was the first to establish a worthwhile training program, a program which served as a model to several other college programs.

Perhaps as a result of the great stimulus to sociological research given by Dr. DuBois and his associates, Monroe N. Work and R. R. Wright, Jr., we note the emergence in the next two decades of the careers of such notable sociologists as Charles S. Johnson, E. Franklin Frazier, Ira DeA. Reid, and Walter Chivers. It is a striking fact that all of these men were graduates of black undergraduate colleges and that they were equally at home in the fields of sociology and social service. Much of their success has been credited to their graduate training in universities such as Chicago and Columbia, but it is as likely that their previous training gave them high motivation.

All of these men were beneficiaries of the stimulus given to professional social work training by Dr. George Edmund Haynes.

> In developing the idea of better training for Negro social workers, Dr. Haynes took advantage of the offer to develop the Department of Sociology at Fisk University, and to establish there a training center for Negro social workers in connection with that University. It was also determined that he should open up an experiment in Nashville, a Southern city, in social service work among Negroes with the idea that graduates of his department at Fisk, giving promise of success in social work, should be brought to New York by the League for further training. In cooperation with the women of the M. E. Church South, and Fisk University, the Bethlehem Training Center was thus developed.[5]

In another training program devised also by Dr. Haynes, the League

> established a system of fellowships which paid enough to meet the modest living expenses of a student who, after qualifying, could obtain free instruction from the School of Philanthropy. The League established also so-called broken or part fellowships to enable a young man or woman, who already had some training, to put in a short period in the head office seeing how the everyday work of such organization was carried on.[6]

Among those who benefited from League fellowships were persons who later became important in social work education, such as Garry W. Moore, previously mentioned, E. Franklin Frazier, Forrester B. Washington, and Inabel Burns Lindsay. Moore, Frazier, and Washington became, successively, Directors of the Atlanta School of Social Work, and Dr. Lindsay was to become founding Dean of the Howard University School of Social Work. Dr. Frazier, as Professor of Sociology, Howard University, played a significant role in the history of both institutions.

Many of the fellows became, as had been anticipated, prominent in the work of the National Urban League itself. Still others such as Ira DeA. Reid, E. Franklin Frazier, and Walter B. Chivers ultimately devoted the major part of their careers to teaching in black colleges and in research and consulting. All came to chair their departments of sociology--Atlanta University, Howard University, and Morehouse College respectively--and were to have a hand in training, along with Charles S. Johnson at Fisk University, the great majority of blacks who were to take the Ph. D. degree in sociology.

The participation of blacks in social work education and in sociological research and education is an unknown footnote in the history of these disciplines. Their record, however, speaks for itself, and when it becomes a matter of common knowledge, these men and women will be recognized for the pioneers they truly were.

A graduate of Fisk University, possibly a student of Professor George Edmund Haynes, Mrs. Millie E. Hale, a professional nurse, established a hospital with social services for the black population of Nashville, Tennessee.

Document 28*

John Marshall Ragland, "A Hospital for Negroes with a Social Service Program," Opportunity, I (December, 1923), pp. 370-371.

The problem of hospital care for difficult medical cases is characteristically acute in southern cities where prevailing sentiment bars Negroes from the institutions of the city. It has been so in Nashville, Tennessee, with its Negro population of 35,000. The hospital of the Meharry Medical College has, to some extent, met this need; but aside from its inadequacies for the entire Negro population, it is closed throughout the summer months. This gap has been filled in a remarkable manner by one energetic, socially minded woman, Millie E. Hale, the wife of a prominent Negro physician who is professor of Clinical Medicine and Surgery at the Meharry Medical College. In July of 1916 Mrs. Hale, a graduate of Fisk University, established the first year round hospital for Negroes with 12 beds, 2 nurses in charge, and with herself as the first student nurse, graduating three years later. Incidentally, her average rating of 91 per cent before the Tennessee State Board of Examiners for Nurses was the highest for that year. The institution has grown steadily to accommodate 75 patients and is at present being enlarged to 100 beds. Since its organization 7,000 patients have been registered, and 5,000 operations have been performed with a mortality rate of less than 3 per cent. Dr. J. H. Hale is the surgeon-in-chief. He is employed by his wife and paid a standard fee for all operations performed. Four other house physicians and a corps of 26 nurses are on the payroll of the institution. Dr. Hale's continued studies and annual visits to the Mayo Clinics serve as an aid to the hospital's increased technique.

*Reprinted by permission of the National Urban League.

Perhaps more important still are the social service programs instituted by Mrs. Hale. In addition to being general manager of the hospital, superintendent of nurses, manager of a community grocery store, head of the Ladies Auxiliary, her social service program includes a community house, four large playgrounds well equipped for out-door exercise, and an out-patients' department where more than 2,000 patients were cared for during last year. This work has been gradually extended to include the services of some of the hospital staff and it now reaches a wide and important sector of the Negro population. The home visits are made by the nurses to encourage better housekeeping. Two nurses are assigned to the community for bedside nursing. If necessary, they prepare the family meals, clean the house, and give such other relief as is necessary for the rehabilitation of the family. During June of this year the second annual picnic for children was held. It was attended by more than 5,000 children. The Nashville Electric Railway Company provided, without cost, 16 street cars for the transportation of the children to the parks; citizens of Nashville donated the use of 100 automobiles; the Rev. Preston Taylor gave 100 gallons of ice cream; and the Ladies' Auxiliary donated 300 pounds of barbeque and fish sandwiches.

There are no parks for Negroes in Nashville. Mrs. Hale has purchased four large plots of land in different sections of the city and planted playgrounds for colored children. Three nights a week free band concerts and open air moving-pictures are provided for the children. A physical director and a nurse are in charge of each playground. The 14 room house of Dr. and Mrs. Hale has been converted into a community center where club meetings are held. A pre-natal and baby welfare clinic, a free dispensary and clinic for adults, a class in religious education, free health lectures, and institutes for the benefit of women who wish to become better acquainted with methods of community betterment, are some of the activities held in this center.

A Social Service Institute, or workshop was planned by the Neighborhood Union to provide instruction for their volunteer workers. It was supported by other social work agencies in Atlanta as well. A second institute was held in September of the next year, and, it was successful as a stimulus to the larger undertaking represented in the establishment of the Atlanta School of Social Work.

In the next article, Robert C. Dexter, General Secretary, Associated Charities, Atlanta, Georgia, discusses 1) the need for professionally trained black social workers; 2) the reasons why they should be employed by social work agencies which conduct programs in and for the black community; and 3) most remarkably for his time, the problems imposed upon them by overt and institutional prejudice. In Mr. Dexter's discussion is summarized the kind of thinking which led competent and compassionate social workers like himself to advocate and to support the founding of a school for training blacks to become social work practitioners. Mr. Dexter and Mr. Jesse O. Thomas participated in the discussions at the National Conference of Social Work, April, 1920, and each had a part in making possible the organizational meeting of May 20, 1920, which resulted in the opening in September 1920 of the Atlanta School of Social Service, soon renamed Atlanta School of Social Work. Although this article was published in 1921, it was apparently composed in the late spring or summer of 1920, that is, after the organizational meeting but before the formal opening of the school.

Document 29*

Robert C. Dexter, "The Negro in Social Work," The Survey, Vol. XLVI, (June 25, 1921), pp. 439-440.

What are some of the chief problems of social work with the Negro? First and foremost, the need for trained colored leadership in social work. The colored worker, provided he is properly trained and is allowed to work without too great restraint, is much better suited for family case work, and indeed for all other kinds of social work, with colored people, than is the white worker. My experience with white workers with colored people convinces me that nine out of ten make either one of two mistakes--both fatal. They either insist on the standards of family and social life which they consider those of normal white people; or they believe that because their clients are Negroes they cannot be expected to have much in the way of standards. And the workers are content with the dole, whether of relief or service. The first group of workers are very liable to fail in their attempt and admit finally that the second have the correct attitude. The second method, carried to its logical conclusion, means that there is literally no constructive work done with colored people, and that the ideals of family and community life, economic and moral alike, are uncultivated and unknown.

The intelligent colored worker, on the other hand, knows her people's background. She does not impose on them a standard which is at present impossible; nor--and this is even more important--does she believe them non-moral or unimprovable. There are such subnormal groups among the colored people as among the whites, and possibly more of them because of the later emergence from barbarism, but it is the height of absurdity so to classify the entire race.

There are many elements in this better understanding by col-

*Reprinted by permission.

ored workers of the problems of their people. By no means the least important is the knowledge of the colored community which the worker can bring to bear on the solution of the problems presented. It has been my experience that even the socially-minded man who has lived all his life beside a large colored community has very little knowledge of the resources of that community. Just as in the daily papers the unpleasant features of civic and national life are given prominence, so it is the unpleasant features of the Negro community which the average white person hears about. The fact that the bulk of the men and women are hard workers is unknown or unthought of.

Nor do white people realize the pathetic eagerness for their children's education and general advancement which many--indeed most--colored people feel. No group can be despaired of that will make the sacrifices for education which many of them have made. The dead earnestness in the matter of race and social improvement on the part of the younger and better educated men and women is another unknown factor to white people. All these and many other assets for community and individual betterment are a part of the daily life of the colored social worker, provided--and this is an important proviso--that social workers are secured with the equipment and from the environment that would give them access to and knowledge of these factors in their community life.

It is worth while to emphasize this point. It would seem unnecessary as we have been so long convinced that for social workers generally men and women of intellectual training, progressive outlook and real personality are essential, but too many times and in too many places the colored worker has been chosen because he is esteemed "safe" or "good" with no regard for intellectual qualities or training. Such workers carry no weight with their own people. In North and South alike there is to be found a large number of educated, devoted colored men and women, who, if the opportunity for service in the field of social work is presented, will be glad to enroll and to qualify for such service. The desire for race improvement burns bright in the hearts of colored people and consequently any effort in that direction, if properly led, will not suffer for lack of personnel. This personnel will, of course, need training, and schools both North and South should be available for colored workers. In the South this will call for separate training schools similar to the one being started in Atlanta this year in connection with Morehouse College, or to the school which Community Service conducted for its colored workers at Richmond. In the North a definite attempt should be made to enroll in the schools for social work already established a proportion of colored students sufficiently large to cover the field among their own people. The National Urban League's department of education constitutes an approach to the problem.

Various movements are on foot among the colored people for their own improvement and a social worker who is not in touch with them is probably not of the sort to serve the community best. This does not necessarily mean that the social worker should be sympathetic with every radical movement which is stirring, but it does mean that he should be familiar with those activities which are working toward the advancement of the colored people and be ready to lend every possible assistance to the sound and constructive movements.

One qualification for work with his own people which the colored worker possesses surpasses all others: faith in the ultimate destiny of the Negro race. It is possible for a white man to possess this faith, but it is a more intense reality to the man or woman of African origin. Without such faith social work with any group is bound to be limited, but with it as a fundamental philosophy the work, even if it be at times disappointing, seems ultimately and always worth while.

For the social worker there are two important manifestations of race prejudice to be dealt with: one internal in the welfare organization itself on the part of contributors, board members, executive officers or staff workers; the other external, the result of prejudice in the community--in any community North or South to some extent--which influences the living and working conditions of the colored people. The former is, of course, only a specific illustration of the latter. Though we are social workers we cannot expect to be entirely exempt from the habits of mind of the community in which we live. At the same time any social work organization, worthy of the name, should free itself as much as possible from the baleful effects of prejudice. One Southern city, Chattanooga, has pointed the way; the Associated Charities there has a colored man on its board of directors. Social workers are as a whole relatively free from prejudice, but in offices employing large numbers of people a feeling of race difference is apt to creep in, unless those in charge are careful to establish an atmosphere of real democracy. In dealing with boards and contributors or public governing bodies the difficulty of avoiding prejudice is greater. Here it should be the function of the worker and particularly of the executive to guard against any manifestation of prejudice. Differences in salaries, in office equipment, promotions, or appropriations for departments, and indifference to overwork or poor work are common forms in which this prejudice manifests itself. The genuine social worker will constantly be on the alert to detect beginnings of prejudice and will fight them with all his might.

The effect of prejudice on the colored people is something that many white people, themselves free from prejudice, do not realize. I wish that our northern social workers could see the shacks in the Negro sections of some southern cities--whole rows of buildings with no running water, but plenty standing in the cellars, with leaking roofs, unpaved and improperly lighted streets, absolutely devoid of sanitary necessities--not to speak of comforts--and of everything else that makes for decent living conditions, and replete with everything that makes for disease and degeneracy. They would then understand why it is that the northern Negro is fighting so bitterly the prejudice which is exemplified in the segregation laws.

The colored man, I believe, in common with the other elements which go to make up "our America" will bring his genuine emotional, artistic and spiritual contribution to the better America that is to come.

In his autobiography, Jesse O. Thomas, first Chairman of the Executive Committee of the Atlanta School of Social Service, reprints the minutes of a meeting of concerned citizens to discuss the organization of a school for training blacks in the profession of social work. Those attending later became members of the first Board of Directors of the School. The President of Atlanta University, Myron W. Adams, was unable to commit the resources of Atlanta University prior to a meeting with his Board of Trustees; however, the President of Morehouse College was able to volunteer the services of Professor Garry W. Moore, Professor of Sociology, as Director, and classroom space in Sale Hall for the conduct of the sessions of the school. Mr. Moore, a graduate of Morehouse College, 1912; an Urban League Fellow, 1912-13; a former juvenile probation officer for Fulton County, 1914-15; first Superintendent of Boy's work for the International Committee of the Young Men's Christian Association; and a commissioned officer of World War I, served two years as Director of the School. At a meeting held in September, 1920, Professor Monroe N. Work of Tuskegee Institute and Mr. Walter Hill, State Supervisor of Negro Education for the State of Georgia, were also elected to the Board of Trustees.

Document 30*

Minutes of a Meeting Called to Discuss the Organization of the Atlanta School of Social Work, reprinted in My Story in Black and White, by Jesse O. Thomas, (New York: Exposition Press, 1967), pp. 120-123.

On May 12 a group of citizens met at 23 Cain Street in the office of the Tuberculosis Association at the request of Mr. Jesse O. Thomas. The meeting was called to order by Mr. Thomas, who outlined the purpose of the meeting, which was to consider the establishment of a school of Social Work.

Included among those present were Rev. Russell Brown, Lem-

*Reprinted by permission.

uel Foster, Dr. and Mrs. John Hope, Prof. Garry Moore, Miss Rose Loew, Miss Mary Dickerson, Mr. John W. Logan, Mrs. Hattie Green, Miss Mae Maxwell, Dr. M. W. Martin of Gammon Theological Seminary, President J. H. Lewis of Morris Brown College, Mr. Robert Dexter of the Family Welfare Society, and President M. W. Adams of Atlanta University. A letter of regret was read from President King of Clark University.

Mr. Thomas stated that at the request of Mr. Eugene Kinckle Jones, Executive Secretary of the National Urban League, who had been scheduled to speak at the National Conference of Social Work in New Orleans, on April 14, he had become a substitute. In Mr. Jones' communication he stated that Mr. Thomas, representing the Urban League in the southern territory, might include in his remarks any information pertinent to the work of that section. At that time, Mr. Thomas was having some difficulty in finding a trained social worker to become the executive secretary. Under these circumstances, he decided to point out the need for a training center for Negro social workers in the South. He further stated that at the conclusion of his address in New Orleans, thirteen executive secretaries of Family Welfare Societies across the South invited him to remain for a few minutes and go into further detail about the organization of a school.

At the conclusion of the conference with the executive secretaries he was requested to canvass in the large cities of the South in an attempt to determine in which city there was the best field-work possibilities. When that fact was determined, if he would organize the school, they would each see that a colored person was sent to the school at the expense of their agencies. Mr. Thomas stated that he had written to New Orleans, Jacksonville, Memphis, Nashville, and Birmingham, and when the information concerning the field-work possibilities in those cities were compared with the situation in Atlanta, by all odds Atlanta provided the best possibilities.

He suggested that in order for the matter which he had brought to present to the committee to be properly considered, the group form a temporary organization. On motion of Mr. Lemuel Foster, seconded by Mr. Robert Dexter, it was agreed that the group would form a temporary organization with Mr. Thomas serving as temporary chairman. The temporary chairman suggested that it would be his hope that the organization from the beginning would be interracial, and suggested that one of the white members of the committee be designated as temporary secretary. On motion of Dr. Russell Brown, seconded by Mr. Logan, Miss Mary Dickerson was designated as temporary secretary.

Mr. Thomas stated that inasmuch as Atlanta University had the best library facilities, he had had a conference with President Adams with respect to organizing the school in connection with Atlanta University, and that while President Adams expressed keen interest in the enterprise, he advised Mr. Thomas that he could not take any action until the matter was presented to his Board, which did not meet until June of that year. He then stated that Dr. Hope had offered the use of Prof. Garry Moore as director of the school and classroom space in Sale Hall. In view of the fact that it was desirable to have the decision made before the colleges closed for the year, so that the information concerning the organization of the school could be given to the members of the graduating classes of the various colleges before they left the campuses, it would be advantageous to make a decision before the meeting of the Atlanta University Trustee Board in June.

He, therefore, recommended that Dr. Hope's offer be accepted, which was agreed upon by common consent. In anticipation of favorable reaction to the proposal, Mr. Thomas had written a constitution, copy of which is herewith attached. The reference in the original Constitution referring to qualifications for admission was amended. The original draft said that the qualifications for admission should be graduation from an accredited high school. It was the opinion of Miss Dickerson that that qualification was too high, and she suggested that it be amended to read, "High School or the equivalent." The amendment was adopted and became a part of the original by-laws. Professor Moore, Dr. Hope, and Mr. Thomas were appointed as a committee to get out a bulletin announcing the opening of the school and to select a volunteer faculty.

Upon the motion of Mr. Robert Dexter, seconded by Dr. Hope, the temporary officers were made permanent and other participating members gave their assent to become permanent members of the Board of Directors of the newly established School of Social Work.

There being no further business, the meeting adjourned to be called by the chairman when the need arose for another meeting.

Jesse O. Thomas, Acting Chairman
Mary Dickerson, Acting Secretary

Although they were unreported in its official proceedings, discussions held by Robert C. Dexter and Jesse O. Thomas at the 1920 annual meetings of the National Conference of Social Work, New Orleans, Louisiana, led to the establishment of the Atlanta School of Social Work. In this brochure the title "Atlanta School of Social Service" is employed. This designation is also employed in the Catalogue of Morehouse College for the years 1919-20, 1920-21, and 1921-22. This name links the Atlanta School of Social Work with the Institute of Social Service sponsored by the Neighborhood Union at Morehouse College in 1919 and 1920. The Institute, however, had the character of what is today called a "workshop", and was designed for the instruction of its volunteer matrons. The complete professionalization of the Atlanta School of Social Work occurred with the assumption of its directorship by E. Franklin Frazier in 1922. It was incorporated and chartered during his administration on March 22, 1924.

Document 31

Announcement, Atlanta School of Social Service at Morehouse College, Atlanta, Georgia, 1920.

Executive Committee

Jesse O. Thomas, Chairman
Robert C. Dexter, Vice-Chairman
Rosa Loew, Secretary
John Hope, Treasurer

Dean W. M. Adams
Dr. Plato Durham
Mr. Lemuel L. Foster
Mrs. D. R. Green
Mrs. John Hope
Mr. R. A. Magill
Miss Mae B. Maxwell
Dr. W. F. Penn
Mr. William J. Trent
Mr. J. L. Wheeler
Mr. Hugh M. Willet

Announcement

It is the object of the Atlanta School of Social Service to afford an opportunity for training in the principles and technique of social work to colored young men and women. Trained Negro leadership in solving the social problems of the South is essential and it is to provide an opportunity for such training that this school is established. It is the outgrowth of a feeling which found expression in the National Conference of Social Work at New Orleans of the tremendous need for colored social workers.

Atlanta offers the best opportunity of any city in the South for such a school. It has a large colored population, there is a splendid spirit of co-operation between the races, and there are several excellent schools and colleges. The various social agencies of Atlanta, too, are in the forefront of the South and all of the leading organizations have developed strong colored departments, particularly the Anti-Tuberculosis Association, the Juvenile Court and the Associated Charities; the Southern Headquarters of the Urban League are in Atlanta, as well as one of its best organized branches. The classroom work will be at Morehouse College.

The School is fostered by a group of social workers and people interested in social work throughout the section and has the hearty backing and support of the educational institutions in Atlanta. The plan is to offer a one year course in social theory and practice to qualified students beginning September, 1920 and continuing through the academic year. A statement of the courses offered, the instructors, and the requirements for admission, will be found on the following pages.

Faculty

John Hope, A. M. , President of Morehouse College.

Garry Ward Moore, Director of School, and Professor of Sociology, Morehouse College.
A. B. Morehouse College, 1912; graduate New York School of Philanthrophy, 1913; Juvenile Probation Officer, Atlanta Juvenile Court, 1914-1915; Student Columbia University Summer Sessions, 1913-1915-1917-1920.

Marion C. Pruitt, M. D.
Atlanta School of Medicine, 1911; graduate work in medicine New York, Vienna, Austria and London, England; Fellow of Royal College Physicians and Surgeons Edinburgh, 1917; Major U. S. Army in France, 1918-1919.

Newdigate M. Owensby, M. D.
University of Maryland, 1904; Post-graduate in medicine Berlin, Edinburgh, London; Assistant in Psychiatry, Johns Hopkins Hospital, Baltimore; Professor of Nervous and Mental Diseases, Baltimore University; Major Medical Corps, United States Army.

Robert Cloutman Dexter, Secretary Atlanta Associated Charities.
A. B. Brown University, 1912; A. M. Brown University, 1917; Boston School for Social Workers, 1913-1914; General Secretary Montreal Charity Organization Society, 1915-1918; American Red Cross, 1918-1919; General Secretary Atlanta Associated Charities 1919-.

Jesse O. Thomas, Field Secretary Urban League for Southern States.
Tuskegee Institute, 1907; Field Secretary Tuskegee Institute, 1907-1914; Principal Voorhees Institute, 1914-1918; State Supervisor Negro Economics, New York State, 1918-1919; New York School Social Work, 1919; Field Secretary National Urban League, 1919-.

Mrs. John Hope.
President Atlanta Neighborhood Union; Conducted Training School Hostess House Workers--Y. W. C. A. 1917-1918.

Courses of Study

Course I. ECONOMIC AND SOCIAL THEORY
(a) First half year--economic theory.
(b) Second half year--social theory.
Two hours per week. Prof. Moore.

Course II. MEDICAL-SOCIAL PROBLEMS
(a) First half year, physiology and health problems; including

sanitation, public health, social aspects of tuberculosis, venereal disease, etc.
Two hours per week. Dr. Pruitt.

(b) Second half year, psychology and mental problems; including study of feeble-minded, insanity and the elements of psychology as applied to work with individuals.
Two hours per week. Dr. Owensby.

Course III. SOCIAL CASE WORK

(a) The first half year will be confined mainly to the family and family case work.

(b) The second half year deals with specialized case work--child placing, institutional work, juvenile court, adult probation, and industrial case work.
Two hours per week. Mr. Dexter.

Course IV. COMMUNITY ORGANIZATION

(a) Including publicity and finance, committee organization, social programs, recreation and community movements generally.
Two hours per week. Mr. Thomas and Mrs. Hope.

Course V. STATISTICS AND RECORD KEEPING

This course will be devoted principally to--

(a) Elementary principles of statistics and their application.

(b) Methods of collecting and presenting material in social surveys.

(c) Principles of record keeping as applied to social case records. An original investigation of some phase of Negro life in Atlanta will also be conducted.
Two hours per week. Prof. Moore.

Course VI. FIELD WORK

To be conducted under the auspices of the Anti-Tuberculosis Association, the Atlanta Associated Charities, and the Atlanta Urban League.
Eight hours per week.
In addition there will be a course of ten evening lectures by speakers of note on the general subject, "The Field of Social Work." These lectures will be open to the public but attendance by students in the Course is compulsory. List of lecturers will be announced later.

General Information

Admission:

Students must be at least 20 years of age and be graduates of a high school or equivalent. They must present to the Director satisfactory credentials of character and academic qualifications. The college opens September 28th, 1920.

As the number of students to be enrolled during the coming year will be strictly limited, it is suggested that applications be made at the earliest possible moment to the Director, Prof. G. W. Moore.

Fees and Expenses:

The tuition fee for the year's course will be $25.00, payable in advance semi-annually.

Students can secure board and lodging at reasonable rates.

Certificates:

A certificate will be given at the satisfactory completion of the year's course. During the first year all six courses will be required of each student for a certificate.

Positions for which such a certificate should qualify would be District Agents and Executives in Colored Departments of Associated Charities and similar organizations; probation officers in Juvenile Courts; attendance officers, recreation directors; Urban League Secretaries and assistants; social service departments of churches, Y. M. C. A. 's, Y. W. C. A. 's and welfare workers in industry.

Discipline:

The faculty reserves the right to ask any student to withdraw from the school who shows definite unfitness for social work.

All Correspondence Regarding the School Should Be Addressed To:

Prof. G. W. Moore,
Morehouse College
West Fair Street, Atlanta, Ga.

Professor Garry W. Moore, first to hold the position of Director of the Atlanta School of Social Work, died on April 3, 1923, while on leave to complete his studies for the Doctor of Philosophy degree at Columbia University. He had been replaced for the year 1922-23 by Edward Franklin Frazier who, subsequently, served as Director until 1927. Frazier, a former Urban League fellow, 1920-21, held an M. A. degree from Clark University, Worcester, Massachusetts, 1920, and had just returned to the United States from a year of study overseas at the University of Copenhagen, 1921-22.

In its first years the school was located on the campus of Morehouse College, using space in Sale Hall, but during Frazier's administration it was moved to downtown Atlanta so that it would be more accessible to the agencies in which students did field placements. It should be noted that the charter provides for a school of social work and health, the latter being a prime concern of agencies working in the black communities. Nothing in the way of elaborate development of medical social work took place, but it is of interest to note that, as early as the first year of the school, the curriculum included a course on medical-social problems, half of which dealt with physical health and disease and half with mental health and illness. Also, from the beginning stress was placed on community organization as well as upon social case work in the curriculum.

Document 32*

Charter Incorporating the Atlanta School of Social Work, Superior Court, Fulton County, Georgia, May 22, 1924.

GEORGIA
TO THE SUPERIOR COURT OF SAID COUNTY
FULTON COUNTY

The Petition of
M. W. Adams, W. W. Alexander, John Hope, W. J. King, J. H. Lewis, Joseph Logan, J. O. Thomas, W. J. Trent, Mary Dickinson, Cora Finley, Helen B. Pendleton, Lucy Tapley, Jane Van de Vrede, Ada Woolfolk, all of Fulton County, Georgia, and Edgar H. Johnson, of DeKalb County, Georgia

shows:

1.

Petitioners desire for themselves, their associates, successors and assigns, to be incorporated under the name and style of
ATLANTA SCHOOL OF SOCIAL WORK
for a period of twenty years, with the privilege of renewal as provided by law.

2.

The object of said corporation is educational and philanthropic, and not pecuniary gain. For the accomplishment of its object the corporation will establish and conduct a school of social work and health, with such branches, departments, and courses of study as may be deemed proper or desirable, and with power to confer certificates on graduates, students and others.

3.

The corporation will have no capital stock. The members will not be personally or individually liable for any debts, obligations or liabilities of any kind whatsoever incurred for or by the corporation, its trustees, its officers, agents or employees.

*Reprinted by permission of Atlanta University.

4.

The principal office of the corporation and the seat of said school shall be in Fulton County, Georgia, but the corporation shall have the right to establish branch offices, or schools at such place or places within or without the State of Georgia, as it may desire.

5.

The general powers of the corporation shall be all those belonging to corporations under the laws of the State of Georgia, including the right to sue and be used (sic), to have and to use a common seal, to acquire by purchase, gift, devise, or otherwise, property of every description, including stock of other corporations, and to hold or dispose of the same; to borrow money and execute notes, bonds or other evidences of indebtedness and to secure the same by mortgage or conveyance of its property or otherwise; to make and to change from time to time by laws for the governing of the corporation; to select officers and to name an advisory board.

6.

The affairs of the corporation shall be managed and conducted by the members thereof, who shall be known as trustees. The trustees shall consist of not less than nine nor more than twenty-one, as the by-laws may from time to time designate. At their organization meeting trustees shall divide themselves into three classes, as nearly equal in number as possible, and these classes shall serve as trustees for one, two and three years, respectively. Subsequent elections shall be for the term of three years, except that a vacancy shall be filled for an unexpired term. The new members shall be chosen by the old members as may be provided by the by-laws.

Wherefore, petitioners pray that they may be incorporated under the name and style aforesaid, with all the rights, powers, privileges and immunities prayed for or referred to in the foregoing petition.

Elliott Cheatham
Attorney for Petitioners

GEORGIA
IN THE SUPERIOR COURT OF SAID COUNTY
FULTON COUNTY May Term, 1924.

Whereas
have filed in the office of the Clerk of the Superior Court of said county the foregoing petition which seeks the formation of a corporation, to be known as

ATLANTA SCHOOL OF SOCIAL WORK

for the purpose set out in said petition, and have published the petition and have complied with the statutes in such case made and provided, and the court, upon the hearing of said petition, being satisfied that the application is legitimately within the purview and intention of the Code and laws of the State of Georgia.

It is considered, ordered and adjudged, that the said application be it is hereby granted, and that petitioners and their successors be incorporated under the said name and style of Atlanta School of Social Work, and that said corporation is hereby clothed with all the privileges and powers set out or referred to in said petition and made subject to all the restrictions and liabilities fixed by law.

This 22nd. day of May, 1924.

E. D. Thomas
Judge Superior Court, Atlanta Circuit.

Under the leadership of E. Franklin Frazier, the Atlanta School of Social Service became the Atlanta School of Social Work when it received its charter in 1924. Frazier, an M. A. in psychology, Clark University (Massachusetts), reveals his intellectual competence in this article, as he discusses the social psychology of race prejudice:

> We are concerned here chiefly with the psychological approach to the problem of insanity,--for race prejudice is an acquired psychological reaction, and there is no scientific evidence that it represents the functioning of inherited behavior patterns. Even from a practical viewpoint, as we shall attempt to show, we are forced to regard certain manifestations of race prejudice as abnormal behavior.

The demonstration of the pathological character of prejudice, which Frazier attributed to Southern whites, was not well received in Atlanta. In fact, the Atlanta Constitution took exception to his position. The virulence of public reaction, which of course proved his contention, motivated Frazier to leave Atlanta for Chicago.[7]

Document 33*

Edward Franklin Frazier, "The Pathology of Race Prejudice," Forum, Vol. LXXVII, No. 6, (June, 1927), pp. 856-861.

(The attitude of races to one another has given rise to much speculation, and many writers have maintained that men do not differ greatly from ants in their antipathies. Race hatred is so strong among ants that their battles can be arranged with certainty by entomologists for the movies. A more flattering view of human prejudices is here suggested; for if they are chiefly due to psychopa-

*Reprinted by permission.

thology there is hope that with the progress of science a somewhat more rational attitude may eventually prevail.)

> The Negro-in-America, therefore, is a form of insanity that overtakes white men.
>
> --The Southerner, by Walter Hines Page.

Although the statement above makes no claim to technical exactness, it is nevertheless confirmed by modern studies of insanity. If, in developing this thesis, we consider some of the newer conceptions of mental processes as they apply to abnormal behavior, we shall find in each case that the behavior motivated by race prejudice shows precisely the same characteristics as that ascribed to insanity. This does not refer, of course, to those phenomena of insanity due to abnormalities of the actual structure of the brain, nor does it refer to the changes that come in dementia. We are concerned here chiefly with the psychological approach to the problem of insanity,--for race prejudice is an acquired psychological reaction, and there is no scientific evidence that it represents the functioning of inherited behavior patterns. Even from a practical viewpoint, as we shall attempt to show, we are forced to regard certain manifestations of race prejudice as abnormal behavior.

The conception used to explain abnormal behavior which we shall consider first is dissociation of consciousness. Normally, the mental life appears to be a "homogeneous stream progressing in a definite direction toward a single end," as Dr. Hart puts it. That this apparent homogeneity is deceptive, even in normal minds, is shown by a little observation. Every one has had the experience of performing a task while engaged in an unrelated train of thought. In cases such as this the dissociation is temporary and incomplete, while in insanity the dissociation is relatively permanent and complete. Automatic writing in cases of hysteria, somnambulism, dual personality, and delusions are cases of the splitting off of whole systems of ideas. The conclusion of Hart that "this dissociation of the mind into logic-tight compartments is by no means confined to the population of the asylum" will lead us to those manifestations of race prejudice that show the same marked mental dissociation found in the insane. Herbert Seligman, in his book on the Negro, suggests the insane nature of Southern reactions to the blacks when he says, "The Southern white man puts certain questions beyond discussion. If they are pressed he will fight rather than argue." Southern white people write and talk about the majesty of law, the sacredness of human rights, and the advantages of democracy,--and the next moment defend mob violence, disfranchisement, and Jim Crow treatment of Negroes. White men and women who are otherwise kind and law-abiding will indulge in the most revolting forms of cruelty towards black people. Thus the whole system of ideas respecting the Negro is dissociated from the normal personality and, --what is more significant for our thesis,--this latter system of ideas seems exempt from the control of the personality.

These dissociated systems of ideas generally have a strong

emotional component and are known as complexes. The Negro complex,--the designation which we shall give the system of ideas which most Southerners have respecting the Negro,--has the same intense emotional tone that characterizes insane complexes. The prominence of the exaggerated emotional element has been noted by Josiah Royce in contrasting with the American attitude the attitude of the English in the West Indies, who are "wholly without those painful emotions, those insistent complaints and anxieties, which are so prominent in the minds of our own Southern brethren." Moreover, just as in the insane any pertinent stimulus may arouse the whole complex, so any idea connected with the Negro causes the whole Negro-complex to be projected into consciousness. Its presence there means that all thinking is determined by the complex. For example, a white woman who addresses a colored man as mister is immediately asked whether she would want a Negro to marry her sister and must listen to a catalog of his sins. How else than as the somnambulism of the insane and almost insane are we to account for the behavior of a member of a school board who jumps up and paces the floor, cursing and accusing Negroes, the instant the question of appropriating money for Negro schools is raised? Likewise, the Negro-complex obtrudes itself on all planes of thought. Health programs are slighted because it is argued Negroes will increase; the selective draft is fought because the Negro will be armed; woman suffrage is fought because colored women will vote. In many cases the behavior of white people toward life in general is less consciously and less overtly influenced by the Negro-complex. Bitter memories quite often furnish its emotional basis while the complex itself is elaborated by ideas received from the social environment.

There is a mistaken notion, current among most people, that the insane are irrational, that their reasoning processes are in themselves different from those of normal people. The insane support their delusions by the same mechanism of rationalization that normal people employ to support beliefs having a non-rational origin. The delusions of the insane, however, show a greater imperviousness to objective fact. The delusions of the white man under the influence of the Negro-complex show the same imperviousness to objective facts concerning the Negro. We have heard lately an intelligent Southern white woman insisting that nine-tenths of all Negroes have syphilis, in spite of statistical and other authoritative evidence to the contrary. Moreover, just as the lunatic seizes upon every fact to support his delusional system, the white man seizes myths and unfounded rumors to support his delusion about the Negro. When the lunatic is met with ideas incompatible with his delusion he distorts facts by rationalization to preserve the inner consistency of his delusions. Of a similar nature is the argument of the white man who declares that white blood is responsible for character and genius in mixed Negroes and at the same time that white blood harms the Negroes! Pro-slavery literature denying the humanity of the Negro, as well as contemporary Southern opinion supporting lynching and oppression, utilizes the mechanism of rationalization to support delusions.

Race prejudice involves the mental conflict, which is held to be the cause of the dissociation of ideas so prominent in insanity. The Negro-complex is often out of harmony with the personality as a whole and therefore results in a conflict that involves unpleasant emotional tension. In everyday life such conflicts are often solved by what,--in those following contradictory moral codes,--is generally known as hypocrisy. When, however, the two systems of incompatible ideas cannot be kept from conflict, the insane man reconciles them through the process of rationalization. Through this same process of rationalization, the Southern white man creates defenses for his immoral acts, and lynching becomes a holy defense of womanhood. That the alleged reasons for violence are simply defense mechanisms for unacceptable wishes is shown by a case in which a juror was lynched for voting to exonerate a Negro accused of a crime! The energetic measures which Southerners use to prevent legal unions of white with colored people look suspiciously like compensatory reactions for their own frustrated desires for such unions. Other forms of defense mechanisms appear in the Southerner's sentimentalizing over his love for the Negro and the tendency in the South to joke about him,--which has a close parallel in the humor of the alcoholic. At the basis of these unacceptable ideas, requiring rationalizations and other forms of defense mechanisms to bring them into harmony with the personality, we find fear, hatred, and sadism constantly cropping out.

When one surveys Southern literature dealing with the Negro, one finds him accused of all the failings of mankind. When we reflect, however, that the Negro, in spite of his ignorance and poverty, does not in most places contribute more than his share to crime and,--even in the opinion of his most violent disparagers,--possesses certain admirable qualities, we are forced to seek the cause of these excessive accusations in the minds of the accusers themselves. Here, too, we find striking similarities to the mental processes of the insane. Where the conflict between the personality as a whole and the unacceptable complex is not resolved within the mind of the subject, the extremely repugnant system of dissociated ideas is projected upon some real or imaginary individual. Except in the case of those who, as we have seen, charge the Negro with an inherent impulse to rape as an unconscious defense of their own murderous impulses, the persistence,--in the face of contrary evidence,--of the delusion that the Negro is a ravisher can only be taken as a projection. According to this view, the Southern white man, who has,--arbitrarily without censure,--enjoyed the right to use colored women, projects this insistent desire upon the Negro when it is no longer socially approved and his conscious personality likewise rejects it. Like the lunatic, he refuses to treat the repugnant desire as a part of himself and consequently shows an exaggerated antagonism toward the desire which he projects upon the Negro. A case has come to the attention of the writer which shows clearly the projection of the unacceptable wish. A telephone operator in a small Southern city called up a Negro doctor and told him that some one at his home had made an improper proposal to her. Although the physician protested that the message could not have come from his house the sheriff was sent to arrest him. His record in the town had been conspicuously in accord with the white man's rule about the color line. He had consistently refused to attend white men, not to mention white women, who had applied to him for treatment. Unable, in spite of his record, to escape arrest, he sought the aid of a white physician. The whole matter died down suddenly, the white physician explaining to his colored colleague that he had gone to the operator and found that she was only "nervous" that day. To those who are acquainted with the mechanism of projection, such a word as "nervous" here has a deeper significance.

The mechanism of projection is also seen in the general disposition of Southern white men to ascribe an inordinate amount of fear to Negroes. That the Negro has no monopoly of fear was admirably demonstrated in Atlanta, where, a year or so ago, white people were fleeing from a haunted road while Negroes were coolly robbing graveyards! This same mental process would explain why white men constantly lay crimes to Negroes when there is no evidence whatever to indicate the race of the criminal. Can we not find here also an explanation of the unwarranted anxiety which white men feel for their homes because of the Negro? Is this another projection of their own unacceptable complexes? In the South, the white man is certainly a greater menance to the Negro's home than the latter is to his.

We must include in our discussion two more aspects of the behavior of the insane that find close parallels in the behavior of those under the influence of the Negro-complex. We meet in the insane with a tendency on the part of the patient to interpret everything that happens in his environment in terms of his particular delusion. In the case of those suffering from the Negro-complex we see the same tendency at work. Any recognition accorded the Negro, even in the North, is regarded as an attempt to give him "social equality," the personal connotations of which are familiar to most Americans. In the South, Negroes have been lynched for being suspected of such a belief. Misconstructions such as are implied in the Southern conception of social equality are so manifestly absurd that they bear a close resemblance to the delusions of reference in the insane. Perhaps more justly to be classed as symptoms of insanity are those frequent hallucinations of white women who complain of attacks by Negroes when clearly no Negroes are involved. Hallucinations often represent unacceptable sexual desires which are projected when they can no longer be repressed. In the South a desire on the part of a white woman for a Negro that could no longer be repressed would most likely be projected,--especially when such a desire is supposed to be as horrible as incest. It is not unlikely, therefore, that imaginary attacks by Negroes are often projected wishes.

The following manifestation of race prejudice shows strikingly its pathological nature. Some years ago a mulatto went to a small Southern town to establish a school for Negroes. In order not to become persona non grata in the community, he approached the leading white residents for their approval of the enterprise. Upon his visit to one white woman he was invited into her parlor and treated with the usual courtesies shown visitors; but when this woman discovered later that he was colored, she chopped up the chair in which he had sat and, after pouring gasoline over the pieces, made a bonfire of them. The pathological nature of a delusion is shown by its being out of harmony with one's education and surroundings. For an Australian black fellow to show terror when he learns his wife has touched his blanket would not evince a pathological state of mind; whereas, it did indicate a pathological mental state for this woman to act as if some mysterious principle had entered the chair.

From a practical viewpoint, insanity means social incapacity. Southern white people afflicted with the Negro-complex show themselves incapable of performing certain social functions. They are, for instance, incapable of rendering just decisions when white and colored people are involved; and their very claim that they "know" and "understand" the Negro indicates a fixed system of ideas respecting him,--whereas a sane and just appraisal of the situation would involve the assimilation of new data. The delusions of the sane are generally supported by the herd, while those of the insane are often antisocial. Yet,--from the point of view of Negroes, who are murdered if they believe in social equality or are maimed for asking for an ice cream soda and of white people, who are threatened with similar violence for not subscribing to the Southerner's delusions,--such behavior is distinctively antisocial. The inmates of a madhouse are not judged insane by themselves, but by those outside. The fact that abnormal behavior towards Negroes is characteristic of a whole group may be an example illustrating Nietzsche's observation that "insanity in individuals is something rare,--but in groups, parties, nations, and epochs it is the rule."

In 1927 Forrester B. Washington, Urban League Fellow and Director of the Armstrong Association, Philadelphia, became Director of the Atlanta School of Social Work, succeeding E. Franklin Frazier. Washington held this position as Dean of the Atlanta University School of Social Work until his retirement in 1954. During the twenty-seven years of his administration, the school was accredited by the Association of Schools of Social Work on December 19, 1928; became affiliated with Atlanta University in 1938, being known as the Atlanta University School of Social Work; and in 1947 surrendered its charter to become an integral part of Atlanta University as one of its graduate programs. This enabled students to receive the M. S. W. degree from Atlanta University, which also assumed financial responsibility for the program.

In this essay, written just prior to his coming to Atlanta, Washington discusses the value of professional training for the social worker. The stress on the values of scientific method and research is notable, reinforcing one of the original objectives of the founders.

Document 34*

Forrester B. Washington, "What Professional Training Means to the Social Worker," Annals of the American Academy of Political and Social Science, Vol. CXXVII, (September, 1926), pp. 165-169.

The chief benefit of professional training is that it teaches the social worker to apply the scientific method to his job. The scientific method is that method which underlies all the professions. It is the method which has made a science out of medicine, out of law, out of chemistry, out of biology and the like. It first observes all the known facts about any situation that may come up in its field. It next strives to classify them into series or sequences. Having scrutinized and classified all the elements of a situation, analyzes them according to known laws. When a law is found to which the classification conforms, it is applied to the situation, or, as we would say in social work, to the solution of the problem. Let me quote F. Stuart Chapin here:--

> In this way (according to the scientific method) thinking becomes dynamic, you go from the concrete (observations of facts) to the abstract (principles). Scientific men never make the accumulation of observations an end in itself, but always a means to an end--a general intellectual conclusion.

General Advantages of Scientific Methods

What are the advantages of the scientific method as applied to social work? Let me state in reply, first of all, what the advantages are of the scientific method wherever it is used.

First of all it saves time. One does not follow the system of trial and error to learn the correct solution of a problem. One does not have to learn by his own mistakes. In other words, the trained worker in any field analyzes the situation according to known laws and puts into operation immediately the treatment that he knows is bound to be successful in the particular situation. This, of course, means a saving of time and of energy, both of which can be translated into financial advantage. The scientific method also prevents waste. Waste always results by the old method of trial and error.

Summarizing the advantages of the scientific method, it enables one to analyze the problems which confront him quickly and accurately. He is able to see the situation as a whole. He knows the causes of the conditions which confront him and the probable result of various treatments.

*Reprinted by permission of the publisher.

Advantages of Scientific Method In Social Work

Now let us proceed to a discussion of the advantages of the scientific method in social work. I have shown that saving time is one of the chief advantages of the general use of the scientific method. The saving of time means much to the social worker. In a field where financial support is still forthcoming somewhat grudgingly, money has to go "a long way." The saving of time means that a social worker can get more done for a given expenditure of money.

Secondly, I pointed out that the prevention of waste was another advantage of the general use of the scientific method. What does the prevention of waste mean to the social worker? We know what the prevention of waste means to the chemist, and we know what the prevention of waste means to the skilled machinist whose expert knowledge of the material in which he deals enables him to spoil but a small amount of it. To them it means an economic saving because acids and other raw materials are costly. There is an economic waste in the trial and error method in social work just as there is in the mechanical field. If in the latter field every error means a ruined piece of commodity--which costs money--in the social work field, every individual whom the bungling, untrained social worker fails to restore to normality means an economic loss, for he is not only failing to make a contribution to society but he continues as a burden on society; he must be supported by society and is therefore an economic charge upon society.

But there is something more than the mere economic loss in the prevention of waste in social work. Blind experimentation in social work takes its toll also in the misery caused by the impairment and sometimes destruction of that little appreciated, but most important and most valuable commodity of all--human life.

A Wholesome Philosophy of Life

I also maintain that the scientific method, which is the real basis of professional training, actually gives to the trained social worker another very necessary asset, which strangely enough some people believe professional training takes away from the social worker. It is my opinion that one cannot do effective and worth while social work (whether it be case work in the family or child placement field, or group work in the recreation or some other field), unless one has a workable and wholesome philosophy of life. This wholesome philosophy of life that the successful social worker should have and which I maintain comes out of professional training, consists of two general principles.

The first of these general principles is <u>an abundant but sensible optimism.</u> A social worker cannot do good work unless he believes enthusiastically in the value to society of his individual efforts and those of social workers in general. Few social workers have this optimism permanently unless they are trained. That is because few people are in a position to be optimistic concerning efforts in the field of social work unless they know something of social evolution. Many people, trained as well as untrained, go into social work because of some emotional urge. They are filled with a desire to improve the condition of individuals as well as of society in general. Because general improvements do not occur as swiftly as they had expected, because many individual cases do not improve at all, a large proportion of the untrained social workers come to feel after a while that the effort for the rehabilitation of the individual and society is rather a hopeless task. Many develop the notion that if there is any progress in society at all it is confined to a certain class of super men and women that has borne the same relation in size to the rest of the population ever since the world began.

But the scientific method has taught the trained worker to view the thing in the large. He turns back to his knowledge of the social sciences and finds history telling him that society has progressed favorably not only vertically but horizontally. For instance he learns, according to Todd, that five centuries ago nine-tenths of the population of what is now known as the civilized world lived below the margin of subsistence in the condition which we call poverty. He learns further that not much longer than a century ago more than one-half of this population lived under these conditions. But, on the other hand, he knows that to-day this condition has been reduced until less than one-tenth of this population live in poverty. The trained social worker is therefore much more apt to be optimistic about human progress than the untrained worker, who knows little of the social process.

The second principle of this wholesome philosophy of life is a <u>faith in humans and a knowledge of human frailties.</u>

I maintain that the scientific method has developed both of these characteristics. I can best explain what I mean by an illustration. Most of us who go into social work have certain humanitarian impulses. But in many cases, this humanitarian impulse is limited to certain types of cases. Most new social workers sympathize with the widow, and the orphaned kiddies, the aged, the crippled, the blind and all the other types of cases which are the victim of outside forces. On the other hand, few untrained workers have any sympathy and some have even a distinct abhorrence for such types of cases as the unmarried mother, the paroled prisoner, the venereally infected case, and all the other types that grow out of defects of personality.

But the trained worker is equally tolerant and sympathetic toward this second type of case. The scientific method has taught him that the abnormal behavior of the unmarried mother, the thief, and the like may result from heredity or insufficient glandular secretions or other causes entirely beyond the will and control of the individual concerned. He thinks no more of blaming or condemning these cases for their condition than a physician would think of condemning his patients for becoming ill. He is as impersonal towards them as a chemist towards his acids and alkalis. This attitude of impartiality and of toleration for human weaknesses is necessary in order to successfully treat many types of cases.

In social work, just as in general, the scientific method enables the trained worker to thoroughly analyze the situation which confronts him. He sees the causes of certain problems and he knows the proper treatment for these problems. He sees the bigness and oneness of social work, and yet the complexity of it. He knows where his particular job ends and where the problem should be turned over to some other specialist. The trained worker knows that he cannot do it all. He is not overwhelmed by the situation. He knows just how much he can do, and where some one else can help him of where some one else can take the entire problem over.

The Untrained Worker

The trouble with most untrained workers is that, if they are not overwhelmed by a big situation, they resort to impressions. Let me take an illustration from the field of housing: I have heard social workers express their gratitude that the housing situation is not nearly as bad as it was in Philadelphia because there are numbers of houses for rent. This is faulty reasoning for while there are some houses vacant, there are no more houses available for the man of small income than there were a year ago. He is suffering just as much as ever from overcrowding and its attendant evils, and the social workers' problems have not been eased a bit. The application of a little of the scientific method to this situation would have prevented the circulation of considerable misinformation.

Let me give an illustration of failure to see social problems in the large as the result of the lack of perspective of the untrained worker.

A number of years ago, in a certain southern city, a housing experiment was started at the instigation of one or two well-meaning but untrained social workers. The latter persuaded some equally well-meaning philanthropists to build a number of houses close together in a common neighborhood to be rented at a low price to the small income cases of a certain family welfare agency.

I visited this project recently, and the results are far from what workers who planned it ten or fifteen years ago had expected. The district has become an "area of infection." By throwing a lot of subnormal families together, the founders created an unwholesome atmosphere--a zone of inefficiency. These people should have been scattered among successful families, so that they might have been stimulated toward self-maintenance. As it is, those short-sighted social workers in their endeavor to solve the problems of high rents, created many other problems much more serious. However, it is the tendency of persons with little formal training to see only their angle of the problem. The case worker who has had no experience except in a family agency is apt to overlook the value or even the existence of a housing agency, or a health agency or a recreational agency and vice versa.

Keeping Abreast of The Tide

Our training in social work has taught us that we live in a changing world and that this change is taking place at a faster rate all the time and in the direction of making society and the social process more complex.

Those social workers who have training in the scientific method have learned a method that has prepared them to live in this world of change and to deal with it. It has kept them from accepting any fixed idea of an established system of social work. It has taught them that at the very time they are using methods that have been tested by experience in the past, to be critical of these methods as applied to this changing world.

I know that I would feel lost if I did not have certain professional training in back of me, and I know that I would feel lost if I did not try to keep abreast of the changes in the social process by acquiring from year to year more training.

The trained social worker is prepared to find and expects to find social work extended from year to year to include activities that formerly were not considered social work at all. The untrained social worker as a rule resents the inclusion in the social service field of social reform agencies, of good government leagues, of bureaus of municipal research. But on the other hand the trained worker can visualize the time when social work will comprehend even more than these and he can understand how a progressive welfare federation might include a symphony orchestra in its campaign and could justify it on the basis of its being a social agency doing preventive work.

Great surgeons, constantly experimenting in their fields, have made discoveries that have added years to the span of human life. Engineers working in the field of mechanics have developed transportation to a degree that would have been unbelievable to our ancestors and have so perfected the transmission of messages that they can be sent around the world almost instantaneously.

Does it not seem ridiculous that it has only been within the last twenty years that there has been a curriculum developed to prepare men and women to accelerate human progress? To be master of the process by which social changes take place is the function of the social worker. Only through training in the scientific method can he equip himself for the job.

Excerpts from this Bulletin of the Atlanta School of Social

Work indicate the stage of development which the school had reached in 1929 (the end of the period under discussion, its stated purpose and its status vis-a-vis the other five black educational institutions: Atlanta University, Morehouse College, Spelman College, Clark College, and Gammon Theological Seminary. It was in 1929 that the formal affiliation of Atlanta University, Morehouse and Spelman Colleges into the Atlanta University system began. And, on December 29, 1928, the Atlanta School of Social Work officially came of age, being accredited by the American Association of Schools of Professional Social Work.

Document 35*

Bulletin, Atlanta School of Social Work, 1929-30, Announcements, 1930-31, pp. 9-10, 11, 12-19.

GENERAL INFORMATION

Purpose

The fundamental purpose of the Atlanta School of Social Work is to serve as an institution for the training of Negroes for the profession of social work. It is rapidly becoming in addition, a promotional agency for social welfare work among Negroes over a wide area in the South.

The first function, that of the training of Negroes for social work, grew out of the recognition by a small group of white and colored social workers who attended the National Conference of Social Work at New Orleans in 1920, of the great need for social work among Negroes in the South. They realized that in spite of the war-borne migration the bulk of the 15,000,000 Negroes in America was below the Mason and Dixon line and would remain there for many years to come. They were acquainted by daily experience with the problems of family disorganization growing out of the fact that a tremendously large number of Southern Negro mothers have to work. They knew of the ill health and delinquency which result from the bad housing conditions which Negroes have to combat. They knew of the denial to the Negro of facilities for wholesome recreation. They knew of the other influences retarding the normal development of Negro adults and children not only in the cities but in the rural sections where exist the problems of the Negro tenant farmer. They also knew that the most effective work in solving the social problems that face the Negro could be performed by trained Negro social workers. Successful social work requires knowledge and sympathetic ap-

*Reprinted by permission of Atlanta University.

preciation of the traditions, customs, handicaps, ideals, habits, and, in short, the general social background of a group. There prerequisites could of course be possessed completely by no workers other than members of the Negro race. Moreover, it had been observed that the few Negroes who were trained in social work in the North were either absorbed in that section or did not care to come South.

The second function, that of acting as a center of social work, has largely been thrust upon the School. To understand how this has come about it must be borne in mind that large sections of the South are without Negro social workers or social welfare facilities available to Negroes. In various ways the Atlanta School of Social Work has attempted to fill some of the gaps in a social welfare program for the Negro until existing social agencies could be persuaded to provide the necessary facilities, or new agencies could be formed to carry them on.

These activities of the School involve the conduct of institutes and roundtables on the Negro in social work in areas widely separated from Atlanta; research investigations of Negro communities as a preliminary to plans of social treatment; the inclusion in social programs of persons who are not social workers (in the narrow concept of the word), such as United States Government Home Demonstration Agents and Agricultural Demonstration Agents, workers of the Jeannes and Slater Funds; the bringing to Atlanta on personally supervised observation tours of students in sociology from Negro colleges not located in metropolitan centers; lectures and extension courses given by its teachers to parent-teacher associations, churches, ministerial associations, club women, schools and colleges. Thus the Atlanta School of Social Work acts as a demonstrating agency of social policy and as a clearing house for social service among Negroes over a wide area....

Formal Plan of Cooperation with Local Colleges

There are more Negro colleges in Atlanta of real college grade than in any other city in the country. Under the new raised entering requirements and the new two year curriculum certain possibilities of cooperation between these colleges and the Atlanta School of Social Work presented themselves. Beginning with the year 1928-1929 a plan of cooperation was inaugurated whereby seniors majoring in social science in the five local colleges might take the first year of the two year curriculum of the Atlanta School of Social Work as a part of the requirements for the A. B. degree in their respective colleges. Thus, they could complete the curriculum in social work with one year of post-graduate work in the Atlanta School of Social Work.

Students coming from out of town colleges who have completed courses in case work, community organization and social research as part of their undergraduate work will receive credit for the same at the Atlanta School of Social Work and may complete the curriculum in less than two years. Students with a Bachelor's degree who have not had technical courses in social work will require two years to complete the curriculum.

During the past year students of Atlanta University, Morehouse College, Clark University and Gammon Theological Seminary registered in the Atlanta School of Social Work.

Courses on the Negro

Although the 15,000,000 Negroes in the United States are an integral part of the American people, yet they are separated and segregated to a large degree in the economic, political and social activities which characterize the common life of the nation.

As a result of this separation, the Negro has a different social background which has nothing to do with heredity and a great deal to do with environment. Moreover, he has been forced to develop special group organizations, including social agencies, to solve these special problems which confront him and to take the place of the general community activities from which he is excluded.

Accordingly, the social worker employed in a Negro community finds himself confronted not only with special social problems, but also with either inadequate or unusual resources for dealing with these problems. Nothing that he has been taught in the School of Social Work will tell him how to make up for the deficiencies or how to use the new resources. Everything on the curriculum had been prepared for a community where every resource that existed was available to white clients. Nothing had been taught on the other hand of the entirely different significance of such a community organization as the church in a Negro and in a white community. Social workers among Negroes have developed an elaborate technique to meet these difficulties--but it was not learned in school. They had to acquire it by the trial and error method, and, of course, during the "learning period" the clients were the sufferers.

In order to provide its students with an equipment to meet the special problems that will face them when doing social work in Negro communities, the Atlanta School of Social Work, has introduced a group of courses in social work which, so far as known, are not offered elsewhere in the country. These courses are given in addition to the full amount of technical training given in other schools and with the practical field work experience in Negro neighborhoods of Atlanta, and it is felt that the students will have a better equipment than the graduates of non-racial schools to handle the complex problems of social work in Negro Communities. They are:

"The Technique of Community Work Among Negroes."

"Industrial Problems of the Negro."

"The Conduct of Social Surveys in Negro Communities."

"Housing Problems of the Negro."

"Crime and the Negro."

"Rural Social Work and the Negro."

"Recreation and the Negro."

The School intends from time to time to add other courses to this group.

THE SCHOOL AS A CENTER OF
SOCIAL WORK IN THE SOUTH

Although the school is primarily an institution for the training of social workers it has also become a center for city, county, state, and in some cases, South wide social welfare project among Negroes. Among the social welfare projects in which the Atlanta School of Social Work has taken a leading part during the past year are the following:

Community Activities

Negro Health Week.
The School took an active part in the Atlanta Health Week Campaign for 1929. The director of the Community Work Department of the School served as secretary of the Executive Committee and students of the School assisted with the Clean-up Committee and in other activities.

Recreation Sub-Committee of Committee on Church Cooperation.
The director of the School is chairman of the sub-committee on Recreation of the Church Committee on Cooperation. This committee has made recommendations for increased and improved recreational facilities for Negroes in Atlanta which recommendations are now being acted upon by the municipality. Maps have been prepared by students of the School showing the distribution of Negro children in the city between the ages of 6 to 19, the districts having the highest percentage of Negro juvenile delinquency and other data of value in determining the best locations for Negro playgrounds.

United States Census.
The Research Department cooperated with the directors of the United States census of the Atlanta district by gathering preliminary data and preparing maps showing the distribution of the Negro population which was used as a basis in selecting Negro enumerators.

Atlanta Community Chest Campaign.
The director of the School acted as executive secretary of the colored division of the annual financial campaign of the Atlanta Community Chest for the years 1928 and 1929. The School had charge of a special district in the 1930 drive and the director, teachers and students actively engaged in the campaign.

Participation in this campaign was made the major portion of the field work of the students of the School for the period of each drive. Director, teachers and students took active part in setting up the organization, districting the city, conducting the house-to-house canvas and speaking before Negro churches and fraternal organizations.

Cooperation in Social Research

The Julius Rosenwald Fund.

At the request of the Julius Rosenwald Fund of Chicago, the Research Department of the School, under the direct supervision of the director, made a survey of industrial opportunities afforded Negroes in Atlanta and Columbus, Ga. From this survey in part plans have been worked out by the Rosenwald Fund for assistance to the industrial departments of the Negro high schools in Atlanta and Columbus.

Atlanta Social Research Council.

This body, of which the director of the School is vice-chairman, is composed of representatives of the Sociological Departments of the local colored and white colleges, the Family Welfare Society, the Research Department of the Public Schools, the Gray clinic of Grady Hospital, the Commission on Inter-racial Cooperation, the Atlanta Christian Alliance, the Atlanta Urban League and the Atlanta School of Social Work. Students of the School cooperated in the field work of various studies of living and working conditions of Negroes made by this council.

The Atlanta Negro Business League.

The Research Department of the School conducted a survey of Negro business in Atlanta for the Atlanta Negro Business League.

The Commission on Inter-racial Cooperation.

Students of the School interviewed the Negro families whose homes have been bombed during the past three years in connection with an investigation of these manifestations of racial discord conducted by the Commission on Inter-racial Cooperation.

Atlanta Evening Schools.

At the request of the principal of the Crogman Evening School, the students of the school made a survey of the district surrounding that school.

Fisk University.

At the request of the Department of Economics of Fisk University, the students of the Research Department made a study of the value of the real estate holdings of Negroes in Atlanta.

Informational Service

The Atlanta School of Social Work has one of the most complete files in the South on Social Problems and Social Work among Negroes and receives numerous inquiries concerning these subjects from both local and national organizations and individuals. During the past year the Research Department answered inquiries on housing, occupational distribution, public health work, women in industry, recreational facilities, crime, and juvenile delinquency among Negroes. A large amount of this information was collected by students.

Institutes

The School has conducted various institutes under its own auspices and has supplied social work training in institutes set up by other organizations. Those institutes which the School conducted at Atlanta were held at the School and were attended by its students and a carefully selected group of social workers, public health workers, physicians, ministers, teachers from the local community and advanced students from the local colleges. The special social problems which were the basis of the institutes held by the School at Atlanta were presented by outside experts.

Institutes Conducted By the School

Tuberculosis Prevention, Child Health and the Negro.
The content of the lectures given in this institute is discussed elsewhere in the bulletin under "Special Courses."

Social Hygiene.
The content of the lectures given in this institute is discussed elsewhere in this bulletin under "Special Courses."

Social Work Training for Religious Leaders.
This institute begun two years ago is now conducted annually by the School at Gulfside Association, Waveland, Miss., at the invitation of Bishop R. E. Jones of the Methodist Episcopal Church. It is attended by ministers and other church workers and professional and volunteer social workers from Louisiana and Mississippi. The purpose of this institute is to give these religious and lay social workers an appreciation of the latest developments in the technique of social work.

Institutes in Which the School Cooperated

The Board of Home Missions and Church Extension of the Methodist Episcopal Church, under the immediate supervision of its director of Negro work, Rev. W. A. C. Hughes, conducts in various sections of the South training institutes for rural ministers. For the past two years the Atlanta School of Social Work has been cooperating with Rev. Hughes in supplying social work training for these institutes. One or more teachers from the School have supplied social work instruction at the following institutes:

Daytona Beach, Fla.
Gammon Theological Seminary, Atlanta, Ga.
Waveland, Miss.

Cooperation with Georgia State Conference
of Social Work

The director of the School was a member of the Program Committee of the Georgia State Conference of Social Work for its 1930 conference. The school conducted at the conference a round table on "The Training of Negroes for Social Work." Several board members of the School and other authorities familiar with the need for trained Negro social workers contributed to the discussion.

It is appropriate to close this review of the black heritage in social welfare with this summary article by one of the most distinguished black practitioners, then Executive Secretary of the National Urban League.

Document 36*

Eugene Kinckle Jones, "Social Work Among Negroes," The Annals of the American Academy of Political and Social Science, Vol. CXL, (November, 1928), pp. 287-293.

The modern idea of social work among Negroes is less than twenty years old. The first Negro to set forth in a comprehensive manner an organized social work plan was George E. Haynes who, in 1910, appeared before the Committee on the Improvement of Industrial Conditions of Negroes in New York, an organization founded in 1906, to present at its request a program for investigating social conditions as a basis for practical social service in New York City.

Practical Social Service

From this plan was developed the Committee on Urban Conditions among Negroes which during the same year, 1910, was organized in the home of Mrs. William H. Baldwin, Jr., in New York City for the following purposes:

1. To bring about coordination and cooperation among existing agencies and organizations for improving the industrial, economic and social conditions of Negroes and to develop other agencies and organizations, where necessary.
2. To secure and train Negro social workers.
3. To make studies of the industrial, economic and social conditions among Negroes.
4. To promote, encourage, assist and engage in any and all kinds of work for improving the industrial, economic and social conditions among Negroes.

Also, in 1906, there was organized the National League for the Pro-

---

*Reprinted by permission of the publisher.

tection of Colored Women, which sought to do Travelers' Aid Work among the colored girls and women who were arriving in New York City principally by coastwise steamers seeking employment and better living conditions. The National League for the Protection of Colored Women had branches in Philadelphia under the leadership of Mrs. S. W. Layten and in Baltimore and in Norfolk where travelers' aid was the principal function.

The White Rose Home for Colored Working Girls, organized in 1900 by Mrs. Victoria Earle Matthews, antedated this movement by six years. Prior to the opening of this institution, Mrs. Matthews had with great sacrifice and unselfish devotion conducted volunteer travelers' aid activities in conjunction with colored women's club work.

The first colored woman to be employed as a professional family case worker was Miss Jessie Sleet (now Mrs. J. R. Scales), a trained nurse who was taken on as a case worker in the New York Charity Organization Society in 1902 by Dr. E. T. Devine, then Secretary of the Charity Organization Society. Thus it seems that Dr. Devine was the first white social work executive to realize the value of using competent, trained Negro social workers for work among their own people, whose problems they could understand and whose needs they could well interpret.

Of course, social work, as commonly understood, has been done among Negroes throughout most of the period of the Negro's life in America. As early as 1793, Catherine (Katy) Ferguson, a Negro woman, organized in New York City the first Sunday School in America. During her life she reared or placed in suitable private homes forty-eight children, twenty of whom were white. Possibly, "Katy" Ferguson had no institution to which she could send these helpless little ones, but at least she saw the advantages of the "placing out" system over that of institutional care. During the pre-Civil War anti-slavery agitation period, Isabella, a Negro woman better known as "Sojourner Truth," because of the fact that she was an itinerant lecturer, famed for her frank utterances, was a great woman's suffrage and temperance worker. In 1851, she was found to be working among the wounded soldiers in Washington. The colored orphan home in New York now known as the Riverdale Colored Orphan Asylum and Association for the Benefit of Colored Children was organized in 1838; the Old Folks' Home attached to the Lincoln Hospital was organized in 1839. Anthony Bowen, who was employed in the office of Colonel Chauncey Langdon, founder of the National Convention of the Y. M. C. A. in Boston in 1851, first presented the idea of a Young Men's Christian Association for colored people, the first formal branch of which was organized in 1888 in Norfolk, Virginia, with W. E. Hunton, a young colored Canadian, as the first Secretary. The first colored Young Women's Christian Association was organized in Philadelphia in 1876.

Purpose of Social Work

One usually thinks of social work as an organized community

effort to change social forces so as to reduce the likelihood of individuals becoming handicapped through mental defectiveness, moral delinquency or economic dependency. It comprises not only work of prevention which consumes the major portion of the time of the social worker of today, but also the great volume of social effort prosecuted in connection with family case work organizations, hospital social service and visiting nursing, instruction of the deaf, dumb and blind, training of the feebleminded, psychoanalysis, and other work with abnormal and subnormal persons--the purpose being to restore as nearly as possible to the normal, persons who have congenitally or through accident, become handicapped. The Negro social worker is enlisted in this service, but he has an added responsibility in the task of bringing the whole Negro group as a separate social entity up to a higher level of social status. In order to satisfy the critical Negro public he must show from time to time his success in securing larger opportunity for the Negro as a separate racial group.

The Negro attitude seems paradoxical. The whole idea of racial segregation is obnoxious to him, yet he demands that the Negro social worker specialize in the Negro's peculiar social problems, treat the problems of the Negro as special group problems. He wants the Negro social worker so to handle his cases that he can report on some Negro industrial worker who has a better job than any Negro has before held in a certain industry; some Negro child who is admitted to some institution for training in a field hitherto denied to Negro youth; some hospital to which a Negro patient has been admitted for the first time or to which a young Negro physician is admitted for internship, though barred hitherto; some recreational opportunities provided for Negro youth in a playground or camp or community center not before opened to them.

The most important force at work in interest of the Negro today from the point of view of the social worker is that movement which is active in making communities feel that the Negro is part and parcel of society as a whole, and that general social agencies should always consider the Negro's social needs as proportionate parts of the total social service needs of all of the people.

This would mean that whenever the Boy Scout Movement, the family welfare organization, the health agency and the prison association should begin their activities within any community, there should be a conscious and definite effort on the part of those activities to include in their programs operations within the Negro group that would vouchsafe to the Negro population steady improvement in their boy life, in their family standards, in their health status or in their moral codes. Coincidentally, there should be an extension of the facilities for the training of Negro social workers for these activities and the placing of them in strategic positions with these organizations so that the most effective work may be done.

Complementary to all of this is the demand for accurate and adequate social research and investigations among Negroes so that the actual facts of social conditions among Negroes might be ascertained as bases for intelligent and effective social work. There is hardly a large city today in America with a large Negro population in which the social work movement among Negroes has not become a vital factor in the life of the people. Southern Negro communities still suffer greatly because of the slow growth of social work among the white population, the custom being to postpone the establishment of a social agency among Negroes until a similar activity has gained a foothold among the white population of the community.

Social Work Activities

The national organizations which are most widely established among Negroes are the Young Women's Christian Association with about seventy branches for Negroes; the Young Men's Christian Association with about seventy-five city and industrial branches; the National Urban League with forty-two branches; the Boy Scouts of America with 5,923 colored scouts in 305 troops in 176 cities, and the Playground and Recreation Association with 103 locals doing work among colored people. The American Social Hygiene Association employs a Negro field worker whose health lectures have proved most helpful. (The work of the Young Women's Christian Association is similar to that of the Young Men's Christian Association--an account of whose program is given in another article in this series. I shall therefore confine my statement to the social work activities of other types of agencies.)

The National Urban League makes a specialty of seeking to improve the living and working conditions of Negroes in cities. Its Boards of Control, both national and local, are made up of white and colored citizens. Through its national office, located in New York City, with a southern field office at Atlanta, Georgia, it publishes a monthly magazine, "Opportunity" Journal of Negro Life, which presents results of social investigations and the products of the writings of white and colored persons on the problems relating to interracial contacts or to the Negro. It conducts a Department of Research and Investigations which assembles facts on Negro life which it furnishes to writers, lecturers, and students of race problems. This Department makes surveys of the social conditions among Negroes in the cities, usually under the auspices of local community chests or interracial committees, the findings of which are used by these local committees as bases for inaugurating social service programs in interest of Negro welfare. The Chicago Urban League and the University of Chicago have just completed a cooperative arrangement for maintaining a similar department for local service.

The National Urban League also maintains in New York its National Industrial Relations Department which through publicity of various kinds seeks to bring to the attention of employers of labor the availability and the dependability of Negro labor. In like manner it seeks to bring to the front competent Negro workers who may be available for the jobs that are opened up through this publicity method. This Department conducts intensive industrial campaigns in selected cities to bring Negro workers and employers together, and to bring into helpful cooperation Negro and white workers.

In working with the forty-two local Urban Leagues, this Department of Industrial Relations aims towards standardizing at least the mechanics of the locals' employment service so that there may be uniform records for exchange of information helpful to the workers.

The national office sends out monthly bulletins on the changing employment conditions so that the Negro public may know where there is a shortage of workers and in what communities there is an oversupply of workers. The purpose is to aid in the solution of the unemployment problem.

The National Urban League also maintains fellowships for the training of Negro social workers at leading schools of social work such as the New York School of Social Work, the University of Pittsburgh and the Graduate School of Social Administration of the University of Chicago. The Philadelphia Armstrong Association (the Philadelphia "Urban League") has annual scholarships at the Pennsylvania School of Social and Health Work, and this year for the first time the Columbus Urban League has a Fellow at the Ohio State University.

During the past seventeen years there have been about sixty different Fellows to receive this training through the national organizations--their field work experience being gained in connection with the local Urban Leagues, social service positions being secured for most of them by the Urban League at the conclusion of their training. Many of them are holding most important positions such as social work executives, psychiatric social workers, family case workers, teachers of social sciences, social investigators and recreation supervisors.

The local Leagues have programs to meet the peculiar needs of the communities in which they are located. Practically all of them maintain employment finding facilities for opening up new lines of occupations to Negroes and placing skilled and semi-skilled workers in these positions. They usually become the clearing houses for social service activities among Negroes. They seek to encourage the spirit of cooperation in social work for Negroes. Frequently, their programs include community houses where there are clubs and classes of various kinds for the young and for the old. They conduct health education campaigns and arrange for public interracial meetings. Emphasis is placed on securing publicity in the form of newspaper and magazine articles on Negro life to enlighten the public and to add recruits to the work of furthering interracial good will and understanding.

Community Activities

In the family case work field, Negro workers are increasingly being employed where the Negro case load is high. Boston, Cleveland, Chicago, Atlanta, Detroit, Baltimore, Memphis, Richmond, Tampa, New York, Philadelphia, Columbus, Ohio, St. Louis, Indianapolis, Louisville, Pittsburg, Minneapolis, Cincinnati, and Washington are among the cities which thus far have begun to use from one to six case workers each. Visiting nurses are used in most of the larger cities, and some southern states such as Arkansas, North Carolina, Alabama, Georgia and Virginia have definitely committed themselves to the use of Negro nurses in connection with their statewide work.

Some cities in connection with their health work are using Negro city physicians, and one experiment in community health deserves special mention: that is, the North Carolina Health and Hospital Association, Inc., which is seeking through the organization of the Negro families of Halifax County, North Carolina, to assure to all member-families on the payment of a small monthly fee of less than fifty cents per member free hospital service and medical advice and attention.

The Playground and Recreation Association of America since the World War, when it began its work as the War Camp Community Service, has conducted a special program for the organization of community activities for Negroes. It maintains a summer school for the training of its workers and seeks to provide leisure-time activities in the form of play, choral and pageant work and community house activities.

The work of the visiting teacher is being extended somewhat among Negroes, so that the colored children in many public schools are receiving the benefit of professional advice to parents on the causes of retardation. New York City and Philadelphia are outstanding cases of success in this direction, and the Jeannes and Slater Funds' teachers are being instructed to carry out these ideas in connection with their work.

The outstanding health centers among Negroes is probably the Shoemaker Center in Cincinnati, sponsored by the Public Health Federation and financed by the Cincinnati Community Chest. During the fiscal year closing April 1, 1928, there were 5,248 patients who visited the clinic. The activities consisted of the Family Service Department, Dental Clinic, Baby Clinic and General Health Clinic. The General Health Clinic includes gynecological examinations and venereal disease treatments. The staff of this Center is made up of white and colored physicians, nurses, and case workers.

The Settlement House movement among colored people has never gained very great headway, although there are reputable settlement houses in Boston, Minneapolis, and in Cleveland.

The probation work movement has gained considerable headway, most of the larger cities having Negro probation officers for work with juveniles, and in some cities probation officers are at work in connection with the courts for adults. Birmingham, Atlanta, Savannah, Richmond, Baltimore, New York, Cleveland, Chicago, Louisville are among the cities which have this work.

Child welfare in the form of day nurseries and kindergarten independent of the public school system has been quite widely extended. This year, the first child welfare center, specializing in children between the kindergarten and high school ages, is being inaugurated in New York by the Utopia Neighborhood House developed by a group of Negro Club Women.

Outstanding social housing experiments are the Schmidlapp houses in Cincinnati, a group of five- and six-room duplex homes in a detached section of Walnut Hills; the Dunbar Garden Apartments in New York City, comprising 2,000 families and occupying a whole city block, erected by Mr. John D. Rockefeller, Jr., and sold to the tenants on the cooperative plan; the City and Suburban Homes Company's group of houses in the Columbus Hill section on the west side of New York City, and a Philadelphia Housing Association. With the exception of the Dunbar Garden Apartments, the policy is to rent the houses at a low rental but sufficient to bear a legal rate of interest on the invested funds to allow for amortization.

The cost of social work among Negroes is not nearly as much in proportion as that for whites. Reports from Community Chests in sixteen cities which have member organizations doing specific work for Negroes indicated that last year a total of $367,919.51 was expended through these agencies, and that possibly about $750,000 was expended altogether by these same sixteen agencies for all of their Negro work, including the cost of social service done by white agencies for colored persons.

There are probably as many as 1,500 Negroes in America who are doing some form of social work, although possibly not more than 500 have received any special training in this field. The majority of the social work agencies today, however, are demanding not only that their workers be possessed of a college training, or its equivalent, but that some special training also be secured in the profession.

Twenty family service societies return a total of 9,060 Negro cases during 1927. This is not a full indication of the relief needs of colored families, as these agencies quite uniformly report that the Negro families are the last to apply for relief and the first to become independent again.

Many church organizations are establishing institutional features, although most of these institutional churches confine their social service activities to young peoples' meetings. Several churches have inaugurated very elaborate social service programs. For instance, the Abyssinian Baptist Church of New York City has a $325,000 building including a gymnasium, employment service, Red Cross nurse training center, adult classes and domestic science courses. The St. John's Congregational Church of Springfield, Mass., has a public library, a working girls' home, a boys' club house and a number of apartment houses, and two-family and single-family houses which it lets out at low rentals to its parishioners.

Negro Workers

Negro students in social work are accepted at all of the social service training schools in the North. In the South, there are two training centers, especially designed for Negro workers,--the Atlanta School of Social Work and the Bishop Tuttle Training School for Social Workers connected with the St. Augustine College at Raleigh, N. C. This latter institution specializes in religious workers. The Atlanta School of Social Work is especially designed to train the students for general social service.

There is probably no profession in which Negro members are on as cordial relationships with white members as is that of the social worker. In practically all of the state conferences of social work, whether north or south, there are Negro members. The National Conference of Social Work makes no discrimination in the status of its members as to race or religion. On two occasions, a colored member has been elected to the Executive Board at its annual conferences in the general elections when five members were elected from a slate of fiteen candidates, and on two other occasions Negroes have been nominated for the Board though failing of election, and on one occasion a Negro has been elected to the Board by the Executive Committee to fill out an unexpired term. Negroes have served on five or six of the twelve division committees for the past eight or ten years, and from five to twelve Negro social workers have been speakers on the annual division programs during recent years and frequently on the evening general programs of the Conference.

There is a very close connection between social work among Negroes and the whole problem of race relations in America. Effective social work among Negroes will tend to raise the level of intelligence, of physical vigor and industrial status of the group. It will give them a stronger economic foundation and a better appreciation of social values. It will develop competent and dependable leadership within the racial group. It will bring into closer cooperation white and colored leaders who are concerned about community welfare and will have the effect of making Negroes an articulate group in the community. It will destroy all arguments against giving the Negro his rights on the ground that he cannot use these rights properly. It will remove from the Negro masses the feeling of insufficiency or inferiority which might cause Negroes to hesitate in their yearnings for larger opportunities and their demands for the chance to occupy their rightful place in the life of the nation. It will help to produce a hearty race, a self-contained group, a resourceful people from whom will emerge outstanding characters whose special contributions to the welfare of man will tend to bring more respect for and more confidence in the Negro as a people. And this is the essential element in the solution of what has been described as "America's greatest problem."

NOTES--PART IV

1. Monroe N. Work, ed., The Negro Year Book, 1918-1919, (Tuskegee, Alabama. Negro Year Book Publishing Co., 1919), p. 9.

2. Ibid., p. 12.

3. George E. Haynes, "Negro Migration, Its Effect on Family and Community Life," Opportunity, Vol. II, (October, 1924), p. 305.

4. Guichard Parris and Lester Brooks, Blacks in the City, (Boston: Little, Brown and Co., 1971).

5. L. Hollingworth Wood, "The Urban League Movement," Journal of Negro History, Vol. 9, (1924), p. 118.

6. Ibid., p. 120.

7. Interview with Mrs. Marie Franklin Fundenberg, widow of E. Franklin Frazier, July 17, 1975.

EPILOGUE

The black heritage in social welfare has been revealed, documented and interpreted in the previous pages of this book. The image which it projects on the screen of history may be viewed as the struggle of the black population for survival, for freedom and for equality of opportunity in an alien land among and against an alien people. Beginning with the traumatic experience of forced migration and continuing through the period of involuntary servitude, only to suffer the deprivations imposed by the system of *de jure* segregation in some of the several states and *de facto* segregation in most of the others, the black population began to mobilize itself in order to overcome the hardships and frustrations of second class citizenship.

It was indeed necessary for the black population, as constrained and circumscribed as it was in its development by the almost universal practice of both overt and institutionalized acts of racism, to engage, in the words of Romanyshyn, in "all those forms of social intervention that have a primary and direct concern with promoting both the welfare of the individual and the society as a whole." So motivated, blacks innovated and initiated creative programs, policies and projects in the field of social welfare, benefiting not only themselves, but to the ultimate benefit of all Americans. The record demonstrates that black efforts in the interest of group advancement were not limited to the duplication of social services modeled upon the programs and policies of social welfare devised, organized, funded, controlled and directed by whites. The black heritage is a complex of genuine responses by black people reacting to the need for social welfare services in their own communities. Blacks initiated and formulated policies and programs, mobilized group and community resources, and cooperated collectively in efforts designed to cope with the exigencies of black misery and suffering and to establish the social support and social security to alleviate, if not overcome, that suffering.

This interpretation does not mean to imply that the efforts and contributions of whites were trivial, unnecessary, or insignificant in effect of accomplishment. Rather, it means that collectively, blacks rose above the triple handicaps of slavery, segregation and racism to develop (most often perhaps with the aid, assistance, encouragement, and guidance of some whites,) institutions of social welfare which were most vital to the attainment of an ensurance of their biological, psychological, social, and cultural survival. But beyond survival itself, there was continual effort and enterprise to advance standards of living and to enhance the quality of life.

It has been demonstrated that this required extraordinary efforts on the part of competent individuals supported by well-organized groups. While we recognize similar accomplishments by many white ethnic Americans who migrated voluntarily to these shores, for the most part, they were not subject to de jure segregation and, therefore, did not have to wage a simultaneous struggle for their civil rights. Their struggle was waged primarily in the economic sectors, and the response of the community to their wants and needs was more direct and immediate.

Thus, it was necessary for members of the black population to develop a variety of responses to the manifold needs of social welfare responses which were for altering conditions presented at various times and locales in the course of their history. For example, some took settlement and colonization outside the continental limits of the United States. Despairing of ever attaining their dreams in the land of their birth, utopias were sought in Africa or other parts of the Americas. Others, however, attempted to ameliorate their status in this country by migrating from the locale of slavery to the north and to the west, to those frontiers which offered the potentials for the establishment of all- or majority-black townships and communities. In these communities blacks had hoped that, at least, the control of local government would reside in the members of the black population. Where attempted, this option was generally frustrated by the ultimate dependence of the local community upon the policies of state and federal governments.

Some members of the black population migrated individually, from farm to city; but, most chose to remain in their home communities, utilizing whatever existing resources were available to them and improvising new institutions of social welfare to minister to newly experienced needs. This approach proved intermittently successful, stimulating the development of organizational structures which catered to the needs of black families: children, adults and the aged. Some of these structures are still operative today, remaining viable supports in the black community. In many cases, however, the development in the larger community of Community Chests and Councils after World War I coopted the programs and services initiated and funded by blacks consolidating overall community services but, as a consequence, generating new needs and problems for blacks. Nevertheless, the variety of experiences encountered set the stage and laid the foundations for building a heritage of organizational structures and skills which blacks could call into play whatever the circumstances.

The onset of the Depression in 1929 again necessitated Federal intervention in the social process. Massive Federal programs were devised to stimulate production, decrease unemployment, and provide new forms of public assistance and social security. For the first time since Reconstruction blacks competent in social planning and social administration were enlisted to work in the new agencies and bureaucracies created to promote the general welfare. At the highest level stood those blacks who, collectively, came to be known as "the Black Cabinet" of the Franklin Delano Roosevelt administration. During this period some programs were initiated by executive order, some by congressional legislation, and some by judicial decree, all of which combined to broaden the jurisdiction of the Federal government to act in the interest of the general welfare. For the first time many social problems were recognized as national in scope, requiring a national remedy, and blacks were employed in advisory positions to cope with the special problems and needs of their fellows. The overall intent of federal intervention was to rescue the poor and disadvantaged and to spur the economic recovery of the nation. However, its main effect upon members of the black community was to develop the upward mobility of its middle class, for the exclusionary aspects of federal policies and programs, administered in an environment steeped in institutionalized racism, denied many social welfare benefits to the vast majority of the black population. For instance, while social security was recognized as a form of national insurance, its benefits were initially denied to domestic and farm workers, and it required an additional generation of social struggle to achieve equity.

The economic crisis which spawned the new national welfare policies was alleviated by the onset of World War II. Young black males, and later some females, were inducted into the military services in large numbers, but these services were segregated. Moving black males all over the country and eventually overseas, the military provided them with new opportunities for the evaluation of their position in American society, stimulating in them, to a degree never before possible, demands for first class citizenship and broadened participation in the economy and the polity. Additional social awareness and group identification of blacks as members of a national community was intensified by the co-mingling of black males from farm and ghetto.

Some nine years after the cessation of hostilities the Legal and Educational Defense Fund of the National Association for the Advancement of Colored People (N. A. A. C. P.) directly and successfully challenged the national policy of de jure segregation in the 1954 decision of Brown v. Topeka. This decision overturned the doctrine of "separate but equal" which had prevailed since the Plessy v. Ferguson opinion of the Supreme Court in 1896.

This monumental decision of the Supreme Court of Chief Justice Earl Warren has had the most far reaching consequences of any Federal intervention in the social process. Coupled with the rise of African nationalism, which toppled the colonial regimes of Great Britain, France, and Belgium from 1956 to 1960, it acted as a stimulus to black youth to proudly assume leadership in the civil rights movement, employing on a large scale the strategy of non-violent protest and demonstration so ably articulated and guided by the late Dr. Martin Luther King, Jr. A new ethos of black awareness, consciousness, identity and pride emerged, with the overpowering social and psychological effect of transforming the upward movement of blacks from basically a defensive one to an offensive set of tactics and strategy. Legal efforts to implement the Fourteenth Amendment were transformed in social action movements which asserted, forcefully, the right of blacks not only to aspire to but also to achieve freedom and equality.

These movements catapulted into prominence Dr. Martin Luther King, Jr., and the Southern Christian Leadership Conference (SCLC). He and the organization worked tirelessly to promote group cohesiveness and to push for social legislation of benefit to blacks. At the time of his assassination Dr. King had promulgated plans for uniting all the poor, irrespective of their ethnic origins, in a campaign to combat poverty, neglect, and oppression. Such a union has yet to be achieved, but the black movement for justice has given new birth to the aspirations of other ethnic minorities: the Spanish-speaking Puerto Ricans and Chicanos, the Amerindians, and the Asian-Americans.

All of this transpired between 1935 and 1975, a forty-year period, one-fifth of the life of this nation. As the bicentennial year is celebrated, a new cycle of economic depression threatens the general welfare. However, it is predictable that Americans of African descent in the government and the social welfare services will render distinguished contributions to the efforts to prevail against the tides which threaten to submerge the national cause and heritage.

BIBLIOGRAPHY

PROLOGUE

Armistead, William. Anthony Benezet from the original memoir, revised with additions by Wilson Armistead. London: A. W. Bennett, Bishopsgate Street.

Beasley, Delilah. The Negro Trailblazers of California. Los Angeles, 1919.

Bennett, Lerone, Jr. "The Making of Black America", Part I, XXIV Ebony, June 1969.

_______. "The Making of Black America", Part III, XXV Ebony, August, 1970.

Blassingame, John W. The Slave Community. Plantation Life in the Ante-Bellum South. New York: Oxford University Press, 1972.

Cipolla, Carlo. Guns, Sails and Empires: Technological Innovation and the Early Phase of European Expansion, 1400-1700. New York: Pantheon Books, 1965.

Drake, St. Clair. The Redemption of Africa and Black Religion. Chicago: Third World Press or Atlanta Institute of the Black World, 1970.

DuBois, W. E. B. "My Evolving Program for Negro Freedom" in What the Negro Wants, ed. Reyford W. Logan. Chapel Hill, N. C.: University of North Carolina Press, 1944.

Foster, Lawrence. Negro-Indian Relationships in the Southeast. Philadelphia, 1935.

Gipson, Lawrence Henry. The British Empire Before the American Revolution Vol. II, The British Isles and the American Colonies: The Southern Plantations, 1748-1754. New York: A. A. Knopf, 1960.

_______. The British Empire Before the American Revolution Vol. XIII, The Empire Beyond the Storm, 1770-1776. New York: A. A. Knopf, 1967.

Herskovits, Melville J. The Myth of the Negro Past. New York:

Harper and Brothers, 1941.

Jackson, William S., Joanne V. Rhone and Charles L. Sanders. Social Service Delivery System in the Black Community During the Antebellum Period (1619-1860). Alton M. Childs Series, Atlanta University School of Social Work, 1973.

Klein, Herbert S. Slavery in the Americas, A Comparative Study of Cuba and Virginia. Chicago: University of Chicago Press, 1967.

Miller, Loren. The Petitioners. The Story of the Supreme Court of the United States and the Negro. New York: Pantheon Books, 1966.

Morris, Richard B. Government and Labor in Early America. New York: Octagon Books, Inc., 1965.

Pike, Ruth. "Slavery in Seville at the Time of Columbus," From Conquest to Empire. The Iberian Background to Latin American History, edited with Introduction by H. B. Johnson, Jr. New York, 1970.

Pumphrey, Ralphe and Muriel W., eds. The Heritage of American Social Work. New York: Columbia University Press, 1961.

Romanyshyn, John M. Social Welfare Charity to Justice. New York: Random House and Council on Social Work Education, 1971.

Russell, John H. The Free Negro in Virginia, 1619-1865. New York: Dover Publications, Inc., 1969; originally published in 1913 by the Johns Hopkins Press, Baltimore.

Warner, Robert Austin. New Haven Negroes, A Social History. New Haven: Yale University Press, the Institute for Human Relations, 1940.

PART I

Ames, Mary. From a New England Woman's Diary in Dixie in 1865. Springfield, Mass.: n.p., 1906.

Commager, Henry Steele, editor. Writings of Abraham Lincoln, Constitutional ed., Vol VII cited in Documents of American History. New York: Appleton-Century-Crofts, 1949.

DuBois, W. E. B. Black Reconstruction in America, 1860-1880. New York: Atheneum Press, 1969.

Forten, Charlotte L. The Journal of Charlotte Forten, A Free Negro in the Slave Era, edited with an introduction and notes by Ray Allen Billington. New York: Collier Books, 1958.

Hendricks, George. "Union Army Occupation of the Southern Seaboard, 1861-1865." Abstract, unpublished Ph. D dissertation, Columbia University, 1954.

Hubbard, G. W. History of Colored Schools of Nashville, Tennessee. Nashville, Tenn.: Wheeler, Marshall and Price Printers, 1874.

Letters of Teachers and Superintendents of the New England Educational Commission for Freedmen, Fourth Series. Boston: David Clapp, 1864.

Lindsay, Inabel Burns. "Some Contributions to Welfare Services 1865-1900," Journal of Negro Education, No. 25, Winter, 1956.

Low, W. A. "The Freed Men's Bureau in the Border States," Radicalism, Racism and Party Realignment. The Border States During Reconstruction, ed. Richard O. Corry, Baltimore: The Johns Hopkins Press.

Miller, Loren. The Petitioners, The Story of the Supreme Court of the United States and the Negro. New York: Pantheon Books, 1966.

Pierce, E. L. "The Freedmen at Port Royal," Atlantic Monthly, XXII September, 1963.

Proceedings of the Constitutional Convention of South Carolina, Vol. I Charleston, S. C.: Dening and Perry Printer, 1868.

Stampp, Kenneth M. The Era of Reconstruction 1865-1877. New York: Alfred A. Knopf, 1965.

Taylor, Susie King. Reminiscences of My Life in Camp with the 33rd United States Colored Troops Late 1st S. C. Volunteers. Boston: The Author, 1902.

Wilson, Joseph T. Emancipation Its Course and Progress. Hampton, Va, 1882.

Work, Monroe N. Negro Yearbook 1919. Tuskegee, Ala.: The Negro Yearbook Pub. Co., 1919.

PART II

Arthur, Stanley Cisby. Biographical sketch of Isaiah T. Montgomery, The Item, (New Orleans), September 25, 1922; reprinted in the Journal of Negro History, Vol. VIII, January, 1923.

Barnett, Ida Wells. A Red Record. Chicago: Donahue and Henneberry, 1895.

Bowen, J. W. E., editor. Africa and The American Negro. Atlanta, Ga., 1896.

Carter, E. R. The Black Side. Atlanta, Ga., 1894.

DuBois, W. E. B. "The Study of the Negro Problems," Publications of The American Academy of Political and Social Science, No. 219. An address to the Academy, November 19, 1897.

________. The Philadelphia Negro, A Social Study. Publications of the University of Pennsylvania Series in Political Economy and Public Law, No. 14. Philadelphia: University of Pennsylvania, 1899.

________, editor. Some Efforts of American Negroes for Their Own Social Betterment. The Atlanta University Publications, No. 3, 1898.

Haley, James T., editor. Afro-American Encyclopedia. Nashville, Tenn.: Haley and Florida, 1896.

Hammond, L. H. "A Woman Banker," In The Vanguard of a Race. New York: Friendship Press, 1922.

Leiby, James. "Social Work and Social History," Social Service Review, September, 1969.

Lindsay, Inabel B. "The Participation of Negroes in the Establishment of Welfare Services 1865-1900." Unpublished Ph.D dissertation, University of Pittsburgh, 1952.

O'Leary, Patrick. "The Black Worker and the Trade Union Movement, 1865-1900." Unpublished MS Atlanta University School of Social Work, 1974.

Rippy, J. Fred. "A Negro Colonization Project in Mexico, 1895." Journal of Negro History, Vol. 6, 1921.

Schwendemann, Glen. "St. Louis and the Exodus of 1870," Journal of Negro History, Vol. 46, 1931.

Smith, R. L. "An Uplifting Negro Cooperative Society," World's Work 16(June, 1908).

Work, Monroe N. "The Church and the Negro Community," Southern Workman, XXVII, 37(August, 1908).

Yeatman, James E. Report to the Western Sanitary Commission in Regard to Leasing Abandoned Plantation with Rules and Regulations Governing the Same. St. Louis: Western Sanitary Commission Rooms, No. 10 North 5th Street, 1864.

PART III

Bittle, William E. and L. Gilbert Geis. "Alfred Charles Sam and an African Return, A Case Study in Negro Despair". Phylon, XXIII, 1962.

Bowen, J. W. E. "An Appeal to the King." Address on Negro Day in the Atlanta Exposition, October 21, 1895, Atlanta, Georgia.

Bulletin of National League on Urban Conditions Among Negroes. Report 1912-1913, Announcement 1913-1914, "Foreword," Vol. III, No. 2 November, 1913.

DuBois, W. E. B. "The National Association for the Advancement of Colored People," The Horizon, Vol. VI, No. 2, July, 1910.

_______. "Play for Negroes," World's Work, Vol. 23, January, 1912.

_______. "The Upholding of Black Durham," World's Work, Vol. 23, January, 1912.

Haynes, George E. "Cooperation with Colleges in Securing and Training Negro Social Workers for Urban Centers." Proceedings of the National Conference of Charities and Corrections, Boston, 1911. Fort Wayne, Ind.: Fort Wayne Printing Co., 1911.

Proctor, Henry Hugh. Between Black and White. Boston: Pilgrim Press, 1914.

Shivery, Louie D. The History of Organized Social Work Among Atlanta Negroes 1890-1935. Unpublished Master of Arts Thesis, Department of Sociology, Atlanta University, 1936.

"The Significance of the Niagara Movement," Editorial, The Voice of the Negro, Vol. II, No. 9 September, 1905.

Washington, Booker T. Up from Slavery, An Autobiography. New York: A. L. Burt and Company, 1900.

Williams, Fannie B. "Growth of the Settlement Idea," The New York Age, August 5, 1905.

PART IV

Alexander, Will W. "Phylon Profile XI: John Hope," Phylon, 1947.

Atlanta School of Social Work-- Bulletins, 1920-1931.

Frazier, E. Franklin. "The Pathology of Race Prejudice," Forum,

Vol. LXXVII, No. 6, June, 1927.

________. "The Garvey Movement," *Opportunity*, Vol. IV, November, 1926.

Garvey, Amy Jacques. "Aims and Objects of Movement for Solution of Social Problems," in *Philosophy and Opinions of Marcus Garvey or Africa for the Africans*, N. Y. Universal Publishers of UNIA, 1923.

Haynes, George E. "Negro Migration, Its Effects on Family and Community Life in the North," *Opportunity*, Vol. 2, No. 22, October, 1924.

________. "Negroes Move North. II: Their Arrival in the North," *The Survey*, January 4, 1919.

________. "The Negro Laborer and the Immigrant," *The Survey*, May 14, 1921.

________. "The Church and the Negro Spirit," *Survey Graphic*, 1925.

Hill, T. Arnold. "Recent Developments in the Problem of Negro Labor," *Proceedings of the National Conference of Social Work*, Milwaukee, 1921.

Jackson, J. A. "Colored Actors Union," *The Messenger*, September, 1925.

Jones, Eugene Kinckle. "The Negroes Struggle for Health," *Proceedings of the National Conference of Social Work*, Washington, D. C., 1923.

________. "Building A Larger Life," *Opportunity*, March, 1923.

________. "Social Work Among Negroes," *The Annals of the American Academy of Political and Social Science*, Vol. CXL, November, 1928.

Kellor, Frances A. "Assisted Emigration from the South," *Charities*, Vol. 15, October 7, 1905.

"Letters of Negro Migrants 1916-1918," *Journal of Negro History*, Vol. IV, July, 1919.

Locke, Alain. "The New Negro," *Survey Graphic*, Vol. LIII, 1924-25.

Nelson, Alice Dunbar. "Negro Women in War Work," Chapter XXVII. *The American Negro in the World War* by Emmett J. Scott, 1919.

Powell, A. Clayton. "The Church in Social Work," *Opportunity*, January 14, 1923.

Ragland, John Marshall. "A Hospital for Negroes with a Social Service Program," Opportunity, December, 1923.

Randolph, A. Philip. "The Truth About the Brotherhood of Sleeping Car Porters," The Messenger, February, 1926.

Thomas, Jesse O. My Story in Black and White. New York: Exposition Press, 1967.

Washington, Forrester B. "What Professional Training Means to the Social Worker," Annals of The American Academy of Political and Social Science, Vol. CXXVIII, September, 1926.

Wood, L. Hollingworth, "The Urban League Movement," Journal of Negro History, Vol. 9, 1924.

Woofter, T. J. "Organization of Rural Negroes for Public Health," Proceedings of the National Conference of Social Work, Washington, D. C., 1923.

Work, Monroe. The Negro Year Book. 1918-1919.

________. "Problems of Negro Urban Welfare," The Southern Workman, January, 1929.

INDEX

A. M. A. see American Missionary Association
A. M. E. Churches see African Methodist Episcopal Churches
Abandoned plantations 63ff
Abolitionist movement 4
Abyssinian Baptist Church, New York City 296, 407, 411ff, 462
Adams, Mrs. K. R. 253
  quoted 256
Adams, Myron W. 430, 431
Addams, Jane 204, 206
African continuum 5
African Ecclesiastical Society, New Haven, Conn. 33
African Methodist Episcopal Churches 29, 85, 112, 231
African presence in North America 7
African trading posts 8
Afro-American churches 4, 132
Afro-American Council 199
Afro-Americans
  as social workers 236
  in California 33
  in Durham, N. C. 225ff
  in Kansas 118ff
  in Mexico 113
  in New Haven, Conn. 33
  in St. Louis, Mo. 125
Afro-Spanish artisans 10
Agricultural, Industrial and Colonization Company of Tlahualil, Ltd. (Mexico) 114
Akim Trading Company, Ltd. 187
Alexander, Will W. 374
All-black communities 3, 28, 114, 181, 300
Allensworth, California 189ff
Alpha Suffrage Club, Chicago, Illinois 164
Amalgamated Clothing Workers of America 359
American Colonization Society 28
American Federation of Labor 359
American Missionary Association 62, 76, 80, 87, 252, 253
American Red Cross 385, 399
American Social Hygiene Association 346, 459
Americus Institute, Americus, Ga. 216
Amey, C. C. 228
Anti-Lynching Bureau 163
Armstrong Association, Philadelphia, Pa. 412, 460
Ashley, Simon S. 253
Association for the Protection of Colored Women 379
Atlanta Community Chest 263
Atlanta Constitution (newspaper) 439
  quoted 268
Atlanta Cotton States and International Exposition, 1895 177
Atlanta Inter-racial Committee 251, 257
Atlanta Negro Business League 454
Atlanta Race Riot, 1906 249
Atlanta School of Social Work 434, 426, 430, 444, 463; see also Atlanta University School of Social Work
Atlanta School of Social Work. Charter 437ff
Atlanta Social Research Council 454
Atlanta University, Atlanta, Ga. v, 152, 235, 244, 252, 262, 264, 375, 377, 423, 425, 430, 450
  Conferences 259, 423
  Publications 153ff, 423
  School of Social Work v, 444; see also Atlanta School of Social Work

System 450
Augusta, Alexander T. 77
Ayer, Frederick 253

Baldwin, Maria L. 235
Baldwin, Mrs. William H. 456
Banneker, Benjamin 24
Baptist churches 29
Barnett, Ida B. Wells vi, 162ff
Barton, Bruce, quoted 254ff, 257
Beaufort, S. C. 41, 48, 73, 93
Beaufort County Poor Farm 75
Belcher, May 391
Benezet, Anthony 29
Bennett, Lerone, Jr., quoted 7, 14
Bentley, Charles E. 203
Bethel African Methodist Episcopal Church, Chicago, Ill. 408
Bethune, Mary McLeod 385, 392
Bigham, John Alvin 267
Bird, Crystal 391
Bishop Tuttle Training School for Social Workers, Raleigh, N. C. 463
Black, Charles L. 170
Black churches 296
Black codes 99
Black consciousness 20
Black labor organizations 150
Black philanthropy 31
Black schools in Philadelphia 30
Blassingame, John W., quoted 4
Boley, Okla. 184, 285, 300ff
Bowen, Anthony 457
Bowen, John Wesley Edward 193, 258
quoted 178ff
Bowles, Eva D. 388
Boy Scouts of America 257, 459
Brady, Mabel S. 391
Braithwaite, William Stanley 221
Brotherhood of Sleeping Car Porters 287, 352, 362, 364
Brown, Charlotte Hawkins 385
Brown, John 34, 202, 204
Brown, John M. 120
Brown, Laura 398
Brown, Russell 430
Brown University, Providence, R. I. 379
Brown v. Topeka 468
Bryant, Fletcher 256
Bullock, Matthew W. 402, 423
Bumstead, Horace 152
Burke, Cora 393
Burleigh, Harry Thacker 235, 258
Bush, William 258
Butler, Benjamin Franklin 42, 45, 61, 167

Cabaniss, George W. 402
Cain, Richard H. 103
California Colony and Home Promotion Association 190
Calvary Independent Methodist Church, New York City 407
Cardoza, Francis L. 103, 105
Carey, Alice Dugged 392
Carnegie, Andrew 247
Carr, Julian S. 229
Carrie Steele Pitts Orphans Home, Atlanta, Ga. vi, 254
Carter, Elizabeth 391
Chadwick, Amy 259, 263
Chandler v. Neff 372
Channell, Robert J. 371
Chapin, F. Stuart, quoted 445
Chicago Race Riot, 1919 324, 331ff
Chicago Urban League, Chicago, Ill. 356, 360
Childs, A. Walter 273
Chivers, Walter B. 423, 424
Christophe, Henri 20
Cipolla, Carlo M., quoted 7
Circle of Negro War Relief 395
City and Suburban Homes Company, New York City 462
Civil Rights Act of 1875 167
Claremont Colleges, Claremont, Cal. 378
Clark College, Atlanta, Ga. 244, 450
Clyatt v. U.S. 209ff
Cobb, James A. 371
Cole, Currie Dukes 268
Colored Actors Union 352, 369ff

Colored Men's Protective Association, Atlanta, Ga. 146ff
Colored Nurses Association 385
Colored Protective Association, Atlanta, Ga. 149
Colored Refugee Relief Board, St. Louis, Mo. 128
Columbia University, New York City 238, 243
Commission on Interracial Cooperation 286, 350, 373ff, 375, 454
Committee for Improving the Industrial Condition of Negroes in New York 241
Committee on the Improvement of Industrial Conditions of Negroes in New York 456
Committee on Urban Conditions, New York City 238
Compromise of 1877 170
Congress of Industrial Organizations (CIO) 287
Conservator (newspaper) 164
Convention for the Improvement of Free People of Colour of the U. S., 1833 31
Cook, Amorel 393
Cook, Mrs. George W. 215
Cooley, Rossa B. 210
Cotton States Exposition, 1895 247; see also Atlanta Cotton States and International Exposition, 1895
Council of National Defense 392
Cravath, Erastus 252
Creary, W. F. 404
Creek Indians 27
"Creole" culture 15, 17, 19
Crispus Attucks Circle, Philadelphia, Pa. 395
Cromwell, Mary 390
Cultural survivals 17
Cummings, Ida 393
Curtis, Helen Noble 403, 404
Curtis, James L. 403

Dahomey 17
Daughters of Samaria, Atlanta, Ga. 146
Davenport, Mrs. H. C. 392
Davis, Jackson 215
Davis, Jefferson, former slave 114
Davis Bend, Miss. 114
DeBerry, W. N. 250
DeFrantz, Robert B. 399
Delany, Martin 77, 111, 112
Depriest, Oscar 285
Dericotte, Juliette 391
Dessalines, Jean Jacques 20
Devine, E. T. 457
Dexter, Robert Cloutman 427, 431, 434
Dickerson, Mary 431
Dodge, Cleveland 262
Dodge, Grace 262
Douglass, Frederick 90, 151
Douglass, Joseph 258
Douglass, Louis 205
Dred Scott decision 14
Dublin, Louis I. 295
DuBois, William E. B. vi, 111, 152, 153, 193, 198, 204, 217, 233, 247, 258, 285, 423
    quoted 5
Duke, Washington 229
Dunbar, Paul Laurence 221
Dunbar Garden Apartments, New York City 462
Durham, Plato 257
Dyadic relations 17

East Saint Louis (Illinois) Race Riot, 1917 323
Edisto refugees 52, 55
Educational Commission, Boston, Mass. 47
Eighth Street Colored Baptist Church, St. Louis, Mo. 126
Ellis, H. 114
Emancipation Proclamation, 1863 217
Emigration and migration 13
Evanti, Lillian 258
"Exodusters" vi, 128

Fair Street Clinic, Atlanta, Ga. 268
Family plot system 79
Farmers' Improvement Society of Texas 136ff

Faulkner, William J. 257, 379
Federated Churches of Cleveland, Ohio 295
Federated Women's Club, Chicago, Ill. 232
Ferguson, Catherine (Katy) 457
15th New York Regiment 396
    Women's Auxiliary 396
54th Regiment Massachusetts Volunteers 61
First African Baptist Church, Savannah, Ga. 86
First Congregational Church, Atlanta, Ga. 243, 251, 260
First Regiment of South Carolina Volunteers 59, 73, 75
Fisk University, Nashville, Tenn. 235, 240, 242, 252, 423, 425, 454
    Department of Science and Social Work 237
Fitzgerald, R. B. 228
Foreman, Clark 377
Forten, Charlotte L. 70, 73
Forten, James 70
Fortress Monroe, Va. 42, 144
Fortune, T. Thomas 151, 152
Foster, Manuel 430
Francis, Cyrus W. 252
Frazier, Edward Franklin v, 423, 424, 433, 436
    quoted 439
Free Kindergarten Association for Colored Children, New York City 233
Free Negroes 13, 20
    in North Carolina 20
    in Spain 10
Freedmen's Bureau 63, 74, 76, 77, 96, 103, 105
Freedmen's Hospital, Washington, D. C. 78
Freedmen's Relief Association, New York City 47
Friendship Baptist Church, Atlanta, Ga. 147, 262
Frissell, Hollis Burke 214
Fugitive slave legislature 23
Fugitive slaves 27

Gammon Theological Seminary, Atlanta, Ga. 244, 374, 450
Gandy, John Mercer 215
Garrison, William Lloyd 206
Garvey, Marcus 285, 304, 307
Gate City Free Kindergarten Association, Atlanta, Ga. 258, 264
Georgia Educational League 165
Georgia State Conference of Social Work 456
Georgia State Federation of Colored Women's Clubs 392
Gibson, Truman Kella 258
Gipson, Lawrence H., quoted 8
Grace Congregational Church, New York City 407
Grant, Abram 140
Green, Hattie 431
Green, Sallie 393
Greener, Richard T. 204
Gregory, J. Francis 399
Grimké, Archibald Henry 193
Grimké, Francis James 70, 193, 221
Guinea 20
Guinea, Empire of 8
Guinn v. U. S. 171

Hackley, Azalia 258
Hale, J. H. 425
Hale, Millie E. 425
Haley, Victoria Clay 393
Hampton Institute, Va. 152
Hampton Negro Conference, 1912 214
Hapgood, Emily Bigelow 395
Harben, Robert, Jr. 168ff
Harper, William Rainey 378
Harrison, Hazel 258
Harrison, Richard B. 258
Hart, Albert Bushnell, quoted 440
Hayes, Roland 258
Haynes, George Edmund 180, 216, 217, 235, 249, 292, 293, 385, 423, 456
    quoted 412, 424
Henderson, George W. 245
Herndon, Adrienne 258, 260

Herndon, Alonzo F. 260, 263
Herndon Day Nursery, Atlanta, Ga. 261
Herskovits, Melville J., quoted 5
Higginson, Thomas Wentworth 59, 60, 61, 71
Hill, Gertrude B. 393
Hill, Walter 430
Hilton Head, S. C. 77, 93
Hinsman, Zebedee 191
Hope, John v, 374, 376, 402, 431, 434
Hope, Lugenia (Mrs. John) 180, 260, 265, 269, 374, 385, 431, 434
Hopkins, Charles T. 245
Horizon (periodical) 206
Hospital of Our Lady of the Angels, Seville, Spain 9
Hostess Houses movement 389, 403
House servants 18
Houston Race Riot, 1917 324
Howard, Mrs. David T. 260
Howard, Oliver Otis 76, 93, 97, 98, 104, 106
Howard, Perry W. 364, 365
Howard University, Washington, D. C. 240, 242, 399, 425
  School of Social Work 424
Howell, Clark, quoted 178
Howley, Charles W. 253
Hubbard, G. W. 89
Hunton, Addie Waites 385, 403, 404
Hunton, William Alphaeus 385, 403, 457

I. O. O. F. see Independent Order of Odd Fellows
Ida B. Wells Woman's Club, Chicago, Ill. 164
Indentured servants 11, 13
Independent Order of Good Samaritans, Atlanta, Ga. 146
Independent Order of Odd Fellows
  St. James Lodge No. 1455, Atlanta, Ga. 148ff
  Star of the South No. 1456 149
Independent Order of St. Luke, Richmond, Va. 134
Indians of North America 6
Industrial Workers of the World 359
Institute of Social Service 432
Interracial Committee of Toledo, Ohio 294

Jackson, Mary E. 391
Jackson, William S., quoted 4
Jeanes, Anna T. 211
Jefferson, Thomas 22, 24
Johnson, Andrew 93
Johnson, Charles Spurgeon 423, 425
Johnson, George 191
Johnson, George L. 399
Johnson, J. Rosamond 221
Johnson, James Weldon 325, 377
Johnson, Kathryn M. 404
Jones, Ashby 374
Jones, Eugene Kinckle 240, 431
Jones, Jenkin Lloyd 206
Jones, N. J. 146
Josephine Gray Colored Lady Knitters of Detroit (Mich.) 397
Julius Rosenwald Fund 454

Kealing, Hightower T. 140
Kent, Evart E. 253
Kindle, Ethel J. 391
King, Martin Luther, Jr. 469
Kittrell College, N. C. 391
Klein, Herbert S., quoted 11, 12
Knights of Columbus 405
Knights of Labor 151
Knollenberg, Fred C. 371

Laney, Lucy 385
Langston, John Mercer 77
Legal and Educational Defense Fund of the N. A. A. C. P. 468
Leiby, James, quoted 150
Leonard Street Children's Home,

Atlanta, Ga. 260, 264
Lewis, John H. 431
Liberty Loan Drives 397
"Lightning" Atlanta, Ga. 266
Lincoln, Abraham 47
quoted 99
Lincoln Hospital, New York City 457
Lindsey, Inabel Burns 424
Locke, Alain LeRoy 311
Loew, Rose 431
Logan, Carrie Steele 143ff
Logan, John W. 431
Logan, Rayford W. 111
Lost Creek Settlement, Ind. 28
Louisiana Purchase 23
L'Ouverture, Toussaint 16, 20
Low, W. A., quoted 76
Lynching 320

McEwen, Homer 257
McGhee, F. L. 199
Manumission 12
Maroons 16, 20
Marshall, Louis 371
Martin, M. W. 431
Maryland Mutual Joint Stock Railway Company 91
Matthews, Victoria Earle 457
Maxwell, Mae 431
Mechanics' and Farmers' Bank, Durham, N. C. 228
"Mechanicsville" Atlanta, Ga. 266
Meharry Medical College, Nashville, Tenn. 425
Methodist Episcopal Church, South. Women's Missionary Council 242
Metropolitan Atlanta Association for the Blind, Atlanta, Ga. 257
Metropolitan Baptist Church, New York City 407
Middle passage 15
Migrants, Negro 288ff, 294ff
Miller, Elizabeth 388
Miller, Kelly 221, 310
Miller, Loren, quoted 106, 209
Miller, Thomas E. 88
Miner, Ralph J. 256
Mississippi Constitutional Convention, 1890 171
Montgomery, Isaiah T. 114ff
Moore, Garry Ward 180, 240, 267, 423, 424, 430, 431, 434, 436
Moore, Mrs. Philip North 397
Moorland, Jesse Edward 399, 408
Morehouse College, Atlanta, Ga. 240, 242, 262, 271, 377, 425, 428, 430, 436, 450
Morris, John 191
Morris, Richard B., quoted 13
Morris Brown College, Atlanta, Ga. 244
Mother Zion African Methodist Episcopal Zion Church, New York City 296, 407
Mound Bayou, Miss. 114, 115
Mt. Olive Baptist Church, New York City 407
Mt. Zion Congregational Church, Cleveland, Ohio 296
Mutual aid societies 4, 133
Myers, Isaac 151

N. A. A. C. P. see National Association for the Advancement of Colored People
Nashville, West City Council 88
National Afro-American Council 163
National Alliance of Postal Employees 287
National Association for the Advancement of Colored People 100, 163, 198, 205, 206ff, 286, 304, 319, 351, 365, 370
National Association of Colored Graduate Nurses 388
National Association of Colored Women's Clubs 164, 279, 286, 391, 397
National Child Welfare Association 421
National Colored Labor Union 90
National Colored Press Association 152
National Conference of Social Work 463
National Convention of Congregational Workers Among Colored People 245

National Council of Negro Women 385
National Emigration Aid Society, Washington, D. C. 128
National Independent Political League 206, 207
National Industrial Relations Department 459
National League for the Protection of Colored Women 241, 456
National League on Urban Conditions Among Negroes 216, 239, 240; see also National Urban League; Urban League
National Medical Association 251
National Urban League 241, 286, 304, 351, 365, 398, 417ff, 423, 424, 431, 459; see also Urban League; National League on Urban Conditions Among Negroes
National War Savings Committee 398
Negro Business League 199
Negro Fellowship League 164
Negro migrants see Migrants, Negro
Negro Organizations of Virginia 215
Negro settlements in Spanish Florida 27
Negro social workers see Social workers, Negro
Neighborhood Union, Atlanta, Ga. 240, 264, 265, 270ff, 320, 385, 426, 432
  Aims 275
  Constitution 273ff
  first clinic in Atlanta for Negroes 279
  plan of organization 274
  Surveys 277ff
Nelson, Alice Dunbar 385
New England Suffrage League 199
New Era Women's Club, Boston, Mass. 164
"New Negro," 179, 194, 286, 311, 314ff
New York School of Philanthropy, New York City 238, 243, 424
New York School of Social Work 460
Niagara Movement 180, 197ff
Nixon v. Herndon 370
North Carolina Health and Hospital Association, Inc. 461
North Carolina Mutual and Provident Association 227

Odum, Howard 377
Ohio State University, Columbus, Ohio 460
Olden, Mrs. J. C. 258
O'Leary, Patrick, quoted 152
Olivet Baptist Church, Chicago, Ill. 296, 408
Opportunity, a Journal of Negro Life (periodical) 421, 459
Order of the True Reformers 228
Ovington, Mary White 206
Owen, Chandler 311
Owensby, Newdigate M. 434

Page, Walter Hines, quoted 440
Paine College, Augusta, Georgia 240, 242
Pan Africanism 285
Patterson, Orlando, quoted 17
Payne, William A. 191
Peck, F. J. 149
Penn Industrial Institute, St. Helena Island, S. C. 210
Pennsylvania School of Social and Health Work 460
Peonage 209
Perry, Heman 262
Perry, Ola 261
Phelps Stokes Fund, New York City 256
Philadelphia Housing Association 295, 462
Philadelphia Negro 153, 155ff, 423
Phillis Wheatley Club, Columbia, S. C. 393
Pike, Ruth, quoted 9
Pinyon, Josephine V. 391
Pitts, Mrs. Howard W. 264
Plantation system in Seville, Spain 10
Planter (steamship) 74
Playground and Recreation Asso-

ciation 459, 461
Pleasants, Mammy 33
Plessy v. Ferguson 106, 110, 172ff, 177, 468
Pollard, Claude 371
Port Royal, S. C. vi, 44, 46, 47, 59, 60, 62, 70, 73, 75, 76, 79, 114, 212
Proctor, Henry Hugh 180, 243, 253, 292ff, 402, 406
Proctor, Mrs. H. H. 256
Pruitt, Marion C. 434
Pullman Porters' Benefit Association 368
Pumphrey, Ralph E., quoted 4
Purvis, Charles B. 77

Quarles, Frank "Father" 147
"Quarshie" types 17
Quinn, William Paul 29

Race prejudice 439
Racism 8, 22, 40
Randolph, Asa Philip 311, 365
Ransom, Reverdy Cassius 204
Reconstruction 39
"Red summer of 1919" 324
Reddick, M. W. 216
Reid, Ira DeA. 423, 424
Rhone, Joanne V., quoted 4
Richmond, Lucy B. 391
Riis, Jacob 233
Rite of transition 18
Riverdale Colored Orphan Assylum and Association for the Benefit of Colored Children, New York City 457
Robinson, James H. 412, 417
Robinson, Samuel H. 253
Rockefeller, John D., Jr. 462
Rogers, James Gamble 378
Romanyshyn, John M., quoted 1
Roosevelt, Theodore 250, 387
Rosebud Study Club, Portland, Ore. 393
Royce, Josiah, quoted 441
Ruffin, Adele 391
Ruffin, Josephine St. Pierre 164
Russell, Charles Edward 206
Russell, John H., quoted 14

S. C. L. C. see Southern Christian Leadership Conference
Sage, Dean 378
St. Augustine College, Raleigh, N. C. 463
St. Helena Island, S. C. 52, 56
St. John African Methodist Episcopal Church, Cleveland, Ohio 296
St. John's Congregational Church, Springfield, Mass. 250, 296, 408, 462
St. Luke's Herald (newspaper), Richmond, Va. 135
St. Luke's Penny Savings Bank, Richmond, Va. 133
St. Mark Methodist Episcopal Church, New York City 407
St. Paul African Methodist Episcopal Church, St. Louis, Mo. 126
St. Phillips Protestant Episcopal Church, New York City 407, 410
Salem Methodist Episcopal Church, New York City 406
Sam, Alfred Charles 182ff
"Sambo" types 17
Sanders, Charles L., quoted 4
Savannah Educational Association 86
Schmidlapp Houses, Cincinnati, Ohio 462
Sea Islands, Ga. vi, 41, 46, 50, 60, 75, 95
Second Baptist Church, Detroit, Mich. 408
Segregation 170
    de facto 465
    de jure 465
Seligman, Herbert, quoted 440
Seminole Indians 26
Seminole Wars 26, 27
Sharpe Street Methodist Episcopal Church, Baltimore, Md. 296, 408
Sherman, William Tecumseh 79, 93, 95
Shiloh African Methodist Episcopal Church, Atlanta, Ga. 150

Shivery, Louie D. 263
Shoemaker Center, Cincinnati, Ohio 461
Simmons, D. A. 371
Singleton, Benjamin "Pap" 131ff
Slave codes 11, 21
Slave factories 18
Slave mutinies 16
Slave suicides 16
Slavery
 and the U. S. Constitution 22, 23
 in the Carolinas 27
 in Cuba 11
 in Florida 26
 in Haiti 16, 17
 in Jamaica 17
 in Portugal 9
 in Spain 9
 in the U. S. 6, 11, 15, 26
 in Virginia 20
 in the West Indies 16
Sleet, Jessie 457
Smalls, Hannah (Mrs. Robert) 75
Smalls, Robert 70, 73
Smith, Hannah C. 389
Smith, R. L. 11, 133, 136
Social work 445
Social workers, Negro 424
South Carolina Constitutional Convention, 1868 73, 103
Southern Christian Leadership Conference 469
Spaulding, Charles Clinton 227
Spelman College, Atlanta, Ga. 244, 450
 Nursery school 264
Spingarn, A. B. 371
Spirituals, Negro 15
Stampp, Kenneth, quoted 99
Standard Life Insurance Company, Atlanta, Ga. 262
Stevenson, William 402, 404
Stewart, Maria W. 78
Stokes, Vivian W. 391
Storey, Moorfield 371
Storrs School, Atlanta, Ga. 244, 252
Straight University, New Orleans, La. 245
Stubbs, Blanche W. 393
"Summerhill" Atlanta, Ga. 266
The Survey (periodical) 216

Tabernacle Baptist Church, Augusta, Ga. 250
Talbert, Mary B. 397
"Talented tenth" 181
Tandy, Charlotte H. 126
Tanner, Benjamin Tucker 118
Taylor, Susie King 70, 73
Terry v. Adams 171
Theatre Owners Book Association 369
33d U. S. Colored Troops 73
Thomas, C. B. 388
Thomas, Jesse O. v, 374, 427, 430, 434
Thompson, Augustus 148
Tilford, William H. 415
Trinity College, Durham, N. C. 230
Trinity Mission Settlement, Chicago, Ill. 230, 232
Trotter, William Monroe 193, 199
Truth, Sojourner 77, 457
Turner, Henry McNeal 85, 112, 151
 quoted 112
Turner, John 127
Tuskegee Institute, Ala. 152, 247, 430
Twentieth Century Club, Boston, Mass. 247
Tyler, Ralph W., quoted 404

U. N. I. A. see Universal Negro Improvement Association
U. S. Civil War 39
U. S. Constitution 22
 13th amendment 39, 98, 283
 14th amendment 39, 102, 171, 469
 15th amendment 39, 102, 171, 207, 371
U. S. Constitutional Convention 22
U. S. Supreme Court 106
Universal Negro Improvement Association 285, 304, 305
 Constitution 306
University of Chicago Graduate School of Social Administration 460

University of North Carolina, Chapel Hill 376
University of Pittsburgh, Pittsburgh, Pa. 460
University of Toronto, Canada 378
Urban League 412; see also National Urban League; National League on Urban Conditions Among Negroes
Utopia Neighborhood House, New York City 462

"Vine City" Atlanta, Ga. 266
Virginia Union University, Richmond 243

Walker, Charles T. 250
Walker, Maggie L. 111, 133ff
Walling, William English 206
War Camp Community Service 461
War Work Council 399, 400
Ware, Edmund Asa 252
Ware, Gertrude 260, 264
Washington, Booker Taliaferro 111, 140, 177, 192, 233, 247
"Atlanta Exposition Address," 1895 193ff
quoted 178, 235
Washington, Forrester B. v, 294, 412, 424, 444
Watson, Hattie R. 265
Watts, Nellie 256
Wesley, Charles Harris 399
Western Sanitary Commission, St. Louis, Mo. 63
Whitaker, Mrs. J. W. 392
White, Eartha 392
White Rose Home for Colored Working Girls 457
Whitlock, Brand 206
Wilder, Maria L. 391
Wilkes, W. 374
Willard, Frances 163
Williams Institutional Colored Methodist Episcopal Church, New York City 407
Wilson, Prince E. vii
Winn, Cordelia A. 391
Woods, W. 374
Work, John Wesley 218
Work, Monroe Nathan 423, 430
quoted 100, 283, 335ff
Wright, J. C. 402
Wright, Richard Robert 232
Wright, Richard Robert, Jr. 230, 232, 423

Y. M. C. A. see Young Men's Christian Association
Y. W. C. A. see Young Women's Christian Association
Yergan, Max 399, 402
Young, Charles Noël 287
Young, Whitney M. v
Young Men's Christian Association 399, 412, 457, 459
Young People's Congress, Atlanta, Ga. 245
Young Women's Christian Association 388, 412, 457, 459